D1598107

CURSE ON
THIS COUNTRY

CURSE ON THIS COUNTRY

The Rebellious Army of
Imperial Japan

Danny Orbach

CORNELL UNIVERSITY PRESS **ITHACA AND LONDON**

First published 2017 by Cornell University Press
Printed in the United States of America

Library of Congress Cataloging-in-Publication Data

Names: Orbach, Danny, author.
Title: Curse on this country : the rebellious army of imperial Japan /
    Danny Orbach.
Description: Ithaca : Cornell University Press, 2017. | Includes bibliographical
    references and index.
Identifiers: LCCN 2016041653 (print) | LCCN 2016043609 (ebook) |
    ISBN 9781501705281 (cloth : alk. paper) | ISBN 9781501708336 (epub/mobi) |
    ISBN 9781501708343 (pdf)
Subjects: LCSH: Insubordination—Japan—History. | Military discipline—
    Japan—History. | Sociology, Military—Japan—History. | Japan—History,
    Military—1868–1945.
Classification: LCC UB789 .O73 2017 (print) | LCC UB789 (ebook) |
    DDC 355.00952/09041—dc23
LC record available at https://lccn.loc.gov/2016041653

Cornell University Press strives to use environmentally responsible suppliers and materials to the fullest extent possible in the publishing of its books. Such materials include vegetable-based, low-VOC inks and acid-free papers that are recycled, totally chlorine-free, or partly composed of nonwood fibers. For further information, visit our website at www.cornellpress.cornell.edu.

Defiance of the superior by the subordinate: a deplorable tendency in the fighting services, which proved to be the curse on this country, inviting the misery of today.

—Marquis Kido Kōichi, lord keeper of the privy seal, at the Tokyo Trials

Contents

Acknowledgments

Curse on This Country could not have been written without the generous help of family members, friends, teachers, and colleagues, to whom I owe endless gratitude.

My deep thanks to my dear family, and especially my mother, Lily Orbach, who advised and encouraged me so much. Next, I owe a great debt of gratitude to my sensei, the teachers, professors, and academic advisors who guided me through this arduous journey. Irit Averbuch from Tel Aviv University opened my first window into Japanese history. Andrew Gordon carefully read each chapter and offered extensive comments and guidance. I especially thank him for his endless patience and help in shaping my haphazard ideas into a coherent argument. David Howell gave me penetrating criticism, a wakeup call that helped me trim redundant material and hone my argument. Cathal Nolan's wise comments, support, and insights on the larger context of global military history were invaluable. Niall Ferguson helped with his sharp feedback and also through his teaching, instruction, and original ideas on military affairs, political dynamics, and the philosophy of history.

Andrew Lownie, my dedicated agent, cleverly navigated the stormy water of the international literary market to get this book published. Ned Pennant-Rea, one of the best language editors I've ever encountered, worked very hard on some of the chapters. I am also deeply indebted to the publishing team of Cornell University Press, and especially my editor, Roger Malcom Haydon, who believed in this book from the early stages of the revision and tremendously improved its quality.

When I first went to Japan for archival research, I encountered a tremendous linguistic problem. Many primary sources, especially documents from the nineteenth century, were almost inaccessible to me. Though I had a working knowledge of modern Japanese, these old texts were written in archaic language and often in an illegible scribble. I owe boundless gratitude to the friends and teachers who helped me master the primary documents. Nojima-Kato Yōko, the noted military historian from Tokyo University, was the first to help me to find my way in the maze of primary and secondary sources. Her graduate student, Dandō Mitsuki, graciously initiated me into the complicated but fascinating world of nineteenth-century Japanese, helped me to decipher difficult handwriting, and introduced me to numerous subtleties of the mentality of the time.

Wesley Jacobsen, Udagawa Aya, and Yoshie Hirokazu helped me solve difficult linguistic problems.

I also thank scholars who helped me with specific chapters. Ogawara Masamichi, an expert in Japanese religious and military history, was my first guide to the world of the *shishi*. Reinier Hesselink and Carter Eckert generously gave me original documents from their own collections, which contributed greatly to my research on the same subject. Without their help, it is hard to imagine the first chapter of this book, which served as the basis for much of the rest. Sven Saaler, an expert on pan-Asianism and the history of the modern Japanese army, gave me precious clues and ideas on the Taishō political crisis. Cemil Aydin helped to shed some light on Hashimoto Kingorō, the leader of the Sakura-kai, and his Turkish connections.

Oleg Benesch gave invaluable advice for the manuscript revision stage. My friends Konrad Lawson, D. Colin Jaundrill, Jeremy Yellen, Birgit Tremml, Yoshie Hirokazu, Tina Li, Jolyon Thomas, Wai-Yee Chong, John Lee, Reut Harari, Emer O'Dwyer, Maren Ehlers, and Andrew Levidis gave helpful support and constructive criticism. I am grateful for their insights and ideas, which helped me sharpen and enrich my own arguments. Astghik Hovhannisyan helped me obtain material from Tokyo when I was in the United States and unable to travel. Tatiana Simbirtseva helped me to obtain Russian primary sources on the assassination of Queen Min. Yoichi Funabashi, the former editor of *Asahi Shinbun*, introduced me to the world of Japanese publishing houses, and Vera Baranova graciously assisted me in deciphering the handwriting in several Russian documents.

I thank the staff members of the various archives, libraries, and institutions who helped me in my day-to-day research—first and foremost Kuniko McVey and the other staff members of Harvard Yenching Library, Widener Memorial Library, and Lamont Library. I also owe gratitude to numerous archivists, librarians, and staff members of Tokyo University Library, the National Diet Library (especially the special collections), the National Institute for Defense Studies, the Archive of the Japanese Foreign Ministry, the National Archives in Tokyo, the National Archives in Kew, the National Archives in Washington, DC, and many other institutions.

Finally, I would also like to thank the academic foundations and institutions that generously supplied me with grants and research fellowships: the Reischauer Institute for Japanese Studies, the Asia Center and the Davis Center for Russian and Euroasian Studies (all at Harvard University), as well as the Japan Foundation.

All of the people and institutions mentioned above share in the merits of this book. The responsibility for any faults or errors, however, is exclusively my own.

Note on Names and Dates

All Japanese, Chinese, and Korean names in this book are written according to the East Asian convention of last name first (e.g., Takasugi Shinsaku, Zhang Zuolin). The only exception is East Asian authors who published in Western languages (e.g., Eiko Ikegami). As in most contemporary works, Chinese names and terms are transliterated according to Pin-Yin conventions, instead of the Wade-Giles romanization rules common in earlier books. The exception are names of famous historical figures known in the Wade-Giles version of their names (e.g., Chiang Kai-Shek) or Chinese authors who transliterated their names in Wade-Giles (e.g., Hsien-T'ing Chen).

For the sake of clarity, dates of the old Japanese and Russian calendars (prior to January 1, 1873, and February 1, 1918, respectively) are converted throughout this book to Gregorian dates. The conversion was made with the Funaba Calendar Application, http://www.funaba.org/calendar-conversion.

CURSE ON
THIS COUNTRY

Introduction

> **Duty is weightier than a mountain, while death is lighter than a feather.**
>
> —The Imperial Rescript for Soldiers and Sailors

Many people in the West associate the Imperial Japanese Army with blind obedience to authority. Notorious for following superiors to certain death, Japanese soldiers in the Pacific War evoked among their enemies unsavory images such as "cattle," "herd," or "beehive." In one example among many, an Australian war correspondent wrote that "many of the Japanese soldiers I have seen have been primitive oxen-like clods with dulled eyes. . . . They have stayed in their positions and died simply because they have been told to do so, and they haven't the intelligence to think for themselves."[1]

Leaving the extreme rhetoric aside, there is some truth to the myth of blind discipline. Japanese military ideology did indeed emphasize unconditional obedience toward the orders of superiors. The "Imperial Rescript for Soldiers and Sailors," a seminal document that every soldier, especially from the mid-1920s, had to memorize and be ready to recite at a moment's notice, warned that "soldiers and sailors should consider loyalty their essential duty. . . . With a single heart fulfill your essential duty of loyalty, and bear in mind that duty is weightier than a mountain, while death is lighter than a feather."[2] Officers, too, often rushed toward death without thinking twice when ordered to do so, as exemplified by the relatively high rate of officer casualties in almost all Japanese wars.[3] The penal code of the imperial army, first published in the 1880s, threatened any soldier or officer, regardless of rank, with severe punishment for any act of disobedience.[4]

And yet, the imperial Japanese army was arguably one of the most disobedient armed forces in modern history. Japanese officers repeatedly staged coup d'états, violent insurrections, and political assassinations, phenomena that peaked in the 1870s and in the 1930s. Between these two periods, other officers incessantly resisted orders given by both government and high command. As Craig M. Cameron has written, the phenomenon of *gekokujō*, "the low overthrowing the high," was "a crucial and unique concept shaping Japanese military culture. . . . Mid-level staff officers, by defying their superiors, transformed national policy. . . . Repeatedly, from Emperor Hirohito through the military high command, superiors tolerated insubordination [and] allowed their hands to be forced without reasserting their authority."[5]

This tradition began very early in modern Japanese history. The 1870s were an age of chaos, when rebellious officers, statesmen, and former samurai regularly hatched assassination plots, mutinies, and at times even open rebellions. In the late nineteenth century, and again during the 1910s and 1920s, officers assassinated foreign leaders and overthrew civilian cabinets in moments of political crisis. The 1930s gave rise to a particularly chaotic form of disobedience. In 1931, a military terror organization named the Sakura-kai (Cherry Blossom Society) attempted to annihilate the entire Japanese cabinet with an air strike. A few months later, rebellious officers assassinated Prime Minister Inukai Tsuyoshi. The ensuing coup d'état failed but led to a series of further violent upheavals, both inside and outside the army. In 1935, a leading general was slashed to death by a junior officer because of a factional rivalry.

And finally, in February 1936, state control monetarily collapsed during a massive military insurgency. More than a thousand troops took to the streets, and several Japanese leaders were murdered in their mansions. In a classic book written during the Second World War, the British correspondent Hugh Byas coined the term "government by assassination." Officers of the 1930s, according to Byas, terrorized the civilian cabinet by way of repeated assassinations. Through their ability to inflict lethal violence, they took control of foreign policy, pushing timid and terrified leaders toward a course of unbridled military expansion, and finally, into the disaster of the Pacific War.[6]

The few English-languages studies about Japanese military disobedience have focused on rebellions in the 1930s, probably because of their drama, intensity, and proximity to the Second World War. As all of these books have shown, rebellions and assassinations became an essential feature of Japanese political life during this period.[7] None of these authors, however, has been able to explain the apparent normality and widespread acceptance amongst the elite of such thoroughly abnormal behavior. In 1935, the junior officer who had murdered a general attempted to go on to his next assignment, as if nothing had happened.[8]

The people the conspirators of the Sakura-kai had planned to kill "punished" them with only twenty-five days' confinement to an inn. Indeed, the perpetrators enjoyed widespread sympathy both in the officer corps and from the general public. And yet, it is highly probable that most of these supporters were unfamiliar with the complicated military debates and factional strife that had led to some of the assassinations. It was the "pure motives" of the assassins which mattered to sympathizers.[9] In Japan of the early 1930s, violent acts of officers, as far as they were motivated by "sincere" patriotism, were admired in and of themselves.

As a leading historian of the Japanese army admitted recently, the reasons underlying the rebelliousness of the imperial armed forces in the 1930s are still a mystery.[10] The key to unlocking it lies in the developments of prior decades. In order to understand how Japan became a country in which it was normal for soldiers to rebel, resist, assassinate, and conspire, a history of military insubordination is necessary. Such a long-term history has never been written in English. The present book is an attempt to do so.

Incidents of military insubordination were neither sporadic nor random, I will argue, but rather based on a deep-rooted historical pattern, a culture of rebellion and resistance that was an integral part of Japanese military life from the 1860s to the 1930s. Tracing the roots and the development of this culture, I will demonstrate that it had four major features. First, it was made possible by structural faults in the Japanese polity, comparable to "bugs" in a computer code. Second, its development was an unintentional result of seemingly reasonable decisions made by policymakers trying to achieve other goals. Third, it was doubled-edged, combining violent rebellions with more subtle resistance to state authority. Fourth, rebellion and resistance alternated over the years, nurturing and re-creating each other in a reciprocal way.

Computer bugs are used here as a metaphor denoting basic structural flaws in the political system. Just like bugs in software, they did not prevent the state from running. Only in certain situations, under specific conditions, did they cause severe failures that eventually undermined the entire system. The first bug formed a perpetual niche for rebellion and resistance in the Japanese polity and related to the essence of the Japanese monarchy. As recognized by many historians of modern Japan, the authority of the emperor, absolute in theory, was very limited in practice. For reasons we shall discuss in detail, the emperor, hidden from public view, could not make policy decisions of his own. Yet, as his "will" was the supreme emblem of political legitimacy, a handful of leaders (widely known as the "Meiji oligarchs") were able to use his name to govern unofficially from behind the throne.

However, this ruling group faced a problem. Officially, the emperor was the one who made decisions, and the oligarchs were merely his advisors. So, in order to maintain the image of imperial supremacy, they did not legitimize their own position as the de facto rulers of the country. This situation gave an inexhaustible source of ideological ammunition for dissenters in the military and beyond. Such dissenters could always claim that they, rather than the people who unofficially held power, represented the hidden will of the emperor. As we shall see later, they did so on several occasions, starting with the Satsuma Rebellion in 1877 and ending with the coup d'état of February 26, 1936. These military uprisings, like other acts of insubordination, were directed against the people who ruled the country, but almost never against the emperor or the state. Even in their most violent forms, rebellion and resistance in the army remained monarchic and patriotic.

The second bug, which made such rebellion and resistance harder to contend with, related to a certain feature of official state ideology. The Meiji regime had always been based on a progressive movement of expansion on all fronts: richer country, stronger army, bigger empire. Therefore, disobedient military elements could express their opposition by independently moving along the road of imperial expansion faster and more resolutely than the government. Often, such behavior took the form of unauthorized military operations against other countries. Because state ideology dictated constant territorial expansion, it did not make sense for the government to undo the "achievements" of disobedient officers, even if the political leadership abhorred the way in which they had been obtained. It was difficult to punish such "patriots," who after all were striving for the same goals as the government.

The third bug, which further radicalized this form of insubordination, derived from another feature of the state ideology: its basic ambiguity. It was clear to almost all actors involved that Japan harbored a mission to become richer, stronger, and larger, but it was never clear to what extent. National policy was often interpreted as an ideology of endless imperial growth. Therefore, the thirst of restive elements in the army could never be quenched, and their dreams could never be satisfied. No matter how much the Japanese empire expanded, disgruntled officers could always claim that further expansion was needed. Hence, the three bugs mentioned above created room, ideological encouragement, and endless pretexts for rebellion and resistance in the imperial Japanese army.

However, these bugs only set the stage. They increased the probability of insubordination but did not make it inevitable in itself. The actual development of rebellion and resistance was an unintended consequence of numerous policy decisions taken by different people over a long period of time. Had some of these decisions been different, the developments could well have been slowed or even curbed. The different actors, whether officers, politicians, or law enforcement personnel, always intended to solve problems, not foster insubordination. Yet their actions had consequences they did not foresee.

The insubordination unintentionally created by these actors' decisions took two forms: violent rebellion and resistance to government policy, each dominant at different times. The alternation between rebellion and resistance chronologically frames this book in a period of seventy-six years, from 1860 to 1936, the eve of the Second Sino-Japanese War. In the 1860s, the Tokugawa regime was overthrown by a revolutionary coalition, abetted by samurai terrorists known as *shishi* (warriors of high aspirations). The ideology and organizational patterns of these unruly samurai were adopted by generations of disobedient officers in Japan. Most of all, they influenced violent rebels who, for various reasons, turned against the new regime in the 1870s. Insubordination in this early, formative period was unsurprising, as the regime was new and weak, and its political hierarchy was still fluid and untested.

Ironically, it was the response of the government to the upheavals of the 1870s that made it possible for these patterns of insubordination, established when the regime was weak, to endure even after its solidification. Reforms in the army, implemented after the suppression of a major rebellion in 1877, helped to curb rebellious insubordination for decades, but had an unexpected outcome, nurturing a tendency of resistance to state authority, either in the form of unauthorized military operations (1895, 1928) or as bloodless coups d'état (1912). This resistance preserved, in a dormant form, some of the basic features of the past's violent rebellions. Gradually, it became more radical in nature, until it exploded in a new wave of violent rebellions from 1931 to 1936. In essence, this book answers the questions of why and how the phenomenon of violent insubordination, powerfully curbed after 1877, exploded again fifty years later, contributing to the deterioration of Japan into militarism, unbridled expansion, and world war.

This book is the result of encounters with fifteen archives in four different countries, as well as letter collections, testimonies, police transcripts, court documents, diplomatic cables, historical newspapers, memoirs, interviews, and other forms of primary material in Japanese, English, Chinese, German, and Russian. Some of the incidents explored in the book, such as the Saga Rebellion, the assassination plots of 1874, and the murder of the Korean queen in 1895, have rarely been studied in detail, so the primary materials are of paramount importance. Other incidents, such as the Taishō political crisis (1912–1913) and, especially, the military revolt of February 26, 1936, have been analyzed before by a handful of scholars in English and Japanese, so I have been able to make use of their studies as well as the primary sources.

I have reconstructed and analyzed the incidents in each chapter as products of their time and place, and also as phases in the process that ultimately led Japan to the Pacific War. But every narrative has its limitations, both in the events it covers and the themes it considers. So this book is by no means a comprehensive history of modern Japan. It focuses only on events which are of relevance to major incidents of rebellion and resistance. Other events and developments, even those of great significance to Japanese history, I either mention in passing or not at all.

Nor is this a comprehensive account of dissent in the Japanese empire. There were many disobedient groups in Imperial Japan, such as popular rights activists, restive peasants, unruly students, political ruffians, workers who organized strikes, anarchists, and communists. This book's subject, however, is insubordination in the army's officer corps and other closely related groups. In some of the earlier chapters, we deal at length with mutinies and assassination plots staged by disgruntled samurai, even when they did not officially belong to the officer corps, for three main reasons. First of all, in the first decade of the Meiji era, the borderline between officers and samurai was still blurry. In addition, early Meiji samurai mutineers displayed many patterns later evident among officers. Finally, and most important, the government's reaction to these mutineers led to unintended consequences that shaped military insubordination for the rest of the period, up to the eve of the Pacific War. In the margins of the story, we deal also with the Imperial Navy, which experienced rebellion and resistance only in two short periods (1912–1913 and 1930–1932). Rebellion and resistance among rank-and-file soldiers and civilian adventurers are mentioned only when these people worked with, were allied with, or colluded with officers.

In the following pages I do not tell a story that is unique to Japan. Military disobedience, both in the form of rebellion and defiance, existed at the same time in numerous other countries, particularly in East and South Asia, southern and eastern Europe, sub-Saharan Africa, the Middle East, and Latin America. Other countries also experienced one or more of the "three bugs," albeit in somewhat different forms.

The first bug certainly existed elsewhere. Tsar Nicholas II and Kaiser William II failed to demonstrate leadership at crucial junctures in their reigns. Even such a theoretically omnipotent dictator as Adolf Hitler often did not interfere in key decisions. He expected instead that his subordinates would fight and debate with each other over the "true" meaning of his will ("working toward the Führer," as Hitler biographer Ian Kershaw phrased it).[11] None of these rulers was as hidden as the Japanese emperor, but their failure to lead did allow some room for factional infighting and at times encouraged military insubordination.

An expansionist ideology that was both vague and boundless, which constitutes the second and third bugs, was also far from unique to Japan. Take the infamous Hawaii coup d'état of 1893 as an example. In that year a group of American citizens and officers conspired with the US ambassador to Hawaii to overthrow the queen and establish a phony republic, so as to pave the way for the island to be annexed by the United States. They acted independently, without asking for permission and against the will of President Elect Grover Cleveland. Yet their "patriotism" won them enormous support and made the coup extremely difficult to reverse. Five years later, the United States annexed Hawaii.[12]

So while Japan was not unique in general terms, the way the three bugs combined in the country did make its story different from that of Russia, Germany, or the United States. The challenges Japan faced were also different, as were the responses of policymakers to those challenges. The distinct legacy of the Japanese past, especially the shishi and their ideology, played a particularly important role. Japanese military insubordination, notwithstanding its similarity to cultures of disobedience in other countries, is therefore an independent historical phenomenon. How it came about is the question that this book tries to answer.

WARRIORS OF HIGH ASPIRATIONS

The Origins of Military Insubordination,
1858–1868

In this floating world, life is not worth more than three pennies.

—Takasugi Shinsaku

Lieutenant Colonel Hashimoto Kingorō was an officer in the General Staff of the Imperial Japanese Army. In October 1931, he planned to annihilate the Japanese prime minister and his cabinet ministers with machine-gun fire, poisonous gas, and naval bombers. Defending his behavior, he wrote that he felt he had to follow the footsteps of the "warriors of high aspiration" from the 1860s, known in Japanese as shishi.[1] Hashimoto's close ally, Captain Chō Isamu, justified his cohort's wild drinking habits with the argument that once, seventy years ago, the behavior of the shishi had been very much the same.[2]

Symbols are important, and in more than one way. The shishi were a crucial example used by military rebels all throughout modern, prewar Japanese history. Their myth was the thread that tied the knots of Japanese military disobedience together. Specifically, the shishi had their impact felt on future rebels in three different dimensions, each of them crucial to the development of military insubordination in the Japanese Army. Rebels from 1868 to 1936 chose to imitate the shishi because of their proven, spectacular success. Shishi ideals, reinterpreted and removed from their original context, inspired them well into the twentieth century. Additionally, some of the organizational patterns of these terrorist groups "migrated" into the Japanese Army, becoming an institutional grid on which future insubordination would grow. Finally, the shishi's activity gave rise to a chain of events, reactions, and counterreactions, making the army and the Japanese imperial state more vulnerable to the influence of military rebels. History never has a clear beginning or end, but every historical account is effectively a narrative. As such, it cannot do without chronological boundaries. And for the purpose of our story, the shishi are the point where it had all began.

Before the Shishi: The Twilight of Tokugawa Japan

In 1600, Japan was unified after a prolonged war between numerous independent lords. In order to keep the country united, Shogun Tokugawa Ieyasu and his successors redesigned it as a sophisticated mix between feudalism and central rule. Using the emperor in Kyoto as a rubber stamp, the Tokugawa governed the realm from the city of Edo, living in coexistence with a large number of lords (daimyo), each of them ruling his own domain. The daimyo had to surrender several important prerogatives to the Bakufu, as the shogun's regime was known.[3] First of all, the Bakufu held about one fourth of the country, including large swaths of land in central Japan and the strategic towns of Edo, Osaka, Kyoto, and Nagasaki. In addition, it held, with several exceptions, a monopoly over the highly limited relations that Japan had with foreign countries.[4] Furthermore, the shogun was responsible for upholding peace in the country, including subjugation of violent conflicts between and within domains.

Each daimyo had considerable autonomy to run his own affairs without interference, but significant interactions with other domains were rarely allowed to exist without Bakufu approval. The daimyo were not allowed to enter Kyoto, even less so to approach the emperor.[5] Internal networking between the domains was dangerous, because they could upset the balance and expose the basic weakness of the Bakufu. The shogun and his government, after all, did not possess enough troops, lands, or funds to subdue the entire realm. In order to restrain a rebellious domain, the Bakufu had to borrow power from the other lords. Coalitions between domains, upsetting this balance, were therefore strongly discouraged.

Ideologically speaking, the Tokugawa order was based on the ideal of balance. The government in Edo, the various daimyo, and many of the period's intellectual luminaries believed in a model of harmonious stability between shogun and daimyo, lords and retainers, higher samurai and lower samurai, warriors and commoners, peasants and merchants. Each group was deemed to have its own role in the harmonious structure of the realm.[6] But this balance, like any balance, was an ideological one, never completely aligned with reality on the ground. Throughout the period, individuals from different domains and status groups became interconnected through common social, commercial, literary, and scholarly pursuits.[7] By the turn of the nineteenth century these circulation networks, connecting the various domains with the big cities and with one other were already dense, developed, and highly sophisticated.

Samurai, officially confined to their own domains, also became increasingly interconnected as the nineteenth century progressed. The encroachment of foreign ships led some daimyo to encourage practical education in martial arts. As a result, talented samurai students began to journey, with the blessings of their lords, to the renowned fencing schools of Edo. Others were sent to study various useful subjects, such as musketry, coastal defense, fortification, and Western military organization. Some schools had also taught Confucianism or different strands of Japanese nativism, imbuing their students with deep reverence for the emperor in Kyoto.[8]

Technological developments, especially the proliferation of defensive equipment, made it possible to organize fencing practice bouts, a natural trend given the renewed emphasis on samurai military preparedness. These developments had dramatic ramifications on the growth of samurai networks. Suddenly, fencing tournaments became common and popular, attracting samurai from all across the realm. Both schools and tournaments gave rise to a competitive, bellicose student culture.[9] Indeed, prints in memorial books from the late Tokugawa period vividly show how spirited, violent, and sweaty this culture was, how strong the friendship bonds that it created between warriors from different domains were. These networks formed the basis on which the shishi movement later grew.[10]

The turbulent events of the 1850s had turned some segments of this harmless student culture into a counterculture of dissent. The Shogunate's failure to stop the incursion of Westerners into Japan incensed many daimyo, who were quick to criticize the Bakufu's failure to uphold the "ancestral tradition" of international seclusion. The emperor, for generations relegated by the Tokugawa to the political sidelines, refused to rubber stamp the shogun's policy, proscribing any concessions to the foreigners.[11] Anti-Bakufu elements in Chōshū, a strong domain in western Japan, used the emperor's "order" as a pretext to champion the cause of the foreigners' exclusion, leading to a series of conflicts with the shogun and his government.

This political and social instability proved deeply unsettling to the identity of many young samurai. As the psychologist Erik Erikson has noted, in such situations "youth feel endangered, individually and collectively, whereupon it becomes ready to support doctrines offering an immersion in a synthetic identity (extreme nationalism, racism or class consciousness) and a collective condemnation of a totally stereotyped enemy of the new identity."[12] The arrival of the foreigners to Japan gave these restive elements an enemy to unite against across domainal boundaries. Thus a movement of young samurai, professing hatred of the foreigners, mistrust toward the Bakufu, and increasing anger at the failure of the shogun to protect Japan began to emerge in the late 1850s.[13] It was particularly strong among low- and middle-ranking samurai in Edo, both in fencing schools and other institutions, far away from domainal supervision and imbued with vigor and martial spirit.[14] Finding it easy to hatch conspiracies and brave death along with friends they knew and trusted, many of the samurai students in Edo and the various domains adopted an increasingly rebellious attitude.[15]

Other young samurai, who were not lucky enough to be sent as students to Edo and Kyoto, snuck out of their domains to join the burgeoning samurai counterculture in the big cities. Openly defying the rules of the realm, which strictly forbade such illegal absconding from service, they became *rōnin* or *furō*, masterless samurai, who were effectively wanted criminals.[16] Others established underground cells in their own domains. In Tosa, a fencing master of low samurai status became a leader of a shishi organization known as the Loyalist Party (Tosa Kinnōtō).[17] A miniscule but ultimately influential group of radical samurai also developed in Satsuma, the powerful southern domain.[18]

The movement was strongest in the Chōshū Domain, where it appeared in a private school of martial arts and Confucianism led by the young thinker Yoshida Shōin. A revered spiritual guide of many young samurai within and without his domain, Yoshida distilled the angry mood of many of his peers into scathing criticism of the Bakufu and called his students to actively raise arms against it.[19] A major attempt by the shogun's chief minister to crush the movement in 1858 achieved initial success. But this campaign, known as the Ansei purge, ended abruptly when the chief minister was assassinated on March 24, 1860, by a group of rebellious samurai.[20] This was the first major operation of the shishi movement.

Fools and Madmen: The Shishi Ideology

The term *shishi*, increasingly associated with fugitive samurai who used violence against foreigners, Shogunate officials, and pro-Bakufu elements in the various domains, was adopted from classical Chinese sources. In the *Analects* (15:9), Confucius pointed out that "men of high aspirations would not sacrifice humaneness to remain alive. In certain instances, they would rather sacrifice their own life to uphold humaneness."[21] The term *shishi*, the Japanese reading of the original Chinese *zhi-shi* (men of high aspirations), was familiar to many young samurai from their classical education, though the word *men*, originally referring to scholar officials, was associated in the Edo Period with warriors. Hence the translation of shishi as "warriors of high aspirations." From the late 1850s, nonconformist intellectuals such as Yoshida Shōin began to use it in explicit revolutionary contexts, praising the samurai who raised their swords against the Bakufu and its allies.[22]

In the 1860s, the shishi political platform was summarized by the catchphrase *sonnō jōi*, "revere the emperor and expel the barbarians."[23] The shishi's opposition to the Bakufu rested on its failure to uphold both clauses of the phrase sonnō jōi. By his failure to expel the Western barbarians who polluted the divine Japanese realm, the shogun neglected his duty as the protector of the country.[24] And by refusing to follow the emperor's orders, the Tokugawa house showed irreverence to the throne. Some of the more radical shishi thinkers, such as Yoshida Shōin, went even further and concluded that the Shogunate, by itself, was illegitimate, and the shoguns, from the twelfth to the nineteenth century, were in fact usurpers of imperial power.[25]

The shishi, like all human actors, operated out of a complicated mix of personal and ideological motives. Self-interest was certainly part of the picture. Particularly, the shishi, predominantly young, lower-, and mid-ranking samurai, were resentful of a social order which destined them to live in poverty and obscurity, denying them the right to influence the affairs of the realm.[26] Sakamoto Ryōma from Tosa contrasted, in a famous letter, the exciting adventures he had as a shishi with "a place like home, where you can't have any ambition and you spend your time in stupid ways like an idiot."[27]

This individualism led many shishi to look down on formal hierarchies and symbols of authority and status. Prevailing social norms dictated differences in speech, dress, and demeanor according to one's hereditary rank. The shishi counterculture, which was a reaction against this strict stratification, was leveling by its very nature. Young samurai activists who escaped their domains were often wild-looking, with long hair and disheveled clothes, expressing revulsion for normal rank and status boundaries.[28] Their meeting places tended to be entertainment establishments of the so-called "floating world": restaurants, brothels, inns, and geisha houses.[29] The red light districts of big Japanese cities, whose clientele was anyway a mixed bag of samurai and townspeople, offered relative anonymity regardless of one's rank and status. There, young shishi could hatch plots, drink, carouse with geisha, and enjoy intoxicating freedom.[30]

Yamakawa Hiroshi, a senior Bakufu police official in Kyoto, recalled that in many cases, the shishi crossed the line into outright criminality. "There were many of them," he wrote, "who, paying lip service to sonnō jōi, robbed money to pay for alcohol and prostitutes."[31] And yet, many shishi were also idealists. The rejection of self-interest in favor of public concerns, for example, was dominant in both their oral and written discourse.[32] As even some of their sworn enemies from the Bakufu camp admitted, they "left both lord and family" and took great personal risks to save the realm from an impending crisis.[33]

The urgency of this crisis prompted many shishi leaders and activists to forgo caution and planning, resorting instead to violent direct action. In fact, lack of planning had become an ideal in and of itself. As part of the shishi's protest against the established order, they did not accept the circumspect, calculated ways of domain and Bakufu bureaucrats. Excessive prudence was suspicious and often perceived as hypocrisy, while intuitive violence was viewed as proof of sincerity and purity of heart.[34] This ideology was not merely expressed in failure to plan ahead, but also in self-destructive recklessness.[35] When some Chōshū shishi raided the British Legation (then under construction) in January 1863, they spent the hours before the operation "drinking heavily and singing loudly" in a pub. The fact that they were indeed able to set fire to the legation was indicative of the inadequacy of Bakufu defenses more than of their own operational capabilities.[36]

The metaphors often used at the time to describe such behavior were "madness" (kyō) and "foolishness" (gu), terms signifying readiness to kill and be killed without thinking twice for the sake of the final goal. A madman, explained one shishi thinker, "must break through the stagnation of established procedure to pursue his own version of reality."[37] Sometimes this madness was quite literal. In late 1862, when a detachment of Tosa shishi was making its way from their domain to Edo, some members wanted to disembowel themselves to push the others to greater heroism, "and were talked out of it only with difficulty."[38] That is not to say that all, or most shishi were indeed insane, and many were quite pragmatic. Often, however, even these pragmatic warriors revered the ideal of madness. Yamagata Aritomo and Kido Takayoshi of Chōshū, both of them future national leaders known for their pragmatism, had also shown their respect to this ideal by adopting the ideogram kyō (crazy), into their own nicknames.[39]

The admiration of "madness" was related to yet another key component of the shishi mindset—the tendency to judge one's actions based on the purity of motives, not objective results.[40] To borrow the catchphrase of Jean-Francois Lyotard, the foreigners' arrival in Japan was akin to an earthquake which destroyed "not only lives, buildings and objects but also the instruments used to measure earthquakes."[41] The forced presence of the strange, threatening foreigners, the advance of public discussion, and the paralysis of Bakufu and domain authorities placed a red glowing question mark over accepted values and social hierarchies. In a rapidly changing world with few certainties, one could never be sure what kind of results a specific action would bring. But even in such an uncertain world, the shishi still had full control over their motives. Therefore, it became natural to celebrate the motive itself, an "intuitive sense of what was relevant and appropriate," as the major way to assess the merit of an action.[42]

Itō Hirobumi, a Chōshū shishi later to become a celebrated national leader, wrote retrospectively that "if one speaks logically of the things [that happened then], they are impossible to understand . . . but emotionally, it had to be that way."[43] If one's state of mind was patriotic, pure, and free of selfish considerations, all actions could be justified a priori regardless of success, failure, or future ramifications. The shishi, therefore, was expected to act out his emotions in both expression and deed: behaving violently when angry, bursting out when feeling righteous indignation, celebrating when happy, and shamelessly crying when sad—all of these reactions signified his sincerity and purity of emotions.[44] The emphasis on recklessness, sincerity, and purity of motives, as we shall see, would retain its viability among military rebels many decades after the shishi ceased to exist.

Comrades: The Shishi As an Organization

The shishi gangs were never organized as a tight-knit national movement, but as one historian noted, they operated within "well-developed networks of communication that linked hundreds of their sympathizers. . . . Information moved rapidly among them in such a way as to make joint action possible," sometimes "within hours" of major political developments.[45] Their speed stood in stark contrast to the slowness of official communication channels between domains, devoid of personal rapport and managed by high-ranking and more cautious officials.[46]

Crucially, the shishi operated along private networks of loyalty, standing in increasing opposition to the official networks of the Bakufu and the domains. Unlike the official networks, premised on strict, vertical hierarchies of rank, the private networks of the shishi tended to be more horizontal, loose, and voluntary. The shishi had leaders, too, but they were respected because of their charisma, dedication, and military prowess, not due to bureaucratic, formal, or inherited status.[47] In such private networks, communication took place by means of *kōgi yoron* (public discourse) and *shoshi ōgi* (private opinionating). The adherents of shoshi ōgi valued direct speech over the structured, polite discourse retainers were expected to use when speaking with their domain superiors.[48] Instead, the shoshi ōgi scene became known for ferocious political debates accompanied by enormous amounts of sake drinking. The wild drinking habits of the shishi, a key component of shoshi ōgi, contributed as well to the blurring of internal hierarchies, hereditary status, and other differences between them.

Joining a group was a voluntary but binding act, and deserters risked the death penalty. The commitment was often sealed with a blood oath, a well-known ritual in classical Chinese and Japanese culture. In a solemn oath before the Gods, the shishi injured themselves, mixed their blood with wine and drank it together, thus cementing their inseparable bond. Accordingly, they usually referred to one another as comrades (*dōshi*), a term denoting equality in a common struggle. Loyalty to comrades, as long as they did not betray the group or the cause, was supposed to be fierce and until death. Communication was often made in encoded language, a security measure contributing its own share to the in-group feeling of comradeship-in-arms.[49]

The shishi groups, however, significantly differed from each other in their organizational patterns. Domainal gangs were shishi groups whose membership came, exclusively or at least overwhelmingly, from a single feudal domain. Domain ancestry was very important for most shishi, and many of the gangs, especially in Edo, were based on such ties.[50] These gangs, however, had a larger ideological commitment, sonnō jōi, which made it easier for them to ally with other shishi gangs throughout the realm. Commitments to domain and lord were important, but only as long as they did not collide directly with that cause.[51] Sakamoto Ryōma, the most famous of the Tosa shishi, wrote in a letter that serving the realm must take precedence over both family and domain.[52] The leader of the Chōshū shishi wrote to his counterpart from Tosa that the cause of sonnō jōi had to be pursued "even if both of our domains are destroyed."[53] These shared ideas made it easier for many shishi to organize themselves in mixed gangs, whose members came from various domains. Such gangs were more common in Kyoto, a shogunal city with relatively weak police force which belonged to no domain in particular.

An important characteristic of the mixed gangs was their relatively loose organization. As individual bravery was deemed more admirable than careful calculation, the ability of the leaders to control their hot-headed activists was very limited, especially when impromptu acts of bravery were considered. When Takechi Zuizan, a Tosa shishi leader who was dominant for a while in the Kyoto mixed gangs, wanted to convince some of his activists not to assassinate a certain nobleman, he had to resort to trickery and tiresome negotiations.[54] The mixed gangs were rarely limited to samurai and were often linked with allies from across the social spectrum. Court aristocrats, affluent commoners, geisha, and priests often worked with the shishi as spies, informers, mediators, and financial patrons.

The two patterns mentioned above, the domainal and mixed gangs, were the prevalent organizational structures of the shishi in their early years. Their transformation into militarized gangs, and finally into the alliance which overthrew the Bakufu, was intimately related to the rise and fall of shishi terror in Edo, Yokohama, and Kyoto.

Heavenly Punishment: The Rise and Fall of the Mixed Gangs

In the early 1860s, Kyoto, Edo, and Yokohama were certainly dangerous cities to live in, if one were a Bakufu official, foreigner, merchant doing business with foreigners, or any Japanese friendly to the Westerners.[55] The thoroughfares and small streets near Edo Castle, Kyoto's narrow alleyways, and Yokohama's international quarters were filled with domainal and mixed gangs of shishi, all bellicose and ready for a fight. They were lurking in inns, drinking and hatching plots, sometimes going around the city and picking fights with random people.[56] It can hardly be realized," recalled the British Envoy, "... what it is ... for years and years, to live under a perpetual menace of assassination. . . . Never to put foot in stirrup without consciousness of impending danger; never to sleep without feeling, as your eyes close, that your next waking hour may be your last, with the vengeful steel at your throat, and the wild slogan of murderers in your ear."[57]

Assassinations, declared as "heavenly punishment" (*tenbatsu, tenchū*), were usually carried out by means of an ambush at a late hour. In most cases, the attacks were designed to have a theatrical impact. The bodies or heads of the victims were exposed in public spaces with placards describing their crimes and the reasons for the "heavenly punishment." This was "terrorism" in the literal sense of the word, a strategy of the weak "designed to harm the enemy by spreading fear, confusion and embarrassment."[58] The American envoy, Townsend Harris, was so stricken with fear, as to "drink himself into a stupor" and hardly set foot outside his quarters.[59] Indeed, in 1860 foreigners were attacked frequently, a violent year that ended with the well-known murder of an interpreter in the American Legation. This operation was launched by a mixed gang named Kobi no Kai (Association of the Tiger's Tail), one of the most active shishi groups in Edo. Foreshadowing the reckless optimism of future assassins, these shishi believed that by assassinating this minor American diplomat, they would "sweep the barbarians out of Japan in one stroke."[60]

It was, however, in Kyoto, not in Edo, that the mixed gangs reached their zenith between 1862 and 1864. There were no foreigners in the Imperial capital, so jōi attacks were not an issue. Sonnō, revering the emperor, became instead the slogan uniting the fragile coalition of Chōshū shishi leaders, masterless samurai from other domains, court nobles, geisha, and other commoners. Despite the emperor's distrust of the shishi riffraff, his famous hatred to the foreigners gave them a feeling, false as it was, that the throne was on their side. At the same time, the support the shishi received from a group of radical court nobles gave them indirect access to the palace. In addition, they were backed by the Chōshū Domain, the main rival of the Bakufu. Shogunal policemen could not enter the Chōshū compound in Kyoto, and it had quickly become a safe haven for shishi from various domains. The Kyoto mixed gangs, loosely led by famous shishi such as Kusaka Genzui from Chōshū and the Shinto priest Maki Izumi, had a ubiquitous threatening presence in the imperial capital.[61]

The shishi, like everyone else, knew well that Emperor Kōmei's wish was to expel the Westerners, and the disregard of this wish by the shogun was considered proof of his disloyalty. Claiming they were merely enforcing the imperial will, the shishi proceeded to "punish" the "traitors" who failed to follow the orders of the emperor. In the spring and summer of 1862, there was certainly no lack of volunteers, as the ranks of the local shishi were swelled by a new influx of samurai. Journeying in southwestern Japan, one of the shishi leaders spread rumors that the Bakufu planned to force the emperor to abdicate. The alarm raised by this news brought many radical samurai from Kyushu to the imperial capital.[62] Their influx had turned Kyoto, formerly a relatively calm community, into a dangerous, terror-haunted town, where, according to a Bakufu police commissioner, "residents were suspicious of each other and closed their doors as soon as night fell. They took their startled escape [upon hearing a sound], be that the hustle of the wind or the cry of the crane."[63]

If ordinary residents of Kyoto felt themselves in danger, then officials had much better reasons to be afraid. In Kyoto, the new terror spree, called by its initiators "a blood festival" (*chimatsuri*), was directed first and foremost toward Bakufu bureaucrats who were deemed guilty of disrespectfulness to the court.[64] Police officials who bore responsibility for the Ansei purges (1858–1859), the wave of government repression against the shishi and other opposition forces, were especially high on the kill list, as well as moderate court officials who advocated some form of rapprochement with the Bakufu. Even dignitaries who supported the shishi were marked for assassination, if they dared to turn back on their commitments. Suspicion of duplicity was adequate enough to sentence a suspect to "heavenly punishment," and even shishi leaders were forced at times to hide from particularly zealous activists. According to Thomas Huber, from August 1862 to July 1864, the period in which the Kyoto mixed gangs were most active, political assassinations were almost a biweekly occurrence, with over seventy assassinations in total.[65]

The first prominent victim of the Kyoto shishi, a court servant accused in spying for the authorities, was murdered on July 20, 1862, in his bathtub by a mixed band of masterless samurai. This servant's head was displayed publically near the river bank, with a placard denouncing him as a "great traitor."[66] The head of another court "villain" was set in front of the residence of the shogun's senior representative in Kyoto. "This head," disclaimed the attached placard, "is extremely unsightly, but we offer it for your viewing pleasure as a token of the blood festival for expelling the barbarians." The hands of the victim were thrown into the compounds of two other court nobles, to terrorize them from further cooperation with the Bakufu. This ghastly theater was highly effective. Pro-Bakufu nobles were terrorized, and some of them preferred to resign in order not to end up as the next target. Radical nobles replaced them in court, working there to protect the shishi and lobby for their political demands.[67]

By mocking and provoking the Bakufu in such a way, the shishi were making a statement of disdain to all established hierarchies, declaring their refusal to recognize any authority but that of the emperor. As they did not really receive orders from the throne, this new situation legitimized them to act freely at their own discretion. Official hierarchies, whether of Bakufu, domain, or even court, did not count any longer—only the private networks of their own gangs. Indeed, the samurai terrorists behaved as if *they* were the government. To finance their activity they relied not only on donations but also levied rice and money ("war funds," or *gunshikin*) from wealthy peasants.[68] When they cut down a woman who participated in pro-Bakufu political maneuvers, they had written on the attached placard that "her confession of guilt reopened the investigation and led to her being severely punished."[69] Terms such as *investigation* and *punishment* evoked the language of authority, emphasizing the shishi's pretense to serve as the legitimate government of Kyoto.

The outnumbered and overwhelmed Bakufu guard, always fearful of being attacked from the shadows, virtually dissolved, its commissioners finding refuge in the surrounding countryside. The disappearance of these "wimpy samurai" (*koshinuke bushi*), as they were mockingly called, left the entire stage open for the shishi and their sympathizers.[70] The Bakufu's attempts to bring reinforcements to Kyoto and even to organize progovernment gangs of shishi garnered only meager results at first, and throughout 1862 the terror of the mixed gangs in the capital continued unabated.

Things began to change only in spring 1863, when the Bakufu forces in Kyoto were joined by a formidable detachment from the Satsuma Domain, eight hundred men strong.[71] The regent of Satsuma, Lord Shimazu Hisamitsu, had finally reached an understanding with the weakened Bakufu and consented to put an end to the scourge of the shishi. Alarmingly for the shishi, this move was supported by the emperor, who was deeply suspicious of the court radicals and their shishi allies. The sovereign, terrorized and furious at the radical court nobles who dared to ally with the shishi and forge imperial edicts at their pleasure, implored Lord Hisamitsu to do something about them.[72] On September 30, 1863, in the dead of night, Satsuma and Aizu forces took control of the Imperial Palace. Barring the gates, they expelled the Chōshū guards and denied entry to the radical court nobles. Sanjō Sanetomi, the head of the pro-shishi court faction, was put under house arrest along with his principal accomplices.[73]

The decisive action of Aizu and Satsuma was a hard blow for the shishi, who in one day had lost their control over the emperor, their most important ideological asset. Sanjō Sanetomi, who was able to escape arrest, withdrew with six of his peers, as well as the Shinto priest Maki Izumi and a large crowd of shishi, to Chōshū. Many of those who failed to leave on time were methodically rounded up by Satsuma and Aizu troops, arrested, and sent back to their domains.[74] Similar purges against shishi were launched in the large domains, particularly Tosa, an important stronghold of the movement.[75] The following summer, on July 8, 1864, the *Shin-sengumi*, the Bakufu's own shishi gang, gave yet another blow to the gangs in the capital, launching a devastating surprise attack on their meeting at the Ikedaya Inn.[76] The situation was only significantly different in Chōshū. There, in the last domain friendly to the shishi, the band of noble and samurai fugitives regrouped at a tea house in the town of Mitajiri. Their gang effectively metamorphosed into a military community, its members living, studying, and exercising together.[77]

This new pattern went hand in hand with a transition in the shishi's method of operation. Members of mixed gangs, whether in Mitajiri or in other places, reorganized in military structures, replacing their old hit-and-run tactics with open mutinies. The outline of this strategy, designed to "seize power for the throne with a small band of 'loyal patriots' by lightning violence," was developed by the Shinto priest Maki Izumi.[78]

In the summer of 1864, the military gangs made their first serious strike. The shishi refugee community in Chōshū, led by Kusaka Genzui and Maki Izumi, attempted to launch an offensive toward Kyoto in order to seize the Imperial Palace. This time, they acted as part of a Chōshū-led military expedition. The shishi, a few hundred in number, were organized as a unit in the Chōshū army, led by a samurai official from the domain. Imprudently, the leaders of this new shishi force ignored all pleas for caution and decided to launch an immediate "heroic" attack on the gates of the Imperial Palace in order to abduct the emperor to Chōshū. "What kind of thing is it to hesitate to attack," the commander of the force said angrily, rebuking his associates for their tepidness.[79] As expected, the commander had his way, demonstrating that ideals such as reckless bravery, characteristic of the mixed gangs, had also not disappeared in the new, militarized gang structure.

Consequently, the shishi suffered a crushing defeat in a battle known as the "Incident of the Forbidden Gate" (*kinmon no hen*). The results were disastrous for the shishi leadership: Kusaka Genzui and Maki Izumi took their own lives, while thirty shishi and their supporters were beheaded, their bodies exposed for three days in front of the palace gates.[80] Yet even this defeat did not put an end to the shishi movement, nor to its ongoing process of militarization.

Takasugi Shinsaku and the Chōshū Wars: The Heyday of the Militarized Gangs

After the Incident of the Forbidden Gate, the mantle of leadership of the Chōshū shishi passed to Takasugi Shinsaku, a middle-ranking samurai whose unusual career had marked a sea change in the history of the shishi movement. At the time he took power, conditions in Chōshū and in the Japanese realm at large had changed dramatically. The defeat of the shishi movement in Kyoto dashed the hope of bringing a radical change in the realm through seizure of the palace. The combined army of Satsuma and Aizu, allied with the Bakufu, was just too strong for the shishi to defeat.

Worse than that, Chōshū, the most radical domain and the shishi heartland, found itself caught in a pincer between the foreigners and the Bakufu. In September 1864, only a few weeks after the defeat near the Forbidden Gate, Britain, France, the Netherlands and the United States decided to teach Chōshū what they considered a long-deserved lesson. Incensed by the shelling of Western ships by Chōshū batteries, the four powers dispatched a punitive expedition and dealt a devastating blow to the domain's army.[81] The leaders of the Bakufu, too, wanted to settle a score with the rebellious domain whose endless provocations, they believed, were driving the country into chaos. Not only had the Chōshū's daimyo and his councilors defied the Bakufu and exposed it to Western retaliations by attacking the foreigners, it had also given shelter to dangerous shishi and radical fugitives from the Imperial Court. And the attack on the Imperial Palace could certainly not be tolerated without punishment. On August 29, 1864, the shogun's emissaries in Kyoto, with Satsuma support, were able to procure an edict from Emperor Kōmei authorizing a punitive expedition against Chōshū.[82]

Takasugi Shinsaku, the most influential military leader in Chōshū since the Incident of the Forbidden Gate, had to devise a strategy to cope with the new situation. With a direct style, a predilection for bold action, and a proven ability to gulp impressive amounts of sake, Takasugi was highly popular among the shishi in and beyond Chōshū.[83] And yet, as a curious, quick-witted, and creative leader, he was much less committed to the expulsion of the foreigners than his predecessors. Instead, he preferred to concentrate on "revering the emperor" and fighting the Bakufu by harnessing the shishi fugitives in new, organized military structures under Chōshū supervision. For that purpose, he was more than ready to learn military science from the foreigners.[84]

The first product of Takasugi's creativity was the Kiheitai, a mixed unit of commoners and samurai led by officers from Chōshū and the shishi gangs. Along with similar Chōshū units, it was organized in line with Western military patterns and armed with modern rifles. Promotion was based on merit, not status, and indeed about 60 percent of its members were peasants and other nonsamurai commoners.[85] Success, however, did not come immediately. In the first Chōshū War (late 1864), Chōshū was too isolated to score a victory, and the domain had to surrender to a combined Bakufu-Satsuma army. The Bakufu forced three domain elders to commit suicide. In addition, it forced Chōshū to expel the radical court nobles, install a collaborationist government, and disband the Kiheitai.[86]

But the Bakufu, slow as usual in understanding the intricacies of the new reality, concentrated in punishing the high-ranking offenders. All the while, they ignored the real leader, Takasugi, who was of lower rank and thus operated "beneath the radar." The shishi leader was therefore able to escape, finding shelter with a sympathetic Buddhist nun. A short while later he reappeared to lead a countercoup against Chōshū's collaborationist government. In doing so, he brushed aside the prudent objections of other commanders, who saw no chance in fighting the overwhelming force of the Bakufu and its Chōshū collaborators. But keeping to the shishi tradition of recklessness, Takasugi started a rebellion on his own, carrying the other reluctant commanders in his wake. And this time, it worked. Within a few months of brilliant campaigning, Takasugi was able to retake the government of the domain.[87] Chōshū and the Bakufu were yet again preparing to fight one another, while Satsuma, the great power of the South, watched the emerging conflict and calculated its future steps.

Chōshū, Satsuma, and the Birth of the Interdomainal Alliance

After Chōshū's defeat in late 1864, the Shogunate's relationship with Satsuma quickly deteriorated. The shogun's advisors saw the victory in Chōshū as an opportunity to impress Bakufu superiority on all intransigent domains. First of all, they imposed highly humiliating conditions on Chōshū, contemptuously ignoring Satsuma's advice to behave more moderately. The arrogant policy of the Bakufu not only humiliated the regent of Satsuma, Shimazu Hisamitsu, and his vassals but also created a strong impression that the shogun had no intention of sharing power with the great lords.[88] After Takasugi and his radicals overthrew the collaborationist domain government, the Bakufu planned yet another punitive expedition against Chōshū, which was announced on March 6, 1865. For Satsuma, this was too much. Many Satsuma retainers believed, perhaps justly, that their domain might be the next victim of Bakufu bullying, and the shogun's decision to import arms and military technology from France gave further credence to this threat. Therefore, a reconsideration of the relationship between Satsuma and Chōshū no longer seemed unreasonable.

As a first step, Saigō Takamori and Ōkubo Toshimichi, Lord Hisamitsu's senior advisors, quietly helped Chōshū to overcome the Bakufu blockade and procure arms from Western traders. This gesture opened the way for further negotiations between the two domains.[89] The task of negotiations was assigned by Takasugi to his right-hand man, Kido Takayoshi, who succeeded him later in the leadership of Chōshū's shishi movement. In February 1866, Kido secretly traveled to

Kyoto to meet with Satsuma's Saigō Takamori. But the deep mistrust between the two domains, who had been bitter enemies, made the negotiations extremely difficult, especially as neither of them wanted to lose face by being the first to propose an alliance.[90]

In that crucial moment, connections forged by the pan-Japanese shishi network could achieve what traditional domain-to-domain negotiations could not. Luckily for both Chōshū and Satsuma, shishi from Tosa and Fukuoka, who had excellent connections in both camps, intervened in the stalled negotiations in order to bring them to fruition.[91] Acting as vital keystones, they were able to bridge the gap between the two sides, locking the connection between them. In this context, the credit had gone especially to Nakaoka Shintarō and Sakamoto Ryōma, two Tosa shishi with rich experience in battles, assassinations, and other adventures.[92] Sakamoto, a naval hand and in later days, one of the most celebrated figures of the period, functioned as Satsuma's secret emissary to Chōshū, brokering rice and arms deals. Subsequently, he and Nakaoka were able to smooth away misunderstandings, explain away insults and facilitate a secret alliance between the two domains.[93]

That was also the birth of the final pattern of shishi organization, the interdomainal alliance, connecting Chōshū, Satsuma, Tosa, and other domains in a common, anti-Bakufu partnership. Its architects were not the daimyo, but former shishi and other lower- and mid-ranking samurai who held key positions in their domains. Their wide-ranging connections in the pan-Japanese shishi network helped them to communicate with greater ease with their colleagues from across the realm. This interdomainal alliance was a hybrid creature: its different segments behaved as leaders and representatives of their domains and lords, but still felt, in the tradition of the shishi movement, as servants of a higher pan-Japanese cause.[94]

The interdomainal alliance was the force for change that finally overthrew the Tokugawa Bakufu and pushed Japan into a new phase in its history. On January 3, 1868, the leaders of the interdomainal alliance, now standing in the top leadership positions of their respective domains, took control of the Imperial Palace in a quick coup d'état. Subsequently, they sealed the gates and prevented all Bakufu supporters, both daimyo and court nobles, from entering. Finally in control of the person of the young emperor, the ringleaders, assisted by their court allies, managed to secure two imperial edicts, one depriving the shogun of his titles, lands, and court ranks, and the other declaring him a rebel and enemy of the court.

The shogun, deprived of the ability to maneuver, was like a fish out of water. Hesitant, crestfallen, and disheartened, he withdrew to Osaka.[95] His forces on the ground were defeated shortly after, in the two decisive battles of Toba and

Fushimi. A civil war ensued, but the army of the shogun was leaderless and disconcerted. Edo fell to the forces of the interdomainal alliance later that year, and the last remnants of the Bakufu army were routed in Hokkaido in 1870. That succession of military-political events was the Meiji Restoration, the momentous change which opened the curtain on the history of modern Japan.

Mimesis: Afterlife of the Shishi

A few years after 1868, the shishi ceased to exist as a distinct group. Those who survived the wars of the Restoration either returned to their domains or served the new government in different capacities. Others, who attempted to cling to their rebellious way of life and defy the new imperial regime, were quickly apprehended, tried, and executed. But the shishi had a much longer career in the Japanese imagination. Over the years, they became cultural heroes and role models for countless intellectuals, patriotic organizations, nationalistic societies, and crucially, military groups.[96]

Partially, this was a result of government action. While flesh and blood shishi were often persecuted, imprisoned, and executed, the Meiji government idolized the fallen heroes of the 1860s in extensive commemoration campaigns. In 1875, only eight years after the Meiji Restoration, the Home Ministry ordered all provinces to commemorate the "martyrs" (jun'nansha) of the Restoration, even if they had violated the laws of their domains. Some even received posthumous court ranks. Starting in 1875, hundreds of shishi from all across the realm were enshrined in Yasukuni, the main worship venue for the nation's war dead. Gradually, there was popular demand from below to enshrine even shishi and rebels executed by the Meiji government, as long as they were motivated by sincere patriotism. The Home Ministry often refused such requests (not without prolonged deliberations), but the public debate engraved the memory of patriotic rebels in the popular mind.[97] At times, local governments valorized local shishi on their own initiative. Even more than the Tokyo government, local authorities used shishi memory as a symbol of imperial loyalty, inadvertently legitimizing disobedient behavior as long as its motives were sincere, patriotic, and pure.[98]

In 1913, in response to a petition from a Diet member, the government agreed to enshrine in Yasukuni even pro-Bakufu samurai who fought against the shishi, as long as they sincerely believed that by obeying the orders of their domains they followed the emperor's will. These people, the government decided, would be recognized posthumously as shishi. However, Bakufu allies whose actions were "completely" against the imperial cause, that is—people who knowingly disregarded the emperor's will, would not be recognized. Here, as usual, intentions were the most important benchmark for recognition. Pure-hearted warriors who revered the emperor were shishi, even when they fought on the wrong side, and even if they killed imperial loyalists.[99]

The emerging popular press joined the fray, often using the term *shishi* and its equivalents to praise contemporary activists for their patriotism.[100] Relatively quickly, the myth of the shishi became popular enough to be used for commercial purposes. Popular biographies of individual shishi were advertised in the press, and in 1885 a multibranch book shop specializing in patriotic literature called itself "Shishi must reads: The Soul of Japan."[101] Decades later, in the 1920s and 1930s, the *shishi* were already part of curriculum in military institutions. The preparatory course of the military academy published a collection of exemplary student essays, some of which praised the "warriors of high aspirations" as a model for inspiration and emulation. Their sacrifice, wrote one student, formed the basis for the "glorious reigns" of Emperor Meiji and his successors. He therefore called his peers, and all other Japanese nationals, to follow in the footsteps of the *shishi*'s selfless loyalty to the fatherland and the emperor.[102]

The fact that the shishi were valorized by the government, the army and the press certainly contributed to their renown and made it much easier for dissidents to follow their example without being branded as traitors. This valorization fused with a process known as mimesis, people who operate in conditions of uncertainty tend to imitate "proven" models that worked in the past. Sociologists Walter Powell and Paul DiMaggio have written that "when goals are ambiguous, or when the environment creates symbolic uncertainty, organizations may model themselves on other organizations. The advantages of mimetic behavior in the economy of human actions are considerable; when an organization faces a problem with ambiguous causes or unclear solutions . . . [mimetic imitation] may yield a viable solution with little expense."[103]

Indeed, rebels in the early Meiji era operated under conditions of extreme uncertainty. The old Tokugawa system had disappeared and could not be restored. The new system was still fluid, untested, and constantly changing. The goals of early Meiji rebels were also ambiguous, unclear, and always controversial. In such ideological, political, and emotional mist, it was easy to cling to the shishi movement, its ideology, and organizational patterns, as a respected and legitimate rebel movement that had won an astounding success.[104]

Ideologically speaking, ideas such as bravery, sincerity, self-sacrifice, disdain for authority, and readiness to brave death without thought and calculation were a major part of the ideological discourse of the shishi. Did Takasugi not score a brilliant victory in winter 1864–1865 when he "leaped" into the dark against the Chōshū collaborationist government, brushing aside the prudent advice of his colleagues? Recklessness worked, and was thus deserving of imitation. In the following chapters, we shall see that rebellions and other acts of radical insubordination were, from 1868 to 1936, all too often, reckless, impulsive, unplanned and poorly coordinated.[105] This is a direct result of the mimesis process.

At the organizational level, the shishi had also offered perpetually attractive models for future rebels, in the early Meiji era and beyond. Private networks centered on a charismatic leader, the sworn brotherhoods united by common ideals, as well as the fluidity of the organizational structure—all would be enduring characteristic of rebellious groups in Japan.[106] In other words, the mimesis of the shishi was one of the most important factors shaping the character of Japanese military insubordination for the entire period covered by this book. Just as the original shishi movement has been born in times of ambiguity, uncertainty, and crumbling political order, so too was their mimesis by rebels in early Meiji. But, and this is crucial, that mimesis would endure long after its original political context had ceased to exist, long after the government in Japan had stabilized, long after the political order had crystallized and became much less ambiguous.

Finally, the shishi movement, by creating the interdomainal alliance that took over the country in 1868, constituted the first chapter in the story of modern Japan. Many former shishi became military officers, and the leaders of the interdomainal alliance were the architects of the Meiji regime and the modern Japanese army. This new political order and its eventual breakdown were the most important condition that molded the development of military rebellion and resistance in the years to come.

Part I
AGE OF CHAOS
1868–1878

JEWEL IN THE PALACE
The New Political Order, 1868–1873

> **The administration of government is not difficult: it consists in not offending the great families.**
>
> —Mengzi

In early January 1868 the defeated former shogun, Tokugawa Yoshinobu, convened the foreign diplomats for the last time at Osaka Castle. "One could not but pity him," wrote Ernest Satow of the British Legation, certainly not a friend of the Bakufu. "So changed he was from the proud, handsome man of last May. Now he looked thin and worn, and his voice had a sad tone." The retired shogun, though, did not really believe that the new leaders in Kyoto would be able to form a viable administration without him. To the question of the British Envoy, "as to the form of government that had been set up at Kyoto, he replied that the *mikado* [emperor] ruled nominally, but that Kyoto was occupied by a set of men who did nothing but quarrel among themselves, anything but govern. Yet he did not appear to claim that he himself possessed any authority."[1]

Yoshinobu was not wide off the mark, and in fact noticed, as early as in January 1868, a permanent weakness running through the early Meiji era: the vertical government structure of the Bakufu had been destroyed, but the imperial hierarchy emerging in its stead was weak, confused and slow to coalesce into permanent governing institutions. Important decisions were not reached through formal state hierarchy but rather evolved as a result of deliberations and quarrels in a small network of leaders. The new government, in other words, presumed to be a vertical hierarchy, but in fact was a horizontal network in which power was shared between equals: the leaders of the interdomainal alliance. "There are many individuals," wrote Iwakura Tomomi, a key figure in the new government, "each with his own reasons to start debates, and of course it is impossible to convince them all. [... but only if] the government was as unshakable as a mountain, would it be able to acquire true authority."[2] Yet neither he nor his friends were in a position to create such "unshakable" authority at the time.

In those times of instability, the mere survival of the new regime depended on a fragile balance between the individuals in power and their respective factions. In an interdomainal alliance, it was all but natural that such factions would be based on domain identity. Among the domains that shared power in the new government, the most important were Chōshū, led by Kido Takayoshi, and Satsuma, represented by Saigō Takamori and Ōkubo Toshimichi. Two smaller domains with a significant role were Saga and Tosa, whose representatives in the government were later renowned as the founding fathers of Japanese liberalism. Another crucial component of the government was the group of court nobles led by Sanjō Sanetomi and Iwakura Tomomi. However, individual leaders allied with others not only according to domain, but also based on ideological, political, and personal preferences, and these alliances shifted quite often.

The frantic attempts to keep the balance between these factions shaped the character of the imperial regime in the first few years of its existence. The situation was delicate, as the interdomainal alliance faced threats right from the start, whether in the form of persistent shishi groups, peasant rebellions, or samurai uprisings. However, as long as the balance between the factions was intact, it was difficult for these rebellious elements to gather support and momentum. In order to legitimize their rule, the leaders of the interdomainal alliance made a crucial decision, to "hide" their power behind the prestigious institution of the emperor, without giving this inexperienced monarch real power. Unforeseen by most people at the time, this decision created a "bug" in the system that precipitated the growth of military insubordination for the next seventy years. That became clear already in autumn 1873, when the interdomainal alliance collapsed, leaving in its wake formidable waves of military insurgency.

Jewel in the Palace: The Japanese Emperor as a Hazy Center

Following the Meiji Restoration, the official ideology placed the emperor at the head of the new hierarchy, as the center of sovereignty. Reality on the ground, however, was very different. In 1868, the Meiji emperor was still a sixteen-year-old youth, unaccustomed to political power. Worse, he did not have any retainers loyal only to himself and had no way of obtaining information from the provinces except through the leaders of the interdomainal alliance and their confederates. As Ōkubo himself admitted, the decision to transfer the capital from Kyoto to Osaka, and later (September 1868) to Tokyo was intended first and foremost to remove the emperor from the closed sanctuary of the Kyoto court. Concurrently, Iwakura, Kido, and Ōkubo reformed the court, purging it of "feminine," redundant, and antiquated elements.[3]

As several scholars have already noted, these measures were intended to masculinize the emperor, replacing his feminine and conservative image with one of an up-to-date, manly, and modern monarch.[4] They had, however, the side effect of diminishing the chances of him ever accumulating real power. The overhaul of the court, the sweeping changes in personnel, even more so the relocation of the capital, radically reshuffled the emperor's existing ties in court, preventing him from utilizing them to form independent networks of information.[5] Effective rule, however, always presupposes a private "telescope," autonomous channels of communication and intelligence.[6] The Meiji emperor did not possess such channels, becoming therefore completely dependent on the leaders around him.

The emperor, in Kido's apt definition, was akin to a "jewel" held by the leaders of the government—well respected, but devoid of real power.[7] As noted by several scholars, his presence on the throne during the crucial years of the early Meiji era shaped the imperial institution as a system with a hazy center.[8] The theoretical authority of the emperor, never disputed by anyone, kept all other factors of power gravitating around him like planets surrounding a star. Therefore, the emperor constituted a universally agreed-on center of power, which prevented the system from disintegrating into its components. This political center, however, was hazy, in the sense that the precise role of the emperor, and more important, his wishes, were often hidden and open to debate and interpretation.[9]

Here, a major "bug" in the new regime came into view, one of the structural problems that allowed military insubordination to grow into a pervasive malaise from the early 1870s up until the 1930s. Every actor in the system had to take the imperial "wish" into account, but as this "wish" was usually expressed in decrees formulated by advisors, marginalized actors could always argue that the emperor was "manipulated" by the people around him. "An unjust imperial edict is not an imperial edict at all and should not be obeyed," wrote Ōkubo to Saigō in 1866 in an attempt to justify their refusal to obey an imperial edict procured by the Bakufu.[10] It is important to note that Ōkubo did not merely say that "an unjust imperial edict should not be obeyed," but rather denied its very nature as an imperial edict, because the emperor's will, by definition, could not be unjust. Indeed, the attempt to "guess" what the person at the hazy center really wanted was to be an enduring element in most cases of rebellion and resistance from early Meiji times until the 1930s.

It might have been that a stronger, more dominant individual could have filled the hazy center with real power, utilizing his enormous symbolic capital to form independent networks of information, building his own structure of power while getting rid of troublesome advisors. But given the tender age, character, upbringing, and immediate surroundings of the Meiji emperor, such a result was less than likely. As Ernest Satow remarked, had Meiji's father, Emperor Kōmei, not died prematurely at age forty-one, things could have been very different.[11] Obstinate, conservative, and implacably xenophobic, Kōmei never failed to utter complaints, drag feet, and even defy the Bakufu openly.[12] Such a man was hardly equipped to rule the country after 1868, but it defies reason to believe that he would have been utilized so easily by the leaders of the new regime as a silent, malleable symbol of power. Kōmei's untimely death and his succession by Meiji were a necessary condition for the formation and development of the Meiji system: an interaction of a hazy center, a weak state hierarchy, and the fragile inter-domainal alliance revolving around it.

Juggling: The Ruling Coalition and the Meiji Reforms

The Meiji regime was established through a series of decisive reforms, all of which rested on two major pillars: the symbolic authority of the hazy imperial center and a consensus between the different components of the interdomainal alliance. First, in 1869, the domain lords "volunteered" to "return" their registers (i.e., lands and population) to the emperor "to distribute or retain them at his pleasure."[13] Then, in summer 1871, the Imperial government dismissed all daimyo and reorganized the domains into administrative prefectures.[14] As the central government was still weak and unstable, both of these decisions could not be reached through top-down orders. Rather, they were made through horizontal cooperation between the leaders of the factions from the court, Chōshū, Satsuma, and some other domains.[15]

But the leaders knew well that their power would only last as long as the factions of the interdomainal alliance continued to cooperate with one another. True, the domains were formally abolished, but they still existed as political units and powerful sources of identity. A high officer from Tosa, for example, recalled that he had "prepared the military force of Tosa for the day when hell breaks loose between Satsuma and Chōshū."[16] Aware of the danger, Ōkubo appealed to his Satsuma clansmen to keep amicable relations with Chōshū. "The two domains," he wrote in an open letter, "turned into one for the sake of the Imperial Country . . . together they are its cornerstone."[17] Therefore, he implored his fellow Satsuma samurai to forgo their narrow interests and cherish this cooperation, lest "the domains fight among themselves, each for its own sake . . . and all achievements of the Restoration are lost. . . . Close your eyes and think about it well. [All past achievements] may come to naught in a single moment."[18]

Meanwhile, interdomainal cooperation, tense as it was, bore substantial fruits. These days were exciting, brimming with a breathless series of reforms. The title of samurai was abolished on August 2, 1869, and the former warriors were renamed *shizoku*, or "samurai families."[19] In 1870 the government allowed all commoners to use surnames in public, a measure followed by the establishment of mandatory education, conscription, and other reforms. The leaders, however, knew they were walking on a tight rope.[20] The reforms were all based on collaboration between the rival factions of ruling coalition. As Ōkubo warned his clansmen, internal discord between these factions could bring all of these efforts "to naught." The Meiji government, formed under the aegis of the imperial throne in the early 1870s, was designed to keep the balance between the factions in order to prevent this dreaded outcome.

Government, Army, and the Chōshū-Satsuma Rift

In the new Meiji order, finally stabilized in August 1871, the emperor was formally the head of state and "imperial rule" was to be assisted by the Grand Council of State (Dajōkan), led by a chief minister.[21] Though his powers were theoretically similar to those held by Western prime ministers of the time, Chief Minister Sanjō, a courtier and a former ally of the shishi, was a weak and indecisive politician. As a result, his office was not invested with significant authority. Decisions were actually made by the minister of the right, Iwakura Tomomi, in conjunction with the leaders of the interdomainal alliance who took the title of imperial councilors. These councilors, along with Sanjō and Iwakura, formed the Imperial Cabinet.[22] To add confusion to an already muddled system, government portfolios were not held by members of the cabinet, but by other officials known as lords (*kyō*).[23] The lords did not sit in the cabinet, the main executive body of the new regime, unless they were concurrently appointed as imperial councilors.

In autumn 1871, not long after the stabilization of the Dajōkan system, prominent cabinet members and other dignitaries left for the West in the famous Iwakura Expedition, led by the minister of the right. The large group of Japanese leaders spent almost a year and a half abroad, and visited the United States, Great Britain, France, Germany, Austria-Hungary, Russia, and other European countries.[24] Meanwhile, from late 1871 to autumn 1873, the absence of so many prominent leaders left Japan in the hands of a caretaker government. In Iwakura's absence, Chief Minister Sanjō remained alone at the top of an increasingly unstable ruling elite. Being weak and indecisive, he found it difficult to constantly balance the different forces in the government. Real power rested with Saigō Takamori, imperial councilor and lord of the treasury, who was also in charge of internal administration. But even the admired Satsuma leader, sick, under pressure from all sides, and emotionally unstable, could only barely balance the system and keep it intact.[25]

The rifts and rivalries of the interdomainal alliance were evident, most of all, in the torturous process leading up to the formation of the early Meiji army. It was certainly paradoxical, for the project of the Imperial Army, from its very inception, presumed cooperation between the restoration domains and beyond, paving the way for national unity. The early Meiji army, however, was one of the major venues of feuds between officers and power holders on domainal grounds.

In February 1871, Yamagata Aritomo from Chōshū, Takasugi Shinsaku's lieutenant in the restoration wars, had told Saigō, his Satsuma counterpart, that as long as the central government was not backed by military force, the Restoration was only "nominal." Using an economic metaphor, he reiterated that the government was "gambling with borrowed money." Saigō agreed, and the two decided to establish a central military force (Goshimpei), composed of troops taken from the three major restoration domains, Chōshū, Satsuma, and Tosa.[26] In his negotiations with his non-Chōshū counterparts, however, Yamagata made it clear that the new force belonged to no domain, but to the central government alone. Soldiers, he maintained, may have to fight on command even the lords of their own domains.[27] On February 12, 1872, the Goshimpei were renamed the Imperial Guard (Konoe), investing them with the prestige of direct service to the emperor. Yamagata, promoted in summer 1871 to deputy lord of war, was the strong man in the ministry, as his lord, an imperial prince, was absent from office most of the time.[28]

However, the Imperial Guard was very difficult to control. It was almost exclusively comprised of shizoku, many of them notoriously unreliable, rebellious, and mutinous former samurai from Satsuma and Tosa. Worryingly, some of them were also involved in attacks against foreigners, endangering Japan's delicate relations with the Western powers.[29] As Kido suspected, it was not easy to secure cooperation between soldiers from different domains, each with its own unique traditions, customs, identity, and dialect.[30] According to Hsien-T'ing Chen, the troops were "deeply imbued with the old *han* [domain] loyalties: they regarded themselves as the soldiers of Satsuma, or Chōshū or Tosa, rather than as the soldiers of Japan, the nation."[31] The Imperial Guard units were only formally subordinate to Yamagata and his Army Ministry but actually obeyed individual imperial councilors who had led them during the restoration wars.[32] In an attempt to cope with this situation, Yamagata proceeded to create another military force, exclusively subordinate to his ministry. These were the military garrisons across Japan, beefed up and augmented by the Conscription Act of October 10, 1873.[33]

In order to appease the restive officers of the Imperial Guard, the government had to tap on the influence and prestige of Saigō Takamori. In October 1872, Saigō was appointed by the cabinet as "leading imperial councilor," commander in chief of the Imperial Guard and field marshal of the army, the only one to hold this rank at the time.[34] Under such conditions, the domainal fault lines in the armed forces were becoming increasingly clear: Yamagata and the Chōshū faction controlled most garrisons across the country, while Saigō presided over the Imperial Guard and the National Police.[35] Thus, coming full circle, Satsuma and Chōshū held again their own independent military forces, exactly replicating the situation which the founders of the Imperial Army had intended to avoid.

Collapse: Korea and the End of the Interdomainal Alliance

It was this situation of fragmentation and severe imbalance that faced Iwakura and Ōkubo when they finally returned from Europe around September 1873. The first issue that they had to tackle, however, was not related to internal reforms but rather to foreign policy. It was this problem which led to the most acute government crisis the Meiji system had known since its inception, to the final collapse of the interdomainal alliance, and to strong outbreaks of insubordination inside the army.

The question of how to respond to Korean behavior, deemed offensive and disrespectful by the Japanese leadership, had been on the agenda of the cabinet for quite a while. Since Japan had embarked on Western-style reforms, the Koreans viewed it as a "lawless state," and their harassment of Japanese traders and diplomats was growing by the day. In response, a high official in the Foreign Ministry proposed that a delegation escorted by an armed contingent be sent to Korea in an attempt to force the kingdom to change its ways.[36] Following a debate, the cabinet decided to accept the compromise proposed by Saigō Takamori: he would personally travel to Korea as an envoy to remonstrate with the Koreans on their evil ways. In a letter, which has been both famous and controversial ever since, he assured that his real intention was to have himself murdered by the Koreans, thus providing an excuse for a punitive war against this country.[37]

It is controversial whether Saigō really wanted a war, but he was certainly under immense pressure by his followers in Satsuma and Tosa to do something about the Korean issue.[38] Restive warriors from both domains were looking for employment in a military campaign. Saigō, in any case pressured to the breaking point, was anxious to find a way to appease his supporters. His proposal was endorsed by the cabinet, and as time wore on, he was more and more anxious to set sail.

When Iwakura finally returned to Japan in early September, Saigō was expecting an immediate decision on his delegation, but as he later wrote with great dismay, the minister of the right took his time.[39] For Iwakura, the Russian threat and the internal problems were much more tangible and important. As Saigō kept on pushing, Iwakura became more and more apprehensive toward the entire idea. He, Ōkubo Toshimichi, Kido Takayoshi, and Itō Hirobumi formed a makeshift "returnees" faction, bringing forward the perspective of diplomatic prudence, based on their experience in the West. More than anything, they argued against a military expedition to Korea.[40]

In his famous "Seven Points Speech," Ōkubo tried to convince the councilors that due to the country's lack of military preparedness and tenuous diplomatic position, an expedition to Korea was imprudent.[41] But he failed. The formation of the "returnees" faction had indeed upset the balance in the cabinet, yet nevertheless it was still controlled by Saigō's allies from Satsuma, Saga, and Tosa. Ōkubo formally submitted his resignation, but diligently outmaneuvered his rivals behind the scenes. In a quick move, famously referred to as the "secret plot" (hissaku), he, Itō and Iwakura formed an alliance with the lord of the Imperial Household. This high courtier, who was close to the emperor, was able to procure an imperial edict postponing Saigō's mission to Korea.[42]

With one stroke, Ōkubo destroyed the precarious balance and toppled the interdomainal alliance like a house of cards. He overturned decisions not by turning to the cabinet, which was supposed to be the omnipotent executive branch. Nor did he take his power from the ministries or the former domains.[43] Outmaneuvering all other power factors in the government, Ōkubo utilized the emperor, the "hazy center," and secured a decision by a ploy not dissimilar to the 1868 palace coup which brought about the Meiji Restoration. His move taught all other actors in the system that, in a country controlled by a hazy center, all calculations could be upset should this center unexpectedly interfere in decision making. Ōkubo, a government official competing with colleagues for power and influence, was certainly not a rebel. But after him, rebels and other disobedient elements would exploit the haziness of the imperial center to have their way in politics, and the result would always be disastrous.

Ōkubo's "secret plot" left the government in tatters. Angry, humiliated, and sicker than ever, Saigō Takamori resigned, returning his government salaries, rewards, and titles, except the rank of field marshal. He promptly left to Kagoshima, the capital of the former Satsuma Domain, in what was seen by all as an angry retirement. His supporters in the cabinet and the government ministries, incensed by Ōkubo's move, resigned as well.[44] The "Occupy Korea" debate was so destructive mainly because one side, that of Ōkubo, scored a knockout victory, causing the other side to lose face. Satsuma and Tosa officers in the Tokyo garrison and National Police, as well as veterans of the Imperial Guard, left Tokyo with Saigō Takamori. Most of them were never to return.[45] Satsuma did not rebel yet, but without "Old Saigō," cooperation between Tokyo and Kagoshima became very difficult. The system became more imbalanced than ever before, and the worst trials were still ahead.

Nevertheless, Saigō Tsugumichi, Takamori's younger brother, did not return to Kagoshima. Instead, he stayed at Yamagata's side, the two men still holding the Army Ministry under their sway.[46] Well before his "secret plot," and certainly after it, Ōkubo lost most of his credibility in Satsuma.[47] It was up to "little Saigō," therefore, to broker between the government and the powerful southwestern domain. Saigō Tsugumichi's sudden rise, born out of the imbalance of the government in late 1873, served as the immediate catalyst for the first major case of military insubordination in modern Japan: the unauthorized Taiwan expedition of spring 1874. A wave of military rebellions would be the result of the breakup of the interdomainal alliance. The Taiwan insubordination, by contrast, would rise from the desperate attempts to hold its broken pieces together.

"BY NOT STOPPING"

Military Insubordination and
the Taiwan Expedition, 1874

**If the lords want to stop Tsugumichi, let them fulfill their duty by
[trying] to stop him, and Tsugumichi will fulfill his duty by not
stopping.**

—Lieutenant General Saigō Tsugumichi, April 1874

On December 17, 1871, two ships from the Kingdom of Ryūkyū were washed
up on the coast of southern Taiwan. The crew of these ships received the same
treatment as all foreign sailors who had landed there since an alleged massacre
committed by European interlopers: they were butchered.[1] Only a handful of
them were able to reach the Qing-controlled part of the island, from where they
were repatriated to Ryūkyū through mainland China.[2]

As Ryūkyū was considered by the Japanese leadership to be a dependency of
the empire, the incident was followed by a two-and-a-half-year debate about
whether Japan should invade Taiwan by itself, or rely instead on Qing China to
punish the wrongdoers.[3] During much of 1873 this debate was overshadowed
by the more urgent Korean question, but after Ōkubo's rise to power in late
October, the hot potato of Taiwan arrived on his desk. An intricate chain of
events, culminating in late April 1874, led to the first important case of military insubordination in modern Japan. The commander of the Taiwan Expeditionary Force, Lieutenant General Saigō Tsugumichi, decided to invade Taiwan
against explicit government orders of which he was well aware.[4] Tsugumichi was
known as a cooperative general. His uncharacteristic resistance to state policy
had important ramifications on the development of military insubordination
in Japan.[5]

"Appeasing Angry Spirits": Ryūkyū and the Satsuma Lobby

To understand Saigō's decision to disobey, one has first to understand why Satsuma potentates reacted so strongly to the murder of the Ryūkyūan sailors. The islands of Ryūkyū had first been invaded by Satsuma in 1609, and by the 1870s it was a tributary state of both Satsuma and China. The Tokugawa Bakufu, which was in any case prone to concentrate specific routes of foreign trade in the hands of selected domains, entrusted Satsuma with Ryūkyū. In practice, the prefecture of Kagoshima dealt with the Qing through the kingdom, and grabbed its own share of the lucrative China trade. Constantly worried about Bakufu and Chinese interference with this substantial source of income, the daimyo ordered the successive kings of Ryūkyū to keep the extent of their "special relationship" with Satsuma secret.[6]

Around late 1871, the Ryūkyū question surfaced in both Japanese and Chinese politics. In August that year, upon the abolition of Satsuma and its replacement with Kagoshima Prefecture, Ryūkyū became a tributary of the imperial Japanese government. The new leaders, at odds over the proper treatment of their new catch, gave Ryūkyū the curious status of domain (*han*)—the only one in a country of prefectures. Still Ryūkyū did not give up its tributary relationship with China.[7] In mid-May the following year, when the Japanese envoy to China heard about the murder of the Ryūkyūan sailors and reported it to Tokyo, it was unclear who among the three patrons of Ryūkyū should bear responsibility: the Japanese imperial government, the Qing government, or the leaders of the former Satsuma Domain.[8] In the event, Satsuma was the first to react.

In summer 1872, rumors about the grisly fate of the Ryūkyūan sailors spread around the prefecture, which was particularly restive at that time. The acting governor of Kagoshima Prefecture, Grand Councilor Ōyama Tsunayoshi, complained that the province was quickly becoming ungovernable. While the local shizoku (former samurai) became increasingly hostile to the government, its representatives, such as Ōyama, found themselves in an unenviable position.[9] Under such conditions, the Taiwan Incident was grasped by Ōyama and some of his associates as manna from heaven. Here at last was an event which they could use to rally shizoku opinion in Satsuma. Ryūkyū was now a domain under the central government and no longer a Satsuma dependency, but it was still temporarily attached to Kagoshima.[10] A prompt reaction to the murder of "their" dependents could bolster Satsuma supremacy over Ryūkyū under the new regime and funnel the dangerous energies of former Satsuma retainers into a foreign military adventure. Ōyama did not hesitate.[11] By August 31, 1872, he had sent the following urgent dispatch to the government in Tokyo: "I, Tsunayoshi, plead for imperial authority to lead an investigation. In order to chastise [the aborigines], I humbly beg to borrow several battleships, destroy their lair, annihilate the ringleaders and spread imperial power across the seas, thus appeasing the angry spirits of the islanders. I humbly beg my request to be granted."[12]

The pressure from the Satsuma lobby was not limited to high-ranking individuals such as Ōyama. There was soon a consensus among Satsuma activists that something had to be done to avenge the Ryūkyūan sailors, but as the hierarchy in the prefecture was muddled, it was unclear on whom this honor should be bestowed. The result was a radicalization of all involved, as Kagoshima officials competed with each other over who would press the central government harder to launch an expedition to Taiwan. It was probably assumed that the first to raise the subject would be the first in line for glorious command posts on the expedition. Therefore, Ōyama and his emissary to Tokyo were immediately joined by other eager lobbyists from the former Satsuma Domain.[13]

The reactions in the central government were more nuanced. Some key figures, especially from the Finance, Army, and Navy ministries, as well as Minister of the Right Iwakura Tomomi, were against the idea of a military expedition.[14] Saigō Takamori, the most senior Satsuma figure in the government, was also unenthusiastic about embarking on a military adventure in Taiwan, though he was finally convinced to support it. In March 1873, however, Taiwanese aborigines robbed and mistreated sailors from Oda. Since Japanese subjects from the core of the empire were now endangered, the position of the proponents of the invasion became stronger.[15]

Prelude to the Expedition:
The Soejima Mission to China

At the end of 1872, a final decision on Taiwan was still pending.[16] Many senior government leaders had traveled abroad as part of the famous Iwakura Expedition, and it was difficult for important decisions to be made in their absence. Hence, the advocates of the invasion and their rivals reached a compromise: to send Foreign Lord Soejima Taneomi, a proponent of the invasion, on a diplomatic mission of inquiry to China. He was ordered to ask the Chinese whether they had jurisdiction over the aboriginal part of Taiwan. If they did, he should demand that they take responsibility and adequately punish the aborigines and compensate the families of the bereaved Ryūkyūan sailors. In case the Chinese did not have sovereignty there, he should ask them whether they had any objections to Japan dispatching a punitive expedition to the southern part of the island.[17]

Soejima and his entourage stayed in China for about four months, from March to July 1873. Most of their time was devoted to diplomatic questions unrelated to

Taiwan. The Taiwan Incident was only mentioned in one meeting, held in August between the councilors of the Qing Foreign Ministry and two of Soejima's aids. The meeting was not recorded by the Chinese, but according to the minutes of the Japanese delegation, the Qing officials were asked whether Taiwan was part of China, and if so, whether the Chinese were ready to punish the wrongdoers and pay compensation. The Chinese side replied that they were not responsible for the "barbarian" part of Taiwan, which was "beyond the pale of civilization." This ambiguous if not careless answer was "understood" by the Japanese as a relinquishment of sovereignty over the "barbarian" part of Taiwan.[18] It is probable that the Chinese officials did not even grasp at the time that their answer left such a dangerous lacuna, as they did not take the Taiwan problem seriously.[19]

Soejima's return to Japan on July 25 reawakened the debate over the invasion of Taiwan. As the Chinese answer was interpreted by the Japanese as a carte blanche to invade southern Taiwan, the main argument against the invasion, the danger of a war with Qing China, seemed less convincing than before. However, the debate on Korea in the summer and autumn of 1873 pushed the Taiwan problem to the sidelines, as the Satsuma lobby, Saigō Takamori, and Soejima Taneomi shifted their attention from Taiwan to the Korean Peninsula.[20] The political crisis in October (described in the previous chapter) resulted in a sweeping overhaul of the government, pushing Saigō, Soejima, and their allies out of national politics.[21]

On the one hand, these developments decimated the Satsuma lobby, as its most important government backers retired from office. On the other hand, they gave disproportionate strength to the few Satsuma leaders who decided to remain in Tokyo. After the retirement of Saigō Takamori and his allies, Satsuma troops were seething with rebellion, and a civil war between Tokyo and Kagoshima seemed closer than ever.[22] Hence, those Satsuma retainers who kept their network connections both in the central government and in Satsuma were urgently needed in the capital. The most prominent of these was Saigō Tsugumichi, Takamori's younger brother, major general and deputy army lord. His position advocating a military expedition to Taiwan had therefore to be treated with the utmost seriousness.[23]

A Hot Potato: The Taiwan Problem under the Ōkubo Administration

Under such conditions the Ōkubo administration could not ignore the pending Taiwan problem when it was raised again before the cabinet in the winter months of 1873–1874.[24] Once again Satsuma officers traveled to the capital to lobby for a military expedition.[25] This time the leaders of the government were responsive. The projected expedition was, after all, dear to many Satsuma retainers. The government leaders thought it best to send at least a few of them abroad, for a while, in hopes of appeasing Satsuma public opinion. It was probably also assumed that the alliance between the government and Satsuma, broken after the debate on Korea, could be restored through such a joint venture.

In a memorandum submitted to the cabinet on February 6, 1874, Ōkubo and the new finance lord, Ōkuma Shigenobu, proposed an outline for a military expedition to Taiwan.[26] In order to solidify Ōkuma's position as the head of the hierarchy, he was put in charge of a new government body, the so-called Bureau of Taiwan Barbarian Affairs (*Taiwan Banchi Jimu Kyoku*), directly subordinated to the cabinet.[27] In mid-March Saigō Tsugumichi himself produced another plan, which implied outright colonization, an idea not uncommon among Satsuma activists.[28] Saigō asked Iwakura and Ōkubo to appoint him as the commander of the expedition and even proposed that discontented Satsuma samurai should settle on the annexed island.[29] Given Ōkubo's delicate relations with his former domain and dependence on Saigō, it was unsurprising that the demand of Satsuma officials to prepare Taiwan for colonization were accepted by the government.[30] Accordingly, Ōkuma began to acquire seeds of European trees for plantation in Taiwan, a clear sign of long-term colonial intentions. The plans were to proceed secretly, most probably so as not to provoke protests from the envoys of the Western powers.[31]

On April 4, Ōkubo and Ōkuma finally decided to appoint Saigō Tsugumichi as the commander in chief of the Taiwan Expedition. The appointment was confirmed by Chief Minister Sanjō and submitted to the throne for final endorsement.[32] An imperial decree immediately followed. Saigō was promoted to the rank of lieutenant general, and nominated Commander in Chief in charge of the Barbarian Part of Taiwan (*Taiwan Banchi Jimu Totoku*), a long title without precedent in the short history of the Meiji army.[33] Two other officers, Vice Admiral Akamatsu Noriyoshi from the navy, and Major General Tani Kanjō from the army, were appointed as his seconds in command.[34] The next day, Saigō received two subsequent imperial edicts, defining his task and scope of authority. The first read:

> Regarding the punishment of the Taiwan barbarians, you, Tsugumichi, are appointed as Commander in Chief of Operations in the Barbarian Part of Taiwan. You are hereby invested with full authority to give rewards and inflict punishments using military and naval force . . . :
> 1. To investigate and punish the crime of murdering our countrymen.
> 2. In case the crime is not compensated, you are to use military force to punish [the guilty parties].[35]

A subsequent order, arriving the next day, defined the scope of the mission, and Saigō's role, in greater detail. This order, it seemed, was formulated specifically to curb the authority of the independent-minded Saigō, as it included a long list of limitations and prohibitions. Above all, he was instructed to concentrate on military operations alone without interfering in diplomacy. "If any protest is lodged by the Chinese government," it was written, "[you] have nothing to do with it. [Such a protest] should be answered by means of diplomatic negotiations conducted by our envoy in Beijing." Furthermore, foreseeing the danger of independent military operations with grave international implications, the order specified that "in any matter related to our relationship with the Chinese government . . . you should appeal to the Imperial Throne for orders."[36]

Saigō, in turn, tried to establish a similar vertical structure of command among his troops. In an undated appeal to his soldiers, probably published in early April, he emphasized the importance of unity and military discipline. The soldiers should always obey their commanders, and while on the ships, adhere to the regulations of the Imperial Navy. Most of all, they must take care to avoid independent actions which might jeopardize the relations of the Japanese with friendly locals. "Do not harm the collective by acting on your own rage," he emphasized, "each one should keep that well in mind. For example, even if you are personally offended, bear it with endurance and do not compromise the important interests of the country." He also warned the shizoku to forgo mutual hostilities, to avoid quarreling, and to "overcome the current tendency of our country for loud rows." Only in that way, he emphasized, "will we not bring the sneer of foreigners upon ourselves." In a force comprising so many former samurai, it was important for Saigō to emphasize that the vertical chain of command, representing the interests of the abstract collective called "Japan," should reign supreme during the expedition.[37]

In addition, Saigō did not dispute his subordination to civilian authorities. In a letter to the expedition's American advisor, he rephrased the official orders. The military force, he emphasized, was not assigned to intervene in diplomacy. In case of difficulties raised by Qing authorities, the commander should "wait for orders from the government."[38] So far, there were no signs of disobedience whatsoever. But the events of April 1874 would dramatically change that.

An Unexpected Turn: The Interference of the Foreign Envoys

In April 1874, while the expeditionary force was waiting in Nagasaki for the final order to set sail, the cards were reshuffled. In spite of Japanese attempts to keep the preparations for the expedition secret, the foreign press in Yokohama had been reporting on the subject for quite some time.[39] On April 9, the British envoy in Tokyo, Sir Harry Parkes, wrote to Terashima Munenori, lord of foreign affairs, and warned him against involving British subjects and ships in any activity "considered hostile by the Chinese government."[40] The Japanese government had many reasons to fear British displeasure, one of which was probably financial: the funds for the expedition were to be transferred through a bank in Hong Kong. British sanctions could place the expeditionary force in severe financial troubles.[41]

While Terashima was trying to deflect pressure from Parkes, another front suddenly opened with the US Legation in Tokyo. Unfortunately for the Japanese government, the State Department ordered the new American envoy, John Bingham, to prevent by any means the participation of US citizens or vessels in the "permanent occupation of the Eastern side of the Island of Formosa." The envoy wrote accordingly to Terashima and advised him that it was his duty to "protest against the employment by Your Excellency's [the Japanese] government of any ship or any citizen of the United States in any military or naval expedition hostile to the Government or authority of China, or to any portion of her people, inasmuch as such employment is expressly forbidden and prohibited by the laws of the United States." The German envoy, Max von Brandt, also tried to talk the Japanese out of the expedition. Along with some other Western diplomats, he warned his counterparts from the Imperial government that the Taiwan adventure was likely to be costly in human life and doomed to failure.[42]

"Not the Tsugumichi of Former Days": The Decision to Disobey

The pressure from the foreign diplomats apparently worked.[43] On April 19 the cabinet met in a partial quorum. Still out of Tokyo, Ōkubo was the most notable absentee.[44] Those assembled, chaired by Chief Minister Sanjō, agreed to postpone the expedition. An urgent telegram was sent to Ōkuma in Nagasaki, and Ōkubo was also brought into the picture upon his arrival in Tokyo. Subsequently, on April 29, he hurried to Nagasaki to speak to Saigō Tsugumichi.[45] A special imperial emissary, Secretary of the Cabinet Kanai Yukiyasu, was dispatched to Nagasaki in order to convey the message in person, and the local governor was ordered to delay the departure of the warships until his arrival.[46]

Prince Iwakura Tomomi, minister of the right, documented the subsequent events in his diary:

> On the 25th, [Kanai] Yukiyasu arrived at Nagasaki harbor. [Ōkuma]
> Shigenobu received and read the letter written by [Sanjō] Sanetomi, and

was informed about the protests of the foreign envoys. Subsequently, he called Tsugumichi and explained the situation. Tsugumichi's reply was that the military spirit was already aroused in the army and the navy, and how could he stop them? At the next day at dawn, Shigenobu went over to Tsugumichi at the camp, and told him to await further orders.[47]

Iwakura noted in his diary that Saigō was furious and promptly refused to follow the orders of the government. As Ōkuma explained to Sanjō later, "the army was brimming with military spirit and there was no way to bring it under control."[48] According to Iwakura's narrative:

> Tsugumichi would not listen. Even at the time of receiving the imperial decree appointing him commander-in-chief, he was afraid that the imperial decision would change midway. . . . Now, Tsugumichi had an imperial command in his hand to launch a punitive expedition without bringing disgrace. Was it possible to discuss such an imperial decree in the government then, when the expedition was on its way and not even a few days had elapsed? Furthermore, should they remain in harbor for more than ten days, the military spirit of the troops may dissipate, so why the hell should they wait for further orders?[49]

Now came the crucial part. Saigō Tsugumichi tapped into the hidden power of the emperor to circumvent established channels of authority. Yet his argument was mixed with practical considerations. The conversation below is based on a report which reached Iwakura and was recorded in his diary:

> Tsugumichi had already received a decree signed by the emperor—he is not the Tsugumichi of former days. Today, even if Chief Minister [Sanjō] comes and hands him an order personally, he will not follow it. To begin with, orders issued by the cabinet are constantly changing, filling the hearts of the people of the realm with confusion and fear. The day of foundation [Meiji Restoration] is not far off in the past. Because the leaders are still not used to handling things, soldiers, though stationed everywhere, are rampant with conspiracies. One wrong move and everything will collapse, never to be brought again under control. Though it would not be difficult for Tsugumichi to placate the troops under his own control, once they are out of these makeshift arrangements, what good would it do? Once the depressed mood is aroused [among the troops] a disaster is to be expected, maybe in a scale no smaller than the Saga Rebellion. He is deeply worried about it.[50]

But according to Iwakura, Tsugumichi had also offered a practical solution:

> If the lords want to stop Tsugumichi, let them fulfill their duty by [try-ing] to stop him, and Tsugumichi will fulfill his duty by not stopping. Would the lords try to force his hand he would still destroy the den of barbarians, hanging the imperial edict around his neck. Only death will stop him. If the Qing Government subsequently opens a conflict, our government may excuse itself, shutting the mouth of the Qing gov-ernment by declaring that Tsugumichi is an escaping pirate who stole battleships.[51]

On April 26 the *Yūkōmaru*, the first ship of the expedition, left Nagasaki Har-bor on route to Amoy. On May 3 it arrived, and Saigō's emissary handed over a formal letter to the local Qing governor. For all practical purposes the expedition was launched against government orders, but Tsugumichi was convinced to delay his own departure until Ōkubo arrived in Nagasaki.[52] However, even Ōkubo, the strong man of the government, could not or did not want to change things. In the evening of May 4, Ōkubo finally met Saigō and authorized the expedition post facto.[53] In an agreement signed by Ōkubo, Ōkuma, and Saigō, the former agreed to take on himself the lion's share of the responsibility.[54] On May 16, almost two weeks later, Chief Minister Sanjō retrospectively authorized the fait accompli through a government order. The leaders of the government agreed that now, with the ships on their way and a formal letter already sent to the Chinese side, the annulment of the expedition would result in substantial embarrassment for the Japanese Empire.[55]

To make sense of Saigō's insubordination, tolerated by Ōkuma and rec-ognized post facto by Ōkubo and Sanjō, it must be understood that Ōkuma, Ōkubo, and Sanjō all shared Saigō's cause.[56] The three politicians and the mili-tary leader agreed on the desirability of invading Taiwan. All of them believed that the expedition was both just and beneficial for Japan. Ōkubo and Ōkuma had no doubt that the Taiwanese "barbarians" had to be chastised, although they did not originally plan to annex Taiwan, and reached that radical conclu-sion only as a result of Satsuma lobbying.[57] As they agreed with Saigō on the righteousness of the cause, neither of them had a deep motivation to stop him. Saigō, to use a German military term, had "escaped to the front." Using the second bug in the Meiji system, the drive for territorial expansion, he disobeyed the government while striving for its own goals, and therefore it was difficult for the same government to restrain or punish him. Indeed, several observers, such as the German envoy Max von Brandt, brushed Saigō's insubordination aside.[58] If Saigō merely did what was expected of him by the leadership, was he being disobedient at all?

Nevertheless, the government did attempt to stop Saigō. Ōkuma gave him an order to postpone the expedition. And a few days later, the same order was personally submitted to him by a special imperial emissary. On April 29, Sanjō instructed Ōkuma yet again, in urgent and unequivocal terms, to stop Saigō and his troops. In his letter he emphasized that there was no way to outwit the foreigners and send the expedition under their nose.[59] Even Ōkuma, an avid supporter of the expedition, initially implored Saigō to follow orders. In addition, Sanjō and Iwakura had viewed the events of late April—both Saigō's insubordination and the reaction of the foreign diplomats—as a failure of their policy and offered their resignations, a move prevented only at the last moment.[60]

Hence the pressure applied by the foreign envoys was strong enough to deter the leaders of the government, at least temporarily, from launching the expedition. However, the counterpressure applied by Saigō Tsugumichi, as the representative of Satsuma, was even stronger. The acute imbalance in the ruling group after the October crisis, combined with the specter of a Satsuma rebellion, empowered Tsugumichi as broker between his domain and the government, making him one of the most influential individuals in the country. Without him, there was no one to connect the government and Satsuma, no way to keep together the broken pieces of the former coalition.[61]

Saigō, however, was neither a political extortionist nor a willing rebel. As argued before, he made sincere efforts to create a functioning chain of command, and even ordered his subordinates to leave all diplomatic issues to civilian authorities. In fact, when approached by Qing officials, he refused to negotiate a settlement and advised his Chinese counterpart to approach civilian diplomats.[62] Nor did he disobey government orders after April 1874. On April 25, however, he was in a very difficult position, peer pressured by other Satsuma volunteers around him. Any retreat might have looked like cowardice and destroyed his status in his home domain. Worse, it might have humiliated him in front of his elder brother, Saigō Takamori, who helped him assemble the volunteer troops. Tsugumichi's warning about a possible uprising of the troops was probably sincere. As the *Japan Daily Herald* commented in an editorial, "Soldiers and ships of war are like sharp tools, dangerous things to handle." Considering the fact that a contingent of former Satsuma policemen was already in Nagasaki, as well as there being incessant petitions of Satsuma and Tosa individuals to participate in the expedition, one could assume that postponement might have been a threat not only for the government, but also for Tsugumichi personally.[63] In a way, he deflected the pressure he felt in the direction of the government.

Finally, in order to justify his resistance to government orders, Tsugumichi utilized the power of the imperial institution, the hidden center of authority at the heart of the Meiji system. He originally received an imperial decree, not an order of the government, to chastise the aborigines in Taiwan. Such a sanctified document could not be revoked by a mere order of the government, not even by the chief minister himself. Tsugumichi's threat to sail to Taiwan against orders with "the imperial decree [hanging] around his neck" was therefore highly symbolic. The decree empowered him. It became almost an amulet of resistance. In many later cases of insubordination, defiant officers resorted to "reinterpretation" of the hidden imperial will as a pretext to resist orders or government policy. In 1874, such a move was unnecessary, as the government did not procure an imperial decree to postpone the mission. The fact that Tsugumichi had received his orders in the form of a decree, and their revocation in a mere government instruction, meant he could utilize the authority of the emperor for his own purposes.

Saigō Tsugumichi and His Army in Taiwan: Diffusion of Insubordination?

Having sorted out the difficulties with Ōkubo, Tsugumichi embarked for Taiwan on May 17, reaching the island five days later.[64] He arrived in time for the grand encounter of the expedition, the Battle of Sekimon (Stone Gate), where the Japanese expeditionary force smashed the armed units of the tribe responsible for the murder of the castaway sailors. After another large battle, Saigō could declare, on June 4, that the aborigines had been subdued. The chief, his son, and fifty-three of his warriors lay dead, some of them slaughtered when wounded, their heads and arms severed and put on display by the victorious Japanese. The leaders of other tribes hastened to surrender to Tsugumichi, who seemed to enjoy the role of the benevolent victor.[65]

As far as discipline was concerned, Saigō repeatedly warned his soldiers not to loot, rape, or harm "innocent aborigines." Indeed, there were much stronger efforts of the high command to prevent atrocities than in any subsequent Japanese campaign in China or Taiwan, and the brutality of the Japanese Army in 1874 could not be compared to its ruthlessness in the First Sino-Japanese War (1895), and certainly not to the mass atrocities of the 1930s. Saigō's orders, however, were not always obeyed, as seen by the way his lieutenants, Major General Tani and Vice Admiral Akamatsu, admonished the troops. In these circulars they decried mistreatment of civilians, particularly Taiwanese coolies, "shameful illicit relationships with women," brawls, and violation of orders. All of this behavior was not surprising in a mixed, heterogeneous force comprising garrison soldiers and bellicose Satsuma volunteers.[66]

The force was also plagued by another, more dangerous kind of insubordination, exercised by enlisted men and junior officers alike. Douglas Cassel and James Wasson, the American military advisors, did not fail to notice that both junior officers and enlisted men often broke ranks and attacked the enemy against orders. In his report to Ōkuma, Wasson complained about the "want of order among the troops. The companies had been properly formed in camp on starting but in a short time the ranks were broken and when the rivers were crossed those that got out first dashed ahead without waiting to reform ranks and the march out soon became a mere race to see who would reach the scene of action first."[67]

Cassel, who had a more comprehensive view of the situation, understood that the root of the problem was less the disobedient troops, and more the sanction given by junior officers to such insubordination. Often they authorized and even led private operations against the orders of the generals. This put the sensitive negotiations with the aboriginal tribes at risk:

> But there was and is one evil which I have ever been unable to prevent, and that is the unauthorized movements of small parties of officers and men into the country. I say, "unauthorized," but after all, in many cases no doubt these expeditions have been undertaken under the orders of the comd'g officers. The first which came to my notice was a party of six officers who penetrated the southern country as far as South Bay [...] As I much feared that anything like a collision with any savages in the South would seriously endanger our relations with Esa, Tok-e-tok [Tokitok—the leader of the confederated tribes—D.O.] and the rest of the people with whom we had made friends, I made the strongest representations that such conduct must be discontinued. But as the officers seem to have little or no control over their men, my advice produced but little effect.[68]

Cassel's confusion as to the question of whether these raids were "authorized" or not touched on the heart of the problem: the junior officers had a larger measure of control over the troops than their seniors. Many ambitious officers staged private, uncoordinated operations, which were diplomatically hazardous and resulted in unnecessary loss of life. When a crucial order not to intimidate a delegation of aboriginal chiefs was enforced, Cassel described it as a "wonder."[69] According to his description, even the decisive battle at Stone Gate began when a Japanese company attacked the enemy after being ordered to retreat. The American advisor, who wanted to draw more enemy forces into a trap, felt that the unauthorized advance at Stone Gate frustrated his plans and bitterly complained to Vice Admiral Akamatsu. Dumbfounded, the admiral replied "that the men had acted without orders." Cassel's distrust of the troops was so great that he advised the Japanese commanders to order an immediate attack: "Otherwise in their discontent at inactivity, they will undertake something foolish which may result in disaster."[70] In other words, the junior officers were in need of constant action. Idleness was likely to make them uncontrollable.[71]

Some of the senior officers had a troublingly similar state of mind. In a memorandum sent to the government (probably to Ōkuma), Major General Tani Kanjō proposed attacking the Qing part of Taiwan, using the aborigines, no less, as Japanese shock troops, settling them in the island's capital and turning the whole of Taiwan into an imperial possession. Later, he wrote, Japan would gradually send "robbers to instigate rebellions" throughout China, form alliances with local forces and use the chaos to take over chunks of the country.[72] This wild fantasy, similar as it was to what Japan actually did in the 1930s, opens a window on Tani's unruly mentality. The Taiwan envisioned by him was not an organized colony but rather a private fiefdom of samurai of his kind (most probably from Tosa and Satsuma), constantly employed in private raids and exciting adventures in mainland China. That one of the expedition's top commanders harbored such ideas makes it small wonder that the illicit private operations of junior officers were tolerated. Saigō Tsugumichi explicitly forbade such behavior in his orders, but his ability to fully control the junior officers was no greater than the government's ability to control him. By 1874 the Meiji army was still unable, even at the level of the officers, senior and junior alike, to turn unruly warriors into obedient soldiers.

Did Saigō's insubordination in late April diffuse downward among the troops, causing the officers to imitate the disobedient behavior of their commander? Indeed, the foreign press in Yokohama was well informed about the events of April 25, with the *Japan Daily Herald* condemning the leaders of the expedition as pirates and mutineers. Yet it is unclear whether most of the troops, except for a handful of insiders, were fully aware that Saigō had defied government orders. Even Vice Admiral Akamatsu, who fleetingly mentioned the government order to stop the expedition in his diary, did not remark on the refusal of his commander in chief to obey it, though rumors were certainly widespread.[73] Still, though we cannot say for sure that Saigō's insubordination diffused downward, the junior officers did disobey orders for reasons similar to his. Just like Saigō, they had grown up with a tradition of direct action, personal bravery, and individual honor. Due to the lack of military resources, it was also difficult to replace them with others, and that gave them leverage over their commanders. Therefore, they could not have been easily punished, even if their superiors had wanted to discipline them in the first place.

End of the Taiwan Expedition

Spring gave way to summer, and the drenching heat of Taiwan took its toll on the Japanese troops. Leaking tents made it difficult for them to sleep at night, and their encampment was often flooded by rain. Food and ammunition supplies were sometimes disrupted, and individual units suffered from hunger. According to several estimates, 70 to 80 percent of the troops, including Saigō himself, had contracted tropical diseases, mainly due to consumption of bad food and water.[74] As Mōri Toshihiko argued, Saigō's militant state of mind withered away during the summer, and he was merely looking for an honorable excuse to leave Taiwan altogether.[75] Under such conditions the plan to settle former Satsuma samurai in the island had to be abandoned.

The reports of Saigō and Tani to Ōkuma betrayed their increasing dismay. The morale of the troops, according to Tani, had become more sluggish as time went by. The forced idleness, he warned, was filling the soldiers with homesickness and turning their valor into weakness. Tani's urgent plea to send a detachment of military police (Kempei) to Taiwan indicates that the discipline among the troops had deteriorated as well.[76] Many of the Satsuma volunteers, considered at first enthusiastic and tough, were tired of waiting for the endless negotiations with the Qing to end, especially when their hopes of being replaced by fresh troops were dashed.[77] Perhaps they believed, as some scholars assume, that the Taiwan Expedition was just a quick preparatory stage for an invasion of Korea and wanted to return to Japan and participate in the "real thing." Maybe, as the editors of Kagoshima Prefecture's official history have written, the volunteers had just "softened," tortured by blazing heat and debilitating disease. In any case, they were impatient and could not understand why they had to linger in Taiwan after the surrender of the aboriginal tribes.[78]

"At that time, many pranks were born of the determination of the *senpai* [older soldiers] . . . to push for an early retreat [to Japan]," recalled Adachi Tsunayuki, a young former policeman who participated in the expedition as a volunteer. "Whenever Commander in Chief Saigō appeared at the main encampment and asked the soldiers how they fared, . . . [the young soldiers] would compete among themselves in climbing the Banyan trees, then look down on the camp and yell as loud as they could: 'Let's—go—back! Let's—go—back! (*modo-rō! modo-rō!*)." Yet, according to Adachi, there was also a faction of soldiers, admittedly much smaller, that wanted to remain in Taiwan.[79]

Finally, in late October, China and Japan were able to reach an agreement on the Taiwanese question. The Japanese agreed to evacuate and forgo all claims to Taiwan, in return for a series of major Chinese concessions. The Qing Empire paid compensation to the bereaved families of the Ryūkyūan sailors, effectively

putting up with exclusive Japanese sovereignty over the Ryūkyū Islands. In addition, the Chinese formally recognized that the Japanese had the right to chastise
the aborigines in Taiwan, and reimbursed Japan for the bridges and other instal-
lations built across the southern part of the island.[80]

Ōkubo, knowing well that Saigō had disobeyed orders only a few months
earlier, did not repeat the mistakes made in April. Instead, he did his best to
secure the commander in chief's cooperation with the agreement, assuring him
that he was the victor, not the humiliated chief of a retreating force. First of all,
Ōkubo himself arrived in Taiwan, followed by Prince Higashikuze, the grand
chamberlain, who personally delivered an imperial edict ordering Saigō to return
with his troops to Japan. The formal edict endorsed by the grand chamberlain, a
court noble close to the emperor, meant that Saigō could not again use imperial
authority to disobey orders. Ōkubo was wise enough to take with him some of
the most radical Satsuma activists, thus effectively preventing the formation of a
hawkish lobby back home.[81] Saigō, his officers, and his troops were honored with
flowery compliments, lavish gifts, and an enthusiastic mass reception back in
Yokohama Harbor. Later, in Tokyo, the commander in chief and his officers were
given an imperial audience. To Ōkubo's surprised relief, these precautions proved
to be unnecessary. Saigō wanted out of Taiwan and obeyed the order to retreat
without difficulty. His soldiers, sick and disheartened, were gradually evacuated.
But, according to one participant in the expedition, some of the troops, believing
that Japan had "surrendered" to China, were disappointed with the agreement.[82]

The Taiwan Expedition: An Omen
for the Future?

At first glance, it is tempting to argue that Saigō Tsugumichi's decision to sail to
Taiwan against orders served as a precedent, paving the way for insubordination
in future years. This conclusion seems reasonable, as prewar Japanese history is
replete with examples of military insubordination, most of which bear significant similarity to Saigō's behavior in Taiwan. Several of these incidents will be
described in the following chapters.

Parallels between events, however, do not necessarily denote causality, and
the claim that Tsugumichi's behavior served as a precedent for the future cannot
easily be proven. As far as I have been able to establish, there is no evidence that
later disobedient officers ever mentioned Saigō as their role model or discussed
the 1874 Taiwan invasion as an example to be followed. The Taiwan Expedition
did contribute to the development of future insubordination in the army, but in
a roundabout way. It prompted a sense of crisis in the military elites, a feeling that

something in the prevailing form of civil-military relations was fundamentally wrong. Yamagata and some of his confidants believed that the expedition was a folly, a private action born out of illicit connections between Satsuma politicians and private army units. The entire campaign, said Miura Gorō, a burgeoning Chōshū commander, was a "lawless war."[83] The military reforms initiated by Yamagata four years later, in 1878, were intended to solve this problem by cutting all ties between officers and politicians. These very reforms, as we shall see in chapter 5, became a major source of military insubordination later on.

But the Taiwan Expedition, by itself, did not shock the elites strongly enough to precipitate immediate change in civil-military relations, and in 1874 Yamagata and Miura were relatively isolated voices. In order to convince the leaders of the government to reform their relations with the army, a much greater trauma was needed—one that evolved gradually in the years following the Taiwan Expedition. Saigō Tsugumichi, as we have seen, used the second bug in the Meiji system to disobey his superiors by striving to achieve their goals faster and more efficiently than they could have done. The official drive for a richer country and stronger army was increasingly interpreted by many in the elites as diplomatic assertiveness and territorial expansion. When someone strived for this goal by a military expedition abroad it was difficult to stop him, even with government orders. Along with the haziness of the imperial center, that was a major bug in the Meiji system that encouraged insubordination from Tsugumichi's days up to the 1930s.

In the 1870s, however, the government did from time to time try to stop officers and officials, less prominent than Tsugumichi, who defied its will by "escaping to the front." The result, as we shall see in the next chapter, was a series of armed rebellions. It was these rebellions, along with the Taiwan Expedition, which precipitated the military reforms of 1878—the basis on which later military insubordination would grow.

FATAL OPTIMISM
Rebels and Assassins in the 1870s

> **And it is worthy of remark, that although each person present dis-liked the other mainly because he or she did belong to the family, they one and all concurred in hating Mr. Tigg because he didn't.**
>
> —Charles Dickens, *The Life and Adventures of Martin Chuzzlewit*

In October 1876, almost nine years after the Meiji Restoration, it was clear to Kido Takayoshi that something was rotten in the kingdom of Japan. Storm clouds were gathering, people were unhappy and evidence of imminent rebellion seemed to be ubiquitous:

> It is my observation, as I survey the current scene, that everybody in the land is dissatisfied, whether he be peasant, merchant, or *shizoku*. Although the country has been quiet for a time, it is not because the people were contented. The only completely satisfied people are the government officials. The people, therefore, are set to revolt. . . . The government . . . had carried on its administration in an arrogant style, without consideration for the hard life in the remote areas, and without regard for traditions which date back several hundred years.[1]

Kido was right on the mark. As the Meiji reforms endangered and at times even destroyed the livelihood of many, it is little surprise that they often encountered resistance: peasants who rebelled against conscription, mandatory education, and the legalization of Christianity; shizoku who could not sit idle while their domains were abolished and stipends taken away; or former shishi who had fought to expel the foreigners only to be appalled by the pro-Western policy of the government.[2] Furthermore, in a new state such as Meiji Japan that lacked any substantial policymaking tradition, almost every important decision in internal and foreign affairs was bound to evoke controversy and even indignation. People dissatisfied with the chosen course of policy resorted at times to insubordination, either in the form of resistance to state policy, like Saigō Tsugumichi on the eve of the Taiwan Expedition, or armed rebellion.

Saigō Tsugumichi's insubordination was secret, and thus could be smoothed over. But when the challenge was public, the government could not show leniency to rebels without compromising its most sensitive ideological tenet: the monopoly over the imperial throne. The emperor's will, presented to the public through a thick layer of ministers and advisors, was subject to competing interpretations by the government and its enemies. When the state and a group of violent protesters both claimed to represent the emperor, it was clear that only one of them could be right as the emperor could not support two contradictory causes at once. In such confrontations, each side tended to view its own struggle as purely righteous and the other's as irrevocably wicked. Each faction claimed to represent the hazy imperial center and accused its rivals of rebellion against the throne. Enemy troops were not considered legitimate soldiers (*guntai*) but robbers, rebels, and traitors (*zokutō/zokuhei*). The campaign against them was called a punitive expedition *(seitō)* not a war *(sensō)*.[3] In such a zero-sum game no compromises could be made, and the fight was almost always to the death.

The first bug in the Meiji political code, the haziness of imperial authority, allowed mutineers to justify their behavior by "guessing" what the emperor *really* wanted. Seeing themselves as loyal subjects who merely followed the will of their hidden sovereign, most rebels used the second bug in the regime's official ideology to "escape to the front," disobeying the government while striving for national, patriotic goals, allegedly in tandem with the imagined imperial wish. The fuel for such "patriotic" uprisings was a particular kind of optimism, whose presence or absence was a major determinant for military rebellion and resistance up to the 1930s. In this chapter, we shall discuss early Meiji rebellions and conspiracies in order to understand the patterns of escape to the front, reliance on the hazy center, and the optimism that mutated them into active rebellions. Finally, we shall see why the failure of early Meiji rebellions gave the government more than half of a century without further military uprisings. However, the reaction of the army to this crisis opened the door for new, no less dangerous forms of insubordination.

Pessimism, Optimism, and Conspiracy in Tosa

Around December 1873, a few months after the October crisis over the invasion of Korea, the leaders of the Tosa shizoku in Tokyo convened a large meeting of their clansmen. Tosa was an ally of Satsuma during the October crisis, and its two prominent leaders, Itagaki Taisuke and Gotō Shōjirō, resigned from the cabinet with many of their followers after the breakup of the interdomainal alliance. The assembled Tosa shizoku debated whether they should return to their Prefecture (the former Tosa Domain) and work against the government in Tokyo, or remain in imperial service.[4] The mood in the meeting was very rebellious, according to available testimonies, and moderate opinions were ignored, marginalized, or otherwise brushed aside.[5]

The Tosa leaders knew well that their fellow retainers were bubbling with discontent.[6] Itagaki and Gotō, who supported peaceful opposition, used their power to prevent a mass uprising, but their control over the rank and file was imperfect and could not prevent smaller-scale violence. In their homes, as well as in the abodes of other hosts, Tosa shizoku intermingled with each other and with retainers from smaller domains.[7] Just like the fencing students who turned to revolutionary activity during the late Tokugawa period, some of the social connections between Tosa warriors gradually "mutated" into antigovernment conspiracies.[8]

This mutation was by no means inevitable, universal, or even large scale. In fact, it happened in surprisingly small parts of the Tosa network, mainly because Itagaki, Gotō and their collaborators redirected much of the violent energy into peaceful channels by creating schools, parties, and other organizations.[9] However, some retainers were not satisfied with petitions and political activity, opting instead for a more radical breakaway from the government.[10] This situation gave rise to two distinct groups of violent activists. Both were almost exclusively comprised of Tosa retainers who agreed that the ills in the Japanese polity had to be remedied through violence. In both cases, it was the October crisis and the demise of the interdomainal alliance that triggered their decision to rebel.

In the absence of direction by well-informed national leaders, the members of these groups were largely fed by rumors. As decisions had to be made in such conditions of uncertainty, the question of whether the rebels' "gut feelings" were optimistic or pessimistic was of large importance. In this context the words *optimistic* and *pessimistic* signify one's assessment of the prospects of changing society by violent direct action. While rebels with a pessimistic state of mind prioritized action against symbolic targets, optimists more often resorted to assassinations of high-profile government figures.

The Pessimistic Rebels: Sen'ya, Miyazaki, and Toda

Miyazaki Misaki, Toda Kūjirō, and Sen'ya Kiyosato, three young shizoku, met each other around the dinner tables of Itagaki Taisuke and other Tosa hosts. Miyazaki and Sen'ya were from Tosa, and Toda, their accomplice, came from

Niigata. Sen'ya, a highly charismatic figure according to available testimonies, was the dominant character among the three.[11] Miyazaki worked for a while in the Treasury and the Development Agency, but resigned after the October crisis. He was homeless, forced to roam between the apartments of sympathetic hosts. His friend, Sen'ya and Toda faced a similar situation and had to rely on the hospitality of Itagaki and other Tosa leaders.[12] Like many of their clansmen they were incensed by the October crisis and the government's failure to invade Korea, but for them it was merely the tip of the iceberg, part of an all-pervading moral, spiritual, and religious decay. The leaders, they believed, failed to block Christianity, eliminate Buddhism, and elevate the pure, authentic cult of Japan's native gods.

Beginning in the mid-nineteenth century, but especially gaining momentum after 1868, many members of the ruling elites began to advocate for the establishment of Shinto, an eclectic collection of nativist cults, as the "authentic" Japanese religion. These circles, orchestrated by the Council for Divine Affairs (Jingikan), denounced Buddhism as a foreign religion associated with the discredited Tokugawa regime. Bad enough in itself, Buddhism was even worse when mixed with Shinto, polluting the "authentic" creed of Japan with syncretism. As the syncretism of Buddhist and native cults was very much the reality in Japan prior to 1868, some Meiji Shintoists began a campaign to destroy Buddhism or at least separate it from their own creed. The government half-heartedly supported these attempts by creating an institution for state-sponsored spiritual ethics, called the Great Teaching Institute (Taikyōin). For a time it seemed to some foreign observers that Buddhism was about to be "swept out of Japan."[13] The government, however, gradually broke with the anti-Buddhist campaign. In March 1872, the Council for Divine Affairs was abolished and incorporated into the Ministry of Education.[14] Few months later, the government decided to move the Great Teaching Institute to the Buddhist temple Zōjōji, formerly the place of worship of the Tokugawa family.[15]

Seeing the government backing down from its professed ideology, Toda, Miyazaki, and Sen'ya acquired a mentality of "escape to the front": an attempt to pursue national policy better, faster and more decisively than their leadership. They decided to independently proceed in the direction of spiritual purification, once professed by the ruling elites themselves.[16] The failure to invade Korea and the leniency toward Buddhism combined into one spiritual malaise, a Gordian knot which had to be cut by direct action of brave warriors. The poverty of the three activists, combined with their highly bleak view of Japanese spiritual decay, gave rise to a profoundly pessimistic worldview that significantly affected their revolutionary strategy. First of all, they rejected the tactics of assassinating individual leaders. Killing one of them is futile, Sen'ya told a fellow clansman. "If you cut one blade of grass in the morning, another one will grow up in the evening."

The leadership was not only evil and corrupt but well established. Kill one leader, and another one would take his place. The only chance for revival depended on the elimination of the entire ruling group simultaneously. Thus, Sen'ya and Miyazaki proposed setting fire near the temporary Imperial Palace at Akasaka. Then, they imagined, all of the ministers and imperial councilors would go out to examine the scene only to be slaughtered en masse.[17]

In addition, the pessimism of Toda, Miyazaki, and Sen'ya discouraged them from putting the assassination of government leaders as their top priority, because that by itself would not cure Japan's spiritual decay. First, the insult to the Japanese gods had to be remedied. Therefore, before setting fire in the vicinity of the Imperial Palace, the trio decided to torch other, more important targets. The first target for destruction had to be the ultimate abomination, the Great Teaching Institute placed inside a "dirty Buddhist temple."[18] Then they planned to target Buddhism by burning the popular temple of Kannon, the Goddess of Mercy, in Asakusa. According to Toda, this place "was the source of pollution, undermining the mentality of 'love the country, respect the Gods' among the people."[19] Only after removing the spiritual pollution, they would set fire near the Akasaka Imperial Palace in order to kill the Imperial councilors.[20]

The plan of Sen'ya and his two friends was impossibly complicated and out of touch with the limited resources they had. As they failed to coordinate with other groups, they did not have the manpower to torch the three destinations at once and had to destroy them one by one.[21] On New Year's Eve 1874, at around 1:00 a.m., Miyazaki and Sen'ya sneaked into Zōjōji temple and set fire to the Great Teaching Institute. The fire soon spread to the main hall and consumed it.[22] The police, initially suspecting the night watchman, gradually realized that disaffected shizoku were responsible and began to hunt them down.[23] Undeterred, Miyazaki, Sen'ya, and Toda decided to strike again one week later. On January 8 they tried to set fire to the Kannon Asakusa temple, but the sudden appearance of a patrolman foiled the plan.[24] The three hapless shizoku understood they were in grave danger of arrest and gave up the unrealistic plan to assassinate the imperial councilors.

Takechi Kumakichi and His Group: The Optimistic Rebels

Before and during the arson operation, Sen'ya and his two friends were also in touch with another group of conspirators led by Major Takechi Kumakichi, a former officer and employee of the Foreign Ministry.[25] A distinguished veteran of the Restoration War, Takechi was sent to spy in Manchuria in preparation for a prospective expedition to Korea. After the October crisis he and his brother were intensely unhappy with the government's decision to abandon the invasion. In Tokyo they came in touch with a group of seven Tosa retainers. Four of them came from the same artillery unit in the Imperial Guards, one was a student, one a navy policeman, and the last a petty official at headquarters. Most of them resigned as a result of the October crisis, though others left service a few months beforehand.[26] Unlike Sen'ya, Miyazaki, and Toda, none of them was a homeless nomad, and it seemed that they were well off economically. According to surviving testimonies, all nine were frequent patrons of taverns and brothels in the pleasure quarters. Most of them were previously connected to the Takechi brothers and to each other.[27]

In his writings, Takechi denounced the Meiji leaders as incompetents who tyrannized the Japanese people, infringed the rights of Tosa and other former domains but at the same time canceled the invasion to Korea under threat of foreign governments.[28] Takechi himself served as a spy and risked his life for the purpose of invading Korea. Coming back, he was shocked to discover that the project had been abandoned and decided to "push" the country back in the right direction by escaping to the front. That, according to his coconspirator, Iwata Masahiko, could have been done only by direct action of brave warriors.[29] The belief that a private network of assassins was the only way to save the larger body of the nation from corrupted leadership was taken almost "as is" from late Tokugawa shishi traditions.

All of these ideological components—resistance to centralized tyranny, loyalty to Tosa, and nationalism—blended together into an intensely optimistic worldview. Japan's problem, Takechi reasoned, was not an all-pervading social malaise but only the tyranny at the top. Furthermore, this tyranny did not even rest with the entire group of imperial councilors. Instead, evil was sustained by one person alone—Minister of the Right Iwakura Tomomi. As the pollution of the state was represented by an individual politician, he was demonized accordingly. "Most cunning and evil among evil men—that is Iwakura," Takechi had angrily told one of his friends. Iwata Masahiko wrote to his parents that Iwakura had foiled the invasion of Korea "out of his own selfish motives." Only because of him, bemoaned Shimomura Yoshiaki, another coconspirator, had imperial authority not been spread across the seas and Japan been humiliated in front of the world.[30]

Takechi had further assured a friend that after Iwakura's death the other leaders would succumb. They were docile people. Bereaved of their wicked overlord, they would have to make accommodations with Saigō and Itagaki and bring them back into the government. The plans to invade Korea would probably be resumed. In such a case, Takechi assured, he would embrace death with an easy mind. According to the later testimony of his friend, Takechi was so optimistic as to be "elated."[31] Indeed, rebels with such an optimistic mindset were much more likely to resort to the assassination of specific individuals.[32] "As long as Iwakura does not pay for his crime, it is hard to speak of any future prospects for the country," Takechi told his brother.[33] The wicked person at the top was the only barrier to that bright future and therefore had to be removed.

Takechi's own assassination plot, similarly to shishi assassination operations in the 1860s, was justified by reliance on the imperial hazy center. That ideological move was partially a product of the tension between Takechi's Japanese nationalism and his loyalty to the Tosa identity. Without the imperial center, there was nothing to bind Tosa with the national enterprise and the rest of the country. However, the center also had to be hazy, otherwise it could be used by the leadership to justify centralized tyranny. This delicate balance was reflected in Takechi's remark to a friend, that after the assassination, they would take Iwakura's severed head and bow to the Imperial Palace.[34] This ghastly offering signified that the emperor was viewed almost as a Shintō god—important, worthy of the highest reverence, but at the same time physically absent.

Over a few days, during the first two weeks of 1874, the conspirators had collected intelligence on Iwakura's daily routine, above all the route he used to take from his home to the palace.[35] On the evening of January 14, around eight in the evening, six days after the failed attempt to torch the Kannon Asakusa temple, they ambushed his carriage in a hidden plot of grass beside the Kuichigai hill. Spotting Iwakura passing by, they jumped on his carriage, shouting, "Kokuzoku!" (traitor). While some of the assassins were holding the horse, one of them stabbed through the carriage, lightly wounding the minister. Iwakura, however, was able to jump out into a shallow canal. He hid himself in the shadowy water, concealed by the dark, moonless night, while his assailants were searching for him in vain in the vegetation nearby. Finally, after they despaired and ran away, Iwakura was rescued and brought to safety by a passer-by. That same night, the assassins buried their swords in Itagaki's garden and hoped for the best. The next day, they were disappointed to read in the *Tokyo Nichi Nichi Shinbun* that Iwakura was merely wounded. Their plan had come to naught.[36]

The National Police, reformed by Ōkubo under the auspices of the new Home Ministry, made extraordinary efforts to hunt down the assassins, and they were able to arrest Takechi and five of his accomplices three days later, on the seventeenth. The leader of the group, it seemed, was unlucky enough to leave a sandal and a hand towel at the crime scene, and that evidence had quickly put the police on his track. The remaining three conspirators were found in the next two days.[37] They were interrogated, tortured, and then brought, fully willing to confess, in front of a special tribunal convened on January 18.[38] The six judges, after hearing the confessions, convicted the defendants of "political crimes" (kokujihan).

Accordingly, they were expelled from the shizoku class and condemned to death by beheading.[39] In the summer of 1874, Toda, Miyazaki and Sen'ya were also arrested. Just like Takechi and his group they were declassed and executed.[40]

The utter failure of these two groups of assassins had shown that in order to change things in the government, personal, shishi-style terror would not suffice. These groups were too detached from each other, their members too individualistic to work together. Though each group was familiar with the general intentions of the other, each was oblivious to the other's plan. Nor could they rally wider support around them. In order to trigger a large-scale rebellion, someone had to inject a substantial dose of optimism into a large number of people, and only a famous leader could do that. Takechi, Sen'ya, and the others proved unwilling or unable to win over such a person. The rebels in Saga Prefecture, however, succeeded in doing just that at about the same time.

The Saga Rebellion: Mass Optimism and Escape to the Front

Saga Prefecture, one of the four domains that brought about the Meiji Restoration, had become increasingly restive since the summer of 1873. In fact, problems in that area were nothing new: its internal administration had been chaotic and inefficient for many years, officials at all levels were frequently transferred and many of them were absent from their duties. In the summer of 1873, in addition to having to deal with tyrannical headmen, the local peasants were hit by a drought, a typhoon, and controversial agrarian reforms. Rural unrest was rampant throughout the prefecture.[41] In July that year an energetic new governor of Tosa origins, Iwamura Michitoshi, attempted to rationalize and centralize local administration, ease the lot of the peasants, and build a strong police force. His efforts, effective as they were, encountered resistance from local shizoku whose vested interests were undermined by the new policies.[42]

After the October crisis and the breakup of the interdomainal alliance, these shizoku, deeply affected by soaring rice prices, taxation of their stipends, and Iwamura's "tyrannical" administration, made their own contribution to the local chaos. Poor and unemployed, they looked for income and opportunities to prove their merit in a Korean expedition. It is not difficult to understand why they were disappointed when the plan was shelved. In addition, they were angry over the resignation of "their" Saga ministers from the government. Used to being ruled only by Saga officials, their local patriotic feelings were offended by the appointment of two "foreigners," Iwamura and his deputy Mori Nagayoshi, to the two most senior posts in their prefecture.[43]

On the evening of January 16, just two days after the attempt to kill Iwakura, thirteen shizoku forced their way into the mansion of Councilor (Deputy Governor) Mori. Faced with the surprised official, they loudly demanded permission to convene an "occupy Korea" meeting in one of Saga's public halls. Mori refused and had abuse hurled at him by his "visitors." The next day more petitioners came in and voiced the same demands in equally rude language. Mori, dismayed and insulted, stood by his refusal and summoned all unwelcome visitors for a criminal investigation. First they submitted letters of apology, but during the hearing they condemned the government yet again in harsh language, denouncing Iwakura, Ōkubo, and their friends who conspired to thwart the planned invasion of Korea.[44] Every loyal Japanese subject, they insisted, was bound by duty to advocate an expedition to the Korean Peninsula.[45]

In a letter to Ōkuma Shigenobu, lord of the treasury, Councilor Mori admitted that the situation in Saga was getting out of control. "Occupy Korea" meetings, he assumed, were being convened despite his prohibitions throughout the prefecture.[46] One participant in the meetings had later recalled with pride how he and his friends wore large hats in order to hide their faces when they passed by the governor's office (from thence they were nicknamed the "hat troops"— *Bōshitai*).[47] Painfully aware of the shakiness of his authority, Mori cautioned the government that trouble with the local retainers might break out unexpectedly at any moment.[48] By February 4, both Ōkubo and Kido had written in their diaries about violent disturbances in Saga: local shizoku had robbed large sums of government money. Yet this localized violence still fell short of a full-scale rebellion.[49]

Just like other restive shizoku in the prefecture, the petitioners who insulted Councilor Mori displayed a mentality of "escape to the front." They did not see themselves as rebels but as loyal subjects. Fulfilling their duties, they were merely pressing for the just cause of chastising Korea, advocated by the government itself only a short time before.[50] Urged by Saga clansmen who returned from Tokyo after the October crisis, local shizoku began to stockpile arms, ammunition, and provisions, ostensibly in order to prepare for a Korean expedition. On December 23, around one thousand shizoku activists gathered to inaugurate the Seikantō (Occupy Korea Party). They sent a petition to the government and volunteered to serve as a vanguard force if the plans to invade Korea were rekindled.[51] A quantitative study shows that most of these activists were younger shizoku and many were local officials. Nagano Susumu suggests that by the end of January the Seikantō had taken over the administrative apparatus of the prefecture. By that time it was not yet an army of rebels but rather a private network poised to "push" the government forward in the "right direction."[52]

But not all shizoku in Saga Prefecture shared the worldview of the Seikantō. Others, mainly older men, retired office holders from the former domain and residents of branch domains remained very conservative and concerned with internal rather than with foreign affairs.[53] These retainers, robbed of both honor and livelihood by the taxation of samurai stipends, annulment of class distinctions, and the conscription edict, had ample reasons to be dissatisfied with government policy. Inspired by petitions of Satsuma conservatives, they appealed to the government to rescind conscription, recriminalize Christianity, and forbid Western dress. In addition, they demanded that the daimyo and the stipends of the shizoku be restored. The organization formed by these conservatives was called the Yūkokutō (Patriotic Party).[54]

Just like their colleagues from the Seikantō, members of the Yūkokutō did not see themselves as rebels. In their petition to imperial authorities they admitted that unrest was spreading throughout the country but insisted that they were on the government's side. Their platform was supposed to protect the emperor from the unrest by striking at the roots of the problem. "For the Imperial Country, for the old domain . . . how can we not be filled with rage?" they asked rhetorically.[55] In addition to the demands to undo Westernization, the members also resisted the scheme to invade Korea. In the future, they stated, Japan should invade not only Korea but also China and Russia. But as long as there were so many discontented shizoku around the country it was still "too early" to send a military expedition abroad.[56] Like their Seikantō competitors, members of the Yūkokutō had stockpiled weapons and ammunition, allegedly in order to "protect" the emperor and their former daimyo.[57]

Members of both Seikantō and Yūkokutō shared some important similarities despite their political differences. Both parties recognized the hazy imperial center, but they interpreted its role in different ways. For the Seikantō the emperor was a potent symbol of nationalist prestige, military prowess, and overseas expansion. For the Yūkokutō he was a symbol of Japanese tradition whose power should bind Saga and the other prefectures into a loose feudal structure.[58] These differences in interpretation notwithstanding, the utmost respect to the imperial institution still bound both parties to the larger collective called "Japan," and none of them went so far as to demand independence for Saga. Despite the pro-emperor rhetoric of the two parties, however, their base of support was too parochial to allow effective cooperation with shizoku from other domains.[59] Joint action was difficult also inside Saga Prefecture, whose shizoku were divided on political, generational, and factional lines.[60] Therefore, some of the opposition activists understood that in order to overcome their differences they must be led by a national figure, a leader respected throughout the prefecture and even beyond. Without such a leader the localized unrest in Saga could never have developed into prefecturewide, coordinated opposition.

In the early days of January 1874, there was a growing sense in the Seikantō that Etō Shimpei, former justice lord, was the right man for the job.[61] Etō, who resigned with Saigō Takamori during the October crisis, was disgusted both by government corruption and the failure to invade Korea.[62] Quick to notice the former justice lord's frustration, representatives of the Seikantō had been pressuring him to return to Saga.[63] The prefecture was replete with protest, they told him, but without a "senior figure" (*senpai*) it would be difficult to enlarge the movement. For Etō, frustrated and humiliated, the call to lead a party in his home domain was probably too tempting to ignore.[64] Fully aware of the danger of a rebellion led by a national leader, Chief Minister Sanjō tried to convince Etō to remain in Tokyo, but the former justice lord refused.[65] Blinded by the support of the shizoku groups back home, Etō developed an excessively optimistic state of mind and began to believe that Ōkubo and the other government leaders would tremble at the mere thought of him going to Saga.[66] On January 13 he finally decided to leave without getting prior approval from the cabinet. The government leaders were worried and uncertain. "Etō Shimpei left secretly for Saga," wrote Deputy Justice Lord Sasaki Takayuki in his diary. "His intentions are unknown."[67]

It is still unclear whether Etō intended to lead a rebellion when he left Tokyo, as the evidence is not unequivocal.[68] Most probably, he himself did not have a concrete plan. As several observers have noted, the former justice lord was furious with the government and certainly planned to challenge it with his own political force.[69] Gradually he became enamored with the idea of leading a formidable, armed faction. Using his new power, he may have hoped to "escape to the front" by pushing for an invasion of Korea, even if that was illegal by government standards. He did not rule out a rebellion against the government, which he had seen as a new Bakufu, but did not meticulously plan for that possibility either.[70]

Etō's return alone, however, could not tip the entire prefecture into rebellion. Localized unrest notwithstanding, the political differences between the Seikantō and Yūkokutō were still too deep to allow organized, joint military activity. Etō's authority was respected in the Seikantō, but the Yūkokutō lacked a leader who could unite it for action. In addition, neither party was eager to fight an all-out war. As self-perceived loyal patriots who merely escaped to the front by striving for national goals, they needed a government provocation to push them over the edge. Only such provocation could allow them to believe that they were not rebelling but merely defending themselves.[71]

With their policy decisions, however, the leaders of the government finally pushed Saga over the top. While Councilor Mori was trying to hold his ground in the prefecture, Chief Minister Sanjō turned to a peaceful strategy. He decided to send a Saga retainer named Shima Yoshitake, a former government official, to mollify the discontented shizoku in his home domain. Shima, a deeply conservative man whose younger brother was a prominent activist in the Yūkokutō, was supposed to strike a chord with the activists of this party. Unintentionally, Sanjō had provided the Yūkokutō with the leader it needed to unite for action.

Meanwhile, Home Minister Ōkubo planned a strong-handed response to the violations of discipline in Saga, thus giving the local retainers a good reason to rebel.[72] On January 28, he replaced Governor Iwamura Michitoshi with his brother Takatoshi, a Tosa retainer known for his quick temper and uncompromising attitude. In fact, Takatoshi had already volunteered for this role a few weeks beforehand, imploring Ōkubo to send him to overpower the discontented shizoku in Saga by sword and execute their leaders. He warned that if action was not taken at once, the rebellion was likely to spread to neighboring prefectures.[73] Five days later, on February 4, Ōkubo and his staff decided to dispatch garrison soldiers in order to aid the new governor in the subjugation of the Saga shizoku.[74] That harsh response might have been influenced by the nervous mood prevailing in the government after the attempt to assassinate Iwakura.[75] Ōkubo and his colleagues were afraid that this plot was merely the prelude for further assassinations and perhaps even an armed uprising. There were rumors that Kido Takayoshi might be the next target, which moved some loyal shizoku from Chōshū to guard his house.[76] This was certainly not the time to be "soft" toward unrest in Saga. As intelligence continued to flow from neighboring regions on military preparations in the prefecture, there were genuine fears of a revolutionary ripple effect.[77]

As it turned out, the new Saga governor, Iwamura Takatoshi, boarded the same ship as Shima Yoshitake, Sanjō's emissary to the Yūkokutō. During the journey, Shima was infuriated by the disdain Iwamura showed to the Saga shizoku. He also heard that Iwamura was planning to "invade" Saga using "Chōshū troops." Upon his arrival in Nagasaki, Shima joined the central board of the Yūkokutō. On February 11, he and Etō met in a village near Nagasaki, and the two men decided to rally their respective parties to protect Saga from "invasion." A local loyalist leader informed Governor Iwamura about the content of the meeting, implying that he should not enter the prefecture: Etō and Shima would rebel only to protect their parties from arrest by the governor's garrison troops, otherwise peace would be kept. Iwamura, obstinate as ever, decided to enter Saga anyway, making violent confrontation inevitable.[78]

The rebellion did not have one commander but two—Etō and Shima, who kept their forces separated most of the time. The rebel armies were ill-led and discipline was extremely hard to maintain. Indeed, in the regulations published after February 18, Etō and Shima emphasized, in the first two articles, that soldiers were "not allowed to cast off their shoes and run away to their homes" or to "disappear without prior notification."⁷⁹ No efforts were made to eliminate a Saga loyalist faction, misleadingly called the "Neutral Party" (Chūritsutō), which spied for Governor Iwamura and supplied his army with invaluable local guides.⁸⁰

The political preparations were as inadequate as the military ones. Etō failed in his belated, half-hearted attempts to revive segments of the interdomainal alliance and obtain military assistance from Satsuma and Tosa. Hayashi Yūzō, a Tosa shizoku close to Itagaki, visited Etō in early January in an attempt to mediate between Saga and the other two former domains. However, he was taken aback by Etō's cavalier attitude and lack of preparedness, strongly suspecting that the militarily inexperienced Saga leader was manipulated by reckless shizoku activists. When Etō displayed confidence that Satsuma would follow Saga in rebellion, Hayashi had to warn him that Saigō Takamori, whom he had met earlier in Kagoshima, would not budge. The Satsuma leader merely wanted to be left alone. Hayashi could not even promise assistance from his own native Tosa. Therefore, he urged Etō to postpone the rebellion, but the former justice lord refused. After the conversation, he finally understood that Saga would have to fight the government on its own.⁸¹

The political preparations of Etō and Shima were inadequate even inside Saga. They had based their common cause on Saga local patriotism but badly miscalculated the strength of this identity throughout the region. Many local shizoku militias cared about their region above all else and were ready to support either the rebels or the government according to the situation on the ground. A typical example was Takeo, a strategic town located on the road connecting Saga and the government port of Nagasaki. Shima, who understood the strategic importance of Takeo, offered the local leader a lucrative command post. The latter negotiated for a while through proxies but joined the government side on realizing its strength.⁸² Even in the branch domain of Ogi, a stronghold of the Yūkokutō, local shizoku were reluctant to fight battles outside of their home territory.⁸³

This lack of preparation reflected a profound diffusion of responsibility. The rank and file put their hopes in the leaders, while the leaders—who joined the rebellion at the last moment—trusted prior preparations by their rank and file. As a result, no one was adequately prepared.⁸⁴ Etō was led to believe, as he promised to Shima on February 11, that the rebellion had already been prepared by the Seikantō activists, but that was not the case.⁸⁵ The preparations, as far as they existed, were hasty, haphazard, and uncoordinated.

However, Etō and Shima worked quickly and by February 16 were able to muster around twelve thousand men, both shizoku and volunteers from a commoner background. The rebellion began on the same day, after Iwamura entered the Saga castle with a few hundred garrison troops with the declared intention of arresting Etō and Shima. The two leaders decided to act first by raiding the prefectural headquarters in the precincts of the castle.[86] Fully anticipating the rebellion, Ōkubo decided not to rely on Iwamura and the other generals, and departed to Saga himself on February 14, taking the political, judicial, and military authority over the prefecture.[87] Later, Army Lord Yamagata departed to Kyushu as well in order to command the forces in person. An imperial prince was appointed as a nominal overlord.[88]

The government force, composed of around fifty-four hundred garrison soldiers, volunteer shizoku, and Imperial Guard units, advanced on Saga by land from the north.[89] At the same time, additional units were landed by the navy at the rebels' rear in Nagasaki, enveloping them in a pincer movement.[90] That was one of the first confrontations between the centralized government army and a domainal shizoku force. Passing that trial by fire, the new centralized army showed remarkable strength and discipline. The garrison units, for example, included soldiers from Saga who had to fight their friends and relatives.[91] Notwithstanding some cases of disobedience, most Saga soldiers in the government army took part in conquering their own homeland by sword and fire. The project of military centralization, designed in 1871 by Yamagata Aritomo, the Saigō brothers, and their colleagues, had certainly shown signs of success.

The rebels' collapse began in the periphery: some of the allies of the uprising deserted, others were routed. On February 22 the rebel army was defeated in the decisive battle of Mount Asahi, and the way to Saga from the north was opened. At the same time, the decision of Takeo to support the government allowed the Imperial Army to attack from the south as well.[92] Realizing that all was lost, Etō ordered the army to disband, hide in the prefecture "like Takasugi Shinsaku after the first Chōshū war" or find shelter in Satsuma. He himself decided to ask for help in Satsuma and then in Tosa. First he headed to Kagoshima, where Saigō Takamori refused to help him. Then he turned to Kōchi, but did not receive any assistance from the leaders of the Tosa opposition either. Finally he decided to return to Tokyo in order to commit suicide but was arrested on April 2 while looking for a boat.[93]

Bereft of leadership, the two parties finally surrendered on March 2, after the city castle had fallen. According to Kido Takayoshi's diary, fifteen hundred to sixteen hundred soldiers had given themselves up.[94] At first, their representatives did not agree to admit that they had fought against an "imperial" army.[95] As far as they were concerned, they respected and revered the imperial hazy center. "My colleagues and I are imperial warriors through and through," said the emissary of the Yūkokutō. In addition, he wanted to surrender to Ōkubo personally.[96] The implications were clear: the Saga war was not a "rebellion" but a struggle between two factions which were both loyal to the emperor. The Saga faction lost and was ready to admit its defeat to the leader of their enemy faction. The emperor existed as a symbol uniting the Japanese polity, but in the view of the Saga rebels he was so hazy as to be almost nonpresent. That was similar to Takechi Kumakichi's view of the emperor as a spiritual symbol that had to be revered, but not obeyed.

The government, of course, could not accept this view and treated its captives as rebels against the sole legitimate authority. It therefore rejected the letter as well as the other demands of the Yūkokutō. The representatives of the party were not allowed to enter the camp or surrender to Ōkubo personally, and had to submit letters of apology outside the gates. In addition, they were required to reformulate their letter of apology, admitting they were rebels and robbers (*zokutō*), not legitimate enemy soldiers.[97] According to the directions of Ōkubo and his appointed judge, Kōno Togama, when arrested the prisoners were to be divided into four categories: ringleaders, senior followers, middling types, and lowly followers. Etō and Shima, to whom the first category applied, were to be pilloried, and their lieutenants from the second category "merely" executed. Rebels from the third category were spared but condemned to penal servitude for life. Members of the last category were punished only by penal servitude of three to ten years. Shizoku of all categories were to be declassed. Commoners who drifted into the rebels' camp were treated leniently.[98]

On April 13, Etō Shimpei, the architect of Meiji criminal law, was finally led to the execution ground. His attempts to explain his motives to the judge, his former subordinate and protégé ("President Kōno, I. . . ."), were rudely silenced. In his diary, Ōkubo wrote that the former justice lord was "ugly and ridiculous" on the day of his death. Before his execution Etō had cried thrice: "Only the gods of heaven and earth [*Kōten Gōdo*] know my heart."[99] By using the equivocal word *Kōten*, which means both "gods of heaven" and "emperor," Etō might have wanted to profess yet again his loyalty to the hazy imperial center as a spiritual and religious symbol. This feeling of being loyal but misunderstood was characteristic of Japanese rebels who harbored a mentality of "escape to the front." At the end of the day, the government fought them only because it did not understand their intentions and could not realize that by rebelling they intended merely to protect the hazy center and advance the government's (and the nation's) own goals.

Etō's severed head was displayed for three days in Tokyo, the ghastly photographs hung in government bureaus and sold in broadsheets for months throughout the town.[100] Yet despite this public humiliation of the former justice lord, the government proved unable to stifle his subversive narrative. In August 1874, Foreign Lord Terashima told the German envoy that Etō's grave was decorated every day with fresh flowers. "This is not a sign of despising the emperor and the government," he said, "but only an expression of a wider movement in Japan through which every extraordinary act is idolized."[101] The respect for fallen rebels, treated by so many as fallen heroes, was a sign of things to come.

The End of Revolutionary Optimism: Saigō Takamori and the Satsuma Rebellion

Between October 24 and 28, 1876, three and a half years after the end of the Saga Rebellion, shizoku uprisings erupted again throughout western Japan. The first group to raise arms was the Shinpūren (League of Divine Wind), a spiritual organization whose agenda focused on opposing the influence of Western culture. Its members had practiced a technique of divination through which they checked whether they should rebel. During the Saga Rebellion the answer was "no." In late 1876, however, when the government outlawed the carrying of swords and allegedly "planned to send the emperor abroad," the group could not sit idle any longer. Such orders, they believed, were a sacrilege to the holiest values of Japanese tradition. The leaders of the Shinpūren asked their gods again whether to rebel, and this time the answer was affirmative.[102]

Like Sen'ya, Miyazaki, and Toda, the Shinpūren had a deeply pessimistic worldview: they imagined themselves a small island in a sea of toxic Western influence. Therefore, they did not choose to assassinate leaders in faraway Tokyo, aiming instead for the Kumamoto garrison, the most available target at hand. As usual with pessimistic rebels, the attack was not intended to achieve an immediate political goal but rather to make a bold spiritual statement through the language of violence.[103] The Shinpūren were connected with another like-minded group in Akizuki (in neighboring Fukuoka Prefecture) and with a former army deputy lord, the Chōshū leader Maebara Issei. All three groups resisted Western influence, idolized the old samurai spirit, and revered the hazy imperial center. The result was a coalition of three charismatic local leaders, none of whom was prominent enough to gather support for a large-scale rebellion. Their poor coordination was certainly not improved by the refusal of the Shinpūren to use telegraph, a technology of Western origins.

First, on October 24, the Shinpūren raided and massacred soldiers and officials in the Kumamoto garrison and the prefectural government headquarters. The small band of two hundred rebels was eliminated after one day, but their call for a general uprising was answered by their Akizuki comrades. The uprising in Akizuki was crushed as well after several days, its surviving members hunted in the mountains for the next month.[104] Finally, on October 26, Maebara Issei declared a general uprising in Chōshū, but his Hagi Rebellion was also a short-lived, ill-planned affair. Unlike the leaders of the two other groups, Maebara had been a national politician, and therefore was optimistic enough to try and reach Tokyo in order to "personally complain to the emperor." After the failure of his farcical attempt to sail to the capital, Maebara's small army of two hundred Chōshū retainers retreated to Yamaguchi Prefecture and was finally crushed near the Hagi Castle town.[105]

The utter failure of these small shizoku rebellions proved yet again that a widespread rebellion could not break out without a coordinated movement spearheaded by a first-rate national leader. Of the three rebel leaders of October 1876, only Maebara Issei had once been on the national stage, and even his following did not come close to that of a really powerful politician like Etō Shimpei. The optimism he was able to generate was therefore limited to small groups of fanatics and could not inspire a truly large movement.

But by late October 1876, more than ever, the suspicious eyes of the government leaders were focused on Satsuma. As we have seen throughout the previous chapter, a rebellion of the strong, bellicose southern domain was the nightmare of the Meiji leaders throughout the 1870s. To a large extent, this fear guided their behavior, and led them, for example, to tolerate Saigō Tsugumichi's insubordination during the Taiwan Expedition. And over this entire tense atmosphere loomed the character of Tsugumichi's elder brother, the immensely popular Saigō Takamori. It was widely believed at the time that a word from him could spark all the discontented shizoku in Kyushu, perhaps even throughout the country.[106]

When the autumn of 1876 gave way to winter, Satsuma was in many senses already a de facto independent kingdom.[107] Many government orders, such as the regulations banning the wearing of swords and the adoption of the Western calendar, were contemptuously defied in Kagoshima. Governor Ōyama Tsunayoshi did attempt to reform shizoku stipends and to redraw some antiquated rules of land ownership, but his half-hearted efforts drew fire from all quarters. They were not as rapid as the central government would have wished but radical enough to evoke the ire of the local shizoku.[108] Kido Takayoshi, a strong advocate of vertical, centralized government, recognized the danger looming from Kagoshima but was impatient about the preferential treatment of this defiant prefecture. A confrontation with Satsuma, he believed, was bound to happen sooner or later, but tolerating its de facto independence was contrary to the principle of vertical government, the core of the entire Meiji project. "We should always adhere to the principle of impartiality," he told a friend, "[and] we would have [no] regrets even if we were reduced to holding nothing more than the single castle of Tokyo."[109]

Unlike the uncoordinated rebels of Saga, divided as they were into two rival parties, the oppositional shizoku of Satsuma were strongly united under the banner of Saigō Takamori. Since June 1874, with their master's blessing, they had been busy forming an alternative army under the cover of an institution called the Private School (Shigakkō). This network of schools was almost a state within a state poised to take over public life as soon as the government faced a debilitating crisis from the outside. Its avowed principles were devotion to duty, morality, and protection of the common subjects of the emperor, particularly when the country was facing a "national crisis." The curriculum taught at the main school in Kagoshima and its numerous offshoots throughout the prefecture focused on military affairs, but other fields such as classical Chinese studies, Western languages, and ethics were also taught.[110] Students were expected to be unflinchingly loyal to Saigō and the school, and in 1876 they were forbidden to look for jobs or study opportunities in Tokyo. Much of the bureaucracy of Kagoshima Prefecture was hopelessly entangled with the Private School, as many mayors and police officers were selected from its ranks.[111]

The tension building between the central government and the quasi-independent state of Satsuma made a large-scale conflict between the two likely, but not inevitable. True, Tokyo wanted to bring Kagoshima Prefecture in line with the rest of the country—Ōkubo called Governor Ōyama to Tokyo in September 1876 precisely to make this point—but the leaders were also afraid to provoke it.[112] Chief Minister Sanjō contrasted Saigō's peaceful opposition with the violent uprising in Saga, writing to the prefectural governors that since Saigō returned to Kagoshima the province had been completely peaceful.[113]

Indeed, a prefecturewide rebellion could not break out without the cooperation of Saigō Takamori, who was extremely reluctant to tread this dangerous path. As Mark Ravina has remarked, only the most strained reading of the evidence might lead one to believe that Saigō planned a rebellion in either 1874 or 1877.[114] In fact, most of his time was devoted to his favorite hobbies: tilling his field, fishing, making straw sandals, soaking in hot springs, playing with children, and hunting in the hills with his favorite dog.[115] In September 1876 he confessed to Soejima Taneomi, former lord of foreign affairs, that his interest in politics had waned and he was content with the role of an observer.[116] In fact, as his sister-in-law testified, he often tried to avoid visitors who came to consult him about politics.[117] That was certainly not a behavior fitting a would-be rebel leader. Some leaders of the Private School were certainly bellicose, but even they were unwilling to act "prematurely," that is, without Saigō's consent. For that reason, the Private School refused to cooperate with the emissaries of the Shinpūren in October 1876.[118]

Yet, if forced to rebel, Saigō was very optimistic about his chances. He believed that upon his return to Kagoshima "the world would be surprised." Indeed, his later behavior signified that he was almost certain that a word from him could start a successful national rebellion.[119] However, just like during the debate on occupying Korea, Saigō was not ready to start a war without a justified reason, and the government had still not given him one. In any case, he ordered the forces of the Private School to be prepared for a "national crisis," probably a war between Japan and another power.[120] If that happened he would be able to "escape to the front," save the nation through his own independent forces and change the government without direct confrontation.

In order to force a reluctant Saigō to spearhead a rebellion, extreme provocation was needed. Unfortunately, such an event happened in February 1877, prompted neither by Ōkubo nor Saigō but by the Satsuma retainers who served the central government. Naturally, they were seen by many of their clansmen in Kagoshima as traitors.[121] These people, led by Kawaji Toshiyoshi, chief superintendent of the National Police, had their bastion in the burgeoning internal security apparatus of the Meiji state. After the retirement of so many officers and patrolmen during the October crisis, Ōkubo and Kawaji reorganized the police according to a centralized French model under the auspices of the Home Ministry.[122] The force got beefed up after the Iwakura assassination attempt and the Saga Rebellion to guard against further uprisings and assassination plots. As Sanjō advised the provincial governors, it was difficult to know whether more assassins were lurking in the dark. A heavy police presence was therefore required all around the country.[123]

In December 1876 Kawaji decided to do something about the ticking bomb of Satsuma's Private School. After consulting Ōkubo and Iwakura, he dispatched to the prefecture ten policemen, former Satsuma retainers led by an officer named Nakahara Hisao. These policemen were given two main tasks: to collect intelligence about the "real intentions" of the Private School, and to convince as many disciples as possible to defect. On his arrival at Kagoshima, Nakahara recklessly disclosed the plan to several friends, two of whom were informers of the Private School. In a conversation with one of them, he may have bragged that if need be he would not hesitate to fight Saigō to the death.[124]

On February 3rd shizoku from the Private School arrested Nakahara and his fellow policemen. Under torture, Nakahara confessed that his "real orders," given by Kawaji himself, were to assassinate Saigō.[125] Another envoy of the government, who had given himself up the next day, testified that Ōkubo was the real culprit behind the plot.[126] The British diplomat Ernest Satow, then in Kagoshima, recorded rumors that after the assassination, "the army and navy would advance on Kagoshima and massacre the followers of Saigō."[127] The "confessions" were printed in many copies, distributed in the Private School and quickly brought to Saigō's attention. Now, as far as he and his closest confidants were concerned, everything became clear. The Satsuma "collaborators" in Tokyo had traitorously planned to kill him.[128]

A few days before Nakahara's arrest, the government attempted to reclaim the arms in Kagoshima's arsenal with a naval operation. Angry students from the Private School discovered the plan and retook the weapons, and the whole city was seething with rebellion.[129] Saigō had witnessed his supporters gearing up for war. Later, he told Governor Ōyama that the premature action of his disciples had left him no choice but to join them. "Had I been there," he said, "I would have probably stopped the students [from the Private School] from violently robbing the gunpowder, but now the die is already cast."[130] Yet, contrary to the common legend, Saigō was not merely "dragged" to war by the fait accompli of his students.[131] Rather, in the two crucial meetings he had with the leaders of the Private School on February 5 and 6, the main issue on the agenda was not the arsenal raid but the proper response to Nakahara's assassination plot. "The plot of Nakahara and his men," he told Ōyama, "completely exposed the secret intentions of Ōkubo and Kawaji."[132] Only because Saigō believed he was about to be murdered by government hirelings had he allowed himself to drift with his disciples to act against Tokyo.[133]

However, just like other early Meiji rebels, Saigō did not see himself as a rebel but as a loyal retainer of the imperial hazy center. To Admiral Kawamura, deputy navy lord, he had written later that the government leaders themselves were traitors and rebels who distorted the will of the imperial throne.[134] On February 5 and 6, the leadership of the Private School decided to send Saigō to Tokyo. The aim of the journey was to issue a formal complaint to the emperor about the Nakahara plot and to "question the government."[135] Saigō rejected the suggestion of one of his advisors to travel alone—he would travel with an army. As a field marshal, he claimed, he had the legal right to recruit soldiers all around the country.[136] The surviving testimonies on the meeting show that despite the meticulous military training of the Private School, a strategy for a rebellion had not been prepared in advance. That was yet another example of diffusion of responsibility. A strategy could not be devised without Saigō, but he decided to join only at the last moment.[137]

Indeed, the faulty strategy chosen was yet another indication of Saigō's lack of preparedness. Without any intelligence on government formations and intentions, without any serious attempt to win over strategic commanders, Saigō and his senior advisors were certain that all localities would accept them with open arms. The prevailing opinion was also that most navy officers were "partisans of Saigō." So great was Saigō's overconfidence that he did not allow commoners and shizoku from outside of the Private School to accompany him.[138] After all, the Satsuma leaders had seen themselves as a perfectly legal investigation team. The governor of Kagoshima, Ōyama Tsunayoshi, had accordingly requested all prefectures and garrisons to let Saigō through, attaching also the confessions of Nakahara and his fellow "criminals."[139] In a conversation he held with Ōyama, Saigō predicted that by March he and his troops would already be in Osaka, as if his journey was nothing but a pleasant hike around the country.[140]

Saigō's coordination with other opposition figures around Japan was just as faulty. In January 1874 he had snubbed Hayashi Yūzō, the Tosa emissary who tried to unite the opposition groups in some sort of interdomainal coalition.

Saigō "took his time" until he agreed to meet Hayashi, refused to commit himself, and only asked whether Tosa troops would be able to march against the Kumamoto garrison. Hayashi accused Saigō of arrogance and insensitivity toward the interests of other domains. Finally, the meeting terminated without results. Saigō declined the requests of the Saga rebels for help, and three years later did not lift a finger for the uprisings in Kumamoto, Akizuki, and Hagi. Unsurprisingly, apart from a few isolated, small-scale rebellions in Kumamoto and elsewhere, very few shizoku came to Saigō's aid when he himself rebelled in 1877.[141]

At the beginning, Ōkubo and the other leaders of the government were not certain that Saigō himself was leading the rebel troops, even while they were dispatching garrison soldiers to Kyushu to deal with the uprising.[142] Saigō was so awe-inspiring, his power so overestimated, that they were reluctant to believe it for a few days. When the truth finally dawned on them, their reaction was shock and dismay. "His suspicions aroused, he [Saigō] threw away his life and ruined his good name on account of momentary rage," wrote Kido in his diary. "How regrettable this is, the most regrettable thing in my whole lifetime."[143] But when the Satsuma army stepped out of Kagoshima Prefecture and crossed to Kumamoto on its way north, that was already too much for Ōkubo to bear. On the nineteenth the government declared Saigō and his troops "violent rebels." Consequently, Saigō was divested of all his ranks and titles by the court, and Kagoshima's envoys to other prefectures were promptly arrested.[144] At that moment, Tokyo's state hierarchy and Saigō's private network were repositioned into a zero-sum game. In such a state, any concession to Saigō would undermine the government's monopoly on the imperial hazy center, the very basis of its legitimacy to rule.[145]

Saigō Takamori's first challenge was to overcome the Kumamoto garrison.[146] The local commander, Major General Tani Kanjō, was reinforced by six hundred of Kawaji's policemen and eighteen hundred soldiers from Kokura.[147] Tani, a Tosa general who fought both in the Taiwan Expedition and against the Saga Rebellion, was adamant about resisting Saigō to the last, and he and his troops had to withstand a seven-week siege in inhuman conditions.[148] However, their resoluteness had frustrated Saigō's original plan—to swiftly march to Tokyo. The old rebel leader and his officers, their plan disrupted, were at odds about their next steps and finally decided to split forces in a disastrous way. The bulk of them were still besieging Kumamoto Castle, while others were trying to block the advance of imperial forces from the north.[149]

Saigō had no naval power to protect his home base of Kagoshima and failed to leave reserve units in the city, another result of ill planning and overconfidence. On March 7 a government force led by Lieutenant General Kuroda Kiyotaka, a former Satsuma retainer, raided Kagoshima by sea. Kuroda arrested Governor

Ōyama, confiscated all ammunition, and spiked the guns.[150] On March 20, the Satsuma army was defeated at the crucial battle of Tabaruzaka and pushed away from that strategic pass. Kuroda and his naval force sailed to Nagasaki at the rebels' southern rear. Being threatened by Kuroda from the south and the main government force from the north, the rebels were trapped in a pincer. As they were engaging larger and larger government forces, bereft of ammunition and supplies, the siege of Kumamoto had to be abandoned on April 19. During the final months of the war, Saigō and his remaining force, pursued by government troops, moved to and fro throughout their home prefecture. Their last stand, on September 24, was on Shiroyama Hill next to Kagoshima. Saigō himself suffered a bullet wound and was beheaded by one of his closest followers.[151] With his death the Satsuma Rebellion ended.

Misguided Optimism: Shizoku Rebellions and Their Failure

The failure of Saigō Takamori and his Satsuma army had several important ramifications. One of them was to rob potential rebels of the optimism required to stage a mass military uprising again. If "Great Saigō" had failed, who could succeed?[152] And as demonstrated throughout this chapter, the decision to challenge the government militarily was closely related to the measure of optimism felt by each successive group of rebels. The desperation of pessimistic rebels, isolated activists such as Sen'ya, Miyazaki Toda, and the leaders of the Shinpūren, led them to strike symbolic or convenient targets. Other isolated rebels, for example Takechi Kumakichi, were more optimistic about their ability to inflict change but could not garner enough support to challenge the government openly on the field of battle. Therefore, they chose to assassinate key politicians. Only a national leader such as Etō Shimpei or Saigō Takamori could generate enough optimism to mobilize a large number of shizoku for a mass uprising. However, this optimism proved in all cases to be misguided.

At the time, however, it did not seem so, and many rebels believed that they had a good chance of succeeding. After all, the celebrated shishi who defeated the Tokugawa Bakufu in the late 1860s also operated at first as isolated guerilla warriors. That close precedent was well known to early Meiji rebels, some of whom were veterans of the anti-Bakufu struggle. Etō Shimpei, for example, compared Ōkubo's government to the Tokugawa Bakufu and later suggested to his defeated Saga rebels that they should hide as best they could, then strike back at the government just like Takasugi Shinsaku and his celebrated unit did in 1864.

However, to their great misfortune, rebels in the 1870s adopted shishi ways, recklessness and lack of planning, without the prior conditions that facilitated shishi success. In 1866 the two strongest feudal domains, Chōshū and Satsuma, managed to overcome their differences and forged the alliance that finally defeated the Bakufu. To a large extent, this alliance was made possible by an inter-domainal coalition of samurai activists who bridged and mediated between the particular interests of the domains. By 1874, however, this network was already fragmented, and many of its former members supported the Imperial Government. As Hayashi Yūzō, the Tosa retainer who tried to mediate between the rebel groups, discovered to his dismay, Saigō Takamori "did not care about other domains" and was too bound to the specific interest of Kagoshima.[153] Satsuma and Saga did not help each other, and each of them fought and lost in isolation.

In addition, one of the most important reasons for the victory of the shishi between 1866 and 1868 was their increasing control over the imperial hazy center, the most crucial symbol of political legitimacy. Only after they took final control over it in January 1868 were they able to rally most of the country around them. Such a fit was possible only because the imperial capital was in Kyoto, a place not fully controlled by the Bakufu. During the 1870s, however, the emperor was in Tokyo, protected by the Imperial Army and far away from the domainal power bases of rebelling politicians.

In such conditions, the attempt to fight the government without tangible plans in typical shishi recklessness proved disastrous. Contrary to the arguments of some scholars, the revolutionary movements in Saga and Satsuma were not really hierarchical or tightly controlled by their leaders.[154] The control of Etō and Shima over their troops was very shaky and quick to collapse. Saigō had immense prestige and a much tighter command structure, but still his control over strategy was almost nonexistent, and he mostly reacted to decisions made by others. This was a result of the dynamics of "escape to the front" that we have seen throughout this chapter. The leaders had no plans for rebellion, as they initially only intended to "push" the government in the right direction, as in the case of the Saga Rebellion, or chastise it through reliance on the imperial hazy center, as Saigō and his disciples initially tried to do. At the same time, their followers could not gather enough optimism to rebel by themselves and spent precious time waiting for the leaders to move. As a result, responsibility was diffused between leaders and followers, a dynamic that left no one in control.

To make things even more difficult for early Meiji rebels, the regime in the 1870s had substantial advantages over the Tokugawa Bakufu. To begin with, the telegraph network installed throughout the country from 1871 to 1873 enabled the government to rapidly respond to local rebellions before they gathered steam.[155] In addition, unlike the Bakufu, the Meiji government did not have to rely on fickle, semi-independent daimyo—it had its own centralized army, equipped with modern guns and artillery.[156] Crucially, the Meiji government also had unprecedented control of the sea. During the 1860s, shishi leaders were able to quickly form a navy and compete with the shogun on naval supply routes. In the 1870s, however, no antigovernmental private network, not even the most formidable rebel army under Saigō Takamori, was able to build its own naval force. The results of that failure were disastrous. Both in the Saga Rebellion and in the Satsuma Rebellion the government could land forces at the rebels' rear, in Nagasaki or Kagoshima, while the rebels were never able to threaten the government supply lines or the imperial capital of Tokyo.[157]

To their misfortune, shizoku rebels from Etō Shimpei to Saigō Takamori could not understand the extent to which the central government had grown military teeth since 1868. Instead of infiltrating the state hierarchy, filling it with their own agents, and thus disrupting the military capabilities of the central government, they resigned with their men and withdrew to their old power bases in the domains. Saigō's advance, for example, was blocked by the Kumamoto garrison, a place controlled almost completely by his loyalists only a few years before. But as his officers had all resigned, this important fortress proved to be the government's most efficient line of defense. If in 1871 the government in Tokyo was militarily weaker than the private networks in the domains, by 1877 the scales had tipped in Tokyo's favor. By that time, efficient resistance could no longer come from the former feudal domains. The rebel leaders of the 1870s were plagued by basic misunderstanding of the weakness of their position. At the end of the day, their optimism blinded them from noticing their own anachronism.

Thus the monopoly of the state over the power of coercion, produced by the defeat of the private networks in the former domains, had become clear to most by 1878.[158] To make this point even stronger, the government demanded "letters of apology" (*shazai*) from every rebel who wished to surrender and perhaps save his own skin. In the letter, he had to admit his crimes against the sole legitimate authority—that of the emperor.[159] The shazai was an important ideological tool—a document intended to ideologically disarm the rebels and make them renounce any claim to the hazy center by forcing them to admit the monopoly of the state. It took time, but after 1878 the prevailing shishi mentality of competing private networks gave way to a monopoly of the state over political violence. Political challenges from the opposition continued, as well as resistance and even individual terror—Ōkubo himself was assassinated by angry shizoku in May 1878—but it took almost fifty-five years until rebels would gather enough optimism to challenge the government with an organized military uprising again.

A chapter in the history of Japanese military insubordination was closed, but another one was soon to open. In 1878, about one year after the end of the Satsuma Rebellion, the leaders of the army decided to reform the armed services in order to cut the horizontal ties between politicians and military units—the malady of the 1870s. Their success opened a hidden door to new, no less dangerous forms of military insubordination—but that would not become clear until much later.

Part II
AGE OF MILITARY INDEPENDENCE
1878–1913

GOLD-EATING MONSTERS

Military Independence and the Prerogative
of Supreme Command

> **I will add, for my part, that in fact many persons with the rank of general
> have the habit of saying ludicrously: "I have served my sovereign . . ." as
> if they did not have the same sovereign as the rest of us . . . but their
> own special one.**
>
> —Fyodor Dostoevsky, *Demons*

On December 5, 1878, a little more than a year after the end of the Satsuma
Rebellion, the Japanese armed forces underwent a fateful reform based on
cutting-edge Prussian military models. Yamagata Aritomo, lord of the army,
and his protégé, Colonel Katsura Tarō, established an altogether new, powerful
body called the General Staff (*Sanbō Honbu*) and placed it directly under the
imperial throne. Yamagata himself was appointed as the first chief of the new
organization.[1] The General Staff was given responsibility for operational planning and wartime command. At the same time, the Army Ministry was denied
control over operations, but given important powers of military administration,
mobilization, budgetary control, and the right to promote, transfer, and dismiss
officers. One month later, in January 1879, a third important organ, the Army
Inspectorate (Kangun Honbu), was established and eventually given control over
military education.[2] Each member of this military trinity, the General Staff, Army
Ministry, and the Army Inspectorate, was to undergo important reforms over
the years, but in essence they remained the core of military command from 1879
to 1945. The new system was accompanied by an imported Prussian construct
later known as the "prerogative of supreme command" (Japanese: *tōsui-ken*; German: *Kommandogewalt*), securing the independence of the armed forces from
any civilian institution apart from the imperial throne.

In the postwar years, the prerogative of supreme command (hereafter, the
"supreme prerogative") became a bogeyman to be blamed for all disasters from
early Meiji to the end of the Pacific War. In a highly influential essay, the popular

novelist Shiba Ryōtarō likened it to a genetic disorder transmitted through the ages, an ominous force quickly growing in power. The soldiers of the Imperial Army, entrenched within their own "supreme prerogative country," became as wild and murderous as the *Pixiu*, a gold-eating monster from Chinese mythology. All the attempts made since the Restoration to control this monster only made it fiercer until it had swallowed the entire body politic.[3] It could also be said that the legendary taste of the Pixiu for gold was a fitting metaphor for the increasingly budget-hungry Japanese Army.

Notwithstanding some disagreements about details, many historians found Shiba's Pixiu metaphor sound and convincing.[4] Kikuta Hitoshi, for example, conveniently explained almost every development in civil-military relations since the Restoration as a "step forward" in the growth of the supreme prerogative, that is, the takeover of Japan by its armed forces. The culmination of this process, according to Kikuta, was the militarist wartime regime of General Tōjō Hideki (1941–1944). If the army was a "state within a state," then the chief of the General Staff functioned as an all-powerful, inaccessible "inner shrine" (*Oku no in*).[5]

There is indeed no doubt that the supreme prerogative, as we shall see again and again in the following chapters, was used by the army as a major pretext to defy the government and resist state policy. That was, however, as several scholars have noted, very far from the original intentions of its initiators in 1878.[6] Yamagata and the other Meiji leaders could not imagine, back then, that the army might overthrow a government, as it did in the Taishō political crisis of 1912, launch independent attacks on Chinese soil as in 1928 and 1931, or stage coups d'état against the government as in 1936. But institutions rarely develop according to the original intentions of their founders.[7] In fact, the ideology later known as the supreme prerogative developed gradually not as a tool of rebellion and resistance but rather as a remedy to timely problems and was transmuted by events and circumstances into a force its originators could not have foreseen.

The Military Reforms of 1878

The Prussian model of *Kommandogewalt* was imported to Japan by officers who studied abroad in German military institutions. One of the most influential among them was Katsura Tarō, a Chōshū officer who had spent most of the turbulent 1870s in the German Empire.[8] In August 1870 he left for France to study military science at his own expense, but could not reach besieged Paris due to the Franco-Prussian War. Giving up his Paris plans, Katsura proceeded to study in Berlin instead. In late 1873 he returned to Japan and during 1874 helped to organize the newly reformed Staff Bureau, the first incarnation of the General Staff. In 1875 he was nominated as the Japanese military attaché in Berlin.[9] In July 1878 Katsura returned to Japan and immediately advocated sweeping military reforms in the Prussian mold. That dictated, of course, at least gradual abandonment of the then-accepted French military model, evoking a resistance by a well-entrenched cabal of conservative officers.[10] Yet, even these officers did not resist the gist of the reforms, the establishment of a general staff subordinated directly to the emperor. By the end of the Satsuma Rebellion, Katsura won the cooperation of key military officials such as Yamagata Aritomo and his deputy Saigō Tsugumichi, a necessary precondition for acceptance of his proposed reforms.[11]

One of Katsura's main recommendations to his superiors at the Army Ministry was to adopt the Prussian separation between two aspects of military activity: administration and command.[12] Or, in military professional terms, he proposed an abandonment of the "monistic" system, adopted from the French Army, in favor of a Prussian "dualistic" one.[13] These terms are a little confusing. Contrary to what one may assume, they do not signify a contrast between a system controlled by a single military authority (monistic) and a system controlled by two authorities (dualistic). Instead, the terms signify the relationship between the twin dimensions of command and administration. The "monistic" French system unified both aspects under the War Ministry while the Prussian Kingdom, and later the German Empire, drew a line between organs of administration and command.[14]

After Katsura's return to Japan in August 1878 the reforms were carried out in great haste. The Army Ministry submitted a formal proposal to the cabinet in early October, and it was formally accepted two months later, on December 5. The decision was to establish, based on Katsura's recommendations, a military triumvirate composed of a General Staff, Army Ministry and Army Inspectorate à-la-Prussia.[15] As in Imperial Germany, each of the components was made directly responsible to the emperor. The new regulations of the General Staff, published on December 25, 1878, and signed by Minister of the Right Iwakura Tomomi, constituted the foundational document of the new General Staff. Articles 1, 2, and 4 were the most important ones:

1. The General Staff shall be established in Tokyo. The army inspectors, Imperial Guard units and all garrisons are under its direct authority.
2. The chief of the General Staff shall be an officer, appointed by the emperor. He shall be responsible for the affairs [of the General Staff] and serve as a military advisor to the emperor.
4. All military and strategic plans and military orders and regulations related to marching, transfer and stationing of troops . . . are under the

exclusive authority of the chief of the General Staff. These plans, subject
to imperial approval, shall be submitted to the army lord for execution.[16]

The right of the chief of the General Staff to report directly to the emperor
was established in article 2, premised on the exclusive command prerogative of
the emperor as supreme commander in chief.[17] That premise was reflected in
a detailed missive dispatched by the army lord to the cabinet on December 7,
two days after the issue of the regulations. The document stated, in the very
first sentence, that "the [Army] Ministry and the General Staff are both placed
under direct imperial authority.[18] Eleven years later, in 1889, the Meiji constitution reinforced that by stipulating, in articles 11 and 12, that the emperor
had the prerogative to command the armed forces (*tōsui su*) and to regulate
their peacetime structure and organization. Shortly beforehand, at one of the
preparatory constitutional conferences, Army Minister Ōyama Iwao had first
referred to the emperor's prerogative of supreme command by using the term
tōsui no ken, almost a precise translation of the German *Kommandogewalt*.[19] In
the future, this term, shortened to *tōsui ken*, the prerogative of supreme command, acquired notoriety and became fixed in Japanese military, political, and
constitutional discourse as a keyword signifying the independence of the army
from civilian control.

Katsura and Yamagata did not adopt the Prussian Military Cabinet, a palace
organ with crucial power over military promotions and appointments.[20] Instead,
the Army Ministry was allowed to retain this key authority over military personnel. It had the right to appoint, promote, and dismiss military officeholders,
with the important exception of General Staff officers.[21] Since 1888, the army
minister could also report directly to the throne, a practice that quickly became
a routine.[22]

In January 1879, one month after the establishment of the General Staff, the
Army Ministry issued regulations for a new Army Inspectorate. In 1887, based on
the proposals of the German military advisor Jacob Meckel, the inspectorate was
unified under an individual commander and put in charge of the crucial sphere of
military training and education. The powerful commander of the new inspectorate, called the inspector general of military education (*rikugun kyōiku sōkan*), was
considered the equal of the army minister and the chief of the General Staff. He,
too, possessed the right to directly report to the emperor. The ubiquitous Yamagata
Aritomo was appointed as the first inspector general, to endow the new post with
his personal authority, and maybe to ensure control over this crucial component of
the military establishment. Together with the chief of the general staff and the army
minister, the inspector general became a pillar of the powerful triumvirate of the
Japanese Army, a system retained, with certain changes, up to 1945.[23]

The Elephant in the Room: Explaining the Reforms, Overcoming Resistance

Ironically the 1878 reforms, destined to gradually remove the Japanese armed forces from the orbit of civilian control, passed with relatively little resistance. According to the *Meiji Tennō Ki*, an official chronicle of the Meiji reign, the emperor himself had some misgivings. What might happen, he worried, if in the future the Army Ministry and the General Staff quarrel with each other? However, the emperor was quick to succumb. His closest associate, Minister of the Right Iwakura, endorsed the proposals, and Meiji himself was hardly able to resist his senior advisors even in matters related to his own personal life—much less could he dispute professional recommendations on questions of military organization.[24] From the juxtaposition of the *Meiji Tennō ki* and other sources we know that the proposals were submitted to the emperor in the course of a torturous tour to western Japan, during which he suffered from bad weather, difficult road conditions, and a breathless schedule.[25] Under such circumstances, even a stronger ruler could hardly have been in a position to engage in serious discussions on the intricacies of military organization.

It also helped that the military establishment unanimously endorsed the proposals. That was relatively rare, as the late 1870s and the 1880s were characterized in fierce and often venomous intramilitary debates. Even Yamagata's bitter rivals Miura Gorō, Tani Kanjō, Soga Sukenori, and Torio Koyata (known as the "four generals"), did not oppose the proposals of October 1878.[26] They and their followers worked hard to retain French methods of training and field organization, called for a small, defensive army and resisted military expansion. They resisted almost everything proposed by Yamagata in the 1880s—except the establishment of the General Staff. In fact, Yamagata made considerable efforts to implore, indeed, virtually beg, General Torio Koyata, his archrival, to return to Tokyo from his vacation (in fact an angry retirement) so as to be able to participate in the reforms.[27] Another rival of Yamagata, Lieutenant General Tani Kanjō, was urgently summoned to the capital as well.[28] Had they resisted the reforms, it defies reason to believe that Yamagata would have summoned them so energetically to Tokyo.

The available evidence indicates that most potentates in the civilian government did not oppose Yamagata's proposals either. Itō Hirobumi, Ōkubo's successor as Home Lord and the most influential man in the government, was a particularly strong supporter. In a letter to one of his closest political collaborators, he agreed with the army's position that the reforms "would advance the future military power of our country." In fact, as the letter suggested, Itō was aware of the proposals two months before they were formally endorsed and opened informal negotiations with the Treasury in order to obtain the necessary funds. Ōkuma, lord of the treasury, agreed to meet the special expenditure by increasing the taxation on alcoholic beverages.[29]

The correspondence of key government leaders suggests that they were panicked by the mutiny in the Imperial Guard in August 1878 (known as the Takebashi Incident, more on which later) and sought a quick solution to suppress unrest inside the army. The recent assassination of Ōkubo and the continued agitation of the Popular Rights movement contributed to this atmosphere of panic. Reforms in the mutinous army were needed, and to bolster discipline by creating a direct link between the army and the emperor seemed a logical thing to do. The long-term repercussions of the reforms were hardly considered and could hardly be conceived at the time, especially by busy leaders with a mountain of other pressing duties piling up on their desks. Itō, especially, had seen the reforms as a strictly military matter, a timely measure to consolidate the army that had little relevance to the civilian government.[30] Therefore, when the emperor finally returned to the capital in early November, he encountered a consensus of all leaders, civilian and military alike. Under such conditions, it was inadmissible for him to raise further objections.[31]

The General Staff reforms, hastily accepted in autumn 1878, had already become a binding tradition in the 1880s, when the Meiji constitution was being drafted by Itō Hirobumi and his advisors. The army's independence under the imperial throne, as several scholars have suggested, was already ingrained in bylaws, considered almost as a given by the drafters of the constitution.[32] Already in an early draft, submitted in 1880, the advisor Inoue Kowashi proposed that all civilian and military powers should be invested in the imperial sovereign. In a subsequent draft, he wrote that "the emperor personally commands the army and the navy." In his comments to the Japanese translation of Lorenz von Stein's constitutional-military theory, Inoue approved Stein's own justification of the supreme prerogative: unlike military administration, military command demands absolute obedience and cannot be conditioned by normal civilian law. Therefore, only the monarch could unify in his person both of these aspects of military affairs. That amounted not merely to a justification of the supreme prerogative but also of the military presumption to operate independently from the civilian cabinet.[33]

Still, during the 1880s there were some attempts to resist the military's growing involvement in politics. In December 1885, the old government structure was abolished in favor of a Western-style cabinet system. The weak position of the chief minister was replaced with a somewhat stronger prime minister, who was qualified to advise the emperor in "affairs of state." The positions of the minister of the right, the lords, and the imperial councilors were abolished. Instead, the portfolios were manned by Western-style cabinet ministers. Itō Hirobumi, the rising leader of Japan since Ōkubo's assassination, was appointed as the first prime minister.[34]

The government leaders had used this opportunity to restrict the power of Yamagata, who served concurrently in two of the most powerful civilian and military posts: home minister and chief of the General Staff. Already in August, four months before the final inauguration of the cabinet reform, Yamagata was forced to step down from the General Staff—the home minister could not be a military commander, and the two spheres had to be separated. The initiators of the move were probably Itō and Sanjō.[35] That was not, it should be emphasized, an attempt to reverse the clock to pre-1878 conditions by binding the General Staff to the cabinet's control, but to merely to restrain the army by interpreting the reforms in a more literal way: if civilians are not to be involved in military affairs, military men should not be involved in civilian affairs either.

Yamagata, however, continued to alternate between civilian and military posts—a powerful figure meddling in civilian and military affairs alike.[36] The civilian prime minister still retained some control over the army minister, who was a member of his cabinet, but when the constitution was promulgated in 1889, he still had no real authority over the two other crucial elements of the military establishment, the Army Inspectorate and the General Staff. Indeed, the cabinet regulations formally recognized the chief of the General Staff's right to report directly to the emperor.[37]

Far from being a turning point, the Constitution of Imperial Japan was merely another stepping stone in the road for military independence.[38] According to article 11, "The Emperor has the supreme command of the Army and Navy," (*Tennō wa Rikukaigun o tōsui su*), and article 12 endowed him with the privilege to determine "the organization and peace standing of the Army and Navy." Article 67 determined that "those already fixed expenditures based by the Constitution upon the powers appertaining to the Emperor . . . shall be neither rejected nor reduced by the Imperial Diet, without the concurrence of the Government," thus significantly reducing the leverage the parliamentarians might have had over the army's budget. In his official commentaries on the constitution, Itō Hirobumi emphasized that the emperor had personally led his army since antiquity, and that "a General Staff Office has been established for His Imperial Majesty's personal and general direction of the Army and Navy."[39]

Nakano Tomio, a jurist who criticized the army's independence in the turbulent era of the 1930s, may have been right in his interpretation that, legally, the constitution did not permit the military to run its affairs outside of the cabinet's scope of control.[40] However that did not matter much. As Nakano himself admitted, the constitution was not the turning point in civil-military affairs—only another milestone, and not the most important one, in the process of military empowerment that began in 1878.[41] Seen as such, it was all but natural that the constitution would often be interpreted in a way supportive of the army's point of view.

In 1891, for example, the leaders of the army were able to block an attempt by several veterans of the "four generals" faction, now entrenched in the House of Peers, to undo the supreme prerogative by abolishing the independent General Staff altogether. The initiator of the attempt, former deputy chief of the General Staff Ozawa Takeo, was accused of violating the constitution. As a result his initiative failed dismally, and he almost had his military rank and pension taken away.[42]

The Riddle of the Military Reforms

Why were these complicated and awkward reforms initiated by the military establishment in the first place? What were the motives of their initiators? According to popular wisdom, the Japanese leadership decided to replace the French military model with the Prussian one after the end of the Franco-Prussian war, and the establishment of a General Staff, the institution most associated with Prussia, was part of that process.[43] However, the Franco-Prussian War ended in 1871 and the Japanese General Staff was established only seven years later, in 1878. In fact, before that date the armed forces were run according to the French monistic model: all power was concentrated in the Army Ministry. Though Yamagata, then in a minority opinion, was known to favor the Prussian model, there was no sign prior to 1878 that he planned to establish an independent General Staff.[44] Contrary to that, all of his efforts until the Satsuma Rebellion were directed to augment, not to decrease, the authority of the Army Ministry. The Staff Bureau, an embryonic General Staff, was established in 1871 as a section of the ministry. At no time before 1878 was there an attempt to place it directly under the imperial throne.[45] Katsura may have supported such reforms already in 1875, but by that time he was still powerless. It is reasonable to assume, therefore, that the Satsuma Rebellion was the main catalyst for the reforms of 1878.

But what actually happened during the Satsuma Rebellion that convinced Yamagata to change his previous line of military policy? In the memoirs of Katsura and the memoranda of Yamagata, as well as in the official histories of the Army Ministry and the General Staff, several explanations for the reforms are offered. A key position paper drafted by Yamagata and signed by Saigō Tsugumichi explained that the times had changed: the armies of European countries had become more "developed," and Japan had to keep itself up to date by reinforcing the General Staff.[46] Neither here nor in his other writings, however, did Yamagata explain why exactly the General Staff had to acquire independent status from the civilian government.

In his memoirs, as well as in several letters to policymakers, Katsura Tarō tended to repeat the reasons outlined above, in addition to another important argument. The Satsuma Rebellion, he argued, proved that Japanese military command was inadequate and faulty. Here, Katsura had probably referred to the lack of coordination between the detachments of Yamagata and Kuroda during the war against Saigō Takamori and his rebel army. The official history of the Army Ministry, written at the beginning of the twentieth century under Yamagata's direction, provided a variation of the same argument. A system divided into three professional organs, a General Staff, Army Ministry, and Military Inspectorate, each responsible for its own sphere, was far more efficient, far more able to quickly cope with unforeseen military challenges.[47] That argument is partially true: the lessons of the Satsuma Rebellion were certainly an important impetus for reform. Still, even though it may explain why three such organs of command were established, it still does not explain why they had to be independent of civilian control and subordinate directly to the throne.[48]

In fact, the explanations in the official sources make so little sense that some historians resorted to the personal level in order to explain the events of autumn 1878. The reforms, according to Hata Iikuhiko and Kurono Taeru, were designed first and foremost to satisfy Yamagata's unbridled craving for power.[49] Apart from being yet another example for the almost universal animosity Yamagata evokes among historians, this argument makes little sense. Yamagata was certainly an ambitious person, but if he merely wanted to enhance his own power, why did he have to curtail the authority of the Army Ministry, fully controlled by himself and his cronies, in favor of the newly established General Staff? In addition, even the General Staff was not made omnipotent, as its power was limited and circumvented by the Military Inspectorate. And some of the military inspectors, men such as Tani Kanjō and Miura Gorō, were rivals, not allies of Yamagata.[50] The reforms, therefore, increased Yamagata's power at certain levels, but decreased it at others. In order to understand what he intended to achieve, it is necessary to take a step back and reflect, yet again, on the dynamics of early Meiji politics and their convergence with the events of 1878.

The Logic of the Reforms: Consolidation and Dispersion of Power

In his account of early restoration politics, Michio Umegaki has argued that throughout the first decade of the Meiji era, the Restoration government was working on two seemingly contradicting dynamics. On the one hand, its members were mostly lower- and middle-ranking samurai from peripheral domains, people who would never have been entrusted with national power under the Tokugawa regime. Therefore, their rule over the new system was based on *dispersion* of power, namely—opening the gate of national power to newcomers and sharing it between them, for one of the things elite groups most fear is being tyrannized by one of their members. On the other hand, while in the government, they scarcely wanted to share their newly won power with every claimant, and that necessitated *consolidation* of power in the hands of a few. These contradicting dynamics of dispersion and consolidation, according to Umegaki, characterized the Restoration government from its inception.[51]

In fact, every historical junction in the early Meiji years involved intricate renegotiations on the balance of dispersion and consolidation of power. Some actors were eliminated or excluded, others were strengthened, and yet others were readmitted to the ruling elites along with their allies. The military reforms of 1878 were in fact Yamagata's attempt to settle between these two contradicting dynamics inside the army, to reprogram the dispersion and consolidation of power in order to remedy what he had seen as severe deficiencies in the military system of the 1870s.

The official explanations provided by Yamagata and Katsura for the reforms, as we have already seen, were obscure, partial, dishonest, or otherwise unsatisfactory. Why did they divide military command between three different powers and subordinate each of them separately to the imperial throne? The first and easiest thing to notice is that a major result of the reforms was consolidation of the military elite. The word *consolidation* is used here in Michio Umegaki's sense: by creating the principle of the supreme prerogative, Yamagata and his advisors concentrated military power in the hands of a smaller number of people, while an entire category of power holders—civilian leaders—were excluded as much as possible.

Since he had created the Imperial Guard along with the Saigō brothers, Yamagata was constantly troubled with civilian interference in military affairs. In spring 1873, the cabinet attempted to grab the rudder of military power from the Army Ministry and centralize it under their own control. Yamagata and his deputy lord, Saigō Tsugumichi, had bitterly resisted this move. The joint memorandum written by both men showed their deep disdain for "civilians" and their belief in the superiority of the army's meritocratic system.[52] Yet the leaders of the government insisted on retaining military control. To Yamagata's great dismay, Home Lord Ōkubo, a civilian, took command over all loyalist troops during the Saga Rebellion.[53] Seen from Yamagata's point of view, the Taiwan Expedition was yet another chaotic affair, a strategic folly and an additional indication of the amateurish administration of the army by the civilians in the government.[54] Advising the throne on strategic matters, he had already emphasized in 1874, should have been the prerogative of the army lord.[55]

The amorphous intentions of the government, pushed by the Popular Rights movement, to open some kind of national assembly in future years, further aggravated Yamagata's fears. Given the possibility of the future inclusion of party politicians in the government, there was a danger that such civilians could influence the military through the Army Ministry.[56] Yamagata, it should be noted, was not the only one who feared such an outcome. Even Fukuzawa Yukichi, the leading public intellectual of early Meiji Japan—certainly not a Yamagata admirer—conceded that the Diet had to be kept out of military affairs. Otherwise, he warned, politicians might use armed units and turn the parliament from a venue for public debate into a literal battlefield.[57]

Then there was the issue of military discipline. In his memoirs, in the midst of a typically evasive description of the General Staff reforms, Katsura briefly mentioned the Takebashi Incident of August 23, 1878. The reasons for that incident, he wrote, were well known, and it was needless to elaborate, but along with the lessons of the Satsuma Rebellion they made reform in the army all the more urgent.[58] In that incident, artillery troops from the Imperial Guard rebelled in protest against postponement of payments, murdered some commanding officers, rioted near the Imperial Palace, and even trained their cannons on the official residence of the Treasury Lord. "Even in my wildest dreams I did not except such a serious incident," said Yamagata, obviously shocked. He was aware of the discontent in the Imperial Guard and expected some trouble, but was perhaps surprised by the magnitude.[59] The riots, however, were suppressed on the same day. The authorities suspected that the mutinous troops were influenced by the Movement for Popular Rights, though a close reading of the testimonies of the rebels indicates that such influence, if existent, was meager at best.[60]

For Yamagata, that was yet another validation of warnings he had made since 1873. Even before the October 1873 crisis he was unable to control the Imperial Guard units, who had shown more loyalty to politicians of their former domains than to their formal commander.[61] Military mutinies were rampant, and many of them, like the Saga and Satsuma rebellions, were caused by illicit horizontal connections between politicians and armed units. Already in January 1878, a short time after the end of the Satsuma Rebellion, Yamagata warned that the discipline of the soldiers had to be improved.[62] After the Takebashi Incident, however, he began to strongly associate these disciplinary problems with seditious civilian, political influence on the troops. Any political involvement in the armed forces was seen as a sure recipe for chaos and rebellion, and the leaders of the army were afraid that another uprising may occur at a moment's notice.[63]

Based on this experience, Yamagata became certain that something had to be done to isolate the army from politics and keep civilians out of military affairs. "If reform is not done," Yamagata wrote Itō Hirobumi a short time before the

92   CHAPTER 5

Takebashi Incident, "I am deeply worried that the future goal of upholding military discipline is very much in doubt."[64] The drive for consolidation was comprised of two elements: building a supreme authority of military command and excluding civilians (i.e., politicians), both in the government and in the future parliament, from military decision making.[65] This argument did not appear in Yamagata's formal position papers to the government, for obvious tactical reasons, but his intentions were betrayed by his request that the Imperial Rescript for Soldiers and Sailors would not pass through the hands of the Chief Minister, as was usually the case. It had to be given to the troops directly by the emperor. Even the most venerable civilian politician was not allowed to interfere in military affairs.[66]

In 1881 yet another impetus occured prompting Yamagata to take a radical approach to depoliticize the army. His archrivals, the "four generals," submitted a strong-worded petition to the government against a corrupted deal, selling Hokkaido territories to private Satsuma businessmen at bargain prices.[67] That affair was a part of a major political crisis, which ended with the dismissal of Treasury Lord Ōkuma Shigenobu from the government. The "four generals," Tani Kanjō, Miura Gorō, Soga Sukenori and Torio Koyata, were blamed by Yamagata and his cronies for taking Ōkuma's side in that political debate.[68] That was yet another incentive to tighten and consolidate the military elite, barring and forbidding any political involvement of military leaders (with the sole exception of Yamagata and his closest cronies). Miura, narcissist as always, wrote in his memoirs that Yamagata's moves were done solely in order to "shut him up."[69] That is naturally exaggerated. Yamagata had bigger worries than Miura and his three friends, loud and troublesome as they might have been. Still, there is no doubt that their oppositional activity inside and outside the army was yet another symptom of the phenomena of horizontal political connections he was set to fight against.[70]

Yamagata's message did not remain only at the level of bylaws and regulations and was also strongly expressed in two seminal ideological documents submitted to the troops in 1878 and 1882, respectively. The first, "Admonitions to Soldiers" ("Gunjin Kunkai"), was written by Yamagata's close colleague, Nishi Amane, and the civilian councilor Inoue Kowashi in the wake of the Takebashi Incident. The army, it warned the officers, was still in its infancy. Its body strength was growing, true, but the prevalent problems of discipline indicated that its spirit was yet underdeveloped. And without proper military spirit, the body is nothing but an empty shell. The need of the hour was to instill the old samurai values of loyalty, courage, and obedience in the mass of soldiers of commoner background. Obedience, even to unreasonable orders, should be unconditional, and that was impossible without total detachment between the soldier and the seditious world of popular rights and civilian politics. Most of all, soldiers were forbidden to petition the authorities together or form parties or factions of any kind. Crucially, the appeal reminded the soldiers that in the glorious past the armed forces were "above politics" and answered directly to the imperial throne. The text implied that no civilian "politician," presumably not even the leaders of the government, had the right to give orders to the soldiers of the emperor.[71]

The "Imperial Rescript for Soldiers and Sailors," jointly written by Nishi Amane and Inoue Kowashi and then revised by Yamagata, conveyed the same message even more explicitly. Much of it repeated the gist of the "Admonitions," implicitly suggesting that the first document was not effective enough. Unlike the stylized prose of the "Admonitions," however, it was written in a clear, simple language that every recruit (or so it was hoped) could understand. And indeed, the "Rescript" became mandatory reading material that every soldier and sailor, especially since the mid-1920s, was expected to know inside out.[72] After a short paragraph summarizing the history of the Meiji Restoration, the "Rescript" reached its main point: the troops are the emperor's, and they should be under exclusive imperial control. Rectitude, honor, duty, condemnation of private violence, and distaste of politics—all were strongly tied with the figure of the emperor, the *dai gensui*, supreme commander in chief. That message was even incorporated into the drama of the promulgation. Officially, the emperor "granted" the document to Army Lord Ōyama in a special ceremony.[73] He, the monarch, gave the message to the soldiers in the first person:

> Soldiers and sailors! We are your supreme commander in chief. Our relations with you will be most intimate when We rely upon you as our limbs and you look up to Us as your head. . . . The soldiers and sailors should consider loyalty their essential duty . . . *a body of soldiers or sailors wanting in loyalty, however well-ordered and disciplined it may be, is in an emergency no better than rabble.* Remember that, as the protection of the state and the maintenance of its power depend upon the strength of its arms, the growth or decline of this strength must affect the nation's destiny for good or for evil; *therefore neither be led astray by current opinions nor meddle in politics, but with single heart fulfill your essential duty of loyalty,* and bear in mind that duty is weightier than a mountain, while death is lighter than a feather. Never by failing in moral principle fall into disgrace and bring dishonor upon your name. . . . If you affect valor and act with violence, the world will in the end detest you and look upon you as a wild beast. Of this you should take heed.[74]

Yamagata's move had far-reaching ideological repercussions. The warning against disciplined but disloyal troops was probably directed against units who joined forces with rebellious politicians, for how else, except for such illicit connections, could they be both disciplined and wanting in loyalty?[75]

It is important to note, however, that Yamagata's drive was to consolidate, not to isolate, military power. The two spheres, as Katsura wrote Kido already in 1876, were interconnected.[76] Unlike Kido Takayoshi, Yamagata and Katsura never resisted involvement of military men in civilian life—as long as this involvement was restricted to their own small group of leaders.[77] They themselves constantly meddled in politics, even while they stopped politicians from meddling in their own affairs. Indeed, on numerous occasions during the 1880s Yamagata, Saigō, Ōyama, and Katsura had held civilian portfolios concurrently with their military assignments. Most crucially, Yamagata and Ōyama were both members of the powerful Genrō Council, who had decisive influence over the appointment of prime ministers during the 1890s and to a certain degree up until the 1920s.[78]

That did not mean, however, that Yamagata projected or wanted the army to stage its own foreign policy or to independently attack other countries, as occurred in later decades. Limiting political involvement to himself and his cronies was perhaps the most crucial goal of the project of military consolidation. Other generals were ordered to not act independently in defiance of political authorities. Indeed, Yamagata attempted to counter such a danger by especially strict prohibitions included in the military penal code of 1881. According to article 110, soldiers and officers were forbidden to speak in political conventions or submit political petitions.[79] The articles under the heading "arbitrary use of power" (senken) had stipulated, among other things, that "when a commanding officer has engaged in combat after having received notification of an armistice or peace, he shall suffer death" (69); "when a commanding officer has arbitrarily moved troops against orders or outside of the scope of his authority, except in cases when this is unavoidable, he shall suffer death" (70).[80]

And yet, punishment of insubordination, just like other crimes committed by military personnel, fell under the exclusive jurisdiction of the army and was out of bounds for civilian courts. This was true even when soldiers and officers committed civil crimes, such as murder.[81] Military leaders had therefore the power to whitewash the delinquency of their comrades, including "arbitrary use of power." The real test of Yamagata's regulations was in their enforcement when violated by a senior commander—and that would not happen for the next decade or so.[82]

The drive of military consolidation, therefore, consisted of a systematic attempt to exclude politicians, even of ministerial rank, from military affairs, and bar soldiers and officers from political involvement. However, the reforms staged by Yamagata and Katsura in 1878 included a seemingly contradictory drive of power dispersion—a point usually ignored by most historians.[83] Just like many similar moves during the first decade of the Meiji era, the reforms of 1878 had excluded some people from the room, but dispersed the remaining power more evenly among those who remained. The General Staff, Army Ministry, and Army

Inspectorate were independent of each other in the sense that none of their chiefs had a clear authority to either appoint or dismiss the others, a source of incessant factional strife in future years.[84] Far from centralizing power in the hands of one person, Yamagata had consolidated it and dispersed it at one and the same time, a complicated system that only he could control—and even that not perfectly.[85] There were no absolute power holders in the Imperial Japanese Army.

Lost in Translation: What Went Wrong?

The dramatic Prussian-German influence on the Japanese political structure in the prewar years is almost undisputed among scholars of modern Japanese history. Some, like Bernd Martin, even believe that by choosing the "wrong" model, that of Germany, Japan went halfway down the road of militarism, aggression, and national catastrophe.[86] Such claims are undoubtedly exaggerated: Japan was as influenced by other Western countries, especially France but also Britain and the United States, and this influence was never completely superseded.[87] Nor does it make sense to blame Prussian influence for everything that went wrong in Japan. In that context, it is instructive to note that the Prussian Army, the forerunner of the mature Meiji army, did not develop such severe tendencies of blatant, violent insubordination as its Japanese counterpart. One reason was that the emulation of the Prussian model was never as "broad, deep and faithful" as some historians would like us to believe.[88] In retrospect, learning from Imperial Germany was a fateful decision, not necessarily because it was "the wrong model," as Bernd Martin has suggested, but because some of the crucial components were lost in translation.[89] Borrowing the explanation offered by Eleanor Westney in her discussion of French influences on the early Meiji police force, one might say the Imperial Japanese Army's understanding of the Prussian model was based on "imperfect information, in the sense of information on the formal system but not the informal."[90]

Katsura advocated the Prussian model to the Japanese government as early as August 1875, but his reports focused on certain aspects and not on others. As he admitted later, his missives were intentionally concise, in order not to evoke redundant arguments among his influential readers in Japan. The main thrust of his argument was focused on the merits of Prussian dualism: the separation between military command and military administration. Katsura's time in Germany was mostly spent in the Inspectorate of the Third Prussian Army and in the War Ministry. Both of these organs had daily dealings with the General Staff, and it is therefore natural that Katsura became interested in the trinity of staff, ministry, and inspectorate.[91] These three institutions, as we have seen, were adopted root and branch by the Japanese Army. In Germany, as in Japan, the military inspectors, chief of the General Staff, and the war minister had every right to directly report to the emperor (*Immediatstellung/Immediatrecht*). All of them were directly subordinate to the supreme command of the monarch (*Kommandogewalt*), a construct from which the Japanese supreme prerogative developed.[92]

However, there were some key differences between Germany and Japan of which Katsura and his fellow reformers might have been unaware. First of all, the Prussian *Kommandogewalt* and the Japanese supreme prerogative developed under different historical conditions, substantiated by different basic cultural, military, and political assumptions. In fact, the concept of *Kommandogewalt* was born, in its modern form, out of a series of debates between Otto von Bismarck, minister-president of Prussia (after 1871, Reich chancellor) and Helmuth Graf von Moltke, chief of the General Staff. Both men, like other key figures in the Prussian ruling elites, agreed that the parliament should be excluded as much as possible from military affairs.[93] The question of the civilian government's right to be involved in military operations was, however, more complicated.[94] In the Austro-Prussian war of 1866, Moltke recommended occupying Vienna, and in the Franco-Prussian war of 1871 he strongly advised an advance into the south of France. In both cases his goal was to utterly destroy the fighting force of the enemy. Bismarck adamantly resisted these plans, as he feared that they might have precipitated the intervention of foreign powers or undermined his diplomatic efforts. In the end, in both cases, bitter debates ensued but Bismarck won the day.[95] Moltke, the chief of the General Staff, had written in disappointment to the emperor: "Up till now, I have considered that the chief of the General Staff (especially in war) and the federal chancellor are two equally warranted and mutually independent agencies under the direct command of Your Royal Majesty."[96]

The words "especially in war" were crucial: Moltke did not dispute the supremacy of the civilian government in peacetime. Indeed, he did not even dispute that setting political goals to the army is the exclusive prerogative of the civilian government, and his only request from the minister-president was not to meddle in "professional" military issues in the course of a campaign. Bismarck, by contrast, believed that as a minister-president he had the right to veto operational moves with unwelcome political repercussions. Both he and Moltke, however, worked under the assumption that the military and the cabinet operate in parallel professional spheres, and the debates were mainly on the question of where to draw the borderline between the two.[97]

The first crucial difference between Germany and Japan, in that sense, was a sociological one. In Prussia, many civilian and military leaders might have originated from the landed nobility, but as far as life experience and educational background were concerned they were two distinct groups. Politicians studied law and economics in state universities, while military men grew up in specialized army environments. They had different backgrounds, and therefore it made sense to assign each of them a separate sphere of activity. The struggles between them, at least until the First World War, tended to be merely on the proper division of labor between the two spheres.

In the early Meiji era the distinctions between the two groups were not as clear, as almost all potentates of the first generation of political leaders originated from the same cohort of Restoration leaders and their immediate cronies. Chief of the General Staff Yamagata, Home Lords Ōkubo and Itō, even Itagaki, leader of the opposition—all began their careers as domainal samurai, bureaucrats, and military leaders at one and the same time. It was a novel idea, therefore, to define Ōkubo and Itō as "civilians" who had exclusive prerogative to take foreign-policy decisions, and Yamagata as a "military man" whose responsibility should be confined to military operations alone. Itō and Yamagata, after all, had served together as commanders under Takasugi Shinsaku in 1864. None of them could be defined as more "soldierly" than the other.[98] Even when such ideas were imported to Japan from Germany, they had weak roots and were more easily violated.

Before 1878, the border between the military and civilian spheres was violated from both sides: Ōkubo involved himself with military command, while Yamagata interfered in politics. However, after the General Staff reforms, the military enjoyed institutional safeguards which effectively closed it to civilian influence. The leaders of the army, by contrast, still felt themselves competent to interfere in state affairs. Yamagata never used this leverage to stage a completely independent foreign policy, but with the next generation of not-as-careful military leaders, that was merely one step away.

Second, and this was a crucial problem, the position and political role of the emperor was very different in Germany and Japan. The Prussian model was based on the notion of an enlightened monarch delegating powers to educated bureaucrats.[99] The General Staff, fashioned by Helmuth von Moltke and his colleagues as an elite body directly subordinate to the throne, presumed an active monarch taking independent decisions based on professional advice. The power of the monarch was strengthened by the institution of the Military Cabinet, part of the palace apparatus that controlled the promotions of military personnel. Its orders were binding even without a countersignature by the war minister, that is—it was independent of both the government and the General Staff.[100] Had Yamagata and Katsura established a powerful military cabinet inside the palace, preferably headed by a nobleman with military experience, the emperor might have gained a better institutional leverage over his armed forces. But they did no such thing. During his sojourn in Prussia, Katsura did not have access to the Imperial Palace in Berlin and was naturally not exposed to the daily activity of the Military Cabinet. Therefore, it is not surprising that this institution was not emphasized in the reports he sent back to Japan.[101]

Lacking institutional leverage such as an independent palace military cabinet, the Japanese emperor's day-to-day authority was never as strong, clear, or active as the German emperor's. Malleable as he might have been, Emperor William I was a de facto ruler. His was the last word, and even Bismarck, at times, had to work hard to persuade him.[102] The Japanese emperor, by contrast, remained a hazy center up to 1945. The emperor, wrote Inoue Kowashi in a secret position paper, "governs the people, [but] does not personally administer the government." Inoue's position might have been related to the resolution of the Meiji leaders not to involve the emperor in political debates which might undermine his prestige.[103] The emperor reigns over the realm, wrote Fukuzawa Yukichi, but he does not rule it. "It is disadvantageous for the country to involve our imperial house directly in politics."[104] As Hata Ikuhiko has noted, "In the debates and disputes about the supreme prerogative, there are no examples of cases when the opinion of the emperor or his interpretation were quoted."[105]

The passivity of the emperor made Yamagata's General Staff not only independent but also fragmented, because the various independent military organs did not have a strong monarch able to call them to task.[106] Just like in Germany, they struggled with each other to gain more influence and power, but as the final arbitrator at the throne was rarely active, settlements between them had to be made, as usual in Meiji Japan, through horizontal negotiations. As a result, the military establishment became dominated by an incessant factional struggle—usually between Yamagata's "Chōshū clique" (more a social than a geographical concept) and a successive line of rival factions. The struggle went on even after the gradual demise of the Chōshū clique in the 1920s between a whole plethora of successive cliques and subcliques. Fed by the weakness of the imperial center, debilitating factionalism remained an incurable problem of the Japanese armed forces up to 1945.

Future Repercussions

The supreme prerogative system created in 1878, with all of its flaws, was not an accident but rather a rational, effective solution to the problems of the preceding decade. For the future, it was to become virtually impossible for civilian politicians such as Etō Shimpei to rally military units. The chances that one general, such as Saigō Takamori, would be able to accumulate enough power to overthrow the entire system became less likely as well. The peculiar kind of rebellious insubordination which plagued Japan before 1878, based on illicit horizontal connections between politicians and army units, disappeared for a long time. Indeed, it was almost fifty-five years until a rebellious group attempted to overthrow a government by a violent military revolt again.

For that reason, it would be wrong to draw a straight line between the defiance of Saigō Tsugumichi in 1874, during the Taiwan Expedition, and future, supreme prerogative–based resistance to state authority. It is tempting to draw such a line, as both Saigō and later practitioners of military resistance utilized the imperial hazy center in order to justify their behavior. But in 1874, Saigō Tsugumichi did not argue that the army had a special tie to the emperor, or that the government did not have the right to issue orders to the army. He merely claimed that his orders were given in the form of an imperial rescript, and therefore must be rescinded only by such a rescript—not by a mere cabinet order. In practice, however, he was moved to resistance by the pressure of Satsuma interest groups and armed shizoku volunteers, just the kind of illicit connections that Yamagata tried (with great success) to eliminate in 1878.

In the short run, it also seemed that supreme prerogative ideology helped to counter disobedience through strong emotional and mental inhibitions. Commanders constantly made clear to their soldiers that they were the soldiers of the emperor. Every command of a superior officer was a personal, direct order from the emperor, and as such could not be questioned "regardless of circumstances." If the order was illegal, a soldier still had to obey, though he was allowed to complain after the fact.[107] Even routine ceremonies were imbued by the imperial halo. When officers, for example, were transferred from one role to another, it was announced that they moved to their new duty "following the emperor's order." Testimonies show that such ceremonies had strong and long-lasting emotional influence on the officers and soldiers involved.[108]

But the remedy Yamagata had used had unexpected side effects and his system, as time went on, became increasingly shaky and difficult to control. After he and the first generation of leaders departed from the scene, there was virtually no one with adequate social capital to orchestrate all of its components.[109] The peculiar formula of dispersion and consolidation of power chosen by Yamagata, Katsura, and others, based on their imperfect understanding of the Prussian model, created a rich background for the future development of military insubordination. The military establishment was consolidated in such a way as to minimize civilian involvement in its professional sphere, without renouncing its right to have its own say in affairs of state.[110] That, in the future, enabled the army leadership to institutionally defy the cabinet.

On the other hand, and this has not yet adequately recognized, power was also dispersed inside the military establishment, because the reformers failed to create a clear-cut vertical hierarchy. One's direct superior was the representative of the emperor and had to be obeyed, but the leaders of the army were equals, and there was no clear hierarchy among them. In the future, this failure would precipitate the phenomena of insubordination inside the officer corps itself, as it was sometimes highly tempting to defy a commander from a rival military faction.[111] Every faction could claim that it alone understood the will of the hazy imperial center, and there was no strong overlord to arbitrate between these factions or to bind them to a clear-cut, central authority. The result, as events in the next decades would prove, was a military system prone to the evils of factionalism, resistance, and finally, also assassination and terror.

THREE PUFFS ON A CIGARETTE

General Miura Gorō and the
Assassination of Queen Min

> **This was a matter which I decided in the space of three puffs on a cigarette, . . . whether my behavior was right or wrong, only Heaven can judge.**
>
> —Lieutenant General Miura Gorō

At dawn on October 8, 1895, the Royal Palace of Seoul was surrounded by Japanese and Korean troops hoping to seize the reins of power from the queen of Korea and her family. They escorted an elderly Korean prince into the palace grounds, where he stood waiting. Once the palace was surrounded, a group of Japanese officers, policemen, and civilians, broke into the private apartments of Queen Min, hacked her to death with swords, slew several of her court ladies and burned their bodies on the lawn. The minister of the royal household was also slain, and the crown princess was beaten. All of this happened in front of the stupefied king of Korea.

This act of coup d'état and regicide was cold bloodedly planned by the Japanese envoy, Lieutenant General Miura Gorō, along with his legation staff and the owner of the local Japanese newspaper. Not only did Miura fail to ask the permission of the Japanese Government for such a dramatic operation, he worked hard to keep it in the dark, excluding even the consul of his legation from the plot. After the deed he concealed the truth about his own involvement from the Foreign Ministry for as long as possible. For this blatant defiance of government authority, Miura and his group of cutthroats were ordered back to Japan, arrested, and placed on preliminary trial on charges of conspiracy to murder and murder. The Hiroshima Court for Preliminary Inquiries, however, ruled that the evidence was "insufficient" to open formal proceedings.

The murder of Queen Min was far from the worst atrocity committed by the Japanese Empire, even by the standards of the Meiji period. Only shortly beforehand, during the First Sino-Japanese War, General Ōyama's Second Army had perpetrated a massacre in the Chinese city of Port Arthur, in which several thousand civilians were killed.[1] But unlike the nameless victims of Port Arthur, Min was a famous queen. Her brutal murder, along with those of her female attendants, struck a loud chord with contemporary and later Western observers, perhaps because of its "damsel in distress" connotations. In recent decades the queen has increasingly been depicted as a martyr in South Korean popular culture as well, being the subject of novels, movies, a television drama, and even a musical.[2]

Yet the historical importance of the events of October 8, 1895, far exceeds their sensational character. That fateful autumn morning brought together, with dire consequences, two distinct roads of military resistance to state policy. One, from above, was the supreme prerogative tradition, brought to Korea by Miura Gorō, a former general who led, to a large extent, his own private foreign policy. Miura—a person known for his consistent opposition to the Meiji leaders—had given the supreme prerogative tradition a twist of defiance. His attitude converged with the altogether different tradition of resistance from below, of the shishi rebels and assassins, whose political optimism led them to believe that problems could and should be solved by the elimination of prominent individuals.

Supreme prerogative resistance from "above" combined with the resistance of shishi copycats from "below" in a joint operation of "escape to the front"—an attempt to honor the emperor and fulfill the goals of national policy more efficiently than the allegedly hesitant Tokyo government would allow.[3] This, as we shall see, had ominous consequences for the future, as it blurred the borderline between the army and grassroots violent activists, resulting in the delegation of military power into the hands of dubious private agents.

Setting the Stage: The Korean Monarch as a Disrespected Center

The drama of October 10, 1895, needs to be understood within its historical and political context. Korea had been ruled for several decades by King Gojong, who took the throne in 1864. As he was merely a boy of twelve at the time, the affairs of the kingdom were managed by his blood father, Heungseon, better known by the official title, *daewongun*. Ten years later, at age twenty-two, Gojong officially became a ruling king.

In theory, the Kingdom of Choson, as Korea was known at the time, was an absolute monarchy. Ruled for centuries by the Yi dynasty, it was a suzerainty of China, but according to established tradition the Chinese rarely interfered in its day-to-day affairs, entrusting them instead to the discretion of the king. But from the moment he took the throne, Gojong was known as a weak individual, "more or less a nonentity," as Itō Hirobumi put it later.[4] Replacing the formal regency of the daewongun, the king "ruled" the country but in practice was the puppet of court factions, powerful ministers, his first consort Queen Min (Myeongseong), and her family members. "Unfortunately for the land," wrote the British observer Isabella Bird, "he [the king] is persuadable by the last person who gets his ear."[5] Once the country was forcibly opened by the Japanese in 1876, foreign envoys—Japanese, Chinese, Russian, and American—joined the struggle for hegemony in Seoul.

The "opening of Korea" resulted in a game of musical chairs between the foreign powers, with each dominating the court in turn. The Japanese gradually gained a foothold in the early 1880s, but were almost expelled by the Chinese in 1884, only to return a decade later as a result of the Sino-Japanese War (1894–1895). By then the Russian Empire had emerged as a dominant power and squabbled with the Japanese over the Korean spoils. But even during the decade of Chinese dominance, and certainly afterward, no single power was ever able to dominate Korea entirely. Several government ministries as well as military units were always controlled by different countries or foreign advisors, who had their own independent agendas.

But the Korean game was internal as well as external. Almost every foreign power had its Korean allies, and the alliances between internal factions and foreign countries constantly shifted and changed. Indeed, the royal weakness expressed itself not only in foreign policy but also internally. There was rarely a time when the king dared to resist a faction that controlled the palace. Occupying it became a routine way of taking power. In 1882, traditionalist forces led by the daewongun moved into the palace and executed their rivals.[6] In 1884 reformist groups, with the support of elements from the Japanese Legation and idealist students from Keiō University repeated this exercise, treating their rivals in the same murderous manner.[7] And in some of these cases, confidants, ministers, and close advisors of the king were executed on the palace grounds, before his very eyes.[8]

The manifest weakness of the royal center had given rise to a factionalism even more debilitating than the one in Japan. As there was nothing to bind the Korean factions to each other—neither a strong state hierarchy nor even the myth of an omnipotent imperial center—factional strife in late Choson Korea was governed by the rule of "winner takes all."[9] The ambition of each faction, wrote Homer Hulbert, an American missionary with an intimate knowledge of the Seoul court, "was to gain a place where, under the protection of the government, he might first get revenge upon his enemies and then, secondly, seize upon their wealth."[10] That was true to varying degrees for almost all factions, reformist and conservative alike, regardless of their affiliation and declared ideals.

Yet the system of the disrespected royal center had other peculiarities that gave Queen Min certain advantages over rival faction leaders. Disrespected as he was, the king remained at the center. The power of Queen Min derived from the fact that she was constantly close to him. Other factions may have controlled the cabinet, but she had dominance over the Royal Court.[11] Even the most powerful minister, the king's own father, the daewongun, could be exiled either inside or outside Korea (which happened several times). The queen, by contrast, could not be separated for long from the king unless she was demoted to the status of a commoner, and it was difficult to convince Gojong to do that.[12]

Queen Min evoked contradictory feelings, but no one doubted the force of her personality. "She was wise and highly energetic," wrote the Russian envoy Karl Weber.[13] The traveler Isabella Bird, who met her several months before her death, remembered that her "eyes were cold and keen, and the general expression [was] one of brilliant intelligence."[14] By her cunning and charisma she obtained constant access to those at the center and was able to exercise political influence—by no means absolute, and varying according to circumstances, but always significant.[15]

By 1894 there were numerous political factions in Korea, forming a highly complicated map of rivalries and shifting alliances. Factions constantly split, individuals moved from one group to another, and the groups were aligned toward different foreign powers at different times. The Min faction, centered around the queen and her family, were dominant. They cooperated closely with the Chinese and later tilted toward an alliance with Russia.[16] The reformists, who had seen Japan as a model for the future development of Korea, had not recovered since the failure of their coup d'état in 1884. Their exiled leader, Park Yonghyo, was still in Japan as a political fugitive. Finally, there was the faction of the daewongun, the old archconservative, marginalized, frustrated, and practically confined to his rural villa in Kongdok-ri. Formerly an implacable enemy of Japan, by 1895 the daewongun was glad to cooperate with anyone ready to restore his former power.[17]

The Impending Crisis: Japan's Dilemma in Korea

With the failure of the pro-Japanese coup of 1884, Japan became a relatively marginal factor in Korean politics, though it retained a strong economic foothold in the country. The Tianjin Agreement, signed in April 1885, secured Korean "independence," and China and Japan agreed to consult each other before sending troops to the kingdom. However, China did not honor the agreement and dominated Korean politics throughout the decade.[18] The Japanese, increasingly unhappy with that arrangement, were reluctant to confront China on the peninsula. In 1894, however, a peasant rebellion led by a xenophobic religious sect called the Donghak (Eastern Learning), reshuffled the cards of the Korean game. Though the Donghaks were supported by a number of Japanese adventurers, they were in essence deeply hostile to Japan. Their military achievements, therefore, alarmed the Japanese government, which dispatched an expeditionary force to check their advance. The risky attempt of Japan's foreign minister, Mutsu Munemitsu, to use this as an opportunity to challenge Chinese dominance in the peninsula resulted in a war between the two powers.[19]

After a chain of military victories on land and sea, Japan won the war with China in the spring of 1895, but the Chinese departure from Korea left the Japanese statesmen in a dilemma about their future policy. Japan probably did not have a plan to annex Korea, though this option was growing in popularity among the Japanese elites.[20] The military consensus in Japan, shaped by strategic thinkers such as Yamagata Aritomo, had seen Korea as a security threat, "a dagger pointed at the heart of Japan." And therefore Japan was unwilling to see a foreign power, such as China or Russia, dominating Korea politically or militarily. The thinking went that because the chaos in Korea was likely to tempt such foreign powers to intervene, Japan was obliged to insist on far-reaching reforms in order to safeguard Korea's "independence." In this context, as Peter Duus has noted, "independence" meant Korea's disengagement from any foreign power apart from Japan.[21]

During the war, in the summer of 1894, the Japanese envoy to Korea, Ōtori Keisuke, decided to overthrow the Korean government, dominated as it was by the queen and her pro-Chinese Min faction. He therefore struck a deal with the daewongun, allowing him to occupy the royal palace with the assistance of Japanese troops. The attack matched up with previous Japanese foreign policy and was nothing new or surprising—the palace had been occupied several times in the recent past by various factions. The king and the queen were unharmed, and Ōtori's emissary, first secretary of the legation Sugimura Fukashi, even turned down the daewongun's request to assassinate his Min rivals.[22] But the old prince, ossified conservative that he was, failed to satisfy Japanese demands for reform, and the queen quickly regained her former influence. His policy in shambles, Ōtori was replaced by former foreign minister Inoue Kaoru, one of the founding fathers of the Meiji regime and an experienced politician with immense prestige.[23]

Inoue attempted an altogether different strategy to Ōtori's. A short while after his arrival, he proclaimed that he would force the king to exclude *both* the queen and the daewongun from politics.[24] However, the astute Inoue soon recognized that, unlike the daewongun, the proximity of the queen to the throne could not be ignored, so he shifted gears. Giving up on his insistence that the queen should be excluded, he now attempted to co-opt her into his plans, creating a delicate balance between her and the other political factions.[25] On the one hand, as a token of reconciliation, he offered her a large monetary endowment and promised her Japanese protection whenever she felt herself in jeopardy. Unlike other male diplomats, Inoue was also able to meet the secluded queen face to face.[26] On the other hand, to balance her power, he brought the leader of the reformist faction back from his exile in Japan and installed him as home minister and later as prime minister. All in all, he strived toward the same goals as his predecessors: reforming Korea in order to forestall future rebellions and "secure its independence" from any foreign power except Japan.[27]

In spring 1895, however, Inoue's policy encountered difficulties. Things had initially been going well, with Japan winning decisive military victories over Qing China, culminating in the removal of Chinese influence in Korea via the Shimonoseki Treaty of April 17, 1895. But Japanese power on the peninsula suffered a setback six days later, when the empire had to bow to the "Triple Intervention" of Russia, France, and Germany and give up the Liaotung Peninsula, the main territorial gain obtained in the wake of the Sino-Japanese War.[28] Souring the impression of Japanese victory, the Triple Intervention prompted the queen to turn to Russian help and advice to counter the Japanese.[29] At the same time, the influence of the Japanese advisors in the various Korean ministries quickly diminished, and they found themselves more or less ignored. They started appealing to the legation to do something to improve their standing.[30]

Meanwhile, the security situation in the country went from bad to worse. Not only was the countryside extremely difficult to control, plagued as it was by incessant violence, floods, and cholera, but the Korean Army itself had not a semblance of unity.[31] Different units were loyal to different factions, and even worse, to different foreign states and foreign advisors. Two battalions of the army, known as the Hullyeondae, were trained and held by the Japanese. The Palace Guard and the police, by contrast, were loyal to the Min faction. Their relationship with the Hullyeondae was strained. Clashes between the police and Hullyeondae troops became common throughout the summer of 1895.[32]

The Beginning of a Plan: Dissent of the Professionals

Sugimura Fukashi, who was legation first secretary and acting envoy by the summer of 1895, had been a dominating presence in the Seoul legation since the early 1880s. A veteran of the Taiwan Expedition, he gradually won a reputation as an experienced Korean hand, and his name was widely known in Japanese foreign policy circles. His constant presence in Seoul contributed to his renown.[33] Accordingly, when Sugimura turned against Inoue and his conciliatory policy, the latter's status in Seoul became difficult to maintain.[34] Unlike Inoue, Sugimura had constantly advocated a relentless struggle against the Min faction—which he saw as the source of all evil, corruption, and tyranny in Korea—and to defeat the queen he was even ready to ally with the conservative daewongun, Japan's former enemy.[35]

Another related group of key actors was the cohort of Japanese advisors to the Korean court and government ministries. These people were closely tied to the Japanese legation—so closely tied, in fact, that they must be seen as an integral part of their country's diplomatic corps, in comparison to other foreign advisors, from Germany or America, for example, who were more independent.[36] The most influential member of this group was Okamoto Ryūnosuke, veteran of the Satsuma Rebellion. In 1878, as a battalion commander, he became complicit in the Takebashi Incident, a soldier's uprising that shook the Japanese leadership. After the uprising had failed, Okamoto survived a suicide attempt.[37] He was not executed, but barred from ever joining the army or the civil service again. In 1895, however, he had played an altogether different role as advisor to the Korean court.[38] Later defined by Miura as an "expert to the daewongun," he was the contact person between the Japanese legation and the discredited prince, keeping the communication channels between the two sides intact. "Without Okamoto," Miura had said, "it was impossible to do anything with the daewongun, everybody knew that."[39] But as long as Inoue was the envoy, Okamoto could not convince the legation to form such an alliance. The advisor, therefore, was greatly frustrated with the envoy's policy of balance. As he testified later, "It was inadvisable to wait for Inoue to make up his mind."[40]

Events in the summer of 1895 gave the plan an air of urgency. In July, Inoue returned to Tokyo for consultations, and his policy, already in difficulties, quickly collapsed in his absence. The pro-Japanese, reformist prime minister, feeling, as Sugimura had put it, that he was "sitting on a volcano," decided to act on his own accord against the Min faction.[41] But his plot was discovered, and the coup plan soon collapsed. The prime minister was subsequently dismissed by the king and he escaped to Japan.[42] Inoue hurried back to Korea and attempted to reinstate working relations with the queen, but his time was running out. In fact, Okamoto had secretly written to Tokyo and asked that Inoue be replaced by someone like Lieutenant General Tani Kanjō or Lieutenant General Miura Gorō.[43] Both men, members of the conservative opposition, were political rivals of Inoue and the other Meiji oligarchs. After some debates, the government accepted Okamoto's plea and replaced Inoue with Miura.

Why exactly Miura Gorō was appointed envoy to Korea is a matter of serious controversy among historians. The fact that Inoue, his predecessor, warmly recommended him was interpreted by some as "proof" of Inoue's complicity in the plot to kill the queen, but this assumption cannot be substantiated.[44] Inoue was probably looking for someone inexperienced and easy to manipulate behind the scenes, as he indeed tried to manipulate the new envoy, unsuccessfully, in the first weeks of September.[45] Foreign Minister Mutsu strongly resisted the appointment, other cabinet ministers supported it, and finally Prime Minister Itō decided to approve it, based on a recommendation from Lieutenant General Tani, Miura's colleague in the conservative opposition.[46]

Tani's responsibility for Miura's appointment is tinged with sad irony. A hero of the Taiwan Expedition and the Satsuma Rebellion, he had called for an occupation of Taiwan and South China in 1874. Since then, however, he had become a staunch anti-imperialist, the only major military figure consistently opposed to territorial expansion.[47] In his letter to Prime Minister Itō, Tani emphasized the need for Miura to stop interfering in Korean affairs, the need to restrain the *sōshi*—the Japanese political ruffians who roamed the Korean countryside—and to stop treating Korea as if it belonged to Japan. Additionally he emphasized that Miura was to be accompanied by a worthy advisor, the writer, journalist, and Harvard graduate, Shiba Shirō.[48]

Thus, when Miura arrived in Seoul in September, he carried with him contradictory expectations. Lieutenant General Tani, his friend in the conservative opposition, had hoped he would be softer than Inoue. Softer, that is, to the Koreans, and stricter with the lawless elements in the Japanese community.[49] Okamoto, however, expected him to be more hawkish, bellicose and "resolute" than Inoue was. It was up to the new envoy and his advisor, Shiba, to decide which role to play.

Navigating without a Compass: Miura Gorō in Seoul

Miura Gorō, originally a Chōshū retainer, began his political career as a protégée of Kido Takayoshi. The embittered, ailing Chōshū leader saw great promise in his young colleague. "Miura is a sincere man, reserved in speech, my true friend," he wrote in his diary in 1877, pleased with his protégée's military success in the war against Saigō Takamori, "and he reveres me as an elder brother. I have long deplored that his ability has remained undiscovered while sycophants of clever words were promoted in office." Kido was particularly impressed by the fact that Miura was the only commander who was able to keep "strict discipline" in his camp.[50] The excerpts from Kido's diary are interesting, as his impressions of

Miura run contrary to others' in later years. Miura became universally known for his crude and direct style. One may guess that Yamagata, whose policy Miura attacked by every possible means, would not have described him as "disciplined" either. Perhaps Miura had been tactfully restraining himself in front of his former teacher, biding his time before showing his true colors.

Known to later generations mainly for his involvement in the Queen Min assassination affair, Miura is widely perceived as a staunch military expansionist. In fact, he was not. During the 1880s he was one of the bitterest opponents of the government's policy of military expansion, calling instead to keep the army as a small defensive force.[51] Like his colleagues in the "four generals" faction and the conservative opposition in general, he was highly antagonistic both to the Popular Rights movement and the government of the Meiji oligarchs, but it seems that his criticism was mostly reserved for the latter. The tradition of Kido Takayoshi, his beloved late teacher, was interpreted by him as a vow to eradicate the Chōshū and Satsuma cliques (*hanbatsu*), and to work for the nation as a whole without any partisan interests. Though he never called to resist the government violently and did not overstep the boundaries of loyal opposition, Miura had always seen the politicians in power as nothing but string pullers of sinister and selfish "cliques." In addition, being an outspoken man, he never hid his opinion even during his years in active service. For these reasons Yamagata had foiled an attempt of the conservative opposition, supported by the emperor, to appoint him as the chief of the General Staff.[52]

It is therefore unsurprising that such a man was unenthusiastic about following orders from leaders he had loathed and disrespected. "This was a matter which I decided in the space of three puffs on a cigarette," he admitted later in his memoirs, when referring to the assassination of the queen. "I made my decision and resolutely carried it through. I was surprisingly unconcerned about the government at home. . . . Whether my behavior was right or wrong, only Heaven can judge."[53] Even when he worked for national goals, Miura was always an oppositionist at heart, subordinate to Heaven and the emperor, not to the government. And that is the key to understanding his later behavior as diplomatic envoy in Seoul.

Why was a man of such a character, ostensibly with minimal diplomatic skills, put in charge of the Korean situation under almost impossible conditions?[54] Miura himself recognized the insurmountable difficulties and his own inability to solve them. He therefore refused the post three times, just as he had turned down a previous request to serve as an envoy in France.[55] He warned his superiors that he had no knowledge of the current trends in global politics, lacked diplomatic skills, and felt that a clear line of national policy was essential for any chance of success. The Foreign Ministry failed to answer or send Miura policy instructions, probably because its leaders, too, were not sure where they were headed. As if anticipating the negligence of the ministry, Miura complained that he was going to Korea as a sailor forced to "navigate the sea without a compass in a moonless, starless night."[56]

Upon his arrival, Miura had to decide how to deal with Queen Min. In his memoirs, he recalled that she was a "highly talented" woman who, bypassing her husband, served as the "true monarch of Korea." At his first royal interview, he noticed that the queen spoke to the king from a rear room behind the throne.[57] During that interview, Miura declared that unless summoned by the royal couple, he would remain in the legation, copy holy sutras, and enjoy the natural beauty of Korea.[58] Beyond the niceties, Miura suspected that the queen looked down on him as a dim-witted soldier and planned to take advantage of his weakness to disband the Hullyeondae.[59] If that was indeed the case, his declared intention of turning the legation into a Buddhist retreat certainly strengthened that impression. Needless to say, unlike Inoue, Miura had no chance to personally negotiate with the secluded queen. He recognized her power but could not approach her—and therefore felt clueless and helpless.[60] Two other possible solutions, employing a woman to negotiate with the queen or keeping Inoue Kaoru as a diplomatic tutor, were rejected. The idea of using a woman was, according to Miura, "rejected from above," and Inoue was pushed back to Japan. The new envoy was too haughty to accept tutelage.[61]

The Japanese position in September 1895 was therefore one of weakness. The legation was headed by an inexperienced and ignorant personality. The cohort of professional diplomats and advisors, devoid of leadership, felt powerless to remedy the constantly worsening situation. Okamoto, for one, believed that a violent showdown was likely to take place sooner or later.[62] Barred from the palace, estranged from the queen, lacking allies and outsmarted by the Russians, they were constantly afraid that their last vestige of power, the Hullyeondae battalions, would be destroyed altogether, thus sweeping away the remnants of Japanese influence in Korea.[63] As a result, they yearned for strong measures against the Min faction to prevent the looming disaster. Miura, aggressive by nature, concurred. But for anything, any measure at all, Korean allies were needed, and they were in short supply.

The Korean Counterparts: Miura and the Daewongun

It was clear to Miura, his colleagues, and the Japanese advisors in the Korean government that nothing could be done in that country without an alliance with at least one Korean faction, preferably more. The most natural allies of the Japanese were the soldiers and officers of the Hullyeondae. They were trained by Japan, and their very livelihood was dependent on close cooperation with that country. As they were universally seen as a pro-Japanese force, it was clear that they owed their existence to Japanese bayonets.[64] Colonel Woo Beomseon, commander of the Hullyeondae's Second Battalion, was a particularly trusted ally of the Japanese.[65] The commander in chief of the force, however, was not as reliable. Colonel Hong Kyedong was a confidant of the queen.[66]

But officers of the Hullyeondae, useful as they might have been, could not take the wheel of the government in Korea. For that purpose, an alliance with a senior Korean politician was necessary. The Japanese were finally able to secure the cooperation of some cabinet ministers, including the newly appointed prime minister, but that did not seem to be enough. It was questionable whether such people could do anything by themselves.[67] The Japanese therefore had to acquire an ally with a strong influence over the court, and that could only be the daewongun. He was eager to find new allies and a channel of communication was created with him through intermediaries such as Okamoto and the deputy consul of the Japanese Legation. The latter communicated with the classically educated daewongun by exchanging essays and poems in literary Chinese.[68]

According to his own version, Miura was very reluctant to cooperate with the daewongun at first, and it took some effort to convince him to confirm the alliance.[69] But as he came with little knowledge of Korea, it was natural that his decisions would be dependent on the consensus already formed by the legation staff. Like Sugimura and the other diplomats he felt the pressure of fast unfolding events. If he dallied, the Hullyeondae or the daewongun might start a rebellion by themselves, leaving the Japanese on the sidelines. The daewongun, Miura emphasized, was also in a dire financial situation, so the time was ripe to pressure him into concessions.[70]

Indeed, only the weakness of the Japanese position in Korea and the sense of emerging catastrophe, combined with Okamoto's persuasive power and prior knowledge of the daewongun, could justify such an alliance. The daewongun, after all, was a highly unattractive ally. An attempt to join forces with him had failed miserably only a year before, after he reneged on his promises and secretly tried to collaborate with the Chinese. It was this betrayal that had prompted Inoue to halt the cooperation with the old prince, a xenophobe with a proven record of guile and lies. The Japanese, Sugimura cautioned Miura, had "got their fingers burned" with the daewongun before. Now, however, Miura, Sugimura, and their colleagues believed they had no choice. The alliance was an act of desperation.[71]

And, as Sugimura told one of the Japanese advisers, it had to be accompanied by "decisive action"—words would not do.[72] Pieces of the puzzle seemed to fall into place, as the other allies of the Japanese, such as the prime minister and senior officers in the Hullyeondae, agreed to cooperate in reinstating the daewongun to power.[73] The negotiations with the old prince took some time, and their final result is still a matter of controversy. Kim Moonja and Tsunoda Fusako may be right in arguing that a solid written agreement with the daewongun was never signed, and the text of the agreement, as it appears in Miura's private papers, may not be authentic. Certainly, Miura and his advisors had an interest in overplaying the daewongun's involvement in order to legitimize their own deeds as mere attempts to help him.[74] But the daewongun's eagerness to exploit the results of the coup after the assassination of the queen disproves such apologetics. The daewongun was not forced by the Japanese to cooperate, and he had formed a sort of alliance with them—hazy and unwritten, maybe, but an alliance all the same. In any case, it was not until October 5 that the Japanese believed they had won over the daewongun. By that time, the decision to kill the queen had already been made.[75]

The Fox Hunters: Seoul's Sōshi and the Decision to Kill the Queen

Regicide was not an inevitable part of the plan devised by "professionals" such as Sugimura and Okamoto. The daewongun, after all, could be installed in the palace without much bloodshed, as he had been the year before. In fact, the idea of killing Queen Min did not originate in the Japanese Legation but rather among a motley group of Japanese adventurers affiliated with a nationalist organization known as the Tenyūkyō (Heavenly Grace and Chivalry) and with a Seoul-based Japanese newspaper.[76] The plot of October 1895 came into being only when this idea, which came from below, converged with the plans from above, devised by Miura and his colleagues.

The people who finally killed the queen were known in the Japanese legation and community as sōshi, literally "manly warriors." However, in the 1880s, it became a common tag for "young, politically engaged men who took up the cause of expanding popular rights," most prominently by violent means.[77] The sōshi, described by the contemporary press as youths with torn clothes, shabby long hair, and dirty countenances, traced their ideological ancestry both to the shishi of the 1860s and the rebels of the 1870s, such as Saigō Takamori's Satsuma Army. However, unlike the shishi, the term *sōshi* often carried negative connotations closer to the English word *thugs*.[78] No longer interested in full-scale rebellion against the system, the sōshi worked for politicians in the Movement for Popular Rights, guarding their assemblies, collecting intelligence, and using violence against political rivals of all kinds. Politically, they were associated with two of the guiding ideas of the Movement for Popular Rights: greater political participation for the Japanese people at home and an assertive foreign policy abroad. Indeed many of them preferred to see themselves as "heroes" (*yūshi*) or as "commoner shishi" (*minkan shishi*), a term that carried clear oppositional, anti-establishment connotations.[79] As a group with ambiguous goals and unclear means, it was natural for them to imitate the shishi both ideologically and organizationally. They too were violent, optimistic, looked down on careful planning, and adored alcohol and adventure.

During the 1880s several sōshi immigrated to Korea under the aegis of a local Japanese law firm, in fact a center for nationalist ruffianism. There, in the new Japanese settlement, the social gap between the sōshi and the other settlers was not as large as in Japan, and their bravado in a dangerous world earned them much greater prestige. Japanese in Korea possessed the right of extraterritoriality, so the sōshi were not bound to Korean law. Members of the Tenyūkyō roamed the Korean countryside, helped antigovernment rebels, and engaged in brawls, often treating the local villagers roughly. The Korean countryside was lawless in any case, and the local police did not have any right to arrest or to try them. As the Japanese Legation and army command recognized their usefulness as freelance intelligence agents, Japanese law enforcers turned a blind eye to their activities. After they robbed explosives from a Japanese-owned mine, for example, the legation denounced them as brigands, but did nothing tangible to stop them.[80]

Many of the sōshi were educated professionals of samurai background: pharmacists, monks, teachers, lawyers, martial artists, and writers. Others were simply unemployed adventurers or professional toughs in the "silent house" (*Museikan*), the sōshi band of the opposition's Freedom Party.[81] A significant number were journalists in Seoul, working in a Korean-Japanese bilingual propaganda newspaper, published by the reporter Adachi Kenzō under the auspices of the Japanese Legation.[82] The reporters and editors of *Kanjō Shinpō*, led by Adachi and his chief editor, Kunitomo Shigeaki, were socially tied to members of the Tenyūkyō.

Importantly, most of them came from Kumamoto, a Kyushu city looking toward Korea from the other side of the narrow sea. Influenced by the strong imperialist sentiments prevalent in this prefecture, the Kumamoto sōshi were known to be relentless advocates of military expansionism, associated with the nationalist Kumamoto Kokken-tō (Kumamoto State Power Party).[83] Adachi and his toughs had a rich history of violence. Being involved in the antigovernment campaign during the debate on the unequal treaties, they changed sides in 1892 and employed violence against oppositionists on behalf of the Home Ministry. During the Sino-Japanese War, Adachi, with some fellow military correspondents, was reportedly involved in a massacre of Chinese merchants.[84] Now, the newspaper *Kanjō Shinpō* became a new center for ruffianism. The Harvard graduate Shiba Shirō, Miura's personal advisor, joined the newspaper as a reporter. Not only did he not help his boss to fight the sōshi, as Tani Kanjō had expected, but he ended up becoming a sōshi himself.[85]

The sōshi had long clamored for a more hawkish policy and were highly unsympathetic to Inoue's conciliatory diplomacy.[86] Closely following the tradition of shishi political optimism, they had no patience for the complicated strategies of professional diplomats. Korea, as far as they were concerned, was a depraved society without effective laws, fallen from its past grandeur, full of evil and corruption that had to be eradicated by force. It was also, however, a civilization similar to that of Japan, a sister country that had to be redeemed.[87] Just like the assassins of Iwakura in 1874, the sōshi believed that radical change for the better could be made by getting rid of specific individuals, who were demonized accordingly. For the journalists of the *Kanjō Shinpō* and their friends, the demon was Queen Min.[88]

Political concerns mixed with misogyny, as the powerful woman was seen not only as a political rival about to "sell" Korea to the Russians, but also as an otherworldly, demonic presence.[89] Adachi Kenzō, the owner of *Kanjō Shinpō* and the leader of this group of sōshi, described her in his memoirs as "that bewitching beauty, who cunningly, ubiquitously and treacherously manipulated virtuous men for over a generation."[90] Kikuchi Kenjō wrote about her in the same vein, as the "wickedness at the King's side" (*Ōgawa no Kanja*) that had to be swept away.[91] According to the retrospective account of the nationalist organization Kokuryūkai, a society closely associated with the Tenyūkyō and one of the best sources for understanding the sōshi mentality of the time, the queen was a "vampire woman" (*yōfu no jōsei*), "a master of plots, sly, jealous and cruel." The account admitted that the queen was "one of these rare heroic and strong women of East Asia," but painted her power as selfish and destructive, feminine in the worst sense of the word. In the same vein, Kobayakawa Hideo described the queen as the "greatest woman in our generation," stronger even than the "heroic" daewongun, but also as a puppet master of an entire country and the source of all evil ("the evil root") in Korea.[92] This peculiar combination of admiration and hatred of the queen's supernatural presence was best reflected in a bizarre description offered by the sōshi Kikuchi Kenjō. After the queen had died, he wrote, her blood soaked into the earth, flowers fell from the trees, and the "wind was crying through the pines," either from sorrow or glee.[93]

Already in the summer of 1895, in a meeting with Okamoto, some sōshi and their allies were advocating "settling scores" with the queen. Their language was even clearer than that. In his testimony Okamoto said that the "Japanese sōshi maintained that XX had to be eliminated." The name of the victim was censored in the report, but given the intention of "settling scores" mentioned earlier, it is not difficult to understand to whom they referred.[94] That may be interpreted as an attempt by Okamoto to shift his own guilt to the sōshi, but in their own account they wrote about the matter in almost identical terms. "The only way to save Korea was to bury Queen Min. Slaughter Queen Min! Bury Queen Min!"[95] That sentiment also took the form of an "escape to the front" opposition based on the second bug of the Japanese political system, as many sōshi believed they merely had to strengthen the resolve of their "soft," "cowardly and timid" government.[96] While Inoue and his superiors in Tokyo hesitated, the sōshi gave their enthusiastic support to the daewongun, hailed by Kikuchi and Kobayakawa as the "old hero."[97] And they eagerly waited for an opportunity to strike.

This energy from below converged with the plans hatched in the legation. Upon his arrival in Seoul, Miura was quickly connected with the sōshi through his advisor Shiba Shirō. In any case, Miura was known as a person with strong ties in the sōshi world.[98] Around September 19, the connection was reinforced when the new envoy met Adachi Kenzō for a working session. Adachi was well acquainted with Miura, as they were both active in the movement against the government's plan to revise the unequal treaties in the late 1880s. Therefore, the newspaper owner, fed up with the "failure" of Inoue's policy, was greatly heartened to see Miura in Seoul.[99]

In their talk, the new envoy asked Adachi whether he had any young men available for a "fox hunt." Adachi understood the metaphor immediately: fox spirits disguised as cunning, evil and beautiful royal women were common stock in Japanese, Chinese, and Korean folklore. The description sat nicely with the misogynist views espoused by Adachi and his fellow sōshi. Their cooperation with Miura, it seemed, was a natural one.

According to Adachi's own testimony, "his heart leaped with joy" when he heard about the plan. Before they parted, Miura warned him that the matter was of the utmost secrecy.[100] Adachi cautioned Miura that his employees in the newspaper were gentle by nature, and thus it might be advisable to recruit more appropriate people from Kumamoto. Miura answered that it was out of the question— Adachi needed to rely on his own resources.[101] In response, the newspaper owner recruited a group of sōshi, including all the reporters and editors from his newspaper. These people, essentially private citizens, were responsible for the bloodiest part of the mission: to kill the queen herself. Miura's advisor, Shiba Shirō, served as the point of liaison between his boss and Adachi's sōshi.[102]

The optimism of the sōshi, mixed as it was with the demonization of the queen, created a bloodthirsty enthusiasm unmatched by anyone else in the legation. One of the sōshi, Hirayama Iwahiko, told Adachi's wife a short time before the operation that "you must be sorry you were born a woman," because she could not take part in the exciting "manly" adventure. Another reporter, Kobay-akawa Hideo, almost burst in tears when told by Adachi to remain behind and watch the production of the next day's newspaper. Had he missed such an oppor-tunity, he said, he would regret it throughout his life. During the raid, he felt that he and his friends were just like "heroes of a novel."[103] The exuberance of the sōshi was so great that Okamoto had feared that, if left to themselves, they would get out of hand and might confront the Korean government independently.[104]

According to the verdict of the preliminary court in Hiroshima, the decision to kill the queen was formally proclaimed in a meeting held at the Japanese Lega-tion on October 3 between Miura, Sugimura, and Okamoto. Having "received a request from the daewongun," the envoy and his two advisors decided not merely to force the latter's entry into the palace but to kill Queen Min.[105] In implementing the plan, they decided to use all means at their disposal—Japa-nese soldiers, Korean Hullyeondae, and of course the sōshi—"the young men who deeply lamented the course of events."[106] Three days later, Miura had given similar orders to Colonel Mayahara, one of the instructors of the Hullyeondae.[107]

Originally, Miura had scheduled the plan for mid-October. Events, however, interfered, as the queen prepared her own strike. For several days, officers of the Hullyeondae, especially the commander of the Second Battalion Woo Beomseon, visited the legation and warned that an action against them by the queen was imminent.[108] On the seventh, the Korean war minister visited the Japanese Lega-tion, and advised Miura that the court had decided to finally disband the Hul-lyeondae. The king, he said, was sick of their constant squabbles with the Seoul police. However, the royal center did not have the power to actually disband the units, and therefore the minister duly implored Miura to do so. The irascible Japanese envoy, unable to control his rage, shouted "You fool! Never!" and kicked "that fellow" out of the room.[109] According to Miura, the minister conceded to Sugimura, who waited for him on the first floor, that the Min faction had also planned to assassinate leading pro-Japanese politicians and "take Russia's side." The visit of the war minister, in any case, convinced the plotters that the opera-tion had to be carried through sooner than planned.[110] The raid on the palace was scheduled for the morrow, October 8.[111]

At the final hour, there was a last-ditch attempt by Inoue Kaoru to prevent disaster. The former envoy, who felt that something was about to go wrong in Seoul, telegraphed Miura and implored him to go to the palace, speak with the king and queen and "try to control the violence of the court," that is, to negotiate to keep the Hullyeondae together. Sugimura and Miura, however, gave an eva-sive reply. They wrote that "warnings will not be effective. The situation is very dangerous, and it is difficult to know when an incident will occur."[112] From that Inoue could probably understand that Miura planned to act violently, perhaps even occupy the palace, but he could not have guessed that Miura's real intention was to kill the queen whom he, Inoue, had personally offered Japanese protection if she was ever in danger.

The Assassination

Okamoto was given, as usual, the responsibility of liaising with the daewongun. Okamoto, Deputy Consul Horiguchi, Police Inspector Ogiwara and his troops, made their way together to the former regent's residence. Before setting out, Ogiwara had instructed his men to change into civilian clothes, that is, to turn themselves effectively into sōshi. Okamoto strictly warned the sōshi, whom he had seen as rude and untrustworthy, to keep completely silent during his discussion with the daewongun.[113]

The operation formally began in Kongdok-ri, the rural abode of the daewongun. Around 2:00 a.m., upon arrival at the daewongun's villa, Okamoto, Ogiwara, and Horiguchi went in for a talk, accompanied by some of the Koreans.[114] It took a long conversation of "two or three hours" to convince the old man to come along, but Okamoto finally succeeded in this task.[115] The group united with another squad of sōshi en route to the palace, and the whole force of thirty-odd sōshi and Korean civilians, accompanied by Hullyeondae, Japanese army officers, and consular policemen, headed to the royal quarters. The sōshi were dressed in a motley of Korean, Western, and Japanese clothes. According to the account of the *Kokuryūkai*, "some were armed with swords, some with sticks and some with pistols . . . indeed they looked like a gang of highway robbers. But in the midst of this chaos there was unity and a resoluteness of mind and action." Near the palace, the assault teams were joined by Japanese soldiers from the Consulate Guard Unit.[116]

At around 5:00 a.m., when the raid was about to begin, the Korean collaborators inside the palace fulfilled their own part of the plan. As if playing the role of a Shakespearian villain, the vice minister of agriculture, and a favorite of the queen, convinced her that no harm would come to her from the Japanese. Had not Inoue promised to protect the safety of the royal couple in times of need? He advised her to therefore neither hide nor flee.[117] Other collaborators, no less dangerous, made sure that the Palace Guards were neutralized. Under the noses of the two foreign advisors, the American general William McDye and the Russian Afanasii Seredin-Sabatin, soldiers were quietly removed from the guard to other assignments, modern weapons were taken away and officers were won over. Crucially, no guards were posted on the path leading to the quarters of the queen. The later testimonies of Seredin-Sabatin, McDye, and others portrayed a scene of utter incompetence and chaos.[118]

The king, alarmed by the noise outside, quickly dispatched one of his confidants to alert the American and Russian envoys and ask for their help.[119] At around 5:00 a.m., some of the Japanese policeman climbed the walls using folding ladders and opened the gates from the inside.[120] Colonel Hong Kyedong, the commander of the Hullyeondae, was one of the plot's first victims. Not privy to the conspiracy and loyal to the queen, he tried to stop his own troops and was shot to death by a Japanese officer.[121] There were some shots exchanged, but soon the rest of the Palace Guard officers abandoned their men, who, now leaderless, tried simply to run away and save their lives. The road, according to the sōshi Kobayakawa, was littered with discarded caps, weapons, and uniforms. General William McDye, the American advisor of the Guard, tried to rally a few dozen troops in a small alleyway, but they were "too excited" to obey him.[122] The Japanese soldiers reformed in military order inside the palace, surrounding the inner chambers and blocking all escape routes. Having their way cleared, the sōshi went in for the kill, accompanied by some Japanese officers, probably clad in civilian attire.[123] According to the official Korean investigation report: "The Japanese sōshi, numbering thirty or more, under the leadership of a head Japanese, rushed with drawn swords into the building, searching the private rooms, seizing all the palace women they could catch, dragging them round by the hair and beating them and demanding to know where the queen was."[124] According to Takahashi Genji, the two main political groups of sōshi, the Freedom Party and the Kumamoto Party, had competed with each other over who would find the queen first, a competition which no doubt contributed to the brutality of the entire operation.[125] The Russian advisor Seredin-Sabatin, fearful for his life, asked for Japanese protection, which was given to him, and had to witness the invaders pushing the hapless court ladies out of the low windows and dragging them by their hair across the mud.[126]

All the while the sōshi had sought by a literal process of elimination to locate the queen. "The heroes of Korea," wrote Kikuchi Kenjō, "thinking of these long years of silent pain, were looking for the queen across the halls."[127] Initially the suspicion fell on two of the court ladies, who were slashed by swords. The minister of the royal household, trying to protect the ladies' quarters with his body, was killed by a Japanese officer.[128] The queen was subsequently found in a room by one of the sōshi, maybe Takahashi Genji (or, according to another version, an army lieutenant).[129] The killer threw her down, jumped on her breast three times with his shoes and then hacked her with his sword. Satisfied with their deed, the sōshi took the body of the queen to the lawn and burned her with kerosene.[130]

When the editors of the local English language journal, the *Korean Repository*, hastened to the scene they found that the "great front gate was guarded by Japanese troops, and more could also be discerned inside. A surging crowd of Koreans could be seen at the far end . . . and among them were the palace women."[131] The American envoy, who arrived with his Russian colleague, witnessed "evil look-ing Japanese with disordered clothes, long swords and sword canes" hurrying around.[132] Sugimura's fervent request to conceal Japanese involvement was in vain. The sōshi were just too proud of what they were doing.[133]

Amidst the carnage, the daewongun, backed by Hullyeondae and Japanese bayonets, emerged to take control of the palace. According to Miura, who met him a short time later, the old prince was "beaming with delight."[134] In two proc-lamations, signed by the Committee of National Independence, he vowed to "aid His Majesty, expel the low fellows . . . save the country and introduce peace."[135] In an especially cruel gesture, he tried to force the king to degrade his slain consort into the rank of a commoner. Probably, as the British Legation assumed, the pur-pose was to block the future way of her son to the throne, clearing the way for the daewongun's own grandson. Gojong, however, in a rare display of courage, told his father that "you can cut my fingers off, but I will not sign your proclamation." The daewongun was forced to issue the edict without the royal seal, endorsed only by the ministers of the new, pro-Japanese cabinet. Most of the foreign dip-lomats in Seoul refused to recognize it as a royal act.[136]

After the assassination, Miura and his accomplices seem to have panicked at the results of their own deeds. At first, even the king did not suspect Miura him-self, and believed, according to a report submitted by the Russian Legation, that the assassination was an initiative of Okamoto and the other Japanese advisors. While a trail of evidence led to the legation, Miura tried to cover himself as much as possible by lying to the representatives of the other powers.[137] His attempts at a whitewash, however, were poor at best. Apart from the fact that so many observers, Korean and Western alike, had seen the Japanese troops and the sōshi in the palace, Miura and Sugimura left a trail of evidence regarding their own involvement. Indeed, when Korean royal emissaries hurried to the Japanese Lega-tion to urgently summon Miura to the palace, they found him with Sugimura dressed and with sedan chairs ready and waiting outside the door, suggesting that they knew something was amiss.[138] Everything in their behavior that morning smacked of complicity.

In the afternoon, speaking in an emergency meeting of the diplomatic corps, Miura was confronted with accusations from the other envoys, especially those from Russia and America. When the Russian Envoy, Karl Ivanovich Weber, insisted that Japanese with naked blades were seen at the crime scene, Miura lamely replied that some Koreans may have donned Japanese garb and used Japa-nese swords.[139] The next day, he employed the newly installed Korean cabinet in his attempt at a cover-up, arranging an assurance from the new war minister that some Korean rebels were dressed in Japanese clothes, and that "no Japanese" were present at the disturbances. Three Korean scapegoats were chosen for the executioner's axe.[140]

Miura's blatant lies not only to the Koreans and the other envoys but also to his own government proved that he had not acted under explicit or implicit instructions from Tokyo.[141] On the same morning, at eight o'clock, he had already telegraphed Acting Foreign Minister Saionji Kinmochi and assured him that the whole incident was a fight between Korean troops. The fate of the queen, he emphasized, was still unknown.[142] It is astounding that Miura, as a diplomat working for the Japanese government, held his own government in such a low regard that he would feed it the same lies as he did the foreign envoys that same day. As Consul Uchida Sadatsuchi, the supreme Japanese judicial authority in Seoul, wrote in rage, Miura treated everyone outside his circle of conspirators as an outsider, whether he was a foreign diplomat or a member of his own government.[143]

Saionji suspected foul play and asked Miura whether Japanese subjects were involved in the killing of the queen.[144] In response, Miura said that the queen "might have been" killed, but that the alleged involvement of Japanese subjects was still "under investigation." In the evening, Miura went a step further, and conceded to Saionji that some Japanese might have been involved as minor players but "did not do violence." He condemned yet again the evil of the queen's influence, a disease that afflicted the entire Korean system and hinted that something had to be done to stop the disbandment of the Hullyeondae and the total expulsion of Japanese influence from Korea. All the while, Miura pretended that he was investigating the affair, "updating" his minister every few hours, as if he was not the main initiator of the plot. His whole writing style, admitting the facts in small increments while repeatedly insisting on the legation's innocence, resembled a delinquent schoolboy stretching his rhetorical powers to postpone an inevitable confession.[145]

Even the Japanese government, rarely keen to punish its own offenders, could not ignore the growing evidence indicating Miura's complicity. Consul Uchida Sadatsuchi was not privy to the conspiracy and was horrified when he found out that Japanese subjects were involved in it. He was even more chagrined that his own subordinates from the police had plotted with Miura behind his back.[146] Uchida's original instinct was to whitewash the entire affair to save embarrassment for his government, especially because at first he was not completely certain that Tokyo was not behind the operation.[147] But when he was convinced that the assassination was Miura's private venture, particularly after a senior diplomat, Komura Jūtarō, was sent by Tokyo to investigate, Uchida knew he could not conceal facts from his own superiors at Miura's behest.[148]

Thus, following a common pattern for organizations being investigated, the investigator from outside (Komura) forged a natural alliance with the outsider of the organization (Uchida). To assist Komura, the consul conducted his own thorough investigation of the affair, and on November 15 released to Tokyo a detailed, candid report incriminating Miura, the legation staff, and the sōshi alike, with an explicit recommendation to punish them accordingly.[149] Uchida, who decided to expel some of the sōshi from Korea, had to endure violent threats from elements in the Japanese community. A highly unpopular figure among the sōshi, he was seen as a whistleblower because he was the only truly obedient official in the Japanese Legation.[150] He felt himself committed to the formal hierarchy of the Foreign Ministry more than to the private network centered on the unholy trinity of sōshi, diplomats, and advisors in the Japanese Seoul community.

Response under Fire: The Trial in Hiroshima

The foreign envoys in Seoul did not try to violently engage the Japanese, but they certainly showed signs of discontent. No one believed the denials of Miura and his Korean allies, and soon it became common knowledge that the incident was planned by the Japanese Legation.[151] A few days after the assassination of the queen, in a joint show of forces, the Russian and American envoys landed a small number of marines from their men-of-war in the harbor "in order to protect the King."[152] On February 11 the king and the crown prince, hidden in women's sedan chairs, escaped to the Russian Legation and "ruled" the country under Weber's warm embrace.[153] With the Russian envoy's cooperation, the king restored the queen to her former exalted status, overthrew the pro-Japanese cabinet, and declared Japan's leading collaborators to be traitors.[154] The pro-Japanese prime minister and some of his colleagues were subsequently lynched by an angry mob, along with some Japanese civilians.[155] A short era of Russian dominance began in Korea.

The Japanese government, taken aback by the international turmoil, disavowed all responsibility for the event. In a conversation with Ernest Satow, the British envoy in Tokyo, two days after the assassination, Acting Foreign Minister Saionji assured him that "the Japanese Government would view with the greatest displeasure the participation of Japanese subjects in a treasonable conspiracy against the sovereign of a friendly state."[156] In addition, the acting foreign minister was afraid lest Miura or the "criminal sōshi" initiate a battle with Russian and American troops, and he ordered the envoy to restrain the ruffians and keep the Japanese troops inside their barracks.[157] For the same reason, the home minister proposed that Prime Minister Itō issue an imperial edict, preventing additional sōshi ("rowdy folk") from traveling to Korea.[158]

Soon, both Komura in Seoul and the authorities in Tokyo understood the extent of Miura's complicity, and he was recalled to Japan along with Sugimura, Okamoto, and the sōshi.[159] Many of them, according to later testimonies, believed that a prize was waiting for them at the harbor. Others had dreams of rallying the Tokyo sōshi in support of the daewongun's government.[160] Upon their arrival in Hiroshima, however, they were arrested on charges of murder and conspiracy to commit murder.[161] A confession admitting personal involvement in the killing caused the public prosecution to indict one of the sōshi, Hirayama Iwahiko, on a charge of "willful homicide," and Takahashi Genji admitted killing at least one woman.[162] The preliminary trial, similar in nature to a grand jury process in the United States, took place before Justice Yoshioka Yoshihide in the Hiroshima Court for Preliminary Inquiries.

The decision of the Hiroshima court, published on January 20, is a curious document. Its description of the events up to the entry of the Japanese sōshi to the palace is surprisingly honest, so that even the Korean Committee of Inquiry, established by the king under Russian auspices on February 11, used it as a source for the facts of the case. That is strange because if the Japanese judge had wanted to hush up the affair completely, he could have accepted the numerous excuses Miura made after the assassination. Instead the court report described the events accurately and ascribed to Miura a clear-cut intention to commit homicide. However, as the Korean committee rightly stated, "The judgment of the Japanese Hiroshima court, after stating that 'about dawn the whole party ... entered the palace ... and at once proceeded to the inner chambers,' stops abruptly in its statement of facts, but says, 'notwithstanding these facts there is no sufficient evidence to prove that any of the accused actually committed the crime originally mediated by them.'"

All defendants were acquitted on the grounds of insufficient evidence.[163] Their acquittal was based, according to the verdict, on Article 165 of the Meiji Code of Criminal Procedure (Keiji Soshōhō). This article endowed judges with a sweeping power to acquit a defendant whenever they believed that the evidence for the case was inadequate.[164] The Meiji judicial system empowered the magistrates with considerable authority to evaluate which evidence was "sufficient" and which was not, based on the judicial principle of "common sense" (dōri).[165] In an apologetic document, drafted after the trial either by the court or the Japanese government, the court's decision was defended by purely legalistic arguments. The evidence, according to this document, had proved that the defendants entered the palace with the "determination" to kill the queen, but did not prove that they were the ones who killed her. In addition, several people had already been condemned by a Korean court for the same offence.[166]

The construct separating "determination," "result," and "action" was awkward to say the least, and court's arguments seem to defy reason.[167] The facts mentioned at the verdict certainly supported the conspiracy indictment, and as for the act of homicide itself, there was solid evidence against at least four of the sōshi and two of the policemen.[168] Consul Uchida, eager to incriminate the defendants, had sent ample additional evidence to the court.[169] Furthermore, Judge Yoshioka did not invite key foreign witnesses, nor even consider their written testimony, meticulously taken by Uchida.[170] Therefore, the fact that Yoshioka acquitted *all* defendants of *all* charges cannot be explained exclusively through recourse to the legal realm.

Did the government interfere to save the defendants? Most authors tend to take this as self-evident.[171] But we have no documentation to prove it, and by 1895 governmental interference in the work of the courts was far from universally accepted. Only four years before, in 1891, the president of the Supreme Court parried the pressure of the government to condemn to death a policeman who assaulted the Russian crown prince, sentencing him to life imprisonment instead.[172] A year later, the government had the president sacked for improper behavior (gambling in a tea house). Both incidents provoked sharp controversy, public attention, and press coverage. Therefore, by 1895, the independence of the courts was still a matter of contention that could arouse public ire.[173] If the government indeed interfered in Yoshioka's work, it probably did so very secretly and no evidence remains. Furthermore, some of the correspondence between Saionji and his diplomats expressed a consensus that adequate punishment, rather than whitewashing, might have served the reputation of the government better.[174] Miura might have been excused for political reasons, but exonerating the sōshi was not necessarily in the Japanese government's best interest. Therefore, the assumption that the verdict was engineered by the Japanese government, while impossible to dismiss, has to be seriously doubted.

Another possibility, no less probable, is that the acquittal was solely the decision of Judge Yoshioka. Certainly it was not his initial intention, as the investigation he conducted was serious and resolute. He could have changed his mind, or got cold feet somewhere in the middle, whether due to his appreciation of the perpetrators' patriotism and pure motives, fear of being assassinated himself, or a certain unwillingness to sour the relationship between Japan, the daewongun, and the new puppet regime in Korea.[175]

A short time beforehand, a military tribunal of the Hiroshima Fifth Division had acquitted all the military personnel involved, and its story, almost untold until now, seems rather different from that of the Hiroshima court. Throughout October, the military investigators seemed quite willing to believe that the officers and soldiers on trial were not involved in the killings. Gradually, however, they felt that there were substantial contradictions in their testimonies, and asked the Army Ministry for permission to send investigation teams abroad in order to interrogate military personnel stationed in Korea.[176] But in early November, the investigators began to express increasing sympathy for the defendants and their families, especially because they acted under orders, and Japanese martial law was unclear on the question of whether subordinates had the right or duty to disobey illegal orders.[177]

Finally, after consulting the Army Ministry, the tribunal decided to acquit all defendants of murder, conspiracy to murder, and infringement of authority, because they acted under orders which seemed to them legitimate. Surprisingly, the judges emphasized that subordinates must refuse orders that are clearly illegal, unjust, or for which the commander has no authority, and if they obey, they cannot be exempted from criminal responsibility. Yet, in the face of the evidence in its possession, the court ruled that the military defendants neither heard about a plan to kill the queen nor had a hand in such a plan—their role was merely to safeguard the gates and ease the daewongun into the palace. If the ruling of the Hiroshima court was politically motivated, then its military counterpart preferred to whitewash the affair in order to reinforce its view of military obedience. Had there been any illegality here, it was implied, the responsibility rested not with the soldiers, but with Miura.[178]

An Echo for the Future: The Purchase Power of Optimism

The assassination of Queen Min was a unique event, first of all because it was successful. Failed attempts to kill Queen Min had been made in the abortive coups d'état of 1882 and 1884. Violent occupation of the palace, ending with executions of ministers, happened every few years in late Choson Korea, and the Japanese had been involved in some of these actions. Envoy Ōtori, as we have seen, orchestrated a successful palace raid only a year before, in 1894, again in collaboration with the daewongun. But previous attempts to kill the queen had been made by Koreans. The Japanese, on the other hand, took great care not to harm members of the royal family when they occupied the palace in 1894. In other words, it was the combination of regicide *and* Japanese involvement which made the Queen Min Incident unprecedented.[179] It is therefore instructive to make sense of the underlying factors behind it and the long-term ramifications of it.

There are several ways to do this and all are related to the intricate relationships between the perpetrators and their attitude toward their victim. First, there is a gender issue, which is almost always overlooked by authors and observers.

Not a few writers have been outraged by the fact that a "defenseless" woman was murdered by a gang of male cutthroats, but little attempt has been made to understand this horrific event in the context of the prevailing gender ideology of the time.[180] The politics of Meiji Japan were based on a clear separation between men and women. The former belonged to the public realm and the latter to the domestic realm. After the Meiji Restoration, almost all major leaders agreed that the emperor must "reform" himself as a manly ruler.[181] The way to do that, of course, was to remove him from the influence of the court ladies in Kyoto. Feminine involvement in politics was seen as backward and evil—part and parcel of Japan's "feudal" past.

Korean court culture also demanded strict seclusion of women. In a sense this tradition was more stringent than in Japan, as the court ladies were not to be seen by male guests. Still, that culture did allow a handful of elite women, such as Queen Min, to be involved in politics in the coulisses. It was just this sort of involvement that gave the Japanese considerable difficulties. On the one hand, as Miura and his staff fully recognized, the queen was one of the most powerful politicians in the country. On the other hand, she was hidden and Japanese diplomats could scarcely even speak with her, let alone apply crude pressure as they frequent did with Korean male politicians. By applying careful diplomacy, Inoue was able to approach the queen; Miura could scarcely do the same. Of course, the Japanese could have sent a woman to negotiate with her, as the Russians and the Americans did. Miura recognized that possibility in his memoirs, but as he said, "it was rejected from above."[182] The gender ideology of the Japanese did not permit them to employ women in sensitive political roles, and therefore barred them from communicating with the queen.[183]

Failures of communication, which are common in such cases, bred growing anger, resentment, and hatred, as seen in almost all accounts of the Japanese who were involved in the assassination.[184] The daewongun betrayed and harmed Japan at least as much as the queen, but he was never as maligned by the Japanese. In fact, after the event he was lionized by sōshi such as Kikuchi Kenjō as the "old hero" and even compared to Napoleon.[185] Combined with the misogynist ideology of manly brotherhood concocted by Adachi and his fellow sōshi, it was natural to demonize a powerful female as a "bewitching beauty," "fox," or "vampire woman." As "decent women" remained at home, the political woman had to be a fantastical monster. Killing her was not murder but a form of exorcism. The sōshi referred to the murder using the verb *hōru* (to slaughter an animal), in another example of dehumanization.[186] This misogyny goes a way to explaining the fury of the killers and their brutality during the operation.[187]

The second important factor, also almost always overlooked, was the unique personal background of the major architect of the conspiracy, Miura Gorō. In one of his apologetic statements to the court, the former envoy had written that it defied reason to assume that he, a man with "military habits," would behave in such an "erratic and unrestrained way" (*fukisoku hōjū no kōi*).[188] But in fact, Miura's erratic and unrestrained behavior was in perfect harmony with his military habits. Unlike his predecessors in the Seoul Legation, he was a product of the disobedient "habits" groomed by the supreme prerogative tradition: disdain of civilian superiors and the absence of a clear hierarchy within the officer corps itself.

Indeed, Miura did not have much respect for superiors, either in the military or outside it, especially when they did not bother to give him explicit instructions.[189] As a member of the losing military faction of the "four generals," he loathed the leaders of the army and the government, looking down on them as selfish "clique leaders." Only someone like him could tell a subordinate such as Consul Uchida that the perpetrators would keep the matter secret, "even when questioned in a court of law."[190] Only such a man could negotiate directly with imperial headquarters in defiance of diplomatic procedure, pressure the government to give him the right to mobilize troops in order to suppress bandits, and then use this privilege to murder the queen of another country.[191] And all of this was done in the space of "three puffs on a cigarette," without pausing even once to consider the foreign policy of his own government.[192]

But Miura did not operate in a vacuum. The key issue here was that an official representative of the Japanese state, a diplomat and former general, had used a group of civilian riffraff to go his own way. That was a symptom of a historical process with far-reaching consequences: the gradual disappearance of the gap between "resistance from above" and "resistance from below."[193] Both roads of insubordination had their roots as far back as the late Tokugawa period. During the 1860s, the gap between the rank-and-file shishi and their political leaders was not as great, as they all belonged to the same networks of conspirators. In the next decade the gap grew wider, as the leaders became more entrenched in their positions with every failed revolution or assassination attempt. It was easier for rank-and-file samurai to communicate with leaders such as Takasugi Shinsaku and Kido Takayoshi in the 1860s, harder but still possible to have a dialogue with Ōkubo or Saigō in the 1870s, and extremely difficult to approach Itō or Yamagata in the 1880s and 1890s, except for a few well-connected individuals. Resistance from above, based the supreme prerogative, remained the prerogative of an exclusive group of top military commanders.

Grassroots militants, reincarnated as sōshi, had their own assigned place in the new world of oligarchic rule and party politics. They could use violence against political rivals, operate under the protection of party leaders and generally enjoy themselves in a rowdy sort of way. But as "professional" political bullies, they could no longer hope to substantially change the system by sheer force, except perhaps through a handful of powerful bosses who gradually became part of the political elite. Their influence still existed, but it was limited. Though the police tolerated their violence, they were often punished, especially when they "crossed the line" by engaging in truly dangerous activities such as assassination attempts.[194] Their belief in their ability to change the system through resistance or rebellion from below had disappeared. Had optimism been a currency, then one may say that its "purchase power" substantially decreased in the Japanese mainland throughout the late 1880s and early 1890s.

In Korea, however, the situation was very different. There, as Takahashi Genji put it, he and his friends could "work for the country without atoning for one's sins and be cleared of all charges."[195] As we have seen, the power, influence, and self-confidence of the sōshi significantly increased upon their arrival in that troubled kingdom, where they enjoyed extraterritoriality, immunity from the law, and could be violent with impunity. Useful to the army as intelligence agents, the sōshi also were treated leniently by the Japanese Legation, the only authority which could punish them, which turned a relatively blind eye to their behavior, giving them much greater freedom of action than they ever had in Japan. In the general lawlessness of Korea, a country ruled by feuding, and sometimes warring factions, violence was frequent in any case. Crucially, it gave birth to the same process we witnessed in 1870s Japan: the belief that through assassination of specific "demonic" individuals the political Gordian knot could be disentangled. In other words, the currency known as "violent optimism" had much more purchase power in Korea than it did in Japan.

The result was a similar process to that defined by Prasenjit Duara as "state involution," the entrustment of state authority to private agents acting on behalf of the state and yet not an official part of its apparatus. The constant association of state and private agents in these transactions of power prompts the former to fall into the influence of the latter, as the official and private realms bleed into each other.[196] In the specific case of Japan, the constant use made by military officials, either active or retired (such as Miura), of sōshi as cutthroats and intelligence agents in Korea and Manchuria, formed such strong connections between the foreign policy establishment, the army, and the private nationalist organizations that in future years it became very difficult to draw clear boundaries between these three authorities.

During the assassination of Queen Min this process was made manifest when Ogiwara's policemen and the Guard's officers shed their uniforms and virtually blended with the sōshi. As the newspaper *Tōhoku Nippō*, put it, "For the sake of our country, we must deeply regret the fact that some of our diplomats and soldiers adopted the behavior of sōshi," a complaint echoed by Consul Uchida.[197]

There is no better example of this hybridity than Okamoto Ryūnosuke, a former rebellious officer who led the sōshi into action. He was a quasi-establishment figure, an advisor to the Korean government unofficially affiliated with the Japanese Legation. With the passage of time, individual army officers became associated with wild, private nationalist societies more than with their official commanders, re-creating the horizontal bonds between army units and politicians that Yamagata Aritomo strove to eliminate throughout the 1880s.

That process certainly did not begin in 1895, and one can find its roots as far back as the cooperation between Keiō students, and the Japanese Legation in the Korean abortive coup of 1884. The Queen Min assassination suggests a road not taken, and herein lies its importance. Its exceptional nature had given the Japanese government the opportunity to punish the perpetrators severely, thus slowing down the process of involution, halting or even reversing it. The failure of Judge Yoshioka to do so, whether due to his own discretion or government interference, obliterated this golden opportunity. Thus the latent structure of involution kept its existence, a ticking time bomb destined to explode in the late 1920s. First came Korea. Next was Manchuria.

COUP D'ÉTAT IN THREE ACTS
The Taishō Political Crisis, 1912–1913

> **Soldiers and ships of war are like sharp tools—dangerous things to handle.**
>
> —*Japan Daily Herald*, July 1874

Political, military, and institutional power, convincing as it may be in theory, is never fully realized until tested in a confrontation of some kind. The emperor, for example, theoretically possessed unlimited authority to command the army, but as the Meiji and Taishō emperors never forced the hand of military leaders, their power was never tested. In the same vein, Japan may have been building its military capabilities throughout the Meiji era, but until tested on the ground against China (1894–1895) and Russia (1904–1905), the empire was not yet considered a first-rate military power by other countries.

The same also applied to the independence granted to the military establishment under the prerogative of supreme command. True, individual military leaders made use of it, but occasionally and sparingly at the very best. The successful attempts of the military leaders to block constitutional challenges to the supreme prerogative system in the 1880s and 1890s involved a brutal struggle with the "four generals" faction and its allies but did not overstep the boundaries of legality. Individual army commanders behaved independently, at times, during the First Sino-Japanese War, but that could be ascribed to faulty communications and misunderstandings more than to outright insubordination.[1] The Queen Min Incident, despite its international ramifications, was still on the margins of the empire, and furthermore, it was engineered by an individual general and not by the army as an institution. In the Meiji era, the army had never tried to make use of the full extent of its autonomous power, or to overthrow a cabinet which defied its will. Apparently, the military leaders were too cautious to rock the boat in such a way.[2]

Such a move against a reigning cabinet, which amounted almost to a bloodless coup d'état, was first attempted in 1912. This event was the opening act of a major upheaval known as the Taishō political crisis. Crucially, the sensational events of this crisis were fueled by a process with dramatic ramifications for the future. The rank of officers involved in military resistance became increasingly lower as time went by. The senior generals, who were in firm control of the army in the Meiji era, lost much of their influence to midlevel bureau chiefs by 1912. These midlevel officers, in turn, were later pushed aside by even younger peers. This process, akin to a progressive democratization of military disobedience, made the army unrulier and more difficult to control. Eventually, it emerged as the key to the tragedies of later years.

A Short Blanket: The Squabble over the Budget in the Late 1900s

After the Russo-Japanese War, the growing complexity of the state became alarmingly evident in Japanese governing circles. The *genrō*, Meiji oligarchs such as Itō Hirobumi, Yamagata Aritomo, and Inoue Kaoru, were slowly but steadily withdrawing from the scene, leaving it open to the next generation of leaders. Itō was assassinated by a Korean nationalist in 1909, and advancing age gradually eroded the power of both Yamagata and Inoue.[3] Katsura Tarō and Saionji Kinmochi, the protégées of Yamagata and Itō, respectively, were the most prominent representatives of the new generation of leaders, and during the first decade of the twentieth century they took turns at the helm of the government. These two leaders, more than their predecessors, faced considerable difficulties controlling the entire breadth of an increasingly convoluted government apparatus.

Some of the complication arose from the sheer number of groups vying for power. Business circles, growing in influence, demanded the ear of policymakers. The army, no longer fully under Yamagata's control, was insistent about keeping its power intact. The Imperial Navy, emboldened by its achievements in the Russo-Japanese War, demanded its own share of the pie after long, painful years in the shadow of the army. Influenced by the expansionist ideology of the American naval thinker A. T. Mahan, the navy advocated making sea power the foundation of national defense, even to the degree of making the war fleet an independent force under the emperor.[4] Different segments of the bureaucracy, especially in the Home Ministry and the Treasury, were powerful actors, which statesmen could ignore only at their own peril.

This situation, difficult in any case, was further complicated by the entrance of the political parties into the intricate power struggle. The old Freedom Party, reincarnated in 1900 as Rikken Seiyūkai (Association of Friends of Constitutional Government, hereafter "Seiyūkai) abandoned its uncompromising oppositional attitude to the government and the bureaucracy. In that year, it formed a political alliance with Itō Hirobumi, considered the more moderate of the Meiji oligarchs, and later accepted the nominal leadership of his protégée, Saionji Kinmochi. The real leader of the party, however, was the chairman of its executive body, the shrewd politician Hara Kei (Takashi). Though leading a policy of compromise with the ruling establishment, Hara strove steadily to increase the power of the Seiyūkai at the expense of the oligarchs and their "cliques," with a single goal in mind: a government fully controlled by political parties and lower house majorities.[5]

All the power factors described above, the Genrō, businessmen, generals, admirals, bureaucrats, and party politicians, were tied to each other in informal groups, yet another manifestation of the phenomenon of private horizontal networks prevalent in Japanese politics since the late Tokugawa period. True, the hierarchy of the state was much stronger in 1912 than in the 1870s, but at certain points in time it could not withstand the pressure exercised by private civilian and military networks. The Taishō political crisis of 1912 was one of these seminal moments.

Around 1912, the weakness of the system as a whole emanated from the basic contradictions between plans, visions, and ambitions held by members of different factions, often intensely hostile to each other. As the imperial center was, as always, hazy and hidden, there was no one who could serve as a final arbitrator to solve the contradictions between the different visions for future national policy. While each vision could, perhaps, be implemented in isolation from the others, they could not exist in unison. The problem was first and foremost economic: these plans required funds—enormous amounts—and the state did not have the ability to finance all of them at the same time.[6]

Hara Kei, the driving spirit behind the first Saionji cabinet of 1906, wanted to build a power base for the Seiyūkai by forming a strong network of patronage in the provinces, his famous "pork barrel" policy. In order to forge ties between the local branches of the Seiyūkai and influential strongmen throughout Japan, he had promised an abundance of "candies" to local allies in form of schools, bridges, dams, and most of all—train stations and railway lines. These expensive plans, known at the time as Hara's "positive policy," became the core strategy of the Seiyūkai.[7]

The armed services, however, had their own costly plans. After the Russo-Japanese War the empire had solidified its control over Korea, which was finally annexed in 1910, and in addition extracted a wide array of privileges and concessions in South Manchuria. Three years before, without consulting the government, the General Staff devised a "national defense plan" for operations in the continent, requiring four additional divisions. These plans bore the signature of Emperor Meiji and thus were seen by the army as sanctified and unchangeable. The navy, painfully aware of the technological obsolescence of its fleet and worried about a possible confrontation with the United States, advocated even more expensive schemes for naval enlargement.[8] The army received two of the four divisions in 1907, but the first Saionji cabinet (1906–1908), as well as the subsequent second Katsura cabinet (1908–1911), dillydallied with the army's demands for two additional divisions on one hand, while brushing off the navy with the other.[9] The plans, however, were never rejected altogether, in order to prevent a complete break with the armed services. Instead, they were delayed on an annual basis.[10] Similar to the interdomainal alliance of the early 1870, the late Meiji political game was based on a delicate balance between different factions. A grave insult to one of them, especially the army or the navy, could result in damage to that balance, leading to unexpected and probably disastrous results.

The situation, however, became truly impossible during the second Saionji cabinet, which came to power in August 1911. During that year the external debt of Japan, already high after the Russo-Japanese War, skyrocketed.[11] Prime Minister Saionji and his finance minister realized that a policy of fiscal retrenchment was inevitable. Both leaders decided to accompany the new policy with tax cuts, as demanded by large segments of the business community and the population at large.[12] That, of course, made it more difficult to find any funds for Hara's "positive policy," and the leader of the Seiyūkai, entrenched in his powerful position as home minister, resisted. As usual, a compromise was reached: government expenses would be cut, but without obliterating the railway projects, indispensable to the maintenance of the Seiyūkai's patronage networks in the provinces.[13]

This compromise had to leave somebody unhappy, probably an actor lacking strong presence at the negotiation table. In 1912, the army was designated by the government leaders to play such a role—and the two major policymakers, Hara and Saionji, decided to postpone, yet again, the authorization of the long-promised two divisions.[14] The decision seemed to be politically feasible at the time. Urban public opinion, influenced by the economic slump and the liberal press, was increasingly hostile to the army's endless demands for more funds. The rivals of the army were by no means pacifist, but they were ready to limit the empire's expansion and believed that economic prosperity was more important than military strength.[15] There was hardly a time in prewar Japanese history, perhaps except 1921–1922 (the last years of the failed Siberian Intervention) when public opinion was so critical of the army, although this antiarmy attitude was more common in the big cities than in the countryside.[16] Hara had probably seen it as a signal to strongly resist the establishment of the new divisions in fiscal year 1912.

In addition, during 1912, Prime Minister Saionji diverged from the defense policy of previous cabinets in a fateful way. While previous cabinets brushed off the demands of navy and army alike, Saionji decided to veto the army's plans, while giving generous budgetary handouts to the navy.[17] This decision, yet again, bowed to public opinion as expressed in the liberal press: the exploits of the navy in the Russo-Japanese War had gradually endeared it to significant parts of the press.[18] A commentator in the journal *Taiyō*, for example, had noted that Japan's national defense had to be based first and foremost on sea power. The demands of the army for expansion were not related to legitimate security concerns, only to "daydreams of aggressors and imperialists."[19] This kind of mood made it easier for the government to turn down the army's request, while promising to use the money saved through the retrenchment to gradually fulfill the navy's plan. The intense interservice rivalry made this struggle especially bitter and emotionally charged.[20]

The army could not stomach a situation where the navy got all it wanted while its own plans were constantly frustrated.[21] The preference for one armed service and discrimination against the other undermined the balance, and for that reason, it became increasingly difficult to delay a confrontation over the budgetary issue as in previous years. A feeling of a looming zero-sum struggle slowly pervaded the minds of decision makers in the army, navy, cabinet, and Seiyūkai alike.[22]

A good example of that feeling, from the army's side, was a series of memoranda written by Major General Tanaka Giichi, the influential chief of the Military Affairs Bureau in the Army Ministry. In these letters, Tanaka bemoaned the passive attitude of the government in face of the chaos created in China by the republican revolution of 1911. The Russians were advocating their own rights in Manchuria, and for the Japanese it was a golden opportunity to demand a larger slice of the Chinese melon. To fortify Japan's "special rights" in Manchuria and Mongolia, as well as to guard against a potential Russian attempt to restage the conflict with the Japanese Empire, the army had to obtain two more divisions.[23]

These professional arguments, however, were not the main problem. Rather than dealing with the issue as a legitimate debate about defense policy, Tanaka and his colleagues began to regard it as a conspiracy hatched by a malicious, cunning enemy.[24] How else could one explain the government's animosity to the army and its preferential treatment of the navy and the political parties? The "antimilitarist politicians" in the parties and the cabinet, claimed Tanaka's colleague, Colonel Ugaki Kazushige, did not share the army's foresight for the nation's "posterity," being obsessed instead with private interests, the greed of businessmen, and "economic trifles."[25] As a result, Tanaka complained that the "deteriorating fortress" of the army was about to give in to the government's "assault," a lethal blow against the imperial regime itself.[26] What was at really at stake here was military independence from civilian rule, the supreme prerogative ideology that had stood at the basis of military thinking since 1878. The appropriate response in such a case, according to Tanaka, was to "manufacture an excuse precipitating the mass resignation of the cabinet."[27] If the government was an enemy, then it had to be defeated by a formidable countermove—a military coup d'état of one form or the other.

In order to understand the nature of the army's scheme, which stood at the heart of the bloodless coup d'état that followed, we must pause and take a look at a peculiar system that had developed since 1900, an offshoot of the supreme prerogative ideology. It was this system, called the "active duty rule," and the political tools it had generated, which turned the budgetary disputes of autumn 1912 into a government crisis, and finally, into a military coup d'état.

A Sword Wielded by the Army:
The Rule of Active Duty

The basic framework of the army's scheme was based on a footnote to an imperial ordinance from 1900, known as the "rule of active duty ministry" (*Gen'eki Bukansei*, hereafter, "rule of active duty"). This footnote stipulated that the army and navy ministers had to be generals and admirals on active duty.[28] The law was far from being revolutionary. Prior to this, army and navy ministers (with one exception) were selected from the active duty roster, but in 1900 this custom was turned into law.[29]

In face of the increasing influence of the Seiyūkai and other political parties in the civilian cabinet, the active duty rule not only tightened the control of the military establishment over its ministers, but also gave the generals and the admirals a handy tool to threaten unfriendly cabinets. As generals and admirals on active duty were relatively susceptible to pressure applied by military power holders, the army or navy could theoretically withdraw their minister and refuse to appoint a new one, thus forcing the cabinet to resign. Before 1900, the government could, again theoretically, counter that threat by appointing a retired general or admiral, but the active duty rule made that impossible. However, until 1912, the army and the navy never dared to precipitate a crisis by withdrawing their own ministers. In that year, both services did just that against two successive cabinets, thus throwing the entire state into a prolonged, bitter political crisis.

How could the army and navy *actually* prevent an active duty general or admiral from serving as a minister? We shall discuss this crucial question further below, but for now it may be instructive to examine the process by which army ministers were appointed shortly prior to the crisis. As the active duty rule did not ascribe a precise procedure for this process of selection, the decision about which general to appoint was made collectively inside the military elite, along the unofficial lines of the private, horizontal network that governed the army. As we have seen in chapter 5, power in the military establishment was dispersed between different agencies, and no single individual was completely in charge. Figures like Yamagata were highly respected, but they did not make decisions without giving due weight to the consensus formed by the senior generals. In practice, deliberations about the appointment of new ministers were made along the lines of a formidable but informal network, commonly known as the Chōshū Clique.

It is important to note that the name of this group is somewhat mislead-ing. The former Chōshū Domain, a feudal entity roughly equivalent to today's Yamaguchi Prefecture in western Japan, was one of the domains which led the Meiji Restoration in 1868. The private, horizontal network of generals, bureau-crats, politicians, and journalists known as the Chōshū Clique, however, was not a regional organization. It differed greatly from the domain cliques of the 1870s, organizations such as Saigō Takamori's faction, which truly represented the spe-cial interests of former domains and geographical regions (for example Chōshū, Tosa, or Satsuma). The Chōshū Clique, as it had evolved since the 1880s, had little to do with the regional interests of the residents of Yamaguchi Prefecture. Instead, it was a group of highly placed individuals who had known and trusted each other for many years. This clique had strong presence in the bureaucracy and in both houses of the Imperial Diet. It had some allies in the conservative segments of the press and, crucially, also in the Army Ministry, the General Staff, and the higher echelons of the officer corps, where it concentrated around the figures of Field Marshal Yamagata and his protégée, former Prime Minister Kat-sura Tarō.[30]

Most, but not all, members of the group hailed from the Chōshū Domain, and they were usually united by a common political outlook. All of them ven-erated Yamagata, supported expansion to the Asian mainland in some form or another, believed that the army should be independent from the government, and resisted the influence of political parties in military affairs.[31] Crucially, they had all advocated a hard-line position in the debate about the two divisions. Because the Chōshū Clique still stood at the center of military decision making in 1912, new army ministers could not be appointed without its support. Accord-ing to Major General Tanaka Giichi, the head of the Military Affairs Bureau at the Army Ministry and a key figure in the clique, the minister had to be a per-son whose "military views" and "political views" harmonized, a general sound in body and mind, able to represent the interests of the army in a "close fight" with the government. Tanaka and his Chōshū Clique colleagues, in other words, were not electing a leader for the military establishment, a man who could create and implement policy, but rather a mouthpiece for the consensus already formed inside the army.[32]

In April 1912 Army Minister Ishimoto passed away, opening a period of deliberations inside the Chōshū Clique about the choice of his successor. Tanaka and his close colleague, the governor-general of Korea Terauchi Masatake, discussed the appropriate qualifications for the new minister. Then the matter was raised before Field Marshal Yamagata, who proposed four possible candidates. The list was subsequently passed to Katsura, who proposed candidates of his own, as well as to Chief of the General Staff Hasegawa and his deputy. Finally, Yamagata, "after careful deliberations," chose one of the candidates, Uehara Yūsaku, a general of Satsuma origins.[33]

To save the face of the prime minister, Yamagata named Uehara along with two other candidates (Nagaoka and Kigoshi). But the prime minister, cordially, overruled only Nagaoka, and left Yamagata the choice between Uehara and Kigoshi. In response, Yamagata nominated Uehara, as agreed beforehand.[34] After being informed about Yamagata's decision, the prime minister formally submitted Uehara's nomination as army minister for the emperor's approval.[35] It is important to keep in mind that several generals were involved in the selection of the minister, and no one could unilaterally dictate the nomination to the others. The collective nature of this process is key to understanding the crisis that followed.

The Taishō Political Crisis—Act One: Saionji against the Army

In early July 1912, Home Minister Hara Kei had good reasons to believe that the resistance of the army to the government's retrenchment policy could well be overcome. The positions, after all, were not so far apart, as the government wanted merely to postpone the formation of the two divisions rather than indefinitely giving them up. It was also possible to deny extra budget to both army and navy, as in previous years.[36] To begin with, Hara did not attach much importance to the crisis, and even a cursory examination of his diary shows that other problems, such as his duties in the Home Ministry and at the Seiyūkai, overshadowed the question of the two divisions in his mind until early autumn.[37] Still, he devoted some attention to the discord with the army. On July 1, Hara had a fruitful conversation with Katsura Tarō, the former prime minister, whose influence in the army was still significant. Katsura openly told his guest that the demands of the army were unrealistic, and the generals were notified accordingly.[38] Hara thus had ample reasons to think that with the support of Katsura, a prominent figure in the Chōshū Clique, the army's influence might well be checked.

Six days later, Katsura embarked on a long-planned tour of Europe with some of his closest advisors.[39] However, this venture proved to be disastrous. Katsura, who had long maneuvered between Yamagata, his erstwhile patron, and Hara's Seiyūkai, had gradually evoked Yamagata's ire.[40] On July 30 Emperor Meiji passed away after a long illness, and Katsura was forced to cancel his trip and hurry back to Japan.[41] When he arrived in Tokyo, on August 11, he was shocked to discover that Yamagata "arranged" a retirement from active politics for him, into the positions of chief chamberlain in the palace and lord keeper of the privy seal.[42] Such roles were customary for retired genrō and other high dignitaries, but Katsura was at the height of his political aspirations (the London *Times* crowned him in July as the "future prime minister of Japan"), and he perceived Yamagata's move as a stab in the back.[43]

The results were unforeseen and far reaching. After his "exile" to the palace, Katsura quickly entered a bitter mood of "if you wanted me to step out of the way then why didn't you say so," and thus became reluctant to mediate between the Seiyūkai and the Chōshū Clique. Perhaps, as Hara assumed at the time, it was also a cool, reasoned calculation on Katsura's part, as a severe political crisis could have served as an excuse for his return to active politics. Whether it was true or not, in the autumn of 1912 Katsura had a perfect excuse not to help Hara: he could always say that his new role in the palace tied his hands from active involvement.[44]

Under such conditions, it was difficult to create functioning channels of communication between the army and the cabinet. One obvious channel could have been formed through Army Minister Uehara, but he was universally seen as a weak figure manipulated by his subordinates, "a horse managed by a skillful circus rider," according to one observer.[45] Certainly, Uehara was neither able nor willing to challenge the army consensus, and therefore Prime Minister Saionji chose to effectively ignore and bypass him. Yamagata, elderly but still active, was another obvious choice, but even his influence was not as strong as it used to be.[46] He could, perhaps, force the army to compromise, had he wished to put his whole weight into the matter. The problem was how to convince him to make such immense efforts for Hara and the Seiyūkai, whom he heartily disliked.

Instead, Yamagata preferred to keep a low profile, though his position was initially moderate (he and his advisors did not wish to see Saionji's cabinet overthrown, at least not until the last stage of the crisis).[47] Accordingly, in his first meeting with the prime minister in August, Yamagata's offer to solve the crisis was to permit the army to use the money saved by the retrenchment to finance the two divisions. This attempt at compromise was, however, rejected by the cabinet. General Terauchi tried, at the last moment, to postpone the crisis by proposing to delay the extra funding for both army and navy, but this plan also failed to elicit a response.[48] One supporter of the government assured the prime minister that if he stopped the funding plan for the navy, the two divisions issue would die out by itself. But for Saionji and Hara that was no longer the issue: they could not surrender to the army's demands without "losing face" and endangering their support from the navy, the Seiyūkai, and public opinion.[49] Some genrō did try their hand at mediation, but their lack of influence in the army turned it into a mockery. Hara, sick and tired of genrō meddling, wrote in his diary that their influence had to be stopped altogether. Above all, he was loath to meet or to negotiate directly with Yamagata, whom he personally detested.[50]

Adding to the difficulty of the entire situation was the fact that the two people who *really* stood at the epicenter of the army's Chōshū Clique, Major General Tanaka Giichi and his direct subordinate, Colonel Ugaki Kazushige, had no official position of leadership.[51] Both worked in the Military Affairs Bureau at the Army Ministry, Tanaka heading the entire bureau, and Ugaki its most important section (confusingly also named Military Affairs Section). Their formal role was certainly not powerful enough to permit frequent talks with the prime minister or other senior political figures. There was a fatal incongruence between the official, vertical network of the army, the normal hierarchy of ranks, which dictated the official rules of conduct, and the private network, the Chōshū Clique, where real power flowed. The result was that the people who could be approached by the government, Katsura, Uehara, and Yamagata, were either unable or unwilling to change the army's consensus, and the people who *could* influence the army, Tanaka and Ugaki, were unapproachable.[52] The government and the army, unable to communicate and riding on the tigers of public opinion and the internal military consensus, were heading toward an inevitable collision. Attempts to negotiate compromise, while not impossible, became increasingly difficult.[53]

The Genrō Inoue Kaoru, whom we met in the previous chapter as the Japanese envoy to Korea, was perhaps the only one who understood that in order to solve the crisis, one had to stage direct negotiations between the people who really mattered in each camp: Hara from the Seiyūkai and Major General Tanaka from the army. And indeed, he made immense efforts to arrange such negotiations at the beginning of November.[54] However, these attempts ended in failure because of Hara's refusal to negotiate with mid-ranking officers. Major General Tanaka, he told Inoue angrily, was not in a position to speak with him. It was unreasonable, scoffed Hara, to be directly approached by a subordinate officer instead of by the army minister.[55] The two meetings held therefore failed to produce substantial results, and that channel of direct negotiations was never reopened.

Meanwhile, the people who were formally in charge of the army were less and less receptive to compromises. Army Minister Uehara, wrote Hara in his diary, "decided to gamble on a stiff approach."[56] But his sharp-worded petition to the government, submitted in November, was in fact drafted by Tanaka and Ugaki.[57] As Katsura told Hara, the minister had become a "prisoner" of his bureau and section heads, who were located at the junction of control over the military establishment.[58]

In early November, there were some failed, last-ditch attempts by Saionji to work out a compromise with Yamagata. Unfortunately, the old field marshal was in no mood for compromise. He insisted on the absolute necessity of forming the additional two divisions, complained about the discrimination toward the army in favor of the navy, and was not even prepared to delay the formation of the divisions. National defense, he said, must be primary, and the economy secondary. If the government continued to discriminate against the army in favor of the navy, there might be "grave consequences" and a "major incident" could occur. Yamagata, in other words, openly threatened to overthrow the government by use of the military. The fact that his position had hardened so much since August indicates that he might have been influenced by hardliners such as Major General Tanaka—whose arguments were explicitly mentioned in the conversation.[59]

In the cabinet meeting of November 22, the army minister refused to speak with the government about the problems or to explain the reasons for the army's demands, unless the prime minister accepted them in advance. When pressured, he gave an offhand presentation, which, according to Hara, "was even more careless than the one given by Tanaka." This presentation was possibly based, yet again, on a radical opinion paper drafted by Colonel Ugaki. Uehara, it seemed, believed that a head-on confrontation was coming and felt reluctant to do anything to avert it. Hara was indignant: "This is not the behavior of a cabinet minister," he wrote in disgust in his diary.[60] Uehara was no longer perceived as part of the government, but rather as the mouthpiece of a hostile power.

"Public opinion," in addition, had made compromise increasingly difficult. In the face of the army's pressure, the cabinet was encouraged by a strong campaign carried out by financial leaders and strong segments of the liberal press. Shibusawa Eiichi, one of the doyens of the Japanese banking system, expressed "utter resistance" to the army's plan, supporting instead retrenchment and tax cuts.[61] Several influential newspapers and periodicals such as *Tokyo Keizai Zasshi*, *Osaka Mainichi*, and *Nihon Oyobi Nihonjin* railed against the "domain cliques" (most predominantly the Chōshū Clique) and the military leaders, attacks which were intensified in late September and throughout October. On October 5, *Tokyo Keizai Zasshi* suggested that the problem of the division increase was a zero sum game, and Prime Minister Saionji had to decide immediately. The correspondent ridiculed the army's arguments and warned that any attempt to "keep the military balance" with Russia by expanding the Japanese army might lead to an arms race and eventual state bankruptcy.[62]

In a particularly blatant article published on October 15, *Nihon oyobi Nihonjin* charged that the two additional divisions were not required on grounds of national security. Instead, the paper argued, the army's ruling "cliques" were asking for new divisions in order to entrench their dominant position, a demand the people must resist, smashing the cliques with an "iron hammer."[63] Four days later, the *Osaka Mainichi*, quoting an American observer, declared that the rule of the Chōshū Clique, Yamagata, and Katsura had to be swept away, just like Bakufu rule was broken during the Meiji Restoration.[64] Still, it is important to note that several newspapers, such as *Kokumin Shinbun*, took the opposite view and supported the position of the army.[65]

Hara made it clear to Inoue, who was still trying to negotiate a solution, that the Seiyūkai members, like the press, were against bowing to the army's demands, while Yamagata assured Saionji that the army could not give up on its two divisions. On November 20, Hara realized that the cabinet might fall over this issue.[66] Six days later, Saionji and the two Seiyūkai party leaders, Hara and Matsuda, decided not to give in to the army even if the cabinet collapsed as a result.[67] In this dire situation, Hara tried to approach Katsura again. A feeler sent by the Seiyūkai leader allegedly ensured Katsura's agreement to broker a last-minute compromise, delaying the establishment of the two divisions for one year. Katsura, however, declined again to intervene, claiming that Hara's emissary had misheard him. Hara began to suspect that Katsura's behavior was motivated by ulterior designs. "I realized," he wrote, "that Katsura had no intentions of bringing about a settlement to the situation. I felt, in short, that Katsura and his ilk hoped to use this issue to topple the cabinet. Thus, I warned him that on another day, a struggle beyond expectation might develop between him and me."[68]

A final attempt to apply pressure to Uehara also failed. On November 28, the army minister initially agreed to compromise with the government by delaying the formation of the divisions for one year. However, a day later he returned to his noncompromising position. Uehara probably did so, as the leading Japanese scholar of the crisis assumes, due to pressure by Tanaka and other subordinate officers.[69] On November 30, Hara conceded to the cabinet that in the absence of a new army minister they would all have to resign.[70] One day later, Saionji formally notified Uehara that the divisional increase plan had been rejected, and the latter offered his resignation "on grounds of illness" through the secretary of the cabinet.[71]

Now, Hara, Saionji, and their allies had to find a new army minister, but that proved to be a daunting challenge: a consensus had formed around the two divisions issue in the army, and it was very difficult for one single general, even one who did not belong to the Chōshū Clique, to cross the picket line in violation of this consensus. The problem with the army lay not only with its unconstitutional authority to overthrow governments, but also with its internal weakness. Military power was dispersed inside the establishment, without a clear person in charge, and no general was ready to appear as "soft" before his peers. Thus the consensus was aligned according to the positions of the most radical actors.

Still, the cabinet tried to find a replacement for Uehara. In the crucial three days between December 2 and 5, the names of two generals (Terauchi and Kamio) were raised as potential replacements, but both were rejected out of hand by Hara.[72] On December 2, Hara decided to make a final appeal to Yamagata to secure a replacement for Uehara, but to no avail. As a result, the collective resignation of the cabinet was finally submitted to the throne three days later, on the December 5.[73] "That was nothing more or less than a strike of military men," wrote one of Saionji's supporters in rage. "There had been instances of change of Ministry brought about by steps taken in the dark, but no instance of a case undertaken so nakedly, so boldly and so relentlessly as this. It was as if they had blocked up the front and the rear gates, bound the hands and the feet of the inmates and were going to set fire to the house."[74] The prerogative of supreme command, designed by Yamagata in order to stabilize the army and keep it away from rebellious activity, now empowered the generals to overthrow a civilian cabinet. That was a new, dangerous stage in the history of Japanese military insubordination.

On December 17, after considering and dropping several candidates, the Genrō Council recommended Katsura to the emperor as the new prime minister of Japan. His nomination was accordingly approved by the throne.[75] Immediately upon his appointment as prime minister, however, Katsura found himself facing a severe political crisis, very similar to the one which had toppled his predecessor. This time, however, the government was challenged by the Imperial Navy.

Act Two: Katsura against the Navy

When Katsura Tarō was appointed by the emperor as the successor of Prime Minister Saionji on January 17, 1913, there were many who viewed him as the "army's candidate." Yet, if the leaders of the army hoped that Katsura would give them their long-sought two divisions, they were bitterly wrong. Upon his ascendance to the prime ministry, Katsura took a reasonable decision that probably would have saved Saionji's cabinet from dissolution: he delayed the delivery of the extra funds to navy and army alike, with the sound argument that one year at least was required to devise an integrated navy-army defense strategy.[76]

However, the army was not in a position to resist the new prime minister. In a political system based on balance, as was the case in early Taishō Japan, a sweeping victory of one faction over the others could well prove to be a pyrrhic one. Indeed, already in September some army planners expressed the fear that using the active duty rule to overthrow a cabinet might lead to negative repercussions in public opinion. In an anonymous memorandum submitted at that time, a high military officer warned that the army "might become the scapegoat for the failure of the administrative reorganization, naval enlargement and tax cuts alike, making the position of the next cabinet difficult." The author of the memorandum made clear that such consequences were a worthy price for two additional divisions, but he and his colleagues may have underestimated the volume of popular rage.[77] "It is well to smile with pity on the stupidity of Saionji's cabinet," wrote one of Yamagata's confidants to the old field marshal on December 7, "but now the blame is shifted to the army, which draws the entire gamut of the people's wrath."[78]

As a result, the army proved unable to resist its "own candidate," Katsura, when he brushed aside the two divisions' plan.[79] The navy, though, was another story. The influence of Satsuma officers, especially the fleet's founding father, Admiral Yamamoto Gonnohyōe, was very high—so high that the navy as an institution became associated with the "Satsuma Clique." Just like the army's "Chōshū Clique," it was not really a regional organization, certainly not one that worked for the interests of Kagoshima Prefecture or an organization representing all Satsuma officers in the armed services. As we have seen, Army Minister Uehara, a former Satsuma retainer, was a key member of the Chōshū Clique, and many so called "Satsuma Clique" officers, like Admiral Saitō Makoto, were actually not from Satsuma. It would be better to define the Satsuma Clique as a counterorganization of officers and civilians who opposed the Chōshū Clique, namely, the influence of Yamagata and his cronies in the armed forces. In late 1912, these people were mostly concentrated in the navy, and their hatred for the Chōshū Clique, increasingly associated with the army, was combined with the traditional hostility between the two armed services.[80]

Some of Yamagata's advisors had hoped that by nominating Katsura to the prime ministry they might bridge the gap with the Satsuma-dominated navy, but this proved to be wishful thinking.[81] The new prime minister, despite the complexity of his relations with the Chōshū Clique, was still strongly associated with it, and the navy was in no mood to compromise with him. The navy minister, Admiral Saitō Makoto, felt as if his cherished plans for naval renewal had slipped from his hands at the last moment.[82] Unlike the army, which was still licking the wounds from its "victory" in December, the navy was the darling of large segments of public opinion, and in addition, enjoyed the formidable support of

Hara and the Seiyūkai.[83] The leaders of the navy were therefore confident enough to warn the new prime minister that any failure to give them the budget promised by Saionji would be at his own peril. In other words, the navy planned to follow the footsteps of the army in a coup d'état against the government. If Katsura failed to give them the funds for naval expansion, the navy minister would be withdrawn and no successor would be found among the admirals, naturally leading to the collapse of the cabinet.[84]

The navy's stance toward Katsura was haughty to such a degree that even the behavior of the army seemed moderate in comparison. The army, as explained above, at least tried to negotiate. The navy, by contrast, was not interested in any parley. Judging by the behavior of its leaders, they longed either for unconditional surrender, or for Katsura's head on a platter. As Admiral Yamamoto Gonnohyōe told the vice minister, that was a matter of honor. A successor must not be appointed because "the navy's competency is questioned here."[85] Immediately after his nomination, the new prime minister frantically searched for Navy Minister Saitō, but the latter, when contacted by telegraph, sent a note to say that he was convalescing from a sickness in Ichinomiya, a town near Nagoya, and was not available for a meeting. In fact, Saitō really had gone to Ichinomiya, but had already returned to Tokyo on the seventeenth. There he hid, guarded by naval officers with express orders to deny all visitors at the door under the pretext that the minister was not at home.[86]

There are multiple ways to explain Saitō's bizarre behavior, but the most probable is also the most simple: the navy minister did not want to make it completely impossible for Katsura to reach him but wanted to play "hard to get." Finally, one day later, Katsura was able to locate Saitō through the records of the telegraph agency and hastened to meet him. The two men spoke as frankly as possible in the given circumstances. Katsura openly confessed his distress and asked for Saitō's help, but the latter told him that his hands were tied by the collective decision of the other admirals who rejected any compromise. "He was not happy," he explained, "with the way in which things were done in the navy," but he had no choice but to "follow the consensus." Yet, Katsura and Saitō were able to forge a temporary agreement, promising the funds to the navy in two installments spread over two years. A day later, however, Saitō apologized, saying that he had to retract the agreement just made. In a meeting convened in the minister's house, the vice minister, the chief of the navy's staff, and other key officers staunchly resisted the proposed solution, and Saitō could not violate the consensus, as he told his vice minister, "without becoming socially dead." When Admiral Yamamoto Gonnohyōe, the most influential figure in the navy, personally intervened against the compromise with Katsura, Saitō felt he had no choice. Consequently, using the usual pretext, the navy minister retired "due to ill health."[87]

Katsura, however, reacted speedily with an unprecedented move. As a politician who had spent several months in the palace at the side of the new emperor, he saw himself as His Majesty's teacher and tutor, referring to him in conversations with foreign diplomats as "my young master" or even "my boy."[88] Therefore, faced by the navy's intransigence, he felt confident enough to draw power from "his boy" on the imperial throne.

On October 21, a day after the final break with Admiral Saitō, Katsura convened the Genrō Council and was able to convince the elders to play along: a request, jointly signed by Yamagata and Inoue, was duly sent to His Majesty, asking for a rescript forcing Admiral Saitō to resume his duties as navy minister. Taking no chances, the prime minister arranged that the rescript would be handed to Saitō himself in the palace.[89] Katsura, one of the few politicians who were intimately familiar with the complicated, dispersed structure of power in the armed services, realized that the imperial card had to be played against Saitō personally. Had the minister resigned, it would have been much more difficult to issue orders to the "navy," because there was no clear individual in charge—whom would one order? But Saitō was an individual, and like any other Japanese subject, he could not refuse an imperial order given personally to him, and nor could the other officers urge him to do so.[90] Katsura, to say it bluntly, had used a nonconventional weapon, his most effective one, in the battlefield of politics.

Saitō, thus, remained in the Navy Ministry, thereby saving the cabinet from dissolution, but the reaction to the nonconventional weapon Katsura had used spread far and wide.[91] In order to consolidate his power, the prime minister had established a new party, the Dōshikai, a step considered as a casus belli by Hara and the Seiyūkai, who loathed losing their dominant position in the political world. From that moment, the Seiyūkai became committed to join the fight against Katsura.

Still, had the prime minister been confronted merely with Hara, the Seiyūkai, and the navy, he might have got away with his unusual utilization of the hazy center. That, however, was far from being the case. In 1912, the Japanese press, much of it sympathetic to the political parties and to the ideology of constitutionalism, was already boisterous and highly influential.[92] Having separation between throne and government as one of their major demands, the liberal papers had been dismayed in August when Katsura was appointed to the dual role of chief chamberlain and lord keeper of the privy seal. Not only had they seen a danger that the Chōshū Clique might take control of the palace through Katsura, his appointment was seen as a dangerous mixture of throne and government.[93] When Katsura actually used the hazy imperial center, as prime minister, to force the navy to comply, these fears were realized and the response was furious, much beyond that Katsura had probably ever imagined.[94]

Thus, from late December 1912 through February of the following year, Japan was swept by a wave of rallies and mass demonstrations. Many were violent, fed by the press and the smooth, well-oiled national organization of the Seiyūkai Party.[95] This impressive outburst of energy, known at the time as the "Movement to Protect Constitutional Government" (*Kensei Yōgo Undō*) was in fact led by a tenuous coalition of businessmen, journalists, and party politicians, silently backed by the navy.[96] Most impressively, it had united the Seiyūkai with its bitter political rival, the Kokumintō (People's Party).[97] In fact, the movement originated "at the fireplace" in a club called the Kōjunsha, a union of graduates from the prestigious Keiō University with ties in the business world, the press, and the Seiyūkai.[98] In organizing a powerful political response in early Taishō Japan, connectivity was everything. Amidst the chaos and mayhem in the streets, the two main leaders of the movement, the Seiyūkai's Ozaki Yukio and Kokumintō's Inukai Tsuyoshi, were crowned by the intoxicated crowds as the "gods of constitutional government."[99]

The wave of violent criticism omitted few people in the establishment. The press reviled the domain cliques (i.e., the Chōshū Clique), the army, and the genrō, who were decried as senile, power-hungry backroom schemers. Yamagata drew a large share of the fire, and there were even strong rumors about an imminent attempt to assassinate him (such an attempt was indeed made, but the inept assassin, a young dental student, failed to reach the field marshal and was quickly arrested).[100] Katsura, however, emerged as the bête noir of the press. Already suspected by many as the mastermind behind Saionji's fall and vulnerable at the top because of his position as prime minister, his person became a convenient target for the public's rage.[101]

Though the campaign officially began with a joint rally of the Seiyūkai and Kokumintō on December 19, two days before Katsura issued the imperial rescript to Navy Minister Saitō, the dramatic use of the imperial hazy center was a crucial contribution to the fanning of the flames. Ozaki Yukio, one of the movement's leaders, publically charged in a Diet speech after the rescript was issued that Katsura and his friends intended to "hide behind the throne, lying in wait to ambush their political foes. They have made the throne their breastplate, and the rescript their bullets to destroy their enemy."[102] According to one witness, the prime minister was shocked by these accusations, as they exposed the basic illusion at the heart of the Meiji system—the "make believe" that the emperor was really ruling the country. "His [Katsura's] face turned deathly pale. I am certain his hands and feet were trembling. His facial expression was like one being sentenced to death. I had never seen such a pitiful figure."[103] Katsura, confronted by such a challenge to the ideological basis of his political power, reacted with panic. Sensing power slipping from his hands, he increasingly drew credit from the only account he had left - the prestige of the emperor, and issued more and more imperial rescripts, thus reinforcing the public rage as in a vicious circle.[104]

Between February 10 and 12, the Movement for the Protection of Constitutional Government was able to foment riots in many of the major cities of Japan, and the government faced a situation which bordered on anarchy.[105] As in the past, the crowds attacked and destroyed police boxes, progovernment newspapers, and other symbols of the much-despised bureaucracy.[106] Part of the violence, at least, was attributed to groups of sōshi of the same sort that took part in the assassination of Queen Min.[107] As usual, the wave of optimism discharged by the frequent upheavals excited violent activists by making them believe they could truly change the country by acts of mayhem.

Initially, Prime Minister Katsura was resolute about standing firm before the rising tide, just as he was able to bend the navy. The frequent overthrow of cabinets, he wrote to Yamagata, was endangering the very basis of the Japanese polity.[108] Katsura could not dissolve the parliament, which had almost declared open warfare against him, because he had little chance to beat the well-organized, immensely popular Seiyūkai at the polls.[109]

In desperation, the prime minister tried to repeat the same trick that had defeated the navy. He convinced the emperor to personally summon Prince Saionji, president of the Seiyūkai, and hand him an imperial rescript with an order to rescind the party's nonconfidence vote in the Diet. Saionji and Hara, like Admiral Saitō before them, felt they had no choice but to comply with the imperial wish, but this time Katsura went too far.[110] The dignity of the imperial rescripts was so impaired by his behavior that the rank-and-file parliamentarians of the Seiyūkai decided to disobey their leaders and ignore the rescript. Faced by such a humiliation of the imperial institution, unprecedented since the Meiji Restoration, Katsura finally gave up.[111] He drew so much credit from the imperial hazy center that even this allegedly omnipotent source of power was on the verge of default, with fateful implications for the imperial regime in its entirety.[112]

On February 10, the navy's leader Admiral Yamamoto Gonnohyōe, smelling blood, came uninvited to Katsura's residence and rudely urged him to resign for the sake of the emperor. In response, the hapless prime minister agreed, and recommended Yamamoto as his successor. In response, the admiral said that he was not the right man for the job, but if the situation absolutely required it, he was ready to take the heavy burden for the sake of the nation.[113]

The Seiyūkai had failed to rule the country, because it was bullied by the army. Katsura, in turn, defeated the navy but was knocked down by the Seiyūkai, the press, and the general public. Now it was the turn of the Seiyūkai to try again, this time in close collaboration with the Imperial Navy.[114] The results, as we shall see, were dramatic for the country as a whole. The third act of the

Taishō political crisis led, against all odds, to the partial undoing of the supreme prerogative system.

Act Three: "Like the Morning Dew"—the Armed Services Cornered

As the new year began, frustration with the wild behavior of the armed services, which led to the downfall of Saionji's cabinet and contributed to the undoing of Katsura's, was prevalent in Japanese political and journalistic circles. In popular newspapers and periodicals, liberal correspondents and politicians had railed against the active duty rule since at least the beginning of the crisis, calling for appointments of civilians as army and navy ministers.[115] These opinions were also accepted among some leading conservatives. On January 8, Prime Minister Katsura himself confided his doubts to a sympathetic member of the House of Peers, and the two men agreed that the rule of active duty had to be abolished. From now on, Katsura said, the army and navy ministers should become civilians.[116] Even conservative politicians understood that if the malady was not uprooted, the army and the navy could overthrow governments at will, practicing coups d'états as a political routine.

Katsura, however, was too distracted by his other troubles and never really acted against the active duty rule. That mission was left to his successor, Admiral Yamamoto, and the leaders of the Seiyūkai. On March 6, a short while after Katsura's downfall, Hara met with Yamamoto and strongly pushed for a decisive move against the rule. He proposed to change the regulations of the army and navy ministries to also allow retired generals and admirals to serve as ministers. Hara assured Yamamoto that this was the position of the Seiyūkai, as well as a "necessary condition" to mollify public opinion. Admiral Yamamoto promised Hara to support and promote his plan. There were advantages, he assured Hara, in having active duty ministers, but there was no reason to set it as law. Yamamoto's motives for adopting a resolution undermining the power of his own navy are not completely clear.[117] Certainly, dependent as he was on the Seiyūkai, he could hardly resist Hara in such an important matter. Probably, as well, now that he had finally acquired power, the national interest was in his mind. After two attempts by the armed services to overthrow cabinets, the first successful, the second a failure, it was clear to most informed observers that these frequent upheavals were dangerous for the stability of the imperial regime.

The main question was, obviously, how to avoid a replication of the previous months' events. The army and the navy, after all, used the rule of active duty to rebel against budget cuts. What would they do if the very basis of their power was at risk? This time, theoretically at least, both services might overcome their differences to protect the rule, the root of their own power. The challenge facing Hara, Yamamoto, and their allies, was how to block the well-known sequence of events leading to a coup d'état: agitation inside the private networks of the army or the navy, led by a hub such as Major General Tanaka, formation of an anti-government consensus, pressure on the minister to resign, and refusal to appoint a successor, pushing the cabinet to an eventual collapse.

In regard to the navy, the challenge facing the cabinet was relatively easy. Admiral Yamamoto, after all, was himself the hub of the navy's private network, the spirit behind the deliberations leading to the attempted coup against Katsura. Even in his position as prime minister, he had preserved his power. Saionji's downfall, as we have seen, was caused in part by the incongruence between the state's formal hierarchy and the army's private network. Because the truly powerful people were officially low ranking, it was difficult to communicate with them, thus encumbering any attempt at negotiations. In spring 1913, however, at least in relation to the navy, there was finally a full congruence between official and private structures of power. Admiral Yamamoto, the person who held the reins of the navy, also held a high formal position as prime minister.[118] This was owed not only to the admiral's illustrious past as the "father of the Japanese Navy," but also to an unusual amount of personal charisma. Yamamoto, as his bitter political rival, Ozaki Yukio, later recalled, was a "magisterial figure." There was something "quite intimidating" about him "that could strike terror into one's heart. Even a man of such a caliber as Yamagata seemed to treat the count with awe."[119] It was not surprising, then, that Yamamoto had an easy time winning over Navy Minister Saitō Makoto, in any case his close ally for many years.[120]

With the army, too, things seemed to go smoothly, at least at first. Yamamoto began his efforts with the new minister, General Kigoshi Yasutsuna, whose readiness to resign was a necessary condition for any military coup d'état. Kigoshi, an officer more moderate and reasonable than Uehara, loathed presiding over the undoing of the active duty rule, but he was also painfully aware of the isolation of the army and the hostility of public opinion.[121] Therefore, on April 8, he told Yamamoto that given the difficult situation, such a reform was "unavoidable."[122] Yet, Kigoshi, like Uehara, was not a powerful figure in the officer corps, and it remained to be seen how the Chōshū Clique would react.[123] Luckily for the government, Major General Tanaka, the spirit of the coup against Saionji, had been transferred from his powerful position at the ministry to a brigade command post, where he could not influence events.[124] With Kigoshi ready for a compromise and the Chōshū Clique scattered and fractured, there was hardly a force inside the Army Ministry that could push for a coup d'état.

Yet power in the army was dispersed between the ministry and two other entities, the General Staff and the General Inspectorate of Military Education. On March 10, the same day that Yamamoto declared in the Diet that he was resolved to abolish the rule of active duty, he cautioned Hara that obtaining the agreement of Kigoshi was not enough: there had to be cooperation with the General Staff and the Inspectorate as well.[125] Again, the dispersion of power in the army and the absence of a clear person in charge, made it difficult to negotiate with this chaotic organization. Yamamoto, who knew more than anyone else how to navigate in the intricate corridors of the services' private networks, kept Hara informed but presided himself over the discreet political maneuvers. On April 18, he told Hara that problems were likely. Chief of Staff Hasegawa and his deputy strongly resisted the plans to abolish the active duty rule. Reserve officers, Hasegawa warned, could leak military secrets to the political parties. The chief of staff began to apply pressure to Army Minister Kigoshi. The cruel wheels of the military consensus were already grinding. The minister, who was crushed between the resistance of his peers and the strong pressure applied by the prime minister, asked Yamagata for his opinion.[126] The old field marshal did not want to see the rule of active duty disappear, but decided to adopt a passive posture. The army's last coup d'état had cost him dear, both in influence and public image, and he was loath to undergo the same experience again.[127]

Prime Minister Yamamoto, fully aware that Kigoshi was being bullied by his peers, had legitimate reasons to fear that he might resign, and the old story of the December coup d'état might repeat itself. After the failure of his attempts to convince the military string pullers, especially Colonel Ugaki, of the necessity of the reform, the shrewd prime minister decided to draw power from the hazy imperial center. But he did so in a much wiser way than Katsura.[128] Knowing full well the extent of public rage aroused by the use of imperial rescripts, he decided to maneuver secretly inside the palace. Using Kigoshi's malleability, he persuaded him to "secretly report" to the throne about the proposed reform.[129] Now the minister was bound in chains, his loyalty to Yamamoto cemented by his own promise to the emperor, and the decision to abolish the active duty rule was passed in the cabinet on May 2.[130]

When the puppeteers in the army realized that they could not achieve their goals by pressuring Kigoshi to resign, the possibility of staging a coup d'état by withdrawing the minister was blocked. Consequently, several officers contemplated using the only means they had left, a direct appeal to the emperor. Chief of Staff Hasegawa, who held, under the supreme prerogative system, the right to an imperial audience, threatened to use this right to resist the cabinet in mid-April.[131] One month later, in May, he submitted a ferocious petition to the throne, drafted by several mid-ranking officers from the General Staff and the Army Ministry, imploring the emperor to preserve the special relationship with his army, as ensured through the supreme prerogative and active duty rule. Colonel Ugaki even threatened not to cosign the government's orders. Finally, he distributed a strongly worded antigovernment tract to the press, a misdeed that forced the deputy army minister to temporarily transfer him from Tokyo, thus removing the most powerful puppeteer from the scene.[132]

Because Yamagata refused to intervene on the army's behalf, there was no one with equal access to the throne who could counter the moves of the resourceful prime minister. Encouraged by this, Yamamoto gave the final coup de grâce to the army on May 8. He met with Emperor Taishō, ensured that it was "against good order" for the generals to speak with him, and strongly advised him to shelve the army's memorandum. The emperor, who had only Yamamoto's opinion to consider, naturally agreed with his prime minister.[133] The officers of the General Staff were powerless to resist, as all channels of influence they formerly possessed, either through the Army Ministry or the throne, were now blocked. The only thing they could do was take personal revenge on Army Minister Kigoshi, which they did, forcing him to resign and practically destroying his military career on June 24.[134]

Now, the army could theoretically still prevent the appointment of a new minister, challenging Yamamoto to appoint a general from the reserves, a dangerous and unprecedented move. However, the prime minister had outsmarted his army rivals once again. Using his position as the hub of the Satsuma Clique, he had formed a secret channel of communication with pro-Satsuma officers in the General Staff. These officers, who hated the Chōshū Clique, used the opportunity to appoint one of their own to the position of army minister. Finally, with Yamamoto's agreement, they had chosen General Kususe Yukihiko, a former Tosa retainer.[135] The appointment of General Kususe (an accomplice in the assassination of Queen Min), finally signaled for whom the bells tolled. Prime Minister Yamamoto had won, and the army's Chōshū Clique was finally defeated.

The lament within the leading circles of the army echoed far and wide, and Field Marshal Yamagata was now seen by many as a declining if not fading power. In a letter sent to Yamagata by General Terauchi on June 20, the governor of Korea lamented the death of the supreme prerogative, the wellspring of the army's vigorousness and power. "In a day," he wrote to Yamagata, "they have destroyed the political structure that you and your colleagues have built for the country over the past decades . . . the army, too, has been under your direction over these years . . . and even this has been destroyed in a single day. Alas, the lifeblood of a hundred years is like the morning dew."[136]

On the Verge of Collapse: Behind the Taishō Political Crisis

Objectively speaking, there was nothing inevitable in the Taishō political crisis. The dispute between the government and the army was quantitative, not qualitative—a squabble over schedule and costs, not essence. The crisis could have been delayed further, as in the past, and there were also numerous proposals for compromise rejected either by the army, the navy, or the cabinets of Saionji and Katsura.[137] The two important questions that have to be asked are why the sides were not able to overcome their differences, and why the confrontation between them, leading to a series of coups d'états, occurred in 1912–1913 and not earlier. Both questions bear direct relevance to the military establishment's increasing tendency to defy and disobey civilian authorities. The answers reveal why the Taishō political crisis had compromised the very essence of the hazy imperial center, bringing the entire Meiji regime to the verge of collapse.

The first question is easier to answer. All of the proposed solutions were rejected because the debate ceased to be about national policy and became instead an emotionally charged confrontation over ideological principles. While for the cabinet and the Seiyūkai, compromising with the army signified recognition of "clique rule" and military supremacy, the army viewed itself as the last bastion of imperial loyalty in a world ruled by traitorous politicians and corrupted businessmen, supported by the navy for its own selfish reasons. Both sides, pushed by their "public opinion," had found themselves locked in a vicious circle of hostility and mutual radicalization.[138]

The second question, as to why the crisis erupted in 1912 and not earlier, is much more difficult. The death of Emperor Meiji, the long-living monarch who held the system together as a potent symbol, is one possible explanation. The emperor was the axis connecting the ruling elites, and his demise threw them off balance, a situation which the new emperor lacked the prestige to remedy.[139]

However, the full answer to the question cannot be reduced to the death of one individual, prominent as he might have been. As a careful examination of the facts might show, the debate became so emotionally charged after the emperor's death because of a basic malfunction in the communication channels between the two sides. Indeed, as Ōtsu Junichirō argued, when two rivals are not communicating, each of them is likely to ascribe the darkest motives to the other ("when the heart is full of doubt, everyone around you is an enemy.") However, Ōtsu, like most other historians, reduced the problem to faulty communication between the three leaders, Katsura, Saionji, and Yamagata, without noticing that the miscommunication was not only between individuals, but first and foremost between groups, two rival networks, the army and the Chōshū Clique on one side, and the cabinet, navy, and Seiyūkai on the other.[140] The reasons for that mis-communication were rooted in the incompatible structure of these two oppos-ing networks. This network incompatibility of the early Taishō system is the key to understanding the events, their disastrous results, and the unique historical dynamics they engendered.

During the Taishō political crisis, the sociological structure of both govern-ment and army was radically different from that existing thirty-four years before, in 1878, when the supreme prerogative system was first established. Back then, the army and the government were controlled by the same group of leaders. With the passing years, the groups had moved apart, and the arteries of communica-tion between them became increasingly calcified.[141] In 1912, that calcification finally reached the level of a heart attack in the form of a debilitating political cri-sis. As we have seen, Hara and Tanaka, the most important actors during the first phase of the crisis, could not really speak with each other, because the networks they were operating in were incompatible. The dissimilarity in the formal posi-tions of the two men, a minister on the one side and a bureau chief on the other, precluded serious conversations between them. There was substantial incongru-ence between image and reality: between the hierarchical, formal network of the state, in which Hara was much superior to Tanaka, and the private networks of power, in which the two were equally strong puppeteers. This fatal incongruence, which prevented meaningful negotiations between the army and the cabinet, is key to the dynamics of the Taishō political crisis.

In fact, this development, allowing mid-ranking generals such as Tanaka to acquire disproportionate power and disrupt the channels of communication with the government, was a result of a long-range historical process of shifting power in Japan's military elite, a process akin to the "democratization" of mili-tary insubordination. The crux of this process was a constant expansion in the circle of actors involved in the shaping of the army's defiant, independent policy. This "democratization" involved a slow, gradual shift in power from the center to the periphery: the rank of the people who advocated insubordination became increasingly lower and distant from the command centers of the army.

This phenomenon, in which subordinates had considerable influence over their superiors, was not in itself new. In 1874, Saigō Tsugumichi had disobeyed the gov-ernment chiefly because of the pressure exercised by low-ranking retainers, and the same could be said of Etō Shimpei and Saigō Takamori. In the 1870s, however, the role of the "subalterns" was confined to pressuring their seniors. The top lead-ers may have been pushed and shoved, but the helm of resistance was still in their hands. In 1895, during the Queen Min Incident, we can see substantial growth in the power of subordinates and subalterns. Miura Gorō, the planner of the assassi-nation, was indeed the highest Japanese officer in charge, and he disobeyed the government at his own discretion. Still, junior officers and civilian nationalist activists like Adachi Kenzō were heavily involved in decision making. In 1912, the locus of power became even more centrifugal, moving to the hands of bureau and section chiefs such as Major General Tanaka Giichi and Colonel Ugaki Kazushige.

This process has not gone unmentioned in the historical literature, but few have gone so far as to explain the deep reasons at its basis. It is well enough to say that subordinates exercised power over superiors (Japanese: *gekokujo*), but why was this the case?[142] A possible explanation might lie with the interrelated parameters of connectivity and access to information. In the second chapter, while analyzing the reasons for the weakness of the imperial center, I maintained that access to independent channels of information is the key for command and control.[143] The Japanese imperial institution did not grow in power during the 1870s, simply because it lacked such independent channels. The person on the throne therefore became isolated and dependent on information controlled by his advisers, who could manipulate him through "counsel" he did not have the ability to counter. Scholars of Chinese history argue that the same was true for weaker emperors in Imperial China. As soon as their access to information was monopolized by a small group of advisors, they became virtually powerless.[144]

In the Japanese Army, too, we can see a variation of such a process. It is no mere chance that in the 1880s, the golden age of Yamagata's power, he constantly moved between powerful roles in the military establishment, sometimes occupying a post for a few months before moving to the next. The frequent moves helped him to maintain his connectivity to different people in the increasingly convoluted military establishment, holding independent channels of information and thereby ensuring effective control. It is again no mere chance that the most serious case of military resistance in the 1890s, the Queen Min Incident, occurred in a peripheral place, Seoul, where the channels of information feeding political and military leaders could be easily blocked by local commanders such as Miura Gorō.

In 1912, however, the structure had already changed. Yamagata's gradual decrease in power could not be attributed to his advancing age alone, as is often done in studies of the period.[145] Rather, with his rise in status, he had moved, in General Uehara's words, to live "beyond the clouds," in various estates in and out of Tokyo.[146] He became less mobile, and thus more dependent on information given to him by guests he trusted, many of whom were subordinate officers. The tendency to refer to the old field marshal by the locations or names of his villas and estates (for example, Mejiro), was yet another sign of his increasing immobility.[147]

As it happened, it was bureau and section heads such as Major General Tanaka who, owing to their comparatively minor status, could move about relatively freely and maintain contact with officers and civilians, thus enjoying increased access to the flow of information that ensured control. It was Tanaka, for example, who distributed the anonymous memorandum about the cabinet's conspiracy against the army to the leadership, which became a foundation stone of military policy and worked relentlessly to convince Yamagata, Inoue, and the other notables of the indispensability of the two divisions. It was again Tanaka who served as the contact between Yamagata and other high officers in the crucial days before and after the resignation of the cabinet. In addition, he had also advocated the cause of the two divisions in meetings with journalists, businessmen, and even members of the Seiyūkai.[148] In 1912, the vague network called the Chōshū Clique was the main hub of information in the army command, and mid-ranking officers who stood at its epicenter had the greatest connectivity, the best access to information, and therefore a crucial influence on the development of events.

A very similar process took place in the navy as well. According to the diary of the navy vice minister, for example, Minister Saitō Makoto could not violate the consensus among the naval officers, the chief of staff, and section heads. Indeed, the record of their conversations prior to Saitō's resignation showed that the minister was imploring his subordinates to change their minds and allow him to remain in the cabinet. Such a miserable impression did he make, that at certain moments he was almost close to tears.[149] Indeed, the dispersion of power in both armed services, accompanied by a dramatic increase in the connectivity of subordinates, had forced both ministers to contend with a status of equality with, and sometimes even utter dependence on, their military inferiors.

Seen in this light, the Taishō political crisis was a historical juncture of two distinct historical processes, the increase in the supreme prerogative confidence of the armed services, and the "democratization of insubordination" inside them. These collided with disastrous results. The problem with the armed services was that they became stronger and weaker at the same time—stronger as institutions, but at the same time more chaotic and difficult to control—hard from the outside, soft and ripe from within. The democratization of insubordination brought about a situation in which the most powerful people in the army were too low in rank to be approached by the government, thus giving rise to the network incompatibility and failure of communication already described above.

Katsura, frustrated by his failure to reach a modus vivendi with an institution like the navy where the real power holders were inaccessible for him, turned to the only resort he had left: the imperial hazy center. But once he had used the first imperial rescript, this easy solution became an addictive drug, and the prime minister acquired the habit of solving his problems by fiat.

The results were disastrous not only for Katsura but for the system as a whole, in a way not yet appreciated by most historians. As a result of Katsura's frequent use, the imperial rescript, as a tool of governance, underwent a process called by the church historian Richard Southern "spiritual inflation." Originally writing about the indulgence bills distributed by the Catholic Church in the era prior to the Reformation, Southern discerned a process akin to economic inflation. Originally, almost everyone respected the church's indulgences, which could "win" heaven even for the most wretched of sinners. However, when the church used this powerful tool too often, society gradually came to respect it less and less, just like a currency devalued by excessive printing of government bills.[150]

Katsura's reckless use of imperial rescripts brought about a very similar result. Once the members of the Seiyūkai had noticed, in the words of Ozaki Yukio, that Katsura "made the throne his breastplate" and used imperial rescripts "as bullets," the imperial rescripts were devalued along with Katsura's prestige, a fact recognized even by some of Katsura's allies.[151] When such a rescript was first issued, on December 21, it was powerful enough to force the hands of the navy. By the following February, it could not even convince the Seiyūkai parliamentarians to withdraw a nonconfidence bill in the Diet. Katsura himself also contributed to this devaluation in other ways, apart from his frequent use of rescripts. When confronted, for example, by the possibility that an imperial rescript might thwart his plans to establish a new party, he haughtily declared that in such a case he would ignore the rescript, discard his title of prince, and "serve the nation as commoner Katsura Tarō."[152]

However, in the beginning of February 1913, Katsura finally noticed that he had brought the entire Japanese system to the verge of an abyss. The crisis was so serious because the transcendence and absolute power of the throne were the basic assumptions underlying the Meiji system. Since the 1870s, the imperial institution was the superglue holding the various private networks to a certain framework, loose and contested as it might have been. Had imperial rescripts became laughing matters which every politician could ignore, the imperial myth in its entirety could be broken. And then, what would hold the system together? In the next crisis, the entire polity could collapse or at least undergo a radical change. To use one of Slavoj Žižek's metaphors, it was akin to that "classic scene in cartoons. The cart reaches a precipice, but it goes on walking, ignoring the fact that there is nothing beneath. Only when it looks down and notices it," in our case, the basic illusion of the imperial system, "it falls down."[153] Rather than risking that, Katsura had prudently preferred to resign.

A Time-Bomb Delayed: Ramifications for the Future

The Taishō political crisis, unlike all other events analyzed in this book, ended in the defeat of the military establishment. Not only did the army fail, at least for a while, to receive its coveted two divisions, it also proved itself unable to prevent the rise of party government, to stop Hara's quest for power, or to bridge the gap with the navy.[154] Instead, Hara was skillfully able to make use of this gap through his alliance with the Satsuma Clique and Admiral Yamamoto Gonnohyōe. Yamamoto, a rare military figure with national responsibility matched by significant political foresight, cooperated with Hara to abolish the rule of active duty, thus disarming both army and navy of their ability to overthrow cabinets.

Furthermore, the resistance in the army to this move, despite being noisy, was relatively feeble and ineffective. Crucially, the military establishment accepted its defeat without resorting to violence. The army's leaders, including hardliners such as Tanaka, were too integrated in the establishment to seriously rock the boat, and their control over their more radical juniors was still sufficient in summer 1913. They may have been ready to stage bloodless coups d'états, but political violence was still out of the question.

For the first time since Yamagata's military reforms in 1878, the structural balance of the country had tipped to the army's disadvantage. In the 1880s and the 1890s, the four generals and other adherents of civilian control in the establishment had failed to limit the growing prerogatives of the army. Through his alliance with Yamamoto and the navy, Hara was able to do just that in 1913. The two allies had used their newly won power to nip military resistance in the bud. When army elements, for example, had attempted to covertly operate in southern China against government orders, Prime Minister Yamamoto forced the leaders of the army to stop them by cutting their budget.[155] The Taishō political crisis could therefore be seen as a first step in a quest to limit the supreme prerogative and subordinate the army to civilian control.

And yet, the victory of the civilian politicians, its significance notwithstanding, was neither decisive nor permanent. The scrapping of the active duty rule remained theoretical, as none of the successive cabinets dared to appoint retired generals and admirals, let alone civilians or party politicians, into the roles of army and navy ministers. This was not completely impossible, as even Katsura, one of the architects of the supreme prerogative system, conceded in 1912 that civilian administrators could be appointed as ministers. The reason for that failure, as Najita Tetsuo has rightly argued, was political: it was difficult to expect that civilians, even retired generals, would be able to influence the military establishment.[156]

In addition, the military leaders quietly transferred much of the power of the Army Ministry to the General Staff, whose supreme prerogative authority remained uncompromised.[157] This would empower the General Staff to pursue an independent policy during the Siberian Intervention (1918–1922), Japan's failed attempt to interfere in the Russian Civil War, a policy that operated in a gray zone of resistance to government's policy and at times even crossed it.[158] The "gold-eating monster" was therefore defeated, but not pursued into its lair. The basic tenets of the supreme prerogative system, releasing the army from civilian control, were curbed but remained essentially uncompromised.

In addition, no one had tried to reform the military establishment itself in a more hierarchical fashion, replacing the private, horizontal networks of the supreme prerogative system with a solid vertical hierarchy. As a result, the fatal network incompatibility in the system continued to hold the potential for military resistance throughout the next decades. Given the right conditions, it would grow again. And these conditions, as we shall see in the next chapter, were not engendered in mainland Japan. As with the Queen Min assassination, they appeared instead in the distant fringes of the empire, in Manchuria. The fact that this chain of incidents, destined to throw the entire country into a whirlwind of military resistance, bloody violence, and political assassinations, appeared so late, in 1928, and so far away from the center, may be ascribed to Hara's victory in the Taishō political crisis. The fact that it appeared at all, however, could be ascribed to the limited, temporary nature of his triumph.

Part III
INTO THE
DARK VALLEY
1928–1936

THE KING OF MANCHURIA

Kōmoto Daisaku and the Assassination of
Zhang Zuolin, 1928

The true thief is the hole, not the mouse.

—Babylonian Talmud, *Kidushin* 56:1

In 1928 the assassination of Queen Min was more than three decades in the past, and the contingency of events that led a Japanese officer to murder a foreign head of state was hardly on anyone's mind. Yet, in that year, the latent structure that allowed military officers to embark on similar adventures of political assassination forcefully reemerged. A group of young Japanese officers successfully plotted the assassination of Zhang Zuolin (Chang Tso-lin), the powerful warlord of Manchuria, occupier of Beijing, and self-declared generalissimo of all China.

At one time, Zhang was renowned as one of the most formidable figures of the warlord era and a serious contender to unify the country. A ruthless military leader, he emerged from an obscure background as a petty brigand chief to lead one of the strongest armies in China. For years Zhang was an ally of Imperial Japan, but from the mid-1920s his relations with the empire rapidly soured. Nevertheless, the man who plotted his assassination, Colonel Kōmoto Daisaku, acted in complete defiance of Japanese government policy. The plot was well designed as a military conspiracy, its conspirators doing their best to cover their tracks and hide their misdeeds from their superiors.

Crucially for the future, Kōmoto's plot was based on an amalgamation of two different military ideas. A reinvigorated version of the supreme prerogative, which came to the fore in the 1920s, motivated the army to defy the government as an institution. At the same time, another idea known as "operational discretion" (*dokudan senkō*), allowed junior officers to take tactical decisions in the field in defiance of their direct superiors. The combination of these two ideas motivated colonels such as Kōmoto to take strategic initiative in defiance of both government and military high command. This synthesis, developed by Kōmoto and his peers in 1928, was the first spark that ignited the military violence of the 1930s.

The New Ideology of the Supreme Prerogative

Since the Taishō political crisis, party politicians such as Hara Kei had steadily striven to limit the supreme prerogative as much as they could, in an open attempt to gradually subject the army to civilian control. Already in 1913, as we have seen in the previous chapter, the rule of active duty was abolished, and the army could no longer overthrow cabinets at will.

During the Siberian Intervention (1918–1922), Japan's failed and costly attempt to interfere in the Russian Civil War, Hara was not able to fully control the army but was able to make some steps in that direction. As an avowed gradualist, he rejected the proposals of his finance minister to strike a death blow at the supreme prerogative system by abolishing the General Staff. Instead, he and his successors constantly gnawed at the power of the General Staff, tightening their grip over the army through relatively collaborative army ministers.[1] More important, Hara enacted some legal reforms designed to weaken the position of the army. In 1919, for example, he abolished the law that gave the army a monopoly over the key colonial posts of governor-general in Korea, Taiwan, and the leased Kwantung area in Manchuria. From then on, civilians could take these posts. Accordingly, the Kwantung governor-generalship was abolished and replaced with an administration headed by a civilian. The assassination of Hara in 1921 by a civilian nationalist failed to forestall these reforms.[2]

The army's response to these moves was to shift its executive power from organs "infected" by civilian control to institutions still enjoying the prerogative of supreme command. From the end of the Taishō political crisis, power shifted from the Army Ministry to the General Staff, whose chief saw himself as an official shielded by the supreme prerogative, and therefore not responsible to anyone but the emperor.[3] In Manchuria the army's policy was similar. Faced for the first time with a Japanese civilian authority, the military reacted by binding all soldiers and railway guards in the area to the Kwantung Army, the Japanese force stationed in the Manchurian territory controlled by Japan. The commander of this force was directly subordinate to the chief of the General Staff in Tokyo.[4] Its subordination to civilian authorities therefore became a matter of constant contention.

The liberal atmosphere of the early 1920s had engendered popular distrust of the army, especially in the major urban centers, which emboldened politicians to publically gnaw at its privileges. Young officers, who were often poor and hungry for prestige and recognition, were shocked by the "disrespect" shown to the army in both government and civil society. Most of them had grown up in specialized military institutions, a closed space in which elitism, esprit de corps, and belief in their own moral superiority were strongly emphasized. The graduates tended to despise "civilian" officials, politicians, and diplomats. As a response to the antimilitarist feelings in urban Japanese society, the military schools conveyed to their students the army's interpretation of the supreme prerogative, namely— total independence from the government and all laws, except the personal will of the emperor.[5] In this atmosphere, generals who opposed civilian control enjoyed immense popularity in the officer corps.[6]

In 1928 the ultimate representative of this new type of popular officer was Lieutenant General Araki Sadao, chief of the First Department (Operations) at the General Staff. Araki was a representative of a group of younger military leaders who were not bound to the old cliques. Though naturally connected to many people in a way reminiscent of the old cliques, he presented himself, through a boisterous public relations campaign, as their implacable enemy. Araki's tactics, indeed, were a novelty fitting to the new age of mass politics. In 1912, during the Taishō political crisis, ringleaders such as Tanaka Giichi could amass enormous power by networking with a number of key people in different branches of the army. Araki, whose views were widely popularized through internal military publications and even civilian newspapers, was popular among the mass of officers who did not know him personally. Many others had been his students in the prestigious staff college, where he served as an instructor and principal in 1914 and 1928. Essentially, Araki was one of the first mass politicians in the Japanese army who had a large constituency of followers.

As is often the way with popular politicians, Araki's views were formulated in the negative. He breathed fire against the Chōshū Clique, communism, Westernization, and Japanese party politics, all of which were tied in a single, vicious bundle that was upheld as an anathema to the noble values of true Japanese officers. The mass of frustrated officers, as well as many elite graduates of the Staff College, appreciated his emphasis on the "Japanese spirit," a power of will leading the army to victories against materially superior enemies. To fill this demagoguery with ideological substance, Araki lionized traditional samurai values. His world was dichotomous: soldierly values, offensive spirit, and the "Japanese soul" were good, while "cliques," "politicians," and civilian officials were bad. That implied strong adherence to the supreme prerogative and the independence of the army, without any regard to political calculations or civilian control of any kind.

Equally dangerously, Araki publically disregarded the authority of the Army Ministry, perceived as a tool of the cabinet to control operations.[7] During the

Jinan Incident, a bloody clash between Chinese and Japanese soldiers in Shandong in early May 1928, the vice minister of the army ordered Araki to obey government orders and withdraw. Even if it violated the supreme prerogative, the vice minister insisted, the army must comply with government policy.[8] The operations chief bellowed in response:

> What kind of nonsense are you giving me? As a soldier you ought to at least know what a matter of command is. How can you stand there and let the things we decided the other day at the marshals and military councilors meeting, in the presence of a royal prince and with the navy attending, be trampled in the dirt so easily, simply on the basis of government opposition? Aren't you a soldier? If we do that, we're making light of the constitution, and it's going to wind up as an unmitigated disgrace.[9]

Araki's power was not as a conspirator but as a propagandist. He rarely planned any acts of resistance himself, but he advocated such acts. And his words, brazen and unabated, strongly appealed to many army officers. In May 1928, for example, Araki threatened the government that if it did not embark on an aggressive policy in Manchuria, "I do not know what would happen, but I, as the operations chief, cannot take responsibility."[10] These words of passive threat were explosive. Without actually being involved in a plot, Araki propagated not only full military independence from civilian control but also utter disregard for internal military discipline. The ongoing process of "democratization of insubordination" was now open for all to see, as a senior officer openly encouraged his juniors to engage in "direct action" and virtually to lead the course of events.

Araki's preaching of insubordination unfortunately fell on fertile soil, fed by incessant factionalism and dispersion of power within the ranks. In 1928, this dispersion was expressed in widespread opposition to the policy of the Chōshū Clique and its leaders, generals Tanaka Giichi and Ugaki Kazushige. Ugaki, when he served as army minister from 1925 to 1927, had compromised with the ruling cabinet and agreed to abolish some military units, using the funds saved to embark on a project of military modernization. Many young officers resented Ugaki for compromising with party politicians, and especially for abolishing units and dismissing officers—a disastrous move for the pride and livelihood of many of their peers.[11]

Even among the narrow stratum of elite officers, many of whom understood the need for modernization, there was strong resistance to Ugaki's policy. Since the early 1920s, such officers, among them future military leaders, regularly met in Tokyo restaurants, running study groups such as the Futabakai (Two Leaves Society), Mokuyōkai (Thursday Society) and Issekikai (One Evening Society).[12]

The members of these groups, abetted and aided by Lieutenant General Araki, had their differences as to the exact nature of the military reforms they advocated, but all agreed on four main points. The first was utter animosity toward the Chōshū Clique, represented by Tanaka and Ugaki. Second, they advocated a reform in appointing military personnel, up to the point of excluding Chōshū Clique officers from the prestigious Staff College. Third, many of them advocated economic planning and "total war" mobilization. Last, they called for a strong, decisive policy in Manchuria. One of the leading members in these oppositional study groups was Colonel Kōmoto Daisaku, the future assassin of Zhang Zuolin.[13] His hatred of the ruling circles of the army, common among members of these groups, would be expressed in his defiant behavior in Manchuria from 1926 to 1928. However, in order to understand Kōmoto's actions, it is important to take a look at the "Manchurian problem" that his plot intended to solve.

The *Manmō* Problem in the Late 1920s

Manmō was the Japanese abbreviation for "Manchuria and Inner Mongolia," and the Manmō problem pertained to the dilemmas faced by Japanese policymakers in these key regions of northeastern China. The history of Japan's involvement in Manchuria, going decades into the past, was hardly new in 1928. In the Portsmouth Treaty of 1905, the peace agreement ending the Russo-Japanese War, Japan acquired the Russian Empire's concessions in southern Manchuria, most prominently ownership of the South Manchurian Railway and a lease over the Kwantung territory. In the same year, the Qing Government recognized these rights in the Treaty of Beijing and agreed not to infringe on the Japanese concessions.[14]

The 1911 Revolution in China, replacing the Qing Dynasty with a fledgling republic, did not prevent Japan from procuring ever more privileges and rights in Manchuria. In January 1915, while the Great War raged in Europe, the cabinet of Ōkuma Shigenobu used the wartime chaos to bully Yuan Shikai, president of the Chinese Republic, to grant Japan additional concessions. They included a renewal of the Kwantung lease; further mining and railway privileges; and the right of Japanese nationals to live permanently, own land, and launch commercial ventures in the Manchurian interior.[15] Throughout the 1920s, Japan held a plethora of economic rights in the Manchurian hinterland, well beyond the borders of the Kwantung leased territory. There were 200,000 Japanese and 1 million Koreans residing in Manchuria, operating mines, factories, and other ventures. The annual volume of trade between Manchuria and Japan amounted to 400 million yen.[16]

Virtually all policymakers saw Manchuria as the "life line" of Japan, a source of vital natural resources, and an important outlet for Japanese immigration. From a strategic point of view, Manchuria was seen as a primary defensive line against Soviet Russia, a shield protecting Korea and the main islands of Japan. Therefore, the army had to keep a strong presence in that crucial gateway to the heartland of the empire. In addition, as Prime Minister Tanaka Giichi explained to the British ambassador in 1928, the ties of Japan to Manchuria were also "sentimental, as it had been the scene of her struggles in the past," pertaining to the empire's vast sacrifices in the Manchurian theater during the Russo-Japanese War.[17]

As usual with the prewar Japanese administration, the empire's different arms in Manchuria were far from operating in accord with one another. From 1919 the leased territory was ruled by a civilian administrator appointed by Tokyo. This governor often stood at odds with the military power on the ground, the Kwantung Army, which answered directly to the Imperial Army's General Staff.[18] The Kwantung Army also ruled over several battalions of railway guards, responsible for securing the tracks of the South Manchurian Railway. According to the rights inherited from Russia, the railway guards could operate in a narrow corridor on either side of the tracks, giving the Kwantung Army access to certain parts of the Manchurian interior.[19] Another key actor, the South Manchurian Railway Company (often known by its Japanese abbreviation, Mantetsu, but hereafter SMR), was a semigovernmental authority holding vast powers in the Kwantung leased territory. An economic empire, the SMR held not only railway-related assets, but also hotels, hospitals, schools, universities, and other kinds of property in Kwantung and throughout Manchuria, especially in the capital, Mukden.[20]

The Japanese inhabitants of Manchuria, many of them poor immigrants who sought a better life at the fringes of their empire, tended to be suspicious of Tokyo but also fearful of the Chinese population around them. Many of them put their hopes in the Kwantung Army, often demanding increased protection from its commanders.[21] Within this population was a group variously known as the "Manchurian adventurers" (*manshu ronin*), "China adventurers" (*shinu rōnin*), or "mainland adventurers" (*tairiku rōnin*). They were yet another reincarnation of the sōshi and the shishi, ruffians and opportunists who often employed political violence in and beyond Japan's borders. In 1895, such people had played a central role in the assassination of Queen Min in Korea.[22]

Just like their predecessors in late nineteenth-century Korea, the China adventurers were bold, violent, and dirt poor. And they cooperated with the Japanese Army and its secret service, the Special Service Organization (Tokumu Kikan), as well as with civilian nationalist organizations such as the Amur River Society (Kokuryūkai). Often well versed in Chinese language, customs, and culture, they wandered the plains of Manchuria, collecting intelligence and working with local

pro-Japanese elements. Many of them were also mired in the lucrative Manchurian opium trade, trafficking, dealing, and operating opium dens in cities such as
Dairen, the capital of the Kwantung Leased Territory. These adventurers enjoyed
the cooperation of key Japanese officials in the Kwantung Army, the SMR, the
civilian government, the judicial system, and above all the Special Service Organization, who actively helped them or turned a blind eye in return for a share of
the drug trafficking revenue.[23]

Despite this extensive Japanese presence, Manchuria beyond the leased territory was still ruled by local strongmen. Since the revolution in 1911, the most
prominent of these was the former brigand leader Zhang Zuolin, also known as
the "Old Marshal." During the Russo-Japanese War, Zhang's gang collected intelligence for the Russian Army. When taken prisoner by Japanese troops he was
almost shot, but was saved at the last moment by Tanaka Giichi, then an operations officer with the General Staff. Tanaka believed Zhang might prove useful
in the future. From then until 1927, when Tanaka became prime minister, Zhang
showed some allegiance to Japan, but always kept a semi-independent stance.[24]

According to the unwritten agreements reached between Zhang and Japan
in the late 1910s, the Old Marshal was supposed to suppress anti-Japanese campaigns among the Chinese population, keep the communists out of Manchuria, uphold the treaties with Japan, and expand the empire's concessions on
demand.[25] In return, the Japanese provided him with formidable financial and
military support. In 1924, when Zhang waged a war against one of his archrivals
on the mainland, the Kwantung Army arranged a substantial bribe for one of
the anti-Zhang warlords, who turned coat and secured the Old Marshal's victory. Crucially, under the pretext of keeping law and order in Manchuria, the
Japanese Army blocked Zhang's rivals from pursuing him into his home territory. That was true for outside warlords as well as for rivals within Manchuria.
In 1925, when one of Zhang's henchmen rebelled against him, the Kwantung
Army blocked his entrance to one of Manchuria's strategic towns, thus nipping
the rebellion in the bud.[26]

However, around 1926 relations between Zhang and Japan began to sour. The
Manchurian warlord, well aware of his image as a collaborator, was under pressure from much of the Chinese population to resist Japan's imperialist encroachment. He was also worried by the powerful anti-Japanese movement, expressed
through demonstrations, boycotts, and other mass campaigns.[27] In response to
popular pressure, he began to assume an uncompromising attitude in his negotiations on further Japanese concessions in Manchuria. Particularly, Zhang refused
to permit the Japanese to lay new strategic railways or to establish a consulate on
the Korean border. Using American capital, he also planned to lay new railway
lines and take market share away from the SMR. Many in the Japanese authorities

also suspected that Zhang was playing a double game by secretly instigating anti-Japanese demonstrations and boycotts in his territory.[28]

Complicating the picture was the volatile military and political situation on the Chinese mainland. In 1927 Zhang Zuolin, who had occupied Beijing and kept it from his rivals, moved to the city and had himself declared generalissimo of all China, performing the imperial rituals as if one of the emperors of old. His rule, however, was challenged by the Chinese Nationalist Party (Guomindang), a revolutionary faction that played a key part in the revolution of 1911. Armed with Soviet equipment and supplied with capable military advisors by Moscow, the Guomindang launched the "Northern Expedition," a campaign for the unification of the entire country. Riding on the anti-imperialist and antiwarlord feelings of the population, the leader of the Guomindang, General Chiang Kai-shek, promised to do away with both warlords and foreign concessions. Though Chiang hinted to the Japanese that he, too, intended to uphold the current treaties with them, Tokyo was naturally mistrustful. As Zhang Zuolin's troops were defeated by the Northern Expedition, Japan was confronted with an urgent question. Should it continue to support Zhang Zuolin, or try to reach an accommodation with the Guomindang instead? Most important, what should Japan do when the fighting reached the borders of Manchuria?[29]

Until 1927 the prevailing view in Tokyo, espoused by the ruling Minseitō Party and Foreign Minister Shidehara, was to minimize Japan's intervention in the Chinese civil war and respect China's sovereignty, as long as Japan's "special interests" in Manchuria were not compromised by the warring parties. Even liberals like Shidehara, known by their diplomatic moderation, were adamant that these "special interests" ought to be protected at all costs.[30] Until the late 1920s, Shidehara, like many others, believed that this should be done through careful cooperation with the Western powers and local Chinese forces, including Zhang Zuolin.

In March 1927, Guomindang and allied communist soldiers raided and looted foreign dwellings and consulates in Nanjing (the so-called Nanjing Incident), wounding and killing Japanese and other foreigners. The Japanese public's outrage, further exacerbated by an economic crisis, forced the Minseitō cabinet to dissolve. As a result, the rival party, Seiyūkai, came to power under the leadership of General Tanaka Giichi. Tanaka, once the prominent figure in the Chōshū military clique and a staunch enemy of the political parties, had changed course, joined the Seiyūkai Party and won the prime minister's office as the party's chairman. Carried to power by a wave of popular nationalism, he was viewed by many as a "strong leader" bound to restore order. Tanaka therefore promised to toughen up Japanese measures on the Chinese mainland through an "active policy," taking the foreign portfolio into his own hands. In practice, day-to-day Manchurian affairs were managed by Vice Foreign Minister Mori Kaku, the strong man in the Seiyūkai and a well-known political hawk. The problem was that no one, least of all Tanaka himself, knew what the new "active policy" meant and how Japan should navigate its way in Manchuria and China as a whole.[31]

The new prime minister, notwithstanding his avowed readiness to wage war to defend Japan's Manchurian interests, still advocated a policy of cooperation with Zhang Zuolin.[32] Intransigent as Zhang might have been, Japan's rights in Manchuria could still be protected through his rule. Therefore, Tanaka had dispatched several emissaries to Zhang in Beijing, including the president of the SMR, in order to convince the Old Marshal to resume cooperation with Japan. Above all, Tanaka and his emissaries attempted to convince Zhang to leave Beijing, abandon the futile struggle with the Guomindang, and entrench himself in his "fortress Manchuria" protected by Japanese bayonets. Tanaka, like many other Japanese policymakers, was worried that Zhang's war with the Guomindang might undermine the local economy and give rise to chaos by provoking rebellions or bringing the civil war into Manchurian territories.[33] But the warlord remained unmoved by Tanaka's attempt to bring him back to Manchuria. In a misjudged attempt to play on the anticommunist fears of his Japanese counterparts, he insisted that the Guomindang were "red," and he was the only one who could stop the communist tide from swallowing the entire country.[34]

Faced by these difficult, seemingly futile negotiations, many people in the Japanese establishment, chief among them Vice Foreign Minister Mori Kaku, advocated a "stronger" policy toward Zhang Zuolin. Sharing the view of many senior diplomats, Kwantung, and SMR officials, Mori believed that Zhang's "ungrateful" attitude to Japan could not be remedied by mere persuasion. The empire, therefore, should force him to cooperate. And if he disagreed, Japan should even get rid of him in one way or another, maybe forcing him to retire in favor of his son or one of his lieutenants. Mori and his associates did not plan, as yet, to rule Manchuria directly, but hoped to put in place another local strongman, more compliant than Zhang.[35]

Crucially, in 1927 Mori's line was supported by many officers in the General Staff and the Kwantung Army. Zhang's intransigence had outraged senior officers, and many of them, especially in Manchuria, began to advocate tougher measures against him in tandem with Mori Kaku's proposals.[36] But even the leaders of the army could not settle on an alternative policy. Among those who wanted to remove Zhang there was no uniform opinion as to who might replace him, but many officers assumed that his successor, whether his son Xueliang or one his senior officers, was likely to be more compliant to Japanese pressure. The various "China experts" in the army, many of whom had worked as advisors for competing warlords, often recommended their own clients as alternatives to

Zhang. Some others supported the Guomindang. Zhang Zuolin's own Japanese advisers naturally backed him, but they were in the minority.[37]

In June and July 1927, Prime Minister Tanaka attempted to tackle the Manmō problem head on by summoning to a conference in Tokyo all Manchuria-related policymakers from the army, the navy, the Kwantung Government, and the Foreign Ministry. But even the results of this so-called "Eastern Conference" were inconclusive. After many weeks of debate, Tanaka summed up the conference in a series of statements which did not offer a clear alternative to the current policy. As a compromise between the moderate and radical proposals, the Eastern Conference did not rule out cooperation with Zhang, but considered the option of his removal too. Crucially, the conference decided that peace and order in Manchuria had to be protected at all costs.[38] A year later, in May 1928, the cabinet decided that if Zhang was routed by the Guomindang, as many expected, and his army returned to Manchuria as a leaderless mob, all of his soldiers should be disarmed, along with their Guomindang enemies.[39]

This decision was soon translated into policy. In a warning sent to Chiang Kai-shek and Zhang Zuolin, commanders of the feuding Chinese armies, the Japanese government stated that it would take "appropriate and effective measures" to prevent war and chaos in Manchuria.[40] In private conversations, Japanese representatives warned Zhang that if he did not withdraw immediately from Beijing his army might well be disarmed.[41] The commander of the Kwantung Army, Muraoka Chōtarō; his chief of staff, Saitō Hisashi; and his senior staff officer, Kōmoto Daisaku interpreted this as an authorization to solve the "Manchurian problem" by getting rid of Zhang, for how could he rule with his troops disarmed? On May 15, troops were summoned from Korea to reinforce the Kwantung Army. In the mind of the Kwantung Army's commanders, an order to march against Zhang could arrive at any moment.[42] Major General Saitō recorded the atmosphere in his diary:

> Mukden, 21 May: On the assumption that the imperial order decreed . . . would become effective at 12:00 noon here, I advised my subordinates to that effect and summoned them at 12:00. But the orders did not come through. I am beginning to think that in all likelihood the [army's prerogative] of supreme command was disrupted by the [government's] policy . . . waited all night, but the orders never arrived.[43]

The government and the General Staff, indeed, still held the Kwantung Army on a leash. On the nineteenth, the troops were ordered not to proceed beyond the SMR railway zone. As Shanhaiguan, the gateway to Manchuria, was beyond this zone, it meant that the Japanese troops were not allowed to wait there in order to disarm Zhang's troops. Two days later the General Staff conceded that such a move could not be made in face of the government, partially acknowledging the supremacy of civilian rule.[44] Indeed, Prime Minister Tanaka decided to go on working with Zhang Zuolin.[45] Major General Saitō was furious. Premier Tanaka had wavered, bowing to the pressure of foreign countries. The Kwantung Army, Saitō wrote, "expecting mobilization at any moment, is in a state of animated suspense. A feeling of antagonism toward the indecisive Tokyo government is mounting daily."[46]

The government canceled the plan to disarm Zhang's troops because it believed it was about to achieve, if not a lasting solution to the Manmō problem, then at least a temporary respite. On June 1, Zhang Zuolin finally agreed to return to Mukden in defeat, his dream of uniting China under his rule irrevocably shattered.[47] Back in Manchuria, he would be completely dependent on Japanese bayonets and was likely to be more compliant.[48] Just at that moment, a group of junior officers from the Kwantung Army, led by Colonel Kōmoto Daisaku decided on their own initiative to cut the Gordian Knot by killing Zhang, thus shattering their prime minister's policy.

The King of Manchuria: Kōmoto Daisaku As Officer and Conspirator

Like many other young Japanese nationalists throughout the generations, Colonel Kōmoto Daisaku was infatuated with Saigō Takamori, that paradigmatic rebel of the 1870s. He often quoted the following excerpt attributed to the great man: "It is difficult to control a man who neither cares about life, status, wealth or honor. Without such unmanageable people, everyone has to suffer and it is impossible to do great things for the country."[49]

This excerpt gives a good glimpse of the personality of Kōmoto and his tendency for insubordination, as well as of the way that memories of earlier uprisings influenced future rebels. Little is known about the colonel's early life, and his biographers are sharply divided in his appraisal. For Sagara Shunsuke, his biographer and admirer, Kōmoto was a brave, creative, and patriotic young officer.[50] Hirano Mineo, a military correspondent and his brother-in-law, however, described him as a corrupt and rude man with a mentality of an adventurer, who had mistresses all over China and Japan, neglected his wife and daughters, and fleeced his poor family to finance his dissolute life.[51]

Still, both biographers agree that he was a shishi type: bold, daring but disobedient, fond of adventures and quickly bored with day-to-day military routine, a picture substantiated by Kōmoto's own testimonies, letters, and interrogation transcripts. The colonel, for example, used to boast that during the Russo-Japanese

War he flatly refused an order to wash himself, and refrained from taking baths all throughout the campaign. Other anecdotes, of uncertain credibility, disclose that as a cadet he led a raid on the barracks of bullying *senpai* (senior cadets) and, later, as an officer, dared to question orders issued by the chief of the General Staff.[52]

Due to his problematic disciplinary record and his low academic achievements, Kōmoto was initially unable to enter the Staff College (Rikudai), the prestigious institution whose graduates staffed the high echelons of the army, and was admitted only after trying twice. His humble origins from a commoner family of distant samurai ancestry, combined with a burning ambition to succeed and prove himself, made him deeply resentful toward the army's reigning Chōshū Clique and the haughty elite of senior officers.[53] Like Miura Gorō, the erstwhile architect of Queen Min's assassination, he was both hypernationalist and oppositional, frustrated and resentful both of Japan's enemies and of its civilian and military leadership. In a distant place such as Manchuria, such a combination could not but invite trouble. There, in the Wild West of the Japanese Empire, Kōmoto could pursue his aspirations to the utmost. According to Hirano's testimony, Kōmoto used to boast that in the future, his dream was to become "the king of Manchuria."[54]

In 1914, after graduating from the Staff College, Kōmoto was sent by the General Staff to the continent as an intelligence operative, expert for covert operations and advisor to several warlords under the Intelligence Department of the General Staff.[55] Kōmoto's expertise in Chinese affairs, just like his adventurist tendencies, were strengthened significantly during his service in the Siberian Intervention, Japan's failed attempt to meddle in the Russian civil war.[56] In 1923 he returned to Japan as an officer in the China Section of the Intelligence Department, and thus became acquainted with a group of China experts destined to play an important role in his subsequent plots.[57] Another important venue for networking was the Futabakai, the elite study group of aspiring military reformers. Hirano recalled that Kōmoto, known as a bon vivant, was well liked by the other members because of his boisterous generosity. He regularly lent money to his friends and lavishly wined and dined them, thus oiling his exclusive network of connections among his peers.[58] In 1926 he returned to China for his final posting, this time as a senior staff officer with the Kwantung Army. Despite his numerous connections in high places, his stormy character and a series of disagreements with superiors had led to his removal from the General Staff. Under such conditions, exile to Manchuria seemed to be a convenient solution for all.[59]

In Manchuria, the unruly Kōmoto could operate in ideological conditions that proved to be a perfect nurturing ground for his plots. The military strategy of the Japanese empire was based on short, decisive wars fought in enemy territory. When one wants to move quickly and seize opportunities, it is inadvisable to depend on cumbersome military bureaucracy for each and every decision. The constant need for up-to-date intelligence engendered a tradition of covert intelligence operations empowering low-level agents to take independent decisions in the field.[60]

Military and civilian observers often called such behavior *dokudan senkō*, roughly translated as "operational discretion." It was in fact similar to the phenomenon of "escape to the front," discussed in earlier chapters. In the 1920s, the textbook of the prestigious Staff Collage condoned it as means to make lightning decisions during rapid wars of movements.[61] According to Suzuki Teiichi's memoirs, many officers agreed that "when an action is beneficial, you must go ahead without asking the opinion of your superiors."[62] In a time of pressing need, wrote General Ugaki in his diary, an obedient soldier would sacrifice everything, while the practitioners of operational discretion would ignore everything, even authority, in doing what is right. "That is the highest freedom," wrote Ugaki, "the basis for the soldier's spiritual life." And in any case, a soldier could never hesitate. Whether to obey or disobey had to be decided in an instant, according to the requirements of the moment.[63]

For Kōmoto, killing Zhang Zuolin was a legitimate exercise of operational discretion based on urgent military needs. According to Sagara's account, supported by the retrospective testimony of Kōmoto himself, that decision gradually crystallized during two consecutive solo trips in Manchuria, the last of which took place around New Year 1928. Kōmoto had traveled in normal trains, dressed as a Chinese, and used his fluent language skills to "test the ground." To his dismay, he discovered that the population hated Zhang and Japan almost to the same degree and saw both as merciless oppressors and exploiters. As the cause of Japan was, for Kōmoto, inherently righteous, local resistance to the empire had to come from either misunderstanding or maliciousness. The people of Manchuria, he believed, were not inherently anti-Japanese, as they were very friendly to the soldiers of the Imperial Army during and after the Russo-Japanese War. Ergo, they were being misled by someone—and that someone, he believed, was Zhang Zuolin.[64] Zhang, unlike the common people, resisted the righteous cause of Japan out of wickedness, simply to "spread his individual power and that of his military clique and enrich himself at the public's expense."[65]

The decision was finally made, according to Kōmoto's biographer, while the colonel was walking with his daughters in Mount Nirei, a military cemetery near Dairen. While there, he claimed to have undergone something akin to a mystical experience, a spiritual encounter with the souls of the heroes fallen in the Russo-Japanese War. He had to do something, he decided, to save Manchuria, won by their blood.[66] Given the "spineless" policy of the government, the only way was to "escape to the front," eliminating Zhang by independent, direct action.[67] A short time before the assassination, on April 18, 1928, Kōmoto explained his motives in an unusually blunt letter to a coconspirator, a China expert in the army.[68] Due to its paramount importance, this letter deserves to be quoted at some length:[69]

> As for me, I am not highly evaluated at the central quarters. . . . *But as I have ample experience with the criticism of little men and selfish superiors, I do not pay it much attention.* . . . There is no need to cling to our beloved military jobs. It may well be the time to choose another trade, far away [from military life], as to give our superiors (these dull people!) a reason for self-reflection. . . .
>
> As for the situation in Manchuria, there are many who find it difficult to ignore the increasing tyranny of the Chinese side. *The reason underlying it, however, is that they* [Zhang's government] *are being bolstered by the Japanese military cliques—and that is hateful.* Nobody is able to solve the *Manmō* problem by reasoning. The strategy of exchanging little favors is useless. There is no way but force, and it is essential to choose the right pretext and battle standard while doing so. At this point, in the face of even the slightest provocation, we should deal them a devastating blow and force them to change their attitude toward Japan.[70]

Kōmoto elaborated on railway conflicts and on the futility of current Japanese countermeasures in relation to Zhang Zuolin, and then proposed his own solution:

> Wouldn't it be advisable if Zhang Zuolin and maybe one or two others die on the road? This time, by all means, I am going to do it. *Even if they try to stop me, I'll do it at all costs.* To take a life in order to solve the *Manmō* problem, that's our greatest hope. That is the honorable thing to do. . . . last year and the year before, the plans to do something great were stopped in the midst. This year I'm going to score a hit by all means. My plan to cleanse Manchuria and Inner Mongolia with torrents of blood may be, I believe, a fundamental solution to the problem.[71]

As we can see in the italicized sentences, Kōmoto was not ashamed and was even proud in his resistance to state policy. The culture of military insubordination, gradually taking root in the Japanese army since the early Meiji period, was so ingrained now as to seem self-evident to people like him. Moreover, the colonel associated the military "cliques" and their quintessential representative, Prime Minister Tanaka, with Zhang Zuolin. All enemies, internal and external, were tied together in a single, distasteful bundle.[72]

Many years later, Kōmoto told his Chinese captors that he and his friends could not procure an imperial rescript, as such a move had to involve the prime minister as well.[73] Devoid of real access to the emperor, Kōmoto imagined himself as operating according to his will. By doing that, he was taking advantage of the first bug inherent the modern Japanese polity, the haziness of the imperial center. In addition, he was working in accord with General Araki's radical interpretation of the supreme prerogative, positioning the army as completely independent of the government and justifying disregard of internal hierarchies as well.[74] As Yoshihisa Tak Matsusaka argues, Kōmoto's conspiracy was directed not only against Zhang but also against Prime Minister Tanaka, designed to humiliate and force the hand of a man he hated and distrusted.[75] That was an expression of the second bug in the Japan's political structure. "Escaping to the front," or charging independently in foreign battlefields, was perceived as a way to express opposition to the government at home.

The atmosphere of panic in the Kwantung Army headquarters had certainly contributed to the sense of urgency Kōmoto felt. Confronted on a daily basis with the anti-Japanese feelings of the local Chinese population, boycotts, and other displays of hostility, Kōmoto felt, in his own words, that he and his colleagues "were hemmed by enemies from all sides."[76] The scene was dynamic and constantly changing. Chiang Kai-shek was advancing from the south, fighting with the Japanese Army in Shandong. Zhang Zuolin's forces were likely to escape to Manchuria as an unruly mob. There, joined by local anti-Japanese forces, they could force the Kwantung Army to engage in house-to-house battles in Mukden, with terrible implications for the local Japanese population. The impasse had to be solved at once.[77]

As Kōmoto was heir to the long tradition of militant, rebellious optimism, he believed that by getting rid of one person, Zhang Zuolin, he might well solve this impasse for the benefit of Japan. Killing "the brigand leader" was the only way to solve the Manchurian problem.[78] "If this one individual, Zhang Zuolin, falls down," he later recalled his convictions at the time, "the other generals of the Fengtian clique would scatter to the four winds," as they were tied to him as the boss of their gang. Until a new leader emerged, they would be "at their wits ends," and meanwhile chaos would prevail. Then, probably, someone friendlier to Japan would take the helm.[79] Beyond that, Kōmoto did not plan ahead, but concentrated on the limited objective of killing Zhang. The trouble, as he discovered in the early spring of 1928, was that he was not the only one who planned to do so.

Two Alternative Plots

While planning his own operation, Kōmoto did his best to foil two alternative plots. Their story is important, because it sheds some light on the chaotic structure of command of the Kwantung Army, where insubordination was no longer the exception but the rule. The plurality of plans gradually became a security threat, as dark rumors about a military conspiracy against Zhang began to circulate around Beijing. On June 2, the Japanese envoy in Beijing quoted some rumors that Japanese officers planned to arrest Zhang upon his arrival in Mukden. According to another version, Chinese military policemen were supposed to kill him. Such plans, the envoy warned Prime Minister Tanaka, were bound to create an international scandal. Hearing these rumors, Major General Saitō, chief of staff of the Kwantung Army, wondered whether his subordinates were behind the plot, though he surmised that the military policemen who planned to kill Zhang were Chinese, not Japanese.[80] Indeed, in spring 1928, the commander of the Kwantung Army, Lieutenant General Muraoka Chōtarō, began to think about the possibility of killing the Old Marshal in Beijing. For that purpose, he made contact with Major Takeshita Yoshiharu, the military attaché in Harbin, and summoned him into his headquarters in Mukden.

Kōmoto, who had seen Takeshita in the building and understood that something was afoot, called him to a private conversation, disclosed his own conspiracy and convinced him to scrap Muraoka's plan. Beijing, he said, was well guarded, too crowded with Chinese and foreign troops. It was admirable, Kōmoto told Takeshita, that their commander plotted such an assassination without telling Kōmoto, his senior staff officer—but Muraoka, with all due respect, had to be excluded in order "not to bring him into an unfortunate situation." "I will get rid of Zhang Zuolin," Kōmoto said, "and take all the responsibility upon myself."[81] Later, he recalled his belief that "if the high command had such plans, then we staff officers had to implement them."[82] Sometimes it seems that more than being interested in the results, Kōmoto was attracted to the excitement, honor, and adventure of action. Defiant, independent plotting became a goal for its own sake. Takeshita traveled to Beijing and became Kōmoto's agent in the capital.[83] Muraoka, in turn, was oblivious to the details of Kōmoto's plan but might have guessed that something was going on. Captain Kawagoe Moriji, Kōmoto's right hand man, wrote that the Kwantung Army's commander in chief, "a big boss with a big heart . . . pretended not to know while knowing, and allowed his subordinates to do their part."[84]

But Muraoka's vague plan, hijacked by Kōmoto, was not the only plot to kill Zhang Zuolin. Kōmoto was greatly dismayed to hear about a second plan, independently hatched by two officers from the Special Service Organization.[85] The intelligence officer Doihara Kenji, now serving as an advisor with Zhang's army in Beijing, and Major General Hata Shinji, the Special Service chief in Mukden, operated in concert with other intelligence operatives and China adventurers, all of whom agreed that Zhang Zuolin must go.[86] A key coconspirator was a shadowy figure, a former Japanese officer named Araki Gorō. Araki had retired from the Imperial Army as a lieutenant, traveled to China, and became a notorious adventurer and military advisor. Now he served in Zhang's army with the rank of general under a Chinese name and was responsible for the personal bodyguard of Zhang's son. Doihara and Hata convinced Araki to stage a palace coup, toppling and possibly killing Zhang by means of his own bodyguard, enthroning his son Xueliang instead.[87]

To achieve this goal, however, they needed weapons. They tried to procure them from the Kwantung Army through Kōmoto Daisaku. As with Muraoka's plot, Kōmoto was quick to counteract it. In his letter to his friend from the China Section, already mentioned above, he fulminated against the irresponsibility of Doihara and Hata, who relied on feckless Chinese bodyguards for such a sensitive plan. "I would not dance by Doihara's flute," he wrote, ". . . Therefore, I have canceled the arms shipment to Araki's guard. As they tried to forcefully steal the weapons, I have used military policemen to stop them."[88] Kōmoto was doing his best to protect Zhang Zuolin from all assassins but himself.

Kōmoto's Conspiracy

In January, when Kōmoto began plotting, he revealed the secret to a chosen group of officers, including his personal aide, Captain Kawagoe Moriji, and Nakano Yōhei, a Special Service operative in Tsitsihar, North Manchuria.[89] Kawagoe took on himself the day-to-day management of the plot, kept in touch with other confederates, and procured the necessary explosives. Later, he told Kōmoto that he would keep following the plan even if he were discharged from the army as a result. In a typical mentality of "escape to the front," he believed that "solving the *Manmō* problem" was nothing but revering the emperor by following long-standing national policy.[90] Nakano Yōhei was a very different type of collaborator. He epitomized the deep involution of the Japanese army into the sphere of criminals, brigands, and adventurers. A former China adventurer, he was now leading a band of Chinese brigands collecting intelligence for the Kwantung Army. Kōmoto asked Nakano to employ some of his brigands to blow up segments of the railway in areas not controlled by the Japanese, without actually damaging trains, in order to create an image of popular resistance to Zhang's government. Nakano immediately agreed. "I'm Japanese," he said, "and would like to display my genuine feelings of patriotism." During the winter of 1928, there were indeed several such explosions.[91]

On the ground, a dense web of informers and intelligence operatives, orchestrated by Captain Kawagoe, supplied Kōmoto with information on Zhang's movements and whereabouts. In Beijing, Kōmoto could rely on Major Takeshita and Major General Tatekawa, the military attaché at the Japanese legation.[92] Two Koreans were hired to watch over the train station in order to report the number of departing troops. Using such raw intelligence, Kōmoto was able to assess the Old Marshal's intentions. If he retained a large number of troops in Beijing, it might signal his intention to hold onto the ancient imperial capital. If he did not, then he might go back to Mukden, right to the snare prepared for him. Other operatives were waiting at various stops along the Beijing–Mukden route. The nature of the plot, however, was kept strictly confidential, and most agents, and even some Japanese officers, were not informed about the final goal.[93]

In order to blow up Zhang's train, Kōmoto was in need of professionals. For that purpose, he used his authority as senior staff officer and mobilized the Twentieth Engineer Regiment from Korea.[94] Its commander was let into the plot and agreed to give his assistance. He and a member of Kōmoto's staff were responsible for the technical side of the operation.[95] The conspirators chose a place called Huanggutun, about a hundred miles southwest of Mukden. The Chinese rail tracks, they knew, might be legitimately guarded by Zhang's troops, but according to the treaties, no Chinese soldiers were allowed to go near the tracks of the South Manchurian Railway. In Huanggutun, the Mukden–Beijing train passed beneath a SMR railway bridge, thus providing a weak spot in Zhang's defenses.[96]

The Twentieth Regiment's engineers professionally installed on the Japanese bridge a large quantity of explosives, which could be activated by an electric switch.[97] At the right moment the explosives could bring down the bridge on Zhang Zuolin's head. Captain Tōmiya Kaneo, commander of the railway guards in the Huanggutun sector, was also let into the plot. Under his protection, neither Chinese nor Japanese soldiers could disclose the plotters or disturb them in their deadly work. In case the explosion failed to kill Zhang, one of Kōmoto's staff officers waited with bayonet-armed railway guards, ready to board the derailed train and finish the job.[98]

The Cover-up Plan: Kōmoto and the Adventurers

Kōmoto wanted to disguise the fact that Japanese were behind the assassination in order to save embarrassment for both himself and the Kwantung Army.[99] In order to fabricate a convenient cover story, he cooperated with a Japanese coal merchant named Itō Kenjirō, a shadowy figure connected with the China adventurers. Itō was obsessed with the "Manmō problem," and not only for patriotic reasons. Along with his friends, he suffered from Zhang's economic policy as well as from the anti-Japanese boycotts. An extremist representative of a growing anti-Zhang movement among the Japanese merchants in Manchuria, Itō visited Kōmoto twice in his own initiative and implored him to get rid of Zhang, "the cancer of Manchuria."[100] Just like Adachi Kenzō during the assassination of Queen Min, Itō was not a mere accomplice but a coconspirator and major plotter. According to one of Kōmoto's retrospective testimonies, he was the one who actually suggested Huanggutun as the appropriate place for the assassination.[101]

Itō, well connected with the Manchurian underworld, contacted a notorious adventurer of his acquaintance, and asked him to find "three Manchurians whose lives are worthless." This man, a professional thug, worked part-time for the Mukden Special Service branch and supplied the Japanese spying agency with field intelligence.[102] After a short while, he managed to "hire" three morphine-addicted beggars for a hundred yen each through a Chinese pimp, a former rebel who still hated Zhang Zuolin. The adventurer and the pimp, who received a commission for their services, convinced the three addicts that they were to be employed in a secret operation for the Japanese Army. That was correct, of course, but the three beggars could not guess to what end.[103]

Subsequently, the three addicts were washed in a local bathhouse, groomed, dressed in mufti, given fifty yen each, and then brought to Itō's hideout. One of them, who suspected foul play, escaped his captors, but the other two were led to Kwantung Army headquarters, to be examined by Captain Kawagoe, and then to the railway guards in Huanggutun. There, Tōmiya and his men bayoneted them to death. Some hand grenades were installed in their pockets along with letters of confession (written in Japanese *kanbun* by the adventurers) incriminating the Guomindang in Zhang's assassination. The fact that Kōmoto and his confederates believed that such letters could be mistaken for Chinese documents, as well as that morphine addicts would be confused for Guomindang guerrillas, showed the flimsiness of their cover-up attempts. Later, Kōmoto conceded that he did not pay much attention to the cover-up plan, as he did not believe that the Japanese police would investigate the case seriously.[104]

The Operation

Zhang's private train was ready to depart Beijing around 1:00 a.m. in the early morning of June 4. At the station, among the crowds who came to see the Old Marshal off, Major Takeshita and Major General Tatekawa were also waiting. When they witnessed the train departing, the two sped in their car back to the Japanese legation and cabled Kōmoto in Mukden using coded language: "4th, 1:15 a.m., the special train has left Beijing. It is a cobalt blue train of twenty carriages. That person [Zhang] is in the eighth carriage."[105] At the train's next stop, Tianjin, another conspirator, the commander of the Special Service local branch, updated Kōmoto that things were proceeding according to plan. At the same stop Colonel Machino, Zhang's senior Japanese advisor, disembarked the train, leaving onboard his junior colleague, Major Giga.[106] The major, oblivious of Kōmoto's plan, sat with Zhang and General Wu Junsheng, governor of Heilongjiang Province, in the Old Marshal's own luxurious carriage while the train traveled toward Mukden.[107]

At the Huanggutun railway junction, SMR officials had placed multiple sandbags on the railway bridge in order to block the access of Chinese iron thieves who had been raiding the bridge to steal track components. Lieutenant Tōmiya and his men replaced the sand with explosives from a depot placed in Tōmiya's own house.[108] A wire attached to the sandbags led to a detonation device, hidden in the small cabin of the railways guards. Two engineers sat in the cabin, waiting for Zhang's train to arrive. An electric light pole, placed there in advance, illuminated the darkness of the night, allowing the conspirators to see their target clearly. The bodies of the two bayoneted Chinese were lying on the tracks, "confession" letters attached. Meanwhile, Kōmoto and his right-hand man, Kawagoe, were waiting in their favorite Japanese restaurant, keeping in constant touch with their agents at the different spots along the route. Kōmoto refused to stop the operation even when he learned that Major Giga and Colonel Machino would be on the train. As far as he was concerned, Machino could certainly be blown to pieces. The Japanese officers surrounding Zhang, he told Kawagoe, cared only about money and not about the future of the country. Giga was young and it was a pity, sure, but he and Machino were not really Japanese officers—merely "Zhang's parasitic worms."[109]

At three o'clock in the morning, while Zhang's train was slowly proceeding toward Mukden, a commander of the Chinese military police came to visit his Japanese counterpart, one of Tōmiya's subordinates and advised him that the generalissimo's train was soon to pass through. Therefore, he asked for permission to allow his troops to patrol the railway. The Japanese officer, who knew exactly what was afoot, replied that the current treaties forbade Chinese soldiers to patrol the area directly adjacent to the SMR tracks. Their presence, he said, might cause a "misunderstanding" leading to an incident. Under this pretext he rejected the Chinese request, and kept the would-be crime scene free for the perpetrators.[110] As Zhang's train was running behind schedule, Kōmoto and Kawagoe had second thoughts whether to carry out the assassination even after dawn (4:42 a.m.). There was a danger, after all, that the team would be spotted by unwelcome eyes. Kawagoe traveled to Huanggutun to consult with Tōmiya. "We have to do it anyway, even after dawn," said the commander of the railway guards. "If we miss this opportunity, another one is unlikely to come." In addition, he and his men had already killed the Chinese scapegoats.[111] The operation was therefore resumed.

Two hours later, around 5:20 a.m., Zhang's private train finally reached Huanggutun and passed under the SMR railway bridge. The Old Marshal was still sitting with General Wu, and Major Giga had entered the cabin to greet them. As he spotted Zhang's carriage passing by, Tōmiya signaled to the engineers in the hut, and a second later, one of them pulled the switch.[112] Zhang had neglected his personal security to such a degree as to make his personal carriage evident for all to see. It was a conspicuous, luxurious private car, the others being ordinary first- and third-class compartments.[113] The railway bridge collapsed under the blast, hitting several of the carriages, which promptly began to burn. General Wu died on the spot, and Zhang Zuolin himself was mortally wounded. Giga, helped by Chinese soldiers, carried the Old Marshal out of the train and hurried him to his Mukden home. He died there five hours later, though this fact was concealed until his son, Xueliang, could take over. Giga himself was miraculously able to escape with only minor injuries. At least three other passengers were killed or wounded.[114]

Kōmoto hoped that Zhang's demise would lead to a riot of his troops in Mukden, thus supplying the Japanese with an excuse to take over control of Manchuria. Then, a more compliant puppet could be placed on the Mukden throne.[115] For this task, Kwantung Army troops had been put on high alert, ready to take immediate action. However, Chief of Staff Saitō, completely oblivious to Kōmoto's plan, canceled the high alert immediately after the assassination in order to reduce the risk of a clash with Zhang's army.[116]

Four days later Kōmoto's commander, Lieutenant General Muraoka, attempted to re-create the momentum by approaching the Mukden consul and the Kwantung chief of police. The Japanese, he said, "should abandon their lofty Bushido policy and use the opportunity to solve the *Manmō* problem." This move, however, came too late, and the consul refused to cooperate with a "conspiracy of adventurers."[117] Had Muraoka and Saitō, who shared Kōmoto's goals, coordinated with him, they could have moved swiftly to take advantage of the momentary confusion. But the lack of coordination between them exposed the limitations of Kōmoto's method of operation as a lone wolf. By not incorporating his superiors into the plan, Kōmoto had crippled his own initiative. His optimism and self-confidence were reckless and unjustified. Therefore, the assassination of Zhang Zuolin did not produce any meaningful reaction by the Kwantung Army. That would have to wait three years, for the well-planned Manchurian Incident of September 1931.

Exposure and Investigation

Shortly after the assassination, Kōmoto's cover-up plan collapsed, and information about the plot began to leak from several quarters.[118] First of all, the beggar who escaped was arrested by the Chinese authorities and disclosed the little he had known about the plot. The owner of the bathhouse in which the beggars washed followed them into the scene, recognized the corpses, understood they were killed by the army, and reported this to the Japanese civilian police. The police commissioners, in turn, duly transmitted the information to Tokyo.[119]

Even worse, that same morning, six opposition Diet members (from the Minseitō Party) en route to Changchun, had to disembark their train in Mukden because of the explosion in Huanggutun. One of them, Matsumura Kenzō, hastened to see his old friend, Consul General Hayashi Kyūjirō, and found him confounded and shocked by the news. "This is awful!" the consul said. "The army guys have done it. What a mess!" The ensuing investigation indeed confirmed the initial suspicions. As Matsumura wrote later, such high-quality explosives were used only by the Japanese Army, and even the confession letters on the dead bodies—a well-known habit of Japanese assassins—were not written in authentic Chinese but rather in Japanese-style *kanbun*. When Matsumura returned to Tokyo, he reported these findings to the chairman of his party.[120]

Still, though he knew the truth all too well, Consul Hayashi attempted to whitewash the entire affair. Parroting the official declaration of the Army Ministry, he refrained from accusing the army and insisted that the dead morphine addicts, other Chinese, or mysterious adventurers were the real perpetrators.[121] As his conversation with Matsumura reflected, he must have known who was really responsible, but actively concealed it from Prime Minister Tanaka. In fact, the joint Sino-Japanese investigation conducted under Hayashi's auspices was so biased that the Chinese side refused to sign the report.[122] Hayashi repeatedly lied to Tanaka, his formal superior, in order not to irritate the people who were really in charge, the officers of the Kwantung Army, of whom he was truly afraid.[123] According to Kōmoto, army and police authorities in Manchuria shared Hayashi's sentiment and believed that as the assassination happened outside of their jurisdiction, inside Chinese territory, there was no real need to open an investigation.[124]

The false story invented by Hayashi, most probably in cooperation with Kōmoto and other Kwantung Army officers, is highly interesting and instructive not just for its sensational character. The cover story exposed the implicit basic assumptions shared by Japanese policymakers in Manchuria. According to Hayashi's report, a Chinese man named Ling Yinqing, a former intelligence operative in Zhang Zuolin's army, had decided to get rid of Zhang in collusion with his chief of staff. Their goal was to establish a Manchurian national homeland headed by a former Qing prince. Along with two friends, one Chinese and one Japanese adventurer, Ling met with Kōmoto Daisaku to ensure the Kwantung Army's cooperation. Kōmoto agreed, but, mistrustful of Ling, asked that the former prince should lead the plan. Having secured the consent of the Kwantung Army, Ling had employed two Chinese agents to bomb Zhang's train and kill him, but these Chinese, the same morphine addicts found dead on the tracks, were shot by the Japanese guards.[125] This story is interesting mainly because of the things taken for granted by its fabricators: that Kōmoto colluded in a plan to launch an insurrection in Manchuria without asking anyone's permission. Conspiracy was so habitual among officials in Manchuria that even when they lied to the prime minister they hardly tried to conceal this fact.

Almost simultaneously, Prime Minister Tanaka heard a report from a retired Japanese general, a confidant of the late Zhang Zuolin. The general sniffed around the crime scene, examined the evidence and concluded, beyond doubt, that the perpetrators were Japanese military men.[126] "My work is ruined," Tanaka had reportedly exclaimed, "Damn it! These children don't understand their parent's heart." "If the army takes such measures as that," he told Navy Minister Okada, "we will never be able to develop our plan." The perpetrators, he added, had to be "severely punished to prevent such incidents again on the continent." Military discipline had to be reinforced through a court-martial. Besides, that was the only way to restore Japan's international prestige and the army's honor at home and abroad.[127]

As a first measure, Tanaka angrily turned down the army's request to reinforce the Kwantung Army and deploy it beyond the boundaries of the SMR zone.[128] Next, he convened a special, joint committee of inquiry, composed of high-profile representatives from the army, the Foreign Ministry and the Kwantung Government. Concurrently, the commander of the Military Police was dispatched to Mukden to conduct an investigation on the ground. The military police chief, and the committee members, had at their disposal a letter sent by a certain adventurer, exposing the illicit connections between Kōmoto, the merchant Itō, and the China adventurer who recruited the Chinese morphine addicts. Subsequently, the entire gang of adventurers was interrogated by the Kwantung police. In its findings, the committee implicated Kōmoto in the plot, but declared the merchant Itō and the other adventurers as the ringleaders, thereby mitigating the army's guilt. The members of the committee, especially Vice Foreign Minister Mori Kaku, seemed to be interested in hushing up the affair, not in exposing it. Therefore, they decided to stop the investigation right after their second meeting.[129] The Military Police chief, who discovered the whole truth by interrogating one of the engineers, allegedly released a more candid report, exposing Kōmoto as the chief culprit of the plot.[130]

Tanaka was furious. Prince Saionji, the only surviving Genrō and his erstwhile rival during the Taishō political crisis, now implored him to punish the perpetrators severely so as to uproot military insubordination once and for all. As a former soldier and leader of the all-powerful Seiyūkai, he said, Tanaka was equipped more than anyone else to discipline the army.[131] The prime minister agreed. On December 24, in accordance with Saionji's advice, he reported to the new emperor, Hirohito, that the assassination of Zhang Zuolin was planned by Imperial Army officers. A private assassination plot by Japanese officers against a foreign leader could not be left unpunished, Tanaka retorted. Therefore, the prime minister proposed to punish Kōmoto through a court-martial, thus demonstrating Japan's sincere regret to the Chinese side. In response, Hirohito ordered his premier to investigate and punish the perpetrators.[132] After retiring from the imperial presence, Tanaka summoned his army and navy ministers, ordered an investigation and "strong disciplinary measures in respect to the army."[133]

Resistance on the part of military vested interests was quick to emerge. Immediately after Tanaka's first interview with the emperor, Army Minister Shirakawa expressed strong opposition to opening proceedings. Though he was Tanaka's protégée and childhood friend, he refused to cooperate with the premier because "to take steps to punish those responsible to this event would be to expose to the public something which the army wished at the time to conceal." Shirakawa did promise the emperor he would investigate, but he effectively took measures to whitewash the affair.[134] This attitude was shared by other key officers, including Suzuki Sōroku, chief of the General Staff; General Mutō Nobuyoshi, inspector general of military education; and Uehara Yūsaku, the only field marshal who was still active. General Araki and Kōmoto's friends from the Futabakai study group also vigorously resisted any attempt to launch a real investigation, and even rivals of Kōmoto joined the common effort.[135] The spirit of the Kwantung Army penetrated the entire military establishment—the army minister himself was a former commander of this force. As the commanders themselves had a vested interest in maintaining the chaotic system that ensured their independence, they resisted any measure bound to instill order and discipline into the ranks.

In 1913, during the Taishō political crisis, the Seiyūkai Party had served Prime Minister Yamamoto as a counterweight to the army. Now, Tanaka discovered that he had no such counterweight; his own party was on the army's side.[136] Vice Foreign Minister Mori Kaku and Railway Minister Ogawa Heikichi, the real power holders in the Seiyūkai, sympathized with Kōmoto. Minister Ogawa, who was tied to the China adventurers, recognized that Kōmoto's action was dangerous and contradictory to government policy, yet he could not help but admire his patriotism and bravery. In eastern philosophy, he mused, parents have to protect their children even from the law, and Japanese people have to cover up for each other. In addition, Ogawa was afraid that a military court, open for all to see, might harm Japan's foreign relations and give the Chinese a legitimate reason to demand the expulsion of Japanese troops. It could also provide the opposition with a pretext to demand the resignation of the cabinet. Even worse, such a move might provoke "officers and shishi" to denounce the leaders of the government as traitors and embark on a campaign of assassinations. This, Ogawa reasoned, was an excessive sacrifice to make for the cause of restoring military discipline. As a result, Ogawa and Mori effectively blocked all measures of punishment.[137] And if that was not bad enough, the Minseitō politicians gleefully attacked Tanaka from the opposition side, taking delight in embarrassing him with questions during several parliamentary hearings on the affair.[138]

In the face of such resistance, Tanaka's attempts to form his own bloc of supporters were inadequate. As General Ugaki rightly concluded, the prime minister was too confident of his own influence and power.[139] True, he was able to win the support of his navy minister, Admiral Okada; the venerable elder statesman Prince Saionji; as well as Prince Itō Miyoji, president of the Privy Council, but that could not match the resistance in the army and the Seiyūkai.[140]

General Ugaki, Tanaka's longtime partner and ally since the days of the Taishō political crisis, also refused to lend him any support. Ugaki believed that the assassins were dangerous fools, yet he was not ready to punish them. As his diary suggests, he was reluctant to compromise the army's position in the internal power struggle, maybe because he expected to win the army's support in his future political career. Furthermore, Tanaka was guilty of making a mess of things, and it was a "dirty trick" to shift the blame to the army. It might be better, Ugaki surmised, to overhaul the entire leadership including Tanaka, that "Buddhist icon" sitting idly in the government headquarters in Tokyo. Based on such calculations, Ugaki did not lift a finger to support his erstwhile patron.[141]

And if that was not bad enough, Tanaka had made a crucial mistake which was about to undermine his entire enterprise: he had ordered the home minister to suppress news about the assassination in the press. The event, widely discussed in China and the West, was referred to in Japan only as "a certain grave incident in Manchuria" (Manshū Bōjūtai Jiken). The press did cover the investigation in implicit language, but the reports were weak and diluted. The prime minister could not punish officers except through the army minister, and without creating some momentum through public pressure it was extremely difficult to force the latter's hand.[142] In addition, there are some indications that hostility to the army was still alive among many Seiyūkai activists.[143] Had the affair been published, Tanaka could have bypassed Mori and Ogawa in an attempt to garner support inside the larger circles of his party. Therefore, by keeping the affair secret the prime minister prevented a major crisis with the army, but he also isolated himself from sources of potential support.

Tragically, the shifts in configuration of the power in the 1920s left Tanaka, formerly a strong hub, without any power. Faced with strong resistance from the army, the cabinet, and his own Seiyūkai Party, he found himself completely isolated.[144] His Chōshū Clique, once an all-powerful military network, was now an empty shell, no more than a bogeyman for young officers to rally against. At the very best, it was a system of crony appointments to army posts, and nothing more. As Tanaka moved to the Seiyūkai Party, he had lost much of his military influence. But even inside the party, he was not the hub of the real network of power—Mori and Ogawa were.[145] Bereft of any real network, Tanaka found himself exposed to pressure from all quarters.

In spring 1929, influenced by Mori, Ogawa, and Shirakawa, the cabinet decided to hush up the Zhang Zuolin affair. Most of the ministers believed that exposure would sully the dignity of the emperor, who was the commander in chief of the army.[146] The generals, in turn, began to insist that there was "no evidence" for Japanese involvement in the assassination. With such reluctance, was it possible to convict Kōmoto even had a court-martial been held? Tanaka, reluctant to make the affair public, felt he had no choice but to comply.[147] As Emperor Hirohito's frequent inquiries about the investigation were left unanswered, the monarch made it clear that he was not going to let Tanaka off the hook.[148] On June 27, the prime minister came to report, and admitted that the affair would have to be settled as an administrative manner without resort to a court-martial. Emperor Hirohito, in response, blew up in rage. "I spoke to Tanaka in a harsh tone," he recalled later, "saying: 'is it not different than what you have told me before? How about submitting your resignation?'" Tanaka left the audience in tears.[149]

One day later, Army Minister Shirakawa arrived. He disclosed to the emperor that Kōmoto and Muraoka were guilty, but said it would be inadvisable to open a court-martial, as it would undermine the army's honor and Japan's international prestige. Kōmoto might "expose everything" during the proceedings, putting the country in an unfavorable light. Instead, the army would deal with the guilty parties through administrative measures. Hirohito received this presentation with icy silence, but at the end, he gave Shirakawa permission to discipline Kōmoto and his friends without recourse to a court-martial. In an interview with one of Shirakawa's bureau chiefs, he warned the army never to do such a thing again. But without punishment, the warning was hardly effective.[150]

Isolated, deserted, and bereft of all power, General Tanaka Giichi, the former powerful leader of the Chōshū Clique, resigned. He passed away due to illness, aggravated by depression, three months later, in late September 1929. Kōmoto Daisaku, the chief initiator of the entire affair, was never officially tried. He was, however, strongly encouraged to resign his commission and leave the Imperial Army. His commanders Muraoka and Saitō were quietly retired as well.[151]

Emperor Hirohito's intervention in the Zhang Zuolin affair remains a matter of sharp controversy. Some of Hirohito's defenders, such as Stephen Large, see it as yet another failed attempt of the liberal, moderate monarch to restrain the army.[152] Peter Wetzler make the more sophisticated argument that Hirohito and his advisors were perturbed by the inconsistency in Tanaka's reports to the throne and by the perils to the image of the imperial house.[153] Herbert Bix, always keen to nail Hirohito to the wall, contend that the emperor was actually supportive of the Kwantung Army and therefore got rid of Tanaka, the only man who sincerely tried to uproot military insubordination.[154]

None of these interpretations is sufficient. Large does not really explain the reasons for Hirohito's behavior, while the description offered by Bix is incongruent with the evidence.[155] Wetzler presents a subtler description of Hirohito's complex motives, and his emphasis on the latter's anxiety about the prestige of the Imperial House is certainly well merited. It is also true that Hirohito and his advisors were afraid of the "inflation" of imperial power—excessive involvement of the throne in politics which could expose it to the danger of deprecation, censure, and finally even elimination.[156] This argument, undeniably true, explains why the emperor's involvement had to be limited in scope and nature. It still does not explain, however, why the emperor chose to intervene as he did, by censuring Prime Minister Tanaka and contributing to his downfall.

The real answer may be related to the channels of information, command, and control available to the emperor, a recurring theme in our discussion throughout the previous chapters. The emperor, even when ready to risk "inflation" by interfering in politics, had a limited array of tools at his disposal. He could express his wish to other leaders through his palace advisors, and he could summon the premier or the service ministers to the palace. He could demand explanations from them or, though this was unusual, reprimand them in a way that left them no option short of resignation. What Hirohito could not have done, however, was to act independently and to assume the role of the prime minister or the army minister when they failed to act according to his will.

Perhaps, as Ōe Shinobu suggests, Hirohito could have called the chief of the General Staff, who had direct authority over the Kwantung Army, and personally order him to summon a court-martial.[157] But historical protagonists are not always as wise and free of real world constraints as historians, and such an option was hardly raised by anyone at the time. Even though he was a more vigorous emperor than his father, Hirohito reacted rather than initiated. The emperor did not summon Tanaka, for example, on his own initiative. Tanaka came, reported, and only then received an imperial order. Under such conditions, it was difficult to imagine Hirohito summoning the chief of the General Staff and telling him what he should do. And even had he done so, it was impossible for him to follow and monitor effectively the execution of his order. Naturally, it was very easy for the military bureaucracy to sabotage procedures or, at the worst case, to acquit Kōmoto, as had been the case with the murderers of Queen Min thirty years earlier.

The only way Hirohito could have expressed his displeasure was by an angry reaction, "punishing" the individual who seemed to him most responsible for the debacle. And that, of course, would do little to resolve the issue or to curb the Kwantung Army's insubordination. Even that interference seemed excessive to Hirohito's advisors, whose prime interest was to protect the throne, and they ensured that such a move would not repeat itself, at least not in the following years.[158] Hirohito, in other words, had only one bullet in his gun and he aimed it at Tanaka, the most available target and tragically, also the wrong one.[159] Following this fiasco, which the emperor later ascribed to an excess of youthful vigor, he decided to refrain from vetoing government decisions again and to communicate with the prime minister mainly through his courtiers.[160] As the army chiefs could still access the emperor directly through their supreme prerogative privileges, this decision significantly empowered the generals at the expense of the politicians. The army had therefore emerged victorious out of the Zhang Zuolin affair.

Conclusion: The Hole and the Mouse

The year 1928 was an important historical watershed in the development of Japanese military insubordination. In that year, a senior army leader, Lieutenant General Araki Sadao, called on the army to defy the government during a military crisis. A few months later, Kōmoto Daisaku and his coconspirators assassinated Zhang Zuolin, a foreign head of state—an extreme form of military resistance not practiced since the assassination of Queen Min. The Zhang Zuolin affair was a marker of a new era of chaos, mayhem, and political violence. Two years later, in 1930, senior officers denounced the prime minister as "criminal" because he violated the supreme prerogative by opting for naval disarmament, indirectly leading to his assassination by a civilian nationalist. In 1931, young officers intensified this wave of political violence with a plan to wipe out the entire cabinet, the opening act for five turbulent years of assassinations and coups unprecedented since the 1870s.

It would be much too easy to summarize the Zhang Zuolin affair by throwing all the blame on Kōmoto himself. But as the Talmudic proverb goes, "The true thief is the hole, not the mouse." Ill results do not occur only because there is an individual who wants to perform mischief. Rather, the organizational loopholes and the systemic weaknesses allowing such an individual to operate should be the main focus of examination. Indeed, the assassination of Zhang Zuolin and its historical ramifications could not be understood apart from four ideological, political, and organizational conditions that allowed such an incident to occur.

The "hole" was first and foremost framed by the powerful reemergence of supreme prerogative ideology on the Japanese military scene. In 1928, fifteen years after the army's defeat at the Taishō political crisis, this ideology returned with a vengeance, the aggregate result of military developments unfolding since the undoing of the active duty rule in 1913. During the period of Taishō Democracy (1913–1926), civilian cabinets were able to exercise increasing control over the soldiers through the Army Ministry. Although the army was able to shift some authority from the Ministry to the General Staff, this system of control remained until the mid-1920s. But the unpopular reduction of the army under Minister Ugaki, combined with the influence of Araki's demagoguery and the oppositional study groups, eroded the power of the Army Ministry. As a result, civilian control became increasingly frailer in the years leading to 1928, and the supreme prerogative became equivalent in army circles to total independence from the cabinet.[161]

Tanaka himself, though a victim of these tendencies, had a grave responsibility for kindling the fire. Apart from his propagation of the supreme prerogative throughout his military career, his emphasis on "active policy" naturally empowered the army at the expense of the civilian arms of the government. As the British ambassador in Tokyo noted on the day of Zhang's assassination, without being aware of it as yet, "It was no doubt natural that once General Tanaka decided on active measures to protect Japanese interests, the center of control should pass from the Ministry of Foreign Affairs to the General Staff or the War Office [Army Ministry]."[162] If strong measures were to be taken, it was all but natural that the army should stand at the focal point of policy. That, in turn, empowered Imperial Army elements and increased their boldness to act independently. Officers like Araki, utilizing this situation to their advantage, interpreted the supreme prerogative in a radical way, preaching the virtual independence of the army from any kind of civilian supervision.

The supreme prerogative ideology, allowing the military to take strategic decisions independently of the government, combined with the idea of operational discretion as understood in Manchuria, formed the ideological context for Kōmoto's assassination plot in 1928. The supreme prerogative had been designed to allow the leaders of the army, not every officer, to participate in the making of national strategy. Operational discretion allowed junior officers, most of all in Manchuria, to take independent tactical decisions in the field. The combination of both gave junior officers like Kōmoto legitimation to take *strategic* decisions, including the assassination of a head of state in complete defiance of government policy. While the supreme prerogative increased the power of the army as an institution, operational discretion eroded its internal hierarchy. In other words, it was again that disastrous combination of consolidation and dispersion, outer formidability and internal chaos, which made the Japanese Army prone to insubordination.

A third precondition for Kōmoto's plot was the involution of Japanese military elements into the Manchurian underworld. Nakano Yōhei and Itō Kenjirō, two of Kōmoto's accomplices in the plot, operated through an intricate network of adventurers, pimps, and other Chinese and Japanese criminal elements, all of them associated with the army through the Special Service Organization. The close cooperation between military, nationalist-civilian, and criminal elements was already present at the assassination of Queen Min in 1895, and it did not end with Itō's involvement in the murder of Zhang Zuolin. In fact, the involution of army elements into the nationalist-civilian-criminal sphere, already explained in chapter 6, would intensify in the 1930s, as we shall see in the next chapter.

Finally, the "hole" was also a product of the organizational chaos in the Kwantung Army, a force in which official hierarchies were rarely respected. All three commanders of this army, Muraoka, Saitō and Kōmoto, behaved as if conspiracy, resistance, and operation through private networks were their normal method of operation. Muraoka disclosed his own plan to kill Zhang to Takeshita, a Special Service operative, and not to Saitō and Kōmoto, his direct subordinates in the military hierarchy. On June 3, Chief of Staff Saitō assumed that some people in the Kwantung Army were plotting Zhang's death, but was not disturbed in the least that such a conspiracy was hatched without him being informed.[163] One of Kawagoe's roles was to watch over Muraoka's room, to make sure he was not listening to Kōmoto's conversations.[164] General Hata Shinji, the Special Service chief in Mukden, strongly reprimanded the local police for reporting rumors about the affair to the Tokyo government as such reports could "increase the doubts inside the army."[165]

That conspiratorial atmosphere was enhanced by the peculiar organizational structure of the Kwantung Army. Usually, the commanders of Japanese military units, as in other modern armies, were assisted by a chief of staff. The chief of staff had a certain number of subordinates, each responsible for a particular field, such as operations, intelligence, or logistics. The authority of each staff officer was limited, allowing the chief of staff and the commander to assume responsibility for the entire width and breadth of military activity. In the Kwantung Army, by contrast, apart from the posts of commander and chief of staff, there was a peculiar role of "senior staff officer" (*Kōkyū Sanbō*), held in 1928 by Kōmoto. As senior staff officer, Kōmoto was subordinate to Chief of Staff Saitō, but in fact, he had day-to-day responsibility over all segments of staff work.

Such a reality is dangerous in any organization. As the British management theoretician Northcote Parkinson noted, if a superior has only one subordinate down the hierarchy, then this subordinate, who is doing everything that the superior does, is effectively a competitor.[166] In the Kwantung Army, Kōmoto functioned as an informal chief of staff. But because he was not officially recognized as such, he was operating beneath the radar of the higher echelons. Saitō and Muraoka were constantly pressured and watched by the General Staff, but Kōmoto was not, and thus had ample room to hatch conspiracies and plots.[167] After the assassination, the authorities sharply reduced the powers of the Kwantung Army's staff, precisely in order to prevent the events of June 1928 from reoccurring. But as Kōmoto's old position remained, two powerful personalities, Ishiwara Kanji and Itagaki Seishirō, would soon revive it, making the conspiracy of the "Manchurian Incident" possible.[168] As long as the function of senior staff officer remained intact, it was all but expected that someone would fill it with content. Wherever holes exist, mice will always find a way to creep in.

But apart from "the hole"—the ideological and organizational context –the "mouse" that occupied the post of senior staff officer in 1928, Kōmoto Daisaku, was the worst man in the worst place. Just like Miura Gorō, the officer who assassinated Queen Min more than thirty years earlier, Kōmoto was a contrarian at heart, an officer who despised his commanders as members of tyrannical cliques. On the one hand, as early as 1923, he was in very bad standing with his superiors in Tokyo, and felt rejected and excluded. Because of his estrangement from the "higher echelons" he was not in a position to influence national policy through normal means. Nor, as he bitterly complained, could China experts such as himself expect real avenues of promotion in the military.[169] On the other hand, Kōmoto could use his horizontal contacts throughout the army and beyond to plan illicit operations. Manchuria, like Korea before, was a place where the currency of optimism had still high value, where adventurers and rogue officers could, in the words of Zhang Zuolin's advisor Machino Takema, "do heroic things impossible in Japan."[170] The assassination of Zhang Zuolin, in that sense, was Kōmoto's way of leaving his mark and doing "great things" in the only way his position allowed him—through a conspiracy.

The failure of Japan's imperial government to punish Kōmoto and his confederates set an ominous precedent for the future. As Ōe Shinobu writes, many officers were now led to believe that they no longer needed to wait for imperial orders. Just like Kōmoto, they could resist the orders of both military and civilian authorities unless the emperor told them otherwise.[171] And if assassination plots against foreign leaders remained unpunished, why not use similar violence against Japanese leaders, too, in the name of the emperor and under the same patriotic pretexts? The Japanese government would soon discover, to its horror, that military resistance could not be stopped and brushed aside by giving way. The politicians, said Colonel

Suzuki Teiichi in retrospect, did not understand the army's way of thinking. When the civilian government is strong, it can force the soldiers to retreat from occupied territories for the sake of foreign policy. When the politicians are weak, the soldiers follow their military inclinations and expand without limit.[172] In 1928, the politicians and the emperor were not there to stop the soldiers. They, along with the Japanese Empire, would soon be forced to pay the price.

9

CHERRY BLOSSOM
From Resistance to Rebellion, 1931

Now there was only the hush of blossoms, falling, falling.
—Sakaguchi Ango, "In the Forest, Under Cherries in Full Bloom"

In February 1961, the Japanese journalist Nakano Masao stumbled on a surprising discovery. Tracing for months the faded footprints of army rebels, he discovered a safe house formerly used by the Sakura-kai (Cherry Blossom Society), a clandestine organization whose activities precipitated a wave of military violence in the early 1930s. Inside this safe house, the abode of a female dentist and sympathizer of the group, Nakano was able to unearth a carbon copy of a document universally considered to be destroyed: a secret memoir drafted by Colonel Hashimoto Kingorō, one of the cruelest and boldest military rebels in the history of modern Japan. The colonel, sentenced to life as a war criminal by the International Military Tribunal for the Far East, wrote a lengthy, unapologetic account of his group's activity and made four additional copies for his former confederates in the Sakura-kai's inner circle, maintaining one for himself. All copies, except an extra manuscript secretly copied and kept by this sympathizing dentist, were burned and destroyed during the last phases of the war, or immediately thereafter. Their owners, with one important exception, perished as well.[1] Through Hashimoto's unearthed account, historians were able to reconstruct, almost for the first time, the inner workings of the group whose plotting marked a dramatic, violent change in the history of Japanese military insubordination.

The uniqueness of the Sakura-kai was evident in several respects. First of all, it was, perhaps, the first cross-army conspiratorial group, transcending the usual clique rivalries. Unlike previous oppositional organizations, it was not based on feudal ties such as the Chōshū Clique, nor was it set to fight such feudal

193

organizations. Its concerns were all related to problems facing Japan in the 1930s. In addition, it was the first military group of its kind working in equal partnership with nationalist civilian organizations. And finally, its tactics were unprecedentedly violent, especially toward the end of its short existence when it planned to wipe out the entire Japanese cabinet by means of an aerial bombardment. For the first time since the 1870s, the Sakura-kai escalated the familiar patterns of military resistance into an outright rebellion.

Such extreme violence against Japanese leaders had been truly unheard of for more than half a century. Since the repression of the Satsuma Rebellion in 1878, violent military insurrections had all but disappeared from the Japanese scene. Up until 1931, military insubordination had largely taken the form of resistance to state policy via assassinations of foreign leaders and other unauthorized military operations of strategic importance. The Japanese government was challenged and embarrassed by such acts, but had not been physically threatened. Although they were few and far between, assassinations had occurred. These, however, were the acts of civilian nationalists, not of soldiers. The army had once used its power to overthrow a cabinet, in the Taishō political crisis of 1912, but that was a bloodless, nonviolent coup. The Sakura-kai, established in October 1930, was an organization that, for the first time since 1878, pointed the sword of military violence toward the Japanese government itself. Its activity threw the army into a whirlwind and pushed the government and the different military factions to a violent struggle of all against all.

National Reconstruction: The Rebels Turn to Japan

It is common to see the 1930s as a period of rapid deterioration of the political order. Many authors portray the military and its ideological allies as constantly marching forward, collaborating with civilian cabinets or pushing them aside in a quest for unbridled national power.[2] In autumn 1930, however, mid-ranking officers of the Imperial Japanese Army, colonels, lieutenant colonels, and majors close to the centers of power but not yet in formal positions of leadership, did not see themselves as being in the midst of a triumphant march. As far as they were concerned, their experiences did not constitute an "introduction" to eventual military takeover, but rather were a series of frustrating setbacks, defeats, and dashed hopes. The assassination of Zhang Zuolin in 1928 failed to produce any tangible results. In Manchuria, the Kwantung Army was still held in check by senior generals, diplomats, and civilian politicians. The anti-Japanese movement in China continued unabated, while the Japanese Empire's foreign policy, still managed by relative moderates such as Foreign Minister Shidehara Kijūrō and Prime Minister Hamaguchi Osachi, was ever cautious not to provoke Britain, the United States, or other foreign powers. To add insult to injury, the cabinet refused to increase the budget of the army, cutting officers' salaries and slowing down the military modernization process.[3]

The London Naval Disarmament Treaty was yet another painful blow. The navy had seen the agreement as a blatant violation of the supreme prerogative on the part of the prime minister, as only the admirals were authorized to advise the emperor on matters pertaining to naval security.[4] And yet the government had its way and the treaty was signed. In November 1930 Prime Minister Hamaguchi, denounced by the navy as a "supreme prerogative criminal" (tōsui-ken kanpan-sha), was seriously wounded by a right-wing civilian assassin, leading to the resignation of his cabinet in April of the next year and to his death. But Hamaguchi's Minseitō Party still remained in power. The sole surviving genrō, Prince Saionji, insisted on retaining the ruling party in order not to encourage future assassinations.[5] To the military's great chagrin, Hamaguchi's successor, Prime Minister Wakatsuki Reijirō, upheld his predecessor's cautious foreign policy.

In Japan itself, the economic situation progressively deteriorated as a result of the Great Depression of 1929. The cabinet's policy, based on the two pillars of retrenchment and return to the international gold standard, made things even worse. As prices dived, companies were compelled to reduce wages and lay off workers, slowing the economy down and increasing Japan's vulnerability to the global recession. Many peasants whose livelihoods were dependent on silk prices were devastated by the fall of silk demand in the United States.[6] Mid-ranking and junior officers, many of whom led soldiers from the countryside, were painfully aware of their subalterns' plight.[7]

Many officers, like their peers from the civilian right and the patriotic societies, knew well whom to blame in this situation. For them, the government's weak-kneed policy in China and Manchuria and the neglect of Japan's poor were two sides of the same coin. The officers were forced to witness one corruption scandal after another, delineating the illicit ties of Diet members, palace courtiers, and senior generals with the zaibatsu, Japan's maligned business magnates. At the same time, "dangerous" ideologies such as liberalism, socialism, and individualism infested the streets of big cities such as Tokyo, obfuscating "traditional" Japanese values such as frugality, sacrifice, and pure-hearted faith in the imperial throne. For most officers, the army was the ultimate embodiment of these values, and therefore any resistance to military demands was interpreted as an encroachment on Japanese tradition by dangerous, foreign ideologies.[8]

The prevailing feeling among concerned officers was one of their own incompetence, as nothing they had done to that point had been able to fundamentally alter the situation. The solution, as many of them saw it, was a vague vision, known at the time as the Showa Restoration (*shōwa ishin*) or "national reconstruction" (*kokka kaizō*). These terms were popularized by right-wing ideologues beginning in the late 1920s. They constituted part of a dream to reenact the Meiji Restoration, which had been led astray over the years by the corrupt alliance of party politicians, genrō, capitalists, and military cliques.[9] The "national reconstruction" vision was never clearly articulated, but in general, it included the destruction of party politics, military dominance in national policy, a planned economy instead of "selfish capitalism," "traditional values" in place of liberalism, and unilateral expansion into Manchuria, Mongolia, northern China, and maybe even to the Russian Far East. Many activists, well aware of the fate of the Russian Empire, had deemed such a restoration as the only alternative to an eventual communist revolution.[10]

The means to achieve this restoration, however, were subject to sharp controversy. Some officers were reluctant to violate the law. Others, who were ready to resist the state in order to bring about radical change, did not agree on the best way to break the impasse. Kōmoto Daisaku and his many sympathizers in the officer corps believed that military resistance to the government's policy in Manchuria might be the "game changer," a solid base for the army to gather power and facilitate change in Japan itself.[11] Other officers, however, began to challenge this concept of "Manchuria first." Witnessing Kōmoto's daring going to waste due to the generals' and the politicians' hesitance, they concluded that without a bold step to change Japan from within, the dream of territorial expansion was all but futile.[12] The idea of "Japan First, Manchuria Second" was the ideological tenet underlying the Sakura-kai's foundation.[13]

The Ringleader: Hashimoto Kingorō

The prosecution at the Tokyo Trials proclaimed Lieutenant Colonel Hashimoto Kingorō, former intelligence officer, conspirator, and in later life, an influential nationalist leader, as one of the most dangerous figures in prewar Japan. "This man was no mere rabble-rouser in the streets," wrote a prosecution official in an internal memo, "no mere fanatical hawker of propaganda in the hedgerows and byways of Japan. By 1940 this man was one of the twenty most influential and powerful men in Japan. . . . With his record of organizing and directing ultranationalist societies in mind; with his record of plotting revolutions in mind; . . . can there be any doubt as to the character of his power and influence on the Japanese people, both before the war and during it?"[14]

Even if Hashimoto's influence was less than that imagined by this prosecution official, he was undoubtedly a key figure in the Japanese nationalist scene during the 1930s and the early 1940s. Similar to Kōmoto Daisaku, he was highly talented but impulsive, an "unmanageable" shishi type who worked his way into the military elite but never felt at ease there. Not a man of narrow military pursuits, Hashimoto was also a poet and bon vivant, a drinker and a frequent customer of taverns and geisha houses. Professionally he was a military prodigy and excelled in math and in foreign languages, especially Russian and French. A graduate of the elite Army Staff College, he specialized in artillery and intelligence and served several tours of duty as an operative of the Special Service Organization. In 1928, he was sent to Turkey as a military attaché.[15] There his mission was to spy on Soviet military movements in the Caucasus and to sow anti-Soviet sentiments among Caucasian minorities.[16] Monitoring Turkish politics, Hashimoto was thoroughly impressed with the leadership of Mustafa Kemal "Atatürk," the founder of modern Turkey who expelled the last Ottoman sultan and established a secular, authoritarian republic. The easy-to-impress lieutenant colonel had ardently read Atatürk's speeches and had even met the great man for dinner in the new Turkish capital, Ankara.[17]

Following the rise of strong rulers in Europe and in Asia, men such as Atatürk in Turkey, Mussolini in Italy, Stalin in the Soviet Union, Pilsudski in Poland, and Reza Shah in Persia, Hashimoto believed he was able to find the thread connecting these "national saviors" with one another. Oblivious to the complicated circumstances and the significant differences between these countries, he drew one main lesson from his studies: divided and collapsing nations could be saved by strong leaders, capable of forging national consensus with the backing of patriotic officers. Being "hot-blooded through and through," Hashimoto found it easy to brush aside the warning in the Imperial Rescript for Soldiers and Sailors, which prohibited military personnel from "meddling in politics." The rescript, he wrote later, banned political activity only when such was at odds with one's duty. But a soldier, just like any other imperial subject, was obliged to interfere in politics for the sake of the country. In fact, from the point of view of national defense, such intervention might even be considered an essential part of a soldier's duty.[18]

In 1930, when Hashimoto was finally ordered to return to the General Staff, he spent the lengthy nautical journey home contemplating "how to reform Japan." As a result, he wrote, "I succeeded in drawing a definite plan to a certain degree. And on returning to the General Staff Office, my former haunt, I devised several schemes in order to put my ideas into execution."[19] These "schemes," as expressed in Hashimoto's later essays, were a blend of unbridled territorial ambitions and a call for "national reconstruction at home." The corrupt "liberal" regime, he believed, should be destroyed and replaced by an authoritarian state backed by the army, in which "politics, economics, culture, national defense and everything else [were] all focused on one—the emperor." That unified nation, in turn,

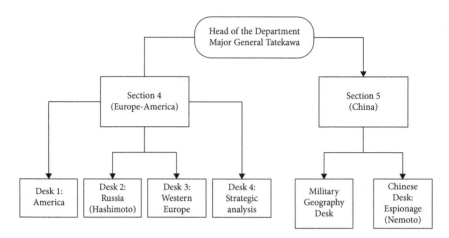

FIGURE 9.1 General Staff Intelligence (Second) Department. The chart is based on the information in Karita, "Jūgatsu Jiken," 1:316.

should "grasp the reins to lead the world in a new world order."[20] With such schemes in mind, Hashimoto returned to Tokyo and was commissioned to lead the Russian desk of the Europe-America section in the Intelligence Department of the General Staff.[21]

Traditionally, the Intelligence Department of the General Staff was entrusted, like similar institutions around the world, with information gathering and special operations in foreign countries. By 1928 the department was already involved in military resistance through cooperation with the assassination plot of Zhang Zuolin. Under the leadership of its new commander, Major General Tatekawa Yoshitsugu (in office since August 1929), it began to meddle in Japanese politics as well.[22] In spring 1930, Major General Tatekawa ordered Hashimoto and his colleague from the China Section, Nemoto Hiroshi, to draft a plan for national reconstruction. By the standards of the time, such a plan could easily have been interpreted as a call for a coup d'état.

Hashimoto wrote later that he and his friends felt that they must act like the shishi of the Meiji Restoration.[23] This was the result of the mimesis process mentioned at the end of chapter 1: the tendency of rebels with ambiguous goals, such as Hashimoto, to imitate the only rebellious model that was both patriotic and successful—that of the shishi. The government, the popular press, and numerous authors unwittingly abetted this process for decades, by praising shishi as patriots, writing about their exploits and enshrining their souls in Yasukuni as national martyrs (*jun'nansha*). In the early Showa period, stories about shishi were also incorporated in the military education system.[24]

The government, naturally, emphasized the shishi's loyalty to the emperor, but others, especially in the radical right and the patriotic societies, fondly remembered also their rebelliousness, unruliness, and drunkenness. Sōshi and other adventurers adopted this ethos by calling themselves "commoner *shishi*."[25] The cooperation between the army and such adventurers, evident since the assassination of Queen Min but much intensified in the late 1920s, instilled the rebellious interpretation of the shishi heritage into the lower echelons of the officer corps. For Hashimoto and his friends, who saw themselves as modern shishi, the government of Japan was just as illegitimate as the Tokugawa Bakufu. Violence against it was permitted, at least in principle.

Hashimoto despised not only the government, but also the army's leadership. His mentality was somewhat similar to that of Kōmoto Daisaku in 1928.[26] Now, however, the Chōshū Clique, that constant anathema of rebellious officers, was all but nonexistent. The question was one of views, and each general was evaluated by his readiness to collaborate with the project of national reconstruction. As most senior officers were reluctant to cooperate, they were denounced by Hashimoto as lazy incompetents. Only a handful, like Major General Tatekawa, were viewed as allies.[27] From the outset, therefore, Hashimoto and his team drew a sharp dichotomy between "us"—the pure-hearted, heroic shishi and their sympathizers—and "them"—corrupt officers who gave their support to the current system. Along with his closest collaborators, Hashimoto swore a solemn oath to brave death for the cause of national reconstruction.[28]

This state of mind, combined with the feeling of urgency, drove Hashimoto to drop all considerations of caution or gradualism. "The dark clouds of the already ossified political world," he wrote, "have to be cleared without a trace, the evil root of the nation has to be removed. With bravery and determination, such would surely be a trivial thing to do."[29] Here we see the same kind of shishi optimism that led Japanese rebels to murder leaders, from the mixed gangs of the 1860s and the plan to assassinate Iwakura, through to the assassinations of Queen Min and Zhang Zuolin to the Sakura-kai: a belief that evil, serious and threatening as it might have been, could be uprooted by one clean sweep, requiring nothing but bravery and determination.

The Cherry Blossom Society and Its Civilian Allies

Tanaka Ryūkichi, an officer who attended the first meeting of Hashimoto's society, held on October 1, 1930, in the Tokyo Officers Club (Kaikōsha), testified later that the participants "did not touch at all on Manchurian problems," because "at that time domestic questions within Japan were extremely acute." According to Tanaka, that first meeting was attended by fifty to sixty officers, including five or six navy officers (delegates of a parallel organization, the Sea and Stars Society), but in the following months the numbers significantly grew.[30] The new group had a unique regulation that limited the membership to relatively junior officers holding ranks of lieutenant colonel and below, and then only if they were "selflessly interested in national reconstruction."[31] Senior officers were formally excluded, though some of them supported the organization from the outside.

The society was nameless for the first few months of its existence. Only in spring 1931 did Hashimoto convince the assembly to approve the name Sakura-kai, Cherry Blossom Society, a known symbol in Japanese military culture that would be used again during the Second World War in reference to the Kamikaze. According to the aesthetic notions of the time, the magnificent but short-lived cherry blossom symbolized the life of the pure and youthful warrior: short, as he was ready to sacrifice it at a moment's notice, and yet resplendent in heroic glamour and unsullied by compromise.[32] This name, too, symbolized Hashimoto's intention to link himself and his society, figuratively and culturally, to the romantic shishi culture of the late Tokugawa and early Meiji periods.[33]

The Sakura-kai's similarity to the shishi was not in name alone. Just as the late Tokugawa rebels were able to overcome the estrangement between the domains by building an interdomainal alliance, the leaders of the Sakura-kai were able to unite officers from various military power centers for common action. That was one of the reasons the Sakura-kai was so dangerous. If previous rebellious cliques inherited the loose structure of the shishi mixed gangs, the Sakura-kai was the first one which, deliberately or unwittingly, imitated the alliance that finally overthrew the Bakufu. Lieutenant General Sotoyama Toyozō, commander of the military police at the time, noticed this and wrote that the intersectional nature of such rebellious networks was the true impetus for the army's "enduring disaster."[34] Had the Sakura-kai been limited to one military power center, for example, to the General Staff, other power centers such as the Army Ministry could have seen it as a selfish, partisan plot to enhance the power of one military institution at the expense of others. Only by overcoming such sectional, factional, and institutional divides was it possible to form a truly effective conspiratorial network.

The three founders of the Sakura-kai, all lieutenant colonels, were Hashimoto from the General Staff, Sakata Yoshirō from the Army Ministry, and Higuchi Kiichirō from the Tokyo Guards Division. Additional cofounders of junior rank, but of no less influence, were Hashimoto's direct subordinates at the Russian Desk: Captain Obara Shigetake, Captain Tanaka Wataru, and Lieutenant Amano Isamu, as well as the China Espionage Desk leader Nemoto Hiroshi. Another key figure was Captain Chō Isamu, also from the Chinese Desk.[35] Chō, destined to be Hashimoto's

General Staff

Army Staff College

Army Ministry

Military Police (Kempeitai)

Toyama Army School (instructors and students)

Inspectorate General

Tokyo Guards Division

Azabu Regiment

Scientific Research Institute

Other military schools (instructors and students)

Imperial Guards

1st Infantry Regiment

Unknown and others

FIGURE 9.2 Sakura-kai membership by unit/branch.

Source: Karita, "Jūgatsu Jiken," 1:327–30.

closest partner in the Sakura-kai's path of terror, was of a very similar character. A notorious drinker and womanizer, he too was talented, quick-witted, but impulsive and cruel, a modern shishi "quick to laugh and cry," prone to outbursts of both glee and outrage.[36] Most rank-and-file members were graduates of the Staff College, that is, they belonged to the narrow elite stratum of officers. The masses of "unit officers" (*taizuki shōkō*) were hardly represented until late March of the following year.[37]

The prominence of Hashimoto, Chō, and their close confederates from the Intelligence Department can be clearly seen in the graph above. The branch in which they served, the General Staff, was in the lead with forty members. The Staff College and the Army Ministry were next in line with fifteen and nine members, respectively. Smaller, but still crucial support came from the Inspectorate General and various regiments and divisions. Ten of the members were students and instructors at the Toyama Army School, an institution specializing in fencing and an important center for nationalist sedition.

Generally, the preponderance of military schools in the Tokyo area gave rise to a rebellious "student culture," somewhat reminiscent of the fencing schools of the late Tokugawa period. In both instances, young and spirited warriors from all across the country could meet each other, socialize, and discuss national reconstruction. This situation made it easy for Sakura-kai leaders such as Captain Obara to recruit new members.[38] Other members of the Sakura-kai were placed in the Military Police, the organization whose duty was to suppress their activity. Possibly these "Trojan horses" kept their superiors in the dark until the last moment.[39] Like Kōmoto Daisaku, the leaders of the Sakura-kai were mid-ranking or junior officers mostly unsupervised by decision makers. But unlike Kōmoto, they served in key areas in and around Tokyo and were, therefore, in positions to aim more precise blows at the civilian cabinet and the ruling elite.

The semipublic section of the Sakura-kai, well-known in army circles, was a study group whose members met monthly to discuss current affairs over dinner.[40] But in fact, this "debate club" was hardly more than a convenient façade. The leaders of the society has also established an inner circle of conspirators, originally known as the "committee of eleven." This group, founded to discuss the means to implement a coup d'état, was led by Hashimoto and Chō.[41]

In its plannings, the committee of eleven could count on the solid support of senior generals in the higher echelons. The Sakura-kai benefited from the patronage of army potentates such as generals Ninomiya Harushige (deputy chief of the General Staff), Sugiyama Hajime (vice army minister), Tatekawa Yoshitsugu (head of the General Staff Intelligence Department), and Koiso Kuniaki (chief of the Army Ministry's Military Affairs Bureau). In this small group of senior schemers, the old clique struggles were still somewhat alive. Generals Ninomiya, Sugiyama, Tatekawa, and Koiso were not members of feudal domain cliques, but they did form a personal clique around general and army minister Ugaki Kazush-ige. These confidants of Ugaki, anxious that their patron was falling in popularity, plotted to make him prime minister in order to revive their power. These political considerations meshed nicely with the ideological goals of the Sakura-kai, moti-vating those high officers to back it up.[42]

The Sakura-kai's military membership was closely allied with civilian nation-alistic societies. Unlike Miura's collaboration with Adachi and his sōshi during the Queen Min assassination, theirs was not an ad hoc alliance but rather a strong, equal partnership. The key person in that alliance was Dr. Ōkawa Shūmei, an intel-lectual for all seasons who wrote extensively on Asian religions, Eastern philoso-phy, economics, law, and pan-Asianism. In addition to serving as the head of the South Manchurian Railway's Research Bureau and being a professor at Takushoku University, he led a long succession of nationalist groupings and organizations. Ōkawa's network of connections extended far and wide, not only in civilian patri-otic societies but also in the higher echelons of the armed services. Indeed, he was even invited to lecture at the General Staff and at the Naval Academy.

Like the Sakura-kai, Ōkawa was interested in "national reconstruction," the destruction of party politics, and a planned economy. Furthermore, he aimed to expand the Japanese Empire into Manchuria and China, an essential step not only in the quest for Japanese economic self-sufficiency but also a precondition to the expulsion of Western imperialism from East Asia. With this expansion in place, Ōkawa hoped, the entire continent might be united under Japanese tute-lage.[43] With such views, it was no wonder that Ōkawa established a good work-ing relationship with the Sakura-kai. In 1931, he held a series of meetings with Hashimoto in a Tokyo tavern to discuss possible actions.[44]

Naturally, in order to finance the coup, Ōkawa had to obtain funds. Initially, 300,000 yen were supposed to come from the Army Ministry, but the flow was soon stopped after a key official got cold feet. Always quick to adapt to shifting circumstances, Ōkawa was able to obtain an even greater sum (500,000 yen) from Marquis Tokugawa Yoshichika, a nationalist peer and the head of the former shogun's household. To keep the matter secret, Tokugawa decided neither to draw money from his bank account nor to sell his stocks. Instead, he sold his private gold bullion reserves and gave the returns to Ōkawa and his partners.[45]

The March Incident

The leaders of the Sakura-kai's radical faction, particularly Hashimoto and Chō, believed that the current system could be changed solely through direct, violent intervention. During the first two months of 1931, they constantly looked for a window of opportunity to catch their opponents unaware. Such an opportunity, unfortunately, was supplied by none other than the organization's arch enemy, Foreign Minister Shidehara. On February 3, during a heated debate in the budget committee of the Imperial Diet, Shidehara (then acting prime minister) defended the London Disarmament Treaty by claiming that it was ratified by the emperor. The Seiyūkai opposition could not miss such a splendid opportunity to rail against the government, accusing Shidehara of evading ministerial responsibility and undermining imperial prestige by dragging the throne into politics.

Imperial authority, as one observer aptly put it, was a "double-edged sword."[46] Just as with Ōkubo in 1873 and with Katsura in 1913, using it for partisan purposes was likely to draw rage from all quarters. The rioting inside the Diet, fanned by Seiyūkai nationalist leaders and led by sōshi from both sides, paralyzed the parliament for about a week. The rage aroused by Shidehara's "slip of the tongue" proved to be a rallying cry for all of the government's enemies, and Ōkawa Shūmei soon noticed an opportunity. Hashimoto, too, was incensed. Shidehara's "shameful" remark, he recalled later, cemented his desire to "eradicate the Diet."[47] In a series of conversations with Hashimoto and his associates, Ōkawa began to develop a plan for action.[48]

This scheme, later known as the March Incident, should be seen as a transitory phase between the bloodless coup d'état of the Taishō political crisis and the new age of violent military rebellions. Indeed, the basic outline was an attempt to reenact the mass "movement to protect the constitution" that overthrew the Katsura cabinet in 1913.[49] Setting the date to March 20, Ōkawa planned to use the nationalists' outrage over Shidehara's "slip" and the Minseitō's Labor Union Bill to organize violent, mass demonstrations in Hibiya Park, a traditional site for popular riots, and march the crowds toward the Imperial Diet. These plans were quite ambitious as the number of the demonstrators was supposed to exceed ten thousand. And to add mayhem to havoc, groups of sōshi were ordered to start fires in different parts of the capital.[50]

This time, though, the mass uprising was to culminate in a coup d'état. For this purpose, Ōkawa attached to the demonstrators special assault teams (Battōtai, "sword-waving squads"; or Kesshitai, "death-defying squads"), staffed by fencing martial artists and armed with sabers. The teams were ordered to storm the prime minister's office and the headquarters of both "established parties," Minseitō and Seiyūkai. A squad of toughs from a nationalistic society was supposed to toss dummy bombs on the Diet buildings. Other groups of rebels were tasked with the occupation of the Metropolitan Police headquarters.[51] The turmoil was designed as an excuse for Sakura-kai-led officers to cordon off the Diet and thereby to block all movement to and from the building, allegedly in order to protect it. Individual ringleaders, with full knowledge of the plan, were supposed to personally lead these officers on the ground, to overpower the guards and to storm into parliament.[52]

Then, the higher-echelon allies of the movement would enter the stage. A certain lieutenant general whose name was kept in secret, was to enter the building with an entourage of officers and confront the cabinet ministers. The text of his speech was drafted in advance by the ringleaders. "The nation," he was supposed to have said, "no longer has faith in the current cabinet. They will have faith only in a cabinet led by General Ugaki. Currently, the country is facing difficult times. Please be kind enough to do the right thing." After this short speech, the cabinet would be forced to resign en masse. Concurrently, Prince Saionji, the only surviving genrō, was to be pressured to "recommend" the army minister, General Ugaki Kazushige, to the emperor as Japan's new premier. The latter, "aided" by Ōkawa Shūmei in the role of kingmaker, was supposed to form a new cabinet, this time without Foreign Minister Shidehara, the bête-noir of the Japanese nationalists. The cabinet would toughen up Japan's Manchurian policy and implement the long-sought-after Showa Restoration.[53]

Just like many other Japanese military conspirators before, Hashimoto and his colleagues were optimistic in the extreme. "Drunk with joy," as their co-conspirator, Captain Tanaka Kiyoshi had put it, they refused to listen to timely warnings. Tanaka, for example, cautioned that their plan was not only hastily drafted but also poorly organized. To begin with, the various units did not have enough coordination, and the plans for the new government were not detailed enough.[54] But the main drawback of the plan, as Tanaka observed, was that it presumed the cooperation of too many unreliable people who were not part of the original circle of conspirators.[55] For example, would Ōkawa and his accomplices be able to rally enough demonstrators at the appointed time? The bombs for the assault teams had to be supplied by the army, but would the conspirators be able to procure them? And the most crucial question of all: Would Ugaki cooperate with the scheme? The army minister's cooperation was indispensable as the entire plan hinged on his readiness to utilize the unfolding mayhem as an excuse to form a new cabinet. And even if that would happen, there was no guaranty that Ugaki would actually make anything more than cosmetic changes to the government policies.

Ugaki's close associates, Tatekawa, Koiso, Sugiyama, and Ninomiya, in association with the Sakura-kai, had "worked" on the army minister at least since January. Indeed, they had a certain basis for optimism. In the past, General Ugaki voiced cautious support for the "Shōwa Restoration" as soon as the majority of the people reached an adequate level of "political awareness." That double game was a mixed bag of opportunism and genuine concerns. Ugaki's own unpublished manuscript shows that he considered using troops to remedy pressing problems such as corruption, the plight of the poor, and the danger of communism, but that he was also afraid of the chaos and disintegration that might ensue.[56]

In early 1931, though still undecided, Ugaki was giving officers around him the feeling that he might support the plot.[57] On January 13 he summoned Koiso, Ninomiya, and other officers, including Sakura-kai leaders such as Hashimoto, to discuss "military reforms." Subsequently, Lieutenant General Ninomiya ordered Hashimoto to "draft a plan for national reconstruction" and to submit it to Ugaki.[58] Major General Tatekawa, Hashimoto's commanding officer in the Intelligence Department, heartily supported the plot, and agreed to apply stronger pressure on Ugaki. No one really seemed to care about the chief of the General Staff, General Kanaya Hanzō, whose reputation as a useless alcoholic was well-known.[59]

The support of senior officers notwithstanding, Ōkawa wanted to be more certain about Ugaki's position. Accordingly a meeting was arranged, presumably after much pleading by Major General Koiso. Here, the testimonies sharply diverge. According to Ōkawa's recollections, Ugaki more or less agreed to cooperate.[60] The army minister, however, strictly denied it. In informal testimony given several months later, he described the meeting with Ōkawa in detail and emphasized that he rejected each and every one of the latter's requests. Ōkawa, according to Ugaki, asked him not to use troops to suppress the demonstrators, to supply them with bombs, and to assume the position of prime minister afterward. In response, the army minister assured Ōkawa that it was the army's duty to keep public order and that he would never assume the prime ministry as his fortunes were strictly tied to the current cabinet.[61] In addition, no bombs could be given to civilians. From these two versions, Ugaki's seems to be more reliable, as Ōkawa's testimony, though not wrong in its entirety, is confused and riddled with outright prevarications.[62]

One thing, however, is clear from both versions. As early as February 11, Ugaki knew about the plot and did nothing to subvert it. Nor did he order an arrest of Ōkawa. At this point, the basic assumptions underlying Japanese discourse at the time should not go overlooked. The fact that the Japanese Empire's army minister met with a notorious conspirator and listened to his plots without having him arrested on the spot, was so self-evident in 1931 that Ugaki could hardly deny it.

However, in an alarming development for the conspirators, an anticoup faction spontaneously formed in the Army Ministry. It was led by some close confidants of Ugaki, and even some Sakura-kai members agreed that Hashimoto and Ōkawa must be stopped. Meanwhile, the supporters of the plot in the Army Ministry began to reconsider. Major General Koiso, for example, was alarmed by the crudeness of Ōkawa's plan. When he heard the details in late February, he denounced it as "childish" and "advised" Ōkawa to retract it. Ōkawa, fearful of the army's fickleness, started to fulminate against the generals.[63] Panicked and close to despair, he sent a highly emotional letter to Ugaki on March 6, cajoling him into spearheading the Showa Restoration to "overcome disorder and vindicate righteousness" as "a great man of ability." But the minister did not react.[64]

Major General Koiso, who was already feeling that the chances to win Ugaki over were slim, started to snub Ōkawa, advising him that Ugaki was too busy and could not meet him again.[65] Accordingly, Koiso dillydallied with the conspirators and refused to give them the bombs he promised. Hashimoto, in response, bypassed Koiso and turned to none other than Kōmoto Daisaku, the former assassin of Zhang Zuolin. However, Kōmoto could not get any bombs either. Major General Tatekawa, who still supported the coup, attempted to procure them through his connections in the infantry school, but that attempt, as well, ended in failure. Finally, a junior officer from the same school secretly got hold of some dummy bombs that were designed to create noise and havoc but nothing more. On March 12 and 13, Hashimoto and another officer carried a large number of these bombs in paper bags to Shimbashi train station, central Tokyo, and handed them over to one of the leaders of Ōkawa's sōshi.[66]

But the plan's complete dependence on Ugaki's cooperation was and remained its most dangerous Achilles heel. The wily military politician, who had changed sides and betrayed his patrons several times in the past, was no person to rely on in an emergency, as Hashimoto and Ōkawa learned several days before launching their plan. Ugaki suddenly ceased his double game and ordered Major General Koiso in unequivocal language to cancel all plans for a coup d'état without delay. In fact, an ulterior political consideration might have been involved. In the beginning of March, as Hashimoto wrote later, rumors began to circulate in the capital that the government might soon resign, and it was likely that Ugaki would be appointed by the throne as Prime Minister Hamaguchi's successor. In such a situation, the army minister would have little reason to join the coup. Why should he risk illegalities when he could get the government on a silver platter? In any case, Koiso ordered Ōkawa to forgo the plan as no military help would be forthcoming.

Initially Ōkawa vowed to continue against all odds, but the prospects of his doing so seemed dimmer by the day. When the demonstrations organized by his allies were finally launched on March 18, they seemed to be disappointingly small.[67] Even Kōmoto Daisaku, the former assassin of Zhang Zuolin, began to plead for caution. He convinced Tokugawa Yoshichika, Ōkawa's financial patron, to tie the latter's hands. The plan, Tokugawa realized, was hopeless and would destroy the army. The marquis, therefore, called on Ōkawa and the other conspirators and "tearfully" implored them to withdraw the plan. Ōkawa insisted for a short while but finally had to give in.[68] As a result, according to Hashimoto,

Minister Ugaki's reputation among the conspirators of the Sakura-kai was crushed in one day.[69] Relying on senior generals was, Hashimoto surmised, a mistake in judgment, not to be repeated again.

The failure of the March Incident, mainly due to the Sakura-kai's higher echelon backers' change of heart, infuriated Hashimoto, Ōkawa, and their friends to no end, which resulted in motivating them to radicalize their goals and means of action. That state of mind, combined with the emboldening effect of the system's failure to punish them, made the next incident almost inevitable.

Ōkawa himself promised Marquis Tokugawa to "regroup for a renewed assault."[70] Accordingly, Hashimoto used the spring and summer months to launch a propaganda campaign for the Sakura-kai, in which he fulminated against the political parties and the government's weak-kneed diplomacy. Lecturing in army venues, including the prestigious Staff College, Hashimoto was "singing the praises" of Mussolini and Atatürk as role models for a military-led restoration of the country.[71] In educational institutions such as the Toyama Army School, the group's coup d'état plans were often discussed by students in quiet corners, and political meetings were held also in the various divisions. The fact that the Sakura-kai's membership significantly grew from fifty to several hundred was surprising, especially after its failure in March. Maybe the newcomers, mostly young officers, were not familiar with the details. In any case, they tended to support Hashimoto's radical views, overpowering the remaining moderates. That was certainly not good news for the government.[72]

Skirmishes in Tokyo: The Government's Reaction

Ugaki's departure for his new assignment as the governor general of Korea did not stop the double-game at the top of the Army Ministry. In fact, the new minister, General Minami Jirō, who assumed office on April 14, was viewed by many as a weaker, duller version of Ugaki. Even more than his predecessor, Minami was reluctant to restrain the young officers in the ranks. During his meeting with Prime Minister Wakatsuki in early September, Minami assured him that enhancing discipline in the army was the utmost need, but as in previous occasions, he emphasized that the provocations of party politicians and their press cronies were driving young officers over the edge. Therefore, Minami cautioned Wakatsuki that in order to uphold discipline, the cabinet had to adjust its policy in tandem with the army's requests. Upon his return to the Army Ministry, Minami was even more brazen. In a conversation with his key subordinates, he said, "The other day, the Premier questioned me concerning the matter of the coup d'état and I threatened him by admitting that such things happen due to the faults of the political parties of today, and that perhaps such incidents may occur again."[73]

The most interesting thing here was that Minami, who used the intransigence of young officers as a tool of political blackmail, did not even pretend to be able to rein them in. And this was not a mere sham. As Prince Saionji's secretary Harada Kumao wrote, the leading generals were truly not in a position to restrain the younger officers. But this was a situation they did not wish to alter. In the absurd situation of 1931, for those in the higher echelons of the army, to relinquish control over juniors was the way to gain greater power.[74]

How normal and blatant the officers' insubordination became in 1931 was evident from a bizarre case, a tempest in a tea cup stirring the Japanese elites in the early days of September. For some time, in fact since the debates on the London Disarmament Treaty, young officers had been openly propagating against the government in public, a campaign orchestrated by the Sakura-kai, by the nationwide organization of reserve soldiers, and by Ōkawa's patriotic societies.[75] Several Diet members, headed by Ozaki Yukio, a veteran critic of the army, sent a bold letter to Minister Minami warning him that such brazen interference in politics was a direct violation of Article 103 in the army's penal code. Minami, of course, ignored the letter, but Prime Minister Wakatsuki did not, and even asked his home minister, Adachi Kenzō, to do something about it.[76] Adachi, greatly perturbed, ordered the police to stop such conventions wherever they were. However, he was far from having an impeccable record of lawfulness himself. Thirty-five years before, in 1895, he had been the leader of the sōshi, thugs who helped Miura Gorō assassinate Queen Min. But now, having climbed to a position of authority, he found himself trying to curb the insubordination of officers who openly attacked his government's policy.

Immediately as the matter became known, Prince Saionji's military contacts bitterly complained to the genrō's secretary about the insult to the army. Koiso and other army leaders demanded explanations from their civilian counterparts. In response, Saionji's secretary, along with Prime Minister Wakatsuki and Foreign Minister Shidehara, denied the entire affair, professing their innocence to the generals. No, it never crossed their minds to propose such an outrageous thing. Pathetically enough, Adachi himself said that he "had no memory" of issuing such orders. Finally, all involved agreed that only the Military Police could discipline officers. And as the Military Police, as usual, did nothing, the Sakura-kai's propaganda campaign continued unabated. Wakatsuki and his ministers were afraid to challenge the army openly, let alone do anything to stop it.[77]

In this tense situation, Saionji wondered whether he should use his prestige as the only surviving elder statesman to "remonstrate with the Army." That was a rather watered-down idea, no more than a timid warning to Army Minister

Minami to "pay extra attention toward maintaining military discipline." Even this idea, however, was soon dropped. Navy Minister Okada assured Saionji and the government that the navy was standing behind them and would even confront the army if necessary. But meanwhile, they should not needlessly provoke the generals. Saionji should keep his interventions for an emergency. The prince finally agreed to wait for a better occasion. "It should be best for me," he told his secretary, Harada, "not to censure the laxity of Army discipline in detail."[78] Saionji could not have known that the situation was grimmer than his worst fears. Hashimoto and Chō, unpunished and undeterred, were constantly plotting, and in Manchuria, the greatest act of military resistance since the Meiji Restoration was about to take place.

The Manchurian Incident

Between March and October 1931, the rebellious movement in the army was constantly swinging between the poles of "Japan first" and "Manchuria first."[79] These factions, though in certain disagreement on tactics, acted in close cooperation with one another. Ōkawa Shūmei, always happy to give his support to any nationalistic venture, was backing and guiding both.[80] After the failure of the March Incident, young officers at the staff of the Kwantung Army decided to put the "Manchuria first" scheme in motion. The ringleaders of the plot were two colonels: Itagaki Seishirō, Kōmoto Daisaku's successor as the Kwantung Army's senior staff officer, and his operation staffer, Ishihara Kanji. Several incidents of Japanese deaths in Manchuria, publicized by propaganda of right-wing societies (including the Sakura-kai) incensed Japanese public opinion, pushing it toward support of military solutions.[81]

This time, the "lone wolf" adventurous mentality of Kōmoto Daisaku was gone without a trace. In its place came a plot, later called the "Manchurian Incident," that was meticulously planned by Itagaki and Ishihara as a team-managed military operation. Hashimoto and Chō, the advocates of the "Japan first" policy, did not try to hinder their colleagues in Mukden, but instead did their best to help and abet them.[82] The plan was, as usual, an initiative from below. As Ōkawa Shūmei testified later, "It wasn't [planned] by high officers. . . . In the Japanese army, high ranking officers do not readily express such opinion. It was decided by the young chief-of-staff conference." The new commander of the Kwantung Army, Lieutenant General Honjō Shigeru, who entered his post in August, was oblivious to the plot.[83]

Unlike the situation in 1928, the military operations in Mukden and other parts of Manchuria were meticulously planned in advance. This time, it was agreed, all contrary orders from Tokyo would simply be ignored.[84] Ishihara darkly warned that in case of persistent, express orders to stop the operation, he and his friends would temporarily give up their Japanese citizenship and occupy Manchuria as stateless adventurers. Chō Isamu, Hashimoto's partner in the Sakura-kai, gleefully disseminated these rumors in the General Staff, deterring the senior generals from any interference with the plot.[85] Ishihara's threat had shown the extent of state involution plaguing the army since the Meiji period. Soldiers and civilian adventurers had collaborated in Manchuria for so long that officers could threaten to become adventurers without raising too many eyebrows. The army minister indeed warned Ishihara "to cease immediately all talk of becoming independent from the Imperial Army or of controlling Manchuria," but no disciplinary steps were ever taken against him.[86]

Foreign Minister Shidehara, who was informed by a mole about the impending plot of the Kwantung Army, decided to stop it before it unfolded.[87] Therefore, he asked Army Minister Minami to send an order to the Kwantung Army to forgo such plans. Minami's emissary was Major General Tatekawa, former plotter of the March Incident and now the commander of the First Department (Operations) at the General Staff.[88] But dispatching Tatekawa to stop the conspirators in Mukden was yet another maneuver characteristic of Army Minister Minami's double game. Tatekawa, later described as "a most enthusiastic advocate of Manchurian independence," was himself privy to the Kwantung Army's conspiracy.

Even worse, under the nose of the army leaders, Hashimoto and his Sakura-kai colleagues established a clandestine network of communication with Mukden. That secret line of communication between Hashimoto and Itagaki, the senior staff officer of the Kwantung Army, effectively functioned as the army's channel of command and control, while the official channel (the army minister/chief-of-staff to Lieutenant General Honjō) was completely dysfunctional. Immediately as Tatekawa was ordered to Mukden, Hashimoto dispatched an urgent, coded message to Itagaki: "The plot is uncovered. Act at once." And then again: "Move before Tatekawa arrives at Mukden."[89]

The rest of the story is well known. Instead of boarding a military airplane, Major General Tatekawa traveled slowly by ferry and train. Upon his arrival, on the night of September 18, Ishihara and his associates arranged for him the merry company of a geisha for the evening. When Tatekawa woke up in the morning, the operation he was ordered to forestall had already launched.[90]

In the dead of night on September 18, a bomb installed by Ishihara's agents on the SMR railway exploded, causing so slight a damage as to allow a Mukden-bound express to pass over without hindrance.[91] Hashimoto Kingorō, red-faced and drunk from joy and sake, stumbled from his favorite pub to the General

Staff, phoned the Kwantung Army and encouraged them to practice "operational discretion" to charge on, regardless of orders.[92] In fact, Itagaki and Ishihara did not even wait for Hashimoto's phone call. The Chinese were promptly blamed for the incident, and in retaliation, Kwantung Army detachments opened fire on the Mukden garrison. The commander of the Kwantung Army, who was also surprised by the incident, authorized their illegal operations in retrospect.[93] A Japanese diplomat who dared to urge restraint was threatened with a naked blade and openly assured that the officers "would kill anyone who endeavored to so interfere."[94]

The main Chinese barracks and Mukden's airfield were both bombarded by heavy field guns, placed by Itagaki in advance with the full knowledge and cooperation of officials in the Army Ministry.[95] The Chinese soldiers, surprised and ill-prepared, retreated from the city. In a few months' time, Japanese forces swept all over Manchuria, overcoming the haphazard resistance of local Chinese commanders, though guerrilla fighting persisted for a longer while. The Kwantung Army was assisted by the SMR, which financed the operation, transported troops and obstructed Chinese troop movements. The leader of China, Chiang Kaishek, surmised that China was still not prepared to resist Japan, and ordered his subordinates to oppose the occupation of Manchuria by diplomatic means alone. The warlord of Manchuria, Zhang Xueliang, hospitalized in Beijing at the time, obeyed the national government's directives and declared a nonresistance policy to the Japanese invaders.[96]

At the same time in Tokyo, Prime Minister Wakatsuki and Foreign Minister Shidehara were horrified by the events, which, as they knew, were a result of well-planned defiance on the part of the Kwantung Army.[97] As they found it impossible to force Itagaki, Ishihara, and their associates to relinquish Mukden, they tried at least to lead a policy of "nonescalation."[98] Consequently, Wakatsuki and Shidehara pressed Army Minister Minami and Chief of General Staff Kanaya to forbid the Korean garrison from reinforcing the Kwantung Army. Without such reinforcements, they knew, it would be impossible to extend operations to the rest of Manchuria. Minami and Kanaya resisted at first but finally succumbed to Wakatsuki's pressure. Consequently, Lieutenant General Hayashi Senjūrō, commander-in-chief in Korea, was ordered not to reinforce the Kwantung Army.[99] But the chief of the General Staff's orders were not merely ignored by the officers on the ground, they were subverted from within. For Hashimoto had sent yet another coded message to Itagaki in Mukden: "The General Staff's orders to stop the army's movements are merely designed to save face in front of the cabinet. There is no real intention to stop."[100] A similar letter was secretly sent to Hayashi. The Korean Army, Hashimoto assured, could safely cross the Yalu River, though in violation of the General Staff's formal orders.[101]

What was astounding about the situation in Manchuria was the lack of any effort on the part of Ishihara, Itagaki, and their friends to conceal their insubordination. Hashimoto recalled later with pride how the General Staff "daily" ordered the Kwantung Army to stop, only to receive mocking replies from Mukden: "When the army deploys forces to fulfill a certain mission, it cannot accept haphazard orders from the General Staff."[102] We have seen before how the senior officers had openly relinquished control over their juniors. Since September 1931, Ishihara and his group of officers came into the open, hardly trying to conceal their pretensions to extend the empire and lead Japanese foreign policy on the ground. In this sense, the true government of the Japanese Empire did not sit in Tokyo but in Mukden, just as the General Staff was managed not from the chief's bureau but from Hashimoto's office.[103] According to Hashimoto, "The fall of prestige of the higher echelons was completely unprecedented in the Imperial Army."[104] Ishihara and his friends, for example, were the ones who debated the future form of government in Manchuria and who finally decided to reestablish the Manchu monarchy.[105]

Prime Minister Wakatsuki, Foreign Minister Shidehara, Prince Saionji, and even the emperor himself were powerless to stop the tide. Refusal to fund the army's expenses, the only measure that could effectively stop its operations, was rejected by the government, probably due to fear of the army and reluctance to bring the civil-military confrontation into the open.[106] With all of its decisions and threats ignored, the Wakatsuki cabinet was even helpless to prevent the movement of troops from Korea to Manchuria, a measure taken illegally without imperial sanction.

The General Staff even gave a formal notification to foreign military attachés that troops were moving to Manchuria, contradicting and shaming the Foreign Ministry, which had promised otherwise. "The situation," testified General Minami, "was always ahead of the government's statement[s], putting me in a very awkward position. This was because [according to the] principle on which the army was established the War Minister could not interfere with military operations. The Kwantung Army, on the other hand, appealed to us that the situation on the spot was such that . . . it was unavoidable for them to take necessary measures of self-defense."[107] The insubordination of the Kwantung Army staff, in other words, was made possible by a fateful amalgamation of supreme prerogative ideology, giving the high command the prerogative to act independently of the government, and operational discretion, endowing junior officers with the right to act independently of the high command. As a result, the entire Manchurian territory passed into Japanese hands and was soon to be followed by the foundation of Manchukuo, a puppet state controlled by the Kwantung Army.

The October Incident

Moving the troops to Manchuria, according to Harada, was already a "sort of a coup d'état."[108] Soon, Saionji's secretary had learned that this "sort" of coup could quickly escalate into a real one. In early October, Harada heard rumors that Ishihara and his group were openly discussing such a possibility. The government in Tokyo, powerless as it was, was still perceived as a nuisance.[109] "Whenever they drank," wrote Harada, "they always boasted that 'this plot was planned long ago. . . . Furthermore, we have succeeded in this plan, therefore when we return to the homeland this time, we will carry out a coup d'état, and do away with the political party system of government. Then we will promulgate a nation of National Socialism with the Emperor as the center. We will do away with capitalists, Mitsui and Mitsubishi, and will carry out the even distribution of wealth."[110]

The true danger, however, came not from Ishihara but from Chō and Hashimoto. The leaders of the Sakura-kai, who, contrary to Ishihara, believed that internal revolution had precedence over outward expansion, were determined to cement the achievements of the Kwantung Army in Manchuria by doing away with the reluctant Wakatsuki cabinet. As Chō disclosed later to a friend, the plan was to "set up a new government, and with the power of the new government to rally the support of the entire population toward the settlement of the Manchurian Incident." Dr. Ōkawa Shūmei, the civilian partner of the conspirators, had even more far reaching plans: to use Manchuria as a springboard for a pan-Asian alliance, driving the Western powers out of the continent.[111] The conspirators kept their more cautious seniors more or less out of the picture. Accordingly, they scheduled a plan for October that was much bolder and bloodier than the abortive March Incident.

In early October, based on tips from his contacts, Harada began to suspect that an "action" by the army was expected in December, during the next session of the Diet.[112] Probably, like a general preparing for the previous war, he predicted a replay of the March Incident. Other civilian leaders sensed the danger of military violence and began to change their colors. Home Minister Adachi, who merely two months earlier had proposed using the civilian police to forcefully disperse military propaganda meetings, openly defended the army's position in the cabinet. "Since then," Harada wrote wryly, "Adachi has been extremely popular with the Army."[113] Adachi, who had some precious firsthand experience in nocturnal assassinations, probably did not want to appear on one of the black lists and end his life as his former victim, Queen Min of Korea, had.

Little did Adachi know that Hashimoto, Chō, and the other ringleaders had no intentions of sparing his life. In fact, as Hashimoto recalled later, a bloodbath was prepared, along with simultaneous liquidation of the entire ruling elite. The list of would-be victims included all cabinet ministers, party leaders, business magnates, genrō, courtiers, and imperial advisors. Even other officers who did not support the Sakura-kai were marked for arrest or elimination. According to Tanaka Kiyoshi, Hashimoto, Chō, and their friends intended to use the execution squads to settle scores with personal rivals in the army.[114]

The Sakura-kai's leaders drew one major lesson from the March debacle. As Ōkawa testified, the setup was supposed to be purely military, without reliance on civilian demonstrators. Ōkawa himself had a significantly lesser role than in March: to occupy the newspapers' editorial offices with some soldiers in order to ensure positive media coverage and to fly a flag with the inscription, "The Imperial Flag Restoration Headquarters" ("Kinki Ishin Honbu") on the roof of the Land Survey Department of the General Staff. Most of all, he was expected to use his considerable charisma to mobilize popular support for the revolution. Other patriotic societies, including the adherents of the nationalistic new religion Omotokyō, would help him by mobilizing their forces throughout Japan, taking over potential bastions of resistance to reduce the possibility for a civil war.[115]

The army, however, was in charge of the lethal part of the plan. According to the recollections of Hashimoto and Tanaka Kiyoshi, the ruling elite was to be massacred using a combined assault force of soldiers from the Twenty-Third Infantry Regiment (Imperial Guards Division), with machine guns, shells, and poisonous gas. The cabinet, as it was planned, would be wiped out during their session by naval bombers. If such a hit became impossible, the ministers were to be killed individually, preferably at the same time.[116]

In such a case, Chō Isamu, perhaps the most bloodthirsty of the rebels, was tasked with the assassination of Prime Minister Wakatsuki. Colonel Sasaki Tōichi, a former accomplice in the plan to kill Zhang Zuolin, was given the honor of liquidating Army Minister Minami. Foreign Minister Shidehara, the symbol of Japan's "weak-kneed" foreign policy and his ministry officials, including the lower ones, were also high on the kill list. Their massacre was entrusted to the squad of Major Noda Kengō. Allies of the Sakura-kai from the navy agreed to assassinate Count Makino, lord keeper of the privy seal, in his Kamakura mansion. The conspirators naturally knew that they had to overrun the Imperial Palace, as no authority could be imagined without possession of the imperial hazy center. That role was given to the infantry unit of Major Tanaka Nobuo. He and his men were ordered to overpower the Imperial Guard, isolate Hirohito from the outside world and surround him with "loyal advisors" from the Sakura-kai. In essence, this was an attempt to reenact the Kyoto coup d'état that launched the Meiji Restoration more than sixty years earlier. Additional teams were tasked with occupying key police stations in the capital.[117]

Intelligence was collected on the main targets by reconnaissance teams who duly noted the locations and whereabouts of their formal residences, private mansions, and even the domiciles of their mistresses in Tokyo and Kamakura. The plan was scheduled for the wee hours of October 24. The code words were "tennō chūshin" (emperor at the center). Flags with symbols and slogans of the Shōwa Restoration were prepared in advance, entrusted to the hands of Dr. Uchida Kinu (Masako), a female dentist sympathetic to the rebels, mentioned in the beginning of this chapter. Following an honored tradition of Chinese and Japanese secret societies (including the shishi gangs), Chō led some of the ring-leaders to a tavern in Shibuya, where they sealed their loyalty to the plot by sign-ing a pledge with their blood.[118]

This time the conspirators decided not to rely on feckless senior officers, but they did hope that some of them would jump on the revolution's wagon once action was taken.[119] Like their role models, the leaders of the Meiji Restoration in 1868, Hashimoto and his friends knew they were too young to lead the new government formally. Consequently, the plan was to use a figurehead of immense prestige, Admiral Tōgō Heihachirō, the elderly hero of the Russo-Japanese War. The admiral was supposed to "advise" the emperor to form a new cabinet, headed by Lieutenant General Araki Sadao with Major General Tatekawa as foreign minister and Ōkawa Shūmei as finance minister. The leaders of the Sakura-kai reserved for themselves the key roles of home minister (Hashimoto Kingorō) and Metropolitan Police commander (Chō Isamu). By holding the formidable internal security apparatus in their hands, they probably intended to control the country from behind the scenes.[120]

Apart from taking power, the conspirators did not have specific plans of how to rule Japan. Like previous rebels, their shishi mentality precluded meticulous planning. They naturally thought to "crush" the corrupt politicians and business magnates, change the course of foreign policy, and support the occupation of Manchuria, but these vague phrases were never translated into precise policy planning. Araki was the designated prime minister, and yet he was never con-sulted nor informed about the plan. In reply to the queries of Captain Tanaka Kiyoshi, who had always been skeptical, Hashimoto and Chō admitted that they were mostly interested in destruction. The construction of the restoration regime, they said, would be left to civilian nationalists such as Ōkawa Shūmei.[121]

But the planning did not go smoothly as the discord and internal feuds, developing in the Sakura-kai since the failure of the March Incident, had now reached a breaking point.[122] Already in the weeks prior to the March Incident, some moderate officers in the organization had been reluctant to launch a violent coup d'état. Tanaka Kiyoshi, for example, had become convinced that the plan was not merely futile but might also wreck the army, without whom national reconstruction was hardly imaginable. In October, this discord spread from the margins to the center, plaguing with doubts even members of the inner circle of the Sakura-kai. Higuchi Kiichirō, one of the founding fathers of the society, tried to convince Hashimoto to abandon the plan, though this had been a futile attempt leading to a "violent debate." Some of the younger officers, though ardent supporters of revolutionary violence, were still disgusted by Hashimoto's and his friends' drunkenness and lewd behavior, by their idolization of foreign role models such as Mussolini and Atatürk, and by their refusal to listen to any opinions but their own.[123] A few months later, Chō Isamu bitterly complained to a friend that "members of the Sakura-kai began to hesitate, and, therefore, he tried forcibly to drag them along toward execution of the plan." Even Ishihara Kanji, the architect of the Manchurian Incident, began to oppose the idea of a coup d'état in Tokyo.[124]

Finally, an unknown person gave up the details of the plan to the authorities.[125] Ōkawa Shūmei and Chō Isamu believed that the traitor was Lieutenant Colonel Nemoto, who had gotten cold feet at the last moment. Some young officers preferred to blame Ōkawa himself. According to another opinion, Hashimoto went too far in his attempts to win over senior officers. He and his friends were extremely negligent about secrecy and openly disclosed their plans in numerous drunken parties. According to two different testimonies, Chō had even bragged about the plan in the middle of Shinjuku station. Completely unaware of the crowds around him, he cried out loud that they would "win the streets of Tokyo with blood and gore," gesturing wildly as if he were sword-fighting.[126] Therefore, it would not be unreasonable to assume that information about the conspiracy simultaneously leaked from several quarters.

In any case, the rumors reached Lieutenant General Araki, the designated prime minister of the rebels, who informed Army Minister Minami. The two consulted about the matter, and Araki, still highly popular among conspirators in the army, decided to use his authority to crush the plan on Minami's behalf. Subsequent events were quick to unfold. Araki later told Saionji's secretary that on October 16 he had surprised the leaders of the conspiracy, Hashimoto, Chō, and the others, in a tavern at Kyōbashi, one of their favorite drinking haunts. At that time, Hashimoto, Chō, and their friends were virtually living in taverns, plotting, drinking, and carousing with geisha. Chō later bragged that by doing this, they imitated their cherished role models, the shishi of the Meiji Restoration. Hashimoto neglected his home life so badly that his wife was seeking a divorce.[127] Lieutenant General Araki, always a champion of austere military morals, was thoroughly disgusted. "Nothing can be effectuated by airing your opinions here while drinking sake and becoming drunk," Araki remonstrated with his juniors. "You must refrain from doing anything violent or thoughtless. The army officers of

Japan are the so-called Kusanagi [Kusunoki] sword; the Kusanagi sword should always be polished, but it should not be indiscriminately drawn from its scabbard. It is almost inconceivable that I should have to come here in military uniform where you are drinking sake in order to [admonish] you on this sort of matter. You must be more discreet."[128]

It is clear from several sources that the conversation in Kyōbashi did take place, but it is difficult to know whether these were the exact words that Araki said, as they appear only in his own testimony to Harada.[129] This dramatic dialogue, indeed, smacks of typical Arakian hyperbole. But whatever Araki's precise words were, his report to Harada exposed important patterns of the army's ideology—the silent basic assumptions that are present even in post facto apologetic accounts. Araki did not treat Hashimoto and his friends as traitors and conspirators but as children who erred in their enthusiasm. He reprimanded them for immoral behavior (drinking sake) and for "thoughtlessly" using violence. Violence in itself was not condemned, as shown by Araki's next two sentences: The sword of the army, associated with the medieval legendary loyalist Kusunoki Masashige, should be "polished" but not "indiscriminately drawn." In other words, Araki had, rather brazenly, suggested to Harada, Saionji, and the other leaders of the government that the sword was there—and that it could be drawn again at will.

The next day, following a decision taken in a nocturnal meeting at the army minister's residence, the conspirators were arrested by military policemen at their tavern. The military police troops, equipped with police cars and accompanied by reporters, surrounded the entire establishment. The commander of Tokyo's Military Police promised to treat the prisoners "according to the spirit of Bushido." The practical meaning of this lofty declaration was to accommodate them in comfortable conditions, with alcohol and Geisha on demand.[130] Hashimoto remained in confinement for twenty-five days, and along with his comrades, was later transferred to a unit far away from Tokyo.

Prime Minister Wakatsuki and his colleagues were, yet again, afraid to confront the army, and therefore allowed the General Staff to whitewash the rebellious plans of its own officers. The perpetrators were anyway out of bounds for the civilian justice system, as a law from 1921 gave the army exclusive jurisdiction over soldiers even when they committed civil crimes.[131] How the Imperial Japanese Army dealt with such political infractions was crystal clear to everyone involved: it did nothing. Certainly, the Military Penal Code, which invoked the death penalty for such cases, was never used against Hashimoto and his friends. As one general told a high court official, "Though they had to be punished according to the Military Penal Code, the fact that most of them repented and reflected on the error of their ways, and in consideration of their motives, their patriotic spirit and the prestige of the army, they were dealt with in an administrative manner."[132] When one member of the Privy Council tried to gently remind Army Minister Minami about the need to punish the rebels, he was rudely brushed aside and told to "leave it to the army." As a result, the counselor backed off without further ado. Inquiries from the Justice Ministry were ignored as well.[133] The commanding generals were afraid of the young officers, and the civilian government feared the army as a whole, shaking from the mere thought of further assassinations and coups d'état.

There was yet another important reason for inaction, a concern that had been plaguing the political system since the assassination of Queen Min in 1895: if the affair became public, the honor of the emperor's army might be sullied. Therefore, everyone cooperated in the cover-up attempts. Senior officers such as Koiso and Tatekawa were naturally unwilling to allow a public trial, in which their own involvement in the March Incident might be exposed.[134] Likewise, generals Minami and Kanaya were reluctant to expose to the world what the government already knew: that they were powerless to control their own army. The leaders of the government had an interest to rein the army in, but (as in 1895 and 1928) not at the price of internationally shaming Japan.

Consequently, even Foreign Minister Shidehara, the moderate politician so detested by the army and whose name appeared in every list of "traitors for elimination," publicly cooperated with the whitewashing. In a conversation with an American diplomat, he said that "the affair was minor and that there had been no danger and insufficient evidence to implicate or justify the prosecution of any civilians. The army he said had its own discipline, which he could not discuss."[135] Based on such information, the American ambassador, W. Cameron Forbes, reported in the beginning of November that "those officers who were put under restraint have now been released, possibly because they could not be punished without the matter becoming public, or possibly because the temper of the army at the present time would render unwise such a procedure."[136] The government had missed yet another chance to discipline the army, opening with its own hands the door to the violent chaos of the early 1930s.

Hashimoto Kingorō and the other leaders of the Sakura-kai resumed their military careers shortly after the affair, some of them later gaining notoriety as war criminals. Hashimoto was involved in the sinking of the US ship *Panay* in 1937, one of the crimes that earned him a life sentence at the postwar Tokyo Trials. Chō Isamu, perhaps the most bloodthirsty member of the Sakura-kai, was one of the masterminds of the Nanjing Massacre in 1937. He ended up committing suicide along with his commanding officer at the close of the Okinawan Campaign. His close colleague Amano Isamu, who had been serving as a colonel in Manchuria in 1945, cold-bloodedly massacred Soviet citizens in response to the Russian declaration of war and then ended his life in a Siberian prison camp.[137]

But Higuchi Kiichirō, the most moderate member of the Sakura-kai's inner circle, was remembered for remarkably different feats. In 1938, as the Special Service chief in Harbin, without securing permission from his superiors, he saved an unknown number of freezing Jewish refugees by admitting them to Manchurian territory. That act of operational discretion was performed in defiance of protests from the Nazi government and the Japanese Foreign Ministry alike. Higuchi, as in the "good old days" of the Manchurian Incident, informed his superiors that they had no right to interfere with his operational discretion. Manchukuo, he wrote rather brazenly, was an independent country, neither a dependent of Germany nor of Japan. As such, it had a full right to make a "sovereign" decision. The commanders of the Kwantung Army, General Ueda Kenkichi and his chief of staff Tōjō Hideki (future prime minister of Japan), refused to punish their defiant subordinate, following a pattern remarkably similar to the whitewashing of military insubordination numerous time before. Instead, they had Higuchi transferred away from Manchuria. In this case, it seems, the Imperial Army's culture of insubordination had taken a uniquely humane form.[138]

Conclusion: From Resistance to Rebellion

The two conspiracies of the Sakura-kai, in March and October 1931, opened a new phase in the history of Japanese military insubordination. After half a century, the powerful lesson of the Satsuma Rebellion was finally forgotten in Japanese military circles. Fifty-three years after Saigō Takamori's death, Japanese officers were again raising the banner of violent rebellion against their own government, and this time with bombs and airplanes.

This return to violence had multiple reasons. As we have seen in previous chapters, the motor of violence among Japanese assassins was optimism: a belief that by removing a small number of people, they could truly make a change. All previous assassins were optimistic, but only in certain respects. Miura Gorō and Kōmoto Daisaku hoped to change Japanese policy, but they could not hope to do so by striking a direct blow at the government. Rather, they attempted to strike at the margins, taking down victims in Seoul and in Mukden, hoping that the indirect effect of their actions would change national policy in the right direction. The optimism of Hashimoto and his friends, however, reached entirely new heights. They had good reasons to believe in their power to take over the government through a concentrated blow at the center. After all, they led the first cross-army conspiratorial organization in the history of modern Japan, and they enjoyed support by senior officers, generous backing of financial patrons, and strong cooperation with a dense web of violent civilian organizations. The decision to turn to violence marked the culmination of accumulated precedents, acts of resistance that remained unpunished. If the assassination of a Chinese leader under "patriotic" pretexts was forgiven so easily, then killing Japanese leaders to pursue similar goals was arguably just a small step further.

Historically speaking, the fiasco of the Sakura-kai had several important ramifications. On the one hand, the failure of the army to punish Hashimoto and his friends encouraged further plotting by subsequent groups. But on the other hand, the events surrounding the defeat of the Sakura-kai's conspiracies shattered the unity of oppositional Japanese officers. The October failure sharpened the lines between officers endorsing the new waves of violence and those opposing it.[139] The action Araki took against the October Incident, the subversion exercised by officers in the Army Ministry, Ugaki's double game, and the rumors that Ōkawa and Hashimoto betrayed the coup to the authorities radicalized the animosity between officers, reshuffling them into new factions that were bitterly hostile to one another.[140]

Ever radicalizing, the army was increasingly defiant of the government as an institution, producing both rebellions and unauthorized operations in Manchuria and in North China. But at the same time, its internal structure had weakened almost to the breaking point. Discipline was extremely tenuous, and control by senior officers over their juniors grew ever weaker.

For years, generals such as Araki, Ugaki, and Minami used the intransigence of their subordinates as a tool of political blackmail against the government. Soldiers could be used against the government in an emergency, wrote Ugaki, but not thoughtlessly or without preparation. "We must control the rash and blind acts of the young officers," he added—lest they be manipulated by right-wing civilian figures such as Ōkawa Shūmei.[141] But neither Ugaki nor his fellow generals could force the genie back into the bottle, nor could they resume the control they had lost. Yet again, the combination of strength and weakness, of outer formidability and internal chaos, was the key to understanding both the dynamics of 1931 and the violent rebellions in the years ahead. More than anything else, it was this combination that rendered the Japanese government completely incompetent in coping with unfolding events. The army, strong in its weakness, was virtually unapproachable. The prime minister had institutional channels to deal with the army minister and the chief of the General Staff, but how could he parley with junior officers in Tokyo or in Manchuria—the people who held actual power? The democratization of insubordination, a process that was moving the focal point of disobedience to increasingly junior officers, calcified the arteries of communication between the civilian and the military elites.

By 1931, the situation had become far worse than it had been during the time of the Taishō political crisis. If Army Minister Uehara, the only person who could be approached by the government in 1912, was a weak leader, his successor in 1931, Minami Jirō, was almost irrelevant. In a cabinet meeting on October 10, Prime Minister Wakatsuki lamented, saying, "When I admonish the War Minister, he always says that he'll immediately warn army officials at the site of the incident; however, army officials in Manchuria are acting arbitrarily in complete disregard of the warnings of the War Minister."[142] Some civilian leaders, such as Saionji's secretary Harada Kumao, placed the blame on General Minami's incompetence. "He is useless," said Harada in frustration, "like beating the air." Chief of the General Staff Kanaya Hanzō, a notorious alcoholic, was also a "misfit," as General Matsui Iwane openly told Harada. Hashimoto, the leader of the Sakura-kai, actually agreed, writing in his secret memoirs that the chief of the General Staff reminded him of a "scarecrow."[143] Nor could the commanders of individual units control their officers any better. Hashimoto wrote that Ishihara, Itagaki, and their friends "naturally" ignored Lieutenant General Honjō, the commander of the Kwantung Army, as if such insubordination was an ordinary law of nature. "Never mind Honjō," Itagaki told a colleague. "It's Ishihara's war."[144] Military resistance to state policy had ceased to be an exception, having become a cultural norm.

The situation only became more aggravated after the dissolution of the Sakura-kai. The failure of mid-ranking officers, elite Staff College graduates such as Hashimoto Kingorō, to overthrow the government deepened the "democratization of insubordination" in the Japanese Army by clearing the stage for younger officers. These people, completely out of touch with senior generals, were far more resolute and difficult to control. Never again would a coup be abolished only because Ugaki had changed his mind, or because Araki had remonstrated the organizers. The deluxe "arrest conditions" of the Sakura-kai leaders, with luxurious inn rooms, sake, and geisha, disgusted many of their younger followers and convinced them that they were merely used by their superior officers.

In the future, said Lieutenant Suematsu Tahei, he would not follow Hashimoto nor anyone else, "only His Majesty the Emperor."[145] Suematsu, a notorious rebel, did not disavow revolutionary violence, which he continued to plot and practice. He was just refusing to accept the leadership of senior officers, leaning instead on the emperor. However, he was not referring to the living individual Hirohito, who was well beyond his reach, but to the imperial hazy center as an idea. By submitting himself to imagined authority, his declaration amounted to a refusal to follow anyone but himself. In the guise of total submission to the emperor, the young officers defied *all* of their superiors, even radicals such as Hashimoto.

From that point on, organized coup plans such as the Sakura-kai's would be denounced by many young officers as "fascism," a term that became code for haughtiness and blind imitation of foreign ideas, just like Hashimoto's endless blather about Mussolini and Atatürk.[146] And as rebellious officers had few effective ways, in the absence of agreed authority, to solve disagreements and conflicts between themselves, the Imperial Japanese Army quickly sunk into its own internal, violent conflict.[147]

Another alarming development in 1931 was the increasing extent of state involution. During the assassination of Queen Min, as we have seen, the cooperation of the army in Korea with civilian sōshi had blurred the distinction between military activists and civilian adventurers. In 1931, this "rotten but unbreakable connection," to use the words of Tanaka Kiyoshi, grew ever stronger. Officers such as Hashimoto were much more influenced by civilian, nationalist gurus such as Ōkawa Shūmei than by their own military superiors.[148]

Hashimoto's recollections of the days subsequent to the Manchurian incidents are quite astounding in this sense. He describes how right-wing political activists, some of them responsible for fomenting and planning terror and rebellion against the Japanese government, were frequent guests in General Staff headquarters, regularly feted, dined, and wined by senior officers. Funds from the General Staff regularly flowed to such activists, never to be seen again. Civilian patriots had even treated military armaments as their private property. Major General Koiso had to implore Ōkawa's sōshi to return the bombs borrowed for the March Incident. Being turned away for months, he was even ready to pay them. Only through the intervention of Marquis Tokugawa Yoshichika, the financial patron of the sōshi, was Koiso able to rescue the bombs from their clutches.[149] The high command of the army was enmeshed with these activists politically, socially, and financially. Even the dissolute shishi culture of the "patriotic societies" had spread to their army allies, as demonstrated by the life-style of debauchery and drinking adopted by Chō, Hashimoto, and the inner circle of the Sakura-kai.[150]

Like a contagious disease, the defiant attitude of the army and its allies from the nationalist societies spread to other parts of the government apparatus until, in the words of one rear admiral, "the whole works went crazy."[151] The nationalist organization Kokuhonsha, headed by Count Hiranuma Kiichirō from the Privy Council, counted prosecutors and Justice Ministry officials among its members. Being intimately connected with nationalist activists, the agents of the Kokuhonsha took care that even assassins would be treated leniently by the courts. Bribes were distributed lavishly by such societies, as well as by the Kwantung Army, further corrupting the civilian apparatus.[152] Senior officials such as Home Minister Adachi increasingly drifted to the side of the rebellious officers. In mid-October, after Hashimoto and his friends had been arrested by the Military Police, even young officials from the Foreign Ministry "seemed to have become more sympathetic with the army and they talked as though they felt that there was nothing dangerous in the present situation."[153]

Even Harada Kumao, Saionji's right-hand man and certainly not an admirer of the army, was inadvertently influenced by this process of state involution. As part of his duties to gather intelligence for his boss, he regularly met with officers in order to become acquainted with the situation inside the army. However, the information conveyed by these sources was neither neutral nor innocent. Harada's eyes inside the army certainly gave him important knowledge, but they also distorted his view, by giving him manipulated intelligence that the situation was not as grave as he believed.[154] They cajoled him, and through him also Prince Saionji, not to press for serious action against the military offenders. At the Tokyo trials, Marquis Kido Kōichi, lord keeper of the privy seal, lamented that military insubordination was a "curse" that brought on Japan the misfortunes of war, defeat, and occupation. If that was so, then Kido, Harada, Saionji, and their government colleagues, by their failure to act, had contributed their own part to its perpetuation.

PURE AS WATER

The Incident of February 1936 and
the Limits of Military Insubordination

**The young officers are pure as water, innocently flowing onwards. If
there is a wave, it is caused by the wind.**

—Lieutenant Colonel Mitsui Sakichi

On February 26, 1936, Captain Yamaguchi Ichitarō, a company commander in
the First Infantry Regiment, was that week's officer on duty. At around 8:00 a.m.,
he visited the official residence of the army minister, General Kawashima Yoshiyuki, and found the place in complete disarray. According to normal military
procedure, a junior officer like Yamaguchi could never speak freely with the minister, who was one of the "big three" of the Imperial Army. But extraordinary
circumstances had led Kawashima to ask Yamaguchi for his advice.

Three hours earlier, a group of radical lieutenants and captains had used the
cover of a snowstorm to mobilize fourteen hundred soldiers, take over large parts
of central Tokyo, and launch attacks on several prominent leaders. The finance
minister, the inspector general of military education, and the lord keeper of the
privy seal had been shot to death and cut down with swords. The previous lord
keeper had barely escaped with his life, and the chief chamberlain of the imperial
court was gravely wounded. Prime Minister Okada Keisuke, the main target of
the day, had hidden in a closet, from where he would later be whisked to safety
by loyal servants.

The mutinous officers had not harmed the army minister, General Kawashima
Yoshiyuki, but had tried instead to entice him over to their side. In the early morning, a unit of around two hundred soldiers and officers, armed with pistols, automatic weapons, and machine guns, had surrounded his residence and invaded
the anterooms. When the minister encountered Captain Yamaguchi in one of the
rooms, he asked him what he, the minister, should do. The rebels had very recently

given Kawashima a list of demands. Most important among them were that they be allowed to remain in their current positions, and that he procure an imperial order proclaiming a new restoration. Captain Yamaguchi, who knew the rebel leaders well and sympathized with their cause, answered Kawashima cautiously. He said that the incident had to be solved quickly, before foreign countries could take advantage of the situation, and preferably without shedding the blood of soldiers and civilians. It was Kawashima's prerogative, he said, to decide whether the troops who surrounded his residence were "righteous" or "rebellious."[1]

The army minister had to decide who stood on which side of this binary. Whether implicitly or explicitly, it was a binary that had accompanied the army's culture of insubordination since the 1870s. Both the government and the insurgents saw themselves as loyal servants of the emperor. But because the hidden monarch could not support two contradicting causes at once, one had to be righteous and the other rebellious. That was, most of all, a power play. "The ones who win," Yamaguchi said later, "are the emperor's soldiers, and the ones who lose are traitors."[2] When insubordination was hidden, the dilemma could be ushered behind closed doors. For that reason, the army had worked hard to keep all prior incidents secret, even the murderous plot of Hashimoto in October 1931. But when a rebellion came into the open, as it had in the Satsuma Rebellion of 1877 and the February Incident of 1936, a decision had to be made.

February 26, 1936, was the day when the army's culture of insubordination, which had been slowly brewing for more than seventy years, finally exploded into full-scale rebellion. This underground culture, long hidden in order to "uphold the honor of the army," came at last into the open, along with the ideological, political, and military structures that had sustained it for so long. The shishi myth of the righteous warrior acting on impulse, without planning or thinking, had finally reached its logical extreme. Ben Ami Shillony, one of the early historians of the incident, wrote that "like a lightning bolt at night, the rebellion illuminated things which had hitherto been shrouded in darkness. Intricate connections, clashing interests, ideological conflicts and factional strife came to the fore, momentarily shattering the image of the harmonious imperial army."[3]

The February coup d'état was also the culmination of another long-term process, the democratization of insubordination, leaving the helm of dissent in the hands of officers of lower and lower rank. Previous dissenters were higher in rank. With the important exception of some of the Sakura-kai's leaders, their radical ideology was mitigated by their age, responsibility, and stakes in the political establishment. The initiators of the February Incident, by contrast, were lieutenants and captains, hot-blooded youngsters with radical ideology and, theoretically, very few restraints. But when the moment of truth came, the rebels' behavior was much more timid than their radical ideology would lead one to assume. In line with the first and second bugs in the Meiji political system, their insubordination was monarchic, that is, dependent on the interpretation of the emperor's will, and patriotic—designed to serve the state. These limitations, combined with their junior rank, paralyzed their willpower and confused their strategy, with disastrous consequences for the rebellion as a whole.

The February Incident was not only a watershed in the history of violent Japanese military insubordination; it exposed its limits and marked the end of its violent phase. Most members of the Japanese leadership, both civilian and military, believed that the rebels had crossed a red line by using rank-and-file troops to attack the government and the army top brass. The punishments dished out to the rebels were so severe that they brought an end to the mutinous movement in the officer corps. But, like Yamagata's reforms in 1878, which had similarly been designed to enforce order and crush insubordination, the reaction of the elites to the February Incident had dangerous side effects. Essentially, it strengthened the army to the extent that it gained decisive dominance over foreign policy decision making. This military dominance heralded the worst for the future.

Shishi and the Privileged Classes: The Passion of the Young Officers

A few days after the failure of the October 1931 Incident, a small group of lieutenants and captains, later known as the Young Officers movement (Seinen Shōkō Undō), met in a private house in order to discuss the setback and draw conclusions. All were marginal figures in the March and October incidents who were looking for new ways ahead after the dissolution of the Sakura-kai. Four of the assembled guests, lieutenants Koda Kiyosada, Muranaka Kōji, Isobe Asaichi, and Kurihara Yasuhide, would be the key ringleaders of the February 1936 Incident.

As Lieutenant Koda testified, the young officers who attended the meeting deeply mistrusted the personality and the motives of Hashimoto and other general staffers in the Sakura-kai. Though they were right to give Hashimoto his chance, the plot was thwarted by the "will of heaven," and rightly so. Koda's close friend and partner, Lieutenant Muranaka Kōji, later wrote that Hashimoto and Chō were con men who used the army's money to finance their dissolute lifestyle. They made their meetings in dark pubs, "put on the posture of shishi, and full of pretentious talk, sang elegies and chattered in drinking parties."[4] But it was not only the drunkenness and debauchery of Hashimoto and Chō that annoyed their younger followers. The elite status of Hashimoto and his friends created an impression that for them, everything was a game. They exploited naïve junior officers for their selfish endeavors, lied about their true intentions, and treated their younger confederates with disrespect. Some of the young officers also believed that Hashimoto himself had leaked the October plot to the authorities. He and Chō's "punishment" in a lavish inn after the failure of the incident certainly strengthened that impression.[5]

Therefore, the founders of the Young Officers Movement decided to take the helm and lead the country toward restoration and for that, Lieutenant Koda recalled, they "had to spill blood."[6] "This was a restoration," Lieutenant Kurihara later explained, "differently than in a war, when the high command issues orders downwards to the staff officers, here we believed that the fire of the restoration has to burn from below and then rise up [to the higher echelons]."[7]

It is important to emphasize that this movement never represented all or most young officers in the army. "The young officers," written with the definite article, refers below to members of the specific group which later organized the incident of February 26, 1936, and not to junior Japanese officers at large. Many officers, in fact, were uninterested in politics, and others were disgruntled but did not cross the line over to illegality.[8] All in all, only twenty-four officers were involved in the February Incident. But the infiltration of their ideology to wider circles, even in the army's leadership, allowed them to operate for a long time with relative impunity. They had influence on wider circles of NCOs and ensigns, with an especially formidable base of support among organized army reservists, who tended to be intensely nationalistic and easily incited.[9]

The social circumstances within the imperial army made violence a logical way to express one's frustration. The young officers, most of whom did not graduate from the elite Staff College and were not likely to be admitted, had little prospect of promotion to positions of high military leadership.[10] Those with rebellious leanings could not participate in open political activity as well. If they were stationed in mainland Japan, they could not express their opposition by way of open defiance. They could not, for example, take part in unauthorized operations in China. Unlike Colonel Ishiwara Kanji, the architect of the Manchurian Incident, they were too junior to plan such endeavors. Clandestine activities, sanctioned by the precedents of previous rebels, were the only way left open to them. Participating in the patriotic quest for a new restoration was an exciting adventure, a way to escape the drab routine of military life. As Lieutenant Tsushima Tsuguo testified later, it was a way to "personally experience the *kokutai* and to implement it." Committed, enthusiastic officers such as he were thus transformed from mere cogs in the immense military machine into actors in a national drama—an exhilarating and empowering experience.[11]

Notwithstanding their hostility to the Sakura-kai, the young officers generally shared much of its ideology, especially the idea of the Showa Restoration. Like their seniors, they wanted a stronger army, more resolute foreign policy, and a political system focused on universal veneration of the emperor. They were even more incensed by the widespread poverty in the country than the Sakura-kai. As junior commanders they were closer to the rank-and-file soldiers and felt the social problems of the country firsthand. Many were horrified to hear from their soldiers about malnourished peasants, rural families crushed by debts, workers who lived in grinding poverty, and sisters sold to urban brothels. In Tokyo, where most young officers later involved in the February Incident served, the gaps between rich and poor were especially striking, and corruption scandals of politicians erupted one after the other.[12] In the young officer's understanding, the resistance of some party politicians to the army's demands for more budget was an essential part of this corruption. The main target of their criticism was the long-serving finance minister, Baron Takahashi Korekiyo, known as one of the staunchest rivals of the army in the cabinet. Takahashi's obstinate refusal to raise the army's budget after the Manchurian Incident was interpreted by many senior and junior officers, and not only members of the Young Officers Movement, as malicious subversion of national defense.[13]

Beneath the darkening sky, the members of the Young Officers Movement looked backward at the Meiji Restoration, when, as one of them put it, "the illustrious heart of the emperor shined unobstructed over the entire world."[14] Fed by nationalist, romantic literature, most of them believed that the restoration was not a historical period of turmoil, civil war, and hesitant experiments in government, but a perfect golden age under the august rule of the emperor, a god in human form. All problems, therefore, could be solved by returning to this golden age of yore and undoing the subsequent decades of deterioration and degeneration. The sorry state of Japan was perceived thus as the evil doing of a new Bakufu, which would be obliterated by a new restoration.[15]

Many junior officers, especially but not exclusively those involved in the Young Officers Movement, admired the shishi of the Meiji Restoration and sought to imitate them. In his court interrogation, Lieutenant Isobe Asaichi related that as a native of Yamaguchi Prefecture, he was always attracted to the stories of the Chōshū shishi, which had inspired him to join the army in the first place. He also quoted shishi thinkers as relevant examples for his defense.[16] Young, rebellious army officers such as Isobe called themselves dōshi (comrades), a term often used as a synonym for shishi in the late Tokugawa period and throughout modern Japanese history. They also used shishi slogans, with slight modifications. Thus the phrase sonnō tōbaku (revere the emperor, destroy the Bakufu) from the Meiji Restoration, was modified by the young officers to sonnō tōkan (revere the emperor, destroy the traitors). Just like the shishi, they believed it was their duty to ignite the new restoration through violence. When they murdered their victims, or justified such murders, they often used the term heavenly punishment as the shishi assassins had before them.[17] "Every time the divine way of Japan was distorted," First Lieutenant Ikeda Toshihiko said, "the sword of divine punishment has been swung."[18]

The word *punishment*, which appeared so often in the discourse of the young officers, may sound strange at first. Usually, punishment is a sanction dished out by a person in authority to a citizen, subject, or subordinate who has violated a law. The young officers, however, were clearly not in a position of authority, and yet believed they had the right to punish their superiors. In their writings, testimonies, and interrogations, they argued that far from being rebels, they were in fact enforcers of imperial law.[19] To illustrate this claim, Lieutenant Suematsu Tahei related the story of a young officer who disobeyed a superior and corrected a falsified battle report that unjustly glorified his unit's battlefield performance. He defied his superior, only because the latter had violated the law. As long as the commander upheld the law, it was mandatory to obey him. When he did not, insubordination became a military duty.[20]

The problem, however, was one of interpretation: how could you *know* that your commander had violated the law? The example brought by Suematsu was deceivingly simple; falsifying a battle report was obviously a crime regardless of rank. Indeed, the young officers never justified disobedience in routine military matters. Things were different, however, when it came to political questions. A long tradition of military insubordination, from the shishi to the Sakura-kai, relied on the haziness of the imperial center, the first bug of the Japanese political system, to "interpret" the emperor's will—the supreme law of the land—according to one's political vision. The young officers, like many of their predecessors, used their interpretation of the hazy imperial will to claim that they understood the essence of the law better than their superiors, and therefore had the right to "punish" violators regardless of rank.

However, the young officers' understanding of the imperial will was subjective. Due to their young age, their inexperience, and their distance from the centers of political power, they perceived the emperor not as a flesh and blood political actor but as a spiritual concept. Hayashi Hachirō believed that a loyal officer had only to sincerely think about the emperor with devotion and reverence—in order to know what to do.[21] Treason against the emperor and supreme prerogative crimes, explained Isobe, were legal according to the letter of the law. Such crimes could be detected only through the intuition of pure-hearted patriots and not in law books.[22] The decision to disobey was no longer based on facts but on feelings.

The young officers consciously imitated the shishi in other respects. They also sanctified intuition and shunned detailed planning.[23] "We thought only about destruction, not about building," said Lieutenant Kurihara after the February Incident.[24] As long as one was motivated by pure-hearted patriotism, then the consequences of an act were less significant. To fight for justice was all that mattered, and sooner or later good would prevail over evil.[25] Kurihara believed that even if he and his friends failed, they would be vindicated by history, just like the shishi after the Incident of the Forbidden Gate (1864), and the assassins of Zhang Zuolin in 1928.[26]

Nevertheless, the young officers' interpretation of shishi ideals was somewhat different to that of their predecessors. First of all, though far from being hermits, they rejected the culture of exaggerated drinking and whoring prevalent in the Sakura-kai.[27] In addition, they rejected the emphasis on individual heroism. Influenced by modern intellectual trends, they accepted Marxist deterministic views about the inevitability of history. The young officers saw themselves not only as a group fighting for righteousness, but as the representatives of an inevitable historical process of restoration.[28] Individual heroism, greatly appreciated by the shishi and almost all rebels until the 1930s, became less significant. Everyone was regarded as an equal fighter under the emperor, regardless of personality or rank. Therefore, the young officers were keen to use NCOs and ensigns in their rebellious activities. The restoration was a project for the entire nation, not only a handful of selected heroes from the officer corps.[29]

Likewise, the enemies of the restoration were described by the young officers in collective terms, such as the "new Bakufu" or the "privileged classes." These derogatory terms referred to a sinister network of bureaucrats, party politicians, journalists, and senior statesmen, believed to be connected in webs of corruption with the *zaibatsu*, Japan's powerful business magnates. The young officers believed that all of the "privileged" had vested interests in maintaining a failed regime that monopolized wealth and power for selfish reasons. In order to ignite the restoration, the leaders of the privileged classes had to be removed with one bold stroke. Only their obliteration could achieve spiritual, social, and political regeneration. This ideological construct, though, did not entirely correspond to reality. Most of the young officers did not know that several business magnates, most prominently from the Mitsui Corporation, distributed handsome monetary handouts to civilian right-wing activists, who agreed to strike their names from assassination lists and presumably take care of their interests in case of a coup. Ironically, some of this money was channeled to the young officers and financed their activities.[30]

Just like their predecessors, Kōmoto Daisaku and Hashimoto Kingorō, the young officers were deeply suspicious about the army's top brass. For them, however, even rebellious staff officers like Hashimoto belonged to the dark side. Instead of performing their duty and acting against the privileged classes, senior military leaders and their backstage manipulators from the General Staff combined forces with the privileged, and especially with the business magnates. Therefore they distorted the prerogative of supreme command, which had originally been designed to put all soldiers in the direct service of the emperor. Using German ideas, they turned instead to a rigid hierarchy of ranks, monopolizing the link with the emperor for their own selfish designs, while excluding soldiers, NCOs, and junior officers. As such, they stopped being imperial officers and became instead "military cliques."[31] Because these cliques deceptively emphasized discipline and control, the young officers also called them *Tōseiha* ("control faction"), a derogatory term that became ubiquitous in later years.[32] Personal jealousy combined with these ideological hatreds. Like many of their peers, the young officers detested the haughty elite of general staffers, graduates of the Staff College who enjoyed prospects for promotion that they, the young officers, never had.[33]

The handful of military superiors whom the young officers respected were generals who supported the vision of the Showa Restoration and showed relative tolerance for oppositional activity in the junior ranks. Such officers, like General Araki Sadao (army minister from 1932 to 1934), and General Mazaki Jinzaburō (inspector general of military education from 1934 to 1936), spoke incessantly of the "imperial way," a vague utopian vision of a militarized Japanese community led by the emperor. Therefore, they were known as the "imperial way faction" (Kōdōha). The Kōdōha leaders, in fact, were the only senior military leaders the young officers were ready to tolerate, and then not as superiors to whom they owed unquestioned obedience, but as political allies.[34]

Through Nishida Mitsugi, an officer demoted for misbehavior, some of the young officers became acquainted with Kita Ikki, an eccentric thinker and spiritualist with messianic ideas. Kita, who drafted a plan for the Showa Restoration, believed that the coup would be a preamble for a utopian world order, led by Japan under the benevolent leadership of the emperor. In his explorations of the "Japanese spirit," he summoned ghosts of previous emperors, using his wife as a medium. Some of the young officers enthusiastically accepted Kita's revolutionary ideas as "their Quran." Lieutenant Isobe Asaichi was probably Kita's most ardent admirer. At the same time, others did not bother reading Kita's books, or remained unimpressed once they had. Yet this strange thinker remained an important confidant of the young officers until the end, and served as their bridge to civilian nationalist organizations.[35]

Taming the Tiger: The Young Officers Seduced

The radical ideology of the young officers was much softer in practice. In May 1932, they still had some inhibitions and restraints. When their major patron, General Araki Sadao, was appointed army minister, they wanted to give him a chance to further the cause of restoration by legal means. Araki, as had been his habit since the late 1920s, cultivated disobedient young officers as clients and allies, a force with which he could threaten civilian politicians. His relations with them were different than with previous rebels. The Sakura-kai leaders acted behind his back, but he could still give them orders, as he did before the October Incident. The young officers, on the other hand, had an unrulier reputation. Given their aversion to "control," any attempt to boss them was likely to backfire. Hence, Araki resorted to tactics of seduction, maintaining and at the same time taming their violent potential. He treated the leaders of the movement, lieutenants and captains who would normally not dream of speaking with the army minister, as his personal friends. Occasionally, he invited prominent ringleaders such as Kurihara into his mansion for sumptuous meals, and gave them monetary handouts through his personal secretary. That money was passed privately without the knowledge of other military authorities. Araki led his young friends to believe that they had to prepare themselves to play a role in the new restoration. The leaders of the Young Officers Movement saw themselves accordingly as the "sacred sword" of the army and the restoration, polished by Araki in order to be drawn in due time. Meanwhile, they were ready to hold on.[36]

However, the delaying strategy of Army Minister Araki could not last for long, and not only because it was dependent on the good will of young, radical officers prone to outbursts of violence. The young officers were ready to wait on the assumption that Araki and others would implement their restoration program. But Araki's vague, or better said, illusionary program could offer nothing except propaganda on the Soviet menace and aphorisms on the "imperial way." Certainly, the army minister did not have any plan which could both alleviate rural poverty and solve the diplomatic impasse of Japan by military expansion, because achieving both goals at once was fiscally impossible.[37] In short, the Showa Restoration was nothing but an empty phrase. That might be the reason why in their court testimonies, Muranaka and Isobe could not explain to their judges what restoration meant, apart from recourse to the usual phraseology of Japan as the land of the gods, of spiritual regeneration, and the "unification of the economy" to alleviate poverty.[38]

It was not clear how they wanted to achieve these goals: Muranaka and his colleagues rejected capitalism, state socialism, and communism alike. No matter what happened, they could not be satisfied, only restrained until their patience ran out. In 1932, however, while they kept on waiting, other rebels decided to take action.

The May Incident

In March 1932, four months after the Sakura-kai's October Incident, another group of violent revolutionaries dealt a blow to the "privileged classes." A nationalistic society called Ketsumeidan (Blood Pledge Society), led by a Buddhist preacher and an eccentric alcoholic named Inoue Nisshō, assassinated a business magnate along with the former finance minister. Initially the trial of Inoue and his disciples seemed to be held according to unusually strict procedures, as the president of the court instructed the defendants to concentrate on the facts of the case instead of giving long speeches about their motives. The defendants and several newspapers immediately denounced the judge as unpatriotic. He suspended the trial and finally resigned, after apologizing to Inoue in his prison cell. His successor took a much more sympathetic approach, allowing Inoue and the other defendants to speak at length on their patriotic passion, sincere motives, and the corruption of the ruling elites. The new judge, an admirer of the shishi, decided not to apply the death penalty.[39]

This lenient sentencing was not much of a deterrence. On May 15, 1932, naval officers who were connected with the Ketsumeidan, assisted by some army cadets and civilian nationalists, launched a well-organized assassination operation. Driving in cabs to the prime minister office, they fatally shot the elderly Inukai Tsuyoshi. The rebellion spilled into factional infighting, as former Lieutenant Nishida Mitsugi, a civilian ally of the young officers, was shot in his hospital bed because he objected to the timing of the insurrection. Nishida survived the attack. The leaders of the Young Officers Movement did not like the attempt to kill one of their allies. But at the same time, they were impressed by the daring act against the government.[40]

The echo of the events was greatly amplified by the press's intense and sensationalist coverage of the trial. As in the Ketsumeidan trial, the defendants and their lawyers used the public proceedings to disseminate their ideas far and wide, knowing full well the extent to which the culture of insubordination had become ingrained among the elites and the public.[41] Army Minister Araki, as usual, rode this public wave by sympathizing with the "pure-hearted patriots" who acted selflessly for the country. His navy counterpart, Admiral Ōsumi, lamented the fate of his officers in similar terms. The defendants even received daily packed lunches from the Navy Ministry.[42] The councilors of the defendants echoed these sentiments. When faced with such noble motives, one of them said, the court had to refrain from applying the law, acknowledging instead that the assassination of the prime minister was driven by fate and the momentum of history. He elaborated on the precedent of the shishi, concluding that pure-hearted loyalty to the emperor was the spirit of the law, a mysterious sentiment that only Japanese subjects could understand. Judging the defendants severely would undermine that lofty spirit, destroying the very basis of Japanese national polity.[43]

At the same time, the trial of the May 1932 assassins had given rise to an unprecedented attempt to uproot the malady of insubordination in the armed forces. Navy Prosecutor Yamamoto Kōji attacked not only the defendants, but the entire culture of insubordination that had generated their motives. In a presentation which provoked blind rage in the navy and in large segments of the mass media and the public, the prosecutor emphasized that political violence should be punished mercilessly regardless of the perpetrators' motives, patriotism, or alleged loyalty to the emperor. In addition, he quoted from the Imperial Rescript for Soldiers and Sailors, and the Navy Penal Code, both of which forbade soldiers to meddle in politics. Finally, Yamamoto urged the court to treat the defendants in the same manner that rebels had been punished in the 1870s. In effect, the prosecutor attempted to wind back the clock, undo the process unfolding since 1878, and reprogram civil-military relations according to the avowed intention of the Imperial Army and Navy's founders: total separation between the armed forces and politics. Prosecutor Yamamoto paid dearly for his bravery. The public censure forced him to resign from the navy, practically destroying his legal career.[44]

The last attempt to restrain the armed forces' culture of insubordination had failed. The navy judges rejected Yamamoto's view, elaborating instead on the pure-hearted patriotism of the defendants. Accordingly, the punishments for the main offenders were relatively lenient: fifteen years in jail, instead of the execution and life imprisonment which the prosecution had demanded. "Although their [the defendants'] criminal culpability is truly significant," ruled the president of the court, "the depth of their patriotism must be acknowledged." The army court was even more lenient, and its emphasis on the defendants' purity of motives was significantly more pronounced.[45] The patterns set in the late Tokugawa period, emphasizing purity of motives over the consequences of one's act, became almost mainstream in the army, navy, and large segments of the public and the press. Accordingly, the example set by the "*shishi* of the May Incident," as well as the frustration caused by their failure, provided inspiration for copycats to try again.[46] And soon they would.

The Military Academy Incident

As long as General Araki was in charge of the Army Ministry, the young officers were under a certain amount of control, feted, financed, and kept by their Kōdōha patrons as an "undrawn sacred sword," a violent reserve force for the future. Araki's position, however, became shakier as time went by. His relentless factional struggles, resistance to military modernization, empty rhetoric on the "imperial way," and reckless talk on war with the Soviet Union, provoked hostility from multiple quarters. On January 23, 1934, Araki was forced to resign due to constant pressure from his Tōseiha rivals, civilian politicians, and the emperor's advisors.[47]

With almost zero achievements to sport, Araki was anyway losing his appeal in the eyes of the young officers. Isobe Asaichi disdainfully said afterwards that he had no power to decide and was fit only to head a "women's committee." Even in 1933, with Araki still in power, Isobe, Kurihara, and some of their colleagues were already toying with the idea of a coup d'état, but planning never got going in earnest.[48] And yet, after Araki's removal, the young officers discovered that they had fallen out of the frying pan and into the fire. The new army minister, General Hayashi Senjūrō, and his key advisor, Major General Nagata Tetsuzan, were much less tolerant of their activity.[49] When the young officers tried to protest about current events, as was their wont, they were brushed off by officials in the Army Ministry. Officers who participated in meetings of the Young Officers Movement began to be transferred out of the mainland, and many such meetings were banned. The young officers' frustration rose along with their feeling of being "persecuted."[50]

The delicate balance between the young officers and the Army Ministry was breached in autumn 1934. During the first two weeks of November, Muranaka, Isobe, and one of their confederates met with cadets in the military academy and discussed plans for an uprising. The drafts never passed the planning stage, but an informer leaked them to the authorities.[51] Nagata and one his assistants, Major Katakura Tadashi, pressed charges against Muranaka, Isobe, and their friend. The military court did not find sufficient evidence for the charge, but the three officers were still suspended from active duty. In August 1935, several months later, Isobe and Muranaka were dismissed altogether, after authoring and distributing an inflammatory pamphlet, in which they exposed embarrassing details about the March and October incidents.[52] As Isobe and Muranaka later put it, they had now become *rōnin*, masterless samurai, and were pushed closer than ever to the use of violence. As it happened, it was an independent initiative of one of their confederates that finally pushed them over the edge.

The Last Straw

In autumn 1935, the atmosphere in the political system generally, and in the army specifically, was extremely tense. Politicians from the Seiyūkai, now in the opposition, collaborated with army officers in a campaign against the "Organ Theory," a constitutional theory that defined the emperor as an "organ of the state," rather than as a divine, all-encompassing sovereign. Many officers, including the leaders of the Young Officers Movement, had seen the theory as sacrilegious and a direct challenge to the kokutai, the vague "national polity" of Japan as an imperial state. Numerous officers enthusiastically participated in a noisy

campaign against the theory, fueled by the national association of army reservists. General Mazaki, the remaining leader of Kōdōha, actively participated in the
campaign, and denounced the theory in his capacity as inspector general of military education. Responding to pressure from below, the army and navy ministers
demanded that the government ban the theory and "clarify the national polity,"
to prevent the reoccurrence of such sacrilege. The government, whose mere existence was threatened by the scandal, finally concurred, and forced the scholar
who invented the theory to resign from his positions in Tokyo University and
the House of Peers. The national campaign for the "clarification of the national
polity" did not stop, however. Many critics of the army in general, and Kōdōha
ideology in particular, were castigated as traitors.[53]

The establishment's response to this scandal was the indirect trigger for the
revolt of February 26, 1936. The affair left many people in the government, as
well as in the Army Ministry, extremely bitter against the rabble-rousers from
the Kōdōha. Sensing an opportunity, Minister Hayashi and Major General
Nagata initiated a sweeping purge against Kōdōha officers. When these personnel
changes were vetoed by General Mazaki, Hayashi and Nagata decided to get rid of
him as well. Supported by the prime minister, Hayashi used Mazaki's "factional
schemes" as a pretext to remove him from his post, an order obtained by way of
a direct appeal by the army minister to the emperor.[54]

Mazaki fought bitterly against the decision, and accused Hayashi and Nagata
that by deciding to transfer him, they were guilty of violating the supreme prerogative. Decisions in the army, he claimed, had to be reached by the consensus
of the "big three," all of whom had direct supreme prerogative privileges. A unilateral removal of one of them, and certainly when done under the influence of
civilian bureaucrats and politicians, was nothing but a crime against the supreme
prerogative and the emperor.[55] Using thinly veiled threats, Mazaki warned his
peers that his transfer would not be taken lightly by the young officers. He knew
that many of them, who had studied in the military academy when he was school
commandant, respected him as teacher and ideological mentor, and implied that
they might unleash violence to protect him.[56] Indeed, on December 24, Mazaki
received two leaders of the Young Officers Movement for a private interview in
his home, in which he bemoaned the "supreme prerogative crimes" of Nagata
and his boss, the army minister. His argument was uncritically accepted by his
guests.[57] Following Mazaki, the young officers started to denounce Minister
Hayashi, Major General Nagata, and General Watanabe Jōtarō, Mazaki's successor, as "supreme prerogative criminals," an accusation with lethal implications.[58]

On August 22, 1935, this instigation was finally translated into action. Lieutenant Colonel Aizawa Saburō, a fencing instructor with a rich record of disobedience and close ties with the young officers, responded to what he later called

"an impulse from on high." Following a long tradition of optimistic assassins, he believed that by killing Major General Nagata, "the headquarters of all the evil," he would solve the problems of the army and the country.[59] A short while before his scheduled transfer to Taiwan, Aizawa came to Nagata's office and cut him down with a sword. Ironically, a few minutes before his death, Nagata was discussing ways to strengthen military discipline. This assassination was so natural for Aizawa, that he did not even see a reason to break up his routine. Before his arrest, he planned to go to the officers' club to buy a new cap (having left the old one in Nagata's office), and then on to his appointment in Taiwan.[60]

In his diary, the dismissed General Mazaki celebrated the "shishi Aizawa," who inflicted "heavenly punishment" on Nagata.[61] The assassination threw the Army Ministry into turmoil. As a senior ministry official wrote in his diary, the atmosphere became very tense, and every corner was "overflowing with gloom."[62] Aizawa's public trial certainly made things worse. The proceedings were used by his defense lawyer, Lieutenant Colonel Mitsui Sakichi, as a platform for propaganda, just like the trials of the Ketsumeidan and the conspirators of May 15, 1932.

Knowing full well that there was no possible legal way to dismiss the murder charges against his client, Mitsui used the same strategy which had worked so well in previous proceedings—the contextualization of Aizawa's crime within a larger framework of national decay. Violence, he said, was the path to spiritual regeneration. Not the crime itself, but the historical process mattered. Accordingly, Mitsui summoned witnesses representing the elites, both politicians and business magnates, in order to cross-examine them on their ties with Major General Nagata. During his testimony, Aizawa yelled at the judge. His defense team presented bountiful letters of support from the public, including one written by high school girls in their own blood, as well as a jar containing a chopped finger, signifying the sender's readiness to die in lieu of the defendant. A Soviet diplomat who attended the trial was astounded that junior officers dared to publically insult the emperor's closest advisors. The trial, he reported, was so crazy as to offer rich research material for psychologists.[63] Indeed, it was difficult for many foreign observers to comprehend how far the culture of insubordination was nestled into Japanese political life.

The sensational trial notwithstanding, the death of Nagata did not drum up the beginning of a wider, more sweeping change, as Aizawa and his sympathizers had hoped. The young officers decided that an assassination of one "evil man" would not suffice. Yet they were inspired by Aizawa, his "beautiful deed" and "total reverence to the emperor." Lieutenant Isobe, always theatrical, took an oath before Aizawa's picture to rebel soon.[64] News that the First Division, to which many of the young officers' units belonged, was about to be transferred to Manchuria, convinced them that they had to act quickly, or not at all.[65]

On February 18, as Aizawa's trial was nearing a climax, Kurihara, Isobe, Muranaka, and another ringleader, Captain Andō Teruzō, met for a crucial conference. All knew that they had to act before the relocation of the First Division. According to Kurihara, all except Andō agreed that there was no other way to launch the Showa Restoration except by direct action. They also decided to use hundreds of rank-and-file troops, NCOs and ensigns, a radical move that only the Sakura-kai had contemplated before.[66] Andō, who still believed the action was premature and was concerned by the lack of concrete planning, hesitated for a few days, but finally accepted the decision of the majority.[67] The action was scheduled for the early morning hours of February 26, with forces from the First and Third infantry regiments (First Division) and the Third Regiment of the Imperial Guard. Captains Andō Teruzō and Nonaka Shirō were company commanders in the Third Infantry Regiment, so they were able to use their established authority to mobilize rank-and-file troops.[68]

The high-priority targets were Prime Minister Okada Keisuke, Finance Minister Takahashi Korekiyo, and several other "traitors around the throne." There was also a list of second-priority "traitors," to be dealt with later.[69] At the last moment, the officers decided to scrap the plan to assassinate Prince Saionji Kinmochi, the only "traitor" who lived in the countryside, far away from Tokyo. The reasons for that decision vary across testimonies. It had strategic meaning, as this key official, the only surviving genrō, was supposed to advise the emperor whom to appoint as prime minister after Okada's demise. Maybe, as Lieutenant Kyohara has related, the conspirators hoped to manipulate or force Saionji, the only still-living participant of the Meiji Restoration, to recommend their own candidate and give a stamp of approval to their new restoration. In any case, Saionji's continued presence on the scene meant that the forces of the old order would still have an important stake in shaping the postcoup reality.[70]

The rebels, with typical optimism, believed that with these "traitors" gone, other senior officers would jump on their wagon. The assumption was not altogether baseless. General Kawashima Yoshiyuki, the new army minister appointed as Hayashi's successor, was backed by Mazaki and had personal ties with the young officers. "My impression from Kawashima," wrote Isobe, "was that if something broke out, he would not repress it."[71]

Besides, there was hope of securing some back channels to the imperial court. Captain Yamaguchi Ichitarō, the young officer sympathizer mentioned at the beginning of this chapter, was the son-in-law of General Honjō Shigeru, the aide-de-camp of Emperor Hirohito. It was expected that after the coup, the rebels would reach the ear of the emperor through Honjō's good services. More important, Prince Chichibu, the emperor's younger brother and a battalion commander in Hirosaki (northeast Japan), knew some of the young officers and sympathized with the idea of the Showa Restoration. However, contrary to the assumptions made by some scholars and observers, the prince was never a true supporter of the Young Officers Movement. Crucially, he never condoned a violent rebellion and did nothing to help the young officers when they rose up.[72]

More fortunate for the rebels was the sorry state of the law enforcement agencies. Although the government knew as least as early as January that the young officers were plotting something, this intelligence was never translated into arrests.[73] The civilian police, which knew a lot about the young officers, had no authority to arrest them—only the military police could do so. But the two organizations were reluctant to share information with each other, and the latter was impotent in any case. Thus, though military policemen had constantly followed Muranaka and Isobe since Nagata was assassinated, the surveillance did not lead to resolute action. Weak, understaffed, and infiltrated by radical officers, the military police had a long tradition of ignoring patriotic insubordination in the ranks.[74]

In order to convince top-level leaders such as the army minister, explain the rebellion, and propagate their vision far and wide, the rebels prepared 150 copies of a short manifesto. The document is typical "Showa Restoration" propaganda and more interesting for its form than its contents. Though it was distributed to soldiers and civilians, its primary audience was not the nation, as was the case with famous revolutionary manifestos in other countries. Instead, it was a formulaic appeal to the higher echelons and to the throne, written in simple yet literary language. The Meiji rebels in 1868 also used the throne as their frame of reference, but they issued declarations on behalf of the throne. They did not appeal to the emperor and certainly not to other superiors, before they launched their coup d'état in 1868. The February 1936 insurgents, by contrast, rebelled against the establishment, but also looked for its approval.[75] This difference is key to the events that followed.

The Incident of February 26: Heavenly Punishment

At 4:30 a.m. on February 26, fourteen hundred troops from the First and the Third infantry regiments of the First Division, as well as from the Third Regiment of the Imperial Guard, left their barracks under the cover of a heavy snowstorm.[76] They carried guns, sub- and heavy machine guns, as well as ample rounds of ammunition, but very little food supplies. The plan was to conclude the operation in one day. Before setting out, the officers read their manifesto to the troops and told them they were going to launch a new restoration. To strengthen this impression, the ringleaders sewed into their caps the "three *sen* stamp," referring to the famous poem of the shishi leader Takasugi Shinsaku, extolling self-sacrifice for a righteous cause. "In this floating world," the poem said, "life is not worth more than three *sen* [pennies]."[77]

Lieutenant Kurihara Yasuhide spearheaded the effort to "eliminate the traitors," the dignitaries whose mere existence made restoration impossible. The most important of these "traitors" was undoubtedly Prime Minister Okada Keisuke. At 5:00 a.m., Kurihara's squad arrived at the prime minister's official residence. Kurihara posted armed soldiers at every exit, and broke into the apartments with his troops. While some of the invaders were fighting the guards, others searched for Okada in the corridors. They didn't have prior intelligence about the contours of the prime minister's sizable residence. When the house staff disconnected electrical power, the invaders had to feel their way in the dark. In the garden they spotted a man in night clothes, Okada's brother-in-law, and shot him. Kurihara examined the slain man and, mistaking him for the prime minister, ordered his soldiers to surround the residence and block all access. From there, he hurried to the army minister's residence. In fact, Okada had been hidden in a closet by one of the servants and was eventually whisked out of the building.[78]

Other squads moved to eliminate other high-priority "traitors." The finance minister, Baron Takahashi Korekiyo, was the easiest to kill. Lieutenant Nakahashi Motoaki and the members of his squad from the Third Imperial Guard assembled near Takahashi's private residence, where the soldiers were briefed on the minister's "crimes," particularly his refusal to raise the army's budget. They found Takahashi asleep. Nakahashi yelled "Heavenly punishment!" and shot the old man, while another officer slashed him with a sword.[79] At the same time, a third squad, led by Lieutenant Sakai Naoshi, murdered Saitō Makoto, former navy minister, prime minister, and lord keeper of the privy seal. Saitō's wife placed herself before her husband and told the rebels to "shoot me instead. The country cannot lose my husband." They wounded her, killed the lord, and then cheered banzai to honor the emperor.[80] Lieutenant Sakai went back to the troops and showed them his hands, dripping with blood. "This," he said, "is the blood of the evil traitor Saitō. All of you, look!"[81]

Two hours later, soldiers and officers from the squad that had murdered Saitō arrived at the house of General Watanabe Jōtarō, the inspector general of military education. When the inspector general's wife appeared, she asked the intruders whether they were Japanese soldiers. "We are not the private soldiers of his excellency [the general]," First Lieutenant Yasuda Yutaka answered, "but the soldiers of his majesty the emperor."[82] Watanabe, who woke up during the commotion, took a futon for cover and tried to shoot at the invaders. But they were too numerous. The inspector general was first hit by two pistol shots and a machine gun, and then, according to the usual protocol, cut with a sword.[83] The other two assassinations were not as successful. Chief Chamberlain Suzuki Kantarō was severely wounded, and his wife convinced the assassins to leave his body alone. The officers, who thought him dead, left, but Suzuki eventually recovered from his wounds. Count Makino Nobuaki, the former lord keeper of the privy seal, escaped through the back door with the help of a nurse, a policeman, and his granddaughter.[84]

In other cases, however, the rebels showed surprising restraint. Later in the morning, after the main wave of assassinations had passed, Kurihara and his mobile team rampaged through the headquarters of *Asahi Shinbun*, a newspaper deemed hostile to the army and the Showa Restoration. They declared that they were going to impose "heavenly punishment" on the newspaper for being "un-Japanese." But instead of killing all the workers, they ordered them to evacuate the building, and then climbed into the second floor and scattered the typing templates.[85] Another squad of rebels, led by Captain Nonaka Shirō, surrounded the building of the Metropolitan Police, where they negotiated with two high-ranking officers and gave them their manifesto. They were not keen to open fire and occupied the building without shedding blood.[86] In this sense, the young officers were much less bloodthirsty than the Sakura-kai, who planned, as mentioned in the previous chapter, to slaughter entire groups of people, for example in the foreign ministry.[87] This curious combination between restraint and deadly violence was a major feature of the events of February 26, 1936.

Flashlight in the Snow: Lieutenant Nakahashi at the Emperor's Doorstep

The rebels, well aware of the significance of the hazy imperial center to Japanese politics, dispatched Lieutenant Nakahashi Motoaki and his unit from Third Imperial Guard to approach the palace and take over one of the entrances, the Sakashita Gate. To justify such a move the young officers could use as a precedent the famous palace coup performed by their role models, the shishi of the Meiji Restoration. Only when the Meiji revolutionaries had controlled the emperor, did they have the power and legitimacy to overthrow the Bakufu and launch the restoration.

According to the plan, Nakahashi was supposed to make use of the ensuing chaos to convince headquarters to let him guard the Sakashita Gate as an emergency relief force, and block the entrance of "evil" courtiers and advisors. According to the regulations, dignitaries could use only the Sakashita Gate for entry, and as they did not know that rebels were stationed there, they had no reason to avoid it. When spotted, they could be greeted by machine-gun fire (though this was not mentioned explicitly by Nakahashi or the other witnesses.)[88] The second phase of the plan was to call reinforcements from other rebels in order to besiege the gates and possibly occupy the entire compound. As Nakahashi had only sixty-two soldiers at his disposal, he could not overcome the palace guard without reinforcements, and had to convince the local commander to tolerate his presence until they arrived. Fortunately for him, his company was on standby duty that day, so his presence at the gate was explainable.[89]

Nakahashi's attempt to install his men near the imperial palace showed initial signs of success. Though the security detail commander, who already knew that imperial guards assassinated the finance minister, suspected Nakahashi due to his mutinous reputation and disorderly appearance, he still allowed him to station his troops near the Sakashita Gate. But the siege was ineffective: several courtiers, including Kido Kōichi, were able to pass through. Then Nakahashi proceeded to the second part of the plan, and tried to call reinforcements from Captain Nonaka in the Metropolitan Police headquarters, only nine hundred meters away on the other side of the palace moat. There, in the watchtower, one of Nonaka's subordinates waited for a signal from the palace. Nonaka was supposed to call reinforcements from Captain Andō, who was waiting with his unit nearby. Why couldn't Nakahashi send an emissary directly to Andō, instead of communicating with him in such a roundabout way through Nonaka? Such an unnecessary complication is yet another indicator of the rebels' failure to make detailed plans in advance.[90]

The attempt to call reinforcements failed. The rebels near the police headquarters did not spot Nakahashi's flashlight signal, probably due to poor visibility caused by the snowy weather. An attempt to send another signal, through a hand flag, failed as well. According to one version, an emissary from Nakahashi reached police headquarters, but Nonaka did not budge due to his reluctance to violate the dignity of the emperor.[91]

Nakahashi, who was probably certain that reinforcements were on their way, walked to the security detail's command post, placed his gun threateningly on the desk and asked for authority over the palace guard. Laying all his cards on the table, he told the commander that the Showa Restoration had been launched, and his comrades would soon be in the palace with troops. The commander, astounded and angry, put Nakahashi under arrest in one of the rooms, but this arrest, it seems, was as inept as Nakahashi's own performance that day. At around 8:30 a.m. Nakahashi was able to escape the palace and join his comrades at the prime minister's residence. His soldiers returned to government control and were released to their barracks several hours later.[92]

Righteous or Rebellious? The Army Minister's Dilemma

While their colleagues were raining "heavenly punishments" on Japan's leaders, Muranaka, Isobe, and Koda approached the compound of the army high command in central Tokyo with detachments of troops, armed with rifles, automatic weapons, and machine guns. Some of the squads occupied the buildings of the General Staff and the Army Ministry, while Muranaka, Isobe, and Koda entered Army Minister Kawashima's official residence. They faced no opposition at the entrance. Once within the building, the officers behaved with relative restraint. As Koda said later, they did not stray beyond the anteroom, in order "not to be rude," and tried not to wake up the ladies.[93] They demanded, however, to see Minister Kawashima right away about an urgent matter. The minister came at 6:30 a.m. and received the officers for an interview. Accompanied by Isobe, Muranaka, and Kurihara, who hurried from the prime minister's residence, Koda read the rebels' manifesto to Kawashima and put forward a series of demands. The army minister was required to sanction their presence in their current positions, arrest or relieve rival officers (including Tōseiha movers and shakers, as well as figures involved with the Sakura-kai and the March and October incidents), and take the first steps to establish a reform cabinet for initiating the Showa Restoration.

Kawashima did not impress the young officers. Due to brain damage he had received in Korea, his speech was mumbled and indistinct. Ignorant about the minister's medical condition, Koda interpreted his speech as fearful and hesitant.[94] Responding to the officers' demands, Kawashima refused to relieve or arrest officers, but praised the motives of the rebels, and promised to submit "most of their demands" to the emperor. Without making a firm decision, Kawashima left his residence at 9:00 a.m. for consultations in the Imperial Palace.[95] A short while after the minister's departure, an incident occurred near the gates of his house. Lieutenant Isobe Asaichi, angry and nervous, spotted Major Katakura, one of the officers responsible for his demotion in the Military Academy incident, and shot him in the face. Katakura was evacuated to a hospital.[96]

With full control over the civilian police headquarters, and in the absence of an efficient, action-ready military police, the rebels had to worry only about other army units, most of all the First Division, to which two of their regiments belonged.[97] The division commander, General Hori Takeo, and members of his staff, consulted with their colleagues in the Tokyo Garrison. Initial plans to violently crush the rebellion were quickly abandoned. Both Hori and his counterpart from the Tokyo garrison, General Kashi Kōhei, loathed to see Japanese soldiers shooting at each other. They also feared that central Tokyo would turn into a battlefield, knowing that such fights could start a fire that might consume large parts of the city. Foreign embassies would probably be hit, causing a diplomatic crisis. Not only civilians would be killed and buildings destroyed, but even worse—stray bullets might hit the Imperial Palace. Therefore, and also out of sympathy to the pure motives of the rebels, Hori and Kashi decided on a strategy of containment.[98]

When the supreme military council—an unofficial body of army elders which also included Kōdōha potentates such as Araki and Mazaki—met in the late morning hours, the containment strategy of Hori and Kashi, mixed with genuine sympathy toward the rebels, produced a relatively favorable result. The council unanimously agreed on a proclamation of martial law, signed by Army Minister Kawashima. The order went into force at 2:50 a.m. the next morning but only in the areas surrounding the rebels' positions. General Kashi was appointed as commander of the martial law headquarters.[99] In a separate note to the rebels, signed by Kawashima, the councilors acknowledged that the young officers' motives were in accordance with the kokutai, promised to convey their demands to the emperor, and made a vague commitment to work toward the realization of their goals.[100]

General Kashi ordered all detachments in the capital not to shoot or confront the young officers. Moreover, he formally integrated them into the capital's defense system and ordered them to retain their present positions. Thus the commander of martial law turned the insurgents, momentarily, from a rebellious army into a loyal force. Kashi even went further: in his statement, dictated by phone, he communicated an earlier, more radical version of the decision draft. In this version, the supreme military council endorsed not only the rebels' motives, but their actions as well. The content of this phone conversation was confirmed by a formal order, released by the Tokyo garrison at 3:20 p.m.[101]

Yamaguchi Ichitarō, the company commander who advised the army minister in the morning to decide whether the mutineers were "righteous" or "rebellious," was sent by his superiors to the rebel positions to convey the good news. Naturally, the young officers felt relieved, and according to some testimonies, declared their victory and spontaneously started to dance. Along with Yamaguchi, they believed that the garrison's order made things clear. They were in imperial service, hence—they were a righteous and not a rebellious army. By 7:00 p.m. the insurgent units were integrated in a newly formed force led by the commander of the First Infantry Regiment and given regular hot meals delivered from headquarters.[102] The official proclamations, though, did not define them as either "righteous" or "rebellious," but in evasive terms such as "activist officers."[103] The final decision between "righteous" and "rebellious" had to wait for later. It was naturally dependent on the power dynamics in the political system and on the ground.

At 9:00 p.m. seven senior generals from the Supreme Military Council, accompanied by several general staffers, traveled to the army minister's residence to meet the ringleaders of the coup. The Kōdōha generals, Araki and Mazaki, talked with the rebel leaders. Lieutenant Koda, who spoke for the young officers, asked again to arrest civilian and military leaders who were hostile to the coup. In addition, he demanded that the generals sack Tōseiha officers, form a "strong cabinet," and declare the Showa Restoration. Araki's answer was polite but stern. It was unseemly, he said, to arrest old and venerable people without a good reason. In addition, cabinets were formed by imperial sanction, and not by the Supreme Military Council. As for the Restoration, Mazaki added that the Supreme Military Council was not qualified to declare it. But, he assured the young officers that he, and presumably the other members of the council, sympathized with their goals. The young officers should unconditionally trust the councilors, their seniors, and leave matters in their hands. Mazaki warned that the final decision rested with the emperor, and anyone who dared to violate an imperial command must be treated as an enemy.[104]

This conversation was held in a tense, unclear political situation. The civilian government was confused and paralyzed. Prince Saionji, who was regularly tasked with recommending a new prime minister to the emperor, refused to risk his life and stayed away from Tokyo.[105] The vacuum was soon filled by other power factors. By the night of February 26, midlevel General Staff officers were beginning to wonder whether they could take the lead. By noon, a high official in the Army Ministry's Military Affairs Bureau ordered some subordinates to draft an imperial rescript for the Showa Restoration.[106] In the evening, Colonel Ishiwara Kanji, the architect of the Manchurian Incident in 1931, Aizawa's lawyer Lieutenant Colonel Mitsui Sakichi, as well as the Sakura-kai's leader Hashimoto Kingorō, met in the Imperial Hotel to discuss the nature of the restoration. All three, who were deeply involved in the army's culture of insubordination, agreed that the army should take over, lead the restoration, and appoint a new prime minister. They failed, however, to agree on a candidate. Mitsui, who was ideologically close to the young officers, believed that General Mazaki should serve as Japan's new prime minister. Hashimoto proposed Lieutenant General Tatekawa, his patron from the days of the March Incident. Ishiwara, by contrast, wanted an imperial prince to take the lead. When the meeting ended, it was clear that Ishiwara, Hashimoto, and Mitsui could not overcome their differences and form a clique that would manage the chaos from behind the scenes.[107]

The failure of the General Staff officers to step forward left the stage empty for the army leaders, who were now relatively free from the influence of junior manipulators and puppeteers. As long as the rebels were armed, and the position of the emperor was still hidden in the confines of the palace, the Kōdōha leaders Araki and Mazaki had a natural advantage over their peers. After all, only they could speak with the armed rebels and use their presence in central Tokyo as a political trump card. The young officers, for their part, were in a vulnerable position. By playing along with the Supreme Military Council, they integrated themselves again into the military hierarchy and bound their fate to the political maneuvers of their top-brass sympathizers. Yet, as Isobe forewarned his friends, this dependency was very dangerous. Even the Kōdōha generals could not be trusted.[108]

The above episode reflects some fundamental flaws of the rebellion. Just like in the rebellions of the 1870s, the absence of active leadership led to a diffusion of responsibility that precluded serious planning and left nobody in control.[109] Even worse, the young officers' strategy was confused. Isobe wrote later that no thorough planning could be made, because the rebels could not foresee the army's reaction to the first wave of assassinations.[110] But that was just the point: he and his friends were caught between two different strategies. The first was to follow the example of the May 1932 Incident, kill some dignitaries, withdraw and hope that the army leadership would do the rest, or in Araki's words, "to be satisfied that their motives were reported to the emperor."[111] For that, only rudimentary planning was needed. Alternatively, the rebels could launch a fully fledged coup d'état and enforce a restoration through their armed presence. Such an elaborate political move, however, required thorough planning. The ringleaders of the February Incident did not really plan ahead and left too much to the discretion of the army leaders, as if they were pursuing the former strategy. And yet they implemented the latter strategy—a coup d'état, without adequate preparations.

Consequently, as a high-ranking officer of the Tokyo Garrison wrote later, the rebels became paralyzed immediately after their first strike.[112] They did not make any attempts to expand the scope of terror by murdering more of their enemies; nor did they take over the military and civilian communication facilities, which were close to the area they controlled; nor force the staff officers to submit orders to the troops in Tokyo which were favorable to the insurgency. Besides, they had failed to mobilize in advance their supporters in the provinces, the Tokyo military schools, the reservist organizations, or the civilian right-wing movements. Nor did they have enough food to withstand a protracted siege. And even if they had had enough supplies, the army authorities could not be expected to tolerate the occupation of central Tokyo indefinitely. The inability of the rebels to disentangle themselves from the military hierarchy put them at a disadvantage. However, the army leadership's fear of a showdown in central Tokyo kept the fragile balance, for now.[113]

The Haze Disappears: Emperor Hirohito's Decision

The British correspondent Hugh Byas, who watched the drama of the incident unfolding, recalled that the capital "was lifeless under the grimy snow. All the familiar figures had vanished from the streets. The schools were closed. No trains were entering the city and no street cars were running. . . . Tokyo was isolated for the last act."[114]

Facing this impasse, all eyes turned to the imperial hazy center. The failure of the rebels to eliminate or arrest the senior courtiers left the emperor surrounded with anti-rebellion advisors.[115] Worst of all, the emperor himself detested the young officers and their Kōdōha patrons because of their high-blown rhetoric and recidivist disobedience.[116] Now, furious at the murder of his closest advisors and worried about adverse impacts on the economy, he was determined to crush the revolt.[117] When Army Minister Kawashima entered into an imperial audience and tried to bring the rebels' demands to the monarch's attention, Hirohito refused to listen. "Whatever their excuses are," he told Kawashima, "I am displeased with this incident. It has brought disgrace on the vital essence of our national character." Avoiding equivocal statements, the emperor ordered Kawashima to arrest the rebels. He summoned his aide-de-camp, General Honjō Shigeru, every twenty or thirty minutes to ask for updates about the measures being taken to subdue the uprising.[118]

The behavior of Emperor Hirohito has to be understood in its political and organizational context. As the imperial hazy center usually reigned, but not ruled, the emperor could push high-ranking officials to act by issuing unequivocal orders, but did not have the organizational tools to manage the process himself. As we have seen in chapter 8, Hirohito could not follow up the implementation of his orders in the wake of the Zhang Zuolin Incident, and those were sabotaged by the army.[119] During the February Incident, however, he could exercise greater control over the situation thanks to several advantages. Apart from the relative paralysis in the usual civilian and military mechanism, which turned attention toward the imperial will, there were enough powerful actors, separate from the emperor's remaining advisors, who were keen to utilize the imperial order to crush the rebellion. The General Staff was dominated by Tōseiha, and the navy was incensed by the rebels' assault on three retired admirals (Okada, Suzuki, and Saitō). Such actors, whom the rebels failed to neutralize, could fill the frame of the imperial will with substance. The rebels' failure to eliminate their rivals in the armed services proved fatal to the prospects of their cause.[120]

And yet the influence of Army Minister Kawashima, Garrison Commander Kashi, and the Kōdōha leaders significantly delayed the execution of the imperial will.[121] February 27 and a large part of the twenty-eighth were spent in endless attempts to negotiate with the young officers and convince them to retreat gradually and peacefully. The emperor urged his hesitant commanders to act immediately by gradually increasing the volume and intensity of his interventions. Again and again he told General Honjō, his aide-de-camp, that if the rebels were not suppressed forthwith, he would take the palace guards and lead the pacification efforts in person.

Honjō, as one may remember, had important stakes in the army's culture of insubordination. In 1931, as the commander of the Kwantung Army, he had sanctioned the Manchurian Incident. Even now he had certain sympathy for the young officers and personal connections with them through his son-in-law, Captain Yamaguchi Ichitarō. In his audience with the emperor, he tried to use the usual arguments. The rebels were wrongheaded, he said, but their motives were patriotic and pure. The emperor angrily rejected these attempts at apology. "How can we not condemn even the spirit of these criminally brutal officers who killed my aged subjects who were my hands and feet? To kill the old subjects whom I trusted the most is akin to gently strangling me with floss-silk." He further professed impatience with General Kashi's policy of negotiation and accommodation with the rebels. "It appears," wrote Honjō, "that His Majesty felt that the chief of the martial law [Kashi] was too cautious and was procrastinating unnecessarily."[122]

Hirohito's frequent and angry interventions shifted the balance in the entire system, gradually but surely. If on the twenty-sixth Mazaki and the other military councilors were still negotiating with the rebels about their political goals, in a second meeting, held in the afternoon of the twenty-seventh, the senior generals did not agree to hearing conditions and demands. Instead, Mazaki tried to convince the young officers to surrender peacefully and "entrust everything into his hands," otherwise he would have to "overcome his sorrow" and punish them severely. The young officers first agreed to surrender and "entrust everything to Mazaki." Later, however, they changed their stance. And yet, generals Kashi and Hori still looked for a way out and delayed the execution of the imperial command.[123]

In the early morning of the twenty-eighth, Hirohito's personal intervention increased yet again in volume and intensity. He submitted an imperial order to the martial law headquarters to force the rebels to abandon their positions forthwith. As this order, however, came through Kashi, Hori, and the First Division, the rebel leaders could still claim it was falsified and cling to their own "interpretation" of the imperial will. Nakahashi told an emissary of the martial law headquarters that the young officers would not withdraw as long as the Showa Restoration remained unlaunched.[124] The imperial order was a fake, a scheme of the "traitors around the throne."[125] In the next few hours, some of the young officers started to fortify their positions, ordered the machine-gun teams to stand on high alert, and prepared for the final showdown.[126]

Lieutenant General Sugiyama, vice chief of the General Staff and one of the young officers' staunchest enemies, tried to give an order to assault, but it was foiled once again by Kashi and some of the military councilors, who believed they could convince the rebels to commit suicide. After some debate, many of the rebels accepted this honorable way out. Kurihara and Koda started crying, and in a tearful voice asked to inform the emperor about their motives. Then, they would take their own lives if an imperial emissary told them to do so.[127] That was not only a means of saving face, but also a desperate appeal to sustain the narrative of a direct connection between the rebels and the emperor, which stood at the basis of their ideology. Hirohito, who understood it well, angrily refused to accommodate the request. "His Majesty," wrote General Honjō, the emperor's aide-de-camp, "was highly displeased and said: 'If they wish to commit suicide, let them do so as they please. It is out of the question to dispatch an imperial agent to such men.'" Hirohito exploded with fury and told Honjō in blunt language that if Hori did not subdue the rebellion immediately, then maybe the First Division should be led by someone else.[128]

In the early morning of the twenty-ninth, the army high command ended all ambiguous talk. Army Minister Kawashima wrote to Hori that there was "no room for discussion" with violators of national law and military discipline.[129] The young officers were no longer defined in watered-down terms such as "activists." Instead, in orders issued by the army minister and the martial law headquarters, they were denounced as rebels who had defied an imperial command.[130] Suddenly, Isobe wrote, the young officers stopped being a righteous army and became rebels and traitors.[131] Even General Araki agreed that the rebellion must be crushed. Accordingly, the First Division stopped bringing food supplies to the rebels' positions.[132]

At the same time, General Kashi found the right strategy to end the rebellion bloodlessly. Instead of holding another round of futile negotiations with the young officers or attacking them upfront, he aimed at their Achilles Heel—the NCOs and ensigns who served under them. The course of action, yet again, was to expose the imperial hazy center. In the early hours of the morning, the imperial order to subdue the rebellion was broadcast to the soldiers by radio and loudspeakers, and also from tanks, airplanes, and an enormous balloon.[133] Only in his famous surrender speech in August 1945, did Hirohito appeal to the public in a more direct way. Faced with the imperial words, the soldiers and NCOs started to desert, and most rebel officers gave up as well. The soldiers, recalled Hugh Byas, "surrendered their arms and were packed into trucks and rushed to their barracks."[134] Captain Andō Teruzō, barricaded in the Sannō Hotel, was the last one to surrender. After a failed suicide attempt he was arrested, along with the others. A head-on charge was no longer necessary, and by 2:00 p.m. on February 29, generals Sugiyama and Kashi could finally report to the emperor that the incident had been settled.[135]

Trial and Punishment

Apart from two young officers, who committed suicide, all of the others were arrested in the late afternoon hours of February 29. The scope of the rebellion, its intensity, the assassinations of advisors close to the emperor, and especially the use of rank-and-file troops, had finally crossed an invisible red line. The February rebels were therefore condemned by all army leaders in harsh language. Army Minister Kawashima, who had encouraged the rebels through his hesitant behavior on February 26, now called their coup "an indelible black mark on the history of the sacred Showa reign." The unequivocal condemnation of the rebels was also expressed in the army's decision to strip them of all commissions, ranks, and honors.[136] Following their interrogations, they were tried relatively quickly and in secret, in order to prevent them from propagating their ideas and encouraging copycats, as the rebels of May 1932 and Lieutenant Colonel Aizawa had done.[137]

The behavior of the army leaders, many of whom had encouraged or tolerated the young officers for several years, seemed hypocritical even to some enemies of the rebellion. General Ugaki Kazushige, the governor-general of Korea who appeared in the young officers' black list, wrote in his diary that it was "disgusting to watch these rascals [the army leaders], holding in one hand the matches and in the other one the water hose, setting fire and putting it out at the same time, inciting the pure young officers, pleading their cause and then claiming credit for having put them down."[138]

In their prison cells, the young officers discovered that they had been abandoned by all of their allies. Isobe hoped that senior Kōdōha officers, such as Mazaki and Kashi, would testify for him and his fellow conspirators. Did they not support the rebellion in the first day? Kashi had even ordered the rebels to assume guard positions as part of the martial rule declared in Tokyo. If the young officers were traitors, Isobe argued, then these generals were implicated to the same degree, and with them the entire army.[139] The interned officers were hurt even more by their designation as rebels, when all they had ever intended was to serve the emperor. Isobe poured his feelings into his diary, unable to understand why the beloved monarch wanted to execute his most faithful servants.[140] And yet many of the young officers still assumed that Hirohito had been duped by traitorous advisors. Their incantations were in vain, as the authorities did everything possible to hush them up. Public sensation, the oxygen which had fed the fire of violent insubordination since 1931, was denied. As a result, the young officers felt helpless and forlorn.

Hatred was all that remained. In his cell, Isobe prayed to the Shinto gods to wreak vengeance on the traitors around the throne, the "unclean staff officers," the generals, the judge—all who had wronged him. The army, he said, was nothing but a conglomeration of military cliques. Araki, Mazaki, and the other Kōdōha leaders were as bad as the others. In order to launch a real restoration, patriots had to destroy the army first.[141] The last words of another rebel, Shibugawa Zensuke, probably represented the feeling of most officers involved in the incident: "Oh nation! Do not trust the Imperial Army."[142]

The severity of the punishments also knew no precedent. This time, there were no free servings of alcohol, no geisha, no luxurious inn rooms, even no lenient jail terms—as there had been in the wake of the May 1932 Incident. According to Isobe's prison diary, the torturous heat in the suffocating cells made one look forward to the gallows.[143] And, indeed, he did not have to wait for long. All rebel leaders, including Kurihara, Andō, Muranaka, Koda and Isobe, were condemned to death and executed, along with their civilian mentor Kita Ikki. Aizawa Saburō, the murderer of Major General Nagata, was shot as well. Several sympathizers who did not participate in the rebellion directly, such as Captain Yamaguchi Ichitarō, were imprisoned for life. Even General Mazaki, formerly one of the "big three" of the army, was tried and held in prison for many months, though he was eventually released.

Insubordination and Its Limits: The Afterlife of the February Incident

The February Incident was allowed to take place, and to go as far it did, only in a society where violent rebellion had stopped being an outlier and become instead an accepted cultural norm. In his court testimony, Lieutenant Nakahashi explained the assassination of ministers as part of his military routine. "As soldiers," he said, "we did not think about the law. We were trained to kill. . . . The most important thing is sincerity. We did not think we were breaking the law."[144] Many officers and soldiers who were not rebels themselves supported the young officers' vision to different degrees. Funayama Ichirō, a paramedic who treated wounded insurgents but was never a rebel per se, confessed in his interrogation that he, too, supported a restoration, the removal of the ruling classes, and a military dictatorship.[145] Many others had resisted the plans of the young officers but still were loathe to inform on them due to camaraderie, fear, or a combination of both.[146]

The young officers did not invent the ideology that justified their cause. Instead, they used ideological tools that had been for years part of the army's culture of insubordination: the imitation of the shishi and mutinous reliance on the hazy center had already become entrenched habits in the 1930s. The prerogative of supreme command, invented by Yamagata Aritomo as a tool to prevent military rebellions in 1878, was used to justify such a rebellion in 1936. Operational discretion, originally devised to allow soldiers to independently solve tactical problems when fighting Japan's enemies, was reinterpreted as carte blanche for officers to assassinate foreign leaders and also "internal enemies"—civilians such as Prime Minister Okada and officers such as General Watanabe.[147] The reoccurring failure of the civilian and military ruling elites to punish officers who used the supreme prerogative and operational discretion as pretexts for insubordination radicalized these concepts, until the young officers were able to use them to legitimize a violent rebellion against their own superiors and the civilian cabinet.

The coup of February 1936 was also the end of another long-term historical process, the democratization of insubordination in the Japanese armed forces. As we have seen, the rank of the officers at the helm of insubordination became lower and lower with the passing of the years: from senior generals like Miura Gorō to bureau chiefs like Tanaka Giichi, staff officers such as Kōmoto Daisaku and Hashimoto Kingorō, and finally young lieutenants and captains like Isobe, Muranaka, and Kurihara. One of the repercussions of this process, touched on in previous chapters, was ongoing ideological radicalization. While senior officers were ready to stage upheavals, their responsibilities made them less willing to rock the boat. For all of his hatred to the Saionji Government in 1911, Tanaka Giichi did not even consider using violence during the Taishō political crisis. Even most members of the Sakura-kai were reluctant to act without the backing of senior officers, as evidenced by the slow dismemberment of the society in the days before the October Incident. The lieutenants and captains of the Young Officers Movement had the most extreme ideology of all. They did not consult senior officers, idolized murderous violence against all perceived "enemies," and saw the mere idea of military discipline in political matters as an abomination.

The young officers' lower status in the system made them the most extreme in theory and yet the most timid in practice. On February 26 they murdered senior statesmen, courtiers, and generals, but they could not operate for a long time outside of the military hierarchy. When confronted with the supreme military council, the difference in age and rank overwhelmed them, and they were too easily convinced to bind themselves again to the military chain of command. Even their manifesto was formulated like a petition, or appeal to the government, and not like a clarion call of independent rebels.[148]

Theoretically, the rebels of February 1936 may have seen themselves as a modern version of the shishi of the Meiji Restoration, but that too fell apart in practice. The original plan of the rebels was to isolate the imperial palace and exclude the "traitors around the throne," but that plan fell far short of the famous palace coup of 1868. The leaders of the Meiji Restoration, after all, had actively taken over the palace. In February 1936, even the limited plan of a partial palace blockade was not implemented. Nakahashi Motoaki, who was responsible for the blockade, behaved irresolutely from the moment he came into the palace gates. When his plan to call for reinforcements failed, he cowed before a senior officer and fled the scene, practically deserting his troops.

That scene reflects the enormous gap between the historical reality of the shishi in the Meiji Restoration, and that of the young officers. The leaders of the Meiji Restoration revered the emperor in theory, but like all informed political actors in the late Tokugawa period, they knew he was a sixteen-year-old puppet, or as Kido Takayoshi had put it, a "jewel" in their hands.[149] The young officers, by contrast, were a product of an education and propaganda system that presented the emperor as an omnipotent god and the embodiment of pure-hearted patriotism.[150] As patriots, the young officers naturally believed that their vision was identical to the emperor's secret wish, and that His Majesty would have supported them, if he had only heard about their motives from General Honjō, General Mazaki, or Prince Chichibu. They could not understand that their beloved monarch was a strong-willed politician who hated them. When imperial hostility came into the open, they became confused and paralyzed.[151] "As soldiers," wrote Captain Nonaka in his farewell letter, "we did not understand the subtleties of high politics. Whether we were fools or lunatics, I don't know."[152] In the conditions of 1936 Japan, junior officers without political acumen and understanding of palace politics were intellectually and psychologically unfit to navigate the corridors of power. Ironically, the democratization of insubordination saved the government.

After the young officers had failed and been severely punished, the momentum of the democratization of insubordination stopped, and the pendulum began to turn back in the other direction. By severely punishing and humiliating the rebels, the army finally put an end to its own culture of violent insubordination. After the incident, Army Minister Kawashima explained that the army would be cleansed and "completely renewed, so that a national army that is truly united and powerful can be built. In this way, the army will comply with the emperor's wishes." The inspector general of military education also emphasized the value of strict discipline in his admonitions of the troops. General Terauchi Hisaichi, Kawashima's successor as army minister, instructed the divisional commanders that officers should cease all political involvement. An officer must express his political opinions only in a petition to the army minister, through his immediate superiors.[153] The Kōdōha faction, implicated in the rebellion, was beaten badly, and its leaders Araki and Mazaki pushed out of the army. Mazaki was also jailed for many months.

As a result, the February Incident opened a power vacuum at the political center. The emperor, who had forcefully intervened to stop the coup, had neither the power nor institutional tools to rule the country directly. The civilian elites were terrified by military violence. In the absence of the other genrō, who were already dead, the ailing Prince Saionji was not the right man to use his privilege to rule de facto from behind the scenes. The shock of the incident forced most members of the supreme military council and most full generals to resign from active service.[154]

The only elite that remained on its feet after the shock waves of the February Incident, were the midlevel staff officers associated with Tōseiha. As several advisors of the emperor suspected, they were the moving force behind the resignation of their seniors, a golden opportunity they were quick to exploit.[155] Even before the incident, they held much of the power in the Army Ministry and the General Staff, manipulating and controlling their seniors. Up until 1936, they had been threatened only by the violence of the young officers. After the February Incident, this violence died out, so, facing no threat, these midlevel Tōseiha officers held all the threads of power in their hands. Even the emperor, who distrusted the army, confided to his aide-de-camp that there was a "need to accommodate the urgent demands of the military to some extent in order to avoid the repetition of a tragedy of this kind."[156]

The Tōseiha staff officers did not lose even one moment in their quest for power. The US ambassador, Joseph Grew, rightly guessed that the new prime minister, Hirota Kōki, would have to "play ball with the army to a certain extent," but Hirota's capitulation to the army went much further than Grew had anticipated.[157] The army leaders hinted to the government that in order to prevent future rebellions such as the February Incident, they should be more receptive to military demands.[158] Immediately after the incident, Hirota reinstated the rule of active duty, thus giving the army the power to overthrow civilian cabinets through the withdrawal of the army minister. That was far from being his only concession. During the formation of the cabinet, Hirota also capitulated to military vetoes on ministers deemed too "liberal" and significantly raised the army's budget.

Later in 1936, midlevel officers led by Colonel Mutō Akira, and the intelligence specialist Doihara Kenji instigated a "Mongolian independence movement," reenacting the Manchurian Incident of 1931.[159] Ishihara Kanji, the architect of the previous incident and now the operations chief at the General Staff, tried to stop the new encroachment. In a rare display of awareness of historical irony, he was told by Mutō, his direct subordinate, that "my current behavior is similar to yours during the Manchurian Incident. I am surprised to hear such things from you now."[160]

Following the process delineated throughout this book, the army became simultaneously stronger and weaker—powerful as an institution within the state, but devoid of any ability to control its own junior officers. The severe repression of the February Incident was indeed effective in curbing violent disobedience, but it did nothing to restrain the tendency of officers to act independently in the field in defiance of higher authorities.

In 1937, Army Minister Terauchi Hisaichi, was insulted by a Diet member and asked the prime minister to dissolve the Lower House. When Hirota refused, Terauchi used the rule of active duty to overthrow the cabinet. In the Taishō political crisis, the army overthrew a cabinet over what it had seen as a matter of cardinal importance. Now, this bloodless coup d'état was repeated at the whim of an insulted general. Military dominance over the country, facing no real competition, became arbitrary in the extreme.[161]

Andrew Levidis, a historian from Cambridge University, has recently found new documents, including neglected private diaries, indicating that the fear of military resistance played a large part in the decision of the government and the General Staff to extend the second Sino-Japanese War. When war broke out after the Marco Polo Incident of July 7, 1937, the government and the General Staff took up several measures that escalated the conflict, including bringing reinforcements to the Shanghai front and refusing to negotiate with the Chinese Nationalist government. This decision, according to Levidis's findings, was motivated in part by the fear of Tōseiha officers in the General Staff, that if the war with China ended too early, disgruntled Kōdōha officers would use their operational discretion to transfer military units to the north and provoke a war with the Soviet Union. As the General Staff believed that Japan was not ready to fight with the Soviet Union, the extension of the war in China was seen as the lesser of two evils.[162]

The specter of military resistance was therefore a constant cloud hovering over the ruling elites and radicalizing foreign policy. Even when there was no actual resistance, it was always a possibility that policymakers had to take into account, as evidenced in their decision to extend the war in China in order to avoid an unauthorized attack on the Soviet Union. However, as so often before, the Japanese leaders could not control the genie they unleashed from the bottle. As the Imperial Army failed to reach clear victory in China, the conflict dragged on, and finally pushed Japan to a disastrous world war with the United States. Japan ended this war as an occupied and impoverished country, its army gone and its empire dismantled. Japanese military resistance, which was intended to serve the army and the empire, finally brought both to an ignominious end.

THE DREADFUL AND THE TRIVIAL

> The author has often observed that in the genesis of great events, men generally possess no inkling of what their actions portend. This problem is not, as one might suppose, a result of men's blindness to the consequences of their actions. Rather it is a result of the mad way the dreadful turns on the trivial when the ends of one man cross the ends of another. . . . In the prosecution of competing human interests, the result is always unknown, and all too often terrifying.
>
> —Scott Baker, *The Prince of Nothing*

This book has established that a culture of insubordination, an ideological pattern of rebellion and resistance, was a constant feature of Japanese military life from the Meiji Restoration onward. Having its roots in the shishi culture of the late Tokugawa period, it migrated into the Meiji era, bloomed in the 1870s, and exploded during the Satsuma Rebellion of 1877. The cures applied by the founders of the Imperial Army, most of all Yamagata Aritomo, solved the problem in the short run, but eventually allowed it to perpetuate in different forms. The culture of insubordination was not extinguished. Rather, when smashed with Yamagata's hammer, it broke into two independent components, which kept on living underground.

The first was elite resistance to state policy, gradually developed through the supreme prerogative ideology. The second, preserved among civilian groups such as the sōshi and adventurers in Korea and Manchuria, as well as patriotic societies in mainland Japan, was the shishi tradition of the mixed gangs. The sōshi espoused an anarchic lifestyle, direct action, and reckless violence in loose, chaotic organizations. For a long time, they were not able to gather enough power to pose a significant risk to the government in Japan, but Korea was another story. In 1895, during the assassination of Queen Min, elite resistance from above and shishi-style resistance from below converged through the cooperation of General Miura and the Seoul sōshi. From that year, through the process of involution, shishi culture slowly crept back from civilian nationalist groupings into the officer corps. While the Taishō political crisis of 1912 was still a pure manifestation of

elite insubordination, the assassination of Zhang Zuolin had a larger shishi component to it, exemplified through Kōmoto's chaotic behavior and his cooperation with the China adventurers. Ironically, the organizational code of the mixed
gangs, imitated again and again by nationalist civilians and officers, was a certain
safety valve for the government. As long as disobedient officers and civilians were
not able to overcome the loose organizational tradition of the shishi, the chance
for methodically organized coups d'état was relatively slim.

And yet, in 1931, the Sakura-kai had tried to do just that. Hashimoto, Chō and
their colleagues attempted to organize conspiratorial groups in a structure akin
to the interdomainal alliance of the late 1860s. They failed, but the increasing tendency of insubordinate officers to organize themselves in competing armywide
alliances boded poorly for the future. In that respect, the two conspiracies of the
Sakura-kai, the March and October incidents, were a turning point. For the first
time since 1877, resistance to state policy escalated into rebellion. That opened
up a violent period of frequent coups, which led up to the outbreak of February
26, 1936. Notwithstanding its severity, this abortive coup demonstrated the limits
of the army's culture of insubordination, as the young officers were too hesitant
and overwhelmed by the military hierarchy to fully implement their radical and
rebellious ideology. After the failure of their plot, the army reacted toughly to
curb its culture of insubordination. Notwithstanding the hesitant behavior of the
young officers when faced with the Supreme Military Council, the act of mobilizing rank-and-file troops to kill the emperor's closest advisors was crossing the
line. The young officers and many of their Kōdōha allies were either executed,
imprisoned, or shown the way out of the army.

But the General Staff, now under uncontested Tōseiha control, was able to use
the events to the army's advantage.[1] The rule of active duty, abolished by Prime
Minister Yamamoto in 1913, was restored, allowing the army to overthrow cabinets again by refusing to appoint a minister. These powers were not merely on
paper: the army leaders used them almost immediately to overthrow Prime Minister Hirota Kōki and to prevent the formation of another cabinet by General Ugaki,
unpopular because of the structural reforms he had led in 1925 and his ambiguous
role in the March Incident. Ugaki, who tried to appeal to the emperor to let him
take the role of army minister, or order a general to accept the appointment by
imperial command, was blocked by court officials. The army, said the lord keeper
of the privy seal, was too strong, and any cabinet opposed by the generals was
doomed from the outset. Ugaki gave up and resigned.[2] Gradually, the power of the
army in successive cabinets increased, and as before, officers led Japanese forces far
deeper into China in defiance of their superiors, civilian and military alike.

The appointment of General Tōjō Hideki to the premiership in 1941 might
be seen as a final attempt to control the army by merging it with the government.

This endeavor proved successful in a certain way, as Tōjō controlled the army as no leader had before, but even then military resistance was not halted.[3] On the eve of the Pearl Harbor attack, for example, two army majors delayed the transmission of a personal appeal for peace from President Roosevelt to Emperor Hirohito, intentionally hiding information from their sovereign in order to ensure that war broke out. This act probably lacked strategic significance, and yet it shows the extent to which military resistance lived on even in 1941.[4] Along with Prime Minister Tōjō, the army and navy led Japan into the Pacific War and finally to the disintegration of the empire which had been built since 1895.

There is an ongoing controversy, quite difficult to solve, about the role of military insubordination in this tragedy. During the Pacific War, the British journalist Hugh Byas, who lived in Japan for many years as a correspondent, published an influential book titled *Government by Assassination*. In his vivid account, Byas argued that the military assassins and their allies from the patriotic societies effectively ruled Japan during the 1930s, pushing timid and cowardly civilian cabinets onto the path of internal dictatorship and international aggression. "The army," wrote Byas, "installed itself in power with the concurrence of a docile nation intoxicated by foreign war, its civilian leaders terrorized by assassination."[5] Some Japanese scholars supported this view. Tanaka Azusa, for example, wrote that the "incidents" engineered by the army manipulated the course of Shōwa history up to the Pacific War.[6]

Other scholars, however, have been more doubtful. James Crowley, a representative of the so-called "realist approach" to international relations, strongly argued that the impact of rebellious officers on national policy was minimal. According to Crowley the assassinations did not significantly influence Japan's foreign policy, which was largely developed in the cabinet and other responsible agencies through legal means. In view of this fact, Crowley concluded that the military rebellions of the 1930s, dangerous as they were to individual Japanese leaders, produced more bark than bite.[7]

However, Crowley had a significant blind spot: he failed to see that foreign policy, indeed, policy in general, is never a linear process. At any given point in time, statesmen are subject to contradictory pressures from multiple quarters, forcing them to decide between different alternatives and to change their plans or compromise. In Japan, just like in any other country, pressures came both from within and without. For example, the Tanaka cabinet was worried about British and American pressure when fishing in Manchuria's troubled waters in the late 1920s. In a world without military insubordination, Japanese statesmen could have responded to similar pressures to degrees which differed according to their perception of the national interest.

But, unfortunately, military insubordination significantly reduced the maneuvering space of the government in the face of external pressure. The variety of blackmail tools available to the army, from the withdrawal of service ministers (dangerous for any cabinet even after the demise of the active duty rule), to independent defiant action, assassinations, and coups d'état, precluded potential compromises with the Westerners and the Chinese. Prime Minister Tanaka Giichi learned this lesson when his attempts to subdue Zhang Zuolin by political means were destroyed by Kōmoto Daisaku's independent action. Shidehara and Wakatsuki had undergone a similar experience during the Manchurian Incident, and Inukai Tsuyoshi's attempt to reach some kind of modus vivendi with China on the Manchurian question had cost him his life during the coup of May 1932. In summer 1937, even the fear of military resistance was adequate to distort decision making, pushing the government and the General Staff to extend the war with China in order to avoid a provoked, unauthorized war with the Soviet Union.[8]

In other words, given the context of rebellion and resistance, it is inadequate to consider, as Crowley does, what Japanese statesmen did in practice. It is equally essential to check what they could not do as a result of military insubordination, and which options were unavailable to them because of military pressure. The army, in this sense, was akin to a shepherd dog running around a herd of sheep and frightening them into going in one direction only. The sheep may or may not have wanted to go elsewhere. In any case, they could not, at least not without exposing themselves to sharp teeth. In the case of Japan, that road led to bitter confrontation with China and finally to a disastrous world war.

But it is also important to note that military insubordination, which led to such disastrous consequences, was far from being the result of a well-planned conspiracy. The process leading to military independence, a country in which "the tail wags the dog," was also not a result of malice, stupidity, or negligence on the part of statesmen, politicians, generals, and bureaucrats. Each leg of this disastrous journey, each policy decision pushing Japan one further mile down the road, was reasonable and understandable in and of itself.

The decision of Saigō Tsugumichi to resist the government's decree in the Taiwan Expedition of 1874 was born out of momentary pressures, not out of malice or an intention to disobey. It was perfectly reasonable for his brother, Saigō Takamori, to rebel in 1877, believing that the government had attempted to assassinate him. Yamagata's response to the events of the time, by conducting the military reforms and building the supreme prerogative system in the 1880s, was a rational countermeasure to prevent the reoccurrence of such rebellions. The decision of Miura and his advisors to assassinate Queen Min was atrocious, indeed, but not out of tune with the political pressures of the time. The Taishō political crisis was also a result of decisions by different political actors, each of them taking care of his own particular interests and none of them planning the final result. Kōmoto's decision to assassinate Zhang Zuolin was based on an already established tradition of supreme prerogative ideology and operational discretion, which endowed resistance with an air of legitimacy in military circles. If senior generals could interfere in politics, and junior officers were allowed to take tactical decisions in the field, it was not unreasonable for Kōmoto to take an independent strategic decision in order to solve the quagmire of the Japanese Empire in Manchuria. And when violence against Chinese leaders could not break the impasse, it took just one small step to use the same ideology to justify violence against Japanese leaders, as the Sakura-kai and the February 1936 rebels had done. It was also reasonable, as far as the General Staff was concerned, to extend the war in China as the lesser of two evils, given the fear of a much more dangerous war with the Soviet Union. Of course, the people responsible for these events could have decided differently. Almost nothing was inevitable. But at no time were their decisions insane or out of tune with the realities they faced.

And yet, despite the fact that each step made a certain amount of sense in and of itself, *all of them together* led to a disastrous result, unimaginable by the people who began the journey. Decisions taken in a certain time and place may lead to altogether different consequences in future years when combined with changing political, military, and social circumstances; different contingencies; and unforeseen decisions of other actors. What Japan lacked, therefore, was not reasonable civilian and military leaders. Its leaders were quite reasonable, in any sense, no less than those of other countries. Instead, it lacked leaders with exceptional foresight—people who could see beyond the immediate, the reasonable, the calculable, and grasp the direction of history. Men who could, in Bismarck's catchphrase, discern the movement of God in history and grasp his coat while He is passing by. But such people are rare indeed, in Japan as in most other countries.

Nothing was predetermined, but still, Japanese insubordination moved in a certain direction. To understand why it ended where it did, the logic of the movement has to be deciphered. And this logic, as explained hereafter, is strongly related to three "bugs" programmed into the political and ideological code of Japan during the Meiji Restoration. All of the three, taken together, allowed the Imperial Army's culture of rebellion and resistance to grow, prosper, and radicalize with the passing years.

The First Bug: Hazy Legitimacy

Political legitimacy may be defined as the ability of a regime to ensure obedience by most people, most of the time, without recourse to coercive means. At root, that is mainly a matter of resources. No regime in the world has enough power to apply constant coercion on everyone. Like a bank, a regime is able to "pay" in the currency of violence to some people. But when too many people have to be "paid," the bank goes bankrupt, and so does the state. Seen in this light, political legitimacy rests on two pillars: intimidation and ideology.[9] Even subjects who dislike the regime may obey most of the time with no need for coercion, because they are afraid of potential sanctions. And yet, especially in modern regimes, this is a necessary but not an adequate condition. Governments usually try to convince most citizens to obey out of their own free will, through multiple ideological agents such as the press, state officials, progovernment social groups, and above all, the education system. In almost any modern state, and Imperial Japan was no exception, political legitimacy rests on the twin pillars of intimidation and ideology.

The new Meiji regime, established after the restoration in 1868, had to rebuild political legitimacy from the ground up, after the demise of the preceding Tokugawa order. As soon as the new leaders took power, they made great efforts to legitimize their new system through intimidation and ideology alike, and were reasonably successful on both counts. By the end of Saigō's rebellion, the military prowess of the regime had been proved beyond reasonable doubt. And, as for ideology, the government also had significant achievements. At least as late as the turn of the century, the vast majority of Japanese had willingly, and sometimes enthusiastically, accepted the centrality and the authority of the emperor, as well as the need of the country to have a strong army, sound economy, and full equality with the great powers of the world. For many people—especially in the army—military prowess was also understood as territorial expansion on the continent. That does not mean that Japan, even if we put aside dissenters, was a monolithic society without debates. The opposite was the case. But imperial patriotism, in the sense of the vision of national power exercised on the continent, was accepted by most Japanese citizens.[10] In that sense, the Meiji regime's ideological quest was a profound success.

And yet, this otherwise immaculate ideological code had a crucial bug programmed into its basic edifice. The oligarchs who had actual, extraconstitutional power in Meiji Japan, the leaders of the interdomainal alliance and their protégées, were never able to ideologically legitimize their own power. In a sense, they did not even try, because that would have undermined the official, absolute authority of the throne. After 1878, they were able to solidify their rule by force of intimidation and clever political compromises, but not through binding legitimacy. In the absence of binding traditions and sophisticated ideological justifications, most components of the government, apart from the emperor, were challenged by rebellious actors at different stages. Why should one obey the genrō? Does the prime minister have power over the army? Should civilian politicians be allowed to exercise majority rule through the Imperial Diet? The hazy, hidden nature of the emperor's power made all of these problems subject to constant negotiations, whose results always, inevitably, left some people unhappy.

These unhappy people, who felt marginalized, exploited, or betrayed by the system, came from many quarters. One group, disgruntled officers of both high and low rank, have been the subject of this book. From 1878 to 1931 they could no longer hope for a successful rebellion, which the government had blocked by way of intimidation. They could also not resist the imperial regime in toto—that road was blocked by state ideology, shared even by those disgruntled soldiers. And yet, the "bug" programmed into the ideological edifice of the regime had left them one main venue to express their frustration, the process we have named "escape to the front": to honor the emperor by striving for territorial expansion, faster, better, and more decisively than the inadequately legitimized government.

Theoretically speaking, this patriotic opposition did not have to amount to international aggression. Lieutenant General Tani Kanjō, hero of the Taiwan Expedition and the Satsuma Rebellion, attacked the imperialistic policy of the government, as he believed that a small Japan would serve the emperor and the nation better. But Tani was a lonely figure in the army, "a flower in a field of grass."[11] Unfortunately, oppositional patriotism was more often expressed by charging ahead against orders to further territorial expansion. This fact was related to a second crucial bug in the political code of modern Japan.

The Second Bug: Territorial Expansion As a One-way Street

Leaving aside outliers such as Lieutenant General Tani, the official state ideology was interpreted in the armed forces, among the ruling elites, and by large segments of the public as national growth, both in the territorial and the financial sense of the term. The costs and the pace were often disputed, but the direction much more rarely so. Spatially speaking, territorial expansion was a one-way street. If the universally accepted ideology was constant growth, it made no sense to reverse achievements once made, even if the fruits of victory were obtained by defiant officers in violation of Japanese law. As shown in both the Queen Min and the Zhang Zuolin affairs, it was also difficult to punish such officers, defiant as they were, because in essence they were advancing along the same road as the government. Misguided they may have been, but their "pure" motives had always evoked the compassion of leaders who sympathized with their goals, if not their means. That was one of the most enduring, and disastrous, legacies of late Tokugawa shishi culture.

In such conditions, the one-way nature of territorial expansion encouraged officers to express their opposition to the government in the form of aggression against other countries and gave them the assurance that their achievements would never be reversed. That feeling of legal impunity and vindication by history, which naturally increased with every failure of the army or the government to punish overt and covert resistance to their orders, created strong optimism in people's ability to change reality through insubordination.[12] And such optimism, as we have seen, had been the fuel of military resistance from the 1870s to the Sakura-kai.

The Third Bug: Territorial Expansion As an Endless Road

What made this rebellious optimism an enduring phenomenon, however, was yet another fatal bug programmed into the ideological code of the imperial Japanese regime. Territorial expansion was not only a one-way road, but an endless one. Unfortunately for Japan, this ideological vision was dangerously vague. When could one know, for example, that the army was strong enough? For military officers, both during the Taishō political crisis and the late 1920s, always wanted more divisions, more funds, and more political influence. How big should the empire have been? Would Korea, Taiwan, and Manchuria suffice, or was further expansion into China required to safeguard the territorial achievements already made? There was no way to know, no objective standard, no agreed-upon measure to ascertain when Japan's destiny was fulfilled, its mission complete. No matter what the government did, no matter how much territory was won, the vague nature of Japanese imperialism had always left much to be desired, and the ideological thirst of civilian and military radicals could never be quenched.

This constant discontent was significantly radicalized in the late 1920s, as the internal situation in Japan increasingly became an additional source of frustration. As Banno Junji noted in his study of the Taishō political crisis, Japanese imperialism suffered from an unsolvable contradiction: Japan, as a country poor in resources, lacked the means to keep a large enough army to maintain the country's dream of being a first-rate empire.[13] Officers such as Hashimoto Kingorō and the rebels of February 1936 were worried both about the poverty in Japan and the slow pace of territorial expansion. Their goal, to create an economically prosperous country with an ever-expanding army and endless military expenditure, could never be met. Therefore, no matter what happened, they were bound to be frustrated.

The ideology of right-wing thinkers such as Ōkawa Shūmei and Kita Ikki enjoyed increasing currency in rebellious military circles from the late 1920s. That made things even worse, as it added a whole new Utopian dimension to the already confused vision of these officers. The dream to fix the entire gamut of military, social, and ideological problems through a "Showa Restoration" was yet again a push toward an unattainable Utopia. Naturally, no one knew how to build such a regime. It was therefore unsurprising that the rebels of February 1936 mainly shrugged their shoulders with indifference when they learned, before being shot, that the army's position was strengthened by their acts. Shibugawa Zensuke implored the nation not to trust the army. Suematsu Tahei, one of the few survivors, wrote in disdain that the army had merely used external aggression to divert attention from Japan's internal problems, even though his friends shot the finance minister who attempted to curb military expansionism abroad.[14] "We did not draw our swords," wrote Muranaka Kōji, "to secure a bigger military budget or to enhance the position of the army. We did it for the sake of the poor farmers, for the sake of Japan, and for the sake of the world."[15] With such ambiguous goals, it was no wonder that Muranaka could not be satisfied. He himself hardly knew what he wanted.

Summing up, the disastrous reality evolved as a result of bugs in the political and ideological edifice of modern Japan. The first bug encouraged disgruntled military elements to express their frustration in perilous ways. The second endowed them with optimism and vindication. The third ensured that they would never be satisfied. And the government or the army leadership could do nothing to appease these constantly frustrated dreamers. Nothing but giving way or fighting back, and that was increasingly difficult as time wore on. The moderate Japanese politicians gave way, in a series of compromises leading them all the way to Manchuria, the Marco Polo Bridge, Nanjing, Pearl Harbor, Saipan, Okinawa, Hiroshima, and Nagasaki. And when they realized in which direction Japan was heading, it was already too late to do anything about it.

Abbreviations

AVPRF	Arhiv Vneshneii Politiki Rossiskei Federatsii (Archive of Foreign Policy of the Russian Federation)
AVPRI	Arhiv Vneshnei Politiki Rossiskoi Imperi (Archive of Foreign Policy of the Russian Empire)
BNA	British National Archives
CKS	*Chōsen Kōshō Shiryō*
CMJP-NAA	China-Manchuria-Japanese Policy, National Archives of Australia
DC-NDL	Digitized Contents: National Diet Library
DES	*A Diplomat in Japan: Diaries of Ernest Satow*
DKN	*Den Kenjirō Nikki*
DKT	*Diary of Kido Takayoshi*
DNGB	*Dai Nihon Gaikō Bunsho*
DSZ	*Dai Saigō Zenshū*
GKSS	*Kindai Nihon Guntai Kyōiku Shiryō Shūsei*
HBDZ	*Heben Dazuo yu Rijun Shanxi "Can Liu"*
HBT	*Hōki Bunrui Taizen*
HSTN	*Hogohiroi: Sasaki Takayuki Nikki*
HTN	*Hara Takashi Nikki*
HULL	Harvard University Lamont Library
IKJ	*Iwakura-Kō Jikki*
IKKM	*Inoue Kaoru Kankei Monjo*
IMTFE	*International Military Tribunal for the Far East Record of Proceedings*
IMTFE-CJEJ	*Court Papers, Journals, Exhibits, and Judgments of the International Military Tribunal for the Far East*
ITKM	*Iwakura Tomomi Kankei Monjo*
JACAR	Japan Center for Asian Historical Record
JANA	Japanese Army and Navy Archives, Library of Congress, Washington DC
KAR	*Korean American Relations*
KBTK	*Kuichigai Bōto Takechi Kumakichi hoka hachi-nin wa Tekiritsu Ukagai*
KNGKSS	*Kindai Nihon Guntai Kyōiku Shiryō Shūsei*
KKN	*Kido Kōichi Nikki*
KKS	*Kagoshima Ken Shi*
KKTD	*Kōshaku Katsura Tarō Den*
KSS	*Kagoshima Seitō Shimatsu*
KTHS	*Katsura Tarō hatsu Shokanshū*
KTKB	*Katsura Tarō Kankei Bunsho* (book form; see bibliography)
KTKM	*Katsura Tarō Kankei Monjo*, original papers, National Diet Library
KTM	*Kido Takayoshi Monjo*
KYAD	*Kōshaku Yamagata Aritomo Den*
LNA-UNOG	League of Nations Archive, Office of the United Nations at Geneva
MBZ	*Meiji Bunka Zenshū*
MGKM	*Miura Gorō Kankei Monjo*

MJPH-NDL	Modern Japanese Political History Materials Reading Room, National Diet Library, Tokyo
MNN	*Makino Nobuaki Nikki*
MT	*Meiji Tennō Ki*
NA-JP	National Archives of Japan
NBHM	*Nakno Bunkō Hōrei Mokuji*
NGB	*Nihon Gaikō Bunsho*
NIDS	National Institute for Defense Studies (Bōeishō Bōei Kenkyūjo)
NKGS	*Nikan Gaikō Shiryō*
NRJ	*Niniroku Jiken*
NRJH	*Niniroku Jiken Hiroku*
NRJKS	*Niniroku Jiken Kenkyū Shiryō*
NRJSK	*Niniroku Jiken Saiban Kiroku*
NSSS-M	*Nihon Seiji Saiban Shiroku*
OHKM	*Ogawa Heikichi Kankei Monjo*
OM	*Ōkuma Monjo*
OSKM	*Ōkuma Shigenobu Kankei Monjo*
OTM	*Ōkubo Toshimichi Monjo*
OTN	*Ōkubo Toshimichi Nikki*
RBOMR-NDL	Rare Books and Materials Reading Room—National Diet Library
RES	*Rikugunshō Enkaku Shi*
RC-ARTIC	Martin A. Ryerson Collection, Art Institute of Chicago
RIK	*Rossiia i Koreia*
SEDS	*Shibusawa Eiichi Denki Shiryō*
SGSS	*Saga Seitō Senki*
SHM	*Saionji-Harada Memoirs*
SHRS	*Sanbō Honbu Rekishi Sōan*
SIKD	*Segai Inoue-Kō Den*
SKTD	*Shōkiku Kido Takayoshi Den*
SOJT	*Sources of Japanese Tradition*
SOJT-B	*Sources of Japanese Tradition*, 2nd ed.
SNKD	*Sainan Kiden*
SPSS	*Shimpen Seinan Senshi*
SRKM	*Sakamoto Ryōma Kankei Monjo*
SSK	*Seisei Senki Kō*
SSKN	*Sanjō Sanetomi-Kō Nenpu*
SSMD	*Shishaku Saitō Makoto Den*
SSN	*Saga Sanenaru Nikki*
SSS	*Saga Seitō Shimatsu*
STD	*Shōwa Tennō Dokuhakuroku*
STDS	*Suzuki Teiichi-shi Danwa Sokkiroku*
STKS	*Saigō Totoku to Kabayama Sōtoku*
STZ	*Saigō Takamori Zenshū*
TGD	*Tanaka Giichi Denki*
TJDH	*Japan Daily Herald*
TKI	*Tani Kanjō Ikō*
TKR	*The Korean Repository*
TMJS	*Tairo Mizuno Jun Sensei*
TMKM	*Terauchi Masatake Kankei Monjo*
TMN	*Terauchi Masatake Nikki*
TSSK	*Tōa Senkaku Shishi Kiden*

TSS-KKJC	*Tokyo Saiban Shiryō Kido Kōichi Jinmon Chōsho*
TTN	*Takarabe Takeshi Nikki*
TYKD	*Tokugawa Yoshinobu-Kō Den*
TWCT-DE	*Tokyo War Crimes Trial: A Digital Exhibition*
UKN	*Ugaki Kazushige Nikki*
US IAJ	US State Department, records related to the Internal Affairs of Japan
YAIK	*Yamagata Aritomo Ikensho*
YAKM	*Yamagata Aritomo Kankei Monjo*
YJKB	Yasukuni Jinja Kaikō Bunkō, Yasukuni Shrine Archives
YKD	*Yuri Kimimasa Den*
ZSK	*Zuihitsu Saionji-kō*

Notes

In the notes, dates are given in the following format: day.month.year (e.g., 22.10.1860).

INTRODUCTION

1. John Dower, *War without Mercy: Race and Power in the Pacific War* (New York: Pantheon Books, 1986, 84).

2. Theodore Wm. De Bary, Gluck Carol, and Arthur E. Tiedermann, eds. *Sources of Japanese Tradition* (2nd ed., New York: Columbia University Press, 2005), 2:705–7. The Japanese original is reproduced in Yui Masaomi, Fujiwara Akira, and Yoshida Yutaka, eds., *Guntai Heishi*, vol. 4, *Nihon Kindai Shishō Taikei* (Tokyo: Iwanami Shoten, 1989), 172–76.

3. See, for example, Ernst L. Presseisen, *Before Aggression: Europeans Prepare the Japanese Army* (Tuscon: University of Arizona Press, 1965), 147.

4. *Rikugun Keihō* (1881), digitized content, National Diet Library, articles 50, 110, http://dl.ndl.go.jp/info:ndljp/pid/794418.

5. Craig M. Cameron, "Race and Identity: The Culture of Combat in the Pacific War," *International History Review* 27, no. 3 (September 2005): 560.

6. Hugh Byas, *Government by Assassination* (New York: Knopf, 1942), 39.

7. Ben Amy Shillony, *Revolt in Japan: The Young Officers and the February 26, 1936 Incident* (Princeton: Princeton University Press, 1973); Sadako Ogata, *Defiance in Manchuria: The Making of Japanese Foreign Policy, 1931–1932* (Berkeley: University of California Press, 1964); Richard Storry, *The Double Patriots: A Study of Japanese Nationalism* (Boston: Houghton Mifflin, 1957); Yale Maxon, *Control of Japanese Foreign Policy: A Study of Civil-Military Rivalry, 1930–1945* (Westport, CT: Greenwood Press, 1973); James B. Crowley, *Japan's Quest for Autonomy: National Security and Foreign Policy, 1930–1938* (Princeton: Princeton University Press, 1966).

8. Fujii Hisashi, *Niniroku Teito Heiran: gunjiteki Shiten kara zenmenteki ni minaosu* (Tokyo: Sōshisha, 2010), 131.

9. David A. Sneider, "Action and Oratory: The Trials of the May 15th Incident of 1932," *Law in Japan* 23, no. 67 (1990): 51–53, 62; Richard Storry, *Double Patriots*, 4.

10. Tobe Ryōichi, "Minshūka no Shiten to Seiji no Henchō—1930 Nendai no Nihon Seiji," keynote address, Modern Japan History Workshop, University of Pennsylvania, Philadelphia, PA, October 18, 2014.

11. Ian Kershaw, *Hitler: A Biography* (New York: W. W. Norton, 2010), 320–58; Marc Ferro, *Nicholas II: Last of the Tsars* (New York: Oxford University Press, 1993), 2; D. P. G Hoffmann, "Kommandogewalt und Kriegsminister," *Zeitschrift für die gesamte Staatswissenschaft /Journal of Institutional and Theoretical Economics* 68, no. 4 (1921): 740–49.

12. Tom Coffman, *Nation Within: The History of the American Occupation of Hawaii* (Kihei, HI: Koa Books, 2009), 109–45.

1. WARRIORS OF HIGH ASPIRATIONS

1. Hashimoto Kingorō, *Hashimoto Taisa no Shuki*, Nakano Masao, ed. (Tokyo: Misuzu Shobō, 1963), 21.

2. "Chō Isamu Shuki," in Ōtani Keijirō, *Rakujitsu no Joshō: Shōwa Rikugunshi* (Tokyo: Yagumo Shoten, 1959), 45.

3. The term *Bakufu* was coined by a small group of nativist scholars in the nineteenth century, and was mainly used as a pejorative by the Shogunate's rivals. It was later picked up and used by many historians of the period. We use it here as a matter of continuity with previous literature.

4. Ronald Toby, *State and Diplomacy in Early Modern Japan: Asia in the Development of the Tokugawa Bakufu* (Stanford, CA: Stanford University Press, 1991), 235–46.

5. Nomura Shinsaku, "Bakumatsu no Goshinpei Secchi ni tai suru Chōshū Han no Kiyo," *Yamaguchi-ken Chihōshi Kenkyū* 110 (October 2010): 32–40.

6. Yamaga Sokō, "The Way of the Samurai," *Sources of Japanese Tradition*, ed. Wm. Theodor de Bary, Carol Gluck and Arthur E. Tiedemann (New York: University of Columbia Press, 2005), 2:662–4 (hereafter cited as *SOJT*).

7. David L. Howell, *Geographies of Identity in Nineteenth Century Japan* (Berkeley: University of California Press, 2005), 24–25.

8. Matsuo Masahito, *Kido Takayoshi* (Tokyo: Yoshikawa Kōbunkan, 2007), 4. Colin Jaunndrill's study of military modernization at the late Tokugawa period has shown the importance of musketry studies in the transitions of the period, but it seems that this specific kind of study did not involve much interdomainal socializing, if at all. See D. Colin Jaundrill, *Samurai to Soldier: Remaking Military Service in Nineteenth-Century Japan* (Ithaca: Cornell University Press, 2016).

9. Cameron Hurst III, *Armed Martial Arts of Japan: Swordsmanship and Archery* (New Haven: Yale University Press, 1998), 83–90; Rainier Hesselnik, "The Assassination of Henry Heusken," *Monumenta Nipponica* 49, no. 3 (autumn 1994): 340; Jansen, *Sakamoto Ryōma and the Meiji Restoration* (Princeton N.J.: Princeton University Press, 1961), 49, 81–89, 115.

10. For a survey of current research in this subject see Chōnan Shinji, "Bunkyūki ni okeru 'Shoshi Ōgi' to Sōmō," *Kokushikan Shigaku* 12 (March 2008): 36–37. An interesting example of the way in which school connections were utilized for rebellious purposes is the case of Orita Toshihide, a Satsuma Samurai retainer and a loyalist. Orita was an expert in fortification science, who, like many other people with useful knowledge, traveled around the realm and taught his field of expertise. Therefore, he had numerous pupils, and every domain, in a sense, was a private interdomainal network which he used to gather intelligence in and around the time of the struggle against the Bakufu in 1868. In this case, a teacher-student network with an interdomainal character was crucial to the war effort as a whole. See Iechika Yoshiki, *Saigō Takamori to Bakumatsu Ishin no Seikyoku* (Kyoto: Mineruva Shobō, 2011), 313, as well as *Orita Toshihide Nikki* in *Tadayoshi-Kō Shiryō*, 7 vols., ed. Kagoshima Ken, Ishin Shiryō, and Hensan Shohen (Kagoshima: Kagoshima Ken, 1974–80), 4:544–55.

11. Donald Keene, *Emperor of Japan: Meiji and his World, 1852–1912* (New York: Columbia University Press, 2002), 39.

12. Erik H. Erikson, *Insight and Responsibility: Lectures on the Ethical Implications of psychoanalytic Insight* (New York: W. W. Norton, 1964), 93.

13. Hesselnik, "Assassination of Henry Heusken," 334.

14. Thomas Huber, *The Revolutionary Origins of Modern Japan* (Stanford, CA: Stanford University Press, 1981), 130; Jansen, *Sakamoto*, 85–86. According to Jansen, some of these students of lower samurai status did not receive boarding at their domain's compound, making it more difficult for domainal authority to monitor their behavior.

15. For theoretical background on the formation of networks of dissent through prior social ties, see, David Knoke, *Political Networks: The Structural Perspective* (Cambridge: Cambridge University Press, 1990), 68.

16. Haga Noboru, *Bakumatsu Shishi no Sekai* (Tokyo: Yūzankaku, 2003), 233–38.

17. Tōta Mitsuhiro, "Tosa Kinnōtō," *Jinbutsu Ōrai Rekishi Dokuhon* 56, no. 6 (June 2011): 86–87. According to Tōta (87), there were 192 sworn members in this party, joined by a larger periphery.

18. Chōnan, "Bunkyūki," 36–69, 37–38.

19. Chōnan, "Bunkyūki," 36; Haga, *Shishi no Sekai*, 21.

20. Yamakawa Hiroshi, *Kyoto Shugoshoku Shimatsu: Kyū-Aizu Rōshin no Shuki*, 2 vols., trans. Kaneko Mitsuharu (Tokyo: Heibonsha, 1965–66), 1:4–5; Keene, *Emperor*, 42–45; Takagi Shunsuke, *Sorekara no Shishi: mō Hitotsu no Meiji Ishin* (Tokyo: Yūhikaku, 1985), 5.

21. The translation from classical Chinese is my own. I decided not to use one of the available excellent translations of the *Analects*, which usually try, legitimately, to translate the term *zhi-shi* in tandem with ancient Chinese meanings or later Chinese Confucian interpretations. Thus often they choose such translations as "gentleman," "earnest officer," or "scholar," which do not fully reflect the particular function of this term in late Tokugawa warrior culture.

22. Haga, *Shishi no Sekai*, 33; Sasaki Suguru, *Shishi to Kanryō: Meiji Shonen no Jōkei* (Kyoto: Mineruva Shobō, 1984), 111; Takagi, *Sorekara*, 2.

23. For more detail on the origins of the term and its usage see Kojima Tsuyoshi, "Chūgoku umare no Shishiteki Shisō," *Jinbutsu Ōrai Rekishi Dokuhon* 56, no. 6 (June 2011): 134–39. See also Sasaki, *Shishi to Kanryō*, 122–23. See also Haga, *Shishi no Sekai*, 233–34; Jansen, *Sakamoto*, 40, 95–96.

24. Nishijima Ryōsaburō, *Nakayama Tadamitsu Ansatsu Shimatsu* (Tokyo: Shinjibutsu Ōraisha, 1973), 39.

25. Kawaguchi, "Shōka Sonjuku," *Jinbutsu Ōrai Rekishi Dokuhon* 56, no. 6 (June 2011): 70–71.

26. Haga, *Shishi no Seikatsu*, 22–25, 33–34; *Dai Nihon Ishin Shiryō*, 3 vols., ed. Shiryō Hensanjo (Tokyo: Tokyo Daigaku Shuppankai, 1959), 3:360–61. See also Jansen, *Sakamoto*, 146; Kido Takayoshi Den Hensanjo, ed. *Shōkiku Kido Kō Den*, 2 vols. (Tokyo: Meiji Shoin, 1927), 1:216 (hereafter cited as *SKTD*); Nishijima, *Nakayama*, 36. When the shishi finally took control of Chōshū in 1865, one of the first reforms they implemented was to end the discrimination against retainers of low rank. See Huber, *Revolutionary Origins*, 193–94.

27. Sakamoto Ryōma to his sister, 22.10.1860, *Sakamoto Ryōma Kankei Monjo*, 2 vols., ed. Nihonshi Sekkyōkai, (Tokyo: Tokyo Daigaku Shuppankai, 1967), 1:136 (hereafter cited as *SRKM*). The English translation is taken from Jansen, *Sakamoto*, 216.

28. See, for example, the description of the Satsuma shishi Imuta in *Shibayama Aijirō Nikki* (unpublished) in Dai Nihon Ishin Shiryō Kōhon, Tokyo University Historiographical Institute (Tokyo Daigaku Shiryō Hensanjo), 79–80 (hereafter cited as *SAN*); Haga, *Shishi no Sekai*, 24–25; Huber, *Revolutionary Origins*, 119.

29. See for example *SKTD*, 1:70–71; Sakamoto to his sister, 22.10.1862, *SRKM*, 1:136, 8.

30. Haga, *Shishi no Sekai*, 198–99, 214; Jansen, *Sakamoto*, 98; Ichisaka Tarō, "Sake to Shishi to Bakumatsu Sōran," *Jinbutsu Ōrai Rekishi Dokuhon* 56, no. 6 (June 2011): 178–83, 178.

31. Yamakawa *Shimatsu*, 1:49. See also Tōyama Shigeki, *Ishin Henkaku no Shosō* (Tokyo: Iwanami Shoten, 1991), 17–18.

32. Itō Seirō, "Tenchūgumi," *Jinbutsu Ōrai Rekishi Dokuhon* 56, no. 6 (June 2011): 106. See also Jansen, *Sakamoto*, 113.

33. Yamakawa, *Shimatsu*, 1:59.

34. See for example *SAN*, 79–80; Sasaki, *Shishi to Kanryō*, 236–37.

35. Harry D. Harutoonian, *Toward Restoration: The Growth of Political Consciousness in Tokugawa Japan* (Berkeley: University of California Press, 1970), 193; Jansen, *Sakamoto*, 98–99, 136; Ernest M. Satow, *A Diplomat in Japan* (Bristol: Ganesha, 1998), 71.

36. This anecdote was told by Itō Hirobumi, who insisted that he, being the only one who refrained from drinking, remembers buying a saw in order to cut the fence. The others, too dazzled by alcohol, had just forgotten it. Itō's self-glorification may be doubted, of

course, but his testimony is very telling as far as the general atmosphere is concerned. See *Itō-kō Chokuwa*, ed. Komatsu Midori (Tokyo: Chikura Shobō, 1936), 104–7. For a detailed description of the legation burning operation, see Nakahara Kunihei, *Inoue-Haku Den* (Tokyo: Tōyō Insatu Kabushiki Kaisha Insatsu, 1907), 1:195–206.

37. Harutoonian, *Toward*, 221–22. And see also Ann Walthall, *The Weak Body of a Useless Woman: Matsuo Taseko and the Meiji Restoration* (Chicago: University of Chicago Press, 1998), 183; Sasaki, *Shishi to Kanryō*, 124–25.

38. Jansen, *Sakamoto*, 136.

39. Harutoonian, *Toward*, 221–22.

40. Harutoonian, *Toward*, 218; Thomas Huber, "Men of High Purpose and the Politics of Direct Action, 1862–64," in *Conflict in Modern Japanese History: The Neglected Tradition*, ed. Tetsuo Najita and J. Victor Koschmann (Princeton: Princeton University Press, 1982), 124; Takagi, *Sorekara*, 4.

41. Jean-Francois Lyotard, *The Differend: Phrases in Dispute*, trans. Georges van den Abbeele (Minneapolis: University of Minnesota Press, 1988), 56.

42. Harutoonian, *Toward*, 232.

43. Albert M. Craig, *Chōshū in the Meiji Restoration* (Cambridge: Cambridge University Press 1961), 198. See also Takii Kazuhiro, *Itō Hirobumi: Japan's First Prime Minister and Father of the Meiji Constitution*, trans. Takechi Manabu (New York: Routledge, 2014), 10.

44. For a few examples out of many, see *SAN*, 79–80; Shimaoka Akira, *Shishitachi no Uta* (Tokyo: Shikuma Shobō, 1942), 30–31; Aoki Shūzō, *Aoki Shūzō Jiden* (Tokyo: Heibonsha, 1970), 65–66.

45. Huber, "Men," 108. See also Jansen, *Sakamoto*, 116. Chōnan Shinji's detailed study of the plots cohatched by Satsuma shishi and Kyokawa's gang is an excellent case study of such network's working mechanism. See Chōnan, "Bunkyūki," 42–55.

46. For an interesting example from Tosa, see the conversation between Takechi Zuizan and the high official of his domain, Yoshida Tōyō. According to this report, Yoshida seemed to be both arrogant and misinformed. The shishi information channels of Takechi were evidently faster and more reliable than the official channels of communications between the domains. See *Ishin Tosa Kinnō Shi*, ed. Zuizankai (Tokyo: Fuzanbō, 1912), 86–88. For a more sustained discussion and analysis of this phenomenon see Chōnan, "Bunkyūki," 59–61.

47. Sasaki, *Shishi to Kanryō*, 124–25, 234–35; Chōnan, "Bunkyūki," 36–37.

48. Chōnan, "Bunkyūki," 36. For a specific example, see the story of Imuta in *SAN*, 80, a shishi who got in trouble with his superior because of "a protest using direct speech" (*chokugen kōgi*).

49. Sasaki, *Shishi to Kanryō*, 124; Jansen, *Sakamoto*, 109; Tōta, "Tosa Kinnōtō," 87. For three examples of such oaths (the blood oath of the Chōshū *Mitategumi* and two another ones) see Haga, *Shishi no Sekai*, 228–33, as well as the text of the *Mitategumi* oath in *Itō Hirobumi Kankei Monjo*, ed. Itō Hirobumi Kankei Monjo Kenkyū Kai, (Tokyo: Hanawa Shobō, 1973–1981), 1:195–99. For further details about the code words, see Haga, *Shishi no Sekai*, 259–60.

50. J. Victor Koschmann, *The Mito Ideology: Discourse, Reform, and Insurrection in Late Tokugawa Japan, 1790–1864* (Berkeley: University of California Press, 1987), 149–52; Takii, *Itō*, 8.

51. Jansen, *Sakamoto*, 116.

52. Ibid., 81, 118.

53. Kusaka Genzui to Takechi Zuizan, 19.2.1862, *Takechi Zuizan Kankei Monjo*, 2 vols. ed. Nihonshi Sekkyōkai, (Tokyo: Nihonshi Sekkyōkai, 1916), 1:60.

54. Keene, *Emperor*, 72–73; Nishijima, *Nakayama*, 34–35. See also Huber, *Revolutionary Origins*, 118.

55. Haga, *Shishi no Sekai*, 244–45.

56. *SAN*, 81–83.

57. Rutherford Alcock, *The Capital of the Tycoon: A Narrative of Three Year's Residence in Japan*, 2 vols. (New York: Harper and Brothers, 1863), 2:47.

58. Yuval N. Harari, "Terror Ma-hu? Mi-Yemei ha-Beinayim ve-ad la-Me'a ha-Esrim ve-Ahat" [What Is Terror? From the Middle Ages to the Twenty-First Century"], *Zmanim* 108 (autumn 2009): 3.

59. Hesselnik, "Assassination of Henry Heusken," 334, 341; Haga, *Shishi no Sekai*, 243–44.

60. *SAN*, 80; Nanbu Yahachirō (Satsuma Edo commissioner) to Kagoshima, 19.6.1862, reproduced in Chōnan, "Bunkyūki," 57.

61. Yamakawa, *Shimatsu* 1:107; Walthall, *Weak*, 187, 202; Jansen, *Sakamoto*, 130–31; Huber, *Revolutionary Origins*, 118.

62. Chōnan, "Bunkyūki," 42–46.

63. Yamakawa, *Shimatsu* 1:44, 107.

64. Ibid., 1:12.

65. Huber, "Men," 109; Huber, *Revolutionary Origins*, 130–31, 162, 198; Yamakawa, *Shimatsu* 1:46–48; Walthall, *Weak*, 148–49; Nishijima, *Nakayama*, 36; Keene, *Emperor*, 67.

66. Huber, *Revolutionary Origins*, 117.

67. Ibid; *SKTD*, 1:216–17, 226; Walthall, *Weak*, 177–78; Haga, *Shishi no Sekai*, 257–58; Kanbashi Norimasa, *Shimazu Hisamitsu to Meiji Ishin: Hisamitsu wa naze, Tōbaku o ketsuishita ka* (Tokyo: Shinjinbutsu Ōraisha, 2002), 119.

68. Yamakawa, *Shimatsu* 1:12. And compare with a similar example from Mito, described in Koschmann, *Mito*, 158.

69. Walthall, *Weak*, 179.

70. Yamakawa, *Shimatsu* 1:12, 38; Huber, "Men," 114.

71. Kanbashi, *Shimazu*, 116.

72. Yamakawa, *Shimatsu* 1:101–3, 186, 89, 91, 203; Kanbashi, *Shimazu*, 121–22.

73. For a detailed account, see Yamakawa, *Shimatsu* 1:191–96. As well as William G. Beasley, *The Meiji Restoration* (Stanford, CA: Stanford University Press), 217; Jansen, *Sakamoto*, 139–40; Kanbashi, *Shimazu*, 117, 23–24.

74. Yamakawa, *Shimatsu* 1:197–200.

75. Beasley, *Meiji*, 217–18.

76. *SKTD*, 1:400–402; Yamamura, "Shinsengumi," *Jinbutsu Ōrai Rekishi Dokuhon* 56, no. 6 (June 2011): 95–96; Keene, *Emperor*, 79.

77. Huber, "Men," 116; Beasley, *Meiji*, 217; Jansen, *Sakamoto*, 197.

78. Harutoonian, *Toward*, 312.

79. Huber, *Revolutionary Origins*, 135–36.

80. Huber, "Men," 120–23; Beasley, *Meiji*, 230–31; Keene, *Emperor*, 79–80; Matsuo, *Kido*, 8–9.

81. Huber, *Revolutionary Origins*, 160.

82. Kanbashi, *Shimazu*, 151; Matsuo, *Kido*, 9.

83. Ichisaka, "Sake," 181–82; Huber, *Revolutionary Origins*, 143, 171–73.

84. Miyake Tsugunobu, "Kiheitai," *Jinbutsu Ōrai Rekishi Dokuhon* 56, no. 6 (June 2011): 100; Huber, *Revolutionary Origins*, 198; Harutoonian, *Toward*, 316, 384, 388–90.

85. Beasley, *Meiji*, 226–27; Miyake, "Kiheitai," 98–99, 102; Takagi, *Sorekara*, 6–8, 16–18; Huber, *Revolutionary Origins*, 120–25.

86. Miyake, "Kiheitai," 100; Iechika, *Saigō*, 113–14; Huber, *Revolutionary Origins*, 166–67.

87. Miyake, "Kiheitai," 101; Kanbashi, *Shimazu*, 154; Jansen, *Sakamoto*, 202–3; Huber, *Revolutionary Origins*, 166, 173–79.

88. Iechika, *Saigō*, 114, 19, 21–22; Jansen, *Sakamoto*, 185, 94–95; Matsuo, *Kido*, 10–11.
89. Kanbashi, *Shimazu*, 156–57; Iechika, *Saigō*, 116 21–22; Jansen, *Sakamoto*, 211–12; Matsuo, *Kido*, 10–11.
90. *SKTD*, 1:595; Iechika, *Saigō*, 123–27; Matsuo, *Kido*, 12.
91. Iechika, *Saigō*, 114–15.
92. Kanbashi, *Shimazu*, 156–57; Matsuo, *Kido*, 10–11.
93. Kanbashi, *Shimazu*, 156–57; Jansen, *Sakamoto*, 217; Matsuo, *Kido*, 11–12; *SKTD*, 1:595–96. The text of the agreement and the history of the negotiations, preserved in a letter sent by Kido to Sakamoto, is fully reproduced in *SKTD*, 1:597–602; see also Iechika, *Saigō*, 127–28.
94. Harutoonian, *Toward*, 392–400; Andrew Cobbing (based on the work of Inuzuka Takaaki), *The Satsuma Students in Britain: Japan's Early Search for the 'Essence of the West'* (Richmond, UK: Japan Library, 2000), 115–16.
95. Matsuo, Kido, 14–15; Satow, *Diplomat*, 302.
96. Sasaki, *Shishi to Kanryō*, 252–57.
97. Takata Yūsuke, "Meiji Ishin 'shishi'-zō no Keisei to Rekishi Ishiki," *Rekishi Gakubu Ronshū: Bukkyō Daigaku Rekishi Gakubu* 2 (March 2012): 43–52, 67–68. The name Yasukuni was adopted in 1879. Until then, the shrine was called Shōkonsha. See also *Yomiuri Shinbun*, 25.10.1876, p. 2; 14.3.1877, p. 1; 21.7.1882, p. 1.
98. See for example the recognition criteria of Yamaguchi Prefecture, reproduced ibid., 66–67, as well as *Asahi Shinbun* (Osaka edition), 16.11.1879, 13.6.1884, p. 2.
99. "Junkoku Shishi Hyōshō Tsuiroku Seigan no Ken," 12.8.1913, National Archives of Japan (hereafter cited as NA-JP), Gyōsei Bunsho, Naikaku Sōrifu, Dajōkan-Naikaku Kankei:1, Kumon Zassan Taishō 2-nen, vol. 35, Teikoku Gikai 2, call number 2A-013–00.
100. For example, the *Asahi Shinbun* (Osaka Edition), 14.11.1980, p. 1, reported that Fukuzawa Yūkichi is convening patriotic shishi (*aikoku no shishi*, i.e., popular rights activists). For similar usage in the same newspaper see also 12.4.1882, p. 1. And compare with *Yomiuri Shinbun*, 16.9.1890, p. 2. A search in the *Asahi Shinbun* database in the first sixteen years of its existence (1879 to 1895, the time span covered by the first six chapters of this book) with four of the most common terms for shishi and similar Bakumatsu patriots (*shishi, yūshi, jun'nansha and sōmō*), produced 1,779 results, distributed throughout the entire period. A similar search in the *Yomiuri Shinbun* database (1874–1895, headlines keyword search) produced 2,148 results. Not all of these articles, however, contain those precise words. In some the quote is paraphrased, and the relevant keywords appear only in the database headlines. In others, especially in the 1870s, synonyms are often used. In addition, in many articles the terms *shishi* or *yūshi* are used to describe not the historical shishi but contemporary patriotic behavior.
101. *Yomiuri Sinbun*, 14.7.1883, p. 4. *Shishi Hitsudoku*: Nihon no Tama. See an advertisement in *Asahi Shinbun* (Osaka Edition), 22.7.1885, 4.
102. Matsumoto Sōji, "Ishin no Shishi o ronzu," in *Seitō Bunsho*, ed. Amakasu Shigetarō (2 vols., Tokyo: Rikugun Yoka Shikan Gakkō, 1937), private collection of Carter Eckert and courtesy of Carter Eckert), 2:7–9. See also Yamashita Fumio's essay in the same collection, 2:13.
103. Paul J. DiMaggio and Walter W. Powell, "The Iron Cage Revisited: Institutional Isomorphism and Collective Rationality in Organizational Fields," *American Sociological Review* 48, no. 2 (April 1983): 151. See also hypotheses A-3 and A-4 in the same paper, 154–55.
104. DiMaggio/Powell, "Iron Cage," 154.
105. Sasaki, *Shishi to Kanryō*, 236–37, 46–47.
106. Ibid., 237.

2. JEWEL IN THE PALACE

The quote given in the epigraph of this chapter comes from *Mencius*, trans. Irene Bloom (New York: Columbia University Press, 2009), 4n6.

1. Satow, *Diplomat*, 302.

2. *Iwakura Tomomi Kankei Monjo*, 8 vols. (Tokyo: Kokuritsu Kobunshokan Naikaku Bunsho Shozō, 1990–91), 4:188 (hereafter cited as *ITKM*).

3. *Ōkubo Toshimichi Monjo*, 9 vols. (Tokyo: Tokyo Daigaku Shuppan-kai, 1967–69), 2:192–93, 301–2 (hereafter cited as *OTM*); *Diary of Kido Takayoshi*, 3 vols., trans. Sidney D. Brown and Akiko Hirota (Tokyo: University of Tokyo Press, 1983–86), 1:120, 125–26 (hereafter cited as *DKT*); Maximilian von Brandt, *Dreihunddreissig Jahre in Ost-Asien: Erinnerungen eines deutschen Diplomaten* (Leipizg: Verlag von Georg Wigand, 1901), 265–66; these reforms were also intended to neutralize the influence of the conservative court faction—people who may have supported the war against the Bakufu, but staunchly opposed Western-style reforms. See Shimoyama Saburō, *Kindai Tennōsei Kenkyū Josetsu* (Tokyo: Iwanami Shoten, 1976), 80–81, 84.

4. Carol Gluck, *Japan's Modern Myths: Ideology in the late Meiji Period* (Princeton, NJ: Princeton University Press, 1985), 73–94; Takeshi Fujitani, *Splendid Monarchy: Power and Pageantry in Modern Japan* (Berkeley: University of California Press, 1996), 174–83; Ben Ami Shillony, *Enigma of the Emperors: Sacred Subservience in Japanese History* (Folkestone, UK: Global Oriental, 2005).

5. *KDT*, 1:72–73; for interesting theoretical insights into the interrelations between relocation and uprooting of old traditions, see Kate Brown, *A Biography of a No Place: From Ethnic Borderland to Soviet Heartland* (Cambridge, MA: Harvard University Press, 2004), 82.

6. Martin van Creveld, *Command in War* (Cambridge: Cambridge University Press, 1895), 65–78, 226–32, 268–77.

7. The translation is taken from Beasley, *Restoration*, 285. For the Japanese original, see *Ōkubo Toshimichi Nikki*, 2 vols. (Tokyo: Tokyo Daigaku Shuppan Kai, 1969), 1:395 (hereafter cited as *OTN*).

8. The concept was already articulated by several scholars, though the term *hazy center* is my own. For an excellent scholarly treatment see, for example, John Haley, *Authority without Power: Law and the Japanese Paradox* (New York: Oxford University Press, 1991), 79–80.

9. For a brilliant contemporary analysis of this phenomenon, see Fukuzawa Yukichi, "Teishitsu-ron" in Fukuzawa, *Nihon Kōshitsu-ron* (Tokyo: Shimazu Shobō, 1987), 22–23.

10. Tōyama, *Ishin Henkaku*, 324. See Harutoonian, *Toward*, 399–400, for analysis and discussion.

11. Satow, *Diplomat*, 192.

12. Keene, *Emperor*, 40–41.

13. Tōyama, *Ishin Henkaku*, 232–33.

14. Michio Umegaki, *After the Restoration: the Beginning of Japan's Modern State* (New York: New York University Press, 1988), 4–5, 8, 35–37.

15. The quote is from *DKT*, 2:61–62; See also *SKTD*, 2:1477–78; Tokutomi Ichirō (Sohō), *Kōshaku Yamagata Aritomo Den* (Tokyo: Yamagata Aritomo-Kō Kinen Jigyōkai, 1933), 134–35.

16. Ōshima Akiko, "Meiji Shoki Dajōkansei ni okeru Seigun Kankei," *Kioi Shigaku* 11 (1991): 10.

17. *OTM*, 3:353, 355.

18. Ibid., 352, 356.

19. The lowest class of Samurai, *sotsu*, was preserved for a while, until it was finally merged with the *shizoku* on 8.3.1872. Shimoyama, *Tennōsei*, 228–34; Wolfgang Schwentkler,

"Die Samurai im Zeitalter der Meiji-Restauration. Einwandel und Modernisierung in Japan, 1830–1890," *Geschichte und Gesellschaft* 28, no. 1 (January–March 2002): 34.

20. For more information of early Meiji reforms, see Sakeda Masatoshi and George Akita, "The Samurai Disestablished: Abei Iwane and his Stipend," *Monumenta Nipponica* 41, no. 3 (autumn 1986): 299–301; Kim, Kyu-Hyun, *The Age of Visions and Arguments: Parliamentarianism and the National Public Sphere in Early Meiji Japan* (Cambridge, MA: Harvard University Asia Center, 2007), 70–80.

21. Reproduced in Yamazaki Tanshō, *Naikaku Seidō no Kenkyū* (Tokyo: Takayama Shoin, 1942), 31.

22. The name of this executive body in Japanese was *seiin* (literally: "Central Chamber"). Since 2.5.1873, the term *cabinet* (*naikaku*) was alternately used. For clarity's sake, I chose to consistently translate as "cabinet."

23. Naikaku Kiroku Kyoku, ed., *Hōki Bunrui Taizen* (Tokyo: Naikaku Kiroku Kyoku, 1889–91), 10:157, 160; 19:2 (hereafter cited as *HBT*); Beasley, *Restoration*, 347; Hsien-T'ing Ch'en, "The Japanese Government and the Creation of the Imperial Army" (Ph.D. diss., Harvard University, 1963), 98. Though most authors translated *kyō* as "ministers," this is highly misleading. The title "minister" (*daijin*) was reserved at the time to the ministers of the right and the left, and was given to officials in charge of portfolios only after the establishment of the cabinet system in 1885. It seems to me, therefore, that translating *kyō* as "minister" might gloss over the uniqueness of the *Dajōkan* system.

24. For a concise description of the expedition, see the introduction to the English version of Kido's diary by the editor and translator, Sidney Brown, *DKT*, 2:xvii–xxxiii.

25. Iechika, *Saigō*, 69–105; Charles Yates, *Saigo Takamori: The Man behind the Myth* (London: Kegan Paul, 1994), 137–39.

26. Ch'en, *Imperial Army*, 55; based on Yamagata's testimony to his biographer. Japanese original in *KYAD*, 2:80; for the text of the order, detailing the exact composition of the assembled force, see *HBT*, 1:43; for discussion see also Umegaki, *Restoration*, 68–69.

27. *KYAD*, 2:80.

28. Ōshima Akiko, "1873 (Meiji Roku-nen) no Shibirian Kontororu: Seikanron Seihen ni okeru Gun to Seiji," *Shigaku Zasshi* 117, no. 7: 1228.

29. Oka Yoshitake, *Reimei ki no Meiji Nihon: Nichi-Ei Kōshōshi no Shikaku ni oite* (Tokyo: Miraisha, 1965), 73–77; Brandt, *Dreihunddreissig Jahren*, 274–75.

30. *Kido Takayoshi Monjo*, 8 vols., ed. Kido-kō and Denki Hensanjo (Tokyo: Nihon Shiseki Kyōkai, 1929–1931), 4:192–93, 196–97 (hereafter cited as *KTM*). In his memoirs, Tani Kanjō recalled that the competition between the three domains inside the force was intense. The Tosa troops, for example, were ordered to "perform better" than their Chōshū and Satsuma counterparts. Nevertheless, they were also warned to keep strict discipline, refraining, for example, from wearing swords. See *Tani Kanjō Ikō*, 2 vols., ed. Nihon Shiseki Kyōkai (Tokyo: Tokyo Daigaku Shuppan Kai, 1975–76), 1:225 (hereafter cited as *TKI*).

31. Ch'en, *Imperial Army*, 83.

32. Ōshima, "Shibirian Kontororu," 1124–26.

33. Tōyama, *Ishin Henkaku*, 244. The garrisons (*chindai*) had been subordinate to the War Ministry (then Army Ministry) since 1871, but at that time they contained relatively few conscripts. Instead, they were filled with shizoku who had volunteered for continued service. These men were considered a major disciplinary problem until they were finally replaced by conscripts, in a process that started with the conscription act of 1873 and ended in the last years of that decade.

34. *DSZ*, 2:663.

35. Nakahara Hidenori, "Sakamoto Sumihiro Rireki Ippan," *Keisatsu Kenkyū* 42, no. 5 (1971): 71–74.

36. Mōri Toshihiko, *Meiji Rokunen Seihen* (Tokyo: Chūō Kōronsha, 1979), 108–10.

37. *DSZ*, 2:736–38.

38. Saigō's real intentions in the Korean issue were a subject of intense debate. Some historians, such as Sidney Brown, the editor of the Kido diaries, depicted Saigō as the head of a "war party," contrasting him with Ōkubo's relative moderation (*DKT*, 2:xxxiii). Kōza School Marxist historians (for example, Tōyama, *Ishin Henkaku*, 309–10) doubted the explanatory power of such distinctions, tending instead to view the differences between Saigō and Ōkubo as rather small: both supported imperialism, and the debate between them was only about timing, internal policy, and the question about who should personally lead the imperialist project. Mōri Toshihiko, by contrast, argued that Saigō did not really want war but actually intended to achieve peace through negotiations. His famous letter to Itagaki, according to Mōri, was merely a tactical ploy to convince his hawkish friend to support the plan. See Mōri, *Seihen*, 112–32. The thesis of Mōri is reservedly supported by several authors, for example Mark Ravina, *The Last Samurai: The Life and Battles of Saigo Takamori* (Hoboken, NJ: John Wiley and Sons, 2004), 189–95. It is, however, strongly criticized by others, most notably Iechika Yoshiki (*Saigō*, 18–23), who believes that Saigō, sick, irrational, and mentally unstable, opted for war as a kind of "escape" from his travails.

39. *DSZ*, 2:787–88.

40. The change was particularly dramatic in the case of Kido, as he used to be an exponent of an aggressive foreign policy towards Korea, see *DKT*, 1:167–68, and compare with his position in 1873, ibid., 2:370–71, 383–84; *KTM*, 8:360–61; Kim, *Age of Visions*, 83–86.

41. For a translation of Ōkubo's "Seven Points Speech," see David J. Lu, ed., *Japan: A Documentary History* (Armonk, NY: M. E. Sharpe, 1997), 325–27.

42. *OTN*, 2:205.

43. In fact, as Tōyama rightly argues, Ōkubo was isolated in his domain even before the Iwakura Expedition. See Tōyama, *Ishin Henkaku*, 331–32.

44. *Sanjō Sanetomi Kō Nenpu*, ed. Kunaishō Zushoryō (Tokyo: Kunaishō, 1901), 27:39a–b (hereafter cited as *SSKN*); *DKT*, 2:385.

45. Nakahara, "Sakamoto Sumihiro," 75.

46. *DSZ*, 2:698 (editor's notes).

47. Umegaki, *Restoration*, 67.

3. "BY NOT STOPPING"

1. Robert Eskildsen, ed., *Foreign Adventurers and the Aborigines of Southern Taiwan, 1867–1874: Western Sources Related to Japan's 1874 Expedition to Taiwan* (Taipei: Institute of Taiwan History, Academica Sinica, 2005), 3–7; Charles LeGendre, "Notes of Travel in Formosa," in *Foreign Adventurers*, ed. Eskildsen, 121–22, 125, 132; *Iwakura-Ko Jikki*, 3 vols. (Tokyo: Kōgo Gūshoku, 1906), 2:1183 (hereafter cited as *IKJ*); Tei Nagayasu (Tei Ei-Nei), "Soejima Taishi teki Shin Gairyaku," in *Meiji Bunka Zenshū*, 32 vols., ed. Meiji Bunka Kenkyū Kai (Tokyo: Nihon Hyōronsha, 1967–74, edition 1955–57, hereafter cited as *MBZ*), 6:63; Paul D. Barclay, "'Gaining Confidence and Friendship in Aborigine Country: Diplomacy, Drinking, and Debauchery on Japan's Southern Frontier," *Social Science Japan* 6, no. 1 (April 2003): 81–82.

2. LeGendre, "Notes," in *Foreign Adventurers*, ed. Eskildsen, 166, 169; *IKJ*, 2:1171; Mizuno Jun, "Taiwan Seiban Ki," in *Tairo Mizuno Jun Sensei*, ed. Yagashiro Hideyoshi (Tokyo: Yuma ni Shobō, 2008), 263 (hereafter cited as *TMJS*). Several testimonies of the survivors, collected by Kagoshima Prefecture officials and reported to the Japanese government, were reproduced in *Saigō Totoku to Kabayama Sōtoku* (Taipei: Saigo Totoku to Kabayama Sōtoku Kinen Jigyō Shuppan Iinkai, 1936), part II, 50–51 (hereafter cited as *STKS*). The different theories on the motives of the perpetrators are analyzed by Ōhama Ikuko. See Ōhama, "'Budansha Jiken Saikō: Naze Paiwan-Zoku wa Ryūkyū Shima-jin wo satsugai shita no ka," *Taiwan Genjūmin Kenkyū* 11 (2007): 203–24.

3. Ōyama Tsunayoshi," Ōyama Kagoshima Ken Sanji Ryūkyū Tōmin Taiwan ni okete Sōgai nit tsuite Monzai no Shi nado nado Jōchin," 31.8.1872, Japanese Army and Navy Archives (Washington DC: Library of Congress), microfilm 5041, reel 34, frame: 44843 (hereafter cited as JANA).

4. Xu Jielin, "Gaisei to Tōchi: 1874-nen Taiwan Shuppei o rei ni shite," in *Gendai Kokka to Kempō no Gerni* (Tokyo: Yūhikaku, 1983), 400.

5. The Taiwan Expedition was already discussed by several scholars, especially Robert Eskildsen, Mizuno Norihiro, and Edwin Pak-Wah Leung, but their discussion focuses on the roots of Japanese Imperialism or Sino-Japanese relations. Japanese language authors, such as Mōri Toshihiko and Xu Jielin, tend to focus on the internal Japanese politics. This chapter, while drawing on the aforementioned studies, is the first to use primary sources to explore the subject from the crucial viewpoint of military insubordination. For the studies mentioned above, see Robert Eskildsen, "Of Civilization and Savages: The Mimetic Imperialism of Japan's 1874 Expedition to Taiwan," *American Historical Review* 107, no. 2 (April 2002): 388–418; Mizuno Norohito, "Early Meiji Policies towards the Ryukyus and the Taiwanese Aboriginal Territories," *Modern Asian Studies* 43, no. 3 (May 2009): 683–739; Leung, Edwin Pak-Wah, "The Quasi-War in East Asia: Japan's Expedition to Taiwan and the Ryūkyū Controversy," *Modern Asian Studies* 17, no. 2 (1983): 257–81; Mōri Toshihiko, *Taiwan Shuppei: Dai Nihon Teikoku no Kaimaku Geki* (Tokyo: Chūō Kōronsha, 1996); Xu, "Gaisei," 389–416.

6. Kagoshima Ken, ed., *Kagoshima Ken Shi* (Kagoshima: Kagoshima Ken, 1967), 2:668 (hereafter cited as *KKS*).

7. Kabayama Sukenori, "Taiwan Kiji," in *STKS*, part II, 144, 47–48; *The Japan Daily Herald*, 7.4.1874 (hereafter cited as *TJDH*); Leung, "The Quasi-War," 258; Tei, "Soejima," in *MBZ*, 6:64. For the debates in the Japanese government on the possible annexation of Ryūkyū to the empire, see *Meiji Bunka Shiryō Sōsho*, 13 vols., ed. Meiji Bunka Shiryō and Sōsho Kankō Kai (Tokyo: Kazama Shobō, 1963), 4:8–9; for analysis, see Kurihara Jun, "Taiwan Jiken (1874 nen): Ryūkyū Seisaku no Tenki toshite no Taiwan Shuppei," *Shigaku Zasshi* 87, no. 9 (1978): 1328–52.

8. Tei, "Soejima," in *MBZ*, 6:63.

9. *OTM*, 3:535; *OTN*, 2:127–28.

10. Tei, "Soejima" in *MBZ*, 6:63.

11. Ōyama, 31.8.1872, JANA, M:5041, R:34, F:33834; Kurihara, "Taiwan Jiken," 1329.

12. Ōyama, 31.8.1872, JANA, M:5041, R:34, F:33834. Iwakura's choice to fully quote Ōyama's letter in his diary (precise date unclear), indicates the influence this letter had on Japanese policymakers. See *IKJ*, 2:1171.

13. Kabayama, "Taiwan Kiji," in *STKS*, part II, 139.

14. *IKJ*, 2:1172; *TJDH*, 7.4.1874; Kobayashi Takao, "Rusu seifu to sei-Tai ronso: Rujandoru oboegaki ni kansuru ichi kosatsu," *Seiji keizai Shigaku* 296 (December 1990): 1–25; Zhang Hu, 'Soejima tai-Shin gaiko no kento,' in *Meiji Ishin to Ajia*, ed. Meji Ishin Shigakkai (Tokyo: Yoshikawa Kōbunkan, 2001), 30–60; Shinobu Seizaburō, *Nihon Seiji Shi*, 4 vols. (Tokyo: Nansōsha, 1976–82), 2:434–35; *DKT*, 3:70–71.

15. Saigō Tsugumichi to Charles LeGendre, 8.4.1874, "Taiwan Joriku ato no Kyōdō oyobi Shinkoku Seifu to no kōshō nado ni kan suru" (Terashima to Parkes, conversation minutes), 7.4.1874, *Dai Nihon Gaikō Bunshō*, 73 vols. (Tokyo: Gaimushō Chōshabu, 1936–40), 7:21–25 (hereafter cited as *DNGB*). For general impressions on the Oda Incident see also Edward H. House, *Japanese Expedition to Formosa* (Tokyo: n.p., 1875), 13; *SEDS*, 3:638.

16. *DKT*, 3:370–71, 3:12, 15, 59–60; *SEDS*, 3:638.

17. *IKJ*, 2:1172–73; *OM* 1:40; *SEDS*, 3:638–39.

18. McWilliams, "East Meets East: The Soejima Mission to China, 1873," *Monumenta Nipponica* 30, no. 3 (autumn 1975): 261–66; The Japanese records, taken by Yanagihara

Sakimitsu and his team, are referred to by Yanagihara and Tei's memorandum in JANA, M:5041, R:34 F:44973, and reproduced in Iwakura's diary (*IKJ*, 2:1174–75) and, in a shortened version, in Tei, "Soejima" in *MBZ*, 6:70–71. For a nearly full English translation (with some unimportant omissions), see Nagao Ariga, "Diplomacy," in *Japan by the Japanese*, ed. Alfred Steed (London, 1904), 161–63. The Japanese "interpretation" of the Qing Foreign Ministry's answer was propagated to the English-speaking world by the *New York Herald*'s Edward House, who served for all practical purposes as the mouthpiece of Soejima and the Foreign Ministry. See House, *Expedition*, 10–11. It was also accepted by *TJDH*, 7.4.1874.

19. This is the assumption of McWilliams, in "East," 268–69.

20. *IKJ*, 2:1176.

21. *SSKN*, 27:39a–b; Ernest M. Satow, *A Diplomat in Japan: The Diaries of Ernst Satow*, 2 vols., ed. Ian Ruxton (Morrisville, NC: Lulu Press, 2009), 2:102 (hereafter cited as *DES*).

22. *OTN*, 2:209, 22; *TKI*, 2:54–55. For historical context, see "Taiwan Shuppei Hōshin to Tenkan to Chōshūha no Hantai Undō," *Shigaku Zasshi* 92, no. 11 (1983): 1774; Shinobu, *Nihon Seiji*, 2:417–18.

23. See for example *OTN*, 2:203–25.

24. *OTM*, 5:234–36; *OTN*, 2:227, 233–36; *Ōkuma Shigenobu Kankei Monjo*, 6 vols. (Tokyo: Nihon Shiseki Kyōkai, 1932–35), 2:235 (hereafter cited as *OSKM*).

25. Kabayama, "Taiwan Kiji," in *STKS*, part II, 281, 314; *IKJ*, 2:1176.

26. "Taiwan Banchi Shobun Yōryaku," 6.2.1874, *DNGB*, 7:1–2. Kabayama, "Taiwan Kiji," in *STKS*, part II, 281. The plan was actually drafted by the envoy to China, Yanagihara Sakimitsu and his right-hand man, Tei Nagayasu, on January 29, 1874, to be revised and submitted later by Okubo and Ōkuma. See JANA, R34-F44973–44979. The colonization plans were also influenced by the reports of spies sent to Taiwan. See Center for Asian Historical Record (hereafter cited as JACAR), http://jacar.go.jp, Ref. A03030073600 (14.6.1875), Ref. AA01100078600, p. 14; Naikaku (December 1874), Ref. C09120280000, Rikugun-shō Dai Nikki (1875), Ref. A03030425400, p. 595.

27. *DNGB*, 7:1–3; *OTM*, 5:343–348; *SSKN*, 27:52a; JACAR, Ref. A03030997600 (5.4.1874), pp. 1–3.

28. *DNGB*, 7:1–3; *OTM*, 5:343–348.

29. Kabayama, "Taiwan Kiji," in *STKS*, part II, 288, 314–16. *TJDH*, 11.4.1874. See also Mōri, *Taiwan Shuppei*, 143–44.

30. *OTM*, 5:468; Kishida Ginkō, 15.5.1874, "Taiwan Shinpō" in *STKS*, part II, 7 (the dates here, and in all other subsequent references to Kishida's articles, are the dates of publication in the *Tokyo Nichi-Nichi Shinbun*, usually two or three weeks after the piece was written.

31. *OTM*, 5:464–69; *OSKM*, 2:283–85; *IKJ*, 2:1179; Ochiai Hiroki, *Meiji Kokka to Shizoku* (Tokyo: Yoshikaewa Kobunkan, 2001), 127; Saigō Jūkō, *Gensui Saigō Tsugumichi Den* (Tokyo: Matsuyō Shobō, 1997), 117. The plan is reproduced in *STKS*, part II, 64, 68. Colonization is explicitly mentioned in the text, as well as the term "colonizing soldiers" (*shokumin-hei*). See also Kabayama, "Taiwan Kiji" in *STKS*, part II, 314, 21.

32. Eskildsen, "Mimetic," 397; *STKS*, part II, 64; House, *Expedition*, 15. For sentiments supporting colonization among Satsuma retainers see also Kabayama, "Taiwan Kiji," in *STKS*, part II, 144. About the seedlings, see Ōkuma to Kido/Kuroda, 10.4.1874, National Archives of Japan (hereafter cited as NA-JP), Gyōsei Bunsho, Naikaku Sōrifu, Dajōkan-Naikaku Kankei:10, Shoban Shorui 2A-033–07, Hitoe 00596100, p. 19.

33. Finance Lord to Lord of Foreign Affairs, 12.4.1874, NA-JP, Gyōsei Bunsho, Naikaku Sōrifu, Dajōkan-Naikaku Kankei:10, 2A-037–00, Hitoe 00977100, pp. 29:d–e; *SSKN*, 27:52a–b; *IKJ*, 2:1179–82.

34. *SSKN*, 27:52a–b; Xu, "Tōchi," 395.

35. *TKI,* 2:65; *IKJ,* 2:1179. Akamatsu Noriyoshi, "Taiwan Seitō no Nikki," in "Akamatsu Noriyoshi Kankei Monjo," Modern Japanese Political History Materials Room, National Diet Library, Tokyo (hereafter cited as MJPH-NDL), p. 1.

36. "Saigō Taiwan Banchi Jimu totoku ni tamawaritaru Shinchoku," 5.4.1874, *DNGB,* 7:18.

37. "Saigō Taiwan Banchi Jimu Totoku ni Tamawaritariru Tokuyu," 5.4.1874, *DNGB,* 7:19; for another version of the order (undated), see *STKS,* part II, 64–70; *IKJ,* 2:1183. This went contrary to the American advisor Charles LeGendre's advice, to concentrate in the hands of one person full authority over both diplomacy and military affairs. See *Ōkuma Monjo* (Tokyo: Waseda Daigaku Shakai Rigaku Kenkyūjo, 1963), 1:42–43.

38. Saigō to the troops, in *STKS,* part II, 70.

39. Saigō Tsugumichi to Charles LeGendre, 8.4.1874, *DNGB,* 7:22.

40. *TJDH,* 6, 7.4.1874. The language of the report indicates that the events were well-known to the readers for quite some time.

41. Parkes to Terashima, 13.4.1874, *DNGB,* 7:31; *OTN,* 2:262.

42. Finance Lord to Lord of Foreign Affairs, 12.4.1874, NA-JP, Gyōsei Bunsho, Naikaku Sōrifu, Dajōkan-Naikaku Kankei:10, 2A-037–00, Hitoe 00977100, p. 29f.

43. Terashima to Bingham, 22.4.1874, Bingham to Terashima, 23.4.1874, *DNGB,* 7:47–48; Brandt, *Dreihunddreissig Jahre,* 302. Brandt's line was also reflected in the foreign press, see *TJDH,* 11.4.1874.

44. Mōri, *Taiwan Shuppei,* 136.

45. *OTN,* 2:256–62.

46. *OTN,* 2:262–63; "Naimu-kyō Ōkubo Toshimichi Kyūshū e mu[ki] shuppatsu todo[ke]," 29.4.1874, NA-JP, Gyōsei Bunsho, Naikaku Sōrifu, Dajōkan-Naikaku Kankei:10, 2A-009–00, Hitoe 01309100, p. 52; *OSKM,* 2:302–3; Akamatsu, "Taiwan Seitō Nikki" in "Akamatsu Monjo," pp. 4–5, MJPH-NDL.

47. *IKJ,* 2:1193; *OSKM,* 2:302–3; Sanjō to Ōkuma, 19.4.1874, JACAR, Ref. A03030120800. Cabinet to Miyakawa, 19, 20.4.1874, JACAR, Ref. A03030122000; *TJDH,* 23, 24.4.1874.

48. *IKJ,* 2:1193–94. Compare with Ōkuma to Sanjō and Iwakura, 20.4.1874, JACAR, Ref. A03030122100, Ōkuma to Sanjō, 2.5.1874, JACAR, Ref. A03030136600; *TJDH,* 7.5.1874.

49. *OSKM,* 2:310. See also Ōkuma to Sanjō and Iwakura, 20.4.1874, JACAR, Ref. A03030122100.

50. *IKJ,* 2:1194. Compare with Ōkuma to Ōkubo, 27.4.1874, JACAR, Ref. A03030131200.

51. *IKJ,* 2:1194–95. And compare with Kabayama, "Taiwan Kiji," in *STKS,* part II, 293.

52. *IKJ,* 2:1195. Ochiai, writing his memoirs after the event, believed that the piracy threat was only a joke, but this is different from the impression conveyed by Iwakura's diary. See Ochiai Taizō, *Seiban Tōbatsu,* 60, in Yasukuni Jinja Kaikō Bunko (Yasukuni Shrine Archives, hereafter cited as YJKB).

53. *IKJ,* 2:1196–97; Kabayama, "Taiwan Kiji," in *STKS,* part II, 319–20; *OSKM,* 2:310; Ōkubo to Sanjō, 29.4.1874, JACAR, Ref. A03030133900; Fukushima to the Bureau of Taiwan Barbarian Affairs, 3.5.1874, JACAR, Ref. A03030137800.

54. *OTN,* 2:266.

55. Ibid.; *IKJ,* 2:1195–99; *OSKM,* 2:307–8, 311–13. The text of the agreement is reproduced in *OSKM,* 2:312–13. Saigō had also agreed to send Wasson and Cassel back to Japan (*OSKM,* 2:311), but that was never done. *TJDH* (25.4.1874), whose editorial line was hostile to the expedition, called LeGendre to follow his newly adopted samurai values to the end, thereby committing *seppuku* to atone for his responsibility to this "very abortive" operation. For the paper's hostility to the expedition and LeGendre alike, see also *TJDH,* 7.5.1874.

56. *STKS,* part II, 75; compare with *IKJ,* 2:1200.

57. Eskildsen, *Foreign Adventurers,* 12; Yasuooka Akio, *Meiji Shoki Nisshin Koshoshi Kenkyu* (Tokyo: Gannando Shoten, 1995), 105; Mōri, *Taiwan Shuppei,* 136–40, 237; Xu "Gaisei," 398; Mizuno, "Early Meiji Policies," 729.

58. Iechika, "Taiwan Shuppei," 1775–76.

59. Brandt, *Dreiunddreissig Jahre*, 303.

60. *OSKM*, 2:305–6.

61. *IKJ*, 2:1203–14.

62. *OTN*, 2:264; *SSKN*, 28:1. *TJDH*, 21 (28.4.1874). So desperate were the leaders of the government that they even tried to summon Shimazu Hisamitsu to Tokyo. He indeed arrived on April 21, and served for a while as the minister of the left. His tenure, however, was stormy and full of fights with other government leaders, most notably his archrival Ōkubo. In 1876, Hisamitsu left the government in disgust, never to return again. See *IKJ*, 2:1207–14. *DKT*, 3:220–21, 38–39; "Naikaku Komon Shimazu Hisamitsu Kagoshima-ken yori ki-Kyō todoke," 22.4.1874, NA-JP, Gyōsei Bunsho, Naikaku Sōrifu, Dajōkan-Naikaku Kankei:10, 2A-009–00, Hitoe 01309100, p. 42.

63. These negotiations are reproduced in the official history of the Taiwan Expedition, "Shoban Shui Sho" in *MBZ*, 6:157. See also the minutes produced by Saigō himself in *STKS*, part II, 104–9, as well as Iwakura's account in *IKJ*, 1203, 24–25.

64. Mizuno Norihito, "Early Meiji Policies," 729; Ochiai Taizō, *Seiban Tōbatsu*, 46–47, YJKB; Mōri, *Taiwan Shuppei*, 137; *TJDH*, 7 (8.5.1874). On May 18, the *Herald* even published a rumor that angry soldiers had threatened to decapitate Saigō if the expedition was canceled. According to Kishida Ginkō, the soldiers waited quietly and obediently at port, but that could well have changed if the expedition had been suddenly canceled. See Kishida, "Taiwan Shinpō," 16.5.1874, in *STKS*, part II, 8.

65. Cassel to LeGendre, 24.5.1873, Wasson to Ōkuma, 1875, in Eskildsen, *Foreign Adventurers*, 203, 237.

66. Saigō to Ōkuma, 7.6.1874, Kabayama, "Taiwan Kiji," in *STKS*, part II, 101–2, 326–27; Cassel to LeGendre, 24, 26.5.1873, Wasson to Ōkuma, in Eskildsen, *Foreign Adventurers*, 209, 12, 36, 39–40, 47–48; Mizuno Jun, "Seiban Ki," in *TMJS*, 228, 81–82; Adachi Tsunayuki, "Watashi no Shosei Jidai no Tsuioku (shita): Adachi Tsunayuki Ō Sōdan," *Jikei* 17, no. 6 (June 1935): 70; Ochiai Taizō, *Seiban Tōbatsu*, 78–79, YJKB. In his memoirs, Ochiai Taizō denies that the Japanese took the heads of the chief and his son, but the testimonies of Wasson, Cassel, and Mizuno indicate otherwise.

67. *STKS*, part II, 179, see also 110–11. Such behavior is also implied in House's account in his *Expedition*, 48, 58. Compare with Adachi Tsunayuki, "Watashi no Shosei Jidai no Tsuioku (shita): Adachi Tsunayuki Ō Sōdan," *Jikei* 17, no. 6 (June 1935): 68–70.

68. Wasson to Ōkuma, 1875, in Eskildsen, *Foreign Adventurers*, 233.

69. Emphasis is mine. Cassel to LeGendre, 24.5.1874, and compare with Wasson to Ōkuma, 1875, in Eskildsen, *Foreign Adventurers*, 207–8, 231–36. Unlike Cassel, Wasson put a greater emphasis on insubordination among the troops.

70. Cassel to LeGendre, 26.5.1874, 212. Cassel's testimony on the disastrous lack of discipline during the Battle of Sekimon is confirmed by the memoirs of Mizuno Jun, "Taiwan Seiban Ki," in *TMJS*, 228. Mizuno also complained that the officers could not control the tendency of soldiers to rush forward, even when such unauthorized moves were dangerous to the war effort. See also hints in the diary of Vice Admiral Akamatsu: Akamatsu, "Taiwan Seitō no Nikki" in "Akamatsu Monjo," 9, MJPH-NDL.

71. Cassel to LeGendre, 24.5.1873, in Eskildsen, *Foreign Adventurers*, 209.

72. See, for example, Eskildsen, *Foreign Adventurers*, 208, 212.

73. *TKI*, 2:71. As usual, Tani had viewed his grandiose schemes on China as means to "sweep away" Japan's "internal trouble" (*naiyū o hakidashi*).

74. *TJDH*, 7.5.1875; *IKJ*, 2:1196, Mōri, *Taiwan Shuppei*, 137; Akamatsu, "Taiwan Seitō Nikki" in "Akamatsu Monjo," 4–5, MJPH-NDL; Kabayama, "Taiwan Kiji," in *STKS*, part II, 324–25. Kishida, "Taiwan Shinpō," 12, 16.5.1874, in *STKS*, part II, 4, 8. The accounts of Mizuno and Ochiai have to be read with caution, as they are influenced by retrospective knowledge. See Mizuno Jun, "Taiwan Seiban Ki," in *TMJS*, 218; Ochiai Taizō, *Seiban*

Tōbatsu, 60–63, YJKB. Edward House, who traveled with the Japanese troops, was completely oblivious of the drama that took place in the Japanese high command, see *Expedition*, 23–24.

75. House, *Expedition*, 53–54, 60; Ochiai Taizō, *Seiban Tōbatsu*, 70–71, 96–97, 110–15, YJKB; Adachi, "Soshei," 71; Wasson to Ōkuma, 1875, in Eskildsen, *Foreign Adventurers*, 250–51; *STKS*, part I, 15–17; Mizuno, "Seiban Ki" in *TMZS*, 291–96; Saigō, *Gensui*, 120. According to Nakahara Hidenori, 561 soldiers died of disease, a very heavy toll for a force of 3,600, especially if one considers that only twelve soldiers actually fell in battle. See Nakahara Hidenori, "Sakamoto Sumihiro Rireki Ippan," *Keisatsu Kenkyū* 42, no. 5 (1971): 77.

76. Mōri, *Taiwan Shuppei*, 145. Eskildsen (*Foreign Adventurers*, 13) argues, without good evidence, that Saigō wanted to remain in Taiwan and opposed the peace agreement with the Qing.

77. *TKI*, 2:68–71, and compare with Kabayama's account, "Taiwan Kiji," in *STKS*, part II, 361–62.

78. Ochiai Taizō, *Seiban Tōbatsu*, 110–16, YJKB.

79. Nakahara, "Sakamoto Sumihiro," 77; *KKS*, 3:867–68. Ochiai Taizō, *Seiban Tōbatsu*, 45, YJKB.

80. Adachi, "Shosei," 70. Compare with Ochiai Taizō, *Seiban Tōbatsu*, 116, YJKB.

81. *SSKN*, 28:1–9; Mizuno Norihito, "Early Meiji Policies," 731–73.

82. Kabayama, "Taiwan Kiji," in *STKS*, part II, 360–66. *OTN*, 2:248–49; Saigō, *Gensui*, 121. About the role of Higashikuze, see especially 362; Ochiai Taizō, *Seiban Tōbatsu*, 134–35, YJKB; Mizuno, "Seiban Ki" in *TMZS*, 297–303.

83. JACAR, Ref. A03031062200 (1874, precise date unknown); *STKS*, part II, 126–27; *OTN*, 2:248–55; *STKS*, part II, 363. According to Ochiai, Saigō was so bored in the last months that he amused himself by watching young, robust soldiers performing sumo wrestling for his pleasure. Even when he heard that Ōkubo was coming, he behaved indifferently and ordered his soldiers to continue the bout. *Seiban Tōbatsu*, 116–17, 130, 33–34, YJKB.

84. *KYAD*, 2:350; Yamagata Aritomo, *Yamagata Aritomo Ikensho* (Tokyo: Hara Shobō, 1966), 57–60. Miura Gorō, *Kanju Shōgun Kaikoroku* (Tokyo: Seikyōsha, 1925), 99–101. Stewart Lone, *Army, Empire, and Politics in Meiji Japan: The Three Careers of General Katsura Tarō* (Basingstoke, UK: MacMillan, 2000), 13. Kurono Taeru, *Sanbō Honbu to Rikugun Daigakkō* (Tokyo: Kodansha, 2004), 28.

4. FATAL OPTIMISM

1. *DKT*, 3:381.

2. Rikujō Jieitai Kita and Kumamoto Shūshinaki, ed., *Shimpen Seinan Senshi*, 2 vols. (Tokyo: Hara Shobō, 1977), 1:23–24 (hereafter cited as *SPSS*); Wagatsuma Sakae et. al, eds., *Nihon Seiji Saiban Shiroku: Meiji*, 2 vols. (Tokyo: Daiichi Hōki Shuppan, 1968–70), 1:402–3 (hereafter cited as *NSSS-M*); Hugh Cortazzi, *Dr. Willis in Japan, 1862–1877: British Medical Pioneer* (London: Athlone Press, 1985), 217–19.

3. Sanbō Honbu Rikugunsha Hensanka, ed., *Seisei Senki Kō* 65 vols. (Tokyo: Sanbō Honbu Rikugunbu Hesanka, 1887), 1:1 (hereafter cited as *SSK*). For an English language example of the government discourse on rebellions see the *Nichi Nichi Shinbun* article, "On Saigō's Rebellion," reproduced by the *Japan Daily Herald*, 3.3.1877. An extreme example of such a Manichean attitude from the rebels' perspective is the Shinpūren manifesto (October 1876), reproduced in *IKJ*, 2:1377–78. See also the crucial discussion of Saigō Takamori, and his lieutenants, described in *SPSS*, 1:117–18. The participants in the discussion described their expedition against the government as an "investigation" (*kitsumon*), as they were the legal authorities and the Tokyo leaders—the criminals. In a

subsequent appeal, the rebels described their mission as a military effort of loyal retainers to "cleanse the evil men" around the throne. See NA-JP, Gyōsei Bunsho, Naikaku-Sōrifu, and Dajōkan-Naikaku Kankei:1, Kōbunroku, *Kagoshima Seitō Shimatsu*, 2A-009–00, 00833100 (hereafter cited as *KSS*), 8:10.

4. Kawata Mizuho, *Kataoka Kenkichi Sensei Den* (Tokyo: Kohokusha, 1978), 248–62; Hayashi Yūzō, *Hayashi Yūzō Jirekidan* (Kōchi: Kōchi Risshimin Toshokan, 1968), 1:53.

5. *Hogohiroi: Sasaki Takayuki Nikki*, 12 vols. (Tokyo: Tokyo Daigaku Shuppan Kai, 1970–79), 5:419 (hereafter cited as *HSTN*).

6. Tani Kanjō to Kataoka Kenkichi, 27.1.1874, reproduced in Kawata, *Kataoka*, 152.

7. See the interrogation of Odate Tomokata, reproduced in Fukushima Nariyuki, *Seikanron no Yobun: Akasaka Kuichigai no Jihen* (Tokyo: Maeda Bajōta, 1927), 108–14.

8. An interesting description of such a process may be found in the police deposition of Odate Tomokata, reproduced in Fukushima, *Akasaka Kuichigai*, 108–14.

9. Hayashi, *Jirekidan*, 1:53; Umegaki, *After*, 202.

10. Ogawara Masamichi, *Seinan Sensō: Saigō Takamori to Nihon Saigo no Naisen* (Tokyo: Chūō Kōron Shinsha, 2007), 10–11. Compare with *HSTN*, 6:16–17.

11. Ogawara Masamichi, "Seikanron Seihen ato no Seifu Tenpuku Keikaku," *Musashino Gakuin Daigaku Kenkyū Kiyō* 3 (2006): 91.

12. *Yūbin Hōchi Shinbun*, 2.10.1875.

13. A. B. Mitford, *Tales of Old Japan: Classic Folklore, Fairy Tales, Ghost Stories, and Tales of the Samurai* (London: Wordsworth Editions, 2000), 313.

14. Helen Hardacre, *Shintō and the State* (Princeton: Princeton University Press, 1989), 30–31.

15. Ogawara Masamichi, *Daikyōin no Kenkyū: Meiji Shoki Shūkyō Gyōsei no Tenkai to Zasetsu* (Tokyo: Keiō Gijuku Daigaku Shuppankai, 2004), 181.

16. "Keishichō Rokuji," *Yūbin Hōchi Shinbun*, 16.9.1874.

17. Take Yoriwake, "Tosa Jinbutsu Hyōron," *Nihon Oyobi Nihonjin* 504 (February 1909), 25.

18. Ibid., 26.

19. *Yūbin Hōchi Shinbun*, 2.10.1875.

20. See the statements of Miyazaki, Senya, and Toda to the police, published in "Keishichō Rokuji," *Yūbin Hōchi Shinbun*, 16.9.1874.

21. Take," Tosa Hyōron," 25.

22. "Shaji Torishirabe Ruisan," 152, reel 50, Rare Books and Old Materials Room—National Diet Library (hereafter cited as RBOMR-NDL).

23. *Yūbin Hōchi Shinbun*, 4.1.1874. For analysis and additional references see Ogawara, *Daikyō*, 184–88.

24. "Keishichō Rokuji," *Yūbin Hōchi Shinbun*, 16.9.1874. Fukushima Nariyuki (*Akasaka Kuichigai*, 58–59) wrongly dates the two incidents to December 20 and January 3, respectively.

25. For information about the contacts between the groups, see Ogawara, "Seikanron Seihen ato," 92–93. And in addition, Takechi Kumakichi's statement, 2, in "Kuichigai Bōto Takechi Kumakichi hoka hachi-nin wa Tekiritsu Ukagai" (hereafter cited as *KBTK*), July 1874, NA-JP, Gyōsei Bunsho, Dajōkan-Naikaku Kankei:1, 2A-009–00, Kō 01237100, part 2.

26. Takechi Kumakichi's statement, p. 2, Yamazaki Norio's statement, p. 1, Iwata Masahiko's statement, p. 1, *KBTK*, July 1874, NA-JP, Gyōsei Bunsho, Dajōkan-Naikaku Kankei:1, 2A-009–00, Kō 01237s100, part 2; Ogawara, "Seikanron Seihen ato," 91.

27. Shimomura Yoshiaki's statement, pp. 2–3, Iwata Masahiko's statement, p. 2, *KBTK*, July 1874, NA-JP, Gyōsei Bunsho, Dajōkan-Naikaku Kankei:1, 2A-009–00, Kō 01237s100, part 2.

28. Fukushima, *Akasaka Kuichigai*, 35–39.

29. Iwata to his parents, 28.3.1874, in Fukushima, *Akasaka Kuichigai*, 121.

30. Based on the memoirs of Hashimoto Hikosuke, quoted in Fukushima, *Akasaka Kuichigai*, 61. Iwata Masahiko to his parents, 28.3.1874, quoted in ibid., 121; Takechi Kumakichi's statement, 2; Takechi Kikuma's statement, 2; Iwata Masahiko's statement, 2–3; Yamazaki Norio's statement, 2; Shimomura Yoshiaki's statement, 1–2 in *KBTK*, July 1874, NA-JP, Gyōsei Bunsho, Dajōkan-Naikaku Kankei:1, 2A-009–00, Kō 01237s100, part 2; *IKJ*, 2:1148; Fukushima, *Akasaka Kuichigai*, 56.

31. Based on the memoirs of Hashimoto Hikosuke, quoted in Fukushima, *Akasaka Kuichigai*, 61–62; compare with Iwata to his parents, 28.3.1874, in ibid., 121. Takechi's denouncement of Iwakura was not uncommon among Tosa retainers at the time. See *HSTN*, 6:16–17.

32. For further elaboration of this idea see Danny Orbach, "Tyrannicide in Radical Islam: Sayid Qutb and Abd a-Salam Faraj," *Middle Eastern Studies* 48, no. 6 (November 2012): 961–72.

33. Kokuryūkai, ed., *Seinanki Den* (Tokyo: Kokuryūkai, 1908–11, hereafter cited as *SNKD*), 2b:235.

34. Hashimoto Hikosuke's memoirs, quoted by Fukushima, *Akasaka Kuichigai*, 61.

35. Takechi's statement, p. 3, Sawada's statement, p. 3, *KBTK*, July 1874, NA-JP, Gyōsei Bunsho, Dajōkan-Naikaku Kankei:1, 2A-009–00, Kō 01237100, part 2.

36. *IKJ*, 2:1146; *OTN*, 2:229–30; Uchida Tomoi, *Itagaki Taisuke kun Denki* (Kōchi: Kumongō, 2009), 2:556–57. In fact, many of them tried to mislead the police and said in their depositions that they had thrown their swords into the river. See Fukushima, *Akasaka Kuichigai*, 127, and compare with Takechi Kumakichi's statement, 4–5; Yamazaki Norio's statement, 5, in *KBTK*, July 1874, NA-JP, Gyōsei Bunsho, Dajōkan-Naikaku Kankei:1, 2A-009–00, Kō 01237100, part 2; Osatake Takeki, "Akasaka Kuichigai no Hen: Iwakura U-Daijin no Kyogeki," *Osatake Takeki cho Sakushū* (Tokyo: Yuma ni Shobō, 2005–6), vol. 5, 151–53; Fukushima, *Akasaka Kuichigai*, 66–68; Sawada to Tsuchiya, 9.2.1874, in *Akasaka Kuichigai*, 124.

37. *OTN*, 2:230–31; Fukushima, *Akasaka Kuichigai*, 89–91; Kaku Kōzō, *Daikeishi Kawaji Toshiyoshi: Bakumatsu Meiji kakenuketa Kyojin* (Tokyo: Shuppan Geijutsusha, 1999), 336–37.

38. Iwata to his parents, 28.3.1874, in Fukushima, *Akasaka Kuichigai*, 122; Uchida, *Itagaki*, 2:557.

39. *KBTK*, NA-JP, Gyōsei Bunsho, Dajōkan-Naikaku Kankei:1, 2A-009–00, Kō 01237100, part 2, pp. 1–2; Osatake, "Akasaka Kuichigai" in Osatake, *Sakushū*, 153–54; *Yūbin Hōchi Shinbun*, 17.1.1874; *NSSS-M*, 1:542.

40. "Keishichō Rokuji," *Yūbin Hōchi Shinbun*, 16.9.1874; Take, "Tosa Hyōron," 26.

41. Nagano Susumu, *Saga no Eki to Chiiki Shakai* (Fukuoka-shi: Kyushu Daigaku Shuppankai, 1987), 116–22, 30–35, 203–4.

42. *NSSS-M*, 1:343; Nagano, *Saga no Eki*, 161–65, 83–85, 90–91.

43. Nagano, *Saga no Eki*, 116–17, 198–204; Ogi-chō (Saga-ken), *Ogi-chō shi* (Ogi: Ogi, 1974), 377.

44. Mori to Ōkuma, 23.1.1874, NA-JP, Gyōsei Bunsho, Naikaku-Sōrifu, Dajōkan-Naikaku Kankei:1, Kōbunroku, *Saga Seitō Shimatsu*, 1:1, 3, 6, 7, 28, 2A-009–00, Kō 01318100 (hereafter cited as *SSS*), 1:10. On the convoluted, chaotic structure of authority in Saga Prefecture, see Nagano, *Saga no Eki*, 114–15.

45. The version of the petitioners is reproduced in Matono Heisuke, *Etō Nanpaku* (Tokyo: Nanpaku Kenshōkai, 1914), 2:403–5. And compare with Mori's letter to Ōkuma, 23.1.1874, NA-JP, *SSS*, 1:10.

46. Mori to Ōkuma, 23.1.1874, NA-JP, *SSS*, 1:10.

47. Matono, *Etō Nanpaku,* 2:405.

48. Mori to Ōkuma, 23.1.1874, NA-JP, *SSS,* 1:10.

49. *OTN,* 2:236; *DKT,* 2:427; *SSSN-M,* 1:344; Nagano, *Saga no Eki,* 209–10.

50. Matono, *Etō Nanpaku,* 2:394.

51. Nagano, *Saga no Eki,* 205; *SPSS,* 1:28.

52. Nagano, *Saga no Eki,* 216, 19–20, 33. See also "Seikan-tō Shuisho," Murachi Masashi's testimony in *Etō Nanpaku,* 2:398–400. For dates and the petition of the Seikan-tō, see Sonoda Hiyoshi, *Etō Shimpei to Saga no Ran* (Tokyo: Shin-jinbutsu Jūraisha, 1874), 150. See also Mori to Ōkuma, 23.1.1874, NA-JP, *SSS,* 1:10. Testimony of Murachi Masashi in Matono, *Etō Nanpaku,* 2:398–400. Maeyama Seiichirō, leader of the loyalist faction in Saga, complained about the presence of Seikan-tō members throughout the administration of the prefecture to Governor Iwamura Takatoshi. See Iwamura to the Lord of Home affairs, 27.2.1874, NA-JP, *SSS,* 2:27(10), p. 2.

53. Sonoda, *Etō,* 130; Nagano, *Saga no Eki,* 233; *Ogi-chō shi,* 377, see also the Ogi diary excerpt reproduced in ibid., 382.

54. NA-JP, *SSS,* 1:26. For the full platform of the Yūkokutō, see "Yūkoku-sha Mōshiaisho" in Matono, *Etō Nanpaku,* 2:429–30; Nakano, *Saga no Eki,* 190–97, 212; Umegaki, *After,* 196–97.

55. "Yūkokusha Mōshiaisho" in Matono, *Etō Nanpaku,* 2:429, and compare with Shima's testimony in ibid., 434.

56. Quoted in Sonoda, *Etō,* 144.

57. Nakano, *Saga no Eki,* 208.

58. Nagano, *Saga no Eki,* 212–13; "Yūkoku-sha Mōshiai-sho," in Matono, *Etō Nanpaku,* 2:429–30.

59. Umegaki, *After,* 207.

60. For quantitative data and analysis about these divisions see Nagano, *Saga no Eki,* 226–35. As Nagano suggests, the data we have about the members of the parties and their distribution is incomplete. See also Iizuka Kazuyuki, "Saga no Ran no zai-Kentō: Shuhen no Shiten kara," *Kyūshū Shigaku* 149 (February, 2008), 28.

61. Testimony of Murachi Masashi, quoted in Matono, *Etō Nanpaku,* 2:395, 401.

62. Etō Shimpei, "Taigai Saku," in *SNKD,* 1A, appendix, 67–69; *NSSS-M,* 1:339.

63. Mashiko Eizu, "Saga Jijō" 1 in *SNKD,* 1B, appendix, 26.

64. Testimony of Murachi Masashi in Matono, *Etō Nanpaku,* 2:397–98, 401; statement of Etō Shimpei to the court, 8–9.4.1874 (hereafter cited as Etō's Statement), reproduced in Matono, *Etō Nanpaku,* 2:555, and compare with the official version of the Army Ministry in Rikugun Sanbō Kyoku, ed., *Saga Seitō Senki* (Tokyo: Rikugun Bunkō, 1875), 2 (hereafter cited as *SGSS*).

65. Sonoda Hiyoshi, *Etō Shimpei to Saga no Ran* (Tokyo: Shin-jinbutsu Jūraisha, 1874), 117. For the account of the conversation between Etō and Itagaki, who tried to convince him to remain in Tokyo, see Matono, *Etō Nanpaku,* 2:410–11.

66. Testimony of Takaki Hidetomi, quoted in Matono, *Etō Nanpaku,* 2:427.

67. *HSTN,* 6:5. See also Etō to the Dajōkan, 9.1.1874, in Matono, *Etō Nanpaku,* 2:406–7; Etō's Statement in ibid., 555; *HSTN,* 6:5; Sonoda, *Etō,* 133.

68. For specific evidence and theories in that regard, see Mōri, *Etō,* 205; *NSSS-M,* 1:341; Iizuka, "Saga no Ran," 16. Compare also with Hayashi, *Jirekidan,* 1:56 (quoted in Matono 418–19); Etō's own Statement is reproduced in Matono, *Etō Nanpaku,* 2:555.

69. Hayashi, *Jirekidan,* 1:53–54.

70. Testimony of Takaki Hidetomi, in Matono, *Etō Nanpaku,* 2:411–12, and the account of the conversation with Itagaki in ibid., 2:409–10.

71. Nakano, *Saga no Eki,* 210.

72. *OTN,* 2-4.2.1874; Shima's testimony in Matono, *Etō Nanpaku,* 2:434.

73. The letter is quoted in *NSSS-M,* 1:342; *SGSS,* 5–6.

74. NA-JP, Gyōsei Bunsho, Naikaku-Sōrifu, Dajōkan-Naikaku Kankei:1, Kōbunroku, *SSS,* 1:1, 3, 6, 7, 28, 2A-009–00, Kō 01318100; *OTN,* 2:236; Mōri, *Etō,* 206.

75. Mōri, *Etō,* 206.

76. *DKT,* 2:420. Compare with *HSTN,* 6:11.

77. *SGSS,* 2, 5–6; Iwakura to Ōkubo, 28.2.1874, reproduced in Matono, *Etō Nanpaku,* 2:568–69; *IKJ,* 2:1157; *NSSS-M,* 1:340; Nagano, *Saga no Eki,* 210. Even as late as March 2, some people in the government were afraid that rebellious troops from Satsuma and Chikuzen might come to the aid of the rebels, although these rumors were quickly refuted. See Fukuoka to Tokyo (telegram), 2.3.1874, NA-JP, *SSS,* 2:68(31), p. 1.

78. Iwamura to the Lord of Home Affairs, 27.2.1874, NA-JP, *SSS,* 2:27(10), pp. 3–4.

79. Etō's Statement in Matono, *Etō Nanpaku,* 2:558. In his testimony, Etō had quoted only these two articles, though he did mention that there were "two or three" additional ones. His emphasis on the prohibitions on desertion show how perennial this problem was in the Saga rebel force.

80. For the reports submitted by the leader of the loyalist faction, Maeyama Seiichirō, to Governor Iwamura see Iwamura to the Lord of Home affairs, 27.2.1874, NA-JP, *SSS,* 2:27(10), 2–3. In addition, see a short statement written by Maeyama, and a letter of his to the Imperial Army, as well as Iwakura's report to Ōkubo: Maeyama Seiichirō, "Sōryūji Shūkai Mōshiaisho," and Maeyama to the Imperial Army, 17.2.1874, Iwakura to Ōkubo, 28.2.1874, in Matono, *Etō Nanpaku,* 2:436–37, 439, 570, and also the testimony of Murachi Masahi in ibid., 438–39, and *SGSS,* 8. For survey and analysis see Sonoda, *Etō,* 157–62; Mōri, *Etō,* 204–5. There were also Saga shizoku who joined the government forces on their own initiative. Even Ogi, a stronghold of the Yūkokutō, had "more than one hundred" allies of the Imperial Army. See *Ogichō-shi,* 377.

81. Hayashi, *Jirekidan,* 1:56–58. For the situation in Tosa, see also *ITKM,* 4:512–13.

82. Shima's testimony in Matono, *Etō Nanpaku,* 2:435–36; Iizuka, Kazuyuki, "Saga no Ran no zai-Kentō: Shuhen no Shiten kara," *Kyūshū Shigaku* 149 (February 2008), 22–24.

83. Iizuka, "Saga no Ran," 28.

84. Eto's Statement in Matono, *Etō Nanpaku,* 2:556–57.

85. Nagano, *Saga no Eki,* 211–12; Mōri, *Etō,* 205. Interestingly enough, this false impression was also shared by Maeyama Seiichirō, the most important supporter of the government in the province. See Shima's testimony in Matono, *Etō Nanpaku,* 2:435; and Maeyama to the Imperial Army, 17.2.1874 in ibid., 439. Compare with Hayashi, *Jirekidan,* 1:56–58, and the testimony of Nakajima Suzutane in Matono, *Etō Nanpaku,* 2:440–41.

86. Chief Minister Sanjō Sanetomi, Dispatch No. 23, 19.2.1874, NA-JP, Gyōsei Bunsho, Naikaku-Sōrifu, Dajōkan-Naikaku Kankei:1, Kōbunroku, February 1874): 8, 2A-009–00, Kō-01016100 (hereafter cited as Kōbunroku 1); *DKT,* 2:433. The number is taken from *NSSS-M,* 1:34515. According to this evaluation, only four or five thousand rebels took part directly in the fighting. See also the report of Nakayama Ichirō to Etō and Shima, 20.2.1874, reproduced in Matono, *Etō Nanpaku,* 2:467–68. For the version of the Yūkokutō, see *Shinbun Zasshi,* 2.4.1874.

87. NA-JP, Kōbunroku 1:11, 13. The Imperial rescript defining Ōkubo's authority is reproduced in Osatake Takeki, *Meiji Bunka Sōsetsu* (Tokyo: Gakugeisha, 1934), 181. See also Chief Minister Sanjō to the Provincial Governors, 17.2.1874, NA-JP, *SSS,* 1:26; *OTN,* 2:237, 40; *NSSS-M,* 1:340. For an English language account, see Masakazu Iwata, *Ōkubo Toshimichi: The Bismarck of Japan* (Berkeley: University of California Press, 1964), 181–82.

88. NA-JP, Kōbunroku 1:17, 18; *OTN,* 2:249; Iwakura to Ōkubo, 28.2.1874, reproduced in Matono, *Etō Nanpaku,* 2:568; NA-JP, *SSS,* 2:33(6); *SGSS,* 27.

89. For precise data on the number of soldiers according to unit and rank see the formal history published by the Army Ministry in 1875: *SGSS,* introduction (page unnamed).

It is not clear whether this number includes the volunteer shizoku or not. For a modern assessment, see *SPSS*, 1:31. About the volunteers, see Kaku, *Daikeishi*, 364–65.

90. *SGSS*, 3–4, 7.

91. Sonoda, *Etō*, 169–70; *DKT*, 2:435. For more information on tactics and the course of fighting, see Edward J. Drea, *Japan's Imperial Army: Its Rise and Fall, 1853–1945* (Lawrence: University Press of Kansas, 2009), 37.

92. *OTN*, 2:242–43; *DKT*, 2:436; Ōkubo to Sanjō, 22.2.1874, NA-JP, *SSS*, 2:29 (2); Drea, *Imperial Army*, 37. For statistics on the Imperial Army's arms see *SGSS*, introduction (page unnamed), 21–23; Iizuka, "Saga no Ran," 24.

93. *OTN*, 2:254; Eto's statement in Matono, *Etō Nanpaku*, 2:559–60; Headquarters to Tokyo (telegram), 2.3.1874, NA-JP, *SSS*, 2:68(31), p. 6.

94. *OTN*, 2:246; *DKT*, 3:4–5, and compare with a telegram to the Army Ministry, 3.2.1874, NA-JP, *SSS*, 2:68(31), p. 13, which similarly estimated the number that surrendered as 1,600. According to the official history of the Army Ministry, there were 358 causalities on the government side, and 323 on the rebels' side—a relatively small number compared to the Satsuma Rebellion, let alone to later wars. See *SGSS*, 38.

95. *Shinbun Zasshi*, 2.4.1874.

96. *SGSS*, 35–36; Quoted also in Sonoda, *Etō*, 192.

97. *SGSS*, 35–36; Nozu to the Army Ministry, 3.2.1874, NA-JP, *SSS*, 2:68(31), p. 10. The original, unrephrased letter is probably the one published in *Shinbun Zasshi*, 2.4.1874. The *Zasshi* correspondent wrote that the letter was left at Saga Castle for the occupying Imperial soldiers. In other words, it was not yet the agreed-upon, formal letter of apology. The revised letter is reproduced in *SGSS*, 35.

98. Sonoda, *Etō*, 217–18; *OTN*, 2:256; *NSSS-M*, 1:350.

99. *OTN*, 2:258; Matono, *Etō Nanpaku*, 2:574–77, 98.

100. *DKT*, 3:19; *NSSS-M*, 1:353; Drea, *Imperial Army*, 38.

101. Brandt, *Dreiunddreissig*, 304. However, some of the government leaders were concerned about popular sympathy for Etō and Shima, especially in the press. See, for example, *OTM*, 5:483

102. *IKJ*, 2:1377; Ogawara, *Seinan*, 34–35.

103. For the manifest of the Shinpūren, see *IKJ*, 2:1377–78; for a partial English translation, see Augustus A. Mounsey, *The Satsuma Rebellion: An Episode of Modern Japanese History* (London: John Murray, 1879), 91–92; *SPSS*, 1:25–28.

104. *DKT*, 3:381; *SPSS*, 1:32–32.

105. *SPSS*, 1:33–34; Kaku, *Daikeishi*, 370–71.

106. *SSK*, 1:13–14; *DKT*, 3:435.

107. Mounsey, *Satsuma Rebellion*, 17, and compare with *DKT*, 3:486. See also Nagano, *Saga no Eki*, 120.

108. Mounsey, *Satsuma Rebellion*, 78–79; James H. Buck, "The Satsuma Rebellion of 1877: From Kagoshima through the Siege of Kumamoto Castle," *Monumenta Nipponica* 28, no. 4 (winter 1973): 429; *Saigō Takamori Zenshū*, ed. Hensan Saigō Takamori Zenshū Henshū Iinkai (Tokyo: Daiwa Shobō, 1976–80), 3:510–12 (hereafter cited as *STZ*); *SSK*, 1:5; *SNKD*, 1b:659–60, 4; *DSZ*, 3:820–81; for discussion about the shizoku stipends and other reforms in Kagoshima, see Tamamuro Taijō, *Seinan Sensō* (Tokyo: Shibundō, 1958), 32–39.

109. *DKT*, 3:401–2.

110. Ogawara, *Seinan*, 15–19; *SNKD*, 1b:652–75; Tamamuro, *Seinan*, 25–32; *SPSS*, 1:45–46.

111. *STZ*, 3:501–2; Ogawara, *Seinan*, 19; *SNKD*, 1b:661, 2a:46–47; Tamamuro, *Seinan*, 15, 30–32; *SPSS*, 1:46.

112. *STZ*, 3:510–11; *SPSS*, 1:49.

113. Chief Minister Sanjō to the Provincial Governors, 17.2.1874, NA-JP, *SSS*, 1:26, 2.

114. Ravina, *Last Samurai*, 192; Charles Yates, "Saigō Takamori in the Emergence of Modern Japan," *Modern Asian Studies* 28, no. 3 (July 1994): 466; John Stephan, "Saigō Takamori and the Satsuma Rebellion," *Papers on Japan* 3 (Cambridge, 1965), 125–61. For an opposite view of historians who believe that Saigō planned a rebellion after his resignation in October 1873, see Tamamuro Taijō, *Seinan*, 12–13; Kaku, *Daikeishi*, 370. This is not dissimilar to the official version of the Army Ministry in *SSK*, 2:5–6.

115. Iwayama Seiko and Iwayama Kazuko, eds., *Saigo san o kataru: Iwayama Toku no Kaisō* (Tokyo: Perikansha, 1999), 56–101.

116. *STZ*, 3:504. See also *HSTN*, 6:2–3, Saigō to Ōyama, 5.4.1875 in *SNKD*, 1b:663–64.

117. Iwayama and Iwayama, *Saigo san*, 192. In his memoirs, Hayashi Yūzō also testified about the difficulties he encountered when trying to meet Saigō in January 1874. See Hayashi, *Jirekidan*, 1:54–55.

118. Testimony of Murachi Masashi in Matono, *Etō Nanpaku*, 2:396–97; *STZ*, 3:507; *SPSS*, 1:25.

119. *STZ*, 3:537.

120. *STZ*, 3:496–97, 509; *HSTN*, 6:2–3; *IKJ*, 2:1396.

121. Kaku, *Daikeishi*, 331–32.

122. *HSTN*, 6:7; D. Eleanor Westney, "The Emulation of Western Organizations in Meiji Japan: The Case of the Paris Prefecture of Police and the Keishi-chō," *Journal of Japanese Studies* 8, no. 2 (summer 1982): 325.

123. Chief Minister Sanjō to the Provincial Governors, 17.2.1874, NA-JP, *SSS*, 1:26, pp. 4–5; *DKT*, 2:428; Westney, "Emulation," 314–16, 22–23.

124. *SPSS*, 1:49; *IKJ*, 2:1399. For a full listing of Nakahara's team as well as brief biographical information, see *SNKD*, 2a:51–53, as well as Taniguchi Tōgorō's testimony, 24.12.1874, in ibid., 36; NA-JP, Ōyama's confession, p. 2. A glimpse into the nature of early Meiji police can be obtained from the regulations drafted by Chief Superintendent Kawaji in January 1874, reproduced in full in Keishichō Shihensan Iinkai, ed., *Keishichō Shi, Meiji Hen* (Tokyo: Keichichō Shihensan Iinkai, 1959), 50–62.

125. Nakahara's confession is reproduced in *SNKD*, 2a:62–64, and the original is in NA-JP, *KSS*, 8:1. See also the denunciation letter that led to his arrest in NA-JP, *KSS*, 8:2. For an English translation of the confession see Mounsey, *Satsuma Rebellion*, 275–78; *SSK*, 1:8–9.

126. This man's name was Nomura Tsuna. His testimony is reproduced in *SNKD*, 2a:73–74.

127. *DES*, 2:232–34. These lines were taken from Nakahara's confession, see in *SNKD*, 2a:63.

128. *STZ*, 3:522–24, 530. Saigō was hunting when he received the news, another indication that he was not prepared for a rebellion. See *SNKD*, 2a:45.

129. *DES*, 2:224–25; *STZ*, 3:523; *SSK*, 2:5; *SPSS*, 1:52–54; *DKT*, 3:435–36. See also the 5.2.1877 diary entry of Ichiki Shirō, op. cit. in *SNKD*, 2a:102–3. For the report of the Imperial Navy about the events see NA-JP, KSS, 8:11.

130. NA-JP, Ōyama's confession, p. 5. The English translation in Mounsey's *Satsuma Rebellion* (282) is inaccurate.

131. Ravina, *Last Samurai*, 200.

132. NA-JP, Ōyama's confession, p. 5.

133. *SPSS*, 1:117–18. For an eyewitness testimony on the state of affairs in Kagoshima in early February, see Cortazzi, *Dr. Willis*, 221.

134. Mounsey, *Satsuma Rebellion*, 175. Compare with Ōyama Tsunayoshi's statement from 28.2.1874. In his public appeal, the governor of Kagoshima Prefecture bemoaned the government's decision to declare Saigō and his troops, loyal subjects all, as rebels to the throne. See NA-JP, KSS, 8:7.

135. *DES*, 2:230; *STZ*, 3:521, NA-JP, Ōyama's confession, p. 5; the term used was "investigation" (*kitsumon*); for detailed descriptions of that crucial meeting in the Private School see *SPSS*, 1:117–18, 23–24, as well as *SNKD*, 2a:104–5 and Ōyama to the police officials, 14.2.1877, NA-JP, KSS, 8:3.

136. *SPSS*, 1:124.

137. Mounsey, *Satsuma Rebellion*, 119–20; *SPSS*, 1:117–18, 23–24; *SNKD*, 2a:104–5.

138. *DES*, 2:230, 4; NA-JP, Gyōsei Bunsho, Naikaku-Sōrifu, Dajōkan-Naikaku Kankei:1, Kōbunroku, 2A-010–00, kō 02170100 (hereafter cited as Ōyama's confession), pp. 11–12; partial English translation in Mounsey, *Satsuma Rebellion*, 288.

139. Ōyama's formal letters are fully reproduced in *SPSS*, 1:125–26, and the originals are in NA-JP, KSS, 8:3. For an English translation see Mounsey, *Satsuma Rebellion*, 138–39. Compare with NA-JP, Ōyama's confession, p. 5; *DES*, 2:230. For the response of the Kumamoto garrison to Ōyama's letter see *SSK*, 21:6–7.

140. NA-JP, Ōyama's confession, 9–10.

141. Hayashi, *Jirekidan*, 1:55–56, 2:1–8; Itagaki's refusal to help Saigō was explicitly declared in a conversation with his (Itagaki's) followers and was reported in the *Tokyo Akebono Shinbun*, 20.6.1877. The article was based on a report by a Tosa retainer, most probably on Itagaki's behest. It seems that the Tosa leader wanted to clarify his position to both Saigō and the government. In any case, according to Uchida (*Itagaki*, 2:619), he told very similar things to the leaders of the Risshisha, his own organization. Tosa was not the puppet of Satsuma, Itagaki emphasized, and would not be dragged after Saigō in his "personal fight" with Ōkubo (*Saigō-Ōkubo no shitō*). Accordingly, Gotō met Kido in Kyoto and secured Tosa's neutrality. Some Risshisha activists, led by Hayashi Yūzō, tried to stage an attack on the Osaka garrison, but their plan was discovered and they were arrested.

142. *SSK*, 1:12–14, 2:5; Hayashi, *Jirekidan*, 2:6–7; *SPSS*, 1:72–74; *OTM*, 7:488.

143. *DKT*, 3:451.

144. *STZ*, 3:538. The original proclamation is reproduced in *SSK*, 1:18, see also 2:6. For an English translation, see Mounsey, *Satsuma Rebellion*, 138; *DKT*, 3:451. About the arrest of the envoys, see NA-JP, KSS, 8:5.

145. *SSK*, 1:18. For detailed statistics on the Imperial punitive force see *SPSS*, 1:57–62.

146. *STZ*, 3:524; Saigō to Ōyama, 12.3.1877, NA-JP, KSS, 8:9.

147. *SSK*, 21:6–7; *DKT*, 3:443; Buck, "Satsuma Rebellion," 434.

148. *SSK*, 2:1–2, 21:6–7.

149. Mounsey, *Satsuma Rebellion*, 158–59; *STZ*, 3:537; *Japan Daily Herald*, 3.3.1877. For statistical data about the two opposing armies, see *NSSS-M*, 1:405.

150. *STZ*, 3:537. Saigō and his officers, it seems, believed that the navy would not attack them. Around February 10, Governor Ōyama told Ernest Satow that the navy would "certainly not" bombard Kagoshima. That self-confidence was misguided. See *DES*, 2:231, 234.

151. An American eyewitness left us a moving testimony of Saigō's last stand, reproduced in Elizabeth Tripler Nock, "The Satsuma Rebellion of 1877: Letters of John Capen Hubbard," *Far Eastern Quarterly* 7, no. 4 (August 1948): 375–60. For information on the myth of Saigō's "suicide" and other legends about his death, see Mark Ravina, "The Apocryphal Suicide of Saigō Takamori: Samurai, Seppuku and the Politics of Legend," *Journal of Asian Studies* 69, no. 3 (August 2010): 691–721.

152. For an alternative explanation rooted in the complex role of domain identity, see Umegaki, *After*, 207–8.

153. Hayashi, *Jirekidan*, 2:1–2. For further discussion on this problem, see *NSSS-M*, 1:374.

154. For a well-argued example, see *NSSS-M*, 1:374.

155. Miyachi Masato, *Bakumatsu Ishinki no Shakaiteki Seijishi Kenkyū* (Tokyo: Iwanami Shoten, 1999), 51; Mounsey, *Satsuma Rebellion*, 109–10.

156. Yates, "Saigō Takamori in the Emergence," 459.
157. Mounsey, *Satsuma Rebellion*, 109–10; *SPSS*, 1:18.
158. Yates, "Saigō Takamori in the Emergence," 461.
159. A good example is the shazai submitted by Kihara Moritada of the Yūkokutō to the Imperial Army on February 28. In the letter, Kihara and his men apologized for their "selfish violence" against the Imperial Army. The letter is reproduced in *SGSS*, 34–35.

5. GOLD-EATING MONSTERS

The epigraph is taken from Fyodor Dostoevsky, *Demons: A Novel in Three Parts*, trans. Richard Pevear and Larissa Volokhonsky (New York: Vintage Books, 1995), 24.

1. *Sanbō Honbu Rekishi Sōan*, 8 vols., ed. Hirose Yoshishirō (Tokyo: Yumani Shobō, 2001), 4:49 (hereafter cited as *SHRS*).
2. Ernst L. Presseisen, *Before Aggression: Europeans Prepare the Japanese Army* (Tucson: University of Arizona Press, 1965), 94.
3. Shiba Ryōtarō, *Kono Kuni no Katachi* (Tokyo: Bungei Shunjū, 1997), 4:134–45. Shiba himself did not mention the gold-eating characteristics of the *Pixiu*. However, as this attribute is strongly associated with this mythical animal, the association could hardly have escaped the author and his readers.
4. For an up-to-date literature survey, see Mori Yasuo, *Nihon Rikugun to Nittchū Sensō e no Michi* (Kyoto: Mineruva Shobō, 2010), 3–8.
5. Kikuta Hitoshi, *Naze 'Sensō' datta no ka: Tōsui-ken to iu Shisō* (Tokyo: Kozawa Shoten, 1998), 74. See also Ōe Shinobu, *Nihon no Sanbō Honbu* (Tokyo: Chūō Kōronsha, 1985), 31–34.
6. Tobe Ryōichi, *Gyakusetsu no Guntai* (Tokyo: Chūō Kōronsha, 1998), 78–80; Yoshimitsu Khan, "Inoue Kowashi and the Dual Images of the Emperor of Japan," *Pacific Affairs* 71, no. 2 (summer 1998): 229.
7. See chapter 8–10, and also Umetani Noboru, "Sanbo Honbu Dokuritsu no Kettei Keii ni tsuite," *Gunji Shigaku*, 9:2:34, 19. See also Umetani's quote in Tobe, *Gyakusetsu*, 90, as well as Peter Wetzler, "Kaiser Hirohito und der Krieg in Pazifik: zur politischen Verantwortung des Tennō in der modernen japanischen Geschichte," *Vierteljahrshefte für Zeitgeschichte* 37, no. 4 (October 1989): 620.
8. Matsushita, *Meiji Gunsei Shiron*, 2 vols. (Tokyo: Yūhikaku, 1956), 2:6–7; Ōtsuka Minao, *Meiji Ishin to Doitsu Shisō* (Tokyo: Nagasaki Shuppan, 1977), 138–40; Presseisen, *Aggression*, 94–95.
9. Katsura Tarō, *Jiden* (Tokyo: Heibonsha, 1993), 73–74, 87–88; Rudolf Hartmann, "Japanische Offiziere im deutschen Kaiserreich," *Japonica Humboldtiana* 11 (2007), 115; Hata Iikuhiko, *Tōsui-ken to Teikoku Rikukaigun no Jidai* (Tokyo: Heibonsha, 2006), 76; Presseisen, *Aggression*, 60–62; Ōtsuka, *Doitsu no Shisō*, 94–95; Stewart Lone, *Army, Empire, and Politics in Meiji Japan: The Three Careers of General Katsura Tarō* (Basingstoke, UK: Macmillan, 2000), 10–11. The Staff Bureau was actually established in 1871 as a section in the Army Ministry (see Presseisen, *Aggression*, 60–62, as well as Katsura, *Jiden*, 81–83). For information on the establishment of the Staff Bureau see Yamagata Aritomo et al., eds., *Rikugunshō Enkaku Shi* (Tokyo: Rikugunshō, 1905), 97–98, 127 (hereafter cited as *RES*), 105.
10. For information on the Japanese adoption of the French model in the 1870s see Presseisen, *Aggression*, 33–45. For information on the French-style buildup of the Army Ministry in 1873, see *RES*, 97–98, 127. About the resistance by conservative officers see ibid., 95, as well as Katsura, *Jiden*, 100; Presseisen, *Aggression*, 95–110; Miura Gorō, *Kanju Shōgun Kaikoroku* (Tokyo: Seikyōsha, 1925), 174–75; and Lone, *Katsura*, 15.
11. Hata, *Tōsui-ken*, 76. On Yamagata's crucial role in the military reform, see also Roger F. Hackett, *Yamagata Aritomo in the Rise of Modern Japan 1838–1922* (Cambridge,

MA: Harvard University Press, 1971), 81–89. On the question of resistance by conservative officers, see also Barbara J. Teters, "The Conservative Opposition in Japanese Politics, 1877–1894" (Ph.D. diss., University of Washington, 1955), 57–58, 65–70.

12. Katsura, *Jiden*, 90–91.

13. Yui Masaomi, "Meiji Shoki no Kengun Kōsō," in *Nihon Kindai Shishō Taikei*, ed. Yui Masaomi, Fujiwara Akira, and Yoshida Yutaka, vol. 4, *Guntai Heishi* (Tokyo: Iwanami Shoten, 1989), 488; Matsushita, *Meiji Gunsei*, 2:3–4.

14. Presseisen, *Aggression*, 61–62; Kino, "Inoue Kowashi," 2:185; Lone, *Katsura*, 12.

15. *SHRS*, 4:17. For an organizational chart of the General Staff in 1878 see ibid., 27. For analysis see Ōe, *Sanbō Honbu*, 35–37. An organizational chart of the General Staff, updated to 1896 (right after the Sino-Japanese War) is in ibid., 61.

16. A facsimile copy of the regulations is fully reproduced in Sanbō Honbu Jōrei, *SHRS*, 4:19–26. For analysis and discussion see Matsushita, *Meiji Gunsei*, 2:11–12.

17. For discussion see Ōe, *Sanbō Honbu*, 33–35.

18. Army Lord to the Cabinet, 7.12.1878 in *SHRS*, 4:17, 33. According to Hata Iikuhiko (*Tōsui-ken*, 63–64) the missive was not drafted by Yamagata but by Saigō Tsugumichi, education lord, who doubled at the Army Ministry during Yamagata's sick leave. For discussion see Matsushita, *Meiji Gunsei*, 2:14–15.

19. Hata, *Tōsui-ken*, 11.

20. For information on the Prussian military cabinet, see Manfred Messerschmidt, "Die politische Geschichte der preussisch-deutschen Armee," in *Deutsche Militär geschichte in sechs bänden 1648–1939*, ed. Militärgeschichtliches Forschugsamt (Munich: Bernard & Graefe Verlag, 1983), 2:297–302.

21. *SHRS*, 4:33; Ōe, *Sanbō Honbu*, 41.

22. The cabinet regulations of 1885 (Dajōkan dispatch no.71) originally allowed such access only through the prime minister, but they were changed three years later. For the original regulations, see Kaneko Kentarō et al., *Itō Hirobumi Den* (Tokyo: Hara Shobō, 1970), 2:485–86. Compare with the *Dajōkan* regulations in Matsushita, *Meiji Gunsei,* 2:15; Mori, *Nihon Rikugun*, 19; Wetzler, "Kaiser Hirohito," 619.

23. For the regulations of the revised inspectorate see *KTKM,* 17:56–58, MJPH-NDL. The power over education was given to the Inspector General on May 31, 1887. See Tomio Nakano, *Origin and Development of So-Called Independence of Supreme Military Command in Japanese Constitution* (Tokyo: Kokusai Shuppan Insatsusha, 1932), 114; Kurono Taeru, *Sanbō Honbu to Rikugun Daigakkō* (Tokyo: Kōdansha, 2004), 5, as well as Kino, "Inoue Kowashi," 2:188; Katsura, *Jiden*, 101; *RES*, 151–52, 217; Hata, *Tōsui-ken*, 62; Ōtsuka Minao, *Doitsu Shisō*, 113–14. Meckel's recommendations are reproduced in Jacob Meckel, "Der organisatorische Aufbau und die Befehlsgliederung der grossen Verbände des japanischen Heeres," in George Kerst, *Jacob Meckel: sein Leben, sein Wirken in Deutschland und Japan* (Göttingen: Musterschmidt Verlag, 1970), 126–27.

24. Kunaichō, ed., *Meiji Tennō Ki*, 13 vols. (Tokyo: Yoshikawa Kōbunkan, 1968–1977), 4:577 (hereafter cited as *MT*); Keene, *Emperor*, 300–302, 583–84.

25. *MT* 4:527–45; *RES*, 148–50; *IKJ*, 2:1604–5; Keene, *Emperor*, 300–302.

26. For a different view, see Teters, "Genrō-in," 367–68. Contrary to Teters's arguments, I have not seen any solid evidence indicating that the "four generals" resisted the establishment of the General Staff. Her source is a 1944 monograph, which indeed tells that Miura and Soga resisted the reforms from the outset—but all of the examples it brings are related to criticism of specific aspects of Yamagata's policy, almost all of them from later years. See Koyama Hirotake, *Kindai Nihon Gunjishi Gaisetsu* (Tokyo: Itō Shoten, 1944), 226–27. An examination of the relevant portions in Tani Kanjō's correspondence, for example, shows that until 1881 his resistance was focused on specific aspects such as the army's pensions' law and not on Yamagata's policy in its entirety. See *TKI*, 2:76–79, and compare with

the editor's introduction to Tani's papers: *Tani Kanjō Kankei Monjo*, eds., Hiroe Yoshihiro, Kobayashi Kazuyuki (Tokyo: Kitazumisha, 1995), 16–17, and with the analysis in Kobayashi, *Tani*, 106–7.

27. See, for example, Torio Koyata's position in Sanjō to Iwakura, 1.12, 1878, reproduced in Umetani, "Sanbō Honbu Dokuritsu," 15, as well as Itō to Inoue, 12.10.1878 in ibid., 5. And also: Ōe, *Sanbō Honbu*, 47–49; Shin'ichi Kitaoka, "The Army As a Bureaucracy: Japanese Militarism Revisited," *Journal of Military History* 57, no. 5 (October 1993): 71–72; Drea, *Imperial Army*, 65–66; Kurono, *Rikugun Daigakkō*, 46–49; Kaneko, *Itō* 2:501–5.

28. Tani Kanjō to Kabayama Sukenori, 2.11.1878 in *TKI*, 2:498.

29. Itō Hirobumi to Inoue Kaoru, 12.10.1878, reproduced in Umetani, "Sanbō Honbu Dokuritsu," 4–5, see discussion and analysis in ibid., 6–7.

30. Umetani, "Sanbō Honbu Dokuritsu," 8–13, compare with the reaction of the leadership as described by Sawachi Hisae, *Hi wa waga Kyōchū ni ari: wasurerareta Konoe Heishi no Hanran Takebashi Jiken* (Tokyo: Iwanami Shoten, 2008), 310–13.

31. In his letter to Inoue Kaoru, Itō made it clear that to keep "due process" they must wait for the emperor's return. However, until that time, Itō ensured the consensus of the entire leadership, so the monarch, upon his return, was faced with a fait-accompli. See Itō to Inoue, 12.10.1878, in Umetani, "Sanbō Honbu Dokuritsu," 5.

32. Katō Yōko, *Sensō no Ronri: Nichi-Ro Sensō kara Taiheiyō Sensō made* (Tokyo: Keisō Shobō, 2005), 143; Nakano, *Origin*, 99; Matsushita, *Meiji Gunsei*, 2:16. See also Ōe, *Sanbō Honbu*, 33.

33. Kino, "Inoue Kowashi," 2:176, 8, 82–83.

34. See the missive of Chief Minister Sanjō in *RES*, 205–6, and the Imperial rescript establishing the cabinet system in ibid., 207–8. For discussion and analysis see Kino Kazue, "Inoue Kowashi no Tōsuiken no rikkenteki Tōgiyo Kōsō (2), " *Geirin* 58 (October 2009): 186–87. See also Itō, *Commentaries*, 89–90; Kaneko *Itō*, 2:484–86; George Akita, *Foundations of Constitutional Government in Modern Japan: 1868–1900* (Cambridge MA: Harvard University Press, 1967), 68; *MT* 6:513–18.

35. *MT* 6:471–72.

36. Nakano, *Origin*, 113; Yui, "Meiji Shoki," in Yui et al., *Guntai Heishi*, 4:492–93; Hackett, *Yamagata*, 91; Ōe, *Sanbō Honbu*, 28, 54, 6–7; Drea, *Imperial Army*, 64; *KYAD*, 2:760.

37. This is the same article that required the army minister to report to the throne only through the prime minister: "Every minister shall report from time to time to the prime minister in matters related to his duty. However, though the Chief of the General Staff shall report directly to the Throne on military matters, the army minister has to report to the prime minister." See Cabinet regulations (1885), article 6, in Kaneko, *Itō* 2:486.

38. Kino, "Inoue Kowashi," 2:189–202 (Itō Myoji is quoted on 201–2).

39. Itō, *Commentaries*, 24–26.

40. Nakano, *Origin*, 99–100. A similar interpretation is offered by Peter Wetzler, "Kaiser Hirohito," 618. According to Wetzler, the direct access of the chief of the General Staff to the throne was only in matters of strict military nature, that is, secret orders, and even such conversations should have been reported later to the prime minister. That may have been true legally, but the most important thing was the way that the army interpreted the legal situation later.

41. Nakano, *Origin*, 100. For a similar perspective see Umetani, *Gunjin Chokurei*, 113, 278.

42. Ōe, *Sanbō Honbu*, 50–51.

43. See for example: Yui, "Meiji Shoki," in Yui et al., *Guntai Heishi*, 4:489; Ōtsuka, *Doitsu Shisō*, 92.

44. Hackett, *Yamagata*, 82; Kurono, *Rikugun Daigakkō*, 20–21; Umetani Noboru, *Gunjin Chokuyu Seiritsushi* (Tokyo: Seishi Shuppan, 2008), 24.

45. *RES*, 97–98, 127.

46. *RES*, 148–50. These arguments were later reproduced in the official history of the general staff (*SHRS*, 4:17), as well as by some historians. See, for example, Matsushita, *Meiji Gunsei*, 2:5.

47. *RES*, 152. See also Kurono, *Rikugun Daigakkō*, 24–25, 8–9; *KTHS*, 165–67, 172, 243. A similar argument was reproduced by Matsushita, *Meiji Gunsei*, 2:3–4.

48. Hata, *Tōsui-ken*, 72.

49. Ibid., 114–17; Kurono, *Rikugun Daigakkō*, 6–7, 28–34. Edward Drea (*Imperial Army*, 50), writes, for example, that the Army Inspectorate was designed by Yamagata to consolidate his own power, and by extension, that of the Satsuma-Chōshu clique. But if that was so, why did the new organ enjoy independent *jōsō* rights? And more than that, why were such rights given to Miura Gorō and Tani Kanjō, Yamagata's implacable enemies?

50. Miura, *Kanju*, 124, 35; Yui, "Meiji Shoki," in Yui et al., *Guntai Heishi*, 4:491–92.

51. Umegaki, *After*, 179–83, 92.

52. Ōshima, "Meiji Shoki Dajōkansei," 27, for analysis and discussion see ibid., 12. Yamagata was to harbor this disdain throughout his life. See Lone, *Katsura*, 23.

53. Lone, *Katsura*, 12; Ōe, *Sanbō Honbu*, 22–24; *KYAD*, 2:334. In the official history of the Army Ministry, compiled in 1905 under Yamagata's auspices, all relevant army commanders are mentioned by name in the section dealing with the Saga Rebellion, but there is not even one word about the overlordship of Ōkubo. See *RES*, 105–6.

54. *KYAD*, 2:350; Lone, *Katsura*, 13; Kurono, *Rikugun Daigakkō*, 28.

55. Yamagata Aritomo, *Yamagata Aritomo Ikenshō* (Tokyo: Hara Shobō, 1966), 57–60 (hereafter cited as *YAIK*, see especially 60); *RES*, 108–9, 119, 131; Hackett, *Yamagata*, 73–74.

56. Hata, *Tōsui-ken*, 71–72; Presseisen, *Aggression*, 61; Kumagai, *Nihongun no Seishin*, 200–201.

57. Fukuzawa Yukichi, "Teishitsu-ron," in Fukuzawa, *Nihon Kōshitsu-ron* (Tokyo: Shimazu Shobō, 1978), 37–40.

58. Katsura, *Jiden*, 94.

59. See Yamagata's letter to Itō, quoted in Umetani, *Gunjin Chokuyu*, 104. For discussion see Sawachi, *Takebashi Jiken*, 312–14.

60. See the verdict of the Military Supreme Court and the letter to Sanjō Sanetomi, quoted in Umetani, *Gunjin Chokuyu*, 104–5, as well as Kurono, *Rikugun Daigakkō*, 26–27; Tobe, *Gyakusetsu*, 66. For a book-length study of the Takebashi Incident, see Sawachi, *Takebashi Jiken*. For a more concise, better documented account of the incident and its legal and political repercussions, see Kumagai, *Nihongun no Seishin*, 66–71; and *NSSS-M*, 1:469–510. The testimonies reproduced in *NSSS-M1*, 483–92 indicate that the catalyst for the incident was discontent over salaries and service conditions, not abstract ideologies or political affiliations.

61. Hackett, *Yamagata*, 71; Umetani, *Gunjin Chokuyu*, 33–34.

62. *RES*, 134.

63. *Katsura Tarō Kankei Monjo*, ed. Chiba Isao (Tokyo: Daigaku Shuppainkai, 2010), 326 (note: this is a book-form selection of Katsura's letters and is different than the archival collection also called Katsura Tarō Kankei Monjo and cited here as *KTKM*); Hackett, *Yamagata*, 83–85; Tobe, *Gyakusetsu*, 67; Fujita Tsuguo, *Meiji Gunsei* (Tokyo: Nobuyamasha, 1992), 81–85. For a different perspective see Hata, *Tōsui-ken*, 97, as well as Umetani, *Gunjin Chokuyu*, 103–4 and Kumagai, *Nihongun no Seishin*, 69–70.

64. Yamagata to Itō, reproduced in *KYAD*, 2:782.

65. Katsura, *Jiden*, 111–12; Hackett, *Yamagata*, 83; Tobe, *Gyakusetsu*, 67; Lone, *Katsura*, 12.

66. Quoted in Hackett, *Yamagata*, 86. Original in Osatake, *Meiji Bunka*, 182. See also *KYAD*, 2:810–12.

67. For a detailed description of the crisis of 1881, see Akita, *Constitutional*, 31–58; Kaneko, *Itō* 2:214–35. Compare with Kurono, *Rikugun Daigakkō*, 39–40.

68. Miura, *Kanju*, 131–34; Tobe, *Gyakusetsu*, 67; Kobayashi, *Tani*, 113–14. For a partial translation and extensive discussion of the four generals' memorial, see Teters, *Conservative Opposition*, 65–70.

69. Miura, *Kanju*, 135.

70. Kumagai, *Nihongun no Seishin*, 184–85, 197.

71. The *Gunjin Kunkai* document is reproduced in full in *YAIK*, 75–83 (see especially 79–82). For discussion, see also Drea, *Imperial Army*, 48.

72. Oleg Benesch, *Inventing the Way of the Samurai: Nationalism, Internationalism, and Bushido in Modern Japan* (Oxford: Oxford University Press, 2014), 177.

73. Keene, *Emperor*, 366.

74. *SOJT*, 2:705–7 (emphasis is mine). The Japanese original is reproduced in Yui et al., *Guntai Heishi*, 4:172–76.

75. Gluck, *Japan's Modern Myths*, 53–54. Tobe, *Gyakusetsu*, 69–71, Yamagata's letter to Itō reproduced in *YKAD*, 2:919–20.

76. *KTHS*, 172.

77. As Shiba Ryōtarō has rightly remarked (*Kono Kuni*, 4:134), Kido was perhaps the only leader who really believed in hermetic separation between the civilian and military spheres. See his strong words in *DKT*, 2:238.

78. *KYAD*, 2:759–60; Hata, *Tōsui-ken*, 112–13; Kurono, *Rikugun Daigakkō*, 31; R. P. G. Steven, "Hybrid Constitutionalism in Pre-war Japan," *Journal of Japanese Studies* 3, no. 1 (winter 1977): 115. The gradual waning in the power of the Genrō is described in ibid., 117–18.

79. Kumagai, *Nihongun no Seishin*, 184. The textbook of the Cadet School from June 1917 made it clear that absolute obedience is a duty of all soldiers and officers, regardless of rank. See Takano Kunio, ed. *Kindai Nihon Guntai Kyōiku Shiryō Shūsei* (Tokyo: Kashiwa Shobō, 2004, hereafter cited as *GKSS*), 4:16.

80. For the original document, see *Rikugun Keihō* (1881), Digitized Content, National Diet Library (hereafter cited as DC-NDL), articles 50, 110, http://dl.ndl.go.jp/info:ndljp/pid/794418. English translation adopted from Maxon, *Control*, 37–38. Maxon has translated the articles from the revised code of 1908. I have changed his translation only in places where the 1881 version was different.

81. Kumagai, *Nihongun no Seishin*, 15, 18–19.

82. In 1908, the army authorities inserted an additional prohibition made increasingly relevant by the expansion of the Japanese Empire. According to the revised Army Penal Code published in that year (article 35), "when a commanding officer has, without reason, initiated hostilities against a foreign country, he shall suffer death." For the original, see *Rikugun Keihō* in *Nakano Bunkō Hōrei Mokuji* (hereafter cited as *NBHM*), http://www.geocities.jp/nakanolib/hou/hm41-46.htm#. The English translation is taken from Maxon, *Control*, 37–38.

83. See, for example, Drea, *Imperial Army*, 50. Kurono Taeru (*Rikugun Daigakkō*, 33–34) describes the establishment of the Army Inspectorate as part of a subchapter entirely devoted to Yamagata's unbridled personal ambition. The fact that by establishing this specific institution Yamagata actually dispersed some power to his rivals seemed to have completely escaped him. Umetani Noboru (*Gunjin Chokurei*, 278) speaks about the system created about 1878 as "Emperor-centered absolutism," ignoring the factionalism, lack of solid hierarchy, and chaotic dispersion of power that characterized it almost to the end. It is indeed a little disconcerting to see how a usually careful scholar such as Umetani is still influenced by some simplistic generalizations characteristic of Japanese Marxist postwar historiography.

84. This definition is adopted from R. P. G. Steven's three conditions for separation of powers, see in "Hybrid," 101–2. See also Miura, *Kanju*, 174–75. The Army Ministry did not have the right to dismiss the officers of the General Staff. See Ōe, *Sanbō Honbu*, 41.

85. *KYAD*, 2:789; Kikuta, *Naze Sensō*, 77–78.

86. Bernd Martin, *Japan and Germany in the Modern World* (Providence, RI: Berghahn Books, 1995), 52–56. For a similar approach, see Chalmers Johnson, *MITI and the Japanese Miracle: The Growth of Industrial Policy, 1925–1975* (Stanford, CA: Stanford University Press, 1982), 36.

87. On French military influence, see Matsushita, *Meiji Gunsei*, 2:6–7; Kerst, *Meckel*, 56–57; Umetani, *Gunjin Chokuyu*, 23–30. For an example of the British and American influence on Japanese constitutional law, see Steven, "Hybrid," 99–133; George Akita, Hirose Yoshihiro, "The British Model: Inoue Kowashi and the Ideal Monarchical System," *Monumenta Nipponica* 49, no. 4 (winter 1994): 117–19.

88. Emily O. Goldman, "The Spread of Western Military Models to Ottoman Turkey and Meiji Japan," in *The Sources of Military Change: Culture, Politics, Technology*, ed. Theo Farrell and Terry Terriff (Boulder, CO: Lynne Rienner, 2002), 53. Otherwise, Goldman's analysis of Japanese military change in light of neo-institutionalist sociological theories is highly illuminating, most particularly her emphasis on interservice rivalry as motive for adoption of foreign ideas.

89. Martin, *Japan and Germany*, 52–56.

90. Westney, "Emulation," 318.

91. Katsura, *Jiden*, 73–74; Matsushita, *Meiji Gunsei,* 2:7. It is very difficult to locate Katsura's original reports from Germany. In the archive of the National Defense Agency, only two short reports survived, and both of them deal with procedural issues related to the Japanese foreign students in Germany. Many reports on relevant issues survived in Katsura's collected papers, but some of them are dated to a later period and many are undated (for example 18:5–7).

92. Gordon A. Craig, *The Politics of the Prussian Army 1640–1945* (London: Oxford University Press, 1964), 218, 23–32; Messerschmidt, "Die politische Geschichte," *Deutsche Militärgeschichte*, ed. Militärgeschichtliches Forschugsamt, 2:299–300; Gerhard P. Gross, *Mythos und Wirklichkeit: Geschichte des operative Denkens im deutschen Heer von Moltke d.Ä bis Heusinger* (Munich: Ferdinand Schöningh, 2012), 59. It is important to note that the handbook "Duties of the General Staff" (*Der Dienst des Generalstabes*), one of the important military guidebooks of the German Imperial Army, offered in its opening chapter a lengthy justification for this privilege as a tradition going back to 1821. See Paul L. E. H. A. Bronsart von Schellendorff, *Der Dienst des Generalstabes* (Berlin: E.S. Mittler und Sohn, 1884), 17–18, 22–25.

93. Craig, *Politics*, 162.

94. Jonathan Steinberg, *Bismarck: A Life* (Oxford: Oxford University Press, 2011), 159–60.

95. Otto von Bismarck, *Briefe an seine Braut und Gattin*, ed. H. Bismarck (Stuttgart: Cotta, 1900), 572–73; Craig, *Politics*, 199–204, 7–15; Azar Gat, *The Development of Military Thought: The Nineteenth Century* (Oxford: Clarendon Press, 1992), 339–41.

96. Translation in Gat, *Military Thought*, 338.

97. For theoretical and historical background on the development of the ideology of military professionalism, see Samuel P. Huntington, *The Soldier and the State: The Theory of Civil-Military Relations* (Cambridge, MA: Harvard University Press, 1957), 7–98. Specifically on Prussia, see ibid., 99–109. One of the best primary sources on the Bismarck-Moltke debate is the War Diary of Crown Prince Friedrich (later Emperor Friedrich III) from the Franco-Prussian War. See Kaiser Friedrich III, *Das Kriegstagebuch von 1870–71*, ed. Heinrich Otto Meisner (Berlin: K. F. Koehler, 1926), 319, 25–26, 483–84, as well as

Otto von Bismarck, *Die Gesammelten Werke* (Berlin: O. Stollberg, 1924), 6b:551–53. For discussion and analysis, see Christopher M. Clark, *Iron Kingdom: The Rise and Downfall of Prussia: 1600–1947* (Cambridge MA: Belknap Press of Harvard University Press, 2006), 515, 28–30; Craig, *Politics*, 195–96, 199–204, 7–15; Gross, *Mythos*, 45.

98. Kitaoka, "Army," 70; Tobe, *Gyakusetsu*, 58–60, 67–68, 161; Huber, *Revolutionary Origins*, 173–75, 205.

99. Tamura Yasuoki, "Sensō-ron no Keifu (2): Tōsuiken Chūritsu o megutte," *Kōchi Daigaku Shakai Kagaku* 98 (July 2010): 2–6, 8–9, 32–33.

100. Steinberg, *Bismarck*, 163; Craig, *Politics*, 162–63; D. P. G. Hoffmann, "Kommandogewalt und Kriegsminister," *Zeitschrift für die gesamte Staatswissenschaft / Journal of Institutional and Theoretical Economics* 68, no. 4 (1921), "Kommandogewalt," 743.

101. There is an undated draft in Katsura's papers specifying the precise roles of the emperor's military adjutant. The author of this short draft (only part of it survived) mentioned several different models of this function, one of which closely resembled the Prussian military cabinet. It is unclear if Katsura himself wrote this note, and if so, when. In any case, the role of the military adjutant as it actually developed was limited to relatively weak liaison functions. See *KTKM*, 16:226, MJPH-NDL.

102. See, for example, Craig, *Politics*, 162–64; Bismarck, *Briefe*, 572–73. For several examples of William II's direct involvement in shaping foreign policy, see Akita and Hirose, "British Model," 416–17.

103. Akira and Hirose, "British Model," 417, compare with Itō, *Commentaries*, 88, warning against a state of affairs as existed in ancient China when "important measures of state were also executed on the authority of an ex-Emperor, of the private wishes of the Emperor, or of written notes of ladies of the Court."

104. Fukuzawa, "Teishitsu-ron," 26–27.

105. Hata, *Tōsui-ken*, 26. For additional discussion of this question, see Wetzler, "Kaiser Hirohito," 616–17; Kitaoka, "Army," 70.

106. See, for example, Lone's description of the emperor's function during the first Sino-Japanese War (*Katsura*, 39). For a brilliant contemporary analysis of the factional fights under the hazy imperial center, see Fukuzawa, "Teishitsu-ron," 22–23. For a discussion on the haziness of imperial authority, see also Haley, *Authority without Power*, 79–80.

107. The quote is taken from instructions on discipline in a textbook of the Cadet School (published June 1917), reproduced in *GKSS*, 4:15–17.

108. Mineo Kyūdai, *Rikugun Sanbō: Erito Kyōiku no Kōzai* (Tokyo: Bungei Shunjū, 1988), 167–69.

109. James Crowley, "From Closed Door to Empire: The Formation of the Meiji Military Establishment," in *Modern Japanese Leadership: Transition and Change*, ed. Bernard S. Silberman and H. D. Harootunian (Tuscon: University of Arizona Press, 1966), 284–85; Ben-Ami Shillony, *Revolt in Japan: The Young Officers and the February 26, 1936 Incident* (Princeton, NJ: Princeton University Press, 1973), 6–7.

110. Kurono, *Rikugun Daigakkō*, 7.

111. Military orders stipulated that a subordinate must obey also a command of an officer who is not his direct superior (*GKSS*, 4:15–16), but as we shall see later, this warning was often unheeded.

6. THREE PUFFS ON A CIGARETTE

The epigraph is taken from Miura, *Kanju*, 341, 47. English translation provided in part by Theodore M. Critchfield, "Queen Min's Murder" (Ph.D. diss., Indiana University, 1975), 94.

1. Drea, *Army*, 86–87.

2. On the reception of Queen Min in contemporary South Korea, see Tatiana Simbirtseva, "Ubiistvo v Dvortse Kyonbokkun," *Vostochnaya Kollektsiya* 3, no. 18

(autumn 2004): 129; Hata Ikuhiko, "Binhi Satsugai Jiken no saikōsatsu," *Seikei Kenkyū* 43, no. 2 (October 2006): 59–61; Shimamura Hatsuyoshi, "Zai Korian no Mune no uchi: Binhi Ansatsu to Seiryaku Kekkon: Chōsen Heigō 100 toshi wo mukae," *Kairo* 3 (2010): 164. The assassination of Queen Min resonated strongly in 1972, almost eighty years later, when the wife of President Pak Chong-hee was shot dead by a Korean resident of Japan. After the event, Korean demonstrators accused Japan of "murdering our empress again." For the testimony of the Japanese ambassador to Korea at the time, see Tsunoda Fusako, *Binhi Ansatsu: Chōsen Ōchō maki no Kokubo* (Tokyo: Shinchō Bunko, 1993), 16–17.

3. "Sugimura Fukashi nado Hikoku Jiken Chijutsusho" (hereafter quoted as "Sugimura Chinjutsusho"), in *Chōsen Kōshō Shiryō*, ed. Itō Hirobumi (Tokyo: Hisho Ruisan Kankōkai, 1936), 2:526–27, 33 (hereafter cited as *CKS*); Kobayakawa Hideo, *Bingō Soraku Jiken*, 35. This handwritten manuscript, a firsthand account written by a participant in the palace raid, was probably composed shortly after the annexation of Korea in 1910. its modern Japanese translation, published fifty years later in a nonfiction collection, was believed by some scholars to be faked (Critchfield, *Murder*, 8–9), but the original was rediscovered later and bequeathed to the National Diet Library by a descendent of Adachi Kenzō. Critchfield argued, among other things, that one of its paragraphs seems to be a paraphrase from Adachi Kenzō's memoir, but the reason is clear: Adachi's notes on the manuscript may show, as Kim Moonja righty assumed (*Chōsen Ōhi Satsugai to Nihonjin: Dare ga shikunde dare ga Jikkō shita no ka* [Tokyo: Kōbunken, 2009], 284–85), that Kobayakawa had used it as a source for his own memoirs. The original prewar Japanese text is kept in the Modern Japanese Political History Materials Reading Room at the National Diet Library, Tokyo, Shushū Bunsho, no.1195.

4. Ernst Satow to Lord Salisbury, 23.10.1895, in George A. Lensen, *Korea and Manchuria between Russia and Japan: The Observations of Sir Ernst Satow, British Minister Plenipotentiary to Japan (1895–1900) and China (1900–1906)* (Tallahassee, FL: Diplomatic Press, 1966), 52. Compare with the description of Isabella Bird, *Korea and Her Neighbours* (Bristol: Ganesha, 1997), 2:43–44.

5. Bird, *Korea*, 2:43–44.

6. Woonsang Choi, *The Fall of the Hermit Kingdom* (Dobbs Ferry, NY: Oceana, 1967), 17–19; Peter Duus, *The Abacus and the Sword: The Japanese Penetration of Korea* (Berkeley: University of California Press, 1995), 54.

7. Choi, *Hermit Kingdom*, 21–23; Critchfield, *Murder*, 31–37.

8. Critchfield, *Murder*, 37.

9. Sugimura Fukashi, *Meiji 28 nen Zaikan Kushinroku* (Tokyo: Hara Shobō, 1981), 146–47.

10. Homer B. Hulbert, *The Passing of Korea* (Seoul: Yonsei University Press, 1969), 47. For a similar description see Choi, *Hermit Kingdom*, 15.

11. For more information of the tension between cabinet and court, see Sugimura, *Zaikan*, 147; Ishizuka Eizō, "Chōsen Jijō Chōsa (Kadai)," in *Miura Gorō Kankei Monjo*, ed. Yamamoto Shirō (Tokyo: Meiji Shiryō Kenkyū Renrakukai, 1960), 72–73 (hereafter cited as *MGKM*).

12. D'Anethan to De Burlet, 10.10.1895, in George A. Lensen, *The D'Anethan Dispatches from Japan, 1894–1910: The Observations of Baron Albert d'Anethan, Belgian Minister Plenipotentiary and Dean of the Diplomatic Corps* (Tokyo: Sophia University Press, 1967), 54; *NSSS-M*, 2:214.

13. K. I. Weber, envoy in Seoul, to the Foreign Ministry, St. Petersburg, 29.11.1895, reproduced in *Rossiia i Koreia : nekotorye stranitsy istorii (konets XIX veka) : k 120-letiiu ustanovleniia diplomaticheskikh otnosheniĭ*, ed. A. V. Turkunov (Moskva: Moskovskiĭ gos. institut mezhdunarodnykh otnosheniĭ (Moscow: Universitet MID Rossii, 2004), 315 (hereafter cited as *RIK*).

14. Bird, *Korea,* 2:39. For a similar description of the queen, see Afanasii Seredin-Sabatin, to the Russian deputy consul in Chifu (Yantai), 30.10.1895, Arhiv Venshneii Politiki Rossiskei Imperii (hereafter cited as AVPRI), fond 143, opis 141, Kitaiskii Stol, attachment to number 121-1895 (hereafter cited as Sabatin's Report AVPRI), 20.

15. Simbirtseva, "Ubistvo," 139.

16. Weber to the Foreign Ministry, 29.11.1895, *RIK,* 315. In the 1890s, as a result of economic interests, the building of the Trans-Siberian railway, and a new, aggressive ideology of manifest destiny (advocated by a school called the "Easterners," "Vostochniki"), Russia became greatly interested in the Far East. Korea, who could supply an ice-free harbor and thus access to the Pacific, was especially important in the larger Russian schemes. For background, see Andrew Malozemoff, *Russian Far Eastern Policy, 1881–1904* (New York: Octagon Books, 1977), 41–93.

17. Duus, *Abacus,* 52–55, 88–89; Critchfield, *Murder,* 60. For a concise description of the sectional map in Seoul by a contemporary witness, see the report of the Russian architect Sabatin, Sabatin's Report AVPRI, 19–21.

18. Malozemoff, *Policy,* 56; Duus, *Abacus,* 54–55.

19. Malozemoff, *Policy,* 52–56; Andre Schmid, *Korea between Empires, 1895–1919* (New York: Columbia University Press, 2002), 25–27; Duus, *Abacus,* 68–70.

20. Duus, *Abacus,* 425. Regarding the development of the idea of annexing Korea, see for example the discussion held on September 26, 1895, between British Envoy Ernst Satow and Prime Minister Itō, Satow to Salisbury, 27.9.1895, reproduced in Lensen, *Satow,* 44–45.

21. Duus, *Abacus,* 49–52, 64–65 (the paraphrase is from 69–70).

22. *NSSS-M,* 2:212; "Sugimura Chinjutsusho," *CKS,* 2:530; Sugimura, *Zaikan,* 46–47, 54, 8.

23. *NSSS-M,* 2:212; Sugimura, *Zaikan,* 71–74, 86–87; "Sugimura Chinjutsusho," *CKS,* 2:533.

24. Sugimura, *Zaikan,* 90–94, 6–7. And see article 4 of the Korean declaration of independence as cabled by the American envoy in Seoul. John M. B. Sill to the Secretary of State, 17.1.1895, *Korean American-Relations: Documents Pertaining to the Far-Eastern Diplomacy of the United States,* ed. George M. McCune (Berkeley: University of California Press), 2:350 (hereafter cited as *KAR*).

25. "Okamoto Jinmon," *CKS,* 2:470; Tsunoda, *Binhi Ansatsu,* 277.

26. Kuzu Yoshihisa (Kokuryūkai), ed., *Tōa Senkaku Shishi Kiden* (Tokyo: Hara Shobō, 1933–36), 1:520 (hereafter cited as *TSSK*); Ko Teung Chai Pan-So, Supreme Court, to Justice Minister Yi Pom Chin, "Official Report on Matters connected with the Events of October 8th, 1895, and the Death of the Queen" (hereafter cited as "Official Korean Investigation"), reproduced in *The Korean Repository,* Seoul (hereafter cited as *TKR*) 3 (1896): 131–32; Adachi Kenzō, *Adachi Kenzō Jijoden* (Tokyo: Shinjusha, 1960), 52.

27. Sugimura, *Zaikan,* 89–105; The gist of Inoue's intended reforms is well illustrated in a memorandum penned by Ishizuka Eizō, a Japanese advisor to the Korean cabinet, written during Inoue's tenure (precise date unknown), "Chōsen Jijō Chōsa (Kadai)," *MGKM,* 72–80.

28. *NSSS-M,* 2:211; Satow to Salisbury, 27.9.1895, in Lensen, *Satow,* 45. On the triple intervention see the detailed description by Malozemoff, *Policy,* 62–68.

29. "Sugimura Chinjutsusho," *CKS,* 2:529; Hata, "Binhi Satsugai," 70.

30. *TSSK,* 1:514–18.

31. Tsunoda, *Binhi Ansatsu,* 276–77.

32. "Hullyeondae Kidō ni tsuite An zen-Gunmudaijin Naihō," 18.8.1895, *MGKM,* 84–85.

33. Duus, *Abacus,* 67.

34. "Sugimura Chinjutsusho," *CKS*, 2:530.

35. Sugimura, *Zaikan*, 89–90.

36. Adachi, *Jijōden*, 53–54; "Sugimura Chinjutsusho," *CKS*, 2:527.

37. Nakusa Morio, *Uyoku Rōnin Tōjō: Okamoto Ryūnosuke no Hikari to Kage* (Tokyo: Sōfūsha, 1980), 27.

38. "Rikugun Shosa Okamoto Ryūnosuke hoka san me no Shokei," 22.3.1879, NA-JP, Gyōsei Bunsho, Naikaku-Sōrifu, Dajōkan-Naikaku Kankei:6, 2A-009-0, Hitoe 00659100; Tsunoda, *Binhi Ansatsu*, 21–24; Yamagata Hojirō, "Chōsen Ōhi Jiken," *Gunji Kenkyū* 3, no. 1 (1938): 45–54 (the testimony of General Kususe Yukihiko, as related to Yamagata), 48.

39. "Miura Jinmon" in *CKS*, 2:420.

40. "Okamoto Jinmon" in *CKS*, 2:455. Regarding the mutual hatred between Inoue and the daewongun, see Horiguchi Kumaichi, *Gaikō to Bungei* (Tokyo: Daiichi Shobō, 1934), 128–29; Nakusa, *Uyoku*, 364.

41. Sugimura, *Zaikan*, 148; Hata, "Binhi Satsugai," 70–71.

42. *NSSS-M*, 2:214–15.

43. "Okamoto Jinmon," "Sugimura Chinjutsusho," *CKS*, 2:462, 529–30.

44. Hata, "Binhi Satsugai," 73.

45. Critchfield, *Murder*, 88.

46. Hata, "Binhi Satsugai," 76–77.

47. Teters, *Conservative Opposition*, 36–38.

48. Tani to Itō, July 1895 (day unclear), *TKI*, 2:599–600. For discussion and analysis, see Kim, *Chōsen*, 104–7; Hata, "Binhi Satsugai," 76–77.

49. After the assassination, Tani was shocked, dismayed, and deeply disappointed by Miura's behavior. See *TKI*; Hata, "Binhi Satsugai," 78–79.

50. *DKT*, 3:477.

51. Kitaoka, "Army," 71–72; Drea, *Imperial Army*, 65–66; Teters, *Conservative Opposition*, 1–20, 36, 53–54, Hata, "Binhi Ansatsu," 77.

52. Miura, *Kanju*, 120–23, 350–51; Teters, *Conservative Opposition*, 58–59, 67–68; Toyabe Shuntei, "Miura," in *Shuntei Zenshū* (Tokyo: Hakubunkan, 1909), 2:178, 80.

53. Miura, *Kanju*, 341, 47 (English translation taken in part from Critchfield, *Murder*, 94). Miura used the character *ten* implying heaven in a transcendental, religious sense.

54. "Sugimura Chinjutsusho," *CKS*, 2:530.

55. Miura, *Kanju*, 319; "Sugimura Chinjutsusho," *CKS*, 2:530–31.

56. Miura, "Taikan Seisaku ni kan suru Miura Shinkōshi, Ikensho: Taikan Seisaku no Kunrei wo matsu," *Nihon Gaikō Bunsho*, ed. Gaimushō (Tokyo: Gaimushō Chōsabu, 1947–53), 28:438–39 (hereafter cited as *NGB*). Compare with Sugimura's version in "Chinjutsusho," *CKS*, 2:530–32.

57. Miura, *Kanju*, 324.

58. Tsunoda, *Binhi Ansatsu*, 283–84.

59. Miura, *Kanju*, 324–25. Adachi Kenzō, as well, recalled that the Korean Court had treated Miura with disrespect, see *Jijoden*, 56.

60. "Okamoto Jinmon," *CKS*, 2:469.

61. Critchfield, *Murder*, 88.

62. "Okamoto Jinmon," *CKS*, 2:470–72.

63. Uchida, "Ōjō Jihen" *NGB*, 28:554.

64. Kobayakawa, *Bingō*, 24–26.

65. Sugimura, *Zaikan*, 179–80.

66. Kikuchi, *Chōsen Ōkoku* (Tokyo: Minyūsha, 1896), 510–11; Tsunoda, *Binhi Ansatsu*, 315. Hong had personally saved the queen during the coup of 1882. See Critchfield, *Murder*, 25.

67. Sugimura, *Zaikan*, 178.

68. Horiguchi, *Gaikō to Bungei*, 120–27; "Miura Gorō Jinmon Chōsho" (hereafter cited as "Miura Jinmon") in *CKS*, 2:409–11, 20. Compare with Sugimura, *Zaikan*, 48; and Uchida Sadatsuchi, "Ōjō Jihen," *NGB*, 555–56 .

69. Miura, *Kanju*, 328–29, 46–47. This version is confirmed by the testimony of Okamoto, who took great pains to convince Miura to work with the daewongun. See "Okamoto Jinmon," *CKS*, 2:470–71, though in Okamoto's testimony Miura seemed a little bit less reluctant to work with the daewongun.

70. "Miura Jinmon" in *CKS*, 2:412–13, "Okamoto Jinmon," ibid., 468–70, 3; Sugimura, *Zaikan*, 171.

71. Sugimura, *Zaikan*, 171–72; Nio Koreshige to the Finance Minister, 11.10.1895, *CKS*, 2:502–4; Kim, *Chōsen*, 326–27.

72. "Okamoto Jinmon," Nio to the Finance Minister, 11.10.1895, *CKS*, 2:471–73, 504; Sugimura, *Zaikan*, 171; The text of the agreement with the daewongun is reproduced ibid., 172–73.

73. Sugimura, *Zaikan*, 178–80.

74. Kim, *Chōsen*, 261–62, 75; Tsunoda, *Binhi Ansatsu*, 287–300. The main primary source for the negotiations is the memoirs of Deputy Consul Horiguchi Kumaichi, but its reliability is certainly open to question. See *Gaikō to Bungei*, 113–34.

75. The Hiroshima court ascribed the decision to kill the queen to the meeting between Miura, Fujimura, and Okamoto on October 3. See "Decision of the Japanese Court of Preliminary Inquiries" (hereafter cited as "Japanese Court Decision"), *TKR* 3 (1896): 123. Compare with "Miura Jinmon" in *CKS*, 2:415. For discussion see Hata, "Binhi Satsugai," 82.

76. According to Tsunoda (*Binhi Ansatsu*, 347) these sentiments had a widespread echo not only among the sōshi, but also in the Seoul Japanese community and among the corps of Japanese advisors. About the formation of the *Tenyūkyō*, see Chae Soo Do, "'Tenyūkyō' ni kansuru ikōssatsu," *Chūō Daigakuin Kenkyū Nenpō: Hōgaku Kenkyūka*. 30 (February 2001): 441–42.

77. Eiko Maruko Siniawer, *Ruffians, Yakuza, Nationalists: The Violent Politics of Modern Japan* (Ithaca: Cornell University Press, 2008), 43. For more information about the term, see Sasaki, *Shishi to Kanryō: Meiji Shonen no Jōkei* (Kyoto: Mineruva Shobō, 1984), 113–15.

78. Sasaki, *Shishi to Kanryō*, 113–16. See especially Tokutomi Sōhō, editorial in *Kokumin no Tomo* 7 (August 1887), "Sōshiron," *Shinonome Shinbun*, 23.1.1888, both reproduced in Sasaki, *Shishi to Kanryō*, 253–57.

79. Kikuchi Kenjō, *Chōsen Ōkoku* (Tokyo: Minyūsha, 1896), 503; *TSSK*, 1:517; Chae, "Tenyūkyō," 440, 45–47. For discussion about the terminology, see Tsunoda, *Binhi Ansatsu*, 302–3. Kobayakawa, for example, had used the terms *dōshi* (brethren), *yūshi* or *minkan shishi* to describe his friends, while the term *sōshi* is used to describe the regular soldiers from both sides. See *Bingō*, 41, 52, 75, 88, 91–92.

80. Chae, "Tenyūkyō," 442, 45; Siniawer, *Ruffians*, 55–56. For good descriptions of the *Tenyūkyō* see also Oleg Benesch, *Inventing the Way of the Samurai: Nationalism, Internationalism, and Bushido in Modern Japan* (Oxford: Oxford University Press, 2014), 68–69; Kang Ching-Il, "Tenyūkyō to 'Chōsen Mondai': 'Chōsen Rōnin' no Tōgaku Nōmin Sensō e no Taiō to kanren shite," *Shigaku Zasshi* 97, no. 8 (1988): 1322–35.

81. Terasaki Yasukichi (alias Takahashi Genji), "Terasaki-shi Sekijitsudan" in Itō Chiyū," *Itō Chiyū Zenshū* (Tokyo: Heibonsha), 12:439–40; Kang, "Tenyūkyō," 1325–26, 42

82. "Sasa Jinmon," *CKS*, 2:487.

83. Kobayakawa, *Bingō*, 41–42, 6–7; Hata, "Binhi Satsugai," 82–83.

84. Kim, *Chōsen*, 298–301.

85. *TSSK*, 1:517; Kobayakawa, *Bingō*, 46–47; Kang, "Tenyūkyō," 1329.

86. *TSSK*, 1:516–17.

87. A good example for this worldview is a book written one year after the incident by Kikuchi Kenjō, one of the sōshi who reinvented himself later as a popular historian of Korea. See *Chōsen Ōkoku*, 159–61, and also Kang, "Tenyūkyō," 1343–45. For the larger context of this type of Japanese image see Schmid, *Korea*, 116–17, 21–23, as well as Duus, *Abacus*, 59–60.

88. Kobayakawa, *Bingō*, 33; Kang, "Tenyūkyō," 1345.

89. Kikuchi, *Chōsen Ōkoku*, 504; Kobayakawa, *Bingō*, 33.

90. Adachi, *Jijoden*, 62.

91. Kikuchi, *Chōsen Ōkoku*, 503.

92. Kobayakawa, *Bingō*, 32–33.

93. Kikuchi, *Chōsen Ōkoku*, 516.

94. "Okamoto Jinmon" in *CKS*, 2:464–65, corroborated by Kobayakawa, *Bingō*, 33. For further evidence see Hata, "Binhi Satsugai," 68.

95. *TSSK*, 1:522.

96. Ibid., 1:538, 45. And compare with Kikuchi, *Chōsen Ōkoku*, 511.

97. Kikuchi, *Chōsen Ōkoku*, 501–3; Kobayakawa, *Bingō*, 34, 6.

98. Uchida, "Ōjō Jihen," *NGB*, 28:559; Critchfield, *Murder*, 81, 147; Hata, "Binhi Satsugai," 77; Nakusa, *Uyoku*, 366.

99. Adachi, *Jijoden*, 54–55. Kobayakawa (*Bingō*, 42) dates the conversation to October 1.

100. Adachi, *Jijoden*, 56–58; Kobayakawa, *Bingō*, 42; Okamoto later tried, disingenuously, to deny the extant of involvement of Adachi's sōshi in the operation, see "Okamoto Jinmon," *CKS*, 2:483. This conversation is reported only by two sources, Adachi and Kobayakawa (the latter does not mention the term "fox hunt"), but its authenticity can still be considered solid. The sōshi undertook the attack on the queen, they were organized by Adachi, and as Sasa testified, believed they were working on behalf of Miura ("Sasa Jinmon," "Shūketsu Kettei Setsumeisho," *CKS*, 2:489, 538). Therefore, a working session between the two men, in which the operation was discussed, most probably took place, and the date offered by Adachi seems very reasonable. In addition, the term *fox* was mentioned by Okamoto again in his operational orders to the troops, as if to mimic's Miura's language (see below).

101. Adachi, *Jijoden*, 56–57.

102. Hata, "Binhi Satsugai," 80.

103. Adachi Yukiko, "Yukiko no Shokanroku," in Adachi, *Jijoden*, 68–69; Kobayakawa, *Bingō*, 59, 81.

104. "Okamoto Jinmon" in *CKS*, 2:451.

105. Uchida, "Ōjō Jihen," *NGB*, 28:559; "Japanese Court Decision," *TKR* 3 (1896): 122.

106. Ibid.

107. Hata, "Binhi Satsugai," 84.

108. Sugimura, *Zaikan*, 176.

109. Miura, *Kanju*, 326, compare with "Miura Jinmon" in *CKS*, 2:417, and An's own version: An Kyong-su, "Hullyeondae Kidō ni tsuki An Zengunmu Daijin Naihō," in *Meiji Shiryō*, ed. Yamamoto Shirō (Tokyo: Meiji Shiryō Kenkyū Renrakukai, 1960), 8:85–86. See also Uchida, "Ōjō Jihen," *NGB*, 28:554, and Sugimura's version in *Zaikan*, 179–80. For a timeline of events on October 7, see Hata, "Binhi Satsugai," 87.

110. "Okamoto Jinmon," *CKS*, 2:474; Sugimura, *Zaikan*, 179–80.

111. "Japanese Court Decision," *TKR* 3 (1896): 123; "Miura Jinmon" in *CKS*, 2:417; Adachi, *Jijoden*, 58–59; Sugimura, *Zaikan*, 181; "Hikoku Kususe Yukihiko Chūsa Kyūjutsu," *Nikan Gaikō Shiryō: Kankoku Ōhi Satsugai Jiken*, ed. Ichikawa Masaaki (Tokyo: Hara Shobō, 1953), vol. 5:132 (hereafter cited as *NKGS*).

112. Sugimura, *Zaikan*, 182.

113. Uchida, "Ōjō Jihen," *NGB*, 28:556; "Japanese Court Decision," *TKR* 3 (1896): 123; "Okamoto Jinmon," *CKS*, 2:475; Kobayakawa, *Bingō*, 56–57; Yamagata, "Chōsen Ōhi Jiken," 48.

114. "Sasa Jinmon," *CKS*, 2:489; Kikuchi, *Chōsen Ōkoku*, 511–13. Okamoto had spent the previous days in Inchon, pretending he was going to depart for Japan, in order to avoid suspicion. See "Okamoto Jinmon," *CKS*, 2:473–76.

115. Uchida, "Ōjō Jihen," *NGB*, 28:556.

116. *TSSK*, 1:528. The Kokuryūkai's description was probably based on the memoir of Kobayakawa, *Bingō*, 81. See also Adachi, *Jijōden*, 58–59; Uchida, "Ōjō Jihen," *NGB*, 28:556. Compare with Sabatin's Report AVPRI, 4.

117. "Official Korean Investigation," *TKR* 3 (1896): 132–33. Seredin-Sabatin did not write about the collaborators, but he did mention that the Palace Guard had dwindled on the crucial night of October 7. Sabatin's Report AVPRI, 3.

118. Sabatin's Report AVPRI, 3–4; Sabatin, "Korea Glazami Rasiyam," *Sankt Peterburskie Vedmosti*, 16.5.1896 (Julian - 4.5), 5–16; Uchida, "Ōjō Jihen," *NGB*, 28:557; "Assassination" in *TKR* 2 (1895): 386–87. General Dye's report is highly apologetic—a spirited defense of his actions as military advisor to the Palace Guard before and during the assassination in response to the accusations of Isabella Bird (*Korea*, 2:73). Still, the utter incompetence of the guard that day was well reflected even in this self-serving testimony. See "General William Dye on 'Korea and Her Neighbors,'" letter to the editor, November 1898, in *TKR* 5 (1898): 440; Kikuchi, *Chōsen Ōkoku*, 515–16; Kobayakawa, *Bingō*, 88–89.

119. Testimony of U Pom-chin, previous Minister of Commerce and Agriculture, in K. I. Weber to Foreign Minister Prince Alexei Lobanov-Rostovskii, 9.10.1895, *RIK*, 283; Allen to the Secretary of State, 10.10.1895, *KAR*, 2:359.

120. Sabatin's Report AVPRI, 3; Adachi, *Jijoden*, 61; "Okamoto Jinmon," *CKS*, 2:477–78; *TSSK*, 1:529–30; Uchida, "Ōjō Jihen," *NGB*, 28:557.

121. Kikuchi, *Chōsen Ōkoku*, 515; Hata, "Binhi Ansatsu," 90.

122. Kobayakawa, *Bingō*, 89; "Assassination" in *TKR* 2 (1895): 387–88; "Official Korean Investigation," ibid., 3 (1896), 142; Sabatin's Report AVPRI, 3–4; "Okamoto Jinmon," *CKS*, 2:477–78. Compare with a much less flattering description by Adachi, leader of the Sōshi (*Jijoden*, 61). According to Adachi, McDye looked and behaved like a pathetic old man, who removed his hat to "give respect" to the invading Japanese troops. For a similar description see also the *Kokuryūkai* version, *TSSK*, 1:529, and Kikuchi, *Chōsen Ōkoku*, 515–16.

123. Hata, "Binhi Satsugai," 92–93. From Japanese testimonies, we know that officers were among the sōshi who entered the inner chambers, but three witnesses, two Koreans and one Russian, testified that the uniformed soldiers surrounded the compound, while nonuniformed men were the ones who went inside. See H. N. Allen to the Secretary of State, 10.10.1895, *KAR*, 2:357–58; Sabatin's Report AVPRI, 4; interrogations of Lieutenant Colonel Yi Ha-gyun, Colonel Hyun In-tak by K. I. Weber, #211 Seoul, October 1895, AVPRI, appendixes 4, 5. However, the Korean investigation report ("Official Investigation Report," 127) argued that uniformed Japanese officers had entered the inner rooms of the palace as well, so it is impossible to be certain about this point.

124. Korean Official Report in *TKR* 3 (1896): 125–26. Compare with the testimony of the Korean crown prince in Weber to Lobanov-Rostovskii, 9.10.1895, *RIK*, 282, and the censored testimony of Okamoto, "Okamoto Jinmon," *CKS*, 2:480–81. The parts related to the murder act were censored, but still, the fact that killing the queen was the mission of the sōshi is relatively clear in context. A fuller, more candid Japanese account, from the sōshi's point of view, can be found at *TSSK*, 1:530, Kobayakawa, *Bingō*, 100; and Kikuchi, *Chōsen Ōkoku*, 516–17.

125. Terasaki (Takahashi), "Setsujitsudan," 442–43.

126. Sabatin's Report AVPRI, 5–7.

127. Kikuchi, *Chōsen Ōkoku*, 516. And compare with a much less flattering description of the carnage in Uchida's report, "Ōjō Jihen," *NGB*, 28:557–58.

128. Prosecutor Kusano to Justice Minister Yoshikawa, 9.11.1895, reproduced in Yamabe Kentarō, "Binhi Jiken ni tsuite," *Koria Hyōron* 6, no. 48 (October 1964), 50; Weber to Lobanov-Rostovski, 9.10.1895, testimony of the Korean crown prince, *RIK*, 277–78, 82.

129. According to Uchida's first report to Deputy Foreign Minister Hara, an army lieutenant killed the queen. See Hara Keiichirō and Yamamoto Shirō, *Hara Kei o meguru Hitobito* (Tokyo: Nihon Hōsō Shuppan Kyōkai, 1981), 152–53; Uchida to Hara, 1.11.1895, *NKGS*, 5:153; Military Police Colonel Hayashi to Deputy Army Minister Kodama, 12.11.1895, *NKGS*, 8:206, implies that he belonged to the secret service and his name was Miyamoto Taketarō. In his formal report to Saionji, Uchida raised the issue again, but as one possibility among many ("Ōjō Jihen," *NGB*, 28:558). Kim Moonja (*Chōsen*, 254–58) has chosen to adopt this version, perhaps uncritically, without paying due attention to the other options (for example Takahashi's incriminating letter, see below).

130. Takahashi remained unrepentant throughout his life, see his "Setsujitsudan," 444–45; Uchida, "Ōjō Jihen," *NGB*, 28:558; Hillier to the Foreign Office, October 1875, British National Archives (hereafter cited as BNA) FO 228 1884, 267. The murder of the queen was described both by the crown prince (Weber to Lobanov-Rostovskii, 9.10.1895, *RIK*, 282, Allen to the Secretary of State, 10.10.1895, *KAR*, 2:358) and by a palace maid, a testimony reproduced in "Assassination," *TKR* 2 (1895): 388–89, and compare with the Kokuryūkai version, *TSSK*, 1:530. Takahashi's identity as the killer of the queen was suggested by Uchida (see above), based on an incriminating letter he had written at the day after the event. But in this letter, Takahashi expressed his fear that he had killed another woman, "a beauty" and the royal household minister, "a loyal retainer," instead of the true enemy—the queen. This letter was not published in *NGB*, but it is kept in Inoue Kaoru's private papers at the National Diet Library. See Takahashi Genji to Suzuki Shigemoto, 8.10.1895, *Inoue Kaoru Kankei Monjo* (hereafter cited as *IKKM*), 58:25, MJPH-NDL. In the ruling Takahashi was referred to by his other name, Terazaki Yasukichi.

131. "Assassination," *TKR* 2 (1895): 390.

132. H. N. Allen to the Secretary of State, 13.10.1895, *KAR*, 2:359 and compare with Satow to Salisbury, 18.10.1895, in Lensen, *Satow*, 50, Saionji to Nishi, 9.10.1895, *NGB*, 8:496–97; Miura, *Kanju*, 338; and Adachi, *Jijoden*, 62; Kobayakawa, *Bingō*, 93; as well as to the report, "Keijō Henji no Kōhō" published in *Tōhoku Nippō*, 24.10.1895. According to this newspaper's report, the swords of the sōshi were "soaked with fresh blood."

133. Critchfield, *Murder*, 135–36.

134. Kikuchi, *Chōsen Ōkoku*, 516–17; Tanaka, "Binhi Ansatsu," 74.

135. Daewongun, proclamation no. 2, reproduced in "Assassination," *TKR* 2 (1895): 389.

136. "Official Korean Investigation," *TKR* 3 (1896): 135. According to another version, also quoted by Weber, the king mentioned his hand, not his fingers. See also, for the absence of the royal seal, in Weber to Lobanov-Rostovskii, 12.10.1895, *RIK*, 290–91; Allen to the Secretary of State, 13.10.1895, *KAR*, 2:362; Testimony of U Pom-chin, in Weber to Lobanov-Rostovskii, 9.10., 7.12.1895, *RIK*, 283, 98–99; Hillier to the Foreign Office, October 1875, BNA FO 228 1884, p. 268–69; Saionji to Hayashi and Nishi, 18.10.1895, *NGB*, 28:520. An English translation of the royal edict was produced ibid., 270–71, as well as in "Assassination," *TKR* 2 (1895): 331. The original, in classical Chinese, is reproduced in *NGB*, 28:505.

137. Weber to St. Petersburg, 9.10.1895, reproduced in *RIK*, 275.

138. "Korean Official Report," *TKR* 3 (1896): 127.

139. Miura, *Kanju*, 338–39. Compare with Weber to Lobanov-Rostovskii, 9.10.1895, *RIK*, 278–80; Kikuchi, *Chōsen Ōkoku*, 517–18.

140. Allen to the Secretary of State, 10.10.1895, *KAR*, 2:361; "Korean Official Report," *TKR* 3 (1896): 129–30; Miura to Saionji, 10.10.1895, 9 a.m., *MGKM*, 91. The correspondence

between Miura and Foreign Minister Kim is reproduced in *NGB*, 28:502–6. Kunitomo repeated the same lie about the Korean dressed in Japanese garb in his interrogation at the Seoul Consulate, 12.10.1895, *IKKM*, 58:27, MJPH-NDL. About the Korean scapegoats see Tsunoda, *Binhi Ansatsu*, 430–31.

141. However, this is far from being uncontested. In October 1895, Seredin-Sabatin had already written to tell the Russian consul in Chifu that the Japanese government was behind the affair (Sabatin's Report AVPRI, 17–18). Kim Moonja, the author of the newest work on the affair in Japanese, believes that Miura and his accomplices had killed the queen according to the will of the Japanese government. Though Kim closely analyzes the evidence and draws on a wide array of primary sources, some of them rare, she is not able to prove her main argument. Nor is she able to explain why Miura lied to Saionji as if he had merely obeyed orders. See Kim, *Chōsen*, 258–59, 360–65.

142. Miura to Saionji, 8.10.1895, 8:00 a.m., *MGKM*, 87.

143. Uchida, "Ōjō Jihen," *NGB*, 28:559.

144. Saionji to Miura, 8.10.1895, 15:00, *MGKM*, 88.

145. Miura to Saionji, 8.10.1895 (3 p.m., 8 p.m., 11 p.m.), 14.10.1895 (3 p.m.), *MGKM*, 87–89, 93; Miura to Itō, 14.10.1895, *NGB*, 28:513–14. Compare with Nio to the Finance Minister, 11.10.1895, *CKS*, 2:502–6.

146. Uchida, "Ōjō Jihen" *NGB*, 28:553–54, 9.

147. In a dispatch to Hara, dated 19.10, Uchida was still uncertain whether the assassination was committed by command from Tokyo, though he assumed that this was not the case. Hara/Yamamoto, *Hara Kei*, 154.

148. Uchida, "Ōjō Jihen," *NGB*, 28:553, 5, 61; Hara/Yamamoto, *Hara Kei*, 152–53.

149. "Ōjō Jihen," *NGB*, 28:252–62. See especially 558–61.

150. Uchida Sadatsuchi, "Taikansha Seimeihyō," *IKKM*, 58:56, MJPH-NDL; Uchida, "Ōjō Jihen," *NGB*, 28:261–62; *TSSK*, 1:537.

151. D'Anethan to de Burlet, 17, 26.10.1895, *D'Anethan Dispatches from Japan*, 54; Weber to Lobanov-Rostovskii, 7.12.1895, *RIK*, 298–99; Nio to the Finance Minister, 11.10.1895, *CKS*, 2:503–4; Komura to Saionji, 17.10.1895, *NGB*, 28:518.

152. Hillier to Foreign Office, 11.10.1875, BNA FO 228 1884, 272; Miura to Saionji, 10.10.1895, 9 a.m., *MGKM*, 91.

153. "The King at the Russian Legation," *TKR* 3 (1896): 80–89; "Official Korean Investigation," ibid., 140–41.

154. "Official Korean Investigation," *TKR* 3 (1896): 80–89.

155. For three eyewitness testimonies of this lynching see "The King at the Russian Legation," *TKR* 3 (1896): 86–89. Tsunoda, *Binhi Ansatsu*, 447.

156. Satow to Salisbury, 16.10.1895, in Lensen, *Satow*, 47. Compare with Saionji to Nishi, 9.10.1895, *NGB*, 28:496–97.

157. Saionji to Miura, 11.10.1895 (3 p.m.), *MGKM*, 91–92.

158. Nomura to Itō, 13.10.1895, NA-JP, Gyōsei Bunsho, Naikaku-Sōrifu, Dajōkan-Naikaku Kankei:6, 2A-011-00, rui 00741100.

159. Saionji to Miura, 17.10.1895 (6pm), *MGKM*, 94–95; *Tōhoku Nippō*, 22.10.1895.

160. *TSSK*, 1:538.

161. *Tōhoku Nippō*, 24.10.1895; "Sasa Jinmon," *CKS*, 2:488.

162. Japanese Court Decision, 20.1.1896, *TKR* 3 (1896): 122–25; Takahashi to Suzuki, 8.10.1895, *IKKM*, 58:25, MJPH-NDL; Kusano to Yoshikawa, 9.11.1895, Yamabe "Binhi Jiken," 50.

163. "Official Korean Investigation," *TKR* 3 (1896): 125; "Japanese Court Decision," *TKR* 3 (1896): 124–25.

164. *Keiji Soshoho* (Osaka: Osaka Asahi Shinbun sha, 1890–1), art. 165, pp. 50–51. For an online version see http://kindai.ndl.go.jp/info:ndljp/pid/795135/33.

165. John Haley argues that "common sense" was often used to adapt the letter of the law to existing values. See Haley, *Authority without Power*, 85.

166. "Okamoto Ryūnosuke hoka 47 mei Yoban Shūketsu Kettei ni Hinan wo hai suru Riyū Setsumeisho" (hereafter cited as "Setsumeisho"), *CKS*, 2:537–39. Ironically, this document was also presented to the public in a censored version, a fact which naturally did not contribute to its reliability and/or persuasive power.

167. For Uchida's description of the events in the palace see "Ōjō Jihen," *NGB*, 28:557–58.

168. Haruta to Kodama, 9, 22.11.1895, *NKGS*, 5:201, 31; Uchida, "Ōjō Jihen," *NGB*, 28:557–58.

169. See for example: Uchida to Hara, 1.11.1895, to Kusano, 12, 19.11.1895, *NKGS*, 5:153, 218, 24, 34–35.

170. See for example General McDye's testimony, taken by Uchida (20.11.1895), *NKGS*, 5:269–74.

171. Critchfield, *Murder*, 229–30.

172. *NSSS-M*, 2:151–55; Teters, *Conservative Opposition*, 111–14.

173. *NSSS-M*, 2:176–94 (see especially pp. 189–91).

174. See for example Kurino to Saionji, 22.10.1895, *NGB*, 28:522–23; Uchida, "Ōjō Jihen," Saionji to the Japanese envoys, "Ōhi Satsugai Jiken Keika Tsūhō no Ken," 8.11.1895, *NGB*, 28:561, 67–68.

175. See especially the first page of the ruling, "Japanese Court Decision," *TKR* 3 (1896): 122. There is evidence, however, that the government took a keen interest in the development of the investigation and in the force of the evidence gathered. See, for example, Justice Minister Yoshikawa to Privy Councilor Kuroda, 10.11.1895, reproduced in Yamabe, "Binhi Jiken," 50.

176. Inoue and Haruta to Deputy Army Minister Kodama, correspondence from October and November, *NKGS*, 5:139–40, 52, 5, 63, 276. The request to send investigation teams to Korea is on 196.

177. This question was discussed in a long letter from Investigator Inoue to Deputy Minister Kodama, 19.11.1895, *NKGS*, 5:228–30, and see also 248–49. About the (lack) of notion of illegal command in the Japanese Army, see Yoshida Yutaka, *Nihon no Guntai: Heishitachi no Kindaishi* (Tokyo: Iwanami Shoten, 2002), 146.

178. On December 19, Inoue asked for permission to return to Tokyo in order to discuss the evaluation of the evidence with the Army Ministry. Possibly, the joint decision to acquit the defendants was made in that meeting. See Inoue to Kodama, 19.12.1895, *NKGS*, 5:274–75. For the final decision of the military tribunal, see ibid., 308–12.

179. That was probably the answer to Sugimura's angry rhetorical question of why the government approved the coup of Ōtori in 1894 but condemned that of Miura at the following year. See "Sugimura Chinjutsusho," *CKS*, 2:533–34.

180. Conroy, *Seizure*, 306–7.

181. Gluck, *Modern Myths*, 73–94; Fujitani, *Monarchy*, 174–83; *DKT*, 1:72–73.

182. Sabatin's Report AVPRI, 21–22; Bird, *Korea*, 2:37, 42, 73; Miura, *Kanju*, 324–25.

183. *TSSK*, 1:522. See also Sabatin's Report AVPRI, 22.

184. *TSSK*, 1:521; Kobayakawa, *Bingō*, 33.

185. Kikuchi, *Chōsen Ōkoku*, 501–2.

186. *TSSK*, 1:522.

187. Bird, *Korea*, 2:65; Uchida, "Ōjō Jihen," *NGB*, 28:557–58; Terasaki (Takahashi), "Setsujitsudan," 442–23. Compare with Sabatin's Report AVPRI, 4–10.

188. "Miura Gorō Jijitsu Teisei Negai," 12.12.1895, *CKS*, 2:524–25.

189. "Sugimura Chinjutsusho," *CKS*, 2:526.

190. Uchida, "Ōjō Jihen," *NGB*, 28–1:560.

191. *Tōhoku Nippō*, 27.10.1895; For discussion on the question of the authority to mobilize troops, see Kim, *Chōsen*, 130–36.

192. The sōshi Kobayakawa Hideo (*Bingō*, 33, 52) rightly defined Miura's decision as a *dokudan* (arbitrary decision made according to one's operational discretion) without the orders or even tacit approval of the Japanese government.

193. Such terms may remind the reader of Maruyama Masao's famous distinction between "fascism from below" and "fascism from above." I have intentionally refrained from using these terms, since in 1895 fascism hardly existed, and it would be both misleading and anachronistic to define either Miura or the sōshi as "fascists." For Maruyama's view, see *Thought and Behavior*, 25–84.

194. Siniawer, *Ruffians*, 54, 87; Kang, "Tenyūkyō," 1341.

195. Terasaki (Takahashi), "Setsujitsudan," 440. See also Kang, "Tenyūkyō," 1341.

196. Prasenjit Duara, "State Involution: A Study of Local Finances in North China: 1911–1935," *Comparative Studies in Society and History* 29, no. 1 (January 1987): 135–36.

197. "Chōsen Kyōhen to Naikaku," *Tōhoku Nippō*, 24.10.1895; Uchida, "Ōjō Jihen," *NGB*, 28:562; "Hikoku Kususe Yukihiko Chūsa Kyūjutsu," *NKGS*, 5:132; Kim Moonja (*Chōsen*, 310) simplified this highly complicated process into a one dimensional conspiracy theory: that the army merely used the sōshi as a smoke screen to hide its activities. This is, however, only a half truth, as the "army" was never a unified body, and the interaction between sōshi and military factions influenced and changed both sides.

7. COUP D'ÉTAT IN THREE ACTS

1. Drea, *Imperial Army*, 89.

2. Tobe, *Gyakusetsu*, 158–59.

3. Peter Duus, *Party Rivalry and Political Change in Taishō Japan* (Cambridge, MA: Harvard University Press, 1968), 11.

4. Tazaki Suematsu, *Hyōden Tanaka Giichi: Jūgonen Sensō no Genten* (Chōfu-shi: Heiwasenryaku sōgō Kenkyūjō, 1981), 1:356–59, 62–63.

5. Najita Tetsuo, *Hara Kei in the Politics of Compromise, 1905–1915* (Cambridge, MA: Harvard University Press, 1967), 105–6, 208–9; Duus, *Party Rivalry*, 3, 8–13, 29–31; Banno Junji, *Taishō Seihen: 1900-nen Taisei no Hōkai* (Kyoto: Mineruba Shobō, 1982), 72; Toshitani Nobuyoshi, "Meiji Kempō Taisei to Tennō: Taishō Seihen Zengo wo chūshin toshite," *Hōgaku Shinpō* 83, no. 10–12 (1977), 72–73; "Hara Naishō no Hirikken," *Osaka Asahi Shinbun*, 20.8.1912.

6. Ōtsu Junichirō, *Dai Nihon Kenseishi* (Tokyo: Hara Shobō, 1969–70), 6:752; Ōe, *Sanbō Honbu*, 127; Banno, *Taishō Seihen*, 9–13.

7. Najita, *Hara*, 60–62; Duus, *Party Rivalry*, 31–33; For a critical contemporary perspective on Hara's policy, see "Hara Naishō no Hirikken," *Osaka Asahi Shinbun*, 20.8.1912.

8. "Chōsen Shidan Secchi," *Osaka Asahi Shinbun*, 20.8.1912; J. Charles Schencking, *Making Waves: Politics, Propaganda, and the Emergence of the Imperial Japanese Navy, 1868–1922* (Stanford, CA: Stanford University Press, 2005), 139; Tazaki, *Tanaka*, 364–65; Toshitani, "Meiji Kempō," 75–76; Ōe, *Sanbō Honbu*, 117–18, 24–25.

9. Yamamoto Shirō, *Taishō Seihen no Kisoteki Kenkyū* (Tokyo: Ochanomizu Shobō, 1970), 43–44; Takakura Tetsuichi et. al., *Tanaka Giichi Denki* (Tokyo: Tanaka Giichi Denki Kankōkai, 1957–58), 2:485–86 (hereafter cited as *TGD*); Schencking, *Waves*, 139–40, 5; Ōe, *Sanbō Honbu*, 118.

10. Uehara to the cabinet, reproduced in *TGD*, 2:492.

11. Banno, *Taishō Seihen*, 10.

12. *Hara Takashi Nikki*, ed. Hara Keiichirō and Hayashi Shigeru, 6 vols. (Tokyo: Fukumura Shuppan, 1965–69), 3:187 (hereafter cited as *HTN*). For details on the retrenchment plans, see the speeches of Saionji and Yamamoto in the Imperial Diet, 23.1.1912,

reproduced in Ōtsu, *Kenseishi,* 6:668–70; Yamamoto, *Seihen,* 179; *TGD,* 2:501; Kaigun Rekishi Hozonkai, ed., *Nihon Kaigun shi* (Tokyo: Kaigun Rekishi Hozonkai, 1995), 2:214; Banno, *Taishō Seihen,* 10.

13. Uehara to Yamagata, 23.10.1912 in *Yamagata Aritomo Kankei Monjo,* ed. Shōyū, Kurabu Yamagata, Aritomo Kankei, and Monjo Hensan Iinkai (Tokyo: Shōyū Krabu, 2004), 1:221–22 (hereafter cited as *YAKM*); *HTN,* 3:254, 9; Gotō to Katsura, 5.9.1912 in *Katsura Tarō Kankei Bunsho,* ed. Chiba Isao (Tokyo: Tokyo Daigaku Shuppankai, 2010), 179–80 (hereafter cited as *KTKB*); Kyofuji Koshichirō to Prime Minister Saionji, 16.11.1912, JACAR, Ref. B03030229900, p. 1.

14. *HTN,* 3:244; Tanaka Giichi, "Zōshi Mondai Keii," in *TGD,* 2:515; Banno, *Taishō Seihen,* 11.

15. See for example: "Rikugun no Kakuchō danjite fuka," *Tōyō Keizai Shinpō,* 15.7.1912, 8–10.

16. About public opinion in the wake of the Siberian Intervention, see Paul E. Dunscombe, *Japan's Siberian Intervention, 1918–1922: "A Great Disobedience against the People"* (Lanham, Md.: Lexington Books, 2001), 4. And see Richard Smethurst data on the greater popularity of the army in rural areas, in Richard J. Smethurst, *A Social Basis for Prewar Japanese Militarism: The Army and the Rural Community* (Berkeley: University of California Press, 1974), 66–71.

17. Uehara to Terauchi, 29.10.1912; Gotō to Katsura, 5.9.1912, *KTKB,* 180–81; *Takarabe Takeshi Nikki: Kaigun Jikan Jidai,* ed. Banno Junji et al. (Tokyo: Yamakawa Shuppansha, 1983), 2:100 (hereafter cited as *TTN*); *HTN,* 3:257; Tazaki, *Tanaka,* 309–10; Schencking, *Waves,* 148–50.

18. Some newspapers, though, were hostile to both armed services. See, for example, "Rikugun no Bōchō danjite fuka," *Tōyō Keizai Shinpō,* 15.7.1912, reproduced in Yamamoto, *Seihen,* 723–75. Even this article, thoroughly hostile to the navy's demands, grudgingly acknowledged their popularity among the public. See also Tazaki, *Tanaka,* 369; Schencking, *Waves,* 138.

19. Jōzai Tagao, "Doku Usoroku," *Taiyō* 1 (August, 1912); 141.

20. "Niko Shidan Zōshi Mondai Oboegaki: Terauchi Naikaku Jitsugen Keikaku," (author unknown, September 1912) in *Terauchi Masatake Kankei Monjo,* ed. Yamamoto Shirō (Kyoto: Kyoto Joshi Daigaku, 1984), 533 (hereafter cited as *TMKM*); *Tokyo Asahi Shinbun,* 26.10.1912; Gotō Shimpei in a conversation with the Russian ambassador: H. A. Malevsky-Malevich to Foreign Minister S. D. Sazonov, 12.12.1912, reproduced in V. E. Molodiakov, ed., *Katsura Taro, Goto Simp ĭ i Rossiia : Sbornik Dokumentov 1907–1929* (Moscow: Dmitriĭ Bulanin, 2005), 87; Hirata Tōsuke to Katsura (December 1912, precise day unclear), *KTKB,* 324–25, and also *TGD,* 2:485.

21. Yamagata-Saionji conversation, 10.11.1912, reproduced in full in *TGD,* 2:495–97, and for Yamagata's version see Irie Kan'ichi, *Taishō shoki Yamagata Aritomo Danwa Hikki: Seihen Omoidegusa,* ed. Itō Takashi (Tokyo: Yamakawa Shuppansha, 1981), 31–34. Compare with the report of an earlier conversation between Yamagata and Saionji, in August, in Gotō to Katsura, 5.9.1912, *KTKB,* 181–82, and with Tanaka's position, "Zōshi Mondai Keii," *TGD,* 2:508, 13. For an insight into feelings in the navy see *TTN,* 2:124.

22. Tanaka to Katsura, 17.12.1912, *KTKB,* 250.

23. Tanaka, "Zōshi Mondai Keii," *TGD,* 2:506–13.

24. Ibid., 2:514–16.

25. Yamamoto, *Seihen,* 176–79; Tanaka Giichi, "Zōshi Mondai no Keii," reproduced in *TGD,* 2:506–7. And compare with Uehara's appeal to the cabinet, reproduced in *TGD,* 2:491–92. See discussion in Ōe, *Sanbō Honbu,* 124–25.

26. Tanaka to Terauchi, 30.3.1912; Terauchi to Katsura, 17.10.1912, *KTKB,* 250, 82–83; Tanaka to Terauchi, 21.2., 30.3.1912; Uehara to Terauchi, 31.3, 29.10, 1912; Uehara to

Katsura, 17.11.1912, *KTKB*, 98–99. "Niko Shidan," *TMKM*, 583–85, for analysis of this position see Yamamoto, *Seihen*, 179.

27. Tanaka to Terauchi, 30.3.1912.

28. "Chokurei dai 193: Rikugunshō Kansei," 19.4.1900, appendix, 15, footnote no.1, JACAR, Ref. A03020460500. For analysis, see Sven Saaler, *Zwischen Demokratie und Militarismus: die Kaiserliche-Japanische Armee in der Politik der Taishō-Zeit, 1912–1916* (Bonn: Bier'sche Verlagsanstalt, 2000), 35–36.

29. Tobe, *Gyakusetsu*, 157. The only exception to that rule was Katsu Kaishū, a civilian but an old naval hand, who served as the lord of the navy (then the equivalent of a minister) from 1873 to 1879, see ibid.

30. Ōtsu, *Kenseishi*, 6:671; Saaler, *Militarismus*, 70–71; Tobe, *Gyakusetsu*, 165; Duus, *Party Rivalry*, 37.

31. Saaler, *Militarismus*, 71–77. See Najita, *Hara*, 233 (note no.10) about the influence of Yamagata as the "glue" holding the network together.

32. Tanaka to Terauchi, 21.2, 30.3 (last lines from the letter). For a different interpretation, see Tobe, *Gyakusetsu*, 175.

33. Oka to Terauchi, 25.3.1912; Uehara to Terauchi, 31.3.1912; Terauchi to Katsura, 6, 14.4.1912, *KTKB*, 278–79.

34. Saionji to Yamagata, 4.2.1912, *YAKM*, 2:147; Oka to Terauchi, 3.4.1912; Lone, *Katsura*, 175–76.

35. Tazaki, *Tanaka*, 295; Takekoshi Yosaburō, *Prince Saionji*, trans. Kozaki Nariyaki (Kyoto: Ritsumeikan University, 1933), 262.

36. *HTN*, 3:264–66.

37. The tendency of the government to delay and ignore the problem until the last moment was bemoaned by General Tanaka, see in "Zōshi Mondai Keii," *TGD*, 2:514.

38. *HTN*, 3:237.

39. *The Times*, 10.6.1912, 15–16.7.1912.

40. Saaler, *Militarismus*, 76; Najita, *Hara*, 93–94; Naitō, Kazunari, "Taishō Seihenki ni okeru Katsura Shintō to Kizokuin," *Shigaku Zasshi* 111, no. 4 (April 2002): 80; Duus, *Party Rivalry*, 39.

41. Kato Takaaki, ambassador to the UK, to Katsura, 3.9.1912, Motono Ichirō, ambassador to Russia, to Katsura, 15.9.1912 *KTKB*, 138–39, 345–46.

42. *Taishō Demokurashii-ki no Seiji: Matsumoto Gōkichi Seiji Nisshi*, ed. Oka Yoshitake and Hayashi Shigeru (Tokyo: Iwanami Shoten, 1959), 3; Katō to Katsura, 3.9.1912, *KTKB*, 138–39; "Yūgo Kōzoku," *Taiyō* 2 (August 1912): 18–19.

43. *The Times*, 18.7.1912; Katō to Katsura, 20.7.1912, Motono to Katsura, 15.9.1912, *KTKB*, 126–28; Lone, *Katsura*, 177; Gotō to Katsura, 5.9.1912, *KTKB*, 178–79.

44. *HTN*, 3:244–45; Katsura's bitterness could be indirectly seen through the letters he received from Yamagata's advisors who promised him repeatedly that there was no attempt to insult or exclude him. See, for example, Gotō Shimpei to Katsura, 28.8, 5.9.1912, *KTKB*, 176–78. It was also reflected in Katsura's later behavior. When he became prime minister again, on December 17, he asked Yamagata, rather rudely, to "rest in his villa" and stop meddling in politics. See Duus, *Party Rivalry*, 39. Still, bitter as he was, in autumn 1912 Katsura did not yet sever the ties with his former friends. Instead, he continued a covert cooperation with Yamagata and the Chōshū clique, even from inside the palace. See, for example, Katsura to Yamagata, 16.10.1912, *KTHS*, 429. In Yamagata's papers (*YAKM*, 1:381–82), this letter is dated 16.10, probably by mistake (15.10 is mentioned in the letter as a future date).

45. Takekoshi, *Saionji*, 267.

46. "Nikko Shidan," *TMKM*, 584.

47. See, for example, the letter sent by Gotō Shimpei, Yamagata's civilian advisor, to Katsura Tarō on 28.8.1912, *KTKB*, 177.

48. *HTN,* 3:250; Hirata Tōsuke (?) to Katsura, December 1912, precise day unclear, *KTKB,* 325, as well as similar ideas (voiced after the fall of Saijonji's cabinet), in Yamagata to Katsura, 10.12.1912, ibid., 447–48, and compare with Yamagata's interview to *Jiji Shinpō,* 11.12.1912, as well as his later version in *Danwa Hikki,* 27–28. This conversation and the interview have to be treated with some caution, as they were apologetic attempts by Yamagata to explain his position post facto. For source analysis, see Itō Takashi, "Taishō shoki Yamagata Aritomo Danwa Hikki," *Shigaku Zasshi* 75, no. 10 (1966): 63–67.

49. Kyofuji to Saionji, 16.11.1912, JACAR, Ref. B03030229900, p. 2. The counterarguments which moved Saionji to stick to his plans to augment the navy are reflected in the petition itself. For the prevailing opinions in Seiyūkai's executive committee at the height of the crisis see also Yamamoto, *Seihen,* 187.

50. *HTN,* 3:257, 64; Katsura to Yamagata, 13.10.1912, *KTHS,* 429; Matsukata to Yamagata, *YAKM,* 3:244.

51. *UKN,* 1:88; *Zuihitsu Saionji-kō,* ed. Koizumi Sakutarō (Tokyo: Iwanami Shoten, 1939), 269 (hereafter cited as *ZSK*); Kobayashi Michihiko, "Taishō Seihenki no Tairiku Seisaku to Rikukaigun: 1912–1914-nen," *Nihonshi Kenkyū* 363 (November 1992): 5; Maeda Renzan, *Rekidai Naikaku Monogatari* (Tokyo: Jiji Tsūshinsha, 1961), 1:412.

52. See for example *HTN,* 3:263–67; Tazaki, *Tanaka,* 330, 4; Uehara to Terauchi, 6.12.1912, reproduced in Yamamoto, *Seihen,* 198–99. On the importance of Hara and Matsuda in the party, see also Ozaki, *Autobiography,* 266.

53. Tanaka to Katsura, 17.12.1912, *KTKB,* 250; Yamamoto, *Seihen,* 170; *TGD,* 2:489; Ōtsu, *Kenseishi,* 6:751; Toshitani, "Meiji Kempō," 81.

54. Tazaki (*Tanaka,* 324) argues that Inoue's mediation was prompted by Tanaka's initiative, an attempt to directly convince the leading members of the *Seiyūkai* of the justice of the army's demands.

55. *HTN,* 3:260, 70.

56. *HTN,* 3:258; Tazaki, *Tanaka,* 334–35.

57. The memorandum is reproduced in *TGD,* 2:491–93, and see note in 493 about authorship. In addition see the analysis in Tazaki, *Tanaka,* 317.

58. The quote is from *HTN,* 3:266. For the failed attempts of Satsuma clique officers to win over Uehara against the Chōshū clique, see Uehara to Terauchi, 6.12.1912 (in this letter, Uehara denied any Satsuma influence on his decisions), reproduced in Yamamoto, *Seihen,* 160, 98–99; Tazaki, *Tanaka,* 331–33.

59. Saionji-Yamagata conversation, 10.11.1912, reproduced in *TGD,* 2:495–97, for Yamagata's version see: *Danwa Hikki,* 31–34. Tanaka, as expected, was staunchly against any delay, see "Zōshi Mondai Keii," *TGD,* 2:509. For interpretation see Tazaki, *Tanaka,* 329. Compare with Yamagata to Katsura, 28.11.1912, *KTKB,* 447. Later, Tanaka himself said that Yamagata was "dragged" into the matter, though he strangely blamed Inoue, of all people, for precipitating the cabinet crisis. See *ZSK,* 269.

60. *HTN,* 3:264; Yamamoto, *Seihen,* 175–76.

61. Yamamoto, *Seihen,* 153.

62. "Chōsen Shidan Mondai no Setsujitsu," *Tokyo Keizai Zasshi,* 5.10.1912.

63. "Tōzai Nanboku," *Nihon Oyobi Nihonjin,* 15.10.1912, 2–3.

64. "Nihon no Zentō wo nani usuru ka III," *Osaka Mainichi,* 19.10.1912.

65. Tazaki, *Tanaka,* 313; Matsukata to Hirata, *YAKM,* 3:244.

66. *HTN,* 3:260–61, 3. As for the importance of the army's feeling of discrimination vis-à-vis the navy, compare with the memorandum submitted to General Terauchi in September, "Niko Shidan," *TMKM,* 533. The resistance in the *Seiyūkai* to the army's demands was also recognized in Yamagata's camp; see Gotō to Katsura, 5.9.1912, *KTKB,* 182.

67. *HTN,* 3:264, 7.

68. *HTN,* 3:267, translation taken from Najita, *Hara,* 98. I have made only one change in Najita's translation, replacing "Katsura and his backers" with "Katsura and his ilk," a somewhat more accurate translation of the Japanese term "Katsura nado."

69. Yamamoto, *Seihen,* 190.

70. *HTN,* 3:269; *Terauchi Masatake Nikki, 1900–1918,* ed. Yamamoto Shirō (Kyoto: Kyoto Joshi Daigaku, 1980), 570–71 (hereafter cited as *TMN*), 568.

71. *HTN,* 3:269–70.

72. *HTN,* 3:270–71.

73. *HTN,* 3:270–71; Tanaka to Terauchi, 4.12.1912, *TMKM,* 587; Tazaki, *Tanaka,* 342. Compare with Yamagata's version in *Danwa Hikki,* 33–34.

74. Takekoshi, *Saionji,* 266.

75. Watanabe to Katsura, December 1912 (precise date unclear), *KTKB,* 492; *TMN,* 570–71; *Den Kenjirō Nikki,* ed. Hirose Yoshihiro (Tokyo: Shōyū Kurabu, Seisaku Fuyō Shobō Shuppan, 2008, hereafter cited as *DKN*), 2:237. For more details about the process of selection see Yamagata's testimony in *Danwa Hikki,* 34–42, as well as Tokutomi Ichirō (Sohō), ed., *Kōshaku Katsura Tarō Den* (Tokyo: Hara Shobō, 1967), 2:613–14 (hereafter cited as *KKTD*). The imperial edict is reproduced in *Danwa Hikki,* 614.

76. Terauchi to Yamagata, 24.12.1912, *YAKM,* 2:401; Tanaka to Terauchi, 27.12.1912, reproduced in Yamamoto, *Seihen,* 300–301; *DKN,* 2:238; *KKTD,* 2:614–15; Schencking, *Waves,* 157. For detailed discussion with numerical data see *Nihon Kaigun shi,* 2:220–22.

77. "Niko Shidan," *TMKM,* 533; Kigoshi to Katsura, 16.2.1913, KTKB, 149.

78. Kiyoura Keigo to Yamagata, 7.12.1912, *YAKM,* 2:79–80; Compare with Uehara to Katsura, 21.12.1912, reproduced in Yamamoto, *Seihen,* 297–99.

79. Tanaka to Katsura, 17.12.1912, *KTKB,* 250–51; Lone, *Katsura,* 182–83.

80. Kiyoura to Yamagata, 16.12.1912, *YAKM,* 2:81; Yamamoto, *Seihen,* 306.

81. Kiyoura to Yamagata, 16.12.1912, *YAKM,* 2:81–82; Gotō's conversation with the Russian ambassador, H. A. Malevsky-Malevich to S. D. Sazonov, 12.12.1912, in Molodiakov, *Sbornik Doukemtov,* 87–88.

82. Even General Tanaka, no friend of the navy, predicted that under such circumstances Admiral Saitō would have to resign—remaining in the cabinet would amount to cowardice. See Tanaka to Terauchi, 27.12.1912, reproduced in Yamamoto, *Seihen,* 301.

83. *HTN,* 3:274; Yamamoto, *Seihen,* 303–4; Kobayashi, "Taishō Seihenki Tairiku," 4.

84. *DKN,* 2:238; *KKTD,* 2:614–15.

85. *TTN,* 2:119.

86. One of the most detailed primary sources for these events is the testimony of Egi Yoku, Katsura's secretary of the cabinet. It is reproduced in *KKTD,* 2:615–18. This testimony is partially confirmed by Saitō's own diary, see the entries for 17–20.12, Saitō Shishaku Kinenkai, ed., *Shishaku Saitō Makoto Den* (Tokyo: Saitō Shishaku Kinenkai, 1941–42), 2:204–7 (hereafter cited as *SSMD*); Yamamoto, *Seihen,* 307–8, as well as by the diary of Navy vice minister Takarabe Takeshi, *TTN,* 2:118–19.

87. Egi's testimony, *KKTD,* 2:616–18; Saitō's diary in *SSMD,* 2:204–7, and the latter's reply to Katsura ibid., 2:205–6; See also Takarabe's diary, *TTN,* 2:119–23, and the discussion in Schencking, *Waves,* 158–59; *Nihon Kaigun shi,* 2:222–25. The key naval officers who were present in the meeting were Admirals Ijūin, chief of staff of the navy; Fujii, his deputy; Matsumoto, chief of the fleet section; and Takarabe, the vice minister (Saitō's diary, 20.12.1912 reproduced in *SSMD,* 2:206). As these names reoccur in the sources, it may be safely concluded that this small group of admirals, along with their mentor Yamamoto Gonnohyōe, held the key for the consensus in the Imperial Navy.

88. Katsura frequently used the German term "mein junger Herr" and once in a while even "mein Junge" (my boy). The conversation was held with the Russian ambassador, and

Katsura, who was fluent in German, used this language as a medium of communication. Malevsky-Malevich to Sazonov, 21.8.1912, Molodiakov, *Sbornik Dokumentov*, 86.

89. *KKTD*, 2:615; *TTN*, 2:123–24; *DDN*, 2:239. The Imperial rescript is reproduced in *SSMD*, 2:211–12.

90. *TTN*, 2:124–25; *HTN*, 3:274–75.

91. Though the navy did get some of the funds for shipbuilding, see *Nihon Kaigun shi*, 2:225–27.

92. For interesting contemporary reflections on the press and its influence on public opinion see the letter sent by the CEO of the *Osaka Mainichi* newspaper, Motoyama Hikoichi, to Communications Minister Gotō Shimpei, 24.12.1912, *KTKB*, 183–84. And compare with Matsukata to Katsura, 20.1.1913, ibid., 340.

93. "Nihon no Zento wo nani usuru ka iii," *Osaka Mainichi*, 19.10.1912; "Yūgo Kōzoku," *Taiyō* 2 (August 1912): 18–19; Yamamoto, *Seihen*, 102–5; Takekoshi, *Saionji*, 266; Hackett, *Yamagata*, 255. Similar feelings prevailed also in the Seiyūkai, see Ozaki, *Autobiography*, 265.

94. *Banshoroku: Takahashi Sōan Nikki*, ed. Takahashi Yoshio (Kyoto: Shibunkaku Shuppan, 1986–90), 1:179; Schencking, *Waves*, 159–66.

95. Though the cooperation of the *Seiyūkai* helped the movement, it was far from being a necessary condition for throwing violent mass demonstrations. In fact, as Andrew Gordon argues, such rallies were often organized against the Seiyūkai, both before and after 1913. See Andrew D. Gordon, "The Crowds and Politics in Imperial Japan: Tokyo: 1905–1908," *Past and Present* 121 (November 1988): 168.

96. *Banshoroku*, 1:235; Hackett, *Yamagata*, 257. For an additional firsthand description by a key participant: Ozaki, *Autobiography*, 267. For analysis see Saaler, *Militarismus*, 84–85.

97. *DKN*, 2:253; Ozaki, *Autobiography*, 266; *HTN*, 3:277–78. For background on the *Kokumintō*, see Duus, *Party Rivalry*, 37.

98. For the disapproval in the Kōjunsha at the very day of Katsura's nomination, see *Banshoruku*, 1:174–75, and for information on the club as the movement's network hub see also ibid., 231–35, 40. The quote about the fireplace is on 235. See also Ozaki, *Autobiography*, 266; Takekoshi, *Saionji*, 270; Duus, *Party Rivalry*, 41.

99. Katsura to Miura Gorō, *KTHS*, 366–67; *DKN*, 2:247, 51; Ozaki, *Autobiography*, 267–68; *HTN*, 3:281; Najita, *Hara*, 102, 17–18; Yamamoto, *Seihen*, 310; Saaler, *Militarismus*, 82.

100. "Chōsen Shidan Mondai," *Tokyo Keizai Zasshi*, 5.10.1912; "Nihon no Zentō wo nani usuru ka III," *Osaka Mainichi*, 19.10.1912; *Banshoroku*, 1:177; *HTN*, 3:274, 6; Yamamoto, *Seihen*, 288–93; Hackett, *Yamagata*, 255.

101. Katsura to Yamamoto, 12.1.1913, *KTHS*, 431; Schencking, *Waves*, 160–66.

102. Ozaki, *Autobiography*, 271. See also *Banshoroku*, 1:235. The original is quoted in Toshitani, "Meiji Kempō," 79.

103. Najita, *Hara*, 147. Compare with *DKN*, 2:261–62, and with Ozaki's version in *Autobiography*, 271. See also Takekoshi, *Saionji*, 274.

104. *DKN*, 2:253; Schencking, *Waves*, 162–63; Toshitani, "Meiji Kempō," 78–79; Funaki Shigeru, *Rikugun Daijin Kigoshi Yasutsuna* (Tokyo: Kawade Shobō Shinsha, 1993), 319–20.

105. Terauchi to Yamagata, 19.2.1913, *YAKM*, 2:401–2.

106. *DKN*, 2:264; Ozaki, *Autobiography*, 273–74; Najita, *Hara*, 160–61; Saaler, *Militarismus*, 87; Hackett, *Yamagata*, 256–57, 62–63.

107. Siniawer, *Ruffians*, 83–85.

108. Katsura to Yamagata, 12.1.1913, *KTHS*, 431.

109. Toshitani, "Meiji Kempō," 79.

110. Ozaki, *Autobiography*, 272; *HTN*, 3:287; Najita, *Hara*, 156; Saaler, *Militarismus*, 86. The original rescript is quoted in Toshitani, "Meiji Kempō," 79.

111. Mochizuki Kotarō to Katsura, 10.2.1913, *KTKB*, 365; *DKN*, 2:263–64; *HTN*, 3:287; Ozaki, *Autobiography*, 273; Saaler, *Militarismus*, 86–87.

112. Najita, *Hara*, 158.

113. *Banshoroku*, 1:233–35. Yamamoto's own version of the events is reproduced in "Hakushaku Yamamoto Gonnohyōe Jikiwa," in *Hakushaku Yamamoto Gonnohyōe Den*, ed. Yamamoto Kiyoshi et al. (Tokyo: Ōban Insatsu Kabushiki Kaisha, 1938), 2:964–65. For discussion see Schencking, *Waves*, 163–65; Saaler, *Militarismus*, 87.

114. *DKN*, 2:264–65; Schencking, *Waves*, 138.

115. "Bukan Seiji Kyōsei," *Osaka Mainichi*, 10.10.1912. See also Jōzai, "doku," *Taiyō* 1 (August 1912): 142; Ozaki Yukio, "Ryōshō ni Bukan Sen'nin no kahi," *Taiyō* 2 (August 1912): 143–46.

116. *DKN*, 2:247.

117. *HTN*, 3:297.

118. Kobayashi, "Taishō Seihenki no Tairiku," 17.

119. Ozaki, *Autobiography*, 280.

120. Kigoshi to Yamagata, 11.3.1913, *YAKM*, 2:24; Funaki, *Kigoshi*, 333.

121. Kigoshi to Yamagata, 11.3.1913, *YAKM*, 2:24.

122. *HTN*, 3:298; Funaki, *Kigoshi*, 334–35.

123. *TTN*, 2:171.

124. *UKN*, 1:88.

125. *HTN*, 3:298; Funaki, *Kigoshi*, 333–34.

126. *HTN*, 3:305–7; *TTN*, 2:169–71; Utsunomiya to Uehara, 20.4.1913, in Yamamoto Shirō, *Yamamoto Naikaku no Kisoteki Kenkyū* (Kyoto: Kyoto Joshi Daigaku, 1982), 187; Funaki, *Kigoshi*, 338–39.

127. Najita, *Hara*, 181–82.

128. *UKN*, 1:87.

129. *HTN*, 3:305–6.

130. *HTN*, 3:308. The original document of the cabinet's decision is reproduced in Yamamoto, *Yamamoto Naikaku*, 190–91.

131. *HTN*, 3:306.

132. *TTN*, 2:175; *UKN*, 1:87; Yamamoto, *Yamamoto Naikaku*, 191.

133. *HTN*, 3:309; *TTN*, 2:175–76.

134. *HTN*, 3:319; *TTN*, 2:188–89; Drea, *Imperial Army*, 131.

135. Utsunomiya to Uehara, 20.4.1913, reproduced in Funaki, *Kigoshi*, 338–39, see also discussion at 340, 50. This channel was maintained by Utsunomiya Tarō, chief of the general staff's second bureau (intelligence), a former Saga retainer and member of the Satsuma clique, and Navy Vice Minister Takarabe, who reported almost immediately to the prime minister. See *TTN*, 2:157, 71, 88–89. For analysis, see Yamamoto, *Yamamoto Naikaku*, 201–2.

136. Terauchi to Yamagata, 20.6.1913, *YAKM*, 2:403. The translation is partially based on Najita's, with some corrections for the sake of accuracy. For Najita's translation of this passage, see *Hara*, 181–82.

137. For details about these proposals, see Yamamoto, *Seihen*, 181–82.

138. *TGD*, 2:489–90; Terauchi to Yamagata, 24.12.1912, *YAKM*, 2:400–401; Tanaka to Terauchi, 15.5.1913, reproduced in Funaki, *Kigoshi*, 346–47; Ugaki, "Rikugaikun Daijin," *UKN*, 1:89–92, 5.

139. Toshitani, "Meiji Kempō," 67, 70, 2–3, 7; *HTN*, 3:245; Frederick R. Dickinson, *Taishō Tennō: Ichiyaku Godaishū wo yūhisu* (Kyoto: Mineruva Shobō, 2009), 88–90; Maeda, *Rekidai*, 1:412, 18–19. Maeda argues (218) that had the Meiji Emperor been alive, he could have summoned Saionji and Yamagata to the palace and lent his prestige in favor of a working compromise.

140. Ōtsu, *Kenseishi*, 6:753–54.

141. Tobe, *Gyakusetsu*, 167–76.

142. For one example out of many for the use of *Gekokujō* in this context, see Funaki, *Kigoshi*, 339.

143. Van Creveld, *Command*, 65–78, 226–32, 268–77.

144. Yuri Pines and Gideon Shelach, *Kol asher mi-taḥat la-shamayim: Toldot Ha-Keisarut Ha-Sinit* (Ra'ananah: Universiṭah ha-petuḥah, 2011), 1:372.

145. Yamagata's English language biographer, Roger F. Hackett, has a more generous evaluation of the field marshal's political power of these years. See Hackett, *Yamagata*, 248–49, and also Duus, *Party Rivalry*, 11.

146. Terauchi to Tanaka, 1.11.1912, reproduced in Yamamoto, *Seihen*, 164.

147. See for example in Uehara to Katsura, 17.11.1912, *KTKB*, 98–99; Hackett, *Yamagata*, 249.

148. Uehara to Katsura, 17.11.1912, *KTKB*, 98–99 ; Uehara to Terauchi, 6.12.1912, reproduced in Yamamoto, *Seihen*, 198–99; Maeda, *Rekidai*, 413; *TGD*, 2:483–84, 8, especially the testimony of Watanabe Yosuke about Tanaka's activity ibid., 520–22.

149. *TTN*, 2:122–23; *SSMD*, 2:216.

150. Richard W. Southern, *Western Society and the Church in the Middle Ages* (London: Penguin Books, 1990), 141–42.

151. Ozaki, *Autobiography*, 271; *DKN*, 2:263.

152. Najita, *Hara*, 138.

153. Slavoj Žižek, "Talk at Occupy Wall St." in "Ecology without Nature," http://ecology withoutnature.blogspot.com/2011/10/zizeks-talk-at-occupy-wall-st.html.

154. Tanaka to Uehara, 15.15.1913, reproduced in Yamamoto, *Yamamoto Naikaku*, 196–97.

155. *HTN*, 5:271, as well as Foreign Minister Makino Nobuaki's Diet speech of 3.2.1917, *Haku Yamamoto Gonnohyōe Den*, 2:992–93. For analysis see Kobayashi, "Taishō Seihenki no Tairiku," 15.

156. Najita, *Hara*, 181.

157. Kobayashi, "Taishō Seihenki no Tairiku," 2.

158. The important affair of the Siberian Intervention, as well as the army's role and behavior, were recently dealt with in Dunscomb's excellent monograph, *Japan's Siberian Intervention*.

8. THE KING OF MANCHURIA

1. Paul E. Dunscomb, *Japan's Siberian Intervention, 1918–1922: "A Great Disobedience against the People"* (Lanham, MD: Lexington Books, 2001), 126–30, 40; Mori, *Nihon Rikugun*, 49, 72–73.

2. Yoshihisa Tak Matsusaka, *The Making of Japanese Manchuria, 1904–1932* (Cambridge, MA: Harvard Asia Center/Harvard University Press, 2001), 233; Kobayashi, "Taishō Seihenki no Tairiku," 2.

3. Kobayashi, "Taishō Seihenki no Tairiku," 2; Mori, *Nihon Rikugun*, 8–9, 28.

4. Ōe Shinobu, *Chō Sakurin Bakusatsu: Shōwa Tennō no Tōsui* (Tokyo: Chūō Kōronsha, 1989), 157.

5. Theodore Cook, "The Japanese Corps: The Making of a Military Elite" (Ph.D. diss., Princeton University, 1987), 86–89. See late editions (the earlier ones did not survive) of the main textbooks used in the prestigious Staff College: "Rikugun Daigakkō Kyōiku Kōryō: Kōmu Saisoku" (June 1907), and "Tōsui Sankōsho Soan Daisan'an" (September 1929), *GKSS*, 7:215, 240–45; Kumagai, *Nihongun no Seishin*, 139–40; Jōhō Yoshio, *Rikugun Daigakkō* (Tokyo: Fuyō Shobō, 1973), 166; Mineo Kyūdai, *Rikugun Sanbō*, 30–31, as well as the testimonies of Arisue Seizō and Imai Takeo, ibid., 294, 305.

6. Leonard A. Humphreys, *The Way of the Heavenly Sword: The Japanese Army in the 1920s* (Stanford, CA: Stanford University Press), 43–50; Benesch, *Inventing the Way*, 170.

7. Kikkawa Manabu, *Arashi to tatakau Tetsushō Araki: Rikugun Uramenshi, Shōgun Araki no shichijū-nen no Gekan* (Tokyo: Araki Sadao Shōgun Denki Hensan Kankōkai, 1955), 80; Ugaki Kazushige, *Shōrai Seidan* (Tokyo: Bungei Shunjū Shinsha, 1951), 321–22; Humphreys, *Sword*, 157–60; Kitaoka, "Army," 79–80; Drea, *Imperial Army*, 156–58; Mori, *Nihon Rikugun*, 72–74.

See also Araki's interview with the League of Nations Commission of Inquiry (Lytton Commission), 5.3.1932, League of Nations Archives, United Nations Office at Geneva (hereafter cited as LNA-UNOG), S29, No. 1 32 Japon, 21.

8. Kikkawa, *Araki*, 80.

9. Translation from Humphreys, *Heavenly Sword*, 151, original in Kikkawa, *Araki*, 80–81. For more details about the background of this dispute see also *TGD*, 2:951–52.

10. Kikkawa, *Araki*, 87.

11. For analysis of Ugaki's policy and its critics, see Humphreys, *Sword*, 79–107; Drea, *Imperial Army*, 151–56; Kitaoka, "Army," 76–79.

12. "Heben Dazuo Kou gong," 4.4.1953, "Pingye Lingfu Zheng ci" (Hirano Mineo's testimony) *Heben Dazuo yu Rijun Shanxi "Can Liu,"* ed. Zhongyang Dang an guan et al. (Beijing: Zhonghua Shu ju, 1995, hereafter cited as *HBDZ*), 7, 68–69; Ōe, *Chō Sakurin*, 33–39, 41–43.

13. "Heben Dazuo Kou Gong," 4.4.1953, *HBDZ*, 18; Ōe, *Chō Sakurin*, 33–39, 41–43. For general discussion of these study groups, see Humphreys, *Sword*, 110–16; Drea, *Imperial Army*, 154–56; Hirano Mineo (Reiji), *Manshū no Inbōsha: Kōmoto Daisaku no unmeiteki na Ashiato* (Tokyo: Jiyū Kokuminsha, 1961), 39–40.

14. Sir Miles Lampson, British Minister in Beijing, to Lord Cushendun, Acting Secretary of State, 19.3.1928, "A Review of the Past and Present Policy of Japan in South Manchuria," "China-Manchuria Japanese Policy, 1923–1932," part I, 152–53, National Archives of Australia, Chin 165 (hereafter cited as CMJP-NAA).

15. Lampson, "Review," CMJP-NAA, 1:155–56.

16. Sir Cecil Dormer, British Ambassador in Tokyo, to Lord Cushendun, 14.8.1928, CMJP-NAA, 1:163.

17. General Honjō Shigeru, General Araki Sadao, interviews with the Lytton Commission, 2.6, 9.10.1932, LNA-UNOG, S31 No.1 31–32 R Manchuria, pp. 1–5, S29 No.1 32 Japon, pp. 3–7; Dormer to Cushendun, 14.8.1928, CMJP-NAA, 1:163. Compare with Tanaka Ryūkichi's testimony, *International Military Tribunal for the Far East*, Record of proceedings, Tokyo, Japan : The United States of America [et al.] against Araki, Sadao . . . Tojo, Hideki [et al.], accused / official court reporters, Jack Greenberg, Chief . . . [et al.] (Microfilm Reels, Center for Research Libraries, Chicago) microfilm reel 2:1958 (hereafter cited as IMTFE). For historical background on the Japanese discourse of "emotional attachment" to Manchuria, see Emer O'Dwyer, *Significant Soil: Settler Colonialism and Japan's Urban Empire in Manchuria* (Cambridge: Harvard University Asia Center, 2015), 138–39.

18. Ōe, *Chō Sakurin*, 123.

19. Matsusaka, *Making of Japanese Manchuria*, 71.

20. IMTFE, R2:1759–60; Ramon H. Myers, "Japanese Imperialism in Manchuria: The South Manchurian Railway Company, 1906–1933," in *The Japanese Informal Empire in China, 1895–1937*, ed. Peter Duus et al. (Princeton, NJ: Princeton University Press, 1989), 101–33.

21. Lampson, "Review," CMJP-NAA, 1:156.

22. For one typical example of shishi influence on a continental adventurer, see Hyō, *Hyōden Munakata Kotarō: Tairiku Rōnin no rekishiteki Yakuwari* (Kumamoto: Kumamoto Shuppan Bunka Kaikan, 1997), 50.

23. Arthur Sandusky (US prosecution), IMTFE, M4:4677–78, 95; O'Dwyer, *Significant*, 109–110; Miriam L. Kingsberg, "The Poppy and the Acacia: Opium and Imperialism in Japanese Dairen and the Kwantung Leased Territory, 1905–1945" (Ph.D. diss., University of California, Berkeley, 2009), 174, 92, 5, 7, 220–25, 31, 7.

24. Lampson, "Review," CMJP-NAA, 1:155; Gavan McCormack, *Chang Tso-lin in Northeast China, 1911–1928: China, Japan and the Manchurian Idea* (Stanford, CA: Stanford University Press, 1977), 1, 12–18.

25. Araki, interview with the Lytton Commission, 9.7.1932, LNA-UNOG, S29, No.1 32 Japon, p. 8, 10; Mizuno Akira, *Tōhoku Gunbatsu Seiken no Kenkyū: Chō Sakurin, Chō Gakuryō no Taigai Teikō to Tainai Tōitsu no Kiseki* (Tokyo: Kokusho Kankōkai, 1994), 366.

26. Kitaoka Shin'ichi, "China Experts in the Army," in Duus, *Informal Empire*, 361–62; McCormack, *Chang Tso-lin*, 146–88.

27. Lampson, "Review," CMJP-NAA, 1:157; McCormack, *Chang Tso-lin*, 223–49; Matsusaka, *Making of Japanese Manchuria*, 312–49 For a list of demonstrations and other anti-Japanese activities, see G. S. Karetina, *Chzhan TSzolin' i politicheskaia bor'ba v Kitae v 20-e gody XX v* (Moskva: Iz-vo Nauka, 1984), 167–70.

28. IMFTE, M2:1752–53; Suzuki Teiichi, *Suzuki Teiichi-shi Danwa Sokkiroku* (Tokyo: Nihon Shiriyō Kenkyūkai, 1971–74), 1:57, 287 (hereafter cited as *STDS*); Kōmoto Daisaku, "Watakushi ga Chō sakurin o koroshita," *Bungei Shunjū* 32 (December 1954): 194, 7. This article is based on an interview with Kōmoto by his brother-in-law, the China correspondent Hirano Mineo, who was a fellow prisoner with him in a Chinese communist prison camp. The transcript of the interview, probably conducted in the late 1930s, was given to Kōmoto's daughter by his private secretary and published in *Bungei Shunju* after the war. See also O'Dwyer, *Significant*, 221–24; "Annual Report on the Kwantung Leased Territory and on Japanese Activities in Manchuria," 1.1.1928, CMJP-NAA, 190 (11), 194 (15).

29. British Secretary of State, cable B55, 19.5.1928, CMJP-NAA, 1:198; Matsusaka, *Making of Japanese Manchuria*, 335–36.

30. Sir Frederick White, "The Drama in Manchuria," *The Times*, 22.2.1928. The author was a political advisor to the Chinese Government. For discussion and analysis of this policy, often defined by scholars as Japan's "new imperialism," see Matsusaka, *Making of Japanese Manchuria*, 267–73. Some scholars, however, believe that the differences between the "new" and the "old" imperialism were not so significant. For example, see McCormack, *Chang Tso-lin*, 134–43.

31. Okada Keisuke's affidavit, IMFTE, M2:1816–17; Dening, British consul in Dairen, in a conversation with Matsuoka Yōsuke, as reported to Sir Cecil Dormer, British Ambassador in Tokyo, 5.6.1928, CMJP-NAA, 1:165; Morishima Morito, *Inbō, Ansatsu, Guntō: Ichi Gaikōkan no Kaikō* (Tokyo: Iwanami Shoten, 1950), 1–8; Matsusaka, *Making of Japanese Manchuria*, 327.

32. Machino, Takema, "Chō Sakurin Bakushi no Zengo," *Chūō Kōron* 64, no. 9 (22.9.1949): 77; Iboshi Ei, "Chō Sakurin Bakusatsu Jiken no Shinsō," *Geirin* (June 1982), 1:8.

33. Okada's affidavit, IMFTE, M2:1817–18; Dening to Dormer (quoting Matsuoka), 5.6.1928, CMJP-NAA, 1:166; *UKN*, 2:689; Inaba Masao, "Chō Sakurin Bakusatsu Jiken" in Sanbō Honbu, ed., *Shōwa Sannen Shina Jihen Shuppeishi* (Tokyo: Gannandō Shoten, 1971, appendix), 3. On the economic aspect of the problem, see Yanagisawa, Asobu, "Hōten ni okeru Hōtenhyō Bōraku Mondai to Futō Kazei Mondai no Tenkai Keika—Chō Sakurin Bakusatsu Jiken no Rekishiteki Zentei," Tokyo Daigaku Keizai Kenkyūkai, *Keizaigaku Kenkyū* 24 (October 1981): 49–50.

34. Yoshizawa to Tanaka, 19.5.1928, *NGB*, Shōwa, 1:1:2, 91; *STDS*, 1:57, 287. Compare with the testimony of Machino Takema, Zhang's advisor, in Machino Takema, "Chō Sakurin Bakushi no Zengo," *Chūō Kōron* 64, np. 9 (22.9.1949): 79.

35. "Pingye Lingfu Zhengci," 21.8.1954, in *HBDZ*, 72; Dening to Dormer (quoting Matsuoka), 5.6.1928, CMJP-NAA, 1:166; Inaba, "Chō Sakurin," 2–3; *TGD*, 2:952–53.

36. Inaba, "Chō Sakurin," 2–3; *TGD*, 2:952–54; Sasaki Tōichi, *Aru Gunjin no Jiden* (Tokyo: Keisō Shobō, 1967), 191.

37. Dormer to Chamberlain, 4.6.1928, Dening to Dormer (quoting Matsuoka), 5.6.1928, CMJP-NAA, 1:165–66, 74–75; Machino, "Chō Sakurin," 76–80; Kitaoka, "China Experts," in Duus, *Informal Empire*, 360, 4–5, 7; Shibutani Yuri, *Bazoku de miru 'Manshū': Chō Sakurin no ayunda Michi* (Tokyo: Kōdansha, 2004), 156–58.

38. William F. Morton, *Tanaka Giichi and Japan's China Policy* (Folkestone, UK: Dawson, 1980), 96–97; For a detailed description of the Eastern Conference, see Matsusaka, *Making of Japanese Manchuria*, 327–40.

39. "Heben Dazuo Bigong," 2.8.1953, *HBDZ*, 39; Dening, Consul in Dairen in a conversation with Matsuoka Yōsuke, as reported to Dormer, 5.6.1928, CMJP-NAA, 1:165; *TGD*, 2:952.

40. Yoshizawa to Tanaka, 15.5.1928, Tanaka to Yoshizawa, 16.5.1928, *NGB* S, 1:1:2, 74–81. See also Tanaka's conversation with Sir Cecil Dormer, British Ambassador to Japan, as reported in Dormer's dispatch to Sir Joseph Austen-Chamberlain (British Foreign Secretary), 4.6.1928, CMJP-NAA, 1:174.

41. Tatekawa Yoshitsugu, military attaché in Beijing, to Army Vice-Minister Hata Eitarō, 18.5.1928, Yoshizawa to Tanaka, 19.5.1928, *NGB* S, 1:1:2, 89–93; Sir Miles Lampson, British Minister to Beijing, conversation with Ou Tching, 23.5.1928, as reported in Lampson to Chamberlain, 23.5.1928, CMJP-NAA, 1:171.

42. *TGD*, 2:954–55; Tanaka Ryūkici's interrogation, IMTFE, M2:1949–52; Iboshi, "Chō Sakurin," 3:40–41. General Saitō's diary entries, 21, 28, 30.5, 1.6, reproduced in Inaba, "Chō Sakurin," 11, 14–15; For detailed analysis of the Kwantung Army's preparations see ibid., 8–9.

43. Original reproduced in Iboshi, "Chō Sakurin," 3:45. I have used the English translation of Leonard A. Humphreys, *Heavenly Sword*, 156–57, with appropriate changes to correct inaccuracies. Compare with Kawagoe Moriji's version in *Chō Sakurin Bakushi Jiken*, 30–34, National Institute for Defense Studies *(Bōeishō Bōei Kenkyūjo)*, Military Archives (hereafter cited as NIDS), itaku no. 251.

44. Chief of the General Staff to Kwantung Army Headquarters, 19.5.1928, Vice CGS to KA Headquarters, 21.5, 1928, Vice Army Minister to KA Chief of Staff, 2.6.1928, reproduced in Inaba, "Chō Sakurin," 10, 16; Kawagoe, "Chō Sakurin" (NIDS), 31.

45. Inaba, "Chō Sakurin," 12.

46. Saitō's diary entries, 23, 25.5, 1.6., reproduced in Inaba, "Chō Sakurin," 14–15. The translation of the direct quote is taken from Humphreys, *Heavenly Sword*, 156. And compare with Kawagoe's description of the atmosphere in the Kwantung Army's staff in *Chō Sakurin* (NIDS), 31–34.

47. Yoshizawa to Tanaka, 1.6.1928, *NGB* S, 1:1:2, 123.

48. *TGD*, 2:954.

49. Sagara Shunsuke, *Akai Yūhi no Manshū Nogahara ni: Kisai Kōmoto Daisaku no Shōgai* (Tokyo: Kōjinsha, 1978), 13.

50. Sagara, *Akai Yūhi*, 11–42. For another favorable assessment of Kōmoto's character see Kawagoe, *Chō Sakurin* (NIDS), 14.

51. Hirano, *Manshū*, 53–63; "Pingye Lingfu Zhengci," 5, 21.8.1954, *HBDZ*, 68–69, 72–73. Similar anecdotes are told by Ozaki Yoshiharu, a staff officer under Kōmoto who had also participated in the murder plot. Even if not entirely reliable in its details, Ozaki's description gives some credence to Hirano's portrayal of Kōmoto, see Ozaki Yoshiharu, *Rikugun o ugokashita Hitobito* (Odawara: Hachishodō Shoten, 1960), 99–102.

52. Sagara, *Akai Yūhi*, 18–26, 40; Hirano, *Manshū*, 20, 52; "Pingye Lingfu Zhengci," 5, 21.8.1954, *HBDZ*, 68–69, 72–73. For Kōmoto's own testimonies see discussion below.

53. "Pingye Lingfu Zhengci," 5.8.1954, *HBDZ*, 68–69; Sagara, *Akai Yūhi*, 19–22, 29–31.

54. "Pingye Lingfu Zhengci," 11.8.1954, *HBDZ*, 6–7; Kawagoe, *Chō Sakurin* (NIDS), 6.

55. "Heben Dazuo Bigong," 27.5.1952, *HBDZ*, 12–13; Hirano, *Manshū*, 50–52.

56. "Heben Dazuo Bigong" (undated), and in 27.5.1952, *HBDZ*, 5, 13; Sagara, *Akai Yūhi*, 40–42.

57. "Heben Dazuo Bigong," 19.4.1953, *HBDZ*, 19.

58. "Pingye Lingfu Zhengci," 11.8.1954, *HBDZ*, 7. Compare with Hirano's description in his book, *Manshū*, 48–49.

59. "Heben Dazuo Bigong," 27.5.1952; Hirano, *Inbōsha*, 65.

60. For background, see James E. Weland, "The Japanese Army in Manchuria: Covert Operations and the Roots of the Kwantung's Army Insubordination" (Ph.D. diss., University of Arizona, 1977), 23–27, 60–63, 81; Officers from the Kwantung Army staff explained this tactical doctrine to the Lytton Commission, 26/27.4.1932, LNA-UNOG, S31 No.1 31–2 R Manchuria, pp. 8–9 (first interview), pp. 4–6 (second interview).

61. Jōhō, *Rikugun Daigakkō*, 229.

62. *STDS*, 1:299.

63. *UKN*, 1:667.

64. Kōmoto, "Watakushi," 194–95, 7, 9.

65. Ibid., 197.

66. Kōmoto, "Watakushi," 194; Sagara, *Akai Yūhi*, 125–30, 148. Kawagoe Moriji, Kōmoto's right hand man, had also mentioned the spirits of the fallen heroes, along with the "imperial will," as one of his sources of inspiration. See Kawagoe, *Chō Sakurin* (NIDS), 78.

67. Kōmoto, "Watakushi," 195.

68. This letter was published in 1992 in the journal *Gendai* by a military correspondent named Sannō Masuhiko. The original was entrusted to the Bōeicho Archive in Tokyo, with very limited access. Still, Kobayashi Kazuhiro, Isogai's biographer, was able to examine it, and compare the raw text with the *Gendai* version. He republished it in full, correcting some of the mistakes in the earlier version. All excerpts here are taken from Kobayashi's version. For more details about this document see Kobayashi Kazuhiro, "*Shina-tsū" ichi Gunjin no Hikari to Kage: Isogai Rensuke Chūjō Den* (Tokyo: Kashiwa Shobō, 2000), 46–47.

69. In the excerpts below, all emphasis is my own.

70. Kōmoto to Isogai, 18.4.1928, reproduced in Kobayashi, *Isogai*, 47–48.

71. Ibid., 48–50. Iboshi Ei, however, interprets this letter somewhat differently. According to his reading, which seems to me somewhat strained, Kōmoto still regarded the assassination at that time as "plan B" in case the Kwantung Army failed to disarm Zhang's army. The decision to kill the Old Marshal, according to Iboshi, was made around May 23. See, Iboshi, "Chō Sakurin," 4:42–44.

72. For very similar criticism against the Japanese military cliques, see Kawagoe, *Chō Sakurin* (NIDS), 78.

73. Heben Dazuo Gongshu," *HBDZ*, 661.

74. "Pingye Lingfu Zhengci," *HBDZ*, 68–71.

75. Matsusaka, *Making*, 346–47; Mori, Katsumi, interview with Kōmoto Daisaku, Dairen, 1.12.1942, in Mori, *Manshū Jihen no Rimenshi* (Tokyo: Kokushu Kankōkai, 1976), 266–67.

76. Kōmoto, "Watakushi," 197, compare with "Heben Dazuo Kou gong," 6.4.1953, *HBDZ*, 33. These arguments were also shared by General Saitō. See his letter to Vice Minister Hata, 20.5.1928, reproduced in Inaba, "Chō Sakurin," 5.

77. Kōmoto, "Watakushi," 196–97; "Heben Dazuo Gongshu," *HBDZ*, 661. According to Iboshi Ei ("Chō Sakurin," 4:44) protecting the local Japanese civilians was one of Kōmoto's

main motives. It seems to me, however, that the importance he ascribes to this particular motive is somewhat exaggerated.

78. Kōmoto, "Watakushi," 197.

79. Ibid., 197. Compare with Kōmoto's Chinese language testimony, "Heben Dazuo Gongshu," *HBDZ*, 661. Also compare with the Ogawa's account in "Manshū Mondai," *Ogawa Heikichi Kankei Monjo*, ed. Oka Yoshitake (Tokyo: Isuzu Shobō, 1973), 1:626–27 (hereafter cited as *OHKM*).

80. Yoshizawa to Tanaka, 3.6.1928, *NGB* S, 1:1:2, 128. Saitō's diary, 3, 6.6.1918, reproduced in Inaba, "Chō Sakurin," 18, 25. These rumors were probably related to Hata's conspiracy (discussed below).

81. Quoted by Sagara, *Akai Yūhi*, 157, and compare with a similar version in Hirano, *Inbōsha*, 79–81; This description is supported by Kōmoto's version in "Watakushi," 198, as well as the version he gave the Chinese authorities, "Heben Dazuo Kou gong" and "Heben Dazuo Gongshu," 6.4.1954, *HBDZ*, 33–34, 660–61 and the interview he gave to Mori Katsumi in 1942 (Katsumi, *Manshū*, 267–28). See also Inaba, "Chō Sakurin," 33. In an interview with Iboshi Ei (19.11.1973), Takeshita denied Kōmoto's version. He admitted that Kōmoto instructed him to collect intelligence on Zhang's movements in Beijing and his imminent departure to Mukden, but denied the story of Muraoka's plot, the details of the conversation with Kōmoto, and any prior knowledge on the latter's real intentions. See, Iboshi, "Chō Sakurin," 1:11. Still, I am inclined to believe Kōmoto's version and reject Takeshita's. First of all, Kōmoto told his story on three different occasions, including to the Chinese investigators. Usually, he tried to take all responsibility upon himself and was proud of his deed. What interest did he have in incriminating Muraoka, who was already dead for almost twenty years? In addition, Kōmoto's version is indirectly supported by Kawagoe's, in Hata, "Chō Sakurin Bakusatsu," 126, and *Chō Sakurin* (NIDS), 36, though the latter reports only on Muraoka's complicity, not on the details of the conversation.

82. "Heben Dazuo Kou gong," 6.4.1954, *HBDZ*, 33–34. For an alternative, but not completely different, interpretation of Muraoka's plot see Iboshi, "Chō Sakurin," 4:48–50.

83. Kōmoto, "Watakushi," 198. Compare with Kawagoe, *Chō Sakurin* (NIDS), 36.

84. Kawagoe, *Chō Sakurin* (NIDS), 77.

85. Sagara, *Akai Yūhi*, 151.

86. Yoshizawa to Tanaka, 16.6.1928, *NGB* S, 1:1:2, 158.

87. Kōmoto, "Watakushi," 200. After the war, however, Araki Gorō argued that he and Doihara knew nothing of Kōmoto's plans. See, *Hiroku Doihara Kenji: Nitchū Yūkō no Suteishi*, ed. Doihara Kenji Kankōkai (Tokyo: Fuyō Shobō, 1972), 238–39. In his letter to Isogai (Kobayashi, *Isogai*, 49), Kōmoto wrote that he indeed concealed the plot from them.

88. Kōmoto to Isogai, 18.4.1928, in Kobayshi, *Isogai*, 48–49. For discussion of the background see Sagara, *Akai Yūhi*, 150–51. And compare with "Heben Dazuo Bigong," 2.8.1953, *HBDZ*, 40.

89. For a full list of the conspirators, see Hata Ikuhiko, "Chō Sakurin Bakusatsu no Zaikōsatsu" *Seikei Kenkyū* 44, no. 1 (May 2007): 124. In Hata's chart, ringleaders are marked with **, and officers who were partly involved with *.

90. Kawagoe, *Chō Sakurin* (NIDS), 14–15, 18–19, 39–40, 78–79. According to Kawagoe's memoirs, this conversation took place on June 2, 1928. And still, Kawagoe asked Kōmoto to give him a "formal order" and was given one, see ibid., 38–39.

91. "Heben Dazuo Kou gong," 6.4.1954, *HBDZ*, 34; Kawagoe, *Chō Sakurin* (NIDS), 15; Sagara, *Akai Yūhi*, 153; Iboshi, "Chō Sakurin," 4:40.

92. Kawagoe, *Chō Sakurin* (NIDS), 36–37; Hata, "Chō Sakurin Bakusatsu," 126.

93. Kawagoe, *Chō Sakurin* (NIDS), 36, 42–48; "Heben Dazuo Kou gong," 6.4.1954, "Heben Dazuo Gongshu," *HBDZ*, 35–36, 662; Sagara, *Akai Yūhi*, 158, 70.

94. Tanaka Ryūkichi's interrogation, IMTFE, M2:1952.

95. "Heben Dazuo Kou gong," 6.4.1954, "Heben Dazuo Gongshu," *HBDZ*, 34, 661. This officer's last name was Kirihara, later changed to Fujii. See Hata, "Chō Sakurin Bakusatsu," 126.

96. Kōmoto, "Watakushi," 198; "Heben Dazuo Kou gong," 6.4.1954, "Heben Dazuo Gongshu," *HBDZ*, 34, 661.

97. Kawagoe, *Chō Sakurin* (NIDS), 43–44.

98. The name of this officer was Major Ozaki Yoshiharu. For his postwar account, see Ozaki, *Rikugun*, 108.

99. Kōmoto, "Watakushi," 198; Kawagoe, *Chō Sakurin* (NIDS), 79.

100. "Special Committee Meeting 2," 23.10.1928, *NGB* S, 1:1:2, 195–96; Sagara, *Akai Yūhi*, 168; "Heben Dazuo Bigong," 2.8.1953, *HBDZ*, 42. For background on the anti-Zhang movement of the Japanese merchants in Manchuria, see Yanagisawa, "Hōten," 48–58.

101. "Heben Dazuo Bigong," 2.8.1953, *HBDZ*, 42. Kōmoto's version is supported by the Japanese Special Committee of Inquiry's findings (second meeting, 23.10.1928), *NGB* S, 1:1:2, 196.

102. Iboshi, "Chō Sakurin," 4:33; Sagara, *Akai Yūhi*, 169.

103. "Special Committee Meeting 2," 23.10.1928, *NGB* S, 1:1:2, 196–97; Ogawa Heikichi, "Manshū Mondai," *OHKM*, 1:627. The name of the pimp was Liu Daiming.

104. "Heben Dazuo Kou gong," 6.4.1954, "Heben Dazuo Bigong," 2.8.1953, *HBDZ*, 36, 42; Yoshizawa to Tanaka, 16.6.1928, *NGB* S, 1:1:2, 158; "Special Committee Meeting 2," 23.10.1928, *NGB* S, 1:1:2, 196–97. According to Kawagoe, the Russian hand grenades were bought in Mukden by General Hata Shinji from the Special Service Organization, who agreed to cooperate with Kōmoto's plot though the latter foiled his [Hata's] own independent operation. See Kawagoe, *Chō Sakurin* (NIDS), 79–81.

105. Yoshizawa to Tanaka, 2.6.1928, *NGB* S, 1:1:2, 125, and compare with a slightly different version in Kawagoe's memoirs, *Chō Sakurin* (NIDS), 40–41. See also Sagara, *Akai Yūhi*, 143; Kōmoto, "Watakushi," 198–99.

106. Machino, "Chō Sakurin," 79.

107. Takamiya Taiehei, *Gunkoku Taiheiki* (Tokyo: Kantōsha, 1951), 46.

108. Kōmoto's interview in Mori, *Manshū*, 268.

109. Kōmoto, "watakushi," 194; Kawagoe, *Chō Sakurin* (NIDS), 40–43, 78–79; Sagara, *Akai Yūhi*, 172–73; "Heben Dazuo Gongshu," *HBDZ*, 661–62; Morishima, "Chō Sakurin," 43. Compare with Hirano, *Inbōsha*, 69–70.

110. Consul General Hayashi to Kwantung Army Chief of Staff Saitō/Vice Army Minister Hata, 16.7.1928, "Ressha Bakuha Jiken ni kansuru Hōten Sōryojikan Chōsa Hōkoku" (author: Consul Uchida Gorō), JACAR, Ref. C04021743400, p. 92 (hereafter cited as "Mukden Consulate Report"); "Chō Sakurin Ressha Bakuha Jiken ni kansuru Shoken" (Kwantung Army to the Army Ministry, undated), reproduced in Inaba, "Chō Sakurin," 62.

111. Kawagoe, *Chō Sakurin* (NIDS), 47–48. The time of sunrise near Mukden (Shenyang) on June 28, 1928, was calculated according to the meteorological data in: http://www.world-timedate.com/astronomy/sunrise_sunset/sunrise_sunset_time. php?month=6&year=1928&sun_param=0&city_id=578. Ozaki Yoshiharu (*Rikugun*, 108–9) argued that Kōmoto asked him whether to cancel the operation. Like Tōmiya, he answered in the negative and urged his commander to act as planned.

112. "Mukden Consulate Report," 82, 87–90; Hata, "Chō Sakurin Bakusatsu," 130; Iboshi, "Chō Sakurin," 4:28.

113. For information about the makeup of the train, see Gong Debo (T.P.K'ung), *The Tragic Death of Chang Tso-lin: A Documentary Survey of a Prelude to the Japanese Invasion of Manchuria* (Peiping, 1932), 8.

114. Sakuma, *Manshū* (NIDS), 4; Hayashi to Tanaka, 4, 5.6.1928, *NGB* S, 1:1:2, 132–33; Inaba, "Chō Sakurin," 19, 21; Takamiya, *Gunkoku*, 46.

322   NOTES TO PAGES 181–183

115. Morishima, "Chō Sakurin," 43; Kōmoto to Araki Sadao and Matsui Iwane, 27.4.1928, Mitani, *Kindai Nihon*, 111–12. The full original, in handwriting, is kept as part of *Araki Sadao Kankei Monjo* in *Tokyo Daigaku Hōgakubu fuzoku Kindai Nihon Hōsei Shiryōbu* (Tokyo University Law Faulty Modern Japan Materials Reading Room) ; Hata, "Chō Sakurin Bakusatsu," 132; Okada's cross-examination, IMTFE, M2:1865.

116. Kōmoto's interview in Mori, *Manshū*, 270; "Heben Dazuo Kou gong," 6.4.1954, *HBDZ*, 36–37. According to Ozaki himself (as confided to Tanaka Ryūkichi in 1929), Saitō reprimanded him because there was no necessity "of using the Kwantung Army against such a weak army as that of the Chinese." See Tanaka Ryūkichi's interrogation, IMTFE, M2:1952, 7.

117. Hayashi to Tanaka, 9.6.1928, *NGB* S, 1:1:2, 142. Morishima Morito, then a diplomat at the Mukden Consulate, recalled that the Kwantung Army approached the consulate several times ("Chō Sakurin, Yō Utei no Ansatsu: Nihon Gaikō no Kaisō [1]," *Sekai* 45 [September 30, 1949], 43). However, Muraoka did not broach the subject in his subsequent conversation with Hayashi. See Hayashi to Tanaka, 13.6.1928, *NGB* S, 1:1:2, 143–44. And compare with subconsul Morishima Morito's account in Morishima, *Inbō*, 24.

118. For details on the cover-up attempts of the conspirators after the assassination, see Kawagoe, *Chō Sakurin* (NIDS), 65–66.

119. "Special Committee Meeting 2," 23.10.1928, *NGB* S, 1:1:2, 197. Morishima, *Inbō*, 25.

120. Matsumura Kenzō, *Sandai Kaikoroku* (Tokyo: Tokyo Keizai Shinpōsha, 1964), 125–29. Kawagoe believed that mistakes done by Hata when procuring Russian bombs for the Chinese decoys, along with the *Minseitō*'s selfish wish to grab power from Tanaka, were responsible for the dismal failure of the cover-up attempt. See Kawagoe, *Chō Sakurin* (NIDS), 79–81.

121. The Army Ministry accused only the addicts. The ministry's release (June 12) is reproduced in Morishima, *Inbō*, 20–21.

122. Hayashi to Tanaka, 4, 8, 13, 21.6.1928, *NGB* S, 1:1:2, 131–32, 9, 44–46, 61–63; Hayashi Kyūjirō, *Manshū Jihen to Hōten Sōryōji* (Tokyo: Hara Shobō, 1978), 21.

123. In their conversation, Hayashi said to Matsumura that he was ready to tell him what really happened, but not in the consulate, "as the army guys are watching." He proposed to have their conversation in a hot spring instead. See Matsumura, *Sandai*, 125.

124. *Muken Consulate Report*, 62–66; "Heben Dazuo Kou gong," 6.4.1954, *HBDZ*, 34; Ōe, *Chō Sakurin Bakusatsu*, 20–23. The concurrent, equally evasive, investigation report of the Kwantung Army ("Chō Sakurin Ressha Bakuha Jiken ni kansuru Shoken," undated) is reproduced by Inaba, "Chō Sakurin," 60–68.

125. Hayashi to Tanaka, 8, 18.6.1928, *NGB* S, 1:1:2, 140–42, 46–50.

126. *TGD*, 2:1028, 30; Ōe, *Chō Sakurin Bakusatsu*, 21–22.

127. *TGD*, 2:1030; Hata, "Chō Sakurin Bakusatsu," 133; Okada's affidavit, IMTFE, M2:1828.

128. "Manshū Chian Iji no tame Kantōgun Shirekan ni ataeru Ninmu nado ni Kansuru Kakugi" (cabinet discussion, 7.6.1928), *NGB* S, 1:1:2, 135–37.

129. "Chō Sakurin Bakusatsu Jiken Chōsa Tokubetsu Iinkai Daichi Kaigi Shinji Jiroku" (hereafter cited as "special committee conference:1"), 22.9.1928, *NGB* S, 1:1:2, 192–93. The committee members were Foreign Ministry: Vice Minister Mori, Head of the Asia Section Arita, Secretary Okazaki; Army: Sugiyama, military affairs bureau chief at the Army Ministry; Kwantung Government: Secretary Ōba (ibid., 192) .

130. Military Police Chief Mine's report is probably irretrievably lost, but General Tanaka Ryūkichi, a Special Service officer who was well acquainted with it, testified about its contents at the Tokyo Trials, see *IMFTE*, M2:1951–60. For further information on the lost report, see Iboshi, "Chō Sakurin," 1:4. This engineering officer, Lieutenant Kirihara, probably spoke about the event in a bar in Seoul, and the rumors reached Mine's ears. See Hata, "Chō Sakurin Bakusatsu," 138.

131. Harada, Kumao, *Saionji-kō to Seikyoku* (Tokyo: Iwanami Shoten, 1950–55), 1:3–4.

132. Had Kōmoto been faced with an effective court-martial, he might have suffered the death penalty under the criminal code of the army (Ōe, *Chō Sakurin*, 123). One of the most important sources for the events that followed is Hirohito's famous "monologue," given in 1946 to one of his courtiers, as well as the diaries and memoirs of various high court officials. See Terasaki Hidenari, *Shōwa Tennō Dokuhakuroku: Terasaki Hidenari Goyōgakari Nikki* (Tokyo: Bungei Shunjū, 1991), 22–23 (hereafter cited as *STD*); Nara Takeji, *Jijū Bukanchō Nara Takeji Nikki Kaisōroku*, vol. 4 (Tokyo: Kashiwa Shobō, 2000); Harada, *Saionji*, 1:4.

133. Okada Keisuke's affidavit, IMFTE, M2:1819–20, 29. For similar remarks by Tanaka in a conversation with his railway minister, Ogawa Heikichi, see "Manshū Mondai," *OHKM*, 1:628, and in an Imperial audience in March quoted in the diary of Count Makino Nobuaki, lord keeper of the privy seal: *Makino Nobuaki Nikki*, eds. Itō Takashi and Hirose Yoshihiro (Tokyo: Chūō Kōronsha, 1990), 350–51 (hereafter cited as *MNN*); Ōe, *Chō Sakurin*, 28, 30.

134. Okada's affidavit, IMFTE, M2:1820; Nara, *Kaisōroku*, 4:151; *UKN*, 2:704; Harada, *Saionji*, 1:5, 8; Drea, *Imperial Army*, 163.

135. Ogawa, "Manshū Mondai," *OHKM*, 1:630; Though Kōmoto complained later that only Araki understood him, he still had many overt and covert supporters in the army. See Kōmoto's interview in Mori, *Manshū*, 271–72; Ōe, *Chō Sakurin*, 31–34, 45–48, 113–14. General Abe Nobuyuki had also participated in the cover-up attempts, though he was an old rival of Kōmoto. About the strained relationship between Abe and Kōmoto, see Hirano, *Inbōsha*, 65.

136. *TGD*, 2:1036.

137. *STD*, 22; Kawai Yahachi, *Shōwa shoki no Tennō to Kyūchū: Jijū Jichō Kawai Yahachi Nikki* (Tokyo: Iwanami Shoten, 1993–94), 3:99 (hereafter cited as *Kawai Yahachi Nikki*). Ogawa was well informed over the affair through his own sources. See his own account: "Manshū Mondai Hiroku-hi," *OHKM*, 1:626–29 (the account is undated, but according to Ogawa's own side note on 627, it must have been written before 1931).

138. *TGD*, 2:1031. For details and partial translation of the parliamentary hearings in both Houses, see Morton, *Tanaka Cabinet*, 153–54; Kung, *Tragic Death*, 20–33.

139. *UKN*, 2:724.

140. *TGD*, 2:1036; Harada, *Saionji*, 3; Okada's affidavit, IMFTE, M2:1820. In a difficult conversation with Ogawa, Saionji decried the poor discipline of the army and the deterioration in state authority. He strongly supported a court-martial. See Ogawa, "Manshū Mondai," *OHKM*, 1:629. Prince Itō's influence was neutralized by pro-army elements at the Privy Council. See Ōe, *Chō Sakurin*, 103. Admiral Okada supported harsh punishment, but without disclosing the event to the public. See Hata, "Chō Sakurin Bakusatsu," 140.

141. *UKN*, 1:689, 704, 12, 24; Ōe, *Chō Sakurin*, 53–56.

142. Tanaka's instructions to the Special Committee of Inquiry, 22.9.1928, *NGB S*, 1:1:2, 195. Okada's cross-examination, IMFTE, M2:1862–63; Harada, *Saionji*, 1:7; O'Dwyer, *Significant*, 226–27.

143. *UKN*, 2:724.

144. Harada, *Saionji*, 1:10.

145. Ōe, *Chō Sakurin*, 115.

146. Harada, *Saionji*, 1:4–5.

147. Ogawa, "Manshū Mondai," *OHKM*, 1:629–30.

148. Nara, *Kaisōroku*, 4:151; *Kawai Yahachi Nikki*, 3:37; *MNN*, 333, 6–7, 43; Harada, *Saionji*, 1:8, 10.

149. *STD*, 22; Harada, *Saionji*, 1:11.

150. *STD*, 23; Nara, *Kaisōroku*, 4:152; *Kawai Yahachi Nikki*, 3:111; *MNN*, 376–78; *Okabe Nagakage Nikki—Shōwa Shoki Kazoku Kanryō no Kiroku*, ed. Shōyū Kurabu (Tokyo: Kashiwa Shobō, 1993), 141–42; *TGD*, 2:1043.

151. Ogawa, "Manshū Mondai," *OHKM*, 1:632; *MNN*, 379.

152. Stephen S. Large, *Emperor Hirohito and Shōwa Japan: A Political Biography* (London: Routledge, 1992), 34–40.

153. Peter Wetzler, *Hirohito and War: Imperial Tradition and Military Decision Making in Prewar Japan* (Honolulu: University of Hawaii Press, 1998), 164. Wetzler's interpretation is supported by Makino's diary, see *MNN*, 377–78.

154. Herbert Bix, *Hirohito Hirohito and the Making of Modern Japan* (New York: HarperCollins, 2000), 217–18.

155. Bix's argument is not supported by any source and is in fact often contradicted by the evidence. See for example Makino's diary entry for 19.1.1929 (*MNN*, 333), where the lord keeper of the privy seal writes explicitly that, in the eyes of the imperial court, the investigation ordered by the emperor was meant to lead to formal and official court-martial. When writing about Hirohito's alleged "acceptance" of the army's position after Shirakawa's audience on March 27, Bix refers to page 350 in Makino's diary (*MNN*), but the source does not lend support to his argument, and neither does the corresponding entry in Okabe's diary (*Okaba Nagakage Nikki*, 74) or Suzuki's testimony (*TGD*, 2:1041). Such problems are unfortunately prevalent throughout Bix's book. See Matsumoto Ken'ichi and Shōji Junichirō, "Critiquing Herbert Bix's 'Hirohito,'" *Japan Echo* 29, no. 6 (December 2002): 65–68.

156. *Okaba Nagakage Nikki*, 141.

157. Ōe, *Chō Sakurin*, 153, 9, 61, 5.

158. Wetzler, *Hirohito*, 156–56.

159. As Ōe Shinobu writes, Hirohito had "pushed the wrong button" (*Chō Sakurin*, 161).

160. *STD*, 23; Ogawa, "Manshū Mondai," *OHKM*, 1:632; Wetzler, *Hirohito*, 165–66.

161. Mori, *Nihon Rikugun*, 72–74.

162. Dormer to Chamberlain, 4.6.1928, CMJP-NAA, 174.

163. Saitō's diary, 3.6.1928, reproduced in Inaba, "Chō Sakurin," 18. The next line in the diary, however, proves that Saitō was not privy to the plot, as he wondered what should be done after Zhang's return. In addition, his diary entry from June 5 shows his lack of acquaintance with the plot (ibid., 25).

164. Kawagoe, *Chō Sakurin* (NIDS), 45–46.

165. Morishima, *Inbō*, 25.

166. Northcote Parkinson, *Parkinson's Law and Other Studies in Administration* (Boston, MA: Houghton Mifflin, 1957), 5.

167. The daily dispatches, telegrams, and letters of the General Staff were burdening Muraoka and Saitō, not Kōmoto. See Inaba, "Chō Sakurin," 9–16.

168. Mark Peattie, *Ishiwara Kanji and Japan's Confrontation with the West* (Princeton, NJ: Princeton University Press, 1995), 93–94.

169. Kōmoto to Isogai, 18.4.1928, in Kobayashi, *Isogai*, 47. See also Kitaoka, "China Experts," in Duus, *Informal Empire*, 339–42, 66–67.

170. Machino, "Chō Sakurin," 76.

171. Ōe, *Chō Sakurin*, 184.

172. *STDS*, 1:292.

9. CHERRY BLOSSOM

The chapter epigraph was translated by Jay Rubin in *The Oxford Book of Japanese Short Stories*, ed. Theodore W. Goossen (Oxford: Oxford Univesity Press, 1987), 205.

1. Nakano Masao comments in Hashimoto Kingorō, *Hashimoto Taisa no Shuki*, ed. Nakano Masao (Tokyo: Misuzu Shobō, 1963, hereafter cited as *Hashimoto Shuki*), 8–10. According to Hashimoto's biographer, Tatamiya Eitarō, the dentist, Uchida Masako

(Kinu), intended to uphold the secrecy of the manuscript, and was cheated by Nakano who "borrowed" and then published it against her will. She never forgave him. For the story, see Tatamiya, *Hashimoto Kingorō Ichidai* (Tokyo: Fuyō Shobō, 1982), 36.

2. Yale C. Maxon, *Control of Japanese Foreign Policy: A Study of Civil Military Rivalry, 1930–1945* (Westport, CT: Greenwood Press, 1973), 72–107; Andrew D. Gordon, *Labor and Imperial Democracy in Prewar Japan* (Berkeley: University of California Press, 1991), 261–69; Elise K. Tipton, *Modern Japan: Social and Political History* (London: Routledge, 2008), 123–52; Gluck, *Japan's Modern Myths*, 282–83. For discussion of this trend in Japanese historiography, see William M. Tsutsui, "The Domestic Impact of War and Occupation on Japan," in *World War Two in Asia and the Pacific and the War's Aftermath, with General Themes: a Handbook of Literature and Research*, ed. Loyd E. Lee (Westport. CT: Greenwood Press, 1998), 138–39.

3. *Kido Kōichi Nikki*, ed. Oka Yoshitake (Tokyo: Tokyo Daigaku Shuppankai, 1966, hereafter cited as *KKN*, 2:147–48; *Tokyo Saiban Shiryō Kido Kōichi Jinmon Chōsho*, eds. Awaya Kentarō et al. (Tokyo: Ōtsuki Shoten, 1987, hereafter cited as *TSS-KKJC*), 43–44.

4. *KKN*, 2:147; Koiso Kuniaki, *Katsuzan Kōsō* (Tokyo: Koiso Kuniaki Jijōden Kankōkai, 1963), 498–500.

5. Kido Kōichi's affidavit, *IMFTE*, reel 23:30, 727–28.

6. Richard J. Smethurst, *From Foot Soldier to Finance Minister: Takahashi Korekiyo, Japan's Keynes* (Cambridge, MA: Harvard University Press, 2007), 243–44, 7–8.

7. Ben-Ami Shillony, *Revolt in Japan: the Young Officers and the February 26, 1936 Incident* (Princeton, NJ: Princeton University Press, 1973), 9–10. Compare with the testimony of Lieutenant Ōkura Eiichi in his memoirs, *Niniroku Jiken e no Banka: Saigō no Seinen Shōkō* (Tokyo: Yomiuri Shinbunsha, 1971), 60.

8. *Hashimoto Shuki*, 15–16; Araki Sadao's interrogation, in *Court Papers, Journals, Exhibits, and Judgments of the International Military Tribunal for the Far East* (Microfilm Reels, Center for Research Libraries, Chicago, hereafter cited as *IMTFE-CJEJ*), reel 11, exhibit 187:T, p. 1; Higuchi Kiichirō, *Rikugun Chūjō Higuchi Kiichirō Kaisōroku* (Tokyo: Fuyō Shobō, 1999), 280–22, 7–8. For more information on the army's pessimistic mood, compare with the detailed annual report of the Soviet Embassy in Tokyo. Written in 1932, it captures well the feeling of ideological decay prevailing in military circles since the 1920s. See "Godovoi Doklad 1932, ob ekonomichesko-politicheskom polozhenii Yaponii," 60, *Arhiv Vneshnei Politiki Rossiskei Federatsii* (Archive of Foreign Policy of the Russian Federation, Moscow, hereafter cited as AVPRF), opis 15, delo 6, popka 149.

9. *Hashimoto Shuki*, 29; Tokugawa Yoshichika, *Saigo no Tonosama: Tokugawa Yoshichika Jiden* (Tokyo: Kōdansha, 1973), 122.

10. Saitō Saburō, "Uyoku Shisō Hanzai Jiken no Sōgōteki Kenkyū: Ketsumeidan Jiken yori Niniroku Jiken Made" in *Kokka Shugi Undō*, ed. Imai Seiichi et al. (Tokyo: Misuzu Shobō, 1963, hereafter cited as "Uyoku Shisō Hanzai"), 4:62; Tokugawa, *Saigo no Tonosama*, 125.

11. Ibid., 62.

12. Ibid., 58; "Minutes of the Third Trial," Ōkawa Shūmei's interrogation in his trial, 1934 (hereafter cited as Ōkawa, 1934 trial protocol), *IMTFE-CJEJ*, reel 24, exhibit 2177A.

13. See the testimony of General Tanaka Ryūkichi in *IMTFE*, reel 2:1962–63. The phrase "Japan First, Manchuria Second" is my own, but its substance is based on Tanaka's testimony.

14. Frank S. Tavenner, Hugh B. Helm, and Arthur Comyns Carr, "Report on the Case against Col. Kingoro Hashimoto," 4, *The Tokyo War Crimes Trial: A Digital Exhibition* (hereafter cited as *TWCT-DE*), University of Virginia Law Library. http://lib.law.virginia. edu/imtfe/content/item-1-report-case-against-col-kingoro-hashimoto-i-j-ret.

326   NOTES TO PAGES 196–200

15. Hashimoto Kingorō's interrogation, *IMFTE-CJEJ*, reel 12, exhibit 258, pp. 1–2; Karita Tetsu, "Jūgatsu Jiken" (1), *Tokyo Tōritsu Daigaku Hōgaku Zasshi* 11, no. 2 (March 1971), 1:319.

16. Hashimoto to General Okamoto Ren'ichirō, Vice Chief of the General Staff, 15.11.1929, *IMTFE-CJEJ*, reel 15, exhibit 734, p. 1. For analysis, see Hiraoki Kuromiya and George Mamoulia, "Anti-Russian and Anti-Soviet Subversion: the Caucasian-Japanese Nexus, 1904–1945," *Europe-Asia Studies* 61, no. 8 (2009): 1421.

17. For discussion on the Turkish influences on Hashimoto, see Tatamiya, *Hashimoto*, 18–32.

18. Higuchi, *Kaisōroku*, 288; Hashimoto Kingorō, excerpts from "The Road to the Reconstruction of the World," "From the Point of View of National Defense, It Is the Duty of the Military to Mix in Politics," *Taiyō Dai Nippon*, 17.3.1937, reproduced in *IMTFE-CJEJ*, reel 11, exhibit 177:1, p. 1; reel 15, exhibit 675:A, p. 2; Tatamiya, *Hashimoto*, 61. In his interrogation, Hashimoto also mentioned Hitler along with the other role-model leaders, but as the latter didn't rise to power until 1933, he could not have influenced the former's state of mind in 1930. See also Karita, "Jūgatsu Jiken," 1:320, as well as Honjō Shigeru to Uehara Yūsaku, 18.8.1931, *Uehara Yūsaku Kankei Monjo*, ed. Uehara Yūsaku Kankei Monjo Kenkyūkai (Tokyo: Tokyo Daigaku Shuppankai, 1976), 452–53.

19. Hashimoto Kingorō, excerpts from "The Road to the Reconstruction of the World," *IMTFE-CJEJ*, reel 11, exhibit 177:1, p. 1.

20. Hashimoto Kingorō, excerpts from "The Inevitability of Renovation," *IMTFE-CJEJ*, reel 12, exhibit 264, pp. 1–2.

21. The Russian desk belonged to Section 4 (Europe and America) in the Intelligence Department. For a thorough analysis on the organizational structure and functions of the department, see Karita, "Jūgatsu Jiken," 1:316–18.

22. "Uyoku Shisō Hanzai," 58; Tanaka Kiyoshi, "Showa 7-nen 1-gatsu, XX Shōsa Shuki, Iwayuru Jūgatsu Jiken ni kansuru Shuki," appendix 5, in Muranaka Kōji and Isobe Asaichi, *Shukugun ni kansuru Ikensho: Shōwa 10-nen 7-gatsu 11-nichi* (Tokyo: self-published pamphlet, 1935, hereafter cited as *Tanaka Kiyoshi Shuki*), 78. The identity of the author, "Major XX," was established by later historians as Tanaka Kiyoshi, captain in 1931. See Tanaka Azusa, "Iwayuru Sangatsu Jiken nit suite: sono Gaiyō to Bunken no Shōkai," *Sankō Shoshi Kenkyū* 16 (June 1978): 9–10. The original manuscript of this source was lost, and it reached us only through a copy made by young officers deeply hostile to the author. Still, Tanaka himself upheld by and large the reliability of the published version after the war. For discussion on the reliability of this source, see Tatamiya, *Hashimoto*, 67–68.

23. *Hashimoto Shuki*, 21; *Tanaka Kiyoshi Shuki*, 78;

24. Matsumoto Sōji, "Ishin no Shishi o ronzu," in *Seitō Bunsho*, ed. Amakasu Shigetarō (Tokyo: Rikugun Yoka Shikan Gakkō, 1937), private collection of Carter Eckert, courtesy of Carter Eckert, 2:7–9. See also Yamashita Fumio's essay in the same collection, 2:13.

For discussion on the process of mimesis, see the last subsection of the first chapter. See also Benesch, *Inventing the Way*, 179, 194.

25. See for example Kobayakawa, *Bingō*, 41, 52, 75, 88, 91–92. For more details see discussion in chapter 6.

26. *Hashimoto Shuki*, 21.

27. Ibid., 21–22.

28. Ibid., 24, 88.

29. Ibid., 30, and see also Nakano's analysis on 60. Compare with Hashimoto's reply to Tanaka in *Tanaka Kiyoshi Shuki*, 89.

30. *IMTFE*, reel 2:1962; *Hashimoto Shuki*, 24–25. Hashimoto's statement is supported by the affidavit of Lieutenant Colonel Wachi Takaji, *IMTFE,* reel 15:19,666. According to

Tanaka Kiyoshi (*Tanaka Kiyoshi Shuki*, 76), the society was founded in late September 1930. See *Tanaka Kiyoshi Shuki*, 79

31. "Uyoku Shisō Hanzai," 58; *Tanaka Kiyoshi Shuki*, 77; Karita, "Jūgatsu Jiken," 1:323.

32. *Hashimoto Shuki*, 25; Karita, "Jūgatsu Jiken," 323.

33. *Tanaka Kiyoshi Shuki*, 98–99. For Tanaka, as the hostile observer he was, the shishi fetish of Hashimoto and his friends was at the root of their recklessness and the main reason for their eventual failure.

34. Sotoyama Toyozō, quoted by Nakano Masao in *Hashimoto Shuki*, 79.

35. "Uyoku Shisō Hanzai," 58; *IMTFE*, reel 2:1962. In his interrogation by the Americans, Hashimoto overemphasized his own role and insisted that the others (most of them already dead at that time) were not founders but merely assistants or secretaries. See Testimony of Hashimoto Kingorō, 17–18.2.1946, *IMTFE*, reel 12:15,647 .

36. Karita, "Jūgatsu Jiken," 1:325. The quote is from the recollections of Chō's close friend Ōkawa Shūmei.

37. *Hashimoto Shuki*, 25, 77–78. The graph represents the membership of the Sakurakai in around the March Incident, before the influx of members in April.

38. "Uyoku Shisō Hanzai," 62; Suematsu Tahei, *Watakushi no Shōwashi* (Tokyo: Misuzu Shobō, 1963), 31, 9.

39. *Tanaka Kiyoshi Shuki*, 97–98; Fujii Hisashi, *Niniroku Teito Heiran: Gunjiteki Shiten kara zenmenteki ni minaosu* (Tokyo: Sōshisha, 2010), 26.

40. *Hashimoto Shuki*, 26–27; "Okamura Memo," op. cit. ibid., 67; *Tanaka Kiyoshi Shuki*, 77; Suematsu, *Watakushi no Shōwashi*, 43. Higuchi Kiichirō, however, claimed in his memoirs that most officers supported his own moderate faction. See *Kaisōroku*, 288. Corroborated by the testimony of another participant, Matsumura Shūitsu, Karita, "Jūgatsu Jiken," 2:276–77. Karita Tetsu believes that was the case until spring 1931 (ibid., 2:277).

41. *Hashimoto Shuki*, 27; *Tanaka Kiyoshi Shuki*, 87.

42. Nakano Masao in *Hashimoto Shuki*, 53, see also Tanaka, "Iwayuru Sangatsu Jiken," 4. For interesting observations on this factional struggle from the point of view of Soviet diplomats, see A. Askov to T. Sokolnikov, 5.5.1934, AVPRI, opis 17, delo 17, popka 158, p. 175 (2).

43. Okada Keisuke's affidavit, Ōkawa, 1934 trial protocol, *IMTFE-CJEJ*, reel 11, exhibit 157, pp. 1, 4; reel 24, exhibit 2177A, pp. 2–10, 14–15, 30–31; Ōkawa Shūmei, *Nihon oyobi Nihonjin no Michi* (Tokyo: Kōchisha Shuppanbu, 1926), 125–26, 42–43; Tanaka, "Iwayuru Sangatsu Jiken," 3–4.

44. Ōkawa, 1934 trial protocol, *IMTFE-CJEJ*, reel 24, exhibiti 2177A, p. 18; Shimizu Gyōnosuke's affidavit, *IMTFE-CJEJ*, reel 11, exhibit 157, p. 1.

45. *TSS-KKJC*, 51. According to Tokugawa's post facto testimony, he gave the money on the condition that "no one would be killed." See *Saigo no Tonosama*, 125–27; "Uyoku Shisō Hanzai," 61. In his secret memoirs, Hashimoto wrote that the money was obtained from a peer but failed to mention his name. See *Hashimoto Shuki*, 61.

46. Tokugawa, *Saigo no Tonosama*, 124.

47. *Hashimoto Shuki*, 45–46. Compare with Koiso, *Katsuzan*, 498–99; Tanaka, "Iwayuru Sangatsu Jiken," 3.

48. Ōkawa, 1934 trial protocol, *IMTFE-CJEJ*, reel 24, exhibit 2177A, pp. 17–18.

49. For the importance of the Taishō political crisis as a precedent for the actors involved in the March Incident, see the analysis of Kobayashi Michihiko, "Sangatsu Jiken Saikō," *Nihon Rekishi* 10 (2007): 1–19.

50. Ōkawa, 1934 trial protocol, *IMTFE-CJEJ*, reel 24, exhibit 2177A, p. 18; *Hashimoto Shuki*, 60–61; *Tanaka Kiyoshi Shuki*, 82–83.

51. *KKN*, 2:147–48; *Hashimoto Shuki*, 61; *Tanaka Kiyoshi Shuki*, 82–83; Shimizu Gyōnosuke's affidavit, *IMTFE-CJEJ*, reel 11, exhibit 157, p. 1. We know that these were

dummy bombs, capable of making noise but with minimal lethal impact, from *Hashimoto Shuki*, 71–72; Koiso, *Katsuzan*, 501.

52. *Hashimoto Shuki*, 61; *Tanaka Kiyoshi Shuki*, 82.

53. *Tanaka Kiyoshi Shuki*, 83. Compare with *KKN*, 2:147; Tanaka,"Iwayuru Sangatsu Jiken," 5.

54. *Tanaka Kiyoshi Shuki*, 82–83. In his trial in 1934, Ōkawa admitted that it was "impossible to draft a concrete plan" for national reconstruction. See Ōkawa, 1934 trial protocol, *IMTFE-CJEJ*, reel 24, exhibit 1175:A, p. 30. Lieutenant Ōkura Eiichi, certainly not a moderate, shared Tanaka's concerns. In his opinion, Hashimoto and Chō were "rushing to a perilous adventure in an intoxicated state of mind." See Ōkura, *Niniroku*, 66.

55. *Tanaka Kiyoshi Shuki*, 83.

56. Karita Tetsu, *Ōkawa Shūmei to Kokka Kaizō Undō* (Tokyo: Ningen no Kagaku Shinsha, 2001), 310–11, Ugaki Kazushige, "Kokka sore ayashi," reproduced ibid., 319–22. This anonymous manuscript was found among Ugaki's papers. Based on its style and content, Karita and other scholars had determined that the general himself was its author (ibid., 307–8, 24). It is dated April 1931, that is, after the March Incident but before the Manchurian and October Incidents. Compare with Ugaki's diary, *UKN*, 1:795–96, in which he documented his intense dissatisfaction with party rule and the deteriorating economic conditions in the country.

57. Karita, *Ōkawa Shūmei*, 310–11; *Hashimoto Shuki*, 56; Koiso, *Katsuzan*, 500–501.

58. *Tanaka Kiyoshi Shuki*, 80.

59. *Hashimoto Shuki*, 47–51; Tatamiya, *Hashimoto*, 59–62. Compare with *KKN*, 2:93.

60. In his memoir (*Katsuzan*, 502–3), Koiso admits he mediated a meeting between Ōkawa and Ugaki, but dates this much later, to late February. He writes that he first met Ōkawa after February 20, refused to cooperate with his plans but still pleaded a meeting between him and Ugaki, which took place a few days later. But according to another source, we know that the meeting between Ōkawa and Ugaki took place on February 11. See Ōkawa, 1934 trial protocol, *IMTFE-CJEJ*, reel 24, exhibit 2177A, pp. 18–19, interview with Nakano Masao, *Hashimoto Shuki*, 59. That, along with Ugaki's testimony to Harada in the latter's memoirs, makes Koiso's version about his refusal to cooperate with Ōkawa a little difficult to accredit. For if he refused, why did he arrange the meeting between Ōkawa and his minister in the first place, and earlier than he would like us to believe? See Harada Kumao, *The Saionji-Harada Memoirs, 1931–1940 [microform]: Complete Translation into English* (Washington, DC: University Publications of America, 1978, hereafter cited as *SHM*), 1:156–57.

61. *SHM*, 1:157–59; Ugaki Kazushige's affidavit, *IMTFE-CJEJ*, reel 11, exhibit 163, p. 1.

62. Ōkawa, 1934 trial protocol, *IMTFE-CJEJ*, reel 24, exhibit 2177A, pp. 19–20. For example (15,583) Ōkawa maintained that he did not intend to destroy parliamentarianism completely, which was an outright lie. Nagata's testimony to Kido Kōichi on his own (Nagata's) conversation with Ōkawa is rather ambiguous about this question. See *KKN*, 2:147. Ugaki's version is supported by *Tanaka Kiyoshi Shuki*, 85; Koiso, *Katsuzan*, 503–4; and Shimizu Gyōnosuke's affidavit, *IMTFE-CJEJ*, reel 11, exhibit 157, p. 1.

63. Okamura memo, op cit. in *Hashimoto Shuki*, 67–68. Corroborated by *Tanaka Kiyoshi Shuki*, 84. Ugaki, "Kokka sore ayashi," reproduced in Karita, *Ōkawa Shūmei*, 321. In his memoirs (*Katsuzan*, 501–7), Koiso described his comments to Ōkawa's plan with the words "illegal and childish" (*Higōhō na, katsu Kodomo-rashi koto*), but the "illegal" part of the phrase seems like a later insertion, as the general had been involved in illegal endeavors at least since January. Perhaps his doubts began to grow after hearing the precise details of Ōkawa's amateurish plan.

64. Ōkawa, 1934 trial protocol, *IMFTE*, reel 12:15,582; Ōkawa to Ugaki, 6.3.1931, *IMTFE-CJEJ*, reel 11, exhibit 163:2, pp. 1–2, for the Japanese original see Tatamiya, *Hashimoto*, 74–75. And compare with Koiso, *Katsuzan*, 509; Tanaka, "Iwayuru Sangatsu Jiken," 7.

65. Koiso, *Katsuzan*, 503–4, 9.
66. "Uyoku Shisō Hanzai," 61; *Hashimoto Shuki*, 71–72; Shimizu Gyōnosuke's affidavit, *IMTFE-CJEJ*, reel 11, exhibit 157, p. 1; Koiso, *Katsuzan*, 502–3.
67. *Tanaka Kiyoshi Shuki*, 85; Ōkawa, 1934 trial protocol, *IMTFE-CJEJ*, reel 24, exhibit 2177A, pp. 18–19; Koiso, *Katsuzan*, 511; Tanaka, "Iwayuru Sangatsu Jiken," 8; Tokugawa, *Saigo no Tonosama*, 130; Hata Ikuhiko, *Gun Fashizumu Undōshi* (Tokyo: Kawade Shobō Shinsa, 1972), 30.
68. Tokugawa, *Saigo no Tonosama*, 130–34. See also Nakano's analysis in *Hashimoto Shuki*, 70; Shimizu Gyōnosuke's affidavit, Tokugawa Yoshichika's affidavit, Ōkawa, 1934 Trial Protocol, *IMTFE-CJEJ*, reel 11, exhibit 157, p. 1, exhibit 158, p. 1; reel 24, exhibit 2177A, p. 20; Koiso, *Katsuzan*, 511–12; Tanaka, "Iwayuru Sangatsu Jiken," 7.
69. *Hashimoto Shuki*, 62. Compare with Okamura memo, ibid., 68.
70. Tokugawa, *Saigo no Tonosama*, 134.
71. Honjō to Uehara, 18.8.1931, *Uehara Yūsaku Kankei Monjo*, 452.
72. "Uyoku Shishō Hanzai," 63; *Hashimoto Shuki*, 77–78; *Tanaka Kiyoshi Shuki*, 85–86; Karita, "Jūgatsu Jiken," 2:283; Honjō to Uehara, 18.8.1931, *Uehara Yūsaku Kankei Monjo*, 452. About the Sakura-kai's activity in Tōyama School see the testimonies of Ōkura Eiichi, *Niniroku*, 61; Suematsu, *Watakushi no Shōwashi*, 39, 42, 4. According to Tatamiya (*Hashimoto*, 52) by September 1931 there were three hundred members in Tokyo alone.
73. *SHM*, 1:43–44, 9 (the quotes are from 49). And compare with Tanaka Ryūkichi's testimony, *IMTFE*, reel 2:2019–20.
74. *SHM*, 1:26, 37.
75. *Hashimoto Shuki*, 146.
76. Citizen's Disarmament League (Ozaki Yukio and six others) to Army Minister Minami, 6.8.1931, *IMFTE*, reel 2:2193–94 .
77. *SHM*, 1:40–41, 5, 50–52.
78. *SHM*, 1:59–61, see also 66.
79. Shimizu Gyōnosuke's testimony in *Hashimoto Shuki*, 76–77, and also Hashimoto's text in 80–81; Honjō to Uehara, 18.8.1931, *Uehara Yūsaku Kankei Monjo*, 453.
80. *IMFTE*, reel 2:1975, 2158–59.
81. Tanaka Ryūkichi's interrogation, *IMFTE*, reel 2:2060–61, 8, 87–96; Morishima Morito's affidavit, Ōkawa, 1934 trial protocol, Hirata Yukihiro's deposition, *IMTFE-CJEJ*, reel 12, exhibit 245, p. 4; reel 24, exhibit 1175:A, pp. 14–15, 17; reel 25, exhibit 2404, pp. 3–7; *Hashimoto Shuki*, 103–5; Ōkura, *Niniroku*, 64.
82. Tanaka Ryūkichi's interrogation, *IMTFE*, reel 2:1966–70, 2015–16; *Hashimoto Shuki*, 84–85.
83. Ōkawa, 1934 trial protocol, Honjō Shigeru, "The True Nature of the Manchurian Incident," written in early October, 1945, *IMTFE-CJEJ*, reel 24, exhibit 2177A, pp. 17, 22; reel 25, exhibit 2403, p. 1; *Hashimoto Shuki*, 127–28.
84. Hayashi to Shidehra, 19 Sept. 1931, *IMTFE*, reel 2:2179–80 ; Mark Peattie, *Ishiwara Kanji and Japan's Confrontation with the West* (Princeton, NJ: Princeton University Press, 1975), 121.
85. *Hashimoto Shuki*, 163; Sadako Ogata, *Defiance in Manchuria: the Making of Japanese Foreign Policy, 1931–32* (Westport, CT: Greenwood Press, 1984), 80, 94; Tanaka Ryūkichi's interrogation, *IMTFE*, reel 2:2017.
86. Peattie, *Ishiwara*, 129.
87. *Hashimoto Shuki*, 119–21.
88. Tanaka Ryūkichi's interrogation, *IMFTE*, reel 2:2006–7.
89. *Hashimoto Shuki*, 120, 22.
90. Tanaka Ryūkichi's interrogation, *IMTFE*, reel 2:1974, 2004–6.

91. V. G. R. B. Lytton et al, *Appeal by the Chinese Government. Report of the Commission of Enquiry* (also known as the Lytton Report, Geneva: League of Nations Publications, 1932), 67–68.

92. *Hashimoto Shuki*, 123.

93. Deposition of Takeda Hisashi, *IMFTE-CJEJ*, reel 25, exhibit 2405, p. 7.

94. Morishima Morito's affidavit, *IMTFE-CJEJ*, reel 12, exhibit 245, p. 6.

95. Tanaka Ryūkichi's interrogation, *IMTFE*, reel 2:1989–90.

96. Shigemitsu to Shidehara, 24.9.1931, *IMTFE-CJEJ*, reel 12, exhibit 246; O'Dwyer, *Significant*, 280.

97. Hayashi to Shidehra, 19.9.1931, *IMTFE*, reel 2:178–79 .

98. Shidehara to Shigemitsu Mamoru, Minister to China, 21.9.1931, *IMTFE-CJEJ*, reel 12, exhibit 246, p. 1.

99. Minami Jirō's deposition, *IMTFE-CJEJ*, reel 25, exhibit 2435, pp. 4–6; Ōkura, *Niniroku*, 65.

100. *Hashimoto Shuki*, 127.

101. *Hashimoto Shuki*, 3–5; See also Tanaka's testimony, *IMTFE*, reel 2:1966–67.

102. *Hashimoto Shuki*, 128.

103. *SHM*, 1:123–24; Forbes to Secretary of State, 7.11.1931, US State Department, Records Related to the Internal Affairs of Japan (hereafter cited as US IAJ), reel 1:321, p. 2. And compare with Ōkawa, 1934 trial protocol, *IMTFE-CJEJ*, reel 24, exhibit 2177A, pp. 21–22; Kido Kōichi's affidavit, *IMFTE*, reel 23:30,738–30,739, 30,746. Hashimoto bragged in 1935 that he and his friends were the "real General Staff." (*Hashimoto Shuki*, 133). In certain respects, he was right.

104. *Hashimoto Shuki*, 128.

105. Katō Yōko, *Manshū Jihen kara Nitchū Sensō e* (Tokyo: Iwanami Shoten, 2007), 17–18.

106. Interrogation of General Araki Sadao, *IMTFE*, reel 2:2220–22. According to Araki, the decision to appropriate the funds to the Kwantung Army was made by the cabinet on December 17, 1931. At that time he had already succeeded Minami as the army minister. See also Araki's interrogation and Minami's deposition, *IMTFE-CJEJ*, reel 11, exhibit 187:S, p. 1; reel 25, exhibit 2435, pp. 6–7.

107. Minami Jirō's deposition, *IMTFE-CJEJ*, reel 25, exhibit 2435, pp. 8–9; Forbes to Secretary of State, 7 Nov. 1931, US IAJ, reel 1:321, p. 2 (hereafter cited as *US-IAF*), HULL.

108. *SHM*, 1:80.

109. Ōkawa, 1934 trial protocol, *IMTFE-CJEJ*, reel 24, exhibit 1175:A, p. 21.

110. *SHM*, 1:97.

111. Tanaka Ryūkichi's interrogation, *IMTFE-CJEJ*, reel 2:1977–80, 2158–59. Compare with *Hashimoto Shuki*, 145–46; Ōkawa, 1934 trial protocol, *IMTFE-CJEJ*, reel 24, exhibit 1175:A, p. 21.

112. *SHM*, 1:105, 116–17. Compare with Kido Kōichi's affidavit, *IMTFE*, reel 23:30,734, 30,737.

113. *SHM*, 1:108. The US Embassy reported that at the time, Adachi was "said to have the largest political following of any one in office." See Forbes to Secretary of State, 24.11.1931, US IAJ, reel 1:323.

114. *Hashimoto Shuki*, 151; *Tanaka Kiyoshi Shuki*, 91, 103.

115. Ōkawa, 1934 trial protocol, *IMTFE-CJEJ*, reel 24, exhibit 2177A, pp. 21–22. Hashimoto possibly told some of his comrades that no civilians were involved and that Ōkawa had no role, see Wachi Takaji's interrogation, *IMTFE*, reel 15:19,680; *Hashimoto Shuki*, 151, 8.

116. *Hashimoto Shuki*, 151; *Tanaka Kiyoshi Shuki*, 76, 89.

117. *Hashimoto Shuki*, 151–57, 60.

118. *Hashimoto Shuki*, 151–60; *Tanaka Kiyoshi Shuki*, 93.

119. Ōkawa, 1934 trial protocol, *IMTFE*, reel 12:15,586–15,587. Compare with Wachi Takaji's affidavit, *IMTFE*, reel 15:19,668; *Tanaka Kiyoshi Shuki*, 90.

120. *Tanaka Kiyoshi Shuki*, 94; Nakano Masao in *Hashimoto Shuki*, 155–57; Araki Sadao's interrogation, *IMTFE-CJEJ*, reel 11, exhibit 187:S, pp. 1–2.

121. Nakano Masao in *Hashimoto Shuki*, 155–57; *Tanaka Kiyoshi Shuki*, 89.

122. *Tanaka Kiyoshi Shuki*, 86, 91–92. Ōkura, *Niniroku*, 64–65; *TSS-KKJC*, 52.

123. *Tanaka Kiyoshi Shuki*, 91–92, 6; Higuchi, *Kaisōroku*, 288–89; Ōkura, *Niniroku*, 64–67; *KKN*, 2:94; "Chō Isamu Shuki," Ōtani Keijirō, *Rakujitsu no Joshō: Shōwa Rikugunshi* (Tokyo: Yagumo Shoten, 1959), 46; Suematsu Tahei complained in his memoirs that the meetings were filled with the "odors" of Mussolini and Atatürk (*Watakushi no Shōwashi*, 43).

124. Tanaka Ryūkichi's interrogation, *IMFTE*, reel 2:2016. Corroborated by "Chō Isamu Shuki," Ōtani, *Rakujitsu*, 46; Ogata, *Defiance*, 98.

125. For some of the theories, according to different testimonies, see Nakano Masao in *Hashimoto Shuki*, 167–68.

126. Ōtani, *Rakujitsu*, 46, "Chō Isamu Shuki," ibid. About Chō's drunken bragging and the Sakura-kai's leaders indiscreet behavior, see Ōkura, *Niniroku*, 65. Corroborated by Suematsu, *Watakushi no Shōwashi*, 52. See also Tanaka Ryūkichi's interrogation, *IMTFE*, reel 2:1981; Araki's testimony, reproduced in *Hashimoto Shuki*, 169; Hashimoto's testimony ibid., 166; *Tanaka Kiyoshi Shuki*, 92, 9; Shillony, *Revolt in Japan*, 28.

127. "Chō Isamu Shuki," op. cit. in Ōtani, *Rakujitu*, 45; *Tanaka Kiyoshi Shuki*, 92; Karita, "Jūgatsu Jiken," 1:319.

128. *SHM*, 1:137–38. Compare with *Tanaka Kiyoshi Shuki*, 97.

129. See for example Wachi Takaji's affidavit, *IMTFE*, reel 15:19,667. According to Wachi, it was Hashimoto who confided the plan to Araki, who told Minami in turn. Hashimoto himself confirmed that Araki acted against the coup and met Chō (not Hashimoto) in the tavern. See *Hashimoto Shuki*, 166. There is also another testimony of Araki, different in details from his confession to Harada, reproduced ibid., 169. Compare to the description of this scene in Chō's memoirs, op. cit. in Ōtani, *Rakujitsu*, 46, as well as *Tanaka Kiyoshi Shuki*, 87. Araki himself stated that he forgot the name of the informer, telling his American interrogators that he was notified by the army minister. See Araki's interrogation, *IMTFE-CJEJ*, reel 11, exhibit 187:S, p. 2.

130. Wachi Takaji's interrogation, *IMFTE*, reel 15:19,679; Suematsu, *Watakushi no Shōwashi*, 53; *KKN*, 2:107; *Hashimoto Shuki*, 167. See also the testimony of Dr. Uchida Masako, reproduced ibid. 172–73; *Tanaka Kiyoshi Shuki*, 97.

131. "Rikugun Gunpō Kaigihō," 26.4.1921, *Kanpō* 63, 26.4.1921. For analysis, see David A. Sneider, "Action and Oratory: The Trials of the May 15th Incident of 1932," *Law in Japan* 23, no. 67 (1990): 14.

132. *KKN*, 2:148. See also Ogata, *Defiance*, 100.

133. "Minutes of the Conference on the China Incident Report dated December 9th 1931," *IMTFE-CJEJ*, reel 24, exhibit 2205:A, p. 2; Sneider, "Action and Oratory," 14.

134. *KKN*, 2:93; *TSS-KKJC*, 49.

135. Edwin N. Neville, Charge d'Affairs (Tokyo) to the secretary of state, 21.10.1931, US IAJ, reel 1:314, HULL.

136. Forbes to Secretary of State, 7.11.1931, US IAJ, reel 1:320, HULL.

137. Wachi Takaji's affidavit, *IMFTE*, reel 15:19,667; Araki Sadao's interrogation, *IMTFE-CJEJ*, reel 11, exhibit 187:S, pp. 1–2; Hashimoto Kingorō's interrogation, *IMTFE-CJEJ*, reel 12, exhibit 258, p. 2; Nakano Masao in *Hashimoto Shuki*, 8–10; Cameron M. Craig, "Race and Identity: The Culture of Combat in the Pacific War," *International History Review* 27, no. 3 (September 2005): 560. Hashimoto was retired from the army in

October 1936, probably as a result of the February Incident. In the following years, apart from a brief return to active service in China between 1937 and 1939, he had a second career as a leading nationalist agitator. See also Amano Isamu's interrogation, *IMTFE-CJEJ*, reel 24, exhibit 2164, pp. 1–2.

138. Ben-Ami Shillony, *The Jews and the Japanese: The Successful Outsiders* (Rutland, Vt.: C.E. Tuttle, 1992), 182–83; Hayasaka Takashi, *Shikikan no Ketsudan: Manshū to Attsu no Shōgun Higuchi Kiichirō* (Tokyo: Bungei Shunjū, 2010), 125–49.

139. *Ogata*, 99.

140. Shillony, *Revolt in Japan*, 28–29; Hata, *Gun Fashizumu*, 31, 41–44.

141. "Kokka sore ayashi," reproduced in Karita, *Ōkawa Shūmei*, 322.

142. *SHM*, 1:116–17.

143. *SHM*, 1:67, 131; *Hashimoto Shuki*, 128. Compare with Wakatsuki Rejirō's affidavit and Araki's interrogation, *IMTFE-CJEJ*, reel 11, exhibit 162, pp. 1–2, exhibit 187:T, p. 2.

144. *Hashimoto Shuki*, 127–28; Peattie, *Ishiwara*, 122–23.

145. Suematsu, *Watakushi no Shōwashi*, 59.

146. Ibid; Suematsu, *Watakushi no Shōwashi*, 43, 53–54, 61.

147. General Ugaki feared such an outcome already after the March Incident. See "Kokka sore ayashi," reproduced in Karita, *Ōkawa Shūmei*, 321.

148. *Tanaka Kiyoshi Shuki*, 85; Araki Sadao's interrogation, *IMFTE-CJEJ*, reel 11, exhibit 187:T, p. 1; Higuchi, *Kaisōroku*, 288. Compare with Ugaki, "Kokka sore o ayashi," reproduced in Karita, *Ōkawa Shūmei*, 321.

149. Tokugawa, *Saigo no Tonosama*, 135–36. See also Tokugawa's affidavit, *IMFTE-CJEJ*, reel 11, exhibit 158, p. 1; Koiso, *Katsuzan*, 512–1; *SHM*, 9:1363; Tanaka, "Iwayuru Sangatsu Jiken," 6. For related correspondence see Karita, *Ōkawa Shūmei*, 331–48.

150. *SHM*, 1:138; *KKN*, 2:147–48; *Hashimoto Shuki*, 134–37; *Tanaka Kiyoshi Shuki*, 86; Ōkura, *Niniroku*, 64–65; Tokugawa, *Saigo no Tonosama*, 140.

151. Taken from a personal letter of this unnamed rear admiral to the American historian Yale Maxon, op. cit. in Maxon, *Control*, 104–5.

152. Maxon, *Control*, 106–7; Ogata, *Defiance*, 94.

153. *SHM*, 1:123–24, 128–29. For similar sentiments among Japanese diplomats, see also Ohashi, Consul General in Harbin, to Shidehara,7 Nov.1931, *IMFTE-CJEJ*, reel 15, exhibit 700, p. 1.

154. *SHM*, 1:31–32, 138.

10. PURE AS WATER

1. Interrogation of Yamaguchi Ichitarō in *Niniroku Jiken Hiroku*, ed. Hayashi Shigeru (Tokyo: Shōgakkan, 1971–72, hereafter cited as *NRJH*), 1:411–12, 416, 429.

2. Hata Ikuhiko, "Niniroku Jiken to Hirohito Tennō," *Seiji Keizai Shigaku* 209 (December 1983): 17. And compare with Matsushita Ichirō, "San'nen okureta Niniroku Jiken," in *Kinpōsan Omoideshū*, ed. Ono Genjirō and Kanashige Ryūsuke (Machida: Kinpōsankai, 1962), 141.

3. Shillony, *Revolt in Japan*, ix.

4. Suzaki Shin'ichi, *Niniroku Jiken: Seinen Shōkō no Ishiki to Shinri* (Tokyo:Yoshikawa Kōbunkan, 2003), 50; Muranaka Kōji, Isobe Asaichi, *Shukugun ni kansuru Ikensho: Shōwa 10-nen 7-gatsu 11-nichi* (Tokyo: self-published pamphlet, 1935), 43; Takumi Chūjō, "Ware Kyūjō o Senkyoseri"—*Niniroku Jiken Hiwa "Kyūjō Sakashita Monnai no Hen"* (Tokyo: Kōyū Shuppan, 1995), 172.

5. Isobe Asaichi, "Denunciation letter of Ugaki Kazushige and nine others" (Ugaki Kazushige nado kyūmei kokuhatsushō), *NRJH*, 4:3–5; Ōkura, *Niniroku*, 68; Muranaka/Isobe, *Shukugun*, 3–4, 43; Suzaki, *Niniroku*, 49–50; Fujii Hisashi, *Niniroku Teito Heiran:*

gunjiteki Shiten kara zenmenteki ni minaosu (Tokyo: Sōshisha, 2010), 96–97. Compare with Suematsu's account in *Watakushi no Shōwashi*, 59–61, 142.

6. Koda's interrogation, *NRJH,* 1:118–19; Muranaka's testimony, *Niniroku Jiken Saiban Kiroku: Kekki Shōkō Kōhantei,* ed. Ikeda Toshihiko (Tokyo: Hara Shobō, 1998, hereafter cited as *NRJSK*), 5. And compare with Muranaka/Isobe, *Shukugun*, 43.

7. Kurihara's interrogation, *NRJH,* 1:129, 131.

8. For a typical testimony of an officer who had a certain ideological affinity with the movement but shunned illegality, see Matsushita, "San'nen okureta" in Ono/Kanashige, *Kinpōsan*, 140–43.

9. *SHM,* 9:1333–34, 1339–44, 1449–50, 10:1410–11. For assessments on the scope of influence of the young officers see the report of the Soviet military attaché to Moscow: I. Rink, Sostoyanie yaponskoi armii k 1/1/1936, godovoi doklad polpregstva SSSR v Yaponii za 1935 god, AVPRF, opis 19, delo 74, papka 174, 85. For a list of all officers involved in the February Incident, as well as their ranks, origins, and eventual punishment, see Fujii, *Niniroku Teito*, 53.

10. Suzaki, *Niniroku*, 100; Fujii, *Niniroku Teito*, 41–42, 47–50.

11. Takeshima's interrogation, Tsushima's interrogation, *NRJH,* 1:142, 145–46.

12. Koda's interrogation, Tsushima's interrogation, Yasuda's interrogation, Ikeda's interrogation, *NRJH,* 1:118, 145, 171, 255; Isobe's testimony, *NRJSK,* 67; Suematsu, *Watakushi no Shōwashi*, 150–51, 260; Isobe, "Gokuchū Shuki," in Takamiya Tahei, *Jungyaku no Showashi: Niniroku Jiken made no Rikugun* (Tokyo: Hara Shobō, 1971), 316; Fujii, *Niniroku Teito*, 61–62, 74.

13. Nakahashi's interrogation, *NRJH,* 1:155; Ōmae Shin'ya, "Rikugun no Seiji Kainyū no Engen ni tsuite: Rikugun Yosan Hensei to Niniroku Jiken," *Seiji Keizai Shigaku* 540, no. 1–12 (2011), 1:6, 10–13. Deposition of Okazaki Koichi, *IMTFE-CJEJ,* reel 31, exhibit 3326, pp. 2–4; Isobe Asaichi, "Kyōdōki" in *Niniroku Jiken: Gokuchū Shuki, Isho,* ed. Kōno Tsukasa (Tokyo: Kawade Shobō Shinsha, 1972, hereafter cited as *NRJ*), 48; Shillony, *Revolt in Japan,* 87–88.

14. Ikeda's interrogation, *NRJH,* 1:255.

15. Suzaki, *Niniroku*, 133–140.

16. Isobe's testimony, *NRJSK,* 63, 76, and see also Matsushita, "San'nen okureta" in Ono/Kanashige, *Kinpōsan*, 140; Shillony, *Revolt in Japan,* 133–34.

17. Nakahashi's interrogation, Yasuda's interrogation, Muranaka's interrogation, Andō's interrogation, *NRJH,* 1:156, 168, 198, 262.

18. Ikeda's interrogation, *NRJH,* 1:255.

19. Isobe's testimony, *NRJSK,* 63, 76.

20. Suematsu, *Watakushi no Shōwashi*, 115–16.

21. Hayashi's interrogation, Ikeda's interrogation, Isobe, "refutation," *NRJH,* 177, 255, 4:19; Isobe, "Gokuchū Shuki," in Takamiya, *Jungyaku,* 314.

22. Isobe, "refutation," *NRJH,* 4:19.

23. Suematsu, *Watakushi no Shōwashi*, 126–27; Isobe, "Kyōdōki," *NRJ*, 54.

24. Quoted in Suzaki, *Niniroku*, 136. See also Suematsu, *Watakushi no Shōwashi*, 111, 258.

25. Nakahashi's interrogation, *NRJH,* 1:158.

26. Kurihara's interrogation, Nakahashi's interrogation, Suzuki's interrogation, Muranaka's interrogation, *NRJH,* 1:135, 157, 189, 208.

27. Muranaka's testimony, *NRJSK,* 23–24.

28. Isobe, "Kyōdōki," *NRJ*, 54–55.

29. Suematsu, *Watakushi no Shōwashi*, 114; Isobe's testimony, *NRJSK,* 64.

30. Mitsui, "summoning," *NRJH,* 1:24; Tanaka's interrogation, Ikeda's interrogation, Isobe, "refutation," *NRJH,* 1:166, 255–56, 4:18; Yugawa (Kiyohara) Yasuhira, "Niniroku

Jiken to Saionji-kō," *Bungei Shunju* 45, no. 6 (June 1967): 326; Shillony, *Revolt in Japan*, 81–95.

31. Yasuda's interrogation, Hayashi's interrogation, Isobe's interrogation, *NRJH*, 1:171, 178, 219–20; Isobe, "Gokuchū Shuki," in Takamiya, *Jungyaku*, 316; Isobe, "Kyōdōki," *NRJ*, 25.

32. Muranaka Kōji, Isobe Asaichi, *Shukugun ni kansuru Ikensho: Shōwa 10-nen 7-gatsu 11-nichi* (Tokyo: self-published pamphlet, 1935), 2.

33. Isobe, "Kōdōki," *NRJ*, 67.

34. Isobe to Mori (from prison, undated), *NRJH*, 4:9; Suematsu, *Watakushi no Shōwashi*, 144, 148. For a typical example of the views prevalent among *Kōdōha* officers, see Mazaki Jinzaburō's interrogation report (Mazaki Jinzaburō chōshusho), *NRJH*, 2:197–98, 212. It is important to note here that both *Tōseiha* and *kōdōha* were not formal organized factions, but brand names given to groups of people who shared similar ideas, often by their antagonists. Furthermore, almost every witness proposed a different map of factions, and also named them differently. As we are interested here in the historical process more than in the complicated nature of Japanese military factionalism per se, we will refer below to three loose groups: *Tōseiha*, *Kōdōha* and the Young Officers Movement.

35. Yasuda's interrogation, Isobe, "refutation letter," *NRJH*, 1:172, 4:13, 19–20; Isobe, "Kyōdōki," *NRJ*, 43; Isobe's testimony, Muranaka's testimony, *NRJSK*, 4, 67–70; Suematsu, *Watakushi no Shōwashi*, 99–100, 105, 152; Fujii, *Niniroku Teito*, 65–66. For my own assessment of Kita Ikki's ideas and influence, see Danny Orbach, "A Japanese Prophet: Eschatology and Epistemology in the Thought of Kita Ikki," *Japan Forum* 23, no. 3 (2011): 339–61.

36. Suzaki, *Niniroku*, 53–54, 62, 67–69; Affidavit of Kido Kōichi, *CJEJ*, reel 31, exhibit 3340, 34–35; Suematsu, *Wakakushi no Shōwashi*, 97–98; Isobe's testimony, *NRJSK*, 72. For the relations between Araki and the young officers, see also the analysis of the Soviet Embassy in Tokyo, in AVPRF, opis 16, delo 12, papka 153, Zheleznyakov, 1th Sekretar nolppredstva to Karaxan, 4.5.1933, 163.

37. Colonel E. A. H James, British military attaché in Japan, to the Foreign Office, 8.5.1936, BNA WO 5585, 4.

38. Muranaka's testimony, Isobe's testimony, *NRJSK*, 13, 77–78.

39. Ōkura, *Niniroku*, 71; Fujii, *Niniroku Teito*, 106; Stephen S. Large, "Nationalist Extremism in Early Shōwa Japan: Inoue Nisshō and the 'Blood-Pledge Corps Incident,' 1932," *Modern Asian Studies* 35, no. 3 (2001): 533–64.

40. Mazaki's interrogation, *NRJH*, 2:215; Muranaka's testimony, Isobe's testimony, *NRJSK*, 15, 71; Isobe, "Kyōdōki," *NRJ*, 43.

41. For historical surveys of the May 1932 Incident, see David Sneider, "Action and Oratory: The Trials of the of the May 15th Incident of 1932," *Law in Japan* 23, no. 67 (1990): 3–9; *NSSS-Showa*, 1:462–551.

42. Fujii, *Niniroku Teito*, 112.

43. Sneider, "Action and Oratory," 32–37.

44. Ibid., 28–32, 40–41.

45. Ibid., 24–25, 37–42.

46. The term "*shishi* of the May Incident" is taken from the interrogation of Sakai Naoshi, see *NRJH*, 1:224; Suzaki, *Niniroku*, 77.

47. James B. Crowley, "Japanese Army Factionalism in the early 1930's," *Journal of Asian Studies* 21, no. 3 (May 1962): 316.

48. Isobe's testimony, *NRJSK*, 77; AVPRF, opis 16, delo 12, papka 153, Zheleznyakov, 1th Sekretar nolppredstva to Karaxan, 4.5.1933, 159; Suzaki, *Niniroku*, 69, 89–91; Fujii, *Niniroku Teito*, 120.

49. Suzaki, *Niniroku*, 95–96.

50. Muranaka's testimony, Isobe's testimony, *NRJSK*, 8–9, 72–73; Suzaki, *Niniroku*, 69, 89–91; Fujii, *Niniroku Teito*, 120; Hata, "Niniroku Jiken to Hirohito Tennō," 5.

51. Suematsu, *Watakushi no Shōwashi*, 130–31; Fujii, *Niniroku Teito*, 50.

52. Muranaka's testimony, Isobe's testimony, *NRJSK*, 9–10, 74; Muranaka/Isobe, *Shukugun*, 15–16, 37–38; Suzaki, *Niniroku*, 96–100.

53. *SHM*, 9:1333–34, 1339–44, 1349–50; Shillony, *Revolt in Japan*, 49–51.

54. Suzaki, *Niniroku*, 70–72; Crowley, "Army Factionalism," 320–21. For thorough analysis of the machinations behind Mazaki's dismissal, see the report of the Soviet military attaché to Moscow: I. Rink, Sostoyanie yaponskoi armii, 80–87.

55. Mazaki, "Testimony in Aizawa's trial," *NRJH*, 1:7–10.

56. Mazaki, "Position Paper," Mazaki's interrogation report, *NRJH*, 1:3–6, 2:201.

57. Mazaki's interrogation, *NRJH*, 2:217. In his diary, Mazaki wrote that he was reluctant to meet Isobe and Kogawa, but finally consented because it was impossible to constantly avoid them. See *Mazaki Jinzaburō Nikki*, ed. Itō Takashi (Tokyo: Yamakawa Shuppansha, 1981–87), 1:327. And compare with Isobe's testimony, *NRJSK*, 77.

58. Muranaka's testimony, Isobe's testimony, *NRJSK*, 12, 15, 75; Isobe, "Kyōdōki," *NRJ*, 48; *Mazaki Nikki*, 1:334; Suematsu, *Watakushi no Shōwashi*, 257.

59. Hugh Byas, *Government by Assassination* (New York: Knopf, 1942), 95, 111.

60. Suematsu, *Watakushi no Shōwashi*, 257; Fujii, *Niniroku Teito*, 125–27, 131; Byas, *Government by Assassination*, 97–98, 115.

61. *Mazaki Nikki*, 1:335.

62. Omae, "Rikugun," 1:15.

63. Yurenev to the deputy people's commissar for foreign affairs, 25.4.1936, AVPRF, opis 19, delo 76, papka 175, 154(4)–155(3). The British journalist Hugh Byas had a similar impression. Though, as an old Japan hand, he was much less surprised. See *Government by Assassination*, 99–100.

64. Yasuda's interrogation, Suzuki's interrogation, *NRJH*, 1:167, 187; Isobe, "Kyōdōki," *NRJ*, 43.

65. Kurihara's interrogation, Nakahashi's interrogation, Muranaka's interrogation, *NRJH*, 1:129, 155, 200; Isobe, "Kyōdōki," *NRJ*, 28. Fujii Hisashi, a military historian and one of the most insightful scholars of the February Incident, argues that the coup was ill-prepared because the ringleaders acted under time pressure. Their movement, which was in decline anyway due to transfers and factional infighting, would have been obliterated by the transfer of the First Division. However, Fujii is only partially right. Failure to plan, as seen earlier in this chapter, was not merely a necessity, but part of the shishi ideology of the young officers. See Fujii, *Niniroku Teito*, 138.

66. For a discussion of the dilemma, see Takumi, *Ware Kyūjō*, 165–67.

67. Kurihara's interrogation, Muranaka's interrogation, Isobe's interrogation, *NRJH*, 1:132, 208, 216–17. Muranaka's testimony, Isobe's testimony, *NRJSK*, 20, 84; Isobe, "Kyōdōki," *NRJ*, 45, 47.

68. Fujii, *Niniroku Teito*, 145.

69. Muranaka's testimony, Isobe's testimony, *NRJSK*, 31, 81–83.

70. Yugawa, "Niniroku Jiken to Saionji-kō," 325; Muranaka's testimony, Isobe's testimony, *NRJSK*, 31, 81–83; Isobe, "Kyōdōki," *NRJ*, 39–40; Shillony, *Revolt in Japan*,

71. Isobe, "Kyōdōki," *NRJ*, 37.

72. The role of Prince Chichibu in the February Incident was always controversial. Ben Amy Shillony may have overemphasized his sympathy to the young officers and accorded too much credibility to post facto rumors. See *Revolt in Japan*, 95–109. For a detailed analysis of Prince Chichibu's behavior before and during the incident, see Hosoka, *Chichibu*, 212–98. The hopes that some of the rebels placed on Chichibu are documented in Hosoka Masayasu, *Chichibu no Miya to Shōwa Tennō* (Tokyo: Bungei Shunjū, 1989), 246–47. See also Hata, "Niniroku Jiken to Hirohito Tennō," 7–8, 14–16. Prince Chichibu's negative attitude toward the rebels was also documented by Baron

Harada Kumao, Prince Saionji's secretary, see *SHM,* 10:1430, and Yugawa, "Niniroku Jiken to Saionji-kō," 323.

73. For prior suspicions in government circles, see *SHM,* 10:1411.

74. Fujii, *Niniroku Teito,* 27–30, 139–41; Shillony, *Revolt in Japan*, 119–20; Isobe, "Kyōdōki," *NRJ,* 26, 36–39. It seems, though, that Isobe overstressed the amount of sympathy the young officers received from Kawashima and his ministry officials before February 26, maybe in order to reinforce the narrative that the young officers were a "righteous army" and not a rebellious one.

75. The manifesto (Kekki Shuisho) is reproduced in full in *NRJ,* 409–11. For a full translation see Shillony, *Revolt in Japan*, 146–48.

76. For precise number of troops and their distribution see Fujii, *Niniroku Teito,* 171–72.

77. Ibid., 173–75; Andō's testimony, *NRJSK,* 287. An informer for the Soviet Embassy, however, reported that the soldiers were misled and told by their officers that they were going to defend the palace or pray in the Meiji Shrine. See Yurenev to the deputy people's commissar for foreign affairs, 25.4.1936, AVPRF, opis 19, delo 76, papka 175, 150 (8). Before the assault on the finance minister, Lieutenant Nakahashi indeed told his troops that they were going to pray in the Meiji Shrine. See Takumi, *Ware Kyūjō*, 202.

78. Kurihara's interrogation, Tsushima's interrogation, *NRJH,* 1:131–32, 147; Joseph Grew, US ambassador, "how Premier Okada escaped assassination," report from Tokyo, 13.3.1936, in Joseph C. Grew, *Ten Years in Japan: a Contemporary Record Drawn from the Diaries and Private and Official Papers of Joseph C. Grew* (London: Hammond, 1944), 177–78.

79. Nakahashi's interrogation, Nakajima's interrogation, *NRJH,* 1:155–56, 230.

80. Yasuda's interrogation, Takahashi's interrogation, *NRJH,* 1:168, 238. Joseph Grew, "Japan's new era begins," report from Tokyo, 1.3.1936, *Ten Years in Japan*, 176.

81. Mugiya's interrogation, *NRJH,* 1:245.

82. Yasuda's interrogation, *NRJH,* 1:169. And for a slightly different version of this exchange, see Takahashi's interrogation, *NRJH,* 1:239.

83. Yasuda's interrogation, *NRJH,* 1:169. And compare with Takahashi's version ibid., 1:239; Shillony, *Revolt in Japan*, 137.

84. Andō's interrogation, *NRJH,* 1:263.

85. Kurihara's interrogation, Nakahashi's interrogation, *NRJH,* 1:131, 156.

86. Tokiwa's interrogation, Suzuki's interrogation, *NRJH,* 1:180, 185; Yugawa, "Niniroku Jiken to Saionji-kō," 322.

87. The young officers criticized the Sakura-kai for their bloodthirstiness, see Muranaka/Isobe, *Shukugun*, 43.

88. Ishibashi Tsuneyoshi, *Shōwa no Hanran: Sangatsu Ku-deta- kara Niniroku Jiken made* (Tokyo: Takagi Shoten, 1979), 2:87.

89. Nakahashi's interrogation, Imaizumi's interrogation, *NRJH,* 1:157, 273; Kurihara's testimony, *NRJSK,* 163, 167; Takumi, *Ware Kyūjō*, 174–75, 193–94, 202–3.

90. Nakahashi's interrogation, *NRJH,* 1:155; Takumi, *Ware Kyūjō*, 224–25. In his trial Nakahashi denied any attempt to occupy the Sakashita Gate or to call for reinforcements, but that contradicted other evidence and testimonies, including Nakahashi's own testimony to the military police (see note above), *NRJSK,* 252, 254, as well as Yugawa, "Niniroku Jiken to Saionji-kō," 322. Nakahashi also contradicts himself in the same testimony, see *NRJSK,* 261–62.

91. First Lieutenant Kiyohara Yasuhira, the officer stationed on the Police Headquarters roof, testified in court that he did not see a signal and implied that he did not expect to see one (Kiyohara's testimony, *NRJSK,* 381). However, in a fuller testimony given after the war, he admitted that such a signal was expected. He waited on the roof

for Nakahashi's flashlight signal, but it never came. See Yugawa, "Niniroku Jiken to Saionji-kō," 322.

92. See Ishibashi, *Shōwa no Hanran*, 2:87–90. Ishibashi's journalistic account is based on conversations with Major Matsumura Hideto and Captain Tanaka Gunkichi shortly after the event. And compare with the slightly different version of Matsushita Ichirō, "San'nen okureta" in Ono/Kanashige, *Kinpōsan*, 146. For a critical survey of the evidence see also Takumi, *Ware Kyūjō*, 210–11, 224–33.

93. Similarly, Kurihara and his troops were careful not to break things in the prime minister's residence, even while they tried to find and kill the owner of the house. See Kurihara's testimony, *NRJSK*, 174.

94. Isobe, "Kyōdōki," *NRJ*, 54–55; Fujii, *Niniroku Teito*, 185.

95. Muranaka's testimony, *NRJSK*, 34–35; Takumi, *Ware Kyūjō*, 215–16.

96. Yamaguchi's interrogation, *NRJH*, 1:417. For Isobe's version, see "Kōdōki," *NRJ*, 63.

97. For the complications, red tape, and other bureaucratic hurdles which slowed down the reaction of the army, see the report of the martial law headquarters' chief of staff, Major General Yasui, "Niniroku Jiken ni kan suru Kaigen Sanbōchō no Shuki," in *Niniroku Jiken Kenkyū Shiryō*, ed. Matsumoto Seichū and Fujii Yasushige (Tokyo: Bungei Shunjū, 1976, hereafter cited as *NRJKS*), 1:19–20.

98. "Kaigen Sanbōchō Shuki," *NRJKS*, 1:20–22. The report of the garrison chief of staff is naturally apologetic. In an attempt to distance Kashi and himself from the rebels, Major General Yasui highlights the "containment" elements of the garrison's strategy and hides the ideological sympathy harbored by Kashi and his officers to the rebels (though there are signs of such sympathy, for example in p. 24). In reality, both elements were probably there. Kashi was indeed afraid of a showdown in the capital and hoped for a peaceful solution, but his patience was also rooted in ideological affinity. It defies reason, for example, to believe that he would have behaved in the same vein had communists taken over parts of central Tokyo.

99. Honjō Shigeru, *Emperor Hirohito and his Aide-de-Camp: The Honjō Diary*, trans and ed. Mikiso Hane (Tokyo: University of Tokyo Press, 1982), 212. For the original text of the martial law orders, see *NRJKS*, 1:147–52.

100. *Honjō Diary*, 209–10; The original draft of the note is reproduced in *NRJ*, 411–12. On the drafting process, see the testimony of General Araki Sadao, "Rikugun daijin kokushi no dekita ikisatsu," *NRJ*, 413–14.

101. *Honjō Diary*, 209. For a transcript of Kashi's phone briefing, see "Kaigen Sanbōchō Shuki," *NRJKS*, 1:21; Fujii, *Niniroku Teito*, 193–94. For the version communicated by Kashi, which became the official one, see reproduction in *NRJ*, 412.

102. Muranaka's testimony, *NRJSK*, 37, 40, 44; Yamaguchi's interrogation, *NRJH*, 1:418; "Kaigen Sanbōchō Shuki," *NRJKS*, 1:23; Yugawa, "Niniroku Jiken to Saionji-kō," 322; Suzaki, *Niniroku*, 197–200, 203–5; Colonel E. A. H. James, "Attempted Coup d'état by Young Officers," 3.3.1936, dispatch no.62, BNA WO 106 5585, 4.

103. *Honjō Diary*, 210; Isobe, "Kōdōki," *NRJ*, 66.

104. Suzaki, *Niniroku*, 209–10, reconstructed the conversation by juxtaposing Yamaguchi's version with other extent sources. For Yamaguchi's detailed recollection of the conversation, see his interrogation in *NRJH*, 1:420–41. For different versions of the conversation, see Isobe, "Kōdōki," *NRJ*, 68–69; Ishibashi, *Shōwa no Hanran*, 2:103–4; and Muranaka's testimony, *NRJSK*, 38–40. Muranaka denied that the rebels ever asked the Supreme Military Council to form a cabinet. They demanded only to arrange the resignation of Okada's government. However, as Muranaka consistently tried to prove that the rebels only wanted to eliminate the traitors without violating imperial orders, his testimony is not completely reliable. Yamaguchi, by contrast, was not one of the rebels but still sympathized them, therefore his testimony seems to be more credible.

105. *SHM*, 10:1425–27; "Kaigen Sanbōchō Shuki," *NRJKS*, 1:20.
106. Iwakuro Erao's testimony, *NRJ*, 414–15.
107. Fujii, *Niniroku Teito*, 210–14.
108. Isobe, "Kōdōki," *NRJ*, 72–73; Suzaki, *Niniroku*, 205; Fujii, *Niniroku Teito*, 173; Takumi, *Ware Kyūjō*, 176–77.
109. Fujii, *Niniroku Teito*, 274.
110. Isobe, "Kyōdōki," *NRJ*, 52–53.
111. Araki, "Rikugun Daijin Kokushi," *NRJ*, 413.
112. "Kaigen Sanbōchō Shuki," *NRJKS*, 1:19–21.
113. For analysis of the strategic failure of the February rebels, see Fujii, *Niniroku Teito*, 263–84. Hata Ikuhiko has surveyed and evaluated the different scholarly opinions on the blunders that led to the failure of the coup's defeat. See Hata, "Niniroku Jiken to Hirohito Tennō," 6. The failure to take over the communication facilities was not unique to the February Incident and could be observed in other countries as well. It was, for example, one of the main reasons for the failure of the coup d'état against Hitler on July 20, 1944. And see my book, *The Plots against Hitler* (New York: Houghton Mifflin Harcourt, 2016), 226–27.
114. Byas, *Government by Assassination*, 125.
115. Muranaka's testimony, *NRJSK*, 43–44; Hata, "Niniroku Jiken to Hirohito Tennō," 10; Hosaka, *Chichibu*, 233–34. Some of these advisors passed by rebel positions without being stopped. See for example *SHM*, 10:1424.
116. Hata, "Niniroku Jiken to Hirohito Tennō," 4.
117. *STD*, 32.
118. Affidavit of Kido Kōichi, *IMTFE-CJEJ*, reel 31, exhibit 3340, p. 47; *Honjō Diary*, 209. And compare to Kido's version in *KKN*, 1:464–65.
119. For another example of this dynamic, see Hata, "Niniroku Jiken to Hirohito Tennō," 4.
120. Hirohito referred to the General Staff channels through which he worked in his famous monologue, *STD*, 32. And see also Yamaguchi's interrogation, *NRJH*, 1:419; *Honjō Diary*, 210; Suzaki, *Niniroku*, 220; Hosaka, *Chichibu*, 234–35; Shillony, *Revolt in Japan*, 167–71.
121. *KKN*, 1:465.
122. *Honjō Diary*, 213. And compare with *SHM*, 10:1428.
123. Muranaka's testimony, *NRJSK*, 46–47; *Honjō Diary*, 213–14, *KKN*, 1:466–67; Isobe, "Kōdōki," *NRJ*, 70–72; Suzaki, *Niniroku*, 240–61, 270–74; Fujii, *Niniroku Teito*, 215–16.
124. Suzaki, *Niniroku*, 270–79; Isobe, "Gokuchū Shuki," in Takamiya, *Jungyaku*, 301–2.
125. *Honjō Diary*, 215; Yugawa, "Niniroku Jiken to Saionji-kō," 323; Suzaki, *Niniroku*, 270–77, 295, 308.
126. Suzaki, *Niniroku*, 296–301.
127. Isobe, "Kōdōki," *NRJ*, 78–79; "Kaigen Sanbōchō Shuki," *NRJKS*, 1:24–25.
128. *Honjō Diary*, 214–16; *STD*, 32–33. And compare with Isobe's version in "Gokuchū Shuki," in Takamiya, *Jungyaku*, 301.
129. Kawashima to Hori, 28.2, 6:00 p.m., *NRJ*, 443.
130. "Gensakurei dai.14," 28.2, 23:00 p.m., *NRJ*, 443–44; *KKN*, 1:468; "Kaigen Shireibu Happyō: Rikugun Daijin Seimei," 29.2.1936, *NRJKS*, 1:155; Hata, "Niniroku Jiken to Hirohito Tennō," 11.
131. Isobe, "Gokuchū Shuki" in Takamiya, *Jungyaku*, 296.
132. Suzaki, *Niniroku*, 302–3.
133. "Kaigen Shireibu happyō: rajio hōsō," 29.2, 8:55 a.m., "Shita shikan hei ni tsugu," *NRJ*, 432, 434; Clive to Foreign Secretary Eden, 30.3.1936, BNA WO 106 5585, 3.
134. Byas, *Government by Assassination*, 125.
135. *Honjō Diary*, 217–18; Isobe, "Gokuchū Shuki," in Takamiya, *Jungyaku*, 301–2; Isobe, "Kōdōki," *NRJ*, 83–84, 87–88.

136. For the army minister's declaration see "Kawashima Rikudaijin seimei," *NRJ*, 418–19. English translation taken from *Honjō Diary*, 219, 223.

137. Hata, "Niniroku Jiken to Hirohito Tennō," 17.

138. Shillony, *Revolt in Japan*, 203.

139. Isobe to Mori Den (from prison, undated), *NRJH*, 4:6–7, 10; Isobe, "Gokuchū Shuki" in Takamiya, *Jungyaku*, 294.

140. Isobe, "Gokuchū Shuki" in Takamiya, *Jungyaku*, 295–96.

141. Isobe to Mori (from prison, undated), *NRJH*, 4:8–9; Isobe, "Gokuchū Shuki" in Takamiya, *Jungyaku*, 293, 297, 318.

142. Suematsu, *Watakushi no Shōwashi*, 153.

143. Isobe, "Gokuchū Shuki" in Takamiya, *Jungyaku*, 293.

144. Nakahashi's testimony, *NRJSK*, 271.

145. Funayama's interrogation, *NRJH*, 1:195; Shillony, *Revolt in Japan*, 133. While it is almost certain, as Shillony writes, that many NCOs supported the coup d'état, the position of the ensigns, many of whom were fresh recruits, is much less clear. The British military attaché, who spoke with some sentries from the Third Infantry Regiment on the twenty-sixth, had the impression that they "did not know what they had been involved in." See Colonel E. A. H James, "Attempted Coup d'état by Young Officers," 3.3.1936, dispatch no.62, BNA WO 106 5585 (cover letter).

146. See for example the testimony of Matsushita Ichirō, "San'nen okureta" in Ono/Kanashige, *Kinpōsan*, 140–44.

147. See for example Yamamoto's interrogation, Isobe, "refutation," *NRJH*, 1:265, 4:19; Muranaka's testimony, *NRJSK*, 39.

148. "Kekki Shuisho," *NRJ*, 409–10. Fujii, *Niniroku Teito*, 274–75.

149. Hata, "Niniroku Jiken to Hirohito Tennō," 19. For the Kido Takayoshi quote see *OTN*, 1:395.

150. Isobe, "Gokuchū Shuki," in Takamiya, *Jungyaku*, 314; "Bushido and a Budget," *The Times* (Tokyo correspondent), 14.7.1936.

151. Yugawa, "Niniroku Jiken to Saionji-kō," 327.

152. Yugawa (Kiyohara) Yasuhira, "Niniroku Jiken to Saionji-kō," *Bungei Shunju* 45, no. 6 (June 1967): 328.

153. Original text in Kawashima, "Rikushō Daijin Seimei," *NRJ*, 419. English translation in *Honjō Diary*, 219, 230–33; Colonel James to the Foreign Office, 8.5.1936, BNA WO 5585, 2.

154. *Honjō Diary*, 225–26, 228–30.

155. Affidavit of Kido Kōichi, *IMFTE-CJEJ*, reel 31, exhibit 3340, p. 52; *Honjō Diary*, 230; Crowley, "Army Factionalism," 320–21.

156. *Honjō Diary*, 221, 226; Ōmae Shin'ya, *Seiji Seiryoku to shite no Rikugun: Yosan Hensei to Niniroku Jiken* (Tokyo: Chūō Kōron Shinsha, 2015), 228–29.

157. Joseph Grew, "Hirota Reorganizes," report from Tokyo, 5.3.1936, *Ten Years in Japan*, 178.

158. Colonel James to the Foreign Office, 8.5.1936, BNA WO 5585, 3.

159. For a study of this incident, see B. Winston Kahn, *Doihara Kenji and the "North China Autonomy Movement," 1935–36* (Tempe: Arizona State University, 1973).

160. Tsutsui Kyotada, *Shōwaki Nihon no Kōzō: sono Rekishi Shakaiteki Kōsatsu* (Tokyo: Yūhikaku, 1984), 97.

161. "Dictatorship in Japan," *Manchester Guardian*, 11.6.1936; Depositions of Tsugita Daisaburō and Tsushima Jūichi, *IMTFE-CJEJ*, reel 31, exhibit 3258, pp. 1–2, exhibit 3324, p. 4; *Honjō Diary*, 224–25; *SHM*, 10:1437–42. For analysis of the shifting balance between the army and the government, see the correspondence of the Soviet Embassy, Stomonyakov to Yurenev, 28.3, 28.6., 1936, AVPRF, opis 19, delo 12, papka 170.

162. Andrew Levidis, "Conservatism and Japanese Army Factionalism, 1937–1939: The Case of Prince Konoe Fumimaro and Baron Hiranuma Kiichirō," talk given at the Forum for US-Japan Relations, Harvard University, November 17, 2015. Levidis's claim is mainly based on two unpublished sources: the diary of General Araki Sadao (late July 1937), and a manuscript written by Colonel Tanaka Shin'ichi (*Shina jihen kiroku*), held in the National Institute for Defense Studies, Tokyo.

CONCLUSION

1. Shillony, *Revolt in Japan*, 209–10.

2. Deposition of Tsugita Daisaburō, *IMTFE-CJEJ*, ree; 31, exhibit 3258, pp. 1–2. See also Shillony, *Revolt in Japan*, 210; Tanaka, "Iwayuru Sangatsu Jiken," 9.

3. Maxon, *Control*, 176, 214–15, 18–19.

4. Iguchi Takeo, *Demystifying Pearl Harbor: A New Perspective from Japan*, trans. David Noble (Tokyo: International House of Japan, 2010), 218–36, 41. For the version of one of these officers, see Tōmura Morio, "Shōwa Tennō eno Shinden wo naze Watashi wa okuraseta no ka?," *Shokun!* 24, no. 2 (February 1992): 206–9. The official at the Japanese embassy in Washington who initiated direct communication between Roosevelt and the emperor as a last ditch attempt to avoid war, was afraid of being killed by radical army elements. See Roger B. Jeans, *Terasaki Hidenari, Pearl Harbor, and Occupied Japan: A Bridge to Reality* (Lanham, MD: Lexington Books, 2009), 115–16.

5. Byas, *Government by Assassination*, 39.

6. Tanaka, "Iwayuru Sangatsu Jiken," 1.

7. James B. Crowley, *Japan's Quest for Autonomy: National Security and Foreign Policy, 1930–1938* (Princeton: Princeton University Press, 1966), 380–84.

8. Joel Joos, "The Liberal Asianism of Inukai Tsuyoshi (1855–1932): Japanese Relations with the Mainland between Opportunism, Pragmatism, and Idealism," *Bulletin of Kochi Woman's University: Series of Faculty of Cultural Studies* 60 (March 2011): 43–46.

9. For theoretical discussion on coercive and persuasive power, see John Scott, "Modes of Power and the Re-conceptualization of Elites," in *Remembering Elites*, ed. Mike Savage and Karel Williams (Malen, MA: Blackwell, 2008), 30. And also Haley, *Authority without Power*, 6–8, 13–14.

10. Gordon, *Imperial Democracy*, 332–33; Gluck, *Modern Myths*, 247–49.

11. Tani was appraised as a "flower in a field of grass" by Mutsu Munemitsu, Japan's foreign minister during the First Sino-Japanese War (1894–95). See Teters, *Conservative Opposition*, 36.

12. For an interesting reflection on this phenomenon, which stood as the basis of the second bug, see the testimony of Imamura Hitoshi in Mineo, *Rikugun Sanbō*, 306–7.

13. Banno, *Taishō Seihen*, 9–13.

14. Suematsu, *Watakushi no Shōwashi*, 153.

15. Shillony, *Revolt in Japan*, 214.

Bibliography

Note: The Japanese term referring to the private or official papers of an individual can be transliterated to English as either *monjo* or *bunsho*. In this book, I have chosen to use the reading monjo, which is more accepted in Japan, though the reading bunsho does appear in many Western library catalogues. However, there is one exception to that rule. I have consulted two versions of the private papers of Katsura Tarō, the originals of which are kept in the National Diet Library, Tokyo, and another version of the papers bound in book form. To differentiate between the two, I have named the original Katsura Tarō Kankei Monjo and the book form *Katsura Tarō Kankei Bunsho*, though in Japanese they are written in the same way.

Archives and Unpublished Primary Sources

Arhiv Vneshnei Politiki Rossiskei Federatsii [Archive of Foreign Policy of the Russian Federation], Moscow

Arhiv Vneshnei Politiki Rossiskoi Imperi [Archive of Foreign Policy of the Russian Empire], St. Petersburg

British National Archives, London

"Court Papers, Journals, Exhibits and Judgments of the International Military Tribunal for the Far East." Microfilm Reels, Center for Research Libraries, Chicago.

Digitized Contents, National Diet Library, Tokyo, http://dl.ndl.go.jp/

"International Military Tribunal for the Far East, Record of Proceedings, Tokyo, Japan": The United States of America [et al.] against Araki, Sadao . . . Tojo, Hideki [et al.], accused / official court reporters, Jack Greenberg, Chief . . . [et al.]. Microfilm Reels, Center for Research Libraries, Chicago.

Japan Center for Asian Historical Record, http://jacar.go.jp

Japanese Army and Navy Archives, Library of Congress, Washington, DC

Kawagoe Moriji. *Chō Sakurin Bakushi Jiken*. National Institute for Defense Studies (see below), itaku no. 251.

Kobayakawa Hideo. *Bingō Soraku Jiken*. Handwritten manuscript, probably composed around the time of the annexation of Korea to Japan in 1911. Its modern Japanese translation, published seventy years later in a nonfiction collection, was considered a fake by some scholars, but the original was rediscovered later and bequeathed to the National Diet Library. The classical Japanese original is kept in the Modern Japanese Political History Materials Reading Room at the National Diet Library, Tokyo, Shushū Bunsho, no. 1195.

League of Nations Archive, United Nations Office, Geneva

Modern Japanese Political History Materials Reading Room, National Diet Library, Tokyo

Nakano Bunko, Hōrei Mokuji, http://www.geocities.jp/nakanolib/hourei.htm

National Archives of Australia

National Archives of Japan, Tokyo

National Institute for Defense Studies [Bōeishō Bōei Kenkyūjo] Military Archive, Tokyo

Rare Books and Materials Reading Room, National Diet Library, Tokyo

Records of the US State Department Relating to the Internal Affairs of Japan, 1930–1939, Harvard University, Lamont Library, Cambridge MA

Ryerson (Martin A.) Collection, Art Institute of Chicago

Sakuma Norizō, *Manshū no Omoide: Chō Sakurin Bakushi Jiken*, National Institute for Defense Studies (see above), itaku no. 245

Tokyo University Historiographical Institute [Tokyo Daigaku Shiryō Hensanjo]

Tokyo University Law Faculty Modern Japan Materials Reading Room [Tokyo Daigaku Hōgakubu fuzoku Kindai Nihon Hōsei Shiryōbu]

The Tokyo War Crimes Trial: A Digital Exhibition, University of Virginia Law Library https://www.google.com/#q=Tokyo+trial%2C+%22hashimoto+kingoro%22

Yasukuni Jinja Kaikō Bunkō [Yasukuni Shrine Archives], Tokyo

Visual Primary Sources

Arai Tomosada (Eizan), ed. *Kwōkoku Bujutsu Eimei Roku.* 1888. Vol. 1. Martin A. Ryerson Collection, Art Institute of Chicago, 761.952, VI 9895.

Katsushika Hokusai. *Hokusai Manga 12560.* Vol. 6. Martin A. Ryerson Collection, Art Institute of Chicago, 0196 RC.

Historical Newspapers, Periodicals, and Bulletins

Asahi Shinbun (Osaka and Tokyo editions)
Kanpō
Nihon oyobi Nihonjin
Osaka Asahi Shinbun
Osaka Mainichi
Shinbun Zasshi
Japan Daily Herald
Korean Repository
Sankt Peterburskie Vedmosti
Taiyō
The Times (of London)
Tōhoku Nippō
Tokyo Akenobo Shinbun
Tokyo Keizai Zasshi
Tōyō Keizai Shinpō
Yomiuri Shinbun
Yūbin Hōchi Shinbun

Published Primary Sources

Adachi Kenzō. *Adachi Kenzō Jijoden.* Tokyo: Shinjusha, 1960.

Alcock, Rutherford. *The Capital of the Tycoon: A Narrative of Three Year's Residence in Japan.* New York: Harper and Brothers, 1863.

Aoki Shūzō. *Aoki Shūzō Jiden.* Tokyo: Heibonsha, 1970.

Banshoroku: Takahashi Sōan Nikki. Edited by Takahashi Yoshio. Kyoto: Shibunkaku Shuppan, 1986–90.

Bird, Isabella. *Korea and Her Neighbours.* Vol. 2. Bristol: Ganesha, 1997.

Bismarck, Otto von. *Die Gesammelten Werke.* Berlin: O. Stollberg, 1924.

——. *Bismarck: Briefe an seine Braut und Gattin.* Edited by H. Bismarck. Stuttgart: Cotta, 1900.

Brandt, Maximilian von. *Dreihunddreissig Jahre in Ost-Asien: Erinnerungen eines deutschen Diplomaten*. Leipizg: Verlag von Georg Wigand, 1901.

Chōsen Kōshō Shiryō. Vol. 2. Edited by Itō Hirobumi. Tokyo: Hisho Ruisan Kankōkai, 1936.

Dai Nihon Gaikō Bunsho. Tokyo: Gaimushō Chōsabu, 1936–40.

Dai Nihon Ishin Shiryō. Edited by Shiryō Hensanjo. Tokyo: Tokyo Daigaku Shuppankai, 1959.

Dai Saigō Zenshū. Edited by Dai Saigō Zenshū Kankō-kai. Tokyo: Heibonsha Hatsubai, 1926–27.

Date Munenari Zaikyō Nikki. Tokyo: Nihon Shiseki Kyōkai, 1916.

Den Kenjirō Nikki. Edited by Hirose Yoshihiro. 3 vols. Tokyo: Shōyū Kurabu, Seisaku Fuyō Shobō Shuppan, 2008.

Diary of Kido Takayoshi. Translated by Sidney D. Brown and Akiko Hirota. 3 vols. Tokyo: University of Tokyo Press, 1983–86.

Eskildsen, Robert, ed. *Foreign Adventurers and the Aborigines of Southern Taiwan, 1867–1874: Western Sources Related to Japan's 1874 Expedition to Taiwan*. Taipei: Institute of Taiwan History, Academica Sinica, 2005.

Friedrich III (Kaiser). *Das Kriegstagebuch von 1870–71*. Edited by Heinrich Otto Meisner. Berlin: K. F. Koehler, 1926.

Fukuzawa Yukichi. "Teishitsu-ron." In *Kōshitsu-ron*. Tokyo: Shimazu Shobō, 1987.

Grew, Joseph C. *Ten Years in Japan: A Contemporary Record Drawn from the Diaries and Private and Official Papers of Joseph C. Grew*. London: Hammond, 1944.

Kindai Nihon Guntai Kyōiku Shiryō Shūsei. Edited by Takano Kunio. 12 vols. Tokyo: Kashiwa Shobō, 2004.

Hara Takashi Nikki. Edited by Hara Keiichirō and Hayashi Shigeru. 6 vols. Tokyo: Fukumura Shuppan, 1965–69.

Harada Kumao. *The Saionji-Harada Memoirs, 1931–1940: Complete Translation into English*. Microform. Washington, DC: University Publications of America, 1978.

——. *Saionji-kō to Seikyoku*. 9 vols. Tokyo: Iwanami Shoten, 1950–56. (Japanese original of the above.)

Hashimoto Kingorō. *Hashimoto Taisa no Shuki*. Edited by Nakano Masao. Tokyo: Misuzu Shobō, 1963.

Hayashi Kyūjirō. *Manshū Jihen to Hōten Sōryōji*. Tokyo: Hara Shobō, 1978.

——. *Hayashi Yūzō Jirekidan*. Kōchi: Kōchi Risshimin Toshokan, 1968.

Heben Dazuo yu Rijun Shanxi "Can Liu." Edited by Zhongyang Dang an guan et al. Beijing: Zhonghua Shu ju, 1995.

Higuchi Kiichirō. *Rikugun Chūjō Higuchi Kiichirō Kaisōroku*. Tokyo: Fuyō Shobō, 1999.

Hiroku Doihara Kenji: Nitchū Yūkō no Suteishi. Edited by Doihara Kenji Kankōkai. Tokyo: Fuyō Shobō, 1972.

Hogohiroi: Sasaki Takayuki Nikki. Edited by Shiryō Hensanjo. Tokyo: Tokyo Daigaku Shuppan Kai, 1970–79.

Hōki Bunrui Taizen. Tokyo: Naikaku Kiroku Kyoku, 1889–91.

Honjō Shigeru. *Emperor Hirohito and his Aide-de-Camp: The Honjō Diary*. Translated and edited by Mikiso Hane. Tokyo: University of Tokyo Press, 1982.

Horiguchi Kumaichi. *Gaikō to Bungei*. Tokyo: Daiichi Shobō, 1934.

House, Edward H. *Japanese Expedition to Formosa*. Tokyo, 1875.

Hulbert, Homer B. *The Passing of Korea*. Seoul: Yonsei University Press, 1969.

Irie Kan'ichi. *Taishō shoki Yamagata Aritomo Danwa Hikki: Seihen Omoidegusa*. Edited by Ito Takashi. Tokyo: Yamakawa Shuppansha, 1981.

Ishin Tosa Kinnō Shi. Edited by Zuizankai. Tokyo: Fuzanbō, 1912.

Itō Hirobumi. *Commentaries on the Constitution of the Empire of Japan.* Translated by Itō Miyoji. Tokyo: Igirisu-Hōritsu Gakko, 1889.

——. *Itō Hirobumi Kankei Monjo.* Edited by Itō Hirobumi Kankei Monjo, Kenkyū Kai. Tokyo: Hanawa Shobō, 1973–81.

Itō-kō Chokuwa. Edited by Komatsu Midori. Tokyo: Chikura Shobō, 1936.

Iwakura-Ko Jikki. 2 vols. Tokyo: Kōgō Gūshoku, 1906.

Iwakura Tomomi Kankei Monjo. Tokyo: Kokuritsu Kobunshokan Naikaku Bunsho Shozō, 1990–91.

Iwayama Seiko and Iwayama Kazuko, eds. *Saigo san o kataru: Iwayama Toku no Kaisō.* Tokyo: Perikansha, 1999.

Lu, David J., ed. *Japan: A Documentary History.* Armonk, NY: M. E. Sharpe, 1997.

Lytton, V. G. R. B., et al. *Appeal by the Chinese Government: Report of the Commission of Enquiry* (also known as the Lytton Report). Geneva: League of Nations Publications, 1932.

Kataoka Kenkichi Nikki. Edited by Risshisha Sōritsu Hyakunen Kinen Shuppan. Kōchi: Kōchi Shimin Toshokan, 1974.

Katsura Tarō. *Jiden.* Tokyo: Heibonsha, 1993.

——. *Katsura Tarō Kankei Monjo.* Edited by Chiba Isao. Tokyo: Daigaku Shuppainkai, 2010. This is a selection of Katsura's letters in book form. It is only a part of *Katsura Tarō Kankei Monjo,* which is kept at the modern Japan political history reading room at the National Diet Library.

——. *Katsura Tarō hatsu Shokanshū.* Tokyo: Tokyo Daigaku Shuppankai, 2011.

Kawai Yahachi. *Shōwa Shoki no Tennō to Kyūchū: Jijū Jichō Kawai Yahachi Nikki.* 6 vols. Tokyo: Iwanami Shoten, 1993–94.

Keiji Soshoh. Osaka: Osaka Asahi Shinbun sha, 1890–91. For an online version, see http://kindai.ndl.go.jp/info:ndljp/pid/795135/33.

Kido Kōichi Nikki. 2 vols. Edited by Oka Yoshitake. Tokyo: Tokyo Daigaku Shuppankai, 1966.

Kido Takayoshi Monjo. 8 vols. Edited by Kido-kō Denki Hensanjo. Tokyo: Nihon Shiseki Kyōkai, 1929–31.

Kikuji Kenjō. *Chōsen Ōkoku.* Tokyo: Minyūsha, 1896.

Kindai Nihon Guntai Kyōiku Shiryō Shūsei. 12 vols. Edited by Takano Kunio. Tokyo: Kashiwa Shobō, 2004.

Koiso Kuniaki. *Katsuzan Kōsō.* Tokyo: Koiso Kuniaki Jijōden Kankōkai, 1963.

Kōmoto Daisaku. "Watakushi ga Chō sakurin o koroshita." *Bungei Shunjū* 32 (December 1954): 194–201.

Korean American-Relations: Documents Pertaining to the Far-Eastern Diplomacy of the United States. Vol. 2. Edited by George M. McCune. Berkeley: University of California Press, 1951.

Machino Takema. "Chō Sakurin Bakushi no Zengo." *Chūō Kōron* 64, no. 9 (September 22, 1949): 72–80.

Makino Nobuaki Nikki. Edited by Itō Takashi and Hirose Yoshihiro. Tokyo: Chūō Kōronsha, 1990.

Matsudaira Shungaku. *Boshin Nikki.* Edited by Iwasaki Eijū. Tokyo: Nihon Shiseki Kyōkai, 1925.

Matsumura Kenzō. *Sandai Kaikoroku.* Tokyo: Tokyo Keizai Shinpōsha, 1964.

Matsushita Ichirō. "San'nen okureta Niniroku Jiken." In *Kinpōsan Omoideshū,* edited by Ono Genjirō and Kanashige Ryūsuke, 136–48. Machida: Kinpōsankai, 1962.

Mazaki Jinzaburō Nikki. Vol. 1. Edited by Itō Takashi. Tokyo: Yamakawa Shuppansha, 1981–87.

Meiji Bunka Shiryō Sōsho. Edited by Meiji Bunka Shiryō Sōsho Kankō Kai. Tokyo: Kazama Shobō, 1963.

Meiji Bunka Zenshū. Edited by Meiji Bunka Kenkyū Kai. Tokyo: Nihon Hyōronsha, 1967–74.

Meiji Shiryō. Edited by Yamamoto Shirō. Tokyo: Meiji Shiryō Kenkyū Renrakukai, 1960.

Meiji shonen Nōmin Sōjō Roku. Edited by Tsuchiya Takao and Ono Michio. Tokyo: Keisō Shobō, 1953.

Miura Gorō. *Kanju Shōgun Kaikoroku.* Tokyo: Seikyōsha, 1925.

——. *Miura Gorō Kankei Monjo.* Edited by Yamamoto Shirō. Tokyo: Meiji Shiryō Kenkyū Renrakukai, 1960.

Mizuno Jun. "Taiwan Seiban Ki." In *Tairo Mizuno Jun Sensei,* edited by Yagashiro Hideyoshi. Tokyo: Yuma ni Shobō, 2008.

Molodiakov, V. E., ed. *Katsura Taro, Goto Simpëi i Rossiia: Sbornik Dokumentov 1907–1929.* Moscow: Dmitriĭ Bulanin, 2005.

Mori Katsumi. Interview with Kōmoto Daisaku, Dairen, December 1, 1942, in Mori, *Manshū Jihen no Rimenshi.* Tokyo: Kokushu Kankōkai, 1976, 262–76.

Morishima Morito. *Inbō, Ansatsu, Guntō: Ichi Gaikōkan no Kaikō.* Tokyo: Iwanami Shoten, 1950.

——. "Chō Sakurin, Yō Utei no Ansatsu: Nihon Gaikō no Kaisō (1)." *Sekai* 45 (September 30, 1949): 41–49.

Nara Takeji. *Jijū Bukanchō Nara Takeji Nikki Kaisōroku.* 4 vols. Tokyo: Kashiwa Shobō, 2000.

Nihon Gaikō Bunsho. 3 vols. Tokyo: Gaimushō Chōsabu, 1947–53.

Nikan Gaikō Shiryō: Kankoku Ōhi Satsugai Jiken. Vol. 5. Edited by Ichikawa Masaaki. Tokyo, Hara Shobō, 1953.

Niniroku Jiken: Gokuchū Shuki, Isho. Edited by Kōno Tsukasa. Tokyo: Kawade Shobō Shinsha, 1972.

Niniroku Jiken Hiroku. 4 vols. Edited by Hayashi Shigeru. Tokyo: Shōgakkan, 1971–72.

Niniroku Jiken Kenkyū Shiryō. 3 vols. Edited by Matsumoto Seichū and Fujii Yasushige. Tokyo: Bungei Shunjū, 1976.

Niniroku Jiken Saiban Kiroku: Kekki Shōkō Kōhantei. Edited by Ikeda Toshihiko. Tokyo: Hara Shobō, 1998.

Ogawa Heikichi Kankei Monjo. 2 vols. Edited by Oka Yoshitake. Tokyo: Isuzu Shobō, 1973.

Okabe Nagakage Nikki—Shōwa Shoki Kazoku Kanryō no Kiroku. Edited by Shōyū Kurabu. Tokyo: Kashiwa Shobō, 1993.

Ōkawa Shūmei. *Nihon oyobi Nihonjin no Michi.* Tokyo: Kōchisha Shuppanbu, 1926.

Ōkubo Toshimichi Monjo. 10 vols. Tokyo: Tokyo Daigaku Shuppan-kai, 1967–69.

Ōkubo Toshimichi Nikki. 2 vols. Tokyo: Tokyo Daigaku Shuppan Kai, 1969.

Ōkuma Monjo. 5 vols. Tokyo: Waseda Daigaku Shakai Rigaku Kenkyūjo, 1963.

Ōkuma Shigenobu Kankei Monjo. 6 vols. Tokyo: Nihon Shiseki Kyōkai, 1932–35.

Ōkura Eiichi. *Niniroku Jiken e no Banka: Saigo no Seinen Shōkō.* Tokyo: Yomiuri Shinbunsha, 1971.

Ozaki Yoshiharu. *Rikugun o ugokashita Hitobito.* Odawara: Hachishodō Shoten, 1960.

Ozaki Yukio. *The Autobiography of Ozaki Yukio: the Struggle for Constitutional Government in Japan.* Translated by Fujiko Hara. Princeton, NJ: Princeton University Press, 2001.

Rikugun Sanbō Kyoku, ed. *Saga Seitō Senki.* Tokyo: Rikugun Bunkō, 1875.

Rossiia i Koreia: nekotorye stranitsy istorii (konets XIX veka) : k 120-letiiu ustanovleniia diplomaticheskikh otnosheniĭ. Edited by A. V. Turkunov. Moskva: Moskovskiĭ gos. institut mezhdunarodnykh otnoshenii (Universitet) MID Rossii, 2004. 275.

Saga Sanenaru Nikki. Tokyo: Nihon Shiseki Kyōkai, 1929–31.

Saigō Takamori Zenshū. 6 vols. Edited by Hensan Saigō Takamori Zenshū Henshū Iinkai. Tokyo: Daiwa Shobō, 1976–80.

Saigō Totoku to Kabayama Sōtoku. Taipei: Saigo Totoku to Kabayama Sōtoku Kinen Jigyō Shuppan Iinkai, 1936.

Saitō Saburo. "Uyoku Shisō Hanzai Jiken no Sōgōteki Kenkyū: Ketsumeidan Jiken yori Niniroku Jiken Made." In *Kokka Shugi Undō*, edited by Imai Seiichi et al. Vol. 4. Tokyo: Misuzu Shobō, 1963.

Sakamoto Ryōma Kankei Monjo. Edited by Nihonshi Sekkyōkai. Tokyo: Tokyo Daigaku Shuppankai, 1967.

Sanbō Honbu Rekishi Sōan. 8 vols. Edited by Hirose Yoshishiro. Tokyo: Yumani Shobō, 2001.

Sanbō Honbu Rikugunsha Hensanka, ed. *Seisei Senki Kō.* 65 vols. Tokyo: Sambō Hombu Rikugunbu Hesanka, 1887.

Sanjō Sanetomi Kō Nenpu. 29 vols. Edited by Kunaishō Zushoryō. Tokyo: Kunaishō, 1901.

Sasaki Tōichi. *Aru Gunjin no Jiden.* Tokyo: Keisō Shobō, 1967.

Satow, Ernest M. *A Diplomat in Japan: The Diaries of Ernst Satow.* Edited by Ian Ruxton. Morrisville, NC: Lulu Press, 2009.

Shibusawa Eiichi Denki Shiryō. 58 vols. Edited by Shibusaya Seien Kinen Zaidan Ryūmosha. Tokyo: Shibusawa Eiichi Denki Shiryo Kankokai, 1955–71.

Sources of Japanese Tradition. Edited by Wm. Theodor de Bary, Carol Gluck, and Arthur E. Tiedemann. New York: University of Columbia Press, 2005.

Suematsu Tahei. *Watakushi no Shōwashi.* Tokyo: Misuzu Shobō, 1963.

Sugimura Fukashi. *Meiji 28 nen Zaikan Kushinroku.* Tokyo: Hara Shobō, 1981.

Suzuki Teiichi. *Suzuki Teiichi-shi Danwa Sokkiroku.* 2 vols. Tokyo: Nihon Shiriyō Kenkyūkai, 1971–74.

Tadayoshi-Kō Shiryō. 7 vols. Edited by Kagoshima Ken Ishin Shiryō Hensan Shohen. Kagoshima: Kagoshima Ken, 1974–80.

Taishō Demokurashii-ki no Seiji: Matsumoto Gōkichi Seiji Nisshi. Edited by Oka Yoshitake and Hayashi Shigeru. Tokyo: Iwanami Shoten, 1959.

Takarabe Takeshi Nikki: Kaigun Jikan Jidai. 2 vols. Edited by Banno Junji et al. Tokyo: Yamakawa Shuppansha, 1983.

Take Yoriwake. "Tosa Jinbutsu Hyōron." *Nihon Oyobi Nihonjin* 504 (February 1909).

Takechi Zuizan Kankei Monjo. 2 vols. Tokyo: Nihonshi Sekkyōkai, 1916.

Tanaka Kiyoshi. "Showa 7-nen 1-gatsu, XX Shōsa Shuki, Iwayuru Jūgatsu Jiken ni kansuru Shuki." Appendix 5 in Muranaka Kōji and Isobe Asaichi, *Shukugun ni kansuru Ikensho: Shōwa 10-nen 7-gatsu 11-nichi.* Tokyo: self-published pamphlet, 1935.

Tani Kanjō Ikō. 2 vols. Edited by Nihon Shiseki Kyōkai. Tokyo: Tokyo Daigaku Shuppan Kai, 1975–76.

Tani Kanjō Kankei Monjo. 15 vols. Edited by Hiroe Yoshihiro and Kobayashi Kazuyuki. Tokyo: Kitazumisha, 1995.

Terasaki Hidenari, ed. *Shōwa Tennō Dokuhakuroku: Terasaki Hidenari Goyōgakari Nikki.* Tokyo: Bungei Shunjū, 1991.

Terasaki Yasukichi (alias Takahashi Genji). "Terasaki-shi Sekijitsudan." In *Itō Chiyū Zenshū.* 30 vols. Tokyo: Heibonsha, 12:439–49.

Terauchi Masatake Kankei Monjo. Edited by Yamamoto Shirō. Kyoto: Kyoto Joshi Daigaku, 1984.

Terauchi Masatake Nikki, 1900–1918. Edited by Yamamoto Shirō. Kyoto: Kyoto Joshi Daigaku, 1980.

Tokugawa Yoshichika. *Saigo no Tonosama: Tokugawa Yoshichika Jiden.* Tokyo: Kōdansha, 1973.
Tokyo Saiban Shiryō Kido Kōichi Jinmon Chōsho. Edited by Awaya Kentarō et al. Tokyo: Ōtsuki Shoten, 1987.
Toyabe Shuntei. *Shuntei Zenshū.* 3 vols. Tokyo: Hakubunkan, 1909.
Uehara Yūsaku Kankei Monjo. Edited by Uehara Yūsaku Kankei Monjo Kenkyūkai. Tokyo: Tokyo Daigaku Shuppankai, 1976.
Ugaki Kazushige. *Shōrai Seidan.* Tokyo: Bungei Shunjū Shinsha, 1951.
——. *Ugaki Kazushige Nikki.* 3 vols. Edited by Tsunoda Jun. Tokyo: Misuzu Shobō, 1968–71.
Yamagata Aritomo. *Yamagata Aritomo Ikenshō.* Tokyo: Hara Shobō, 1966.
Yamagata Aritomo et al., eds. *Rikugunshō Enkaku Shi.* Tokyo: Rikugunshō, 1905.
Yamagata Hojirō. "Chōsen Ōhi Jiken." *Gunji Kenkyū* 3.1 (1938): 45–54 (the testimony of General Kususe Sachihiko, as related to Yamagata).
Yamakawa Hiroshi. *Kyoto Shugoshoku Shimatsu: Kyū-Aizu Rōshin no Shuki.* Translated by Kaneko Mitsuharu. Tokyo: Heibonsha, 1965–66.
Yugawa (Kiyohara) Yasuhira. "Niniroku Jiken to Saionji-kō." *Bungei Shunju* 45, no. 6 (June 1967): 322–28.

Secondary Sources

Akita, George. *Foundations of Constitutional Government in Modern Japan: 1868–1900.* Cambridge, MA: Harvard University Press, 1967.
Akita, George, and Hirose Yoshihiro. "The British Model: Inoue Kowashi and the Ideal Monarchical System." *Monumenta Nipponica* 49, no. 4 (winter, 1994): 413–21.
Akizuki Toshiyuki. "Meiji Shonen no Karafuto: Nichi-Ro Zakkyo o meguru Sho-Mon-dai." *Slavic Studies* 40 (1993): 1–21.
Aoyama Tadamasa. "Jidai o ugokashita 'shishi' tachi no Akira to Yami." *Jinbutsu Ōrai Rekishi Dokuhon* (June 2011): 50–66.
Banno Junji. *Taishō Seihen: 1900-nen Taisei no Hōkai.* Kyoto: Mineruba Shobō, 1982.
Barclay, Paul D. "'Gaining Confidence and Friendship in Aborigine Country: Diplomacy, Drinking, and Debauchery on Japan's Southern Frontier." *Social Science Japan* 6, no. 1 (April 2003): 77–96.
Beasley, William G. *The Meiji Restoration.* Stanford, CA: Stanford University Press.
Benesch, Oleg. *Inventing the Way of the Samurai: Nationalism, Internationalism, and Bushido in Modern Japan.* Oxford: Oxford University Press, 2014.
Berry, Mary Elizabeth. *Japan in Print: Information and Nation in the Early Modern Period.* Berkeley: University of California Press, 2006.
——. "Public Peace and Private Attachment: The Goals and Conduct of Power in Early Modern Japan." *Journal of Japanese Studies* 12, no. 2 (1986): 237–71.
Bix, Herbert. *Hirohito and the Making of Modern Japan.* New York: HarperCollins, 2000.
Bluntschli, J. C. *Das Moderne Völkerrecht der Civilisirten Staten.* Nördlingen: Verlag der C. H. Beck'schen Buchhandlung, 1878.
Brecher, W. Puck. "Down and Out in Negishi: Reclusion and Struggle in an Edo Suburb." *Journal of Japanese Studies* 35, no. 1 (winter 2009): 1–35.
Breen, John. "The Imperial Oath of April 1868: Ritual, Politics and Power in the Restoration." *Monumenta Nipponica* 51, no. 4 (winter 1996): 407–29.
Brown, Kate. *A Biography of a No Place: From Ethnic Borderland to Soviet Heartland.* Cambridge, MA: Harvard University Press, 2004.
Buck, James H. "The Satsuma Rebellion of 1877: From Kagoshima through the Siege of Kumamoto Castle." *Monumenta Nipponica* 28, no. 4 (winter 1973): 427–66.

Burns, Susan L. *Before the Nation: Kokugaku and the Imagining of Community in Early Modern Japan.* Durham, NC: Duke University Press, 2003.

Byas, Hugh. *Government by Assassination.* New York: Knopf, 1942.

Cameron, Craig M. "Race and Identity: The Culture of Combat in the Pacific War." *International History Review* 27, no. 3 (September 2005): 550–66.

Chae Soo Do. "'Tenyūkyō' ni kansuru ikōssatsu." *Chūō Daigakuin Kenkyū Nenpō: Hōgaku Kenkyūka* 30 (February 2001): 439–47.

Ch'en Hsien-T'ing. "The Japanese Government and the Creation of the Imperial Army." Ph.D. diss., Harvard University, 1963.

Chi Hsi-Sheng. *Warlord Politics in China.* Stanford, CA: Stanford University Press, 1976.

Choi Woonsang. *The Fall of the Hermit Kingdom.* Dobbs Ferry, NY: Oceana, 1967.

Chōnan Shinji. "Bunkyūki ni okeru 'Shoshi Ōgi' to Sōmō." *Kokushikan Shigaku* 12 (March 2008): 36–69.

Clark, Christopher M. *Iron Kingdom: The Rise and Downfall of Prussia: 1600–1947.* Cambridge, MA: Belknap Press of Harvard University Press, 2006.

Cobbing, Andrew (based on the work of Inuzuka Takaaki). *The Satsuma Students in Britain: Japan's Early Search for the "Essence of the West."* Richmond, UK: Japan Library, 2000.

Conroy, Hillary. *The Japanese Seizure of Korea, 1868–1910: A Study of Realism and Idealism in International Relations.* Philadelphia: University of Pennsylvania Press, 1960.

Coox, Alvin D. "High Command Field Army: The Kwantung Army and the Nomohan Incident, 1939." *Military Affairs* 33, no. 2 (October 1969): 302–12.

Cortazzi, Hugh. *Dr. Willis in Japan, 1862–1877: British Medical Pioneer.* London: Athlone Press, 1985.

Craig, Albert M. *Chōshū in the Meiji Restoration.* Cambridge, MA: Harvard University Press, 1961.

Craig, Gordon A. *The Politics of the Prussian Army: 1640–1945.* London: Oxford University Press, 1964.

Creveld, Martin van. *Command in War.* Cambridge, MA: Cambridge University Press, 1895.

Critchfield, Theodore M. "Queen Min's Murder." Ph.D. diss., Indiana University, 1975.

Crowley, James B. "Japanese Army Factionalism in Early 1930s." *Journal of Asian Studies* 21, no. 3 (May 1962): 309–26.

——. *Japan's Quest for Autonomy: National Security and Foreign Policy, 1930–1938.* Princeton, NJ: Princeton University Press, 1966.

——. "From Closed Door to Empire: The Formation of the Meiji Military Establishment." In *Modern Japanese Leadership: Transition and Change,* edited by Bernard S. Silberman and H. D. Harootunian, 261–87. Tucson: University of Arizona Press, 1966.

Dickinson, Frederick R. *Taishō Tennō: Ichiyaku Godaishū wo yūhisu.* Kyoto: Mineruva Shobō, 2009, 88–90.

DiMaggio, Paul, and Walter W. Powell. "The Iron Cage Revisited: Institutional Isomorphism and Collective Rationality in Organizational Fields." *American Sociological Review* 48, no. 2 (April 1983): 147–60.

Dower, John E. *Empire and Aftermath: Yoshida Shigeru and the Japanese Experience, 1878–1954.* Cambridge MA: Council on Asian Studies/Harvard University Press, 1979.

——. *War without Mercy: Race and Power in the Pacific War.* New York: Pantheon Books, 1986.

Drea, Edward J. *Japan's Imperial Army: Its Rise and Fall, 1853–1945*. Lawrence: University Press of Kansas, 2009.

Duara, Prasenjit. "State Involution: A Study of Local Finances in North China: 1911–1935." *Comparative Studies in Society and History* 29, no. 1 (January 1987): 132–61.

Dunscomb, Paul E. *Japan's Siberian Intervention, 1918–1922: "A Great Disobedience against the People."* Lanham, MD: Lexington Books, 2001.

Duus, Peter. *Party Rivalry and Political Change in Taishō Japan*. Cambridge, MA: Harvard University Press, 1968.

——. *The Abacus and the Sword: The Japanese Penetration of Korea, 1859–1910*. Berkeley: University of California Press, 1995.

Duus, Peter et al., eds. *The Japanese Informal Empire in China, 1895–1937*. Princeton, NJ: Princeton University Press, 1989.

Erikson, Erik H. *Insight and Responsibility: Lectures on the Ethical Implications of Psychoanalytic Insight*. New York: W. W. Norton, 1964.

Eskildsen, Robert. "Of Civilization and Savages: The Mimetic Imperialism of Japan's 1874 Expedition to Taiwan." *American Historical Review* 107, no. 2 (April 2002): 388–418.

Fairbank, J. K, and S. Y. Teng. "On the Chi'ng Tributary System." *Harvard Journal of Asiatic Studies* 6, no. 2 (June 1941): 135–246.

Fujii Hisashi. *Niniroku Teito Heiran: Gunjiteki Shiten kara zenmenteki ni minaosu*. Tokyo: Sōshisha, 2010.

Fujita Tsuguo. *Meiji Gunsei*. Tokyo: Nobuyamasha, 1992, 81–85.

Fujitani Takeshi. *Splendid Monarchy: Power and Pageantry in Modern Japan*. Berkeley: University of California Press, 1996.

Fujiwara Akira. "Niniroku jiken." *Rekishigaku Kenkyū* 169, no. 3 (1954): 15–25.

——. *Nihon Gunjishi*. Vol. 1. Tokyo: Shakai Hihyōsha, 2006.

Fujiwara Hirosato. "Gijikakumeisha no Yakuwari: Seinen Shōkō, Minkan Uyoku o Chūshin toshita." *Shisō* 355 (1954): 48–75.

Fukushima Nariyuki. *Seikanron no Yobun: Akasaka Kuichigai no Jihen*. Tokyo: Maeda Bajōta, 1927.

Funaki Shigeru. *Rikugun Daijin Kigoshi Yasutsuna*. Tokyo: Kawade Shobō Shinsha, 1993.

Gat, Azar. *The Development of Military though the Nineteenth Century*. Oxford: Clarendon Press, 1992.

Gluck, Carol. *Japan's Modern Myths: Ideology in the Late Meiji Period*. Princeton, NJ: Princeton University Press, 1985.

Goldman, Emily O. "The Spread of Western Military Models to Ottoman Turkey and Meiji Japan." In *The Sources of Military Change: Culture, Politics, Technology*, edited by Theo Farrell and Terry Terriff, 41–62. Boulder, CO: Lynne Rienner, 2002.

Gong Debo (T. P. K'ung). *The Tragic Death of Chang Tso-lin: a Documentary Survey of a Prelude to the Japanese Invasion of Manchuria*. Peiping, 1932.

Gordon, Andrew D. "The Crowds and Politics in Imperial Japan: Tokyo: 1905–1908." *Past and Present* 121 (November 1988): 141–70.

——. *Labor and Imperial Democracy in Prewar Japan*. Berkeley: University of California Press, 1991.

Gross, Gerhard P. *Mythos und Wirklichkeit: Geschichte des operative Denkens im deutschen Heer von Moltke d.Ä bis Heusinger*. Munich: Ferdinand Schöningh, 2012.

Hackett, Roger F. *Yamagata Aritomo in the Rise of Modern Japan, 1838–1922*. Cambridge, MA: Harvard University Press, 1971.

Haga Noboru. *Bakumatsu Shishi no Sekai.* Tokyo: Yūzankaku, 2003.

Haley, John. *Authority without Power: Law and the Japanese Paradox.* New York: Oxford University Press, 1991.

Hara Keiichirō and Yamamoto Shirō. *Hara Kei o meguru Hitobito.* 2 vols. Tokyo: Nihon Hōsō Shuppan Kyōkai, 1981.

Harari, Yuval N. "Terror Ma-hu? Mi-Yemei ha-Beinayim ve-ad la-Me'a ha-Esrim ve-Ahat." *Zmanim* 108 (autumn 2009): 1–15.

Hardacre, Helen. *Shintō and the State.* Princeton, NJ: Princeton University Press, 1989.

Hartmann, Rudolf. "Japanische Offiziere im deutschen Kaiserreich." *Japonica Humboldtiana* 11 (2007): 93–158.

Harutoonian, Harry D. *Toward Restoration: The Growth of Political Consciousness in Tokugawa Japan.* Berkeley: University of California Press, 1970.

Hata Ikuhiko. *Gun Fashizumu Undōshi.* Tokyo: Kawade Shobō Shinsa, 1972, 1–20.

———. "Niniroku Jiken to Hirohito Tennō." *Seiji Keizai Shigaku* 209 (December 1983): 1–20.

———. *Tōsui-ken to Teikoku Rikukaigun no Jidai.* Tokyo: Heibonsha, 2006.

———. "Binhi Satsugai Jiken no saikōsatsu." *Seikei Kenkyū* 43, no. 2 (October 2006): 59–116.

———. "Chō Sakurin Bakusatsu no Zaikōsatsu." *Seikei Kenkyū* 44, no. 1 (May 2007): 101–56.

Hayasaka Takashi. *Shikikan no Ketsudan: Manshū to Attsu no Shōgun Higuchi Kiichirō.* Tokyo: Bungei Shunjū, 2010.

Hesselnik, Rainier. "The Assassination of Henry Heusken." *Monumenta Nipponica* 49.3 (autumn 1994): 331–51.

Hirano Mineo (Reiji). *Manshū no Inbōsha: Kōmoto Daisaku no unmeiteki na Ashiato.* Tokyo: Jiyū Kokuminsha, 1961.

Hirose Yoshihiro. "Binhi Ansatsu Jiken Kankei Shiriyō." *Nihon Kosho Tsūshin* 793, no. 8 (1995): 14–15.

Hoffmann, D. P. G., "Kommandogewalt und Kriegsminister." *Zeitschrift für die gesamte Staatsswissenschaft/Journal of Institutional and Theoretical Economics* 68, no. 4 (1921): 740–49.

Hosaka Masayasu. *Chichibu no Miya to Shōwa Tennō.* Tokyo: Bungei Shunjū, 1989.

Howell, David L. *Geographies of Identity in Nineteenth Century Japan.* Berkeley: University of California Press, 2005.

Huber, Thomas. "Men of High Purpose and the Politics of Direct Action, 1862–64." In *Conflict in Modern Japanese History: The Neglected Tradition*, edited by Tetsuo Najita and J. Victor Koschmann. Princeton, NJ: Princeton University Press, 1982.

———. *The Revolutionary Origins of Modern Japan.* Stanford: Stanford University Press, 1981.

Humphreys, Leonard A. *The Way of the Heavenly Sword: The Japanese Army in the 1920s.* Stanford, CA: Stanford University Press.

Huntington, Samuel P. *The Soldier and the State: the Theory of Civil-Military Relations.* Cambridge, MA: Harvard University Press, 1957.

Hurst, Cameron, III. *Armed Martial Arts of Japan: Swordsmanship and Archery.* New Haven: Yale University Press, 1998.

Hyō Seihō. *Hyōden Munakata Kotarō: Tairiku Rōnin no rekishiteki Yakuwari.* Kumamoto: Kumamoto Shuppan Bunka Kaikan, 1997.

Iboshi Ei. "Chō Sakurin Bakusatsu Jiken no Shinsō, Pt. 1." *Geirin* (June 1982): 2–43.

———. "Chō Sakurin Bakusatsu Jiken no Shinsō Pt. 2." *Geirin* (July 1982), 29–62.

———. "Chō Sakurin Bakusatsu Jiken no Shinsō Pt. 3." *Geirin* (August 1982), 24–66.

——. "Chō Sakurin Bakusatsu Jiken no Shinsō Pt. 4." *Geirin* (September 1982), 27–57.

——. "Chō Sakurin Bakusatsu Jiken no Shinsō Pt. 5." *Geirin* (October 1982), 31–48.

Ichisaka Tarō. "Sake to Shishi to Bakumatsu Sōran." *Rekishi Dokuhon* 56, no. 6 (June 2011): 178–83.

Iechika Yoshiki. "Taiwan Shuppei Hōshin to Tenkan to Chōshūha no Hantai Undō." *Shigaku Zasshi* 92, no. 11 (1983): 1761–89.

——. *Saigō Takamori to Bakumatsu Ishin no Seikyoku*. Kyoto: Mineruva Shobō, 2011.

Iguchi Kazuki. "Shingai Kakumei to Taishō Seihen." In *Kōza Nihonshi*, edited by Rekishigaku Kenkyūkai and Nihonshi Kenkyūkai, 6:317–49. *Nihon Teikokushugi no Keisei*. Tokyo: Tokyo Daigaku Shuppankai, 1970.

Iguchi Takeo. *Demystifying Pearl Harbor: A New Perspective from Japan*. Translated by David Noble. Tokyo: International House of Japan, 2010.

Iizuka Kazuyuki. "Saga no Ran no zai-Kentō: Shuhen no Shiten kara." *Kyūshū Shigaku* 149 (February 2008): 13–35.

Ikegami Eiko. *The Taming of the Samurai: Honorific Individualism and the Making of Modern Japan*. Cambridge, MA: Harvard University Press, 1995.

Inaba Masao. "Chō Sakurin Bakusatsu Jiken." In *Shōwa Sannen Shina Jihen Shuppeishi*, edited by Sanbō Honbu, appendix. Tokyo: Gannandō Shoten, 1971.

Inada Masatsugu. *Meiji Kempō Seiritsu Shi*. Tokyo: Yūhikaku, 1960–62.

Inoue Kiyoshi. *Meiji Ishin*. Tokyo: Chūō Kōronsha, 1970.

Ishibashi Tsuneyoshi. *Shōwa no Hanran: Sangatsu Ku-deta- kara Niniroku Jiken made*. 2 vols. Tokyo: Takagi Shoten, 1979.

Itō Seirō. "Tenchūgumi." *Rekishi Dokuhon* 56, no. 6 (June 2011): 104–10.

Itō Takashi. "Taishō shoki Yamagata Aritomo Danwa Hikki." *Shigaku Zasshi* 75, no. 10 (1966): 63–78.

Iwata Masakazu. *Ōkubo Toshimichi: The Bismarck of Japan*. Berkeley: University of California Press, 1964.

Jansen, Marius B. *The Emergence of Meiji Japan*. Cambridge: Cambridge University Press, 1995.

——. *Sakamoto Ryoma and the Meiji Restoration*. Princeton, NJ: Princeton University Press, 1961.

Jaundrill, D. Colin. *Samurai to Soldier: Remaking Military Service in Nineteenth-Century Japan*. Ithaca: Cornell University Press, 2016.

Jeans, Roger B. *Terasaki Hidenari, Pearl Harbor, and Occupied Japan: A Bridge to Reality*. Lanham, MD: Lexington Books, 2009.

Johnson, Chalmers. *MITI and the Japanese Miracle: The Growth of Industrial Policy, 1925–1975*. Stanford, CA: Stanford University Press, 1982.

Jōhō Yoshio. *Rikugun Daigakkō*. Tokyo: Fuyō Shobō, 1973.

Joos, Joel. "The Liberal Asianism of Inukai Tsuyoshi (1855–1932): Japanese Relations with the Mainland between Opportunism, Pragmatism, and Idealism." *Bulletin of Kochi Woman's University: Series of Faculty of Cultural Studies* 60 (March 2011): 25–57.

Kagoshima Ken, ed. *Kagoshima Ken Shi*. Kagoshima: Kagoshima Ken, 1967.

Kahn, Winston B. *Doihara Kenji and the "North China Autonomy Movement," 1935–36*. Tempe: Arizona State University, 1973.

Kaigun Rekishi Hozonkai, ed. *Nihon Kaigun shi*. Tokyo: Kaigun Rekishi Hozonkai, 1995.

Kaku, Kōzō. *Daikeishi Kawaji Toshiyoshi: Bakumatsu Meiji kakenuketa Kyojin*. Tokyo: Shuppan Geijutsusha, 1999.

Kanbashi Norimasa. *Shimazu Hisamitsu to Meiji Ishin: Hisamitsu wa naze, Tōbaku o ketsuishita ka*. Tokyo: Shinjinbutsu Ōraisha, 2002.

Kaneko Kentarō et al. *Itō Hirobumi Den*. 3 vols. Tokyo: Hara Shobō, 1970.

Kang Ching-Il. "Tenyūkyō to 'Chōsen Mondai': 'Chōsen Rōnin' no Tōgaku Nōmin Sensō e no Taiō to kanren shite." *Shigaku Zasshi* 97, no. 8 (1988): 1321–57.

Kaplan, Morton A. *System and Process in International Politics*. New York: Wiley, 1957.

Karetina, G. S. (Galina Semenova). *Chzhan T S zolin i politicheskai a bor ba v Kitae v 20-e gody XX v*. Moskva: Iz-vo Nauka, 1984.

Karita Tetsu. "Jūgatsu Jiken, Pt. 1," *Tokyo Tōritsu Daigaku Hōgaku Zasshi* 11, no. 2 (March 1971): 299–334.

——. "Jūgatsu Jiken, Pt. 2," *Tokyo Tōritsu Daigaku Hōgaku Zasshi* 12, no. 1 (October 1971): 273–323.

——. "Jūgatsu Jiken, Pt. 3," *Tokyo Tōritsu Daigaku Hōgaku Zasshi* 12, no. 2 (March 1972): 195–227.

——. "Jūgatsu Jiken, Pt. 4," *Tokyo Tōritsu Daigaku Hōgaku Zasshi* 13, no. 1 (October 1972): 83–187.

——. *Ōkawa Shūmei to Kokka Kaizō Undō*. Tokyo: Ningen no Kagaku Shinsha, 2001.

Katō Yōko. *Sensō no Ronri: Nichi-Ro Sensō kara Taiheiyō Sensō made*. Tokyo: Keisō Shobō, 2005.

——. *Manshū Jihen kara Nitchū Sensō e*. Tokyo: Iwanami Shoten, 2007.

Katsuta Masaharu. *Naimushō to Meiji Kokka Keisei*. Tokyo: Yoshikawa Kōbunkan, 2002.

Kawaguchi Masaaki. "Shōka Sonjuku." *Jinbutsu Ōrai Rekishi Dokuhon* 56 no. 6 (June 2011): 68–74.

Kawata Mizuho. *Kataoka Kenkichi Sensei Den*. Tokyo: Kohokusha, 1978.

Keene, Donald. *Emperor of Japan: Meiji and His World, 1852–1912*. New York: Columbia University Press, 2002.

Keishichō Shihensan Iinkai, ed. *Keishichō Shi, Meiji Hen*. Tokyo: Keichichō Shihensan Iinkai, 1959.

Kerst, George. *Jacob Meckel: sein Leben, sein Wirken in Deutschland und Japan*. Göttingen: Musterschmidt Verlag, 1970.

Khan Yoshimitsu. "Inoue Kowashi and the Dual Images of the Emperor of Japan." *Pacific Affairs* 71, no. 2 (summer 1998): 215–30.

Kido Takayoshi Den Hensanjo, ed. *Shōkiku Kido Takayoshi Den*. Tokyo: Meiji Shoin, 1927.

Kikkawa Manabu. *Arashi to tatakau Tetsushō Araki: Rikugun Uramenshi, Shōgun Araki no shichijū-nen no Gekan*. Tokyo: Araki Sadao Shōgun Denki Hensan Kankōkai, 1955.

Kikuta Hitoshi. *Naze 'Sensō' data no ka: Tōsui-ken to iu Shisō*. Tokyo: Kozawa Shoten, 1998.

Kim Kyu-Hyun. *The Age of Visions and Arguments: Parliamentarianism and the National Public Sphere in Early Meiji Japan*. Cambridge, MA: Harvard University Asia Center, 2007.

Kingsberg, Miriam L. "The Poppy and the Acacia: Opium and Imperialism in Japanese Dairen and the Kwantung Leased Territory, 1905–1945." Ph.D. diss., University of California, Berkeley, 2009.

Kino Kazue. "Inoue Kowashi no Tōsuiken no rikkenteki Tōgiyo Kōsō, Pt. 1." *Geirin* 58 (October 2009): 139–71.

——. "Inoue Kowashi no Tōsuiken no rikkenteki Tōgiyo Kōsō, Pt. 2." *Geirin* 59 (April 2010): 172–212.

Kirihara Kenshin. "Bakumatsu Shishi ni okeru Dokuhon: Yoshida Shōin o meguru Dōshiteki Netowoku no Kōchiku." In *Meiji Ishin to Bunka*, edited by Meiji Ishin Shigakukai, 105–26. Tokyo: Yoshikawa Kōbunkan, 2005.

Kitaoka Shin'ichi. "The Army as a Bureaucracy: Japanese Militarism Revisited." *Journal of Military History* 57, no. 5 (October 1993): 67–86.

Knoke, David. *Political Networks: The Structural Perspective.* Cambridge: Cambridge University Press, 1990.

Kobayashi Kazuhiro. *"Shina-tsū ichi Gunjin no Hikari to Kage: Isogai Rensuke Chūjō Den.* Tokyo: Kashiwa Shobō, 2000.

Kobayashi Kazuyuki. *Tani Kanjō: Yūkoku no Meijijin.* Tokyo: Chūō Kōron Shinsha, 2011.

Kobayashi Michihiko. "Sangatsu Jiken Saikō." *Nihon Rekishi* 10 (2007): 1–19.

——. "Taishō Seihenki no Tairiku Seisaku to Rikukaigun: 1912–1914-nen." *Nihonshi Kenkyū* 363 (November 1992): 1–22.

Kobayashi Takao. 'Rusu seifu to sei-Tai ronso: Rujandoru oboegaki ni kansuru ichi kosatsu,' *Seiji keizai Shigaku* 296 (December 1990): 1–25.

Kojima Tsuyoshi. "Chūgoku umare no Shishiteki Shisō." *Jinbutsu Ōrai Rekishi Dokuhon* 56, no. 6 (June 2011): 134–39.

Kokuryūkai, ed. *Seinanki Den.* 6 vols. Tokyo: Kokuryūkai, 1908–11.

Koschmann, J. Victor. *The Mito Ideology: Discourse, Reform, and Insurrection in Late Tokugawa Japan, 1790–1864.* Berkeley: University of California Press, 1987.

Koyama Hirotake. *Kindai Nihon Gunjishi Gaisetsu.* Tokyo: Itō Shoten, 1944.

Kublin, Hyman. "The 'Modern' Army of Early Meiji Japan." *Far Eastern Quarterly* 9, no. 1 (November 1949): 20–41.

Kumagai Teruhisa. *Nihongun no Seishin Kyōiku: Gunki Fūki no Iji Taisaku no Hatten.* Tokyo: Kinseisha, 2012.

Kunaichō, ed. *Meiji Tennō Ki.* Tokyo: Yoshikawa Kōbunkan, 1968–77.

Kurihara Jun. "Taiwan Jiken (1874 nen): Ryūkyū Seisaku no Tenki toshite no Taiwan Shuppei." *Shigaku Zasshi* 87, no. 9 (September 1978): 1328–52.

Kuromiya Hiraoki, and Mamoulia, George. "Anti-Russian and anti-Soviet Subversion: The Caucasian-Japanese Nexus, 1904–1945." *Europe-Asia Studies* 61, no. 8 (2009): 1415–40.

Kurono Taeru. *Sanbō Honbu to Rikugun Daigakkō.* Tokyo: Kōdansha, 2004.

Kuzu Yoshihisa (Kokuryūkai, ed. *Tōa Senkaku Shishi Kiden.* 3 vols. Tokyo: Hara Shobō, 1933–36.

Large, Stephen S. "Nationalist Extremism in Early Shōwa Japan: Inoue Nisshō and the 'Blood-Pledge Corps Incident,' 1932." *Modern Asian Studies* 35, no. 3 (2001): 533–64.

——. *Emperor Hirohito and Shōwa Japan: A Political Biography.* London: Routledge, 1992.

Laurinat, Marion. *Kita Ikki (1883–1937) und der Februarputsch 1936.* Munster: Lit., 2006.

Lee, Loyd E., ed. *World War Two in Asia and the Pacific and the War's Aftermath, with General Themes: A Handbook of Literature and Research.* Westport, CT: Greenwood Press, 1998.

Lensen, George A. *Korea and Manchuria between Russia and Japan: The Observations of Sir Ernst Satow, British Minister Plenipotentiary to Japan (1895–1900) and China (1900–1906).* Tallahassee, FL: Diplomatic Press, 1966.

——. *The D'Anethan Dispatches from Japan, 1894–1910: The Observations of Baron Albert d'Anethan, Belgian Minister Plenipotentiary and Dean of the Diplomatic Corps.* Tokyo: Sophia University Press, 1967.

Leung, Edwin Pak-Wah. "The Quasi-War in East Asia: Japan's Expedition to Taiwan and the Ryūkyū Controversy." *Modern Asian Studies* 17, no. 2 (1983): 257–81.

Lone, Stewart. *Army, Empire, and Politics in Meiji Japan: The Three Careers of General Katsura Tarō.* Basingstoke, UK: Macmillan, 2000.

Maeda Renzan. *Rekidai Naikaku Monogatari*. 2 vols. Tokyo: Jiji Tsūshinsha, 1961.

Malozemoff, Andrew. *Russian Far Eastern Policy, 1881–1904*. New York: Octagon Books, 1977.

Martin, Bernd. *Japan and Germany in the Modern World*. Providence, RI: Berghahn Books, 1995.

Maruyama Kanji. *Soejima Taneomi Haku*. Tokyo: Dainichisha, 1936.

Maruyama Masao. *Thought and Behavior in Modern Japanese Politics*. London: Oxford University Press, 1963.

Matono Heisuke. *Etō Nanpaku*. 2 vols. Tokyo: Nanpaku Kenshōkai, 1914.

Matsumoto Ken'ichi and Shōji Junichirō. "Critiquing Herbert Bix's 'Hirohito.'" *Japan Echo* 29, no. 6 (December 2002): 64–68.

Matsusaka Yoshihisa Tak. *The Making of Japanese Manchuria, 1904–1932*. Cambridge, MA: Harvard Asia Center/Harvard University Press, 2001.

Matsushita Yoshio. *Meiji Gunsei Shiron*. Tokyo: Yūhikaku, 1956.

——. *Chōheirei seiteishi*. Tokyo: Naigai Shobō, 1943.

Maxon, Yale. *Control of Japanese Foreign Policy: A Study of Civil-Military Rivalry, 1930–1945*. Westport, CT: Greenwood Press, 1973.

Mayo, Marlene J. "The Korean Crisis of 1873 and Early Meiji Foreign Policy." *Journal of Asian Studies* 31, no. 4 (August 1972): 793–819.

McCormack, Gavan. *Chang Tso-lin in Northeast China, 1911–1928: China, Japan, and the Manchurian Idea*. Stanford, CA: Stanford University Press, 1977.

McWilliams, Wayne C. "East Meets East: The Soejima Mission to China, 1873." *Monumenta Nipponica* 30, no. 3 (autumn 1975): 237–75.

Meiji Ishin Shigakkai, ed. *Bakuhan Kenryoku to Meiji Ishin*. Tokyo: Yoshikawa Kōbunkan, 1992.

Messerschmidt, Manfred. "Die politische Geschichte der preussisch-deutschen Armee." In *Deutsche Militär geschichte in sechs bänden 1648–1939*, vol. 2, edited by Militärgeschichtliches Forschugsamt. Munich: Bernard & Graefe Verlag, 1983.

Mineo Kyūdai. *Rikugun Sanbō: Erito Kyōiku no Kōzai*. Tokyo: Bungei Shunjū, 1988.

Mitani Taichirō. *Kindai Nihon no Sensō to Seiji*. Tokyo: Iwanami Shoten, 1997.

Mitford, A. B., *Tales of Old Japan: Classic Folklore, Fairy Tales, Ghost Stories, and Tales of the Samurai*. London: Wordsworth Editions, 2000.

Mitsuoka Taeko. *Yuri Kimimasa Den*. Tokyo: Kōyūkan, 1916.

Miyachi Masato. *Bakumatsu Ishinki no Shakaiteki Seijishi Kenkyū*. Tokyo: Iwanami Shoten, 1999.

Miyake Tsugunobu. "Kiheitai." *Jinbutsu Ōrai Rekishi Dokuhon* 56, no. 6 (June 2011): 98–104.

Mizuno Akira. *Tōhoku Gunbatsu Seiken no Kenkyū: Chō Sakurin, Chō Gakuryō no Taigai Teikō to Tainai Tōitsu no Kiseki*. Tokyo: Kokusho Kankōkai, 1994.

Mizuno Norohito. "Early Meiji Policies towards the Ryukyus and the Taiwanese Aboriginal Territories." *Modern Asian Studies* 43, no. 3 (May 2009): 683–739.

Mori Katsumi. *Manshū Jihen no Rimenshi*. Tokyo: Kokushu Kankōkai, 1976.

Mōri Toshihiko. *Meiji Rokunen Seihen*. Tokyo: Chūō Kōronsha, 1979.

——. *Etō Shimpei: Kyūshinteki Kaikakusha no Higeki*. Tokyo: Chūō Kōronsha, 1987.

——. *Taiwan Shuppei: Dai Nihon Teikoku no Kaimaku Geki*. Tokyo: Chūō Kōronsha, 1996.

Mori Yasuo. *Nihon Rikugun to Nittchū Sensō e no Michi*. Kyoto: Mineruva Shobō, 2010.

Morikawa Tetsurō. *Bakumatsu Ansatsushi*. Tokyo: San'ichi Shobō, 1967.

Morimatsu Toshio. *Daihon'ei*. Tokyo: Kyōikusha Rekishi Shinsho, 1980.

Morris, David Morris. "The Problem of the Peasant Agriculturalist in Meiji Japan, 1873–1885." *Far Eastern Quarterly* 15, no. 3 (May 1956): 109–21.

Morton, William F. *Tanaka Giichi and Japan's China Policy*. Folkestone, UK: Dawson, 1980.

Mounsey, Augustus A. *The Satsuma Rebellion: An Episode of Modern Japanese History*. London: John Murray, 1879.

Nagano Susumu. *'Saga no Eki' to Chiiki Shakai*. Fukuoka-shi: Kyushu Daigaku Shuppankai, 1987.

Nakahara Kunihei. *Inoue-Haku Den*. 2 vols. Tokyo: Tōyō Insatu Kabushiki Kaisha Insatsu, 1907.

Naitō Kazunari. "Taishō Seihenki ni okeru Katsura Shintō to Kizokuin." *Shigaku Zasshi* 111, no. 4 (April 2002): 61–85.

Najita Tetsuo. *Hara Kei in the Politics of Compromise, 1905–1915*. Cambridge, MA: Harvard University Press, 1967.

Nakahara Hidenori. "Sakamoto Sumihiro Rireki Ippan." *Keisatsu Kenkyū* 42, no. 5 (1971): 69–86.

Nakano Tomio. *Origin and Development of So-Called Independence of Supreme Military Command in Japanese Constitution*. Tokyo: Kokusai Shuppan Insatsusha, 1932.

Nakusa Morio. *Uyoku Rōnin Tōjō: Okamoto Ryūnosuke no Hikari to Kage*. Tokyo: Sōfūsha, 1980.

Nishijima Ryōsaburō. *Nakayama Tadamitsu Ansatsu Shimatsu*. Tokyo: Ōraisha, 1983.

Nomura Shinsaku. "Bakumatsu no Goshinpei Secchi ni tai suru Chōshū Han no Kiyo." *Yamaguchi-ken Chihōshi Kenkyū* 110 (October 2010): 32–40.

Parkinson, Northcote. *Parkinson's Law and Other Studies in Administration*. Boston: Houghton Mifflin, 1957.

Peattie, Mark. *Ishiwara Kanji and Japan's Confrontation with the West*. Princeton, NJ: Princeton University Press, 1995.

Pines, Yuri, and Shelach Gideon. *Kol asher mi-taḥat la-shamayim: Toldot Ha-Keisarut Ha-Sinit*. Vol. 1. Ra'ananah: Universiṭah ha-petuḥah, 2011.

Presseisen, Ernst L. *Before Aggression: Europeans Prepare the Japanese Army*. Tucson: University of Arizona Press, 1965.

Ochiai Hiroki. *Meiji Kokka to Shizoku*. Tokyo: Yoshikawa Kōbunkan 2001.

O'Dwyer, Emer. *Significant Soil: Settler Colonialism and Japan's Urban Empire in Manchuria*. Cambridge: Harvard University Asia Center, 2015.

Ōe Shinobu. *Nihon no Sanbō Honbu*. Tokyo: Chōkō Shinsho, 1985.

——. *Chō Sakurin Bakusatsu: Shōwa Tennō no Tōsui*. Tokyo: Chūō Kōronsha, 1989.

Ogata Sadako. *Defiance in Manchuria: The Making of Japanese Foreign Policy, 1931–32*. Westport, CT: Greenwood Press, 1984.

Ogawara Masamichi. *Daikyōin no Kenkyū: Meiji Shoki Shūkyō Gyōsei no Tenkai to Zasetsu*. Tokyo: Keiō Gijuku Daigaku Shuppankai, 2004.

——. "Seikanron Seihen ato no Seifu Tenpuku Keikaku." *Musashino Gakuin Daigaku Kenkyū Kiyō* 3 (2006): 89–96.

——. *Seinan Sensō: Saigō Takamori to Nihon Saigo no Naisen*. Tokyo: Chūō Kōron Shinsha, 2007.

Ogi-chō shi. Ogi: Ogi, 1974.

Ōhama Ikuko. "'Bodansha Jiken Saikō: Naze Paiwan-Zoku wa Ryūkyū Shima-jin o satsugai shita no ka." *Taiwan Genjūmin Kenkyū* 11 (2007): 203–24.

Oka Yoshitake. *Reimei ki no Meiji Nihon: Nichi-Ei Kōshōshi no Shikaku ni oite*. Tokyo: Miraisha, 1965.

Ōkubo Toshiaki. *Iwakura Tomomi*. Tokyo: Chūō Kōronsha, 1973.

——. *Meiji Ishin no Seiji Katei*. Tokyo: Yoshikawa Kōbunkan, 1986.

Ōmae Shin'ya. "Rikugun no Seiji Kainyū no Engen ni tsuite: Rikugun Yosan Hensei to Niniroku Jiken." *Seiji Keizai Shigaku* 540, no. 1–12 (2011): 1:1–29.

——. *Seiji Seiryoku to shite no Rikugun: Yosan Hensei to Niniroku Jiken*. Tokyo: Chūō Kōron Shinsha, 2015.

Orbach, Danny. "A Japanese Prophet: Eschatology and Epistemology in the Thought of Kita Ikki." *Japan Forum* 23, no. 3 (2011): 339–61.

——. "Tyrannicide in Radical Islam: Sayid Qutb and Abd a-Salam Faraj." *Middle Eastern Studies* 48, no. 6 (November 2012): 961–72.

——. *The Plots against Hitler*. New York: Houghton Mifflin Harcourt, 2016.

Osatake Takeki. *Meiji Bunka Sōsetsu*. Tokyo: Gakugeisha, 1934.

——. "Akasaka Kuichigai no Hen: Iwakura U-Daijin no Kyogeki." *Osatake Takeki cho Sakushū*. Vol. 5. Tokyo: Yuma ni Shobō, 2005–6.

Ōshima Akiko. "Meiji Shoki Dajōkansei ni okeru Seigun Kankei." *Kioi Shigaku* 11 (1991): 11–27.

——. "1873 (Meiji Roku-nen) no Shibirian Kontororu: Seikanron Seihen ni okeru Gun to Seiji." *Shigaku Zasshi* 117, no. 7 (July 2008): 1219–52.

Ōtani Keijirō. *Rakujitsu no Joshō: Shōwa Rikugunshi*. Tokyo: Yagumo Shoten, 1959.

Ōtsu Junichirō. *Dai Nihon Kenseishi*. Vol. 6. Tokyo: Hara Shobō, 1969–70.

Ōtsuka Minao. *Meiji Ishin to Doitsu Shisō*. Tokyo: Nagasaki Shuppan, 1977.

Raymond, Walter J., ed. *Dictionary of Politics*. Lawrenceville, VA: Brunswick, 1980.

Ravina, Mark. *Land and Lordship in Early Modern Japan*. Stanford: Stanford University Press, 1998.

——. *The Last Samurai: The Life and Battles of Saigo Takamori*. Hoboken, NJ: John Wiley and Sons, 2004.

——. "The Apocryphal Suicide of Saigō Takamori: Samurai, Seppuku and the Politics of Legend." *Journal of Asian Studies* 69, no. 3 (August 2010): 691–721.

Rikujō Jietai Kita and Kumamoto Shūshinaki, ed. *Shimpen Seinan Senshi*. 2 vols. Tokyo: Hara Shobō, 1977.

Rogers, John M. "The Development of the Military Profession in Tokugawa Japan." Ph.D. diss., Harvard University, 1998.

Rudolph, Jennifer M. *Negotiated Power in Late Imperial China: The Zongli Yamen and the Politics of Reform*. Ithaca, NY: East Asia Program, Cornell University, 2008.

Saaler, Sven. *Zwischen Demokratie und Militarismus: Japans Kaiserliche Armee in der Politik der Taisho-Zeit*, 1912–1926. Bonn: Bier'sche Verlagsanstalt, 2000.

——. "Nichidoku Kankei ni okeru Rikugun." In *Nichidoku Kankeishi 1890–1945*, edited by Kudo Akira and Tajima Nobuo, 2:176–228. 2 vols. Tokyo: University of Tokyo Press, 2008.

Sagara Shunsuke. *Akai Yūhi no Manshū Nogahara ni: Kisai Kōmoto Daisaku no Shōgai*. Tokyo: Kōjinsha, 1978.

Saiga Hiroyoshi. *Ōe Ten'ya Denki*. Tokyo: Ōe Futoshi, 1926.

Saigō Jūkō. *Gensui Saigō Tsugumichi Den*. Tokyo: Matsuyō Shobō, 1997.

Saitō Shishaku Kinenkai, ed. *Shishaku Saitō Makoto Den*. 4 vols. Tokyo: Saitō Shishaku Kinenkai, 1941–42.

Sakata, Yoshio, and John W. Hall. "The Motivation of Political Leadership in the Meiji Restoration." *Journal of Asian Studies* 16, no. 1 (November 1956): 31–50.

Sakeda Masatoshi and George Akita. "The Samurai Disestablished: Abei Iwane and his Stipend." *Monumenta Nipponica* 41, no. 3 (autumn 1986): 299–301.

Samuels, Richard J. *Machiavelli's Children: Leaders and Their Legacies in Italy and Japan*. Ithaca: Cornell University Press, 2003.

Sasaki Suguru. *Boshin Sensō: Haisha no Meiji Ishin*. Tokyo: Chūō Kōronsha, 1977.

——. *Shishi to Kanryō: Meiji Shonen no Jōkei*. Kyoto: Mineruva Shobō, 1984.

Sawachi Hisae. *Hi wa waga Kyōchū ni ari: wasurerareta Konoe Heishi no Hanran Takebashi Jiken*. Tokyo: Iwanami Shoten, 2008.

Schellendorff, Paul L.E.H.A. Bronsart von. *Der Dienst des Generalstabes*. Berlin: E. S. Mittler und Sohn, 1884.

Schencking, J. Charles. "The Imperial Japanese Navy and the Constructed Consciousness of a South Seas Destiny, 1872–1921." *Modern Asian Studies* 33, no. 4 (October 1999): 769–96.

Schmid, Andre. *Korea between Empires, 1895–1919*. New York: Columbia University Press, 2002.

Schwentkler, Wolfgang. "Die Samurai im Zeitalter der Meiji-Restauration. Einwandel und Modernisierung in Japan, 1830–1890." *Geschichte und Gesellschaft* 28, no. 1 (January–March 2002): 33–70.

Scott, John. "Modes of Power and the Re-conceptualization of Elites." In *Remembering Elites*, edited by Mike Savage and Karel Williams, 27–44. Malen, MA: Blackwell, 2008.

———. *Social Network Analysis—A Handbook*. London: SAGE Publications, 2009.

Segai Inoue Karo Denki Hensan, ed. *Segai Inoue-Kō Den*. Tokyo: Hara Shobō, 1968.

Shiba Ryōtarō. *Kono Kuni no Katachi*. Vol. 4. Tokyo: Bungei Shunjū, 1997.

Shibusawa Eiichi. *Tokugawa Yoshinobu Kō Den*. Tokyo: Ryūmonsha, 1918.

Shibutani Yuri. *Bazoku de miru 'Manshū': Chō Sakurin no ayunda Michi*. Tokyo: Kōdansha, 2004.

Shillony, Ben Ami. *Revolt in Japan: The Young Officers and the February 26, 1936 Incident*. Princeton, NJ: Princeton University Press, 1973.

———. *The Jews and the Japanese: The Successful Outsiders*. Rutland, VT.: C. E. Tuttle, 1992.

———. *Enigma of the Emperors: Sacred Subservience in Japanese History*. Folkestone, UK: Global Oriental, 2005.

Shimamura Hatsuyoshi. "Zai Korian no Mune no uchi: Binhi Ansatsu to Seiryaku Kekkon: Chōsen Heigō 100 toshi wo mukae." *Kairo* 3 (2010): 158–64.

Shimaoka Akira. *Shishitachi no Uta*. Tokyo: Shikuma Shobō, 1942.

Shimoyama Saburō. *Kindai Tennōsei Kenkyū Josetsu*. Tokyo: Iwanami Shoten, 1976.

Shinjō Katsumi. "'Tōsuiken' e no iwarenaki Godoku no Ketsubetsu: Nihon no Kokunai Seiji ni okeru kono Kotoba no seijiteki oyobi hōteki Yakuwari ni tsuite." *Dōto Daigaku Kiyō: Shakai Fukushi Gakubu* 37 (March 2012): 29–43.

Shinobu Seizaburō. *Nihon Seiji Shi*. Tokyo: Nansōsha, 1976–82.

Simbirtseva, Tatiana. "Ubiistvo v Dvortse Kyonbokkun." *Vostochnaya Kollektsiya* 3, no. 18 (autumn 2004): 127–42.

Siniawer, Eiko Maruko. *Ruffians, Yakuza, Nationalists: The Violent Politics of Modern Japan, 1860–1960*. Ithaca: Cornell University Press, 2008.

Smethurst, Richard J. *A Social Basis for Prewar Japanese Militarism: The Army and the Rural Community*. Berkeley: University of California Press, 1974.

———. *From Foot Soldier to Finance Minister: Takahashi Korekiyo, Japan's Keynes*. Cambridge, MA: Harvard University Press, 2007.

Sneider, David A. "Action and Oratory: The Trials of the May 15th Incident of 1932." *Law in Japan* 23, no. 67 (1990): 1–66.

Sonoda Hiyoshi. *Etō Shimpei to Saga no Ran*. Tokyo: Shin-jinbutsu Jūraisha, 1874.

Southern, Richard W. *Western Society and the Church in the Middle Ages*. London: Penguin Books, 1990.

Suzaki Shin'ichi. *Niniroku Jiken: Seinen Shōkō no Ishiki to Shinri*. Tokyo: Yoshikawa Kōbunkan, 2003.

Steinberg, Jonathan. *Bismarck: A Life*. Oxford: Oxford University Press, 2011.

Steven, R. P. G. "Hybrid Constitutionalism in Prewar Japan." *Journal of Japanese Studies* 3, no. 1 (winter 1977): 99–133.

Takagi Shunsuke. *Bakumatsu no Shishi: Sōmō no Meiji Ishin.* Tokyo: Chūō Kōronsha, 1976.

———. *Sorekara no Shishi: mō Hitotsu no Meiji Ishin.* Tokyo: Yūhikaku, 1985.

Takamiya Tahei. *Jungyaku no Showashi: Niniroku Jiken made no Rikugun.* Tokyo: Hara Shobō, 1971.

Takamiya Taiehei. *Gunkoku Taiheiki.* Tokyo: Kantōsha, 1951.

Takata Yūsuke. "Meiji Ishin 'shishi'-zō no Keisei to Rekishi Ishiki." *Rekishi Gakubu Ronshū: Bukkyō Daigaku Rekishi Gakubu* 2 (March 2012): 43–70.

Takekoshi Yosaburō. *Prince Saionji.* Translated by Kozaki Nariyaki. Kyoto: Ritsumeikan University, 1933.

Takii Kazuhiro. *Itō Hirobumi: Japan's First Prime Minister and Father of the Meiji Constitution.* Translated by Takechi Manabu. New York: Routledge, 2014.

Takumi Chūjō. *"Ware Kyūjō o Senkyoseri"—Niniroku Jiken Hiwa "Kyūjō Sakashita Monnai no Hen."* Tokyo: Kōyū Shuppan, 1995.

Tamamuro Taijō. *Seinan Sensō.* Tokyo: Shibundō, 1958.

Tanaka Azusa. "Iwayuru Sangatsu Jiken nit suite: sono Gaiyō to Bunken no Shōkai." *Sankō Shoshi Kenkyū* 16 (June 1978): 1–18.

Tanaka Hideo. "Binhi Ansatsu no Shin-Han'nin." *Rekishi-tsu* 3 (2012): 72–82.

Tatamiya Eitarō. *Hashimoto Kingorō Ichidai.* Tokyo: Fuyō Shobō, 1982.

Tazaki Suematsu. *Hyōden Tanaka Giichi: Jūgonen Sensō no Genten.* 2 vols. Chōfu-shi: Heiwasenryaku sōgō Kenkyūjō, 1981.

Teng, Ema. "Taiwan As a Living Museum." *Harvard Journal of Asiatic Studies* 59, no. 2 (1999): 445–84.

Terao Miho. "Seichūgumi." *Jinbutsu Ōrai Rekishi Dokuhon* 56, no. 6 (June 2011): 80–86.

Teters, Barbara J. "The Conservative Opposition in Japanese Politics: 1877–1894." Ph.D. diss., University of Washington, 1955.

———. "The Genrō-in and the National Essence Movement." *Pacific Historical Review* 31, no. 4 (November 1962): 359–78.

Thomson, Sandra Caruthers. "Filibustering to Formosa: General Charles LeGendre and the Japanese." *Pacific Historical Review* 40, no. 4 (November 1971): 442–56.

Tipton, Elise K. *Modern Japan: a Social and Political History.* London: Routledge, 2008.

Tobe Ryōichi. *Gyakusetsu no Guntai.* Tokyo: Chūo Kōronsha, 1998.

Toby, Ronald. *State and Diplomacy in Early Modern Japan: Asia in the Development of the Tokugawa Bakufu.* Stanford: Stanford University Press, 1991.

Tokutomi Ichirō (Sohō), ed. *Kōshaku Katsura Tarō Den.* 2 vols. Tokyo: Hara Shobō, 1967.

Tokutomi Ichirō (Sohō). *Kōshaku Yamagata Aritomo Den.* Tokyo: Yamagata Aritomo-Kō Kinen Jigyōkai, 1933.

Toshitani Nobuyoshi. "Meiji Kempō Taisei to Tennō: Taishō Seihen Zengo wo chūshin toshite." *Hōgaku Shimpō* 83, no. 10–2 (1977): 61–91.

Tōta Mitsuhiro. "Tosa Kinnōtō." *Jinbutsu Ōrai Rekishi Dokuhon* 56, no. 6 (June 2011): 86–92.

Tōyama Shigeki. *Meiji Ishin.* Tokyo: Iwanami Shoten, 2000.

Tōyama Shigeki. *Ishin Henkaku no Shosō.* Tokyo: Iwanami Shoten, 1991.

Tripler Nock, Elizabeth. "The Satsuma Rebellion of 1877: Letters of John Capen Hubbard." *Far Eastern Quarterly* 7, no. 4 (August 1948): 368–75.

Tsunoda Fusako. *Binhi Ansatsu: Chōsen Ōchō maki no Kokubo.* Tokyo: Shinchō Bunko, 1993.

Tsutsui Kyotada. *Shōwaki Nihon no Kōzō: sono Rekishi Shakaiteki Kōsatsu.* Tokyo: Yūhikaku, 1984.

Tsutsumi Keijirō. "Saga no Ran to Keishicho Junsa." *Seinan Daigaku Kokusai Bunka Ronshū* 23, no. 2 (February 1999): 161–79.

Tsuzuki Chushichi. "Tenkō or Teikō: The Dilemma of a Japanese Marxist between the Wars." In *Themes and Theories in Modern Japanese History: Essays in Memory of Richard Storry*, edited by Sue Henny and Jean-Pierre Lehmann, 215–30. London: Athlone Press, 1988.

Uchida Tomoi. *Itagaki Taisuke kun Denki*. 3 vols. Kōchi: Kumongō, 2009.

Umegaki Michio. *After the Restoration: The Beginning of Japan's Modern State*. New York: New York University Press, 1988.

Umetani Noboru. "Sanbo Honbu Dokuritsu no Kettei Keii ni tsuite." *Gunji Shigaku* 9, no. 2 (1973): 2–22.

——. *Gunjin Chokuyu Seiritsushi*. Tokyo, Seishi Shuppan, 2008.

Vaporis, Constantine N. *Tour of Duty: Samurai, Military Service in Edo, and the Culture of Early Modern Japan*. Honolulu: University of Hawaii Press, 2008.

Wagatsuma Sakae et al., eds. *Nihon Seiji Saiban Shiroku: Meiji*. 2 vols. Tokyo: Daiichi Hōki Shuppan, 1968–70.

——. *Nihon Seiji Saiban Shiroku: Taishō*. 2 vols. Tokyo: Daiichi Hōki Shuppan, 1968–70.

——. *Nihon Seiji Saiban Shiroku: Shōwa*. 2 vols. Tokyo: Daiichi Hōki Shuppan, 1968–70.

Weland, James E. "The Japanese Army in Manchuria: Covert Operations and the Roots of the Kwantung's Army Insubordination." Ph.D. diss., University of Arizona, 1977.

Welthall, Ann. *The Weak Body of a Useless Woman: Matsu Taseko and the Meiji Restoration*. Chicago: University of Chicago Press, 1998.

Westney, D. Eleanor. "The Emulation of Western Organizations in Meiji Japan: the Case of the Paris Prefecture of Police and the Keishi-chō." *Journal of Japanese Studies* 8, no. 2 (summer 1982): 307–42.

Wetzler, Peter. "Kaiser Hirohito und der Krieg in Pazifik: zur politischen Verantwortung des Tennō in der modernen japanischen Geschichte." *Vierteljahrshefte für Zeitgeschichte* 37, no. 4 (October 1989): 611–44.

——. *Hirohito and War: Imperial Tradition and Military Decision Making in Prewar Japan*. Honolulu: University of Hawaii Press, 1998.

Wigen, Kären. *The Making of a Japanese Periphery, 1750–1920*. Berkeley: University of California Press, 1995.

Yamabe Kentarō. "Binhi Jiken ni tsuite." *Koria Hyōron* 6, no. 48 (October 1964): 47–52.

Yamamoto Kiyoshi et al., ed. *Hakushaku Yamamoto Gonnohyōe Den*. Tokyo: Ōban Insatsu Kabushiki Kaisha, 1938.

Yamamoto Masao. "Kyū Nihongun no Gunpō Kaigi ni okeru Shihōken to Tōsuiken." *Bōeigaku Kenkyū* 42 (March 2010): 67–89.

Yamamoto Shirō. *Taishō Seihen no Kisoteki Kenkyū*. Tokyo: Ochanomizu Shobōkan, 1970.

——. *Yamamoto Naikaku no Kisoteki Kenkyū*. Kyoto: Kyoto Joshi Daigaku, 1982.

Yamamura Tatsuya. "Shinsengumi." *Jinbutsu Ōrai Rekishi Dokuhon* 56, no. 6 (June 2011): 92–97.

Yanagisawa Asobu. "Hōten ni okeru Hōtenhyō Bōraku Mondai to Futō Kazei Mondai no Tenkai Keika—Chō Sakurin Bakusatsu Jiken no Rekishiteki Zentei." Tokyo Daigaku Keizai Kenkyūkai, *Keizaigaku Kenkyū* 24 (October 1981): 48–59.

Yasuoki Tamura. "Sensō-ron no Keifu (2): Tōsuiken Chūritsu o megutte." *Kōchi Daigaku Shakai Kagaku* 98 (July 2010): 1–35.

Yates, Charles. *Saigo Takamori: The Man behind the Myth*. London: Kegan Paul, 1994.

——. "Saigō Takamori in the Emergence of Meiji Japan." *Modern Asian Studies* 28.3 (July 1994): 449–74.

Yoshida Yutaka. *Nihon no Guntai: Heishitachi no Kindaishi*. Tokyo: Iwanami Shoten, 2002.

Yui Masaomi, Fujiwara Akira, and Yoshida Yutaka, eds. *Guntai Heishi*. Vol 4. *Nihon Kindai Shishō Taikei*. Tokyo: Iwanami Shoten, 1989.

Xu Jielin. "Gaisei to tochi: 1874-nen Taiwan shuppei o rei ni shite." *Gendai Kokka to Kenpo no Genri: Kobayashi Naoki Sensei Kanreki Kinen*. Tokyo: Yūhikaku, 1983.

Žižek, Salvoj. "Talk at Occupy Wall St." In *Ecology without Nature*. http://ecologywithout nature.blogspot.com/2011/10/zizeks-talk-at-occupy-wall-st.html.

Index

active duty rule (Gen'eki Bukansei), 134–36, 147, 156
Adachi Kenzō, 113–15, 153, 179, 209, 214, 303n100
Adachi Tsunayuki, 51
Aizawa Saburō, 237–38
    trial of, 238–39
Akamatsu Noriyoshi, 42
Akizuki uprising, 69, 74
Amano Isamu, 200, 219
Andō Teruzō, 239
Ansei purges (1858–59), 11, 17
anti-Bakufu struggle, 10–12, 22, 75
Araki Sadao, 163, 184, 188–89, 216–18, 221–22, 232, 235–36, 245–47
Austro-Prussian war of 1866, 96

Bakufu, 140, 200, 229, 231, 242, 272n3
    anti movement, 10, 12–13, 17–18
    against Chōshū units, 20–22
    criticism of, 10–11
    decline of, 29, 31–32
    prerogatives of, 9
    shishi gang of (Shinsengumi), 19
    shishi's opposition to, 12–21
Battle of Sekimon (Stone Gate), 48–49
Bingham, John, 44
Bismarck, Otto von, 96
Brandt, Max von, 44, 46
Buddhism, 57
    anti-Buddhist campaign of Meiji Shintoists, 57–58
Bureau of Taiwan Barbarian Affairs (Taiwan Banchi Jimu Kyoku), 42
Byas, Hugh, 2

Cameron, Craig M., 2
Cassel, Douglas, 49–50
China adventurers (shina rōnin), 166
Chinese Nationalist Party (Guomindang), 168
Chō Isamu, 8, 200, 202, 210–11, 214–17, 219, 223, 227, 258
Chōshū Clique, 98, 135–36, 138, 141–42, 145, 148, 164–65, 172, 185, 199
Chōshū domain, 10–11, 21–23, 30, 32, 34–35, 53, 65, 69

Chōshū shishi, 13, 15–16, 19, 229
Chōshū Wars, 19–21, 67
Conscription Act of 1873, 35, 278n33

Doihara Kenji, 176, 255
Donghak (Eastern Learning), 105
Duus, Peter, 105

Eastern Conference, 170
Edo (Tokugawa) period (1860s), 9–13, 15–16
Etō Shimpei, 64–68, 75, 77, 98, 152

February coup d'état of 1936 (February Incident), 225–27
    army's reaction to uprising, 244–47
    assassination of Major General Nagata and Aizawa's trial, 238–39
    attempt to secure the Imperial Palace, 242–43
    Emperor Hirohito's interventions, 248–51
    failure and fundamental flaws of rebellion, 246–47
    high-priority targets, 239
    key ringleaders of, 227–28
    political violence, 236–40
    social conditions for, 228
    strategy of containment, 245, 337n98
    trial and punishment, 251–52
    troops involved, 238–40
    uprising, 240–42
    young officers, contribution of (see Young Officers movement [Seinen Shōkō Undō])
First Sino-Japanese War, 1894–1895, 48
Franco-Prussian war of 1871, 96
Funayama Ichirō, 252
Futabakai (Two Leaves Society), 164

Gekokujō (the low overthrowing the high), 2, 153
Germany military model, 95–98
    crucial difference between Japan and, 96–97
    position and political role of the emperor, 97–98
Gojong, King, 102–3, 119
Gonnohyōe, Yamamoto, 142–43, 147–49
Gorō, Araki, 165, 175–77

CPSIA information can be obtained
at www.ICGtesting.com
Printed in the USA
BVOW08*1121211216

471395BV00003B/4/P